# THE PARTNERSHIP ALMANAC

A Sourcebook of
Financial Data, Trends, and
Performance Ratios

# THE PARTNERSHIP ALMANAC

## A Sourcebook of
## Financial Data, Trends, and
## Performance Ratios

*Leo Troy, Ph.D.*

**PRENTICE HALL**
Englewood Cliffs, New Jersey 07632

Prentice-Hall International (UK) Limited, *London*
Prentice-Hall of Australia Pty. Limited, *Sydney*
Prentice-Hall Canada, Inc., *Toronto*
Prentice-Hall Hispanoamericana, S.A., *Mexico*
Prentice-Hall of India Private Limited, *New Delhi*
Prentice-Hall of Japan, Inc., *Tokyo*
Simon & Schuster Asia Pte. Ltd., *Singapore*
Editora Prentice-Hall do Brasil, Ltda., *Rio de Janeiro*

© 1989 *by*

PRENTICE-HALL, INC.
Englewood Cliffs, NJ

10  9  8  7  6  5  4  3  2  1

ISBN 0-13-651464-2

**PRENTICE HALL**
**BUSINESS & PROFESSIONAL DIVISION**
**A division of Simon & Schuster**
**Englewood Cliffs, New Jersey 07632**

Printed in the United States of America

**DEDICATION**

**Dedicated to members of my family:**
**Alex, Dale, and Suzannah B. Troy**

**Also by the author:**

*Almanac of Business and Industrial Financial Ratios*

# The Partnership Almanac:
# Financial Data, Trends, and Ratios

## I. Scope

Although corporations are the most familiar form of business organization, there are actually more unincorporated than corporately organized enterprises. There are over 12 million individual proprietorships and more than 1.7 million partnerships *in which over 13 million partners participate.* By comparison there are nearly 3 million corporations.

Considerable information exists on the performance of corporations, but comparatively little on either individual proprietorships or partnerships. It is the purpose of the *Partnership Sourcebook* to provide users with: (1) comprehensive financial data and ratios on partnerships covering all industries, from Agriculture to Services for the most recent years available (1984 and 1985 in the First Edition); (2) and key financial data showing trends from 1976 through 1985.

The partnerships reported in the *Partnership Sourcebook* include both general and limited partnerships. All industrial classifications are referenced with the Standard Industrial Classification (SIC) of Industries in the Appendix. This enables the user to identify an industry in the *Partnership Sourcebook* and compare it to the SIC's classification.

## II. Financial Data and Ratios

The data and results are presented in three tables. Tables 1 and 2 each present 38 items of financial data and ratios on 89 separate industries for two years, 1984 and 1985. The data and results cover the entire range of industrial and service activity in the economy.

Tables 1 and 2 differ in that Table 1 displays the information for *all partnerships, those with and without net income*; Table 2 reports the same items for *those partnerships which reported a net income.* Thus, the *Partnership Sourcebook* separates those partnerships in each industry which reported net income from the total population of partnerships. In this format, the user can directly compare the results of his/her partnership's performance with all partnerships and separately with those earning a profit, not only in the same industry but also across industries. In addition, the user can easily make a year-to-year comparison on any of the 38 items in Tables 1 and 2.

The number of partnerships varies widely by *industrial sector* of the economy, ranging from over 840,000 in Finance, Insurance, and Real Estate (FIRE, industry 172) to just under 25,000 in Transportation, Communication, and Public Utilities (TCPU, industry 067). By individual industry, the largest number of partnerships are in Operators and Lessors of Buildings (Industry 186) and the smallest number in Poultry and Eggs (Industry 012).

Measured by the number of partners, again the industrial sector of Finance, Insurance, and Real Estate (FIRE) records the greatest number, and, in fact, accounts for more than half

(7.8 million) of all partners (13.2 million). Operators and Lessors of Buildings tally the largest number of partners among individual industries, 5.2 million.

Among the items in Tables 1 and 2 measuring the performance of partnerships are gross and net operating loss or profit, guaranteed payments to partners, other distributions to partners, and changes in partners' capital. In addition, *The Partnership Sourcebook* reports the average earnings per partner and per partnership for each industry for each year.

Partnerships' financial performance is also measured in Tables 1 and 2 by three measures of returns on assets, net income, gross operating profit, and net operating profit. Amounts of gross and net operating profit are also reported. For the total of all industries, agriculture, and finance, insurance, and real estate (FIRE), I have used total receipts instead of operating income; operating income alone would otherwise distort the financial analysis.

Data and ratios cover such key expense items as cost of sales, salaries and wages, interest paid, depreciation, pension and profit sharing, and employee benefit programs. As pointed out in the Highlights section, the role of interest and depreciation have been (and remain even after the Tax Reform Act of 1986) critical to tax sheltering. Additional measures of performance in Tables 1 and 2 are the coverage ratio (times interest earned), inventory turnover, days' sales in inventory, and the average age of the inventory for industries where such information is most applicable.

Table 3 is an historical summary covering the same industries reported in Tables 1 and 2 and encompasses 24 key items affecting partnerships from 1976 to 1985, the most recent year available. These include the number of partners, the number of partnerships, operating income, depreciation, interest paid, payroll, payments to partners, net income less deficits, and average payments per partnership and per partner.

Users should be alerted to some breaks in the series presented in Table 3. The most significant applies to depreciation and affects two industrial sectors particularly, agriculture and real estate. The IRS changed its method of reporting depreciation after 1980 and this profoundly affected the continuity of the depreciation series. Other items affected after 1980 were Taxes Paid and Interest Paid.

Of special note to users is that some of the performance measures of partnerships in Table 3 are converted to *constant dollar terms*, using appropriate price indices, and expressed as index numbers. This presentation may well be the first of its kind.

The sources for the *Partnership Sourcebook* are the tax returns of partnerships filed with the Internal Revenue Service. These are the Partnership Returns of Income, Form 1065. All data processed and made available by the Internal Revenue Service from Form 1065 are utilized in the *Partnership Sourcebook*. Not available from the IRS are balance sheet data except total assets. For 1984, the author calculated the depreciation amounts across all industries, and this is the only figure used which was not supplied directly by the IRS.

## III. Characteristics of Partnerships

The organizational and operational rules for partnerships derive from two sources, law (the Uniform Partnership Act, hereafter the UPA) and contract (the partnership agreement). Partnerships are also affected by numerous enactments and are also subject to the laws of the particular state in which they were formed.

The UPA defines a partnership as "an association of two or more persons to carry on as co-owners of a business for profit." The rights and duties of partners are set forth in the UPA. In those which are general partnerships, each member has a voice in the management of the enterprise and is a co-owner of all property of the partnership, but has no claim on any specific asset. Each partner is entitled to an equal voice unless the partnership agreement provides otherwise. Partnerships are not legal entities, but may carry out any legal activity agreed upon by the partners. A partner has the authority to bind the partnership when dealing with outsiders in the course of business activities. Partners are subject to unlimited liability for debts of the partnership and torts of partners, unless limited by contract. The organization terminates upon the death, withdrawal, or addition of a partner, or earlier by contractual agreement.

Limited partnerships may have both general and limited partners. The latter invest capital and share income or losses, but not share in the management of the organization. Their liability is also limited to their investments in the partnership.

Partnerships are not subject to federal income taxes, but are required to file a Form 1065 for informational purposes. As already stated, the *Partnership Sourcebook* uses the data from these filings with the Internal Revenue Service to calculate and report the financial performance of all partnerships.

The effects of the Tax Reform Act of 1986 on Partnerships will become evident once the data for that year are available. The data and results presented here will prove to be a useful tool in measuring the effects of the Act on partnerships.

## IV. Financial Trends, Factors, and Ratios

Tables 1 and 2 present the following informational, financial, and percentage or ratio data:

1. The number of partnerships.
2. The number of partners.
3. Total assets.
4. Average assets per partnership.
5. Average per partner.
6. Net income, less deficit (Table 1). Net income (Table 2).
7. Average income per partnership.
8. Average income per partner.
9. Operating income.
10. Cost of sales and operations.
11. Salaries and wages (after job credits).
12. Rent paid.
13. Interest paid.
14. Taxes paid.
15. Bad debts.
16. Repairs.
17. Depreciation.
18. Depletion.

19. Pension and profit sharing plans.
20. Employee benefit programs.
21. Other deductions.
22. Total operating costs.
23. Operating income [repeat of item 9].
24. Cost of sales and operations [repeat of item 10].
25. Gross operating profit.
26. Operating costs.
27. Net operating profit.
28. Less: guaranteed payments to partners.
29. Distribution to partners.
30. Other charges.
31. Net change in partners' capital.
32. Coverage ratio: times interest earned.
33. Inventory turnover (times).
34. Days' sales in inventory.
35. Average age of inventory.
36. Return on assets, net income less deficit (or net income only).
37. Return on assets, gross operating profit.
38. Return on assets, net operating profit.

The informational and financial trends presented in Table 3 cover the years 1976–85 inclusive and are:

1. The number of partnerships.
2. The number of partners.
3. Operating income.
4. Depreciation.
5. Taxes paid.
6. Interest paid.
7. Payroll deductions.
8. Payments to partners.
9. Net income, less deficit.
10. Average payment, per partnership.
11. Average payment, per partner.
12. Average income, less deficit, per partnership.
13. Average income, less deficit, per partner.
14. Depreciation as a percentage of operating income.
15. Interest paid as a percentage of operating income.
16. Payroll as a percentage of operating income.
17. Partnership index (1976 = 100): This shows the annual change in the number of partnerships, 1976–85, in index form.
18. Partners index (1976 = 100): This shows the annual change in the number of partners, 1976–85, in index form.
19. Operating income index (1976 = 100): This shows the annual change in partnerships' current dollars.

20. Payments to partners (1976 = 100): This shows the annual change in payments to partners in current dollars.

21. Operating income in constant dollars values showing annual changes in index form (1976 = 100): The actual dollar values of item 19 are adjusted for inflation using the producers' price index (the "cost-of-living" index of business). This shows the annual change in partnerships' operating income in constant (inflation-adjusted) dollars.

22. Payments to partners in constant dollar values, showing annual changes in index form (1976 = 100): The actual dollar values in item 20 are adjusted for inflation, using the consumer price index and expressed in index form to show annual changes.

23. Average payment per partnership in constant dollars (1976 = 100): The actual dollar values in item 10 are adjusted for inflation, using the consumer price index and expressed in index form to show annual changes.

24. Average payment per partner in constant dollars (1976 = 100): The actual dollar values in item 10 are adjusted for inflation, using the consumer price index and expressed in index form to show annual changes.

If the data were not appropriate or unavailable, I have inserted the expression n.a. in the three tables.

**Leo Troy, Ph.D.**
**Rutgers University**

# Highlights, 1984 and 1985

There were 1,643,581 partnerships reporting to the IRS in 1984 and this number rose 4.3 percent to 1,713,603 in 1985. The increase included all industrial sectors, except two. The two sectors with fewer partnerships in 1985 than 1984 were Construction, and Agriculture, Forestry, and Fishing. The largest gain came in Transportation, Communications, and Public Utilities, where the number rose by more than 21 percent, from 20,578 to 24,970 over the two-year period.

Most partnerships in 1985 (843,867), in fact nearly one-half of the total, were in Finance, Insurance, and Real Estate (FIRE). Within this sector, one industry, Operators and Lessors of Buildings, numbered over 582,000 partnerships, or more than one-third of all partnerships. Second in the number of partnerships were Services with 341,000. The smallest number (24,970) were in Transportation, Communications, and Public Utilities (TCPU).

Of the total of 1.7 million partnerships, just under one half (865,000), reported losses, while a slightly larger number, 876,000, reported net income. Combined, the 1.7 million partnerships showed a loss of nearly $9 billion dollars in 1985, an increase over 1984 of $5 billion. (The consolidated 1985 loss is the result of a total loss of nearly $86 billion, reduced by $77 billion in net income.)

The aggregate loss in 1985 (nearly $86 billion) was the largest in the history of the IRS's records on partnerships. The records begin in 1957. It also continues the string of annual losses which have characterized partnerships since 1981.

Partnerships in Finance, Insurance, and Real Estate (FIRE) reported both the largest net income, $30 billion, and the largest losses, $56 billion. Combined, this yielded a net loss for the sector as a whole of $26 billion. (In 1984, the sector produced $19 billion in deficits, so losses increased by $7 billion between the two years.) Within the FIRE sector (Finance, Insurance, and Real Estate), Real Estate partnerships reported the largest losses (net income less deficits), of nearly $30 billion. Most of this loss was reported by Operators and Lessors of Buildings.

Partnerships with net income in the Services sector produced nearly $27 billion in net income, while losers reported deficits of $10 billion. Combining the sector's net income and deficit, Services as a whole showed a net income of $17 billion in 1985. This was the largest profit for any industrial sector.

Within Services the largest profit was registered by partnerships in Legal Services, $11 billion. Medical and Health Services reported $4 billion in profits, and Accounting, Auditing, and Bookkeeping Services $3 billion.

For only the second time in recent years, partnerships in Mining scored a net income (after deficit), some $1.4 billion. Before 1984, partnerships in Mining had not reported positive income since 1968. The turnaround resulted from a reduction in new investment. New investment fell because of depressed prices, especially in petroleum extraction, and this, in turn, reduced the start-up expenses normally required to begin new production fields. Within Mining, Oil, and Gas Extraction, which until 1984 reported losses for nearly a decade, reported income was in excess of $2 billion in 1985.

Some of the foregoing highlights and other financial performances among partnerships are shown in the Chart section of the book.

### The Effect of Tax Shelters on Partnership Income

The Tax Reform Act of 1986 can be expected to have a significant impact on the tax shelter benefits of partnerships. However, comprehensive tax data on the impact are not yet available and will not be for some time. Meanwhile, the *Partnership Sourcebook* offers users an important and unique yardstick for measuring the performance of partnerships prior to the Act. When the 1986 Act data become available, the current *Partnership Sourcebook* will offer an opportunity not only to evaluate past performance but also to enhance planning future financial strategies.

Prior to the 1986 Act, the tax sheltering provisions of the law significantly affected the profits and losses reported by partnerships. Tax shelters offered investors a formula for realizing a profit, while minimizing taxable income. Tax shelters created a relation between income and deductions which produced tax losses and converted ordinary income (which was fully taxed) into tax-favored capital gains income.

Two of the most familiar procedures by which tax sheltering generated deductions and therefore losses for partnerships were borrowing and accelerated depreciation. Borrowing created a deduction for interest paid; acquisition of real property created deductions through accelerated depreciation.

Real estate is singularly well suited for such deductions. Real estate is usually acquired through mortgages and is also entitled to accelerated depreciation deductions. The effects of such tax shelters is to produce losses and this is clearly shown by the statistical data reported in the *Partnership Sourcebook*.

In 1985, all partnerships in the real estate industry produced total net losses of $29.8 billion, of which $26.2 billion was reported by partnerships of Operators and Lessors of Buildings. Over 59 percent of the partnerships in the industry reported losses compared to 42 percent partnerships outside real estate.

The importance of interest and depreciation tax sheltering may be gauged from comparisons of depreciation amounts to operating income. For Operators and Lessors of Buildings, with and without net income, operating income in 1985 totaled $9 billion, interest paid $8 billion (93% of operating income), and depreciation, $5 billion (51% of operating income). Together, these items accounted for nearly $4 billion or 15% of the industry's consolidated deficit of $26 billion. (Losses from rents was the largest expense item in the industry in 1985, amounting to a consolidated total of $28 billion.)

Despite depreciation's impact on tax sheltering as reported on IRS Form 1065 and in the *Partnership Sourcebook*, these figures understate the actual amounts of depreciation available to partnerships, notably in Farming and in Operators and Lessors of Buildings in Real Estate. Partnerships in Agriculture are required to report only net farm profit or loss; partnerships in Real Estate are required to report only net rental income or loss in the income statement on IRS Form 1065. Details for deductions applicable to these two activities are reported on a separate schedule, IRS Form 4562. The IRS does not include these data in the source from which the *Partnership Sourcebook* is drawn. The sector, Finance, Insurance, and Real Estate (most of it in Real Estate), illustrates the true magnitude of the total depreciation available to partnerships. For the (FIRE) sector as a whole, the amount of depreciation available to partnerships on IRS Form 1065 in 1985 was $6 billion, while the amount reported on the real estate expense schedule exceeded $24 billion—four times as much!

There are other tax advantages available to partnerships in addition to the deductions for interest and depreciation. One notable one is favored tax treatment. If a property was held for more than one year, any gains on the property were treated as long-term capital gains and therefore effectively taxed at lower rates.

The net result of these tax shelters was to make partnerships an important vehicle for high income individuals to reduce their tax liabilities.

# Acknowledgements

Thanks are due to several individuals who were instrumental in developing the *Partnership Sourcebook*. In particular I wish to acknowledge the help of Mr. Philip Wilson who was responsible for the programming. For professional help and advice, I wish to thank Professors Neil Sheflin and John Gilmour of Rutgers University; Mr. Dan Goldberg, CPA and Partner of Wiss and Company; Mr. Herb Rosenstein, CPA and a personal friend; students, former and current, Branca Bakardijev, Basit Qayyum, and Sue Ellen Hershman for their steadfastness in inputting so much vital data.

**Leo Troy**

# THE PARTNERSHIP ALMANAC

## A Sourcebook of
## Financial Data, Trends, and
## Performance Ratios

# GRAPHS OF SELECTED RATIOS

## Chart 1: Partnerships, 1976–1985
## All Industries

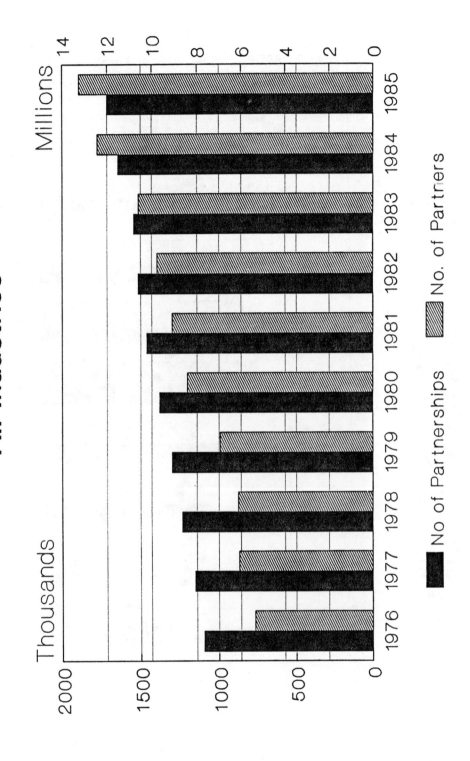

No of Partnerships    No. of Partners

Source:    Table 3

*Page 1*

# Chart 2: Partnerships, 1976–1985
## Finance, Insurance and Real Estate

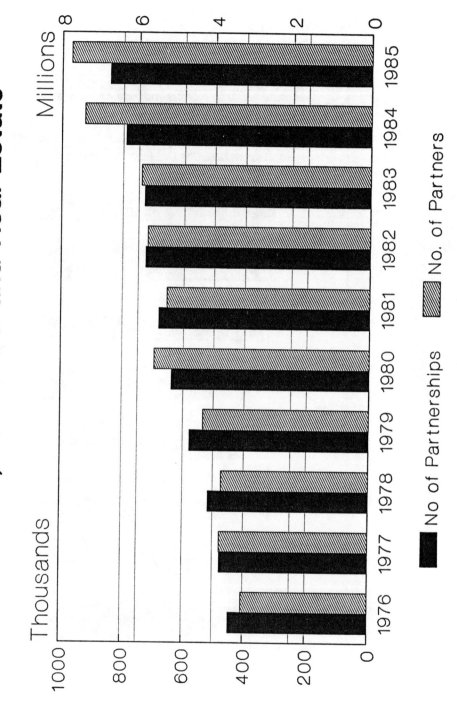

No of Partnerships     No. of Partners

Source: Table 3

# Chart 3: Av Total Assets Per Partnership With and Without Net Income, 1985

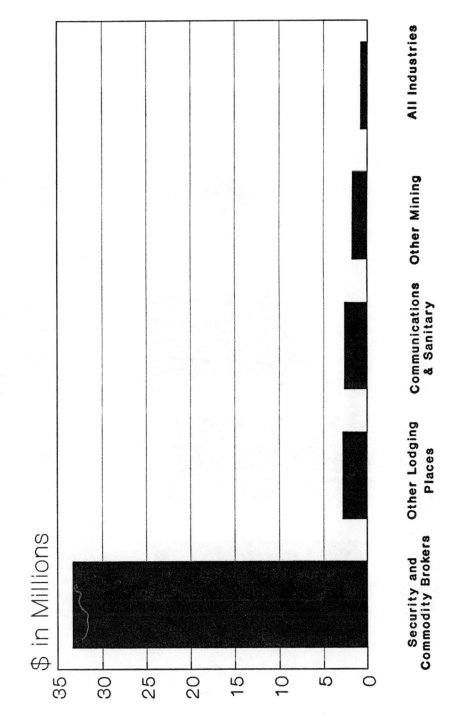

$ in Millions

Source: Table 1

# Chart 4: Earnings Per Partnership With and Without Net Income, 1985

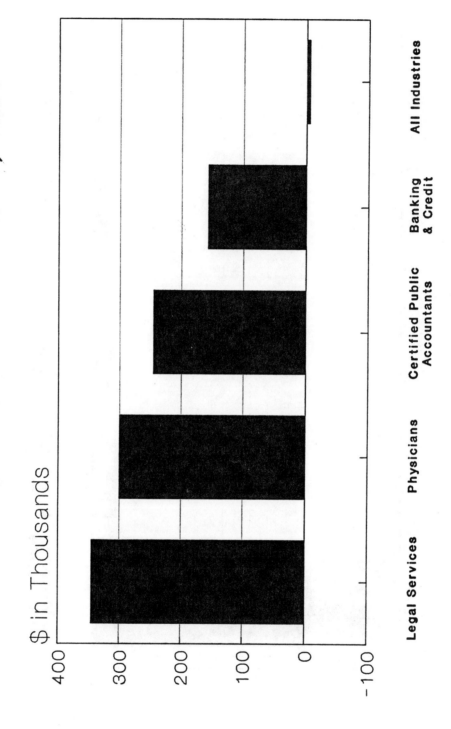

$ in Thousands

| | |
|---|---|
| 400 | |
| 300 | |
| 200 | |
| 100 | |
| 0 | |
| -100 | |

Legal Services   Physicians   Certified Public Accountants   Banking & Credit   All Industries

Source: Table 1

*Page 4*

# Chart 5: Earnings Per Partner
## With and Without Net Income, 1985

$ in Thousands

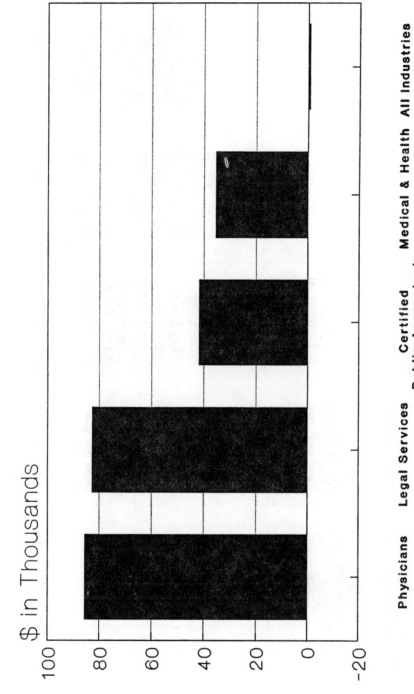

Physicians    Legal Services    Certified            Medical & Health    All Industries
                                Public Accountants

Source: Table 1

*Page 5*

# Chart 6: Cost of Sales
## With and Without Net Income, 1985

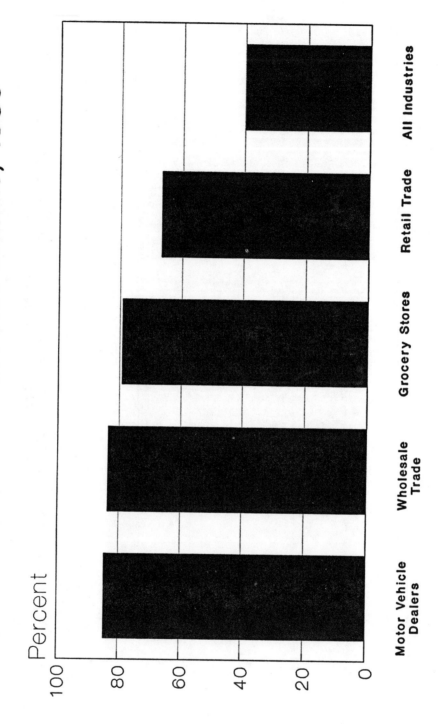

Percent

100 · 80 · 60 · 40 · 20 · 0

Motor Vehicle Dealers · Wholesale Trade · Grocery Stores · Retail Trade · All Industries

Source: Table 1

# Chart 7: Gross Operating Profit With and Without Net Income, 1985

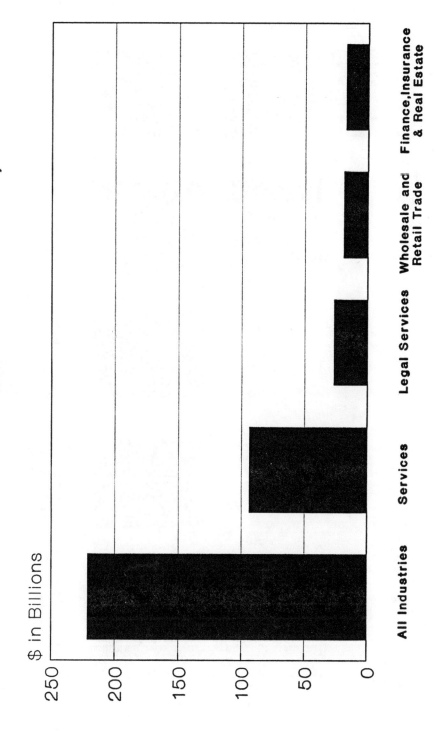

$ in Billions

250
200
150
100
50
0

All Industries    Services    Legal Services    Wholesale and Retail Trade    Finance, Insurance & Real Estate

Source:  Table 1

# Chart 8: Gross Operating Profit With and Without Net Income, 1985

Percent

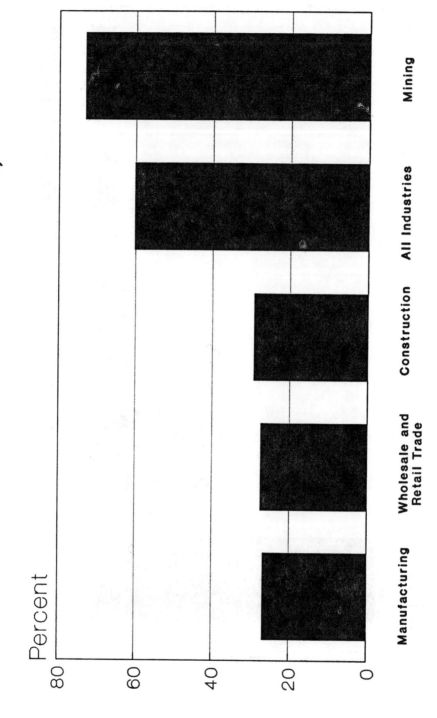

Source: Table 1

*Page 8*

# Chart 9: Net Operating Profit
## With and Without Net Income, 1985

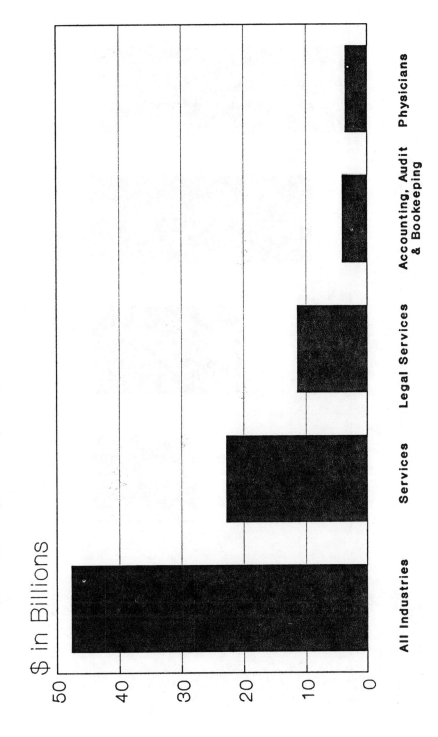

$ in Billions

Source: Table 1

# Chart 10: Net Operating Profit
## With and Without Net Income, 1985

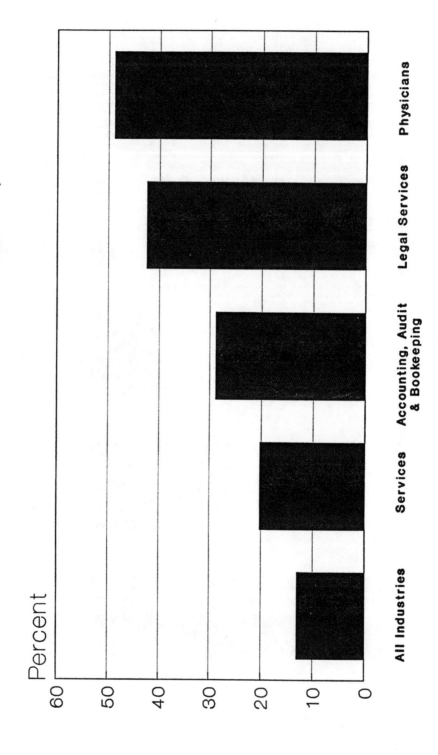

Percent

Source: Table 1

# Chart 11: Distributions to Partners With and Without Net Income, 1985

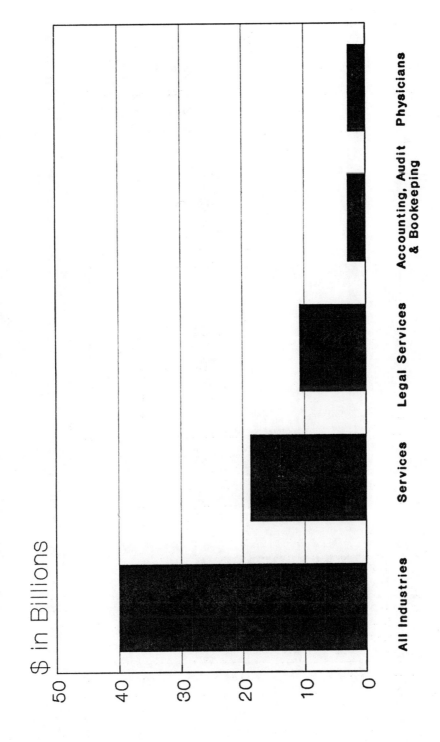

$ in Billions

| | | |
|---|---|---|
| 50 | | |
| 40 | | |
| 30 | | |
| 20 | | |
| 10 | | |
| 0 | | |

All Industries    Services    Legal Services    Accounting, Audit & Bookeeping    Physicians

Source:    Table 1

# Chart 12: Change in Partners' Capital With and Without Net Income, 1985

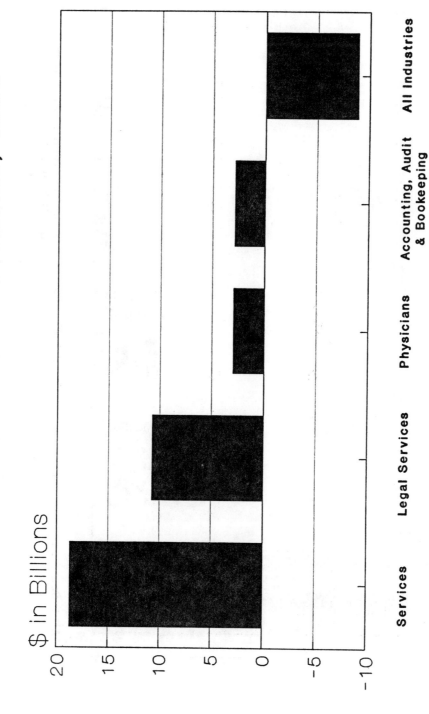

$ in Billions

Source: Table 1

# Chart 13: Losses in Selected Industries
## 1985

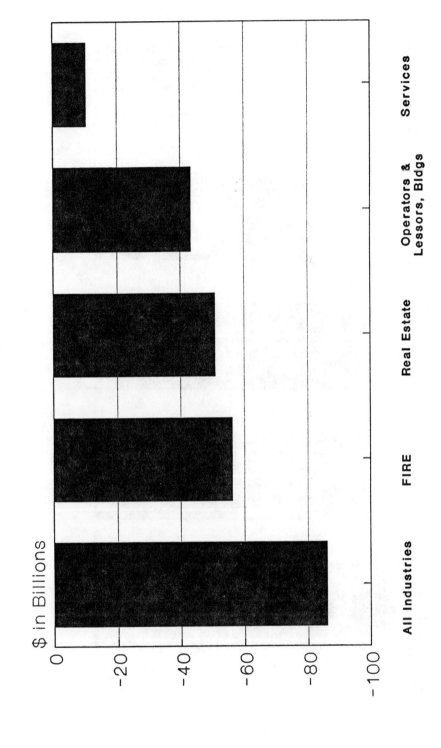

$ in Billions

| | | | | |
|---|---|---|---|---|
| 0 | | | | |
| -20 | | | | |
| -40 | | | | |
| -60 | | | | |
| -80 | | | | |
| -100 | | | | |

All Industries    FIRE    Real Estate    Operators & Lessors, Bldgs    Services

Sources: Tables 1 and 2

*Page 13*

# Chart 14: Return on Assets
## Net Income, 1985

Percent

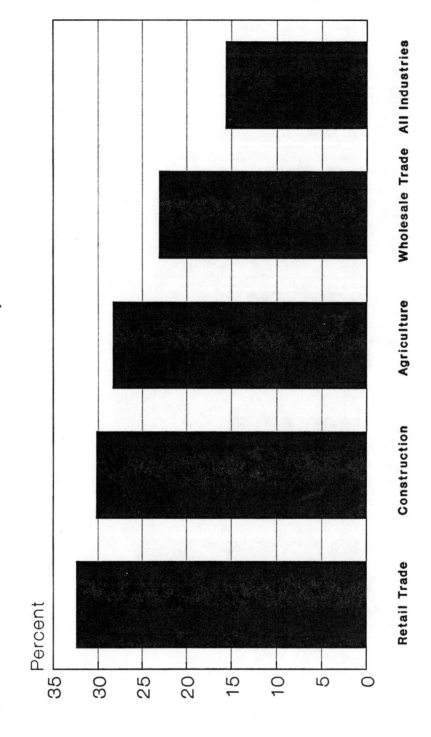

Retail Trade    Construction    Agriculture    Wholesale Trade    All Industries

Source: Table 2

# Chart: 15 Return on Assets
## Net Operating Profit, 1985

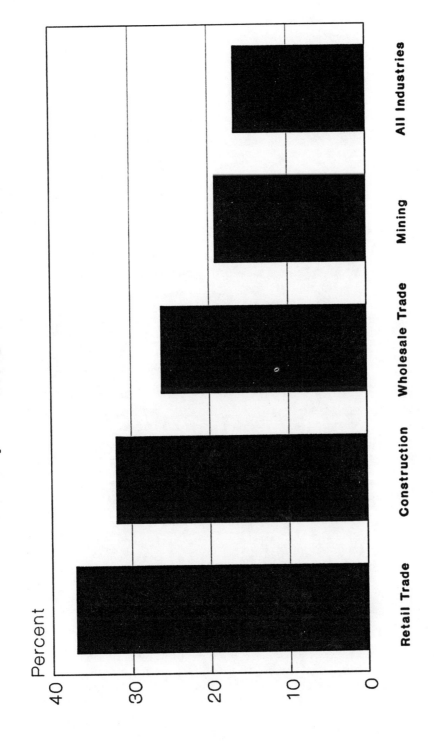

Percent

40 — 30 — 20 — 10 — 0

Retail Trade    Construction    Wholesale Trade    Mining    All Industries

Source: Table 2

*Page 15*

# TABLE 1
## Partnerships with and Without Net Income

Table 1: Partnerships With and Without Net Income: 001. ALL INDUSTRIES

Dollar values in thousands, except averages

|  |  | 1984 |  | 1985 |  |
|---|---|---|---|---|---|
| 1. | Number of Partnerships | 1,643,581 | | 1,713,603 | |
| 2. | Number of Partners | 12,426,721 | | 13,244,824 | |
| 3. | Total Assets | $1,030,848,519 | | $1,269,434,302 | |
| 4. | Average total assets per Partnership | $627,197 | | $740,798 | |
| 5. | Average total assets per Partner | $82,954 | | $95,844 | |
| 6. | Net Income, less Deficit | ($3,500,024) | | ($8,883,674) | |
| 7. | Average per Partnership, total earnings | ($2,125) | | ($5,180) | |
| 8. | Average per Partner, total earnings | ($281) | | ($670) | |
| 9. | Operating Income | $375,192,511 | | $367,117,315 | |
|  | Operating Costs | | | | |
| 10. | Cost of sales & operations | $180,857,822 | 48.2% | $146,315,315 | 39.9% |
| 11. | Salaries and wages | $28,500,111 | 7.6% | $33,867,693 | 9.2% |
| 12. | Rent paid | $7,533,299 | 2.0% | $8,537,160 | 2.3% |
| 13. | Interest paid | $25,437,588 | 6.8% | $28,674,933 | 7.8% |
| 14. | Taxes paid | $6,673,186 | 1.8% | $7,745,756 | 2.1% |
| 15. | Bad debts | $657,156 | 0.2% | $798,293 | 0.2% |
| 16. | Repairs | $2,302,985 | 0.6% | $2,498,020 | 0.7% |
| 17. | Depreciation | $19,782,193 | 5.3% | $22,575,913 | 6.2% |
| 18. | Depletion | $277,521 | 0.1% | $242,097 | 0.1% |
| 19. | Pension & profit sharing plans | $530,116 | 0.1% | $703,297 | 0.2% |
| 20. | Employee benefits programs | $871,296 | 0.2% | $1,019,335 | 0.3% |
| 21. | Other deductions | $58,252,033 | 15.5% | $66,430,128 | 18.1% |
| 22. | Total operating costs | $331,697,821 | 88.4% | $319,424,451 | 87.0% |
|  | Operating Income and Distribution | | | | |
| 23. | Operating Income | $375,192,511 | 100.0% | $367,117,315 | 100.0% |
| 24. | Less: Cost of sales and operations | $180,857,822 | 48.2% | $146,315,315 | 39.9% |
| 25. | Gross operating profit | $194,334,689 | 51.8% | $220,802,000 | 60.1% |
| 26. | Additional operating costs | $150,839,999 | 40.2% | $173,109,136 | 47.2% |
| 27. | Net operating profit | $43,494,690 | 11.6% | $47,692,864 | 13.0% |
| 28. | Less: Guaranteed payments to partners | $7,517,503 | | $7,694,236 | |
| 29. | Distribution to partners | $35,977,187 | | $39,998,628 | |
| 30. | Other charges | $39,499,726 | | $48,898,815 | |
| 31. | Net change partners' capital | ($3,522,539) | | ($8,900,187) | |
|  | Selected Ratios | | | | |
| 32. | Coverage ratio: times interest earned | 0.7 | | 0.7 | |
| 33. | Inventory turnover (times) | 4.5 | | 5.6 | |
| 34. | Days' sales in inventory | 79.6 | | 68.1 | |
| 35. | Average age of inventory (days) | 81.7 | | 65.8 | |
| 36. | Return on assets, net inc., less def | (0.3%) | | (0.7%) | |
| 37. | Return on assets, gross operating profit | 18.9% | | 17.4% | |
| 38. | Return on assets, net operating profit | 4.2% | | 3.8% | |

Table 1: Partnerships With and Without Net Income:  002.  AGRICULTURE, FORESTRY, AND FISHING

Dollar values in thousands, except averages

|    |                                              | 1984 | | 1985 | |
|----|----------------------------------------------|------|------|------|------|
| 1. | Number of Partnerships                       | 139,306 | | 135,909 | |
| 2. | Number of Partners                           | 494,392 | | 584,789 | |
| 3. | Total Assets                                 | $26,738,825 | | $27,026,795 | |
| 4. | Average total assets per Partnership         | $191,943 | | $198,859 | |
| 5. | Average total assets per Partner             | $54,084 | | $46,216 | |
| 6. | Net Income, less Deficit                     | ($749,030) | | ($1;049,433) | |
| 7. | Average per Partnership, total earnings      | ($5,375) | | ($7,719) | |
| 8. | Average per Partner, total earnings          | ($1,515) | | ($1,794) | |
| 9. | Total Receipts                               | $5,885,672 | | $6,528,606 | |
|    | Operating Costs                              |      |      |      |      |
| 10. | Cost of sales & operations                  | $3,498,298 | 59.4% | $3,730,812 | 57.2% |
| 11. | Salaries and wages                          | $378,512 | 6.4% | $544,579 | 8.3% |
| 12. | Rent paid                                   | $76,180 | 1.3% | $70,525 | 1.1% |
| 13. | Interest paid                               | $363,290 | 6.2% | $369,296 | 5.7% |
| 14. | Taxes paid                                  | $88,031 | 1.5% | $101,883 | 1.6% |
| 15. | Bad debts                                   | $19,418 | 0.3% | $16,035 | 0.3% |
| 16. | Repairs                                     | $115,855 | 2.0% | $145,669 | 2.2% |
| 17. | Depreciation                                | $462,002 | 7.9% | $486,141 | 7.5% |
| 18. | Depletion                                   | $12,579 | 0.2% | $31,241 | 0.5% |
| 19. | Pension & profit sharing plans              | $8,185 | 0.1% | $3,387 | 0.1% |
| 20. | Employee benefits programs                  | $6,650 | 0.1% | $5,439 | 0.1% |
| 21. | Other deductions                            | $1,205,369 | 20.5% | $1,404,438 | 21.5% |
| 22. | Total operating costs                       | $6,234,683 | 105.9% | $6,909,489 | 105.8% |
|    | Operating Income and Distribution           |      |      |      |      |
| 23. | Total Receipts                              | $5,885,672 | 100.0% | $6,528,606 | 100.0% |
| 24. | Less: Cost of sales and operations          | $3,498,298 | 59.4% | $3,730,812 | 57.2% |
| 25. | Gross operating profit                      | $2,387,374 | 40.6% | $2,797,794 | 42.9% |
| 26. | Additional operating costs                  | $2,736,385 | 46.5% | $3,178,677 | 48.7% |
| 27. | Net operating profit                        | ($349,011) | (5.9%) | ($380,883) | (5.8%) |
| 28. | Less: Guaranteed payments to partners       | $254,850 | | $327,549 | |
| 29. | Distribution to partners                    | ($603,861) | | ($708,432) | |
| 30. | Other charges                               | $2,753,010 | | $3,258,086 | |
| 31. | Net change partners' capital                | ($3,356,871) | | ($3,966,518) | |
|    | Selected Ratios                             |      |      |      |      |
| 32. | Coverage ratio: times interest earned       | (2.0) | | (2.0) | |
| 33. | Inventory turnover (times)                  | 7.0 | | 4.8 | |
| 34. | Days' sales in inventory                    | 51.4 | | 70.4 | |
| 35. | Average age of inventory (days)             | 52.1 | | 76.4 | |
| 36. | Return on assets, net inc., less def        | (2.8%) | | (3.9%) | |
| 37. | Return on assets, gross operating profit    | 8.9% | | 10.4% | |
| 38. | Return on assets, net operating profit      | (1.3%) | | (1.4%) | |

*Page 17*

Table 1: Partnerships With and Without Net Income:   003.   FARMS

Dollar values in thousands, except averages

|  |  | 1984 |  | 1985 |  |
|---|---|---|---|---|---|
| 1. | Number of Partnerships | 112,817 | | 109,544 | |
| 2. | Number of Partners | 389,673 | | 490,873 | |
| 3. | Total Assets | $22,043,910 | | $22,357,076 | |
| 4. | Average total assets per Partnership | $195,395 | | $204,092 | |
| 5. | Average total assets per Partner | $56,570 | | $45,546 | |
| 6. | Net Income, less Deficit | ($606,945) | | ($854,370) | |
| 7. | Average per Partnership, total earnings | ($5,378) | | ($7,797) | |
| 8. | Average per Partner, total earnings | ($1,557) | | ($1,740) | |
| 9. | Total Receipts | $3,113,091 | | $3,344,233 | |
| | Operating Costs | | | | |
| 10. | Cost of sales & operations | $2,110,767 | 67.8% | $2,227,781 | 66.6% |
| 11. | Salaries and wages | $152,179 | 4.9% | $180,756 | 5.4% |
| 12. | Rent paid | $36,422 | 1.2% | $36,075 | 1.1% |
| 13. | Interest paid | $194,734 | 6.3% | $207,233 | 6.2% |
| 14. | Taxes paid | $40,128 | 1.3% | $44,962 | 1.3% |
| 15. | Bad debts | $17,846 | 0.6% | $10,254 | 0.3% |
| 16. | Repairs | $44,102 | 1.4% | $61,674 | 1.8% |
| 17. | Depreciation | $192,720 | 6.2% | $222,661 | 6.7% |
| 18. | Depletion | $1,351 | 0.0% | $84 | n.a. |
| 19. | Pension & profit sharing plans | $3,856 | 0.1% | $2,478 | 0.1% |
| 20. | Employee benefits programs | $5,701 | 0.2% | $4,497 | 0.1% |
| 21. | Other deductions | $568,098 | 18.3% | $736,562 | 22.0% |
| 22. | Total operating costs | $3,367,915 | 108.2% | $3,735,024 | 111.7% |
| | Operating Income and Distribution | | | | |
| 23. | Total Receipts | $3,113,091 | 100.0% | $3,344,233 | 100.0% |
| 24. | Less:  Cost of sales and operations | $2,110,767 | 67.8% | $2,227,781 | 66.6% |
| 25. | Gross operating profit | $1,002,324 | 32.2% | $1,116,452 | 33.4% |
| 26. | Additional operating costs | $1,257,148 | 40.4% | $1,507,243 | 45.1% |
| 27. | Net operating profit | ($254,824) | (8.2%) | ($390,791) | (11.7%) |
| 28. | Less:  Guaranteed payments to partners | $199,687 | | $250,952 | |
| 29. | Distribution to partners | ($454,511) | | ($641,743) | |
| 30. | Other charges | $2,524,467 | | $2,893,438 | |
| 31. | Net change partners' capital | ($2,978,978) | | ($3,535,181) | |
| | Selected Ratios | | | | |
| 32. | Coverage ratio:  times interest earned | (2.3) | | (2.9) | |
| 33. | Inventory turnover (times) | 5.8 | | 3.6 | |
| 34. | Days' sales in inventory | 64.9 | | 92.4 | |
| 35. | Average age of inventory (days) | 63.2 | | 102.4 | |
| 36. | Return on assets, net inc., less def | (2.8%) | | (3.8%) | |
| 37. | Return on assets, gross operating profit | 4.6% | | 5.0% | |
| 38. | Return on assets, net operating profit | (1.2%) | | (1.8%) | |

Table 1: Partnerships With and Without Net Income:  004.  FIELD CROPS

Dollar values in thousands, except averages

|  | 1984 | | 1985 | |
|---|---|---|---|---|
| 1.  Number of Partnerships | 41,997 | | 44,982 | |
| 2.  Number of Partners | 156,679 | | 159,343 | |
| | | | | |
| 3.  Total Assets | $7,563,058 | | $8,310,489 | |
| 4.   Average total assets per Partnership | $180,086 | | $184,751 | |
| 5.   Average total assets per Partner | $48,271 | | $52,155 | |
| | | | | |
| 6.  Net Income, less Deficit | $392,779 | | $381,496 | |
| 7.   Average per Partnership, total earnings | $9,354 | | $8,484 | |
| 8.   Average per Partner, total earnings | $2,507 | | $2,395 | |
| | | | | |
| 9.  Total Receipts | $891,685 | | $1,345,465 | |
| Operating Costs | | | | |
| 10.   Cost of sales & operations | $445,414 | 50.0% | $808,815 | 60.1% |
| 11.   Salaries and wages | $80,367 | 9.0% | $103,806 | 7.7% |
| 12.   Rent paid | $16,941 | 1.9% | $22,461 | 1.7% |
| 13.   Interest paid | $46,850 | 5.3% | $69,015 | 5.1% |
| 14.   Taxes paid | $22,115 | 2.5% | $27,675 | 2.1% |
| 15.   Bad debts | $1,353 | 0.2% | $8,571 | 0.6% |
| 16.   Repairs | $28,245 | 3.2% | $43,417 | 3.2% |
| 17.   Depreciation | $53,278 | 6.0% | $75,649 | 5.6% |
| 18.   Depletion | $1,320 | 0.2% | $62 | n.a. |
| 19.   Pension & profit sharing plans | $2,536 | 0.3% | $1,730 | 0.1% |
| 20.   Employee benefits programs | $5,010 | 0.6% | $3,435 | 0.3% |
| 21.   Other deductions | $180,148 | 20.2% | $273,779 | 20.4% |
| 22.   Total operating costs | $883,579 | 99.1% | $1,438,417 | 106.9% |
| | | | | |
| Operating Income and Distribution | | | | |
| 23.   Total Receipts | $891,685 | 100.0% | $1,345,465 | 100.0% |
| 24.     Less:  Cost of sales and operations | $445,414 | 50.0% | $808,815 | 60.1% |
| 25.   Gross operating profit | $446,271 | 50.1% | $536,650 | 39.9% |
| 26.     Additional operating costs | $438,165 | 49.1% | $629,602 | 46.8% |
| 27.   Net operating profit | $8,106 | 0.9% | ($92,952) | (6.9%) |
| 28.     Less:  Guaranteed payments to partners | $70,339 | | $129,980 | |
| 29.   Distribution to partners | ($62,233) | | ($222,932) | |
| 30.   Other charges | $643,961 | | $678,333 | |
| 31.   Net change partners' capital | ($706,194) | | ($901,265) | |
| | | | | |
| Selected Ratios | | | | |
| 32.   Coverage ratio:  times interest earned | (0.8) | | (2.4) | |
| 33.   Inventory turnover (times) | 2.6 | | 2.6 | |
| 34.   Days' sales in inventory | 136.2 | | 130.4 | |
| 35.   Average age of inventory (days) | 139.2 | | 138.2 | |
| 36.   Return on assets, net inc., less def | 5.2% | | 4.6% | |
| 37.   Return on assets, gross operating profit | 5.9% | | 6.5% | |
| 38.   Return on assets, net operating profit | 0.1% | | (1.1%) | |

Table 1: Partnerships With and Without Net Income:  005.  VEGETABLE AND MELON

Dollar values in thousands, except averages

| | | 1984 | | 1985 | |
|---|---|---|---|---|---|
| 1. | Number of Partnerships | 1,968 | | 2,497 | |
| 2. | Number of Partners | 5,385 | | 6,204 | |
| | | | | | |
| 3. | Total Assets | $571,935 | | $593,671 | |
| 4. | Average total assets per Partnership | $290,617 | | $237,754 | |
| 5. | Average total assets per Partner | $106,209 | | $95,692 | |
| | | | | | |
| 6. | Net Income, less Deficit | $163,432 | | ($13,118) | |
| 7. | Average per Partnership, total earnings | $83,047 | | ($5,252) | |
| 8. | Average per Partner, total earnings | $30,350 | | ($2,114) | |
| | | | | | |
| 9. | Total Receipts | $71,548 | | $52,861 | |
| | Operating Costs | | | | |
| 10. | Cost of sales & operations | $58,982 | 82.4% | $40,451 | 76.5% |
| 11. | Salaries and wages | $5,663 | 7.9% | $5,344 | 10.1% |
| 12. | Rent paid | $132 | 0.2% | $101 | 0.2% |
| 13. | Interest paid | $1,905 | 2.7% | $3,118 | 5.9% |
| 14. | Taxes paid | $738 | 1.0% | $591 | 1.1% |
| 15. | Bad debts | $7 | 0.0% | $0 | n.a. |
| 16. | Repairs | $854 | 1.2% | $213 | 0.4% |
| 17. | Depreciation | $1,328 | 1.9% | $2,089 | 4.0% |
| 18. | Depletion | $0 | n.a. | $0 | n.a. |
| 19. | Pension & profit sharing plans | $0 | n.a. | $0 | n.a. |
| 20. | Employee benefits programs | $130 | 0.2% | $273 | 0.5% |
| 21. | Other deductions | $7,852 | 11.0% | $26,166 | 49.5% |
| 22. | Total operating costs | $77,600 | 108.5% | $78,346 | 148.2% |
| | | | | | |
| | Operating Income and Distribution | | | | |
| 23. | Total Receipts | $71,548 | 100.0% | $52,861 | 100.0% |
| 24. | Less:  Cost of sales and operations | $58,982 | 82.4% | $40,451 | 76.5% |
| 25. | Gross operating profit | $12,566 | 17.6% | $12,410 | 23.5% |
| 26. | Additional operating costs | $18,618 | 26.0% | $37,895 | 71.7% |
| 27. | Net operating profit | ($6,052) | (8.5%) | ($25,485) | (48.2%) |
| 28. | Less:  Guaranteed payments to partners | $4,856 | | $4,752 | |
| 29. | Distribution to partners | ($10,908) | | ($30,237) | |
| 30. | Other charges | $16,927 | | $100,708 | |
| 31. | Net change partners' capital | ($27,835) | | ($130,945) | |
| | | | | | |
| | Selected Ratios | | | | |
| 32. | Coverage ratio:  times interest earned | (4.2) | | (9.2) | |
| 33. | Inventory turnover (times) | 33.5 | | 4.7 | |
| 34. | Days' sales in inventory | 17.5 | | 87.6 | |
| 35. | Average age of inventory (days) | 10.9 | | 78.3 | |
| 36. | Return on assets, net inc., less def | 28.6% | | (2.2%) | |
| 37. | Return on assets, gross operating profit | 2.2% | | 2.1% | |
| 38. | Return on assets, net operating profit | (1.1%) | | (4.3%) | |

Table 1: Partnerships With and Without Net Income:  006.  FRUIT AND TREE NUT

Dollar values in thousands, except averages

| | 1984 | | 1985 | |
|---|---|---|---|---|
| 1. Number of Partnerships | 11,379 | | 10,409 | |
| 2. Number of Partners | 76,204 | | 94,126 | |
| 3. Total Assets | $4,691,527 | | $4,224,062 | |
| 4. Average total assets per Partnership | $412,297 | | $405,809 | |
| 5. Average total assets per Partner | $61,565 | | $44,877 | |
| 6. Net Income, less Deficit | ($369,356) | | ($385,425) | |
| 7. Average per Partnership, total earnings | ($32,457) | | ($37,027) | |
| 8. Average per Partner, total earnings | ($4,847) | | ($4,095) | |
| 9. Total Receipts | $213,040 | | $212,007 | |
| Operating Costs | | | | |
| 10. Cost of sales & operations | $107,225 | 50.3% | $120,778 | 57.0% |
| 11. Salaries and wages | $11,931 | 5.6% | $11,624 | 5.5% |
| 12. Rent paid | $3,509 | 1.7% | $2,325 | 1.1% |
| 13. Interest paid | $38,372 | 18.0% | $51,597 | 24.3% |
| 14. Taxes paid | $6,856 | 3.2% | $6,604 | 3.1% |
| 15. Bad debts | $104 | 0.1% | $37 | 0.0% |
| 16. Repairs | $2,956 | 1.4% | $3,865 | 1.8% |
| 17. Depreciation | $26,566 | 12.5% | $40,295 | 19.0% |
| 18. Depletion | $0 | n.a. | $2 | n.a. |
| 19. Pension & profit sharing plans | $429 | 0.2% | $76 | 0.0% |
| 20. Employee benefits programs | $57 | 0.0% | $39 | 0.0% |
| 21. Other deductions | $73,944 | 34.7% | $58,677 | 27.7% |
| 22. Total operating costs | $271,949 | 127.7% | $295,925 | 139.6% |
| Operating Income and Distribution | | | | |
| 23. Total Receipts | $213,040 | 100.0% | $212,007 | 100.0% |
| 24. Less: Cost of sales and operations | $107,225 | 50.3% | $120,778 | 57.0% |
| 25. Gross operating profit | $105,815 | 49.7% | $91,229 | 43.0% |
| 26. Additional operating costs | $164,724 | 77.3% | $175,147 | 82.6% |
| 27. Net operating profit | ($58,909) | (27.7%) | ($83,918) | (39.6%) |
| 28. Less: Guaranteed payments to partners | $25,727 | | $16,185 | |
| 29. Distribution to partners | ($84,636) | | ($100,103) | |
| 30. Other charges | $475,983 | | $515,100 | |
| 31. Net change partners' capital | ($560,619) | | ($615,203) | |
| Selected Ratios | | | | |
| 32. Coverage ratio: times interest earned | (2.5) | | (2.6) | |
| 33. Inventory turnover (times) | 5.7 | | 5.0 | |
| 34. Days' sales in inventory | 68.3 | | 84.2 | |
| 35. Average age of inventory (days) | 64.0 | | 73.0 | |
| 36. Return on assets, net inc., less def | (7.9%) | | (9.1%) | |
| 37. Return on assets, gross operating profit | 2.3% | | 2.2% | |
| 38. Return on assets, net operating profit | (1.3%) | | (2.0%) | |

*Page 21*

Table 1: Partnerships With and Without Net Income:   008.   BEEF CATTLE FEEDLOTS

Dollar values in thousands, except averages

|  |  | 1984 |  | 1985 |  |
|---|---|---|---|---|---|
| 1. | Number of Partnerships | 1,646 |  | 1,813 |  |
| 2. | Number of Partners | 6,286 |  | 82,004 |  |
| 3. | Total Assets | $438,539 |  | $657,063 |  |
| 4. | Average total assets per Partnership | $266,427 |  | $362,418 |  |
| 5. | Average total assets per Partner | $69,764 |  | $8,013 |  |
| 6. | Net Income, less Deficit | ($826) |  | $119,944 |  |
| 7. | Average per Partnership, total earnings | ($501) |  | $66,158 |  |
| 8. | Average per Partner, total earnings | ($131) |  | $1,463 |  |
| 9. | Total Receipts | $266,690 |  | $288,162 |  |
|  | Operating Costs |  |  |  |  |
| 10. | Cost of sales & operations | $221,099 | 82.9% | $238,628 | 82.8% |
| 11. | Salaries and wages | $8,234 | 3.1% | $5,611 | 2.0% |
| 12. | Rent paid | $809 | 0.3% | $844 | 0.3% |
| 13. | Interest paid | $3,687 | 1.4% | $7,678 | 2.7% |
| 14. | Taxes paid | $521 | 0.2% | $674 | 0.2% |
| 15. | Bad debts | $0 | n.a. | $251 | 0.1% |
| 16. | Repairs | $1,073 | 0.4% | $1,418 | 0.5% |
| 17. | Depreciation | $2,997 | 1.1% | $1,786 | 0.6% |
| 18. | Depletion | $0 | n.a. | $20 | 0.0% |
| 19. | Pension & profit sharing plans | $29 | 0.0% | $75 | 0.0% |
| 20. | Employee benefits programs | $84 | 0.0% | $176 | 0.1% |
| 21. | Other deductions | $24,478 | 9.2% | $42,345 | 14.7% |
| 22. | Total operating costs | $263,011 | 98.6% | $299,506 | 103.9% |
|  | Operating Income and Distribution |  |  |  |  |
| 23. | Total Receipts | $266,690 | 100.0% | $288,162 | 100.0% |
| 24. | Less: Cost of sales and operations | $221,099 | 82.9% | $238,628 | 82.8% |
| 25. | Gross operating profit | $45,591 | 17.1% | $49,534 | 17.2% |
| 26. | Additional operating costs | $41,912 | 15.7% | $60,878 | 21.1% |
| 27. | Net operating profit | $3,679 | 1.4% | ($11,344) | (3.9%) |
| 28. | Less: Guaranteed payments to partners | $1,722 |  | $1,192 |  |
| 29. | Distribution to partners | $1,957 |  | ($12,536) |  |
| 30. | Other charges | $30,872 |  | $52,967 |  |
| 31. | Net change partners' capital | ($28,915) |  | ($65,503) |  |
|  | Selected Ratios |  |  |  |  |
| 32. | Coverage ratio:  times interest earned | n.a. |  | (2.5) |  |
| 33. | Inventory turnover (times) | 12.0 |  | 5.1 |  |
| 34. | Days' sales in inventory | 30.1 |  | 85.3 |  |
| 35. | Average age of inventory (days) | 30.5 |  | 72.2 |  |
| 36. | Return on assets, net inc., less def | (0.2%) |  | 18.3% |  |
| 37. | Return on assets, gross operating profit | 10.4% |  | 7.5% |  |
| 38. | Return on assets, net operating profit | 0.8% |  | (1.7%) |  |

Table 1: Partnerships With and Without Net Income:  009.  BEEF CATTLE, EXCEPT FEEDLOTS

Dollar values in thousands, except averages

|  | | 1984 | | 1985 | |
|---|---|---|---|---|---|
| 1. | Number of Partnerships | 19,845 | | 15,925 | |
| 2. | Number of Partners | 55,878 | | 60,947 | |
| 3. | Total Assets | $3,633,820 | | $4,270,004 | |
| 4. | Average total assets per Partnership | $183,110 | | $268,132 | |
| 5. | Average total assets per Partner | $65,031 | | $70,061 | |
| 6. | Net Income, less Deficit | ($344,282) | | ($841,298) | |
| 7. | Average per Partnership, total earnings | ($17,347) | | ($52,826) | |
| 8. | Average per Partner, total earnings | ($6,161) | | ($13,803) | |
| 9. | Total Receipts | $535,249 | | $545,091 | |
|  | Operating Costs | | | | |
| 10. | Cost of sales & operations | $449,719 | 84.0% | $412,756 | 75.7% |
| 11. | Salaries and wages | $6,941 | 1.3% | $9,159 | 1.7% |
| 12. | Rent paid | $6,421 | 1.2% | $2,775 | 0.5% |
| 13. | Interest paid | $44,389 | 8.3% | $35,824 | 6.6% |
| 14. | Taxes paid | $2,874 | 0.5% | $2,854 | 0.5% |
| 15. | Bad debts | $2,122 | 0.4% | $76 | 0.0% |
| 16. | Repairs | $3,540 | 0.7% | $5,830 | 1.1% |
| 17. | Depreciation | $26,876 | 5.0% | $20,487 | 3.8% |
| 18. | Depletion | $16 | n.a. | $0 | n.a. |
| 19. | Pension & profit sharing plans | $313 | 0.1% | $147 | 0.0% |
| 20. | Employee benefits programs | $53 | 0.0% | $213 | 0.0% |
| 21. | Other deductions | $96,632 | 18.1% | $140,417 | 25.8% |
| 22. | Total operating costs | $639,896 | 119.6% | $630,538 | 115.7% |
|  | Operating Income and Distribution | | | | |
| 23. | Total Receipts | $535,249 | 100.0% | $545,091 | 100.0% |
| 24. | Less: Cost of sales and operations | $449,719 | 84.0% | $412,756 | 75.7% |
| 25. | Gross operating profit | $85,530 | 16.0% | $132,335 | 24.3% |
| 26. | Additional operating costs | $190,177 | 35.5% | $217,782 | 40.0% |
| 27. | Net operating profit | ($104,647) | (19.6%) | ($85,447) | (15.7%) |
| 28. | Less: Guaranteed payments to partners | $30,386 | | $37,591 | |
| 29. | Distribution to partners | ($135,033) | | ($123,038) | |
| 30. | Other charges | $536,542 | | $884,640 | |
| 31. | Net change partners' capital | ($671,575) | | ($1,007,678) | |
|  | Selected Ratios | | | | |
| 32. | Coverage ratio: times interest earned | (3.4) | | (3.4) | |
| 33. | Inventory turnover (times) | 5.1 | | 2.1 | |
| 34. | Days' sales in inventory | 85.5 | | 131.1 | |
| 35. | Average age of inventory (days) | 72.1 | | 177.5 | |
| 36. | Return on assets, net inc., less def | (9.5%) | | (19.7%) | |
| 37. | Return on assets, gross operating profit | 2.4% | | 3.1% | |
| 38. | Return on assets, net operating profit | (2.9%) | | (2.0%) | |

*Page 23*

Table 1: Partnerships With and Without Net Income: 010.  HOGS, SHEEP, AND GOATS

Dollar values in thousands, except averages

|  |  | 1984 |  | 1985 |  |
|---|---|---|---|---|---|
| 1. | Number of Partnerships | 5,714 | | 4,179 | |
| 2. | Number of Partners | 13,509 | | 11,763 | |
| 3. | Total Assets | $267,581 | | $221,337 | |
| 4. | Average total assets per Partnership | $46,829 | | $52,964 | |
| 5. | Average total assets per Partner | $19,808 | | $18,816 | |
| 6. | Net Income, less Deficit | ($16,480) | | $62,132 | |
| 7. | Average per Partnership, total earnings | ($2,883) | | $14,869 | |
| 8. | Average per Partner, total earnings | ($1,219) | | $5,283 | |
| 9. | Total Receipts | $187,610 | | $169,560 | |
|  | Operating Costs | | | | |
| 10. | Cost of sales & operations | $178,009 | 94.9% | $124,332 | 73.3% |
| 11. | Salaries and wages | $346 | 0.2% | $796 | 0.5% |
| 12. | Rent paid | $91 | 0.1% | $30 | 0.0% |
| 13. | Interest paid | $4,106 | 2.2% | $1,326 | 0.8% |
| 14. | Taxes paid | $118 | 0.1% | $359 | 0.2% |
| 15. | Bad debts | $0 | n.a. | $0 | n.a. |
| 16. | Repairs | $111 | 0.1% | $26 | 0.0% |
| 17. | Depreciation | $105 | 0.1% | $205 | 0.1% |
| 18. | Depletion | $0 | n.a. | $0 | n.a. |
| 19. | Pension & profit sharing plans | $0 | n.a. | $0 | n.a. |
| 20. | Employee benefits programs | $0 | n.a. | $7 | n.a. |
| 21. | Other deductions | $6,851 | 3.7% | $2,305 | 1.4% |
| 22. | Total operating costs | $189,737 | 101.1% | $129,386 | 76.3% |
|  | Operating Income and Distribution | | | | |
| 23. | Total Receipts | $187,610 | 100.0% | $169,560 | 100.0% |
| 24. | Less: Cost of sales and operations | $178,009 | 94.9% | $124,332 | 73.3% |
| 25. | Gross operating profit | $9,601 | 5.1% | $45,228 | 26.7% |
| 26. | Additional operating costs | $11,728 | 6.3% | $5,054 | 3.0% |
| 27. | Net operating profit | ($2,127) | (1.1%) | $40,174 | 23.7% |
| 28. | Less: Guaranteed payments to partners | $6,023 | | $7,078 | |
| 29. | Distribution to partners | ($8,150) | | $33,096 | |
| 30. | Other charges | $59,134 | | $50,391 | |
| 31. | Net change partners' capital | ($67,284) | | ($17,295) | |
|  | Selected Ratios | | | | |
| 32. | Coverage ratio: times interest earned | (1.5) | | 29.3 | |
| 33. | Inventory turnover (times) | 22.2 | | 13.0 | |
| 34. | Days' sales in inventory | 23.9 | | 26.2 | |
| 35. | Average age of inventory (days) | 16.4 | | 28.2 | |
| 36. | Return on assets, net inc., less def | (6.2%) | | 28.1% | |
| 37. | Return on assets, gross operating profit | 3.6% | | 20.4% | |
| 38. | Return on assets, net operating profit | (0.8%) | | 18.2% | |

*Page 24*

Table 1: Partnerships With and Without Net Income:  011.  DAIRY FARMS

Dollar values in thousands, except averages

|  |  | 1984 | | 1985 | |
|---|---|---|---|---|---|
| 1. | Number of Partnerships | 18,328 | | 17,940 | |
| 2. | Number of Partners | 42,257 | | 43,195 | |
| 3. | Total Assets | $2,173,120 | | $1,860,783 | |
| 4. | Average total assets per Partnership | $118,568 | | $103,723 | |
| 5. | Average total assets per Partner | $51,426 | | $43,079 | |
| 6. | Net Income, less Deficit | ($84,740) | | $222,785 | |
| 7. | Average per Partnership, total earnings | ($4,621) | | $12,421 | |
| 8. | Average per Partner, total earnings | ($2,004) | | $5,159 | |
| 9. | Total Receipts | $336,130 | | $184,769 | |
|  | Operating Costs | | | | |
| 10. | Cost of sales & operations | $231,429 | 68.9% | $107,765 | 58.3% |
| 11. | Salaries and wages | $6,640 | 2.0% | $18,166 | 9.8% |
| 12. | Rent paid | $4,440 | 1.3% | $4,243 | 2.3% |
| 13. | Interest paid | $9,424 | 2.8% | $8,650 | 4.7% |
| 14. | Taxes paid | $2,290 | 0.7% | $1,078 | 0.6% |
| 15. | Bad debts | $86 | 0.0% | $1,045 | 0.6% |
| 16. | Repairs | $1,604 | 0.5% | $1,917 | 1.0% |
| 17. | Depreciation | $5,691 | 1.7% | $12,832 | 6.9% |
| 18. | Depletion | $0 | n.a. | $0 | n.a. |
| 19. | Pension & profit sharing plans | $184 | 0.1% | $0 | n.a. |
| 20. | Employee benefits programs | $0 | n.a. | $32 | 0.0% |
| 21. | Other deductions | $16,671 | 5.0% | $29,466 | 16.0% |
| 22. | Total operating costs | $278,459 | 82.8% | $185,194 | 100.2% |
|  | Operating Income and Distribution | | | | |
| 23. | Total Receipts | $336,130 | 100.0% | $184,769 | 100.0% |
| 24. | Less:  Cost of sales and operations | $231,429 | 68.9% | $107,765 | 58.3% |
| 25. | Gross operating profit | $104,701 | 31.2% | $77,004 | 41.7% |
| 26. | Additional operating costs | $47,030 | 14.0% | $77,429 | 41.9% |
| 27. | Net operating profit | $57,671 | 17.2% | ($425) | (0.2%) |
| 28. | Less:  Guaranteed payments to partners | $43,405 | | $42,825 | |
| 29. | Distribution to partners | $14,266 | | ($43,250) | |
| 30. | Other charges | $342,317 | | $177,459 | |
| 31. | Net change partners' capital | ($328,051) | | ($220,709) | |
|  | Selected Ratios | | | | |
| 32. | Coverage ratio:  times interest earned | 5.1 | | (1.1) | |
| 33. | Inventory turnover (times) | 8.0 | | 19.4 | |
| 34. | Days' sales in inventory | 9.0 | | 18.6 | |
| 35. | Average age of inventory (days) | 45.6 | | 18.9 | |
| 36. | Return on assets, net inc., less def | (3.9%) | | 12.0% | |
| 37. | Return on assets, gross operating profit | 4.8% | | 4.1% | |
| 38. | Return on assets, net operating profit | 2.7% | | (0.0%) | |

*Page 25*

Table 1: Partnerships With and Without Net Income:  012.  POULTRY AND EGGS

Dollar values in thousands, except averages

| | 1984 | | 1985 | |
|---|---|---|---|---|
| 1.  Number of Partnerships | 978 | | 732 | |
| 2.  Number of Partners | 2,552 | | 1,951 | |
| | | | | |
| 3.  Total Assets | $542,866 | | $498,649 | |
| 4.    Average total assets per Partnership | $555,078 | | $681,214 | |
| 5.    Average total assets per Partner | $212,722 | | $255,586 | |
| | | | | |
| 6.  Net Income, less Deficit | $7,156 | | $23,955 | |
| 7.    Average per Partnership, total earnings | $7,320 | | $32,731 | |
| 8.    Average per Partner, total earnings | $2,805 | | $12,280 | |
| | | | | |
| 9.  Total Receipts | $324,627 | | $266,575 | |
| Operating Costs | | | | |
| 10.    Cost of sales & operations | $230,516 | 71.0% | $176,933 | 66.4% |
| 11.    Salaries and wages | $8,667 | 2.7% | $7,877 | 3.0% |
| 12.    Rent paid | $1,465 | 0.5% | $1,409 | 0.5% |
| 13.    Interest paid | $7,065 | 2.2% | $3,936 | 1.5% |
| 14.    Taxes paid | $1,168 | 0.4% | $1,164 | 0.4% |
| 15.    Bad debts | $2 | n.a. | $45 | 0.0% |
| 16.    Repairs | $3,413 | 1.1% | $2,716 | 1.0% |
| 17.    Depreciation | $13,267 | 4.1% | $11,002 | 4.1% |
| 18.    Depletion | $0 | n.a. | $0 | n.a. |
| 19.    Pension & profit sharing plans | $122 | 0.0% | $133 | 0.1% |
| 20.    Employee benefits programs | $153 | 0.1% | $224 | 0.1% |
| 21.    Other deductions | $58,006 | 17.9% | $46,157 | 17.3% |
| 22.    Total operating costs | $323,844 | 99.8% | $251,596 | 94.4% |
| | | | | |
| Operating Income and Distribution | | | | |
| 23.    Total Receipts | $324,627 | 100.0% | $266,575 | 100.0% |
| 24.      Less:  Cost of sales and operations | $230,516 | 71.0% | $176,933 | 66.4% |
| 25.    Gross operating profit | $94,111 | 29.0% | $89,642 | 33.6% |
| 26.      Additional operating costs | $93,328 | 28.8% | $74,663 | 28.0% |
| 27.    Net operating profit | $783 | 0.2% | $14,979 | 5.6% |
| 28.      Less:  Guaranteed payments to partners | $2,909 | | $3,780 | |
| 29.    Distribution to partners | ($2,126) | | $11,199 | |
| 30.    Other charges | $23,444 | | $29,728 | |
| 31.    Net change partners' capital | ($25,570) | | ($18,529) | |
| | | | | |
| Selected Ratios | | | | |
| 32.    Coverage ratio:  times interest earned | (0.9) | | 2.8 | |
| 33.    Inventory turnover (times) | 71.5 | | 36.1 | |
| 34.    Days' sales in inventory | 6.9 | | 12.5 | |
| 35.    Average age of inventory (days) | 5.1 | | 10.1 | |
| 36.    Return on assets, net inc., less def | 1.3% | | 4.8% | |
| 37.    Return on assets, gross operating profit | 17.3% | | 18.0% | |
| 38.    Return on assets, net operating profit | 0.1% | | 3.0% | |

Table 1: Partnerships With and Without Net Income:  GENERAL LIVESTOCK, INCLUDING ANIMAL SPECIALTY (013,014)

Dollar values in thousands, except averages

|  |  | 1984 |  | 1985 |  |
|---|---|---|---|---|---|
| 1. | Number of Partnerships | 6,418 |  | 7,479 |  |
| 2. | Number of Partners | 20,607 |  | 22,105 |  |
| 3. | Total Assets | $1,776,755 |  | $1,412,822 |  |
| 4. | Average total assets per Partnership | $276,839 |  | $188,905 |  |
| 5. | Average total assets per Partner | $86,221 |  | $63,914 |  |
| 6. | Net Income, less Deficit | ($319,447) |  | ($365,778) |  |
| 7. | Average per Partnership, total earnings | ($49,772) |  | ($48,907) |  |
| 8. | Average per Partner, total earnings | ($15,502) |  | ($16,547) |  |
| 9. | Total Receipts | $200,974 |  | $199,812 |  |
|  | Operating Costs |  |  |  |  |
| 10. | Cost of sales & operations | $153,158 | 76.2% | $154,050 | 77.1% |
| 11. | Salaries and wages | $9,634 | 4.8% | $5,663 | 2.8% |
| 12. | Rent paid | $961 | 0.5% | $842 | 0.4% |
| 13. | Interest paid | $19,273 | 9.6% | $9,713 | 4.9% |
| 14. | Taxes paid | $1,534 | 0.8% | $1,194 | 0.6% |
| 15. | Bad debts | $14,155 | 7.0% | $76 | 0.0% |
| 16. | Repairs | $1,367 | 0.7% | $1,092 | 0.6% |
| 17. | Depreciation | $37,422 | 18.6% | $30,410 | 15.2% |
| 18. | Depletion | $15 | 0.0% | $0 | n.a. |
| 19. | Pension & profit sharing plans | $221 | 0.1% | $289 | 0.1% |
| 20. | Employee benefits programs | $214 | 0.1% | $97 | 0.1% |
| 21. | Other deductions | $38,967 | 19.4% | $57,806 | 28.9% |
| 22. | Total operating costs | $276,921 | 137.8% | $261,232 | 130.7% |
|  | Operating Income and Distribution |  |  |  |  |
| 23. | Total Receipts | $200,974 | 100.0% | $199,812 | 100.0% |
| 24. | Less:  Cost of sales and operations | $153,158 | 76.2% | $154,050 | 77.1% |
| 25. | Gross operating profit | $47,816 | 23.8% | $45,762 | 22.9% |
| 26. | Additional operating costs | $123,763 | 61.6% | $107,182 | 53.6% |
| 27. | Net operating profit | ($75,947) | (37.8%) | ($61,420) | (30.7%) |
| 28. | Less:  Guaranteed payments to partners | $7,268 |  | $5,670 |  |
| 29. | Distribution to partners | ($83,215) |  | ($67,090) |  |
| 30. | Other charges | $389,365 |  | $398,556 |  |
| 31. | Net change partners' capital | ($472,580) |  | ($465,646) |  |
|  | Selected Ratios |  |  |  |  |
| 32. | Coverage ratio:  times interest earned | (4.9) |  | (7.3) |  |
| 33. | Inventory turnover (times) | 7.9 |  | 10.6 |  |
| 34. | Days' sales in inventory | 79.0 |  | 23.1 |  |
| 35. | Average age of inventory (days) | 46.1 |  | 34.3 |  |
| 36. | Return on assets, net inc., less def | (18.0%) |  | (25.9%) |  |
| 37. | Return on assets, gross operating profit | 2.7% |  | 3.2% |  |
| 38. | Return on assets, net operating profit | (4.3%) |  | (4.4%) |  |

Table 1: Partnerships With and Without Net Income: OTHER FARMS (007,015)

Dollar values in thousands, except averages

| | 1984 | | 1985 | |
|---|---|---|---|---|
| 1. Number of Partnerships | 4,544 | | 3,590 | |
| 2. Number of Partners | 10,316 | | 9,236 | |
| | | | | |
| 3. Total Assets | $684,709 | | $308,197 | |
| 4. Average total assets per Partnership | $150,684 | | $85,849 | |
| 5. Average total assets per Partner | $66,374 | | $33,369 | |
| | | | | |
| 6. Net Income, less Deficit | ($35,178) | | ($59,064) | |
| 7. Average per Partnership, total earnings | ($7,740) | | ($16,452) | |
| 8. Average per Partner, total earnings | ($3,409) | | ($6,395) | |
| | | | | |
| 9. Total Receipts | $85,538 | | $79,932 | |
| Operating Costs | | | | |
| 10. Cost of sales & operations | $35,215 | 41.2% | $43,272 | 54.1% |
| 11. Salaries and wages | $13,756 | 16.1% | $12,710 | 15.9% |
| 12. Rent paid | $1,652 | 1.9% | $1,044 | 1.3% |
| 13. Interest paid | $19,663 | 23.0% | $16,377 | 20.5% |
| 14. Taxes paid | $1,914 | 2.2% | $2,768 | 3.5% |
| 15. Bad debts | $17 | 0.0% | $152 | 0.2% |
| 16. Repairs | $939 | 1.1% | $1,180 | 1.5% |
| 17. Depreciation | $25,190 | 29.5% | $27,907 | 34.9% |
| 18. Depletion | $0 | n.a. | $0 | n.a. |
| 19. Pension & profit sharing plans | $24 | 0.0% | $28 | 0.0% |
| 20. Employee benefits programs | $0 | n.a. | $0 | n.a. |
| 21. Other deductions | $64,548 | 75.5% | $59,445 | 74.4% |
| 22. Total operating costs | $162,918 | 190.5% | $164,883 | 206.3% |
| | | | | |
| Operating Income and Distribution | | | | |
| 23. Total Receipts | $85,538 | 100.0% | $79,932 | 100.0% |
| 24. Less: Cost of sales and operations | $35,215 | 41.2% | $43,272 | 54.1% |
| 25. Gross operating profit | $50,323 | 58.8% | $36,660 | 45.9% |
| 26. Additional operating costs | $127,703 | 149.3% | $121,611 | 152.1% |
| 27. Net operating profit | ($77,380) | (90.5%) | ($84,951) | (106.3%) |
| 28. Less: Guaranteed payments to partners | $7,051 | | $1,900 | |
| 29. Distribution to partners | ($84,431) | | ($86,851) | |
| 30. Other charges | $5,923 | | $5,557 | |
| 31. Net change partners' capital | ($90,354) | | ($92,408) | |
| | | | | |
| Selected Ratios | | | | |
| 32. Coverage ratio: times interest earned | (4.9) | | (6.2) | |
| 33. Inventory turnover (times) | 4.2 | | 11.7 | |
| 34. Days' sales in inventory | 78.4 | | 26.8 | |
| 35. Average age of inventory (days) | 87.1 | | 31.2 | |
| 36. Return on assets, net inc., less def | (5.1%) | | (19.2%) | |
| 37. Return on assets, gross operating profit | 7.4% | | 11.9% | |
| 38. Return on assets, net operating profit | (11.3%) | | (27.6%) | |

*Page 28*

Table 1: Partnerships With and Without Net Income:  AGRICULTURAL SERVICES, FORESTRY AND FISHING (016,022,023)

Dollar values in thousands, except averages

|  |  | 1984 |  | 1985 |  |
|---|---|---|---|---|---|
| 1. | Number of Partnerships | 26,489 |  | 26,365 |  |
| 2. | Number of Partners | 104,718 |  | 93,917 |  |
| 3. | Total Assets | $4,694,915 |  | $4,669,719 |  |
| 4. | Average total assets per Partnership | $177,240 |  | $177,118 |  |
| 5. | Average total assets per Partner | $44,834 |  | $49,722 |  |
| 6. | Net Income, less Deficit | ($142,084) |  | ($195,065) |  |
| 7. | Average per Partnership, total earnings | ($5,362) |  | ($7,396) |  |
| 8. | Average per Partner, total earnings | ($1,356) |  | ($2,076) |  |
| 9. | Total Receipts | $2,772,581 |  | $3,184,373 |  |
|  | Operating Costs |  |  |  |  |
| 10. | Cost of sales & operations | $1,387,532 | 50.0% | $1,503,031 | 47.2% |
| 11. | Salaries and wages | $226,333 | 8.2% | $363,823 | 11.4% |
| 12. | Rent paid | $39,758 | 1.4% | $34,450 | 1.1% |
| 13. | Interest paid | $168,556 | 6.1% | $162,062 | 5.1% |
| 14. | Taxes paid | $47,903 | 1.7% | $56,922 | 1.8% |
| 15. | Bad debts | $1,571 | 0.1% | $5,780 | 0.2% |
| 16. | Repairs | $71,754 | 2.6% | $83,995 | 2.6% |
| 17. | Depreciation | $269,279 | 9.7% | $263,480 | 8.3% |
| 18. | Depletion | $11,229 | 0.4% | $31,156 | 0.10% |
| 19. | Pension & profit sharing plans | $4,329 | 0.2% | $909 | 0.0% |
| 20. | Employee benefits programs | $949 | 0.0% | $942 | 0.0% |
| 21. | Other deductions | $637,272 | 23.0% | $667,880 | 21.0% |
| 22. | Total operating costs | $2,866,768 | 103.4% | $3,174,467 | 99.7% |
|  | Operating Income and Distribution |  |  |  |  |
| 23. | Total Receipts | $2,772,581 | 100.0% | $3,184,373 | 100.0% |
| 24. | Less: Cost of sales and operations | $1,387,532 | 50.0% | $1,503,031 | 47.2% |
| 25. | Gross operating profit | $1,385,049 | 50.0% | $1,681,342 | 52.8% |
| 26. | Additional operating costs | $1,479,236 | 53.4% | $1,671,436 | 52.5% |
| 27. | Net operating profit | ($94,187) | (3.4%) | $9,906 | 0.3% |
| 28. | Less: Guaranteed payments to partners | $55,163 |  | $76,597 |  |
| 29. | Distribution to partners | ($149,350) |  | ($66,691) |  |
| 30. | Other charges | $228,543 |  | $364,646 |  |
| 31. | Net change partners' capital | ($377,893) |  | ($431,337) |  |
|  | Selected Ratios |  |  |  |  |
| 32. | Coverage ratio: times interest earned | (1.6) |  | (0.9) |  |
| 33. | Inventory turnover (times) | 10.4 |  | 9.7 |  |
| 34. | Days' sales in inventory | 30.9 |  | 37.9 |  |
| 35. | Average age of inventory (days) | 35.2 |  | 37.8 |  |
| 36. | Return on assets, net inc., less def | (3.0%) |  | (4.2%) |  |
| 37. | Return on assets, gross operating profit | 29.5% |  | 36.0% |  |
| 38. | Return on assets, net operating profit | (2.0%) |  | 0.2% |  |

*Page 29*

Table 1: Partnerships With and Without Net Income:  026.  MINING

Dollar values in thousands, except averages

|     |                                          | 1984 | | 1985 | |
| --- | ---------------------------------------- | ---------- | ----- | ---------- | ----- |
| 1.  | Number of Partnerships                   | 56,548 | | 62,363 | |
| 2.  | Number of Partners                       | 2,007,460 | | 2,207,066 | |
|     |                                          | | | | |
| 3.  | Total Assets                             | $52,415,093 | | $66,929,582 | |
| 4.  | Average total assets per Partnership     | $926,913 | | $1,073,226 | |
| 5.  | Average total assets per Partner         | $26,110 | | $30,325 | |
|     |                                          | | | | |
| 6.  | Net Income, less Deficit                 | $69,112 | | $1,481,701 | |
| 7.  | Average per Partnership, total earnings  | $1,225 | | $23,761 | |
| 8.  | Average per Partner, total earnings      | $34 | | $671 | |
|     |                                          | | | | |
| 9.  | Operating Income                         | $22,054,470 | | $23,401,721 | |
|     | Operating Costs                          | | | | |
| 10. | Cost of sales & operations               | $5,924,109 | 26.9% | $6,141,962 | 26.3% |
| 11. | Salaries and wages                       | $535,126 | 2.4% | $483,187 | 2.1% |
| 12. | Rent paid                                | $285,384 | 1.3% | $119,000 | 0.5% |
| 13. | Interest paid                            | $1,446,686 | 6.6% | $1,197,096 | 5.1% |
| 14. | Taxes paid                               | $626,753 | 2.8% | $742,756 | 3.2% |
| 15. | Bad debts                                | $30,780 | 0.1% | $45,666 | 0.2% |
| 16. | Repairs                                  | $85,882 | 0.4% | $101,563 | 0.4% |
| 17. | Depreciation                             | $2,949,875 | 13.4% | $3,314,882 | 14.2% |
| 18. | Depletion                                | $204,971 | 0.9% | $179,795 | 0.8% |
| 19. | Pension & profit sharing plans           | $23,366 | 0.1% | $17,045 | 0.1% |
| 20. | Employee benefits programs               | $25,469 | 0.1% | $42,946 | 0.2% |
| 21. | Other deductions                         | $8,946,145 | 40.6% | $8,825,626 | 37.7% |
| 22. | Total operating costs                    | $21,084,775 | 95.6% | $21,211,527 | 90.6% |
|     |                                          | | | | |
|     | Operating Income and Distribution        | | | | |
| 23. | Operating Income                         | $22,054,470 | 100.0% | $23,401,721 | 100.0% |
| 24. | Less: Cost of sales and operations       | $5,924,109 | 26.9% | $6,141,962 | 26.3% |
| 25. | Gross operating profit                   | $16,130,361 | 73.1% | $17,259,759 | 73.8% |
| 26. | Additional operating costs               | $15,160,666 | 68.7% | $15,069,565 | 64.4% |
| 27. | Net operating profit                     | $969,695 | 4.4% | $2,190,194 | 9.4% |
| 28. | Less: Guaranteed payments to partners    | $132,832 | | $96,651 | |
| 29. | Distribution to partners                 | $836,863 | | $2,093,543 | |
| 30. | Other charges                            | $767,979 | | $611,846 | |
| 31. | Net change partners' capital             | $68,884 | | $1,481,697 | |
|     |                                          | | | | |
|     | Selected Ratios                          | | | | |
| 32. | Coverage ratio: times interest earned    | (0.3) | | 0.8 | |
| 33. | Inventory turnover (times)               | 13.0 | | 17.0 | |
| 34. | Days' sales in inventory                 | 29.4 | | 19.6 | |
| 35. | Average age of inventory (days)          | 28.0 | | 21.5 | |
| 36. | Return on assets, net inc., less def     | 0.1% | | 2.2% | |
| 37. | Return on assets, gross operating profit | 30.8% | | 25.8% | |
| 38. | Return on assets, net operating profit   | 1.9% | | 3.3% | |

Table 1: Partnerships With and Without Net Income:  029.  OIL AND GAS EXTRACTION

Dollar values in thousands, except averages

| | | 1984 | | 1985 | |
|---|---|---|---|---|---|
| 1. | Number of Partnerships | 50,980 | | 55,816 | |
| 2. | Number of Partners | 1,883,264 | | 2,130,764 | |
| 3. | Total Assets | $41,265,540 | | $55,759,888 | |
| 4. | Average total assets per Partnership | $809,446 | | $998,995 | |
| 5. | Average total assets per Partner | $21,912 | | $26,169 | |
| 6. | Net Income, less Deficit | $787,343 | | $2,272,782 | |
| 7. | Average per Partnership, total earnings | $15,446 | | $40,721 | |
| 8. | Average per Partner, total earnings | $418 | | $1,067 | |
| 9. | Operating Income | $17,460,989 | | $18,752,076 | |
| | Operating Costs | | | | |
| 10. | Cost of sales & operations | $3,356,057 | 19.2% | $3,550,030 | 18.9% |
| 11. | Salaries and wages | $300,173 | 1.7% | $351,359 | 1.9% |
| 12. | Rent paid | $227,013 | 1.3% | $86,186 | 0.5% |
| 13. | Interest paid | $1,151,108 | 6.6% | $904,948 | 4.8% |
| 14. | Taxes paid | $471,390 | 2.7% | $590,405 | 3.2% |
| 15. | Bad debts | $25,164 | 0.1% | $20,397 | 0.1% |
| 16. | Repairs | $36,498 | 0.2% | $66,472 | 0.4% |
| 17. | Depreciation | $2,331,347 | 13.4% | $2,685,691 | 14.3% |
| 18. | Depletion | $22,642 | 0.1% | $2,892 | 0.0% |
| 19. | Pension & profit sharing plans | $6,677 | 0.0% | $4,270 | 0.0% |
| 20. | Employee benefits programs | $6,184 | 0.0% | $14,288 | 0.1% |
| 21. | Other deductions | $7,932,128 | 45.4% | $7,551,185 | 40.3% |
| 22. | Total operating costs | $15,866,610 | 90.9% | $15,828,123 | 84.4% |
| | Operating Income and Distribution | | | | |
| 23. | Operating Income | $17,460,989 | 100.0% | $18,752,076 | 100.0% |
| 24. | Less:  Cost of sales and operations | $3,356,057 | 19.2% | $3,550,030 | 18.9% |
| 25. | Gross operating profit | $14,104,932 | 80.8% | $15,202,046 | 81.1% |
| 26. | Additional operating costs | $12,510,553 | 71.7% | $12,278,093 | 65.5% |
| 27. | Net operating profit | $1,594,379 | 9.1% | $2,923,953 | 15.6% |
| 28. | Less:  Guaranteed payments to partners | $116,652 | | $84,367 | |
| 29. | Distribution to partners | $1,477,727 | | $2,839,586 | |
| 30. | Other charges | $690,613 | | $566,805 | |
| 31. | Net change partners' capital | $787,114 | | $2,272,781 | |
| | Selected Ratios | | | | |
| 32. | Coverage ratio:  times interest earned | 0.4 | | 2.2 | |
| 33. | Inventory turnover (times) | 17.5 | | 29.8 | |
| 34. | Days' sales in inventory | 22.8 | | 9.7 | |
| 35. | Average age of inventory (days) | 20.9 | | 12.3 | |
| 36. | Return on assets, net inc., less def | 1.9% | | 4.1% | |
| 37. | Return on assets, gross operating profit | 34.2% | | 27.3% | |
| 38. | Return on assets, net operating profit | 3.9% | | 5.2% | |

Table 1: Partnerships With and Without Net Income:  OTHER MINING (027,028,030)

Dollar values in thousands, except averages

|  |  | 1984 |  | 1985 |  |
|---|---|---|---|---|---|
| 1. | Number of Partnerships | 5,568 | | 6,548 | |
| 2. | Number of Partners | 124,196 | | 76,302 | |
| 3. | Total Assets | $11,149,553 | | $11,169,694 | |
| 4. | Average total assets per Partnership | $2,002,434 | | $1,705,818 | |
| 5. | Average total assets per Partner | $89,774 | | $146,388 | |
| 6. | Net Income, less Deficit | ($718,230) | | ($791,082) | |
| 7. | Average per Partnership, total earnings | ($128,990) | | ($120,811) | |
| 8. | Average per Partner, total earnings | ($5,783) | | ($10,368) | |
| 9. | Operating Income | $4,593,481 | | $4,649,645 | |
|  | Operating Costs | | | | |
| 10. | Cost of sales & operations | $2,568,051 | 55.9% | $2,591,931 | 55.7% |
| 11. | Salaries and wages | $234,953 | 5.1% | $131,829 | 2.8% |
| 12. | Rent paid | $58,371 | 1.3% | $32,815 | 0.7% |
| 13. | Interest paid | $295,579 | 6.4% | $292,149 | 6.3% |
| 14. | Taxes paid | $155,363 | 3.4% | $152,351 | 3.3% |
| 15. | Bad debts | $5,616 | 0.1% | $25,268 | 0.5% |
| 16. | Repairs | $49,384 | 1.1% | $35,091 | 0.8% |
| 17. | Depreciation | $618,527 | 13.5% | $629,190 | 13.5% |
| 18. | Depletion | $182,329 | 4.0% | $176,903 | 3.8% |
| 19. | Pension & profit sharing plans | $16,689 | 0.4% | $12,775 | 0.3% |
| 20. | Employee benefits programs | $19,285 | 0.4% | $28,658 | 0.6% |
| 21. | Other deductions | $1,014,017 | 22.1% | $1,274,443 | 27.4% |
| 22. | Total operating costs | $5,218,164 | 113.6% | $5,383,406 | 115.8% |
|  | Operating Income and Distribution | | | | |
| 23. | Operating Income | $4,593,481 | 100.0% | $4,649,645 | 100.0% |
| 24. | Less:  Cost of sales and operations | $2,568,051 | 55.9% | $2,591,931 | 55.7% |
| 25. | Gross operating profit | $2,025,430 | 44.1% | $2,057,714 | 44.3% |
| 26. | Additional operating costs | $2,650,113 | 57.7% | $2,791,475 | 60.0% |
| 27. | Net operating profit | ($624,683) | (13.6%) | ($733,761) | (15.8%) |
| 28. | Less:  Guaranteed payments to partners | $16,181 | | $12,283 | |
| 29. | Distribution to partners | ($640,864) | | ($746,044) | |
| 30. | Other charges | $77,366 | | $45,040 | |
| 31. | Net change partners' capital | ($718,230) | | ($791,084) | |
|  | Selected Ratios | | | | |
| 32. | Coverage ratio:  times interest earned | (3.1) | | (3.5) | |
| 33. | Inventory turnover (times) | 9.8 | | 10.7 | |
| 34. | Days' sales in inventory | 37.9 | | 33.0 | |
| 35. | Average age of inventory (days) | 37.4 | | 34.1 | |
| 36. | Return on assets, net inc., less def | (6.4%) | | (7.1%) | |
| 37. | Return on assets, gross operating profit | 18.2% | | 18.4% | |
| 38. | Return on assets, net operating profit | (5.6%) | | (6.6%) | |

Table 1: Partnerships With and Without Net Income:  031.  CONSTRUCTION

Dollar values in thousands, except averages

|  |  | 1984 | | 1985 | |
|---|---|---|---|---|---|
| 1. | Number of Partnerships | 64,607 | | 56,665 | |
| 2. | Number of Partners | 173,273 | | 134,034 | |
| 3. | Total Assets | $13,783,426 | | $15,007,950 | |
| 4. | Average total assets per Partnership | $213,343 | | $264,854 | |
| 5. | Average total assets per Partner | $79,547 | | $111,971 | |
| 6. | Net Income, less Deficit | $2,193,322 | | $2,207,401 | |
| 7. | Average per Partnership, total earnings | $33,955 | | $38,962 | |
| 8. | Average per Partner, total earnings | $12,661 | | $16,472 | |
| 9. | Operating Income | $23,847,838 | | $22,287,233 | |
|  | Operating Costs | | | | |
| 10. | Cost of sales & operations | $17,192,497 | 72.1% | $15,785,948 | 70.8% |
| 11. | Salaries and wages | $835,984 | 3.5% | $771,503 | 3.5% |
| 12. | Rent paid | $119,355 | 0.5% | $139,605 | 0.6% |
| 13. | Interest paid | $475,227 | 2.0% | $372,977 | 1.7% |
| 14. | Taxes paid | $223,235 | 0.9% | $215,055 | 0.10% |
| 15. | Bad debts | $10,531 | 0.0% | $16,203 | 0.1% |
| 16. | Repairs | $99,231 | 0.4% | $128,004 | 0.6% |
| 17. | Depreciation | $451,520 | 1.9% | $427,186 | 1.9% |
| 18. | Depletion | $745 | n.a. | $356 | n.a. |
| 19. | Pension & profit sharing plans | $8,731 | 0.0% | $9,214 | 0.0% |
| 20. | Employee benefits programs | $10,590 | 0.0% | $12,565 | 0.1% |
| 21. | Other deductions | $1,742,544 | 7.3% | $1,728,206 | 7.8% |
| 22. | Total operating costs | $21,171,286 | 88.8% | $19,607,712 | 88.0% |
|  | Operating Income and Distribution | | | | |
| 23. | Operating Income | $23,847,838 | 100.0% | $22,287,233 | 100.0% |
| 24. | Less: Cost of sales and operations | $17,192,497 | 72.1% | $15,785,948 | 70.8% |
| 25. | Gross operating profit | $6,655,341 | 27.9% | $6,501,285 | 29.2% |
| 26. | Additional operating costs | $3,978,789 | 16.7% | $3,821,764 | 17.2% |
| 27. | Net operating profit | $2,676,552 | 11.2% | $2,679,521 | 12.0% |
| 28. | Less: Guaranteed payments to partners | $405,140 | | $370,549 | |
| 29. | Distribution to partners | $2,271,412 | | $2,308,972 | |
| 30. | Other charges | $79,186 | | $102,461 | |
| 31. | Net change partners' capital | $2,192,226 | | $2,206,511 | |
|  | Selected Ratios | | | | |
| 32. | Coverage ratio:  times interest earned | 4.6 | | 6.2 | |
| 33. | Inventory turnover (times) | 5.4 | | 5.0 | |
| 34. | Days' sales in inventory | 67.7 | | 78.3 | |
| 35. | Average age of inventory (days) | 68.3 | | 73.0 | |
| 36. | Return on assets, net inc., less def | 15.9% | | 14.7% | |
| 37. | Return on assets, gross operating profit | 48.3% | | 43.3% | |
| 38. | Return on assets, net operating profit | 19.4% | | 17.9% | |

*Page 33*

Table 1: Partnerships With and Without Net Income:  GENERAL CONTRACTORS, TOTAL (032,035)

Dollar values in thousands, except averages

| | 1984 | | 1985 | |
|---|---|---|---|---|
| 1. Number of Partnerships | 25,574 | | 20,999 | |
| 2. Number of Partners | 65,095 | | 50,928 | |
| | | | | |
| 3. Total Assets | $11,750,740 | | $12,433,682 | |
| 4. Average total assets per Partnership | $459,480 | | $592,108 | |
| 5. Average total assets per Partner | $180,517 | | $244,142 | |
| | | | | |
| 6. Net Income, less Deficit | $1,113,145 | | $1,213,941 | |
| 7. Average per Partnership, total earnings | $43,536 | | $57,819 | |
| 8. Average per Partner, total earnings | $17,104 | | $23,840 | |
| | | | | |
| 9. Operating Income | $16,326,709 | | $14,193,418 | |
| Operating Costs | | | | |
| 10. Cost of sales & operations | $12,975,383 | 79.5% | $10,992,364 | 77.5% |
| 11. Salaries and wages | $320,774 | 2.0% | $283,368 | 2.0% |
| 12. Rent paid | $65,919 | 0.4% | $60,448 | 0.4% |
| 13. Interest paid | $372,544 | 2.3% | $265,564 | 1.9% |
| 14. Taxes paid | $116,253 | 0.7% | $80,478 | 0.6% |
| 15. Bad debts | $5,799 | 0.0% | $9,089 | 0.1% |
| 16. Repairs | $35,066 | 0.2% | $74,944 | 0.5% |
| 17. Depreciation | $151,180 | 0.9% | $146,842 | 1.0% |
| 18. Depletion | $455 | n.a. | $87 | n.a. |
| 19. Pension & profit sharing plans | $4,636 | 0.0% | $3,949 | 0.0% |
| 20. Employee benefits programs | $5,950 | 0.0% | $4,661 | 0.0% |
| 21. Other deductions | $831,757 | 5.1% | $777,421 | 5.5% |
| 22. Total operating costs | $14,886,074 | 91.2% | $12,699,228 | 89.5% |
| | | | | |
| Operating Income and Distribution | | | | |
| 23. Operating Income | $16,326,709 | 100.0% | $14,193,418 | 100.0% |
| 24. Less: Cost of sales and operations | $12,975,383 | 79.5% | $10,992,364 | 77.5% |
| 25. Gross operating profit | $3,351,326 | 20.5% | $3,201,054 | 22.6% |
| 26. Additional operating costs | $1,910,691 | 11.7% | $1,706,864 | 12.0% |
| 27. Net operating profit | $1,440,635 | 8.8% | $1,494,190 | 10.5% |
| 28. Less: Guaranteed payments to partners | $249,972 | | $196,793 | |
| 29. Distribution to partners | $1,190,663 | | $1,297,397 | |
| 30. Other charges | $77,877 | | $83,469 | |
| 31. Net change partners' capital | $1,112,786 | | $1,213,928 | |
| | | | | |
| Selected Ratios | | | | |
| 32. Coverage ratio: times interest earned | 2.9 | | 4.6 | |
| 33. Inventory turnover (times) | 4.5 | | 4.0 | |
| 34. Days' sales in inventory | 77.5 | | 95.3 | |
| 35. Average age of inventory (days) | 80.5 | | 90.3 | |
| 36. Return on assets, net inc., less def | 9.5% | | 9.8% | |
| 37. Return on assets, gross operating profit | 28.5% | | 25.8% | |
| 38. Return on assets, net operating profit | 12.3% | | 12.0% | |

Table 1: Partnerships With and Without Net Income:  038.  SPECIAL TRADE CONTRACTORS

Dollar values in thousands, except averages

|  | 1984 | | 1985 | |
|---|---|---|---|---|
| 1. Number of Partnerships | 39,001 | | 35,666 | |
| 2. Number of Partners | 108,083 | | 83,106 | |
| | | | | |
| 3. Total Assets | $2,032,516 | | $2,574,268 | |
| 4. Average total assets per Partnership | $52,114 | | $72,177 | |
| 5. Average total assets per Partner | $18,805 | | $30,976 | |
| | | | | |
| 6. Net Income, less Deficit | $1,053,985 | | $993,460 | |
| 7. Average per Partnership, total earnings | $27,029 | | $27,859 | |
| 8. Average per Partner, total earnings | $9,753 | | $11,956 | |
| | | | | |
| 9. Operating Income | $7,483,613 | | $8,093,815 | |
| Operating Costs | | | | |
| 10. Cost of sales & operations | $4,217,114 | 56.4% | $4,793,584 | 59.2% |
| 11. Salaries and wages | $515,210 | 6.9% | $488,136 | 6.0% |
| 12. Rent paid | $53,436 | 0.7% | $79,157 | 0.10% |
| 13. Interest paid | $102,683 | 1.4% | $107,413 | 1.3% |
| 14. Taxes paid | $106,982 | 1.4% | $134,576 | 1.7% |
| 15. Bad debts | $4,732 | 0.1% | $7,115 | 0.1% |
| 16. Repairs | $64,165 | 0.9% | $53,061 | 0.7% |
| 17. Depreciation | $300,343 | 4.0% | $280,344 | 3.5% |
| 18. Depletion | $290 | n.a. | $269 | n.a. |
| 19. Pension & profit sharing plans | $4,095 | 0.1% | $5,265 | 0.1% |
| 20. Employee benefits programs | $4,640 | 0.1% | $7,905 | 0.1% |
| 21. Other deductions | $899,463 | 12.0% | $950,783 | 11.8% |
| 22. Total operating costs | $6,273,891 | 83.8% | $6,908,484 | 85.4% |
| | | | | |
| Operating Income and Distribution | | | | |
| 23. Operating Income | $7,483,613 | 100.0% | $8,093,815 | 100.0% |
| 24. Less: Cost of sales and operations | $4,217,114 | 56.4% | $4,793,584 | 59.2% |
| 25. Gross operating profit | $3,266,499 | 43.7% | $3,300,231 | 40.8% |
| 26. Additional operating costs | $2,056,777 | 27.5% | $2,114,900 | 26.1% |
| 27. Net operating profit | $1,209,722 | 16.2% | $1,185,331 | 14.6% |
| 28. Less: Guaranteed payments to partners | $155,167 | | $173,756 | |
| 29. Distribution to partners | $1,054,555 | | $1,011,575 | |
| 30. Other charges | $1,309 | | $18,991 | |
| 31. Net change partners' capital | $1,053,246 | | $992,584 | |
| | | | | |
| Selected Ratios | | | | |
| 32. Coverage ratio: times interest earned | 10.8 | | 10.0 | |
| 33. Inventory turnover (times) | 11.9 | | 11.0 | |
| 34. Days' sales in inventory | 37.8 | | 39.3 | |
| 35. Average age of inventory (days) | 30.6 | | 33.1 | |
| 36. Return on assets, net inc., less def | 51.9% | | 38.6% | |
| 37. Return on assets, gross operating profit | 160.7% | | 128.2% | |
| 38. Return on assets, net operating profit | 59.5% | | 46.1% | |

Table 1: Partnerships With and Without Net Income:  039.  PLUMBING, HEATING, AND AIR CONDITIONING

Dollar values in thousands, except averages

|  | 1984 | | 1985 | |
|---|---|---|---|---|
| 1. Number of Partnerships | 4,252 | | 3,762 | |
| 2. Number of Partners | 11,279 | | 8,281 | |
| 3. Total Assets | $298,494 | | $329,124 | |
| 4. Average total assets per Partnership | $70,201 | | $87,486 | |
| 5. Average total assets per Partner | $26,465 | | $39,744 | |
| 6. Net Income, less Deficit | $252,801 | | $207,239 | |
| 7. Average per Partnership, total earnings | $59,456 | | $55,090 | |
| 8. Average per Partner, total earnings | $22,414 | | $25,027 | |
| 9. Operating Income | $1,230,657 | | $1,422,554 | |
| Operating Costs | | | | |
| 10. Cost of sales & operations | $716,868 | 58.3% | $954,483 | 67.1% |
| 11. Salaries and wages | $42,040 | 3.4% | $61,407 | 4.3% |
| 12. Rent paid | $14,295 | 1.2% | $19,557 | 1.4% |
| 13. Interest paid | $6,759 | 0.6% | $10,216 | 0.7% |
| 14. Taxes paid | $13,013 | 1.1% | $28,808 | 2.0% |
| 15. Bad debts | $1,900 | 0.2% | $554 | 0.0% |
| 16. Repairs | $3,742 | 0.3% | $4,075 | 0.3% |
| 17. Depreciation | $44,140 | 3.6% | $24,532 | 1.7% |
| 18. Depletion | $0 | n.a. | $0 | n.a. |
| 19. Pension & profit sharing plans | $0 | n.a. | $158 | 0.0% |
| 20. Employee benefits programs | $379 | 0.0% | $1,962 | 0.1% |
| 21. Other deductions | $126,848 | 10.3% | $100,919 | 7.1% |
| 22. Total operating costs | $969,984 | 78.8% | $1,207,296 | 84.9% |
| Operating Income and Distribution | | | | |
| 23. Operating Income | $1,230,657 | 100.0% | $1,422,554 | 100.0% |
| 24. Less: Cost of sales and operations | $716,868 | 58.3% | $954,483 | 67.1% |
| 25. Gross operating profit | $513,789 | 41.8% | $468,071 | 32.9% |
| 26. Additional operating costs | $253,116 | 20.6% | $252,813 | 17.8% |
| 27. Net operating profit | $260,673 | 21.2% | $215,258 | 15.1% |
| 28. Less: Guaranteed payments to partners | $7,686 | | $8,540 | |
| 29. Distribution to partners | $252,987 | | $206,718 | |
| 30. Other charges | $186 | | $104 | |
| 31. Net change partners' capital | $252,801 | | $206,614 | |
| Selected Ratios | | | | |
| 32. Coverage ratio:  times interest earned | 37.6 | | 20.1 | |
| 33. Inventory turnover (times) | 16.1 | | 10.3 | |
| 34. Days' sales in inventory | 29.9 | | 41.7 | |
| 35. Average age of inventory (days) | 22.7 | | 35.3 | |
| 36. Return on assets, net inc., less def | 84.7% | | 63.0% | |
| 37. Return on assets, gross operating profit | 172.1% | | 142.2% | |
| 38. Return on assets, net operating profit | 87.3% | | 65.4% | |

Table 1: Partnerships With and Without Net Income:  040.  PAINTING, PAPER HANGING AND DECORATING

Dollar values in thousands, except averages

|    |                                              | 1984      |        | 1985      |        |
|----|----------------------------------------------|-----------|--------|-----------|--------|
| 1. | Number of Partnerships                       | 6,345     |        | 6,515     |        |
| 2. | Number of Partners                           | 14,156    |        | 15,564    |        |
| 3. | Total Assets                                 | $98,408   |        | $137,242  |        |
| 4. | Average total assets per Partnership         | $15,510   |        | $21,066   |        |
| 5. | Average total assets per Partner             | $6,952    |        | $8,818    |        |
| 6. | Net Income, less Deficit                     | $181,855  |        | $170,053  |        |
| 7. | Average per Partnership, total earnings      | $28,665   |        | $26,102   |        |
| 8. | Average per Partner, total earnings          | $12,848   |        | $10,926   |        |
| 9. | Operating Income                             | $580,228  |        | $773,099  |        |
|    | Operating Costs                              |           |        |           |        |
| 10. | Cost of sales & operations                  | $211,148  | 36.4%  | $309,579  | 40.0%  |
| 11. | Salaries and wages                          | $53,653   | 9.3%   | $81,742   | 10.6%  |
| 12. | Rent paid                                   | $1,063    | 0.2%   | $2,615    | 0.3%   |
| 13. | Interest paid                               | $2,108    | 0.4%   | $4,061    | 0.5%   |
| 14. | Taxes paid                                  | $15,952   | 2.8%   | $14,505   | 1.9%   |
| 15. | Bad debts                                   | $0        | n.a.   | $28       | n.a.   |
| 16. | Repairs                                     | $955      | 0.2%   | $759      | 0.1%   |
| 17. | Depreciation                                | $8,840    | 1.5%   | $34,964   | 4.5%   |
| 18. | Depletion                                   | $0        | n.a.   | $0        | n.a.   |
| 19. | Pension & profit sharing plans              | $0        | n.a.   | $1,772    | 0.2%   |
| 20. | Employee benefits programs                  | $0        | n.a.   | $0        | n.a.   |
| 21. | Other deductions                            | $79,370   | 13.7%  | $151,930  | 19.7%  |
| 22. | Total operating costs                       | $373,089  | 64.3%  | $601,955  | 77.9%  |
|    | Operating Income and Distribution           |           |        |           |        |
| 23. | Operating Income                            | $580,228  | 100.0% | $773,099  | 100.0% |
| 24. | Less: Cost of sales and operations          | $211,148  | 36.4%  | $309,579  | 40.0%  |
| 25. | Gross operating profit                      | $369,080  | 63.6%  | $463,520  | 60.0%  |
| 26. | Additional operating costs                  | $161,941  | 27.9%  | $292,376  | 37.8%  |
| 27. | Net operating profit                        | $207,139  | 35.7%  | $171,144  | 22.1%  |
| 28. | Less: Guaranteed payments to partners       | $25,211   |        | $1,074    |        |
| 29. | Distribution to partners                    | $181,928  |        | $170,070  |        |
| 30. | Other charges                               | $73       |        | $16       |        |
| 31. | Net change partners' capital                | $181,855  |        | $170,054  |        |
|    | Selected Ratios                             |           |        |           |        |
| 32. | Coverage ratio: times interest earned       | 97.3      |        | 41.1      |        |
| 33. | Inventory turnover (times)                  | n.a.      |        | n.a.      |        |
| 34. | Days' sales in inventory                    | n.a.      |        | n.a.      |        |
| 35. | Average age of inventory (days)             | n.a.      |        | n.a.      |        |
| 36. | Return on assets, net inc., less def        | 184.8%    |        | 123.9%    |        |
| 37. | Return on assets, gross operating profit    | n.a.      |        | n.a.      |        |
| 38. | Return on assets, net operating profit      | 210.5%    |        | 124.7%    |        |

Table 1: Partnerships With and Without Net Income:   042.   MASONRY, STONE WORK, TILE SETTING, AND PLASTERING

Dollar values in thousands, except averages

|  | 1984 | | 1985 | |
|---|---|---|---|---|
| 1. Number of Partnerships | 4,199 | | 2,218 | |
| 2. Number of Partners | 9,072 | | 5,012 | |
| | | | | |
| 3. Total Assets | $96,867 | | $85,635 | |
| 4. Average total assets per Partnership | $23,069 | | $38,609 | |
| 5. Average total assets per Partner | $10,678 | | $17,086 | |
| | | | | |
| 6. Net Income, less Deficit | $80,023 | | $50,404 | |
| 7. Average per Partnership, total earnings | $19,064 | | $22,747 | |
| 8. Average per Partner, total earnings | $8,824 | | $10,066 | |
| | | | | |
| 9. Operating Income | $798,252 | | $672,533 | |
| Operating Costs | | | | |
| 10. Cost of sales & operations | $367,445 | 46.0% | $342,727 | 51.0% |
| 11. Salaries and wages | $158,353 | 19.8% | $80,855 | 12.0% |
| 12. Rent paid | $6,750 | 0.9% | $9,232 | 1.4% |
| 13. Interest paid | $12,204 | 1.5% | $6,434 | 0.10% |
| 14. Taxes paid | $12,407 | 1.6% | $9,590 | 1.4% |
| 15. Bad debts | $753 | 0.1% | $670 | 0.1% |
| 16. Repairs | $16,920 | 2.1% | $15,716 | 2.3% |
| 17. Depreciation | $16,755 | 2.1% | $16,397 | 2.4% |
| 18. Depletion | $263 | 0.0% | $235 | 0.0% |
| 19. Pension & profit sharing plans | $1,914 | 0.2% | $1,340 | 0.2% |
| 20. Employee benefits programs | $2,146 | 0.3% | $1,726 | 0.3% |
| 21. Other deductions | $96,877 | 12.1% | $78,835 | 11.7% |
| 22. Total operating costs | $692,787 | 86.8% | $563,757 | 83.8% |
| | | | | |
| Operating Income and Distribution | | | | |
| 23. Operating Income | $798,252 | 100.0% | $672,533 | 100.0% |
| 24. Less: Cost of sales and operations | $367,445 | 46.0% | $342,727 | 51.0% |
| 25. Gross operating profit | $430,807 | 54.0% | $329,806 | 49.0% |
| 26. Additional operating costs | $325,342 | 40.8% | $221,030 | 32.9% |
| 27. Net operating profit | $105,465 | 13.2% | $108,776 | 16.2% |
| 28. Less: Guaranteed payments to partners | $25,431 | | $48,301 | |
| 29. Distribution to partners | $80,034 | | $60,475 | |
| 30. Other charges | $11 | | $10,072 | |
| 31. Net change partners' capital | $80,023 | | $50,403 | |
| | | | | |
| Selected Ratios | | | | |
| 32. Coverage ratio: times interest earned | 7.6 | | 15.9 | |
| 33. Inventory turnover (times) | 21.7 | | 15.7 | |
| 34. Days' sales in inventory | 29.3 | | 36.8 | |
| 35. Average age of inventory (days) | 16.8 | | 23.2 | |
| 36. Return on assets, net inc., less def | 82.6% | | 58.9% | |
| 37. Return on assets, gross operating profit | n.a. | | n.a. | |
| 38. Return on assets, net operating profit | 108.9% | | 127.0% | |

*Page 38*

Table 1: Partnerships With and Without Net Income:  CONTRACTORS NOT ELSEWHERE CLASSIFIED (041,043,044,046,047)

Dollar values in thousands, except averages

|  |  | 1984 |  | 1985 |  |
|---|---|---|---|---|---|
| 1. | Number of Partnerships | 24,206 | | 23,171 | |
| 2. | Number of Partners | 73,577 | | 54,250 | |
| 3. | Total Assets | $1,538,747 | | $2,022,629 | |
| 4. | Average total assets per Partnership | $63,569 | | $87,291 | |
| 5. | Average total assets per Partner | $20,913 | | $37,283 | |
| 6. | Net Income, less Deficit | $539,305 | | $565,764 | |
| 7. | Average per Partnership, total earnings | $22,284 | | $24,422 | |
| 8. | Average per Partner, total earnings | $7,331 | | $10,431 | |
| 9. | Operating Income | $4,874,476 | | $5,225,629 | |
|  | Operating Costs | | | | |
| 10. | Cost of sales & operations | $2,921,653 | 59.9% | $3,186,795 | 61.0% |
| 11. | Salaries and wages | $261,165 | 5.4% | $264,133 | 5.1% |
| 12. | Rent paid | $31,328 | 0.6% | $47,753 | 0.9% |
| 13. | Interest paid | $81,612 | 1.7% | $86,702 | 1.7% |
| 14. | Taxes paid | $65,610 | 1.4% | $81,674 | 1.6% |
| 15. | Bad debts | $2,078 | 0.0% | $5,862 | 0.1% |
| 16. | Repairs | $42,548 | 0.9% | $32,510 | 0.6% |
| 17. | Depreciation | $230,609 | 4.7% | $204,451 | 3.9% |
| 18. | Depletion | $27 | n.a. | $34 | n.a. |
| 19. | Pension & profit sharing plans | $2,180 | 0.0% | $1,994 | 0.0% |
| 20. | Employee benefits programs | $2,115 | 0.0% | $4,217 | 0.1% |
| 21. | Other deductions | $596,368 | 12.2% | $619,101 | 11.9% |
| 22. | Total operating costs | $4,238,031 | 86.9% | $4,535,477 | 86.8% |
|  | Operating Income and Distribution | | | | |
| 23. | Operating Income | $4,874,476 | 100.0% | $5,225,629 | 100.0% |
| 24. | Less:  Cost of sales and operations | $2,921,653 | 59.9% | $3,186,795 | 61.0% |
| 25. | Gross operating profit | $1,952,823 | 40.1% | $2,038,834 | 39.0% |
| 26. | Additional operating costs | $1,316,378 | 27.0% | $1,348,682 | 25.8% |
| 27. | Net operating profit | $636,445 | 13.1% | $690,152 | 13.2% |
| 28. | Less:  Guaranteed payments to partners | $96,838 | | $115,841 | |
| 29. | Distribution to partners | $539,607 | | $574,311 | |
| 30. | Other charges | $1,040 | | $8,798 | |
| 31. | Net change partners' capital | $538,567 | | $565,513 | |
|  | Selected Ratios | | | | |
| 32. | Coverage ratio:  times interest earned | 6.8 | | 7.0 | |
| 33. | Inventory turnover (times) | 10.1 | | 9.9 | |
| 34. | Days' sales in inventory | 43.4 | | 42.7 | |
| 35. | Average age of inventory (days) | 36.3 | | 36.7 | |
| 36. | Return on assets, net inc., less def | 35.1% | | 28.0% | |
| 37. | Return on assets, gross operating profit | 126.9% | | 100.8% | |
| 38. | Return on assets, net operating profit | 41.4% | | 34.1% | |

Table 1: Partnerships With and Without Net Income: 049. MANUFACTURING

Dollar values in thousands, except averages

|  |  | 1984 |  | 1985 |  |
|---|---|---|---|---|---|
| 1. | Number of Partnerships | 29,606 | | 29,980 | |
| 2. | Number of Partners | 93,601 | | 105,007 | |
| 3. | Total Assets | $19,574,057 | | $24,837,834 | |
| 4. | Average total assets per Partnership | $661,152 | | $828,480 | |
| 5. | Average total assets per Partner | $209,122 | | $236,535 | |
| 6. | Net Income, less Deficit | ($1,100,943) | | ($1,085,187) | |
| 7. | Average per Partnership, total earnings | ($37,182) | | ($36,192) | |
| 8. | Average per Partner, total earnings | ($11,761) | | ($10,333) | |
| 9. | Operating Income | $18,944,907 | | $23,139,935 | |
|  | Operating Costs |  |  |  |  |
| 10. | Cost of sales & operations | $14,237,424 | 75.2% | $16,965,616 | 73.3% |
| 11. | Salaries and wages | $927,383 | 4.9% | $1,316,537 | 5.7% |
| 12. | Rent paid | $205,701 | 1.1% | $360,403 | 1.6% |
| 13. | Interest paid | $614,043 | 3.2% | $842,224 | 3.6% |
| 14. | Taxes paid | $209,394 | 1.1% | $250,427 | 1.1% |
| 15. | Bad debts | $37,025 | 0.2% | $44,331 | 0.2% |
| 16. | Repairs | $160,486 | 0.9% | $142,579 | 0.6% |
| 17. | Depreciation | $1,092,447 | 5.8% | $934,692 | 4.0% |
| 18. | Depletion | $37,627 | 0.2% | $7,329 | 0.0% |
| 19. | Pension & profit sharing plans | $24,576 | 0.1% | $41,251 | 0.2% |
| 20. | Employee benefits programs | $62,247 | 0.3% | $98,489 | 0.4% |
| 21. | Other deductions | $2,241,024 | 11.8% | $2,993,173 | 12.9% |
| 22. | Total operating costs | $19,850,749 | 104.8% | $23,999,427 | 103.7% |
|  | Operating Income and Distribution |  |  |  |  |
| 23. | Operating Income | $18,944,907 | 100.0% | $23,139,935 | 100.0% |
| 24. | Less: Cost of sales and operations | $14,237,424 | 75.2% | $16,965,616 | 73.3% |
| 25. | Gross operating profit | $4,707,483 | 24.9% | $6,174,319 | 26.7% |
| 26. | Additional operating costs | $5,613,325 | 29.6% | $7,033,811 | 30.4% |
| 27. | Net operating profit | ($905,842) | (4.8%) | ($859,492) | (3.7%) |
| 28. | Less: Guaranteed payments to partners | $132,861 | | $154,209 | |
| 29. | Distribution to partners | ($1,038,703) | | ($1,013,701) | |
| 30. | Other charges | $63,611 | | $73,861 | |
| 31. | Net change partners' capital | ($1,102,314) | | ($1,087,562) | |
|  | Selected Ratios |  |  |  |  |
| 32. | Coverage ratio: times interest earned | (2.5) | | (2.0) | |
| 33. | Inventory turnover (times) | 7.9 | | 6.6 | |
| 34. | Days' sales in inventory | 53.4 | | 58.7 | |
| 35. | Average age of inventory (days) | 46.0 | | 55.2 | |
| 36. | Return on assets, net inc., less def | (5.6%) | | (4.4%) | |
| 37. | Return on assets, gross operating profit | 24.1% | | 24.9% | |
| 38. | Return on assets, net operating profit | (4.6%) | | (3.5%) | |

Table 1: Partnerships With and Without Net Income:   054.   LUMBER AND WOOD PRODUCTS, EXCEPT FURNITURE

Dollar values in thousands, except averages

|  | | 1984 | | 1985 | |
|---|---|---|---|---|---|
| 1. | Number of Partnerships | 2,162 | | 1,324 | |
| 2. | Number of Partners | 6,534 | | 7,080 | |
| | | | | | |
| 3. | Total Assets | $2,053,582 | | $3,918,992 | |
| 4. | Average total assets per Partnership | $949,853 | | $2,959,964 | |
| 5. | Average total assets per Partner | $314,292 | | $553,530 | |
| | | | | | |
| 6. | Net Income, less Deficit | ($219,853) | | ($151,373) | |
| 7. | Average per Partnership, total earnings | ($101,681) | | ($114,316) | |
| 8. | Average per Partner, total earnings | ($33,645) | | ($21,378) | |
| | | | | | |
| 9. | Operating Income | $2,254,788 | | $2,355,062 | |
| | Operating Costs | | | | |
| 10. | Cost of sales & operations | $1,760,942 | 78.1% | $1,838,378 | 78.1% |
| 11. | Salaries and wages | $69,535 | 3.1% | $80,334 | 3.4% |
| 12. | Rent paid | $27,123 | 1.2% | $21,170 | 0.9% |
| 13. | Interest paid | $146,083 | 6.5% | $145,947 | 6.2% |
| 14. | Taxes paid | $43,364 | 1.9% | $27,943 | 1.2% |
| 15. | Bad debts | $5,919 | 0.3% | $2,036 | 0.1% |
| 16. | Repairs | $74,339 | 3.3% | $24,173 | 1.0% |
| 17. | Depreciation | $120,668 | 5.4% | $118,729 | 5.0% |
| 18. | Depletion | $33,148 | 1.5% | $1,316 | 0.1% |
| 19. | Pension & profit sharing plans | $2,411 | 0.1% | $2,713 | 0.1% |
| 20. | Employee benefits programs | $4,699 | 0.2% | $6,815 | 0.3% |
| 21. | Other deductions | $160,308 | 7.1% | $189,037 | 8.0% |
| 22. | Total operating costs | $2,448,833 | 108.6% | $2,458,886 | 104.4% |
| | | | | | |
| | Operating Income and Distribution | | | | |
| 23. | Operating Income | $2,254,788 | 100.0% | $2,355,062 | 100.0% |
| 24. | Less: Cost of sales and operations | $1,760,942 | 78.1% | $1,838,378 | 78.1% |
| 25. | Gross operating profit | $493,846 | 21.9% | $516,684 | 21.9% |
| 26. | Additional operating costs | $687,891 | 30.5% | $620,508 | 26.4% |
| 27. | Net operating profit | ($194,045) | (8.6%) | ($103,824) | (4.4%) |
| 28. | Less: Guaranteed payments to partners | $18,488 | | $18,994 | |
| 29. | Distribution to partners | ($212,533) | | ($122,818) | |
| 30. | Other charges | $7,615 | | $28,850 | |
| 31. | Net change partners' capital | ($220,148) | | ($151,668) | |
| | | | | | |
| | Selected Ratios | | | | |
| 32. | Coverage ratio: times interest earned | (2.3) | | (1.7) | |
| 33. | Inventory turnover (times) | 8.3 | | 8.9 | |
| 34. | Days' sales in inventory | 44.4 | | 43.7 | |
| 35. | Average age of inventory (days) | 43.8 | | 41.2 | |
| 36. | Return on assets, net inc., less def | (10.7%) | | (3.9%) | |
| 37. | Return on assets, gross operating profit | 24.1% | | 13.2% | |
| 38. | Return on assets, net operating profit | (9.5%) | | (2.7%) | |

*Page 41*

Table 1: Partnerships With and Without Net Income:  056.   PRINTING, PUBLISHING, AND ALLIED INDUSTRIES

Dollar values in thousands, except averages

|  |  | 1984 |  | 1985 |  |
|---|---|---|---|---|---|
| 1. | Number of Partnerships | 4,414 | | 5,634 | |
| 2. | Number of Partners | 19,094 | | 27,677 | |
| 3. | Total Assets | $1,260,481 | | $1,692,079 | |
| 4. | Average total assets per Partnership | $285,564 | | $300,334 | |
| 5. | Average total assets per Partner | $66,015 | | $61,137 | |
| 6. | Net Income, less Deficit | $34,818 | | $118,397 | |
| 7. | Average per Partnership, total earnings | $7,897 | | $21,021 | |
| 8. | Average per Partner, total earnings | $1,826 | | $4,279 | |
| 9. | Operating Income | $1,688,556 | | $2,448,342 | |
|  | Operating Costs | | | | |
| 10. | Cost of sales & operations | $788,160 | 46.7% | $945,419 | 38.6% |
| 11. | Salaries and wages | $227,082 | 13.5% | $329,716 | 13.5% |
| 12. | Rent paid | $20,046 | 1.2% | $67,822 | 2.8% |
| 13. | Interest paid | $42,849 | 2.5% | $57,970 | 2.4% |
| 14. | Taxes paid | $29,026 | 1.7% | $47,020 | 1.9% |
| 15. | Bad debts | $6,245 | 0.4% | $12,263 | 0.5% |
| 16. | Repairs | $5,883 | 0.4% | $11,233 | 0.5% |
| 17. | Depreciation | $40,170 | 2.4% | $55,356 | 2.3% |
| 18. | Depletion | $0 | n.a. | $0 | n.a. |
| 19. | Pension & profit sharing plans | $5,131 | 0.3% | $7,006 | 0.3% |
| 20. | Employee benefits programs | $13,634 | 0.8% | $18,076 | 0.7% |
| 21. | Other deductions | $436,617 | 25.9% | $738,053 | 30.2% |
| 22. | Total operating costs | $1,615,288 | 95.7% | $2,290,594 | 93.6% |
|  | Operating Income and Distribution | | | | |
| 23. | Operating Income | $1,688,556 | 100.0% | $2,448,342 | 100.0% |
| 24. | Less:  Cost of sales and operations | $788,160 | 46.7% | $945,419 | 38.6% |
| 25. | Gross operating profit | $900,396 | 53.3% | $1,502,923 | 61.4% |
| 26. | Additional operating costs | $827,128 | 49.0% | $1,345,175 | 54.9% |
| 27. | Net operating profit | $73,268 | 4.3% | $157,748 | 6.4% |
| 28. | Less:  Guaranteed payments to partners | $38,559 | | $34,597 | |
| 29. | Distribution to partners | $34,709 | | $123,151 | |
| 30. | Other charges | $336 | | $5,415 | |
| 31. | Net change partners' capital | $34,373 | | $117,736 | |
|  | Selected Ratios | | | | |
| 32. | Coverage ratio:  times interest earned | 0.7 | | 1.7 | |
| 33. | Inventory turnover (times) | 18.4 | | 11.3 | |
| 34. | Days' sales in inventory | 20.9 | | 37.3 | |
| 35. | Average age of inventory (days) | 19.9 | | 32.4 | |
| 36. | Return on assets, net inc., less def | 2.8% | | 7.0% | |
| 37. | Return on assets, gross operating profit | 71.4% | | 88.8% | |
| 38. | Return on assets, net operating profit | 5.8% | | 9.3% | |

Table 1: Partnerships With and Without Net Income: 062. MACHINERY, EXCEPT ELECTRICAL

Dollar values in thousands, except averages

|  |  | 1984 |  | 1985 |  |
| --- | --- | --- | --- | --- | --- |
| 1. | Number of Partnerships | 1,018 |  | 317 |  |
| 2. | Number of Partners | 2,299 |  | 1,364 |  |
| 3. | Total Assets | $337,851 |  | $779,782 |  |
| 4. | Average total assets per Partnership | $331,877 |  | $2,459,880 |  |
| 5. | Average total assets per Partner | $146,956 |  | $571,688 |  |
| 6. | Net Income, less Deficit | $39,844 |  | ($77,348) |  |
| 7. | Average per Partnership, total earnings | $39,142 |  | ($243,961) |  |
| 8. | Average per Partner, total earnings | $17,332 |  | ($56,698) |  |
| 9. | Operating Income | $240,360 |  | $517,839 |  |
|  | Operating Costs |  |  |  |  |
| 10. | Cost of sales & operations | $140,619 | 58.5% | $352,000 | 68.0% |
| 11. | Salaries and wages | $5,890 | 2.5% | $35,594 | 6.9% |
| 12. | Rent paid | $1,223 | 0.5% | $6,824 | 1.3% |
| 13. | Interest paid | $11,104 | 4.6% | $41,005 | 7.9% |
| 14. | Taxes paid | $829 | 0.3% | $6,555 | 1.3% |
| 15. | Bad debts | $191 | 0.1% | $1,347 | 0.3% |
| 16. | Repairs | $339 | 0.1% | $2,895 | 0.6% |
| 17. | Depreciation | $7,742 | 3.2% | $61,179 | 11.8% |
| 18. | Depletion | $0 | n.a. | $0 | n.a. |
| 19. | Pension & profit sharing plans | $259 | 0.1% | $1,557 | 0.3% |
| 20. | Employee benefits programs | $102 | 0.0% | $2,548 | 0.5% |
| 21. | Other deductions | $29,753 | 12.4% | $71,232 | 13.8% |
| 22. | Total operating costs | $198,051 | 82.4% | $582,736 | 112.5% |
| | Operating Income and Distribution |  |  |  |  |
| 23. | Operating Income | $240,360 | 100.0% | $517,839 | 100.0% |
| 24. | Less: Cost of sales and operations | $140,619 | 58.5% | $352,000 | 68.0% |
| 25. | Gross operating profit | $99,741 | 41.5% | $165,839 | 32.0% |
| 26. | Additional operating costs | $57,432 | 23.9% | $230,736 | 44.6% |
| 27. | Net operating profit | $42,309 | 17.6% | ($64,897) | (12.5%) |
| 28. | Less: Guaranteed payments to partners | $2,464 |  | $12,451 |  |
| 29. | Distribution to partners | $39,845 |  | ($77,348) |  |
| 30. | Other charges | $0 |  | $0 |  |
| 31. | Net change partners' capital | $39,845 |  | ($77,348) |  |
| | Selected Ratios |  |  |  |  |
| 32. | Coverage ratio: times interest earned | 2.8 |  | (2.6) |  |
| 33. | Inventory turnover (times) | 4.7 |  | 3.3 |  |
| 34. | Days' sales in inventory | 72.9 |  | 116.9 |  |
| 35. | Average age of inventory (days) | 77.1 |  | 111.5 |  |
| 36. | Return on assets, net inc., less def | 11.8% |  | (9.9%) |  |
| 37. | Return on assets, gross operating profit | 29.5% |  | 21.3% |  |
| 38. | Return on assets, net operating profit | 12.5% |  | (8.3%) |  |

Table 1: Partnerships With and Without Net Income:  OTHER MANUFACTURING INDUSTRIES (050,053,055,057-061,063,064,065,066)

Dollar values in thousands, except averages

|    |                                           | 1984 | | 1985 | |
|----|-------------------------------------------|------|-----|------|-----|
| 1. | Number of Partnerships                    | 22,012 | | 22,705 | |
| 2. | Number of Partners                        | 65,673 | | 68,886 | |
| 3. | Total Assets                              | $15,922,143 | | $18,446,981 | |
| 4. |   Average total assets per Partnership    | $723,339 | | $812,463 | |
| 5. |   Average total assets per Partner        | $242,446 | | $267,790 | |
| 6. | Net Income, less Deficit                  | ($955,752) | | ($974,861) | |
| 7. |   Average per Partnership, total earnings | ($43,416) | | ($42,932) | |
| 8. |   Average per Partner, total earnings     | ($14,552) | | ($14,151) | |
| 9. | Operating Income                          | $14,761,203 | | $17,818,692 | |
|    | Operating Costs                           | | | | |
| 10. |   Cost of sales & operations             | $11,547,703 | 78.2% | $13,829,819 | 77.6% |
| 11. |   Salaries and wages                     | $624,876 | 4.2% | $870,893 | 4.9% |
| 12. |   Rent paid                              | $157,310 | 1.1% | $264,587 | 1.5% |
| 13. |   Interest paid                          | $414,007 | 2.8% | $597,311 | 3.4% |
| 14. |   Taxes paid                             | $136,175 | 0.9% | $168,910 | 0.10% |
| 15. |   Bad debts                              | $24,670 | 0.2% | $28,685 | 0.2% |
| 16. |   Repairs                                | $79,925 | 0.5% | $104,278 | 0.6% |
| 17. |   Depreciation                           | $923,861 | 6.3% | $699,428 | 3.9% |
| 18. |   Depletion                              | $4,479 | 0.0% | $6,012 | 0.0% |
| 19. |   Pension & profit sharing plans         | $16,775 | 0.1% | $29,975 | 0.2% |
| 20. |   Employee benefits programs             | $43,812 | 0.3% | $71,050 | 0.4% |
| 21. |   Other deductions                       | $1,614,346 | 10.9% | $1,994,845 | 11.2% |
| 22. |   Total operating costs                  | $15,588,572 | 105.6% | $18,667,214 | 104.8% |
|    | Operating Income and Distribution        | | | | |
| 23. |   Operating Income                       | $14,761,203 | 100.0% | $17,818,692 | 100.0% |
| 24. |     Less:  Cost of sales and operations  | $11,547,703 | 78.2% | $13,829,819 | 77.6% |
| 25. |   Gross operating profit                 | $3,213,500 | 21.8% | $3,988,873 | 22.4% |
| 26. |     Additional operating costs           | $4,040,869 | 27.4% | $4,837,395 | 27.2% |
| 27. |   Net operating profit                   | ($827,369) | (5.6%) | ($848,522) | (4.8%) |
| 28. |     Less:  Guaranteed payments to partners | $73,351 | | $88,167 | |
| 29. |   Distribution to partners               | ($900,720) | | ($936,689) | |
| 30. |   Other charges                          | $55,664 | | $39,594 | |
| 31. |   Net change partners' capital           | ($956,384) | | ($976,283) | |
|    | Selected Ratios                          | | | | |
| 32. |   Coverage ratio:  times interest earned | (3.0) | | (2.4) | |
| 33. |   Inventory turnover (times)             | 7.7 | | 6.4 | |
| 34. |   Days' sales in inventory               | 56.7 | | 60.7 | |
| 35. |   Average age of inventory (days)        | 47.7 | | 57.1 | |
| 36. |   Return on assets, net inc., less def   | (6.0%) | | (5.3%) | |
| 37. |   Return on assets, gross operating profit | 20.2% | | 21.6% | |
| 38. |   Return on assets, net operating profit | (5.2%) | | (4.6%) | |

Table 1: Partnerships With and Without Net Income:  067.  TRANSPORTATION, COMMUNICATION ELECTRIC, GAS, AND SANITARY SERVICES

Dollar values in thousands, except averages

|  |  | 1984 |  | 1985 |  |
|---|---|---|---|---|---|
| 1. | Number of Partnerships | 20,578 |  | 24,970 |  |
| 2. | Number of Partners | 142,091 |  | 186,326 |  |
| 3. | Total Assets | $21,109,071 |  | $26,467,744 |  |
| 4. | Average total assets per Partnership | $1,025,808 |  | $1,059,982 |  |
| 5. | Average total assets per Partner | $148,560 |  | $142,051 |  |
| 6. | Net Income, less Deficit | ($2,007,032) |  | ($3,066,314) |  |
| 7. | Average per Partnership, total earnings | ($97,528) |  | ($122,794) |  |
| 8. | Average per Partner, total earnings | ($14,124) |  | ($16,456) |  |
| 9. | Operating Income | $11,324,902 |  | $11,747,519 |  |
|  | Operating Costs |  |  |  |  |
| 10. | Cost of sales & operations | $5,572,292 | 49.2% | $4,290,900 | 36.5% |
| 11. | Salaries and wages | $687,830 | 6.1% | $799,843 | 6.8% |
| 12. | Rent paid | $189,893 | 1.7% | $243,365 | 2.1% |
| 13. | Interest paid | $1,253,616 | 11.1% | $1,308,508 | 11.1% |
| 14. | Taxes paid | $183,646 | 1.6% | $237,567 | 2.0% |
| 15. | Bad debts | $44,037 | 0.4% | $88,689 | 0.8% |
| 16. | Repairs | $151,040 | 1.3% | $211,784 | 1.8% |
| 17. | Depreciation | $1,872,904 | 16.5% | $2,631,234 | 22.4% |
| 18. | Depletion | $3,848 | 0.0% | $0 | n.a. |
| 19. | Pension & profit sharing plans | $9,273 | 0.1% | $15,205 | 0.1% |
| 20. | Employee benefits programs | $40,050 | 0.4% | $39,515 | 0.3% |
| 21. | Other deductions | $2,961,912 | 26.2% | $4,448,585 | 37.9% |
| 22. | Total operating costs | $12,970,348 | 114.5% | $14,315,360 | 121.9% |
|  | Operating Income and Distribution |  |  |  |  |
| 23. | Operating Income | $11,324,902 | 100.0% | $11,747,519 | 100.0% |
| 24. | Less: Cost of sales and operations | $5,572,292 | 49.2% | $4,290,900 | 36.5% |
| 25. | Gross operating profit | $5,752,610 | 50.8% | $7,456,619 | 63.5% |
| 26. | Additional operating costs | $7,398,056 | 65.3% | $10,024,460 | 85.3% |
| 27. | Net operating profit | ($1,645,446) | (14.5%) | ($2,567,841) | (21.9%) |
| 28. | Less: Guaranteed payments to partners | $102,303 |  | $157,175 |  |
| 29. | Distribution to partners | ($1,747,749) |  | ($2,725,016) |  |
| 30. | Other charges | $259,291 |  | $341,463 |  |
| 31. | Net change partners' capital | ($2,007,040) |  | ($3,066,479) |  |
|  | Selected Ratios |  |  |  |  |
| 32. | Coverage ratio:  times interest earned | (2.3) |  | (3.0) |  |
| 33. | Inventory turnover (times) | n.a. |  | n.a. |  |
| 34. | Days' sales in inventory | n.a. |  | n.a. |  |
| 35. | Average age of inventory (days) | n.a. |  | n.a. |  |
| 36. | Return on assets, net inc., less def | (9.5%) |  | (11.6%) |  |
| 37. | Return on assets, gross operating profit | 27.3% |  | 28.2% |  |
| 38. | Return on assets, net operating profit | (7.8%) |  | (9.7%) |  |

Table 1: Partnerships With and Without Net Income:  TRANSPORTATION, TOTAL (068,071,074,075,076)

Dollar values in thousands, except averages

| | | 1984 | | 1985 | |
|---|---|---|---|---|---|
| 1. | Number of Partnerships | 13,783 | | 17,406 | |
| 2. | Number of Partners | 54,697 | | 61,722 | |
| 3. | Total Assets | $6,385,163 | | $6,932,879 | |
| 4. | Average total assets per Partnership | $463,264 | | $398,304 | |
| 5. | Average total assets per Partner | $116,737 | | $112,324 | |
| 6. | Net Income, less Deficit | $345,598 | | $424,697 | |
| 7. | Average per Partnership, total earnings | $25,080 | | $24,405 | |
| 8. | Average per Partner, total earnings | $6,320 | | $6,882 | |
| 9. | Operating Income | $7,100,782 | | $6,135,591 | |
| | Operating Costs | | | | |
| 10. | Cost of sales & operations | $4,038,167 | 56.9% | $2,576,362 | 42.0% |
| 11. | Salaries and wages | $245,211 | 3.5% | $273,534 | 4.5% |
| 12. | Rent paid | $68,594 | 0.10% | $83,446 | 1.4% |
| 13. | Interest paid | $376,289 | 5.3% | $384,839 | 6.3% |
| 14. | Taxes paid | $72,709 | 1.0% | $89,873 | 1.5% |
| 15. | Bad debts | $4,805 | 0.1% | $3,326 | 0.1% |
| 16. | Repairs | $119,806 | 1.7% | $140,777 | 2.3% |
| 17. | Depreciation | $636,551 | 9.0% | $826,879 | 13.5% |
| 18. | Depletion | $0 | n.a. | $0 | n.a. |
| 19. | Pension & profit sharing plans | $2,539 | 0.0% | $8,320 | 0.1% |
| 20. | Employee benefits programs | $13,855 | 0.2% | $13,799 | 0.2% |
| 21. | Other deductions | $1,026,501 | 14.5% | $1,137,900 | 18.6% |
| 22. | Total operating costs | $6,605,028 | 93.0% | $5,539,217 | 90.3% |
| | Operating Income and Distribution | | | | |
| 23. | Operating Income | $7,100,782 | 100.0% | $6,135,591 | 100.0% |
| 24. | Less:  Cost of sales and operations | $4,038,167 | 56.9% | $2,576,362 | 42.0% |
| 25. | Gross operating profit | $3,062,615 | 43.1% | $3,559,229 | 58.0% |
| 26. | Additional operating costs | $2,566,861 | 36.2% | $2,962,855 | 48.3% |
| 27. | Net operating profit | $495,754 | 7.0% | $596,374 | 9.7% |
| 28. | Less:  Guaranteed payments to partners | $81,447 | | $99,407 | |
| 29. | Distribution to partners | $414,307 | | $496,967 | |
| 30. | Other charges | $68,710 | | $72,432 | |
| 31. | Net change partners' capital | $345,597 | | $424,535 | |
| | Selected Ratios | | | | |
| 32. | Coverage ratio:  times interest earned | 0.3 | | 0.6 | |
| 33. | Inventory turnover (times) | n.a. | | n.a. | |
| 34. | Days' sales in inventory | n.a. | | n.a. | |
| 35. | Average age of inventory (days) | n.a. | | n.a. | |
| 36. | Return on assets, net inc., less def | 5.4% | | 6.1% | |
| 37. | Return on assets, gross operating profit | 48.0% | | 51.3% | |
| 38. | Return on assets, net operating profit | 7.8% | | 8.6% | |

Table 1: Partnerships With and Without Net Income:  071.  TRUCKING AND WAREHOUSING

Dollar values in thousands, except averages

|  |  | 1984 |  | 1985 |  |
|---|---|---|---|---|---|
| 1. | Number of Partnerships | 8,980 | | 12,992 | |
| 2. | Number of Partners | 33,285 | | 41,750 | |
| 3. | Total Assets | $1,561,858 | | $1,610,405 | |
| 4. | Average total assets per Partnership | $173,926 | | $123,954 | |
| 5. | Average total assets per Partner | $46,924 | | $38,573 | |
| 6. | Net Income, less Deficit | $116,856 | | $148,274 | |
| 7. | Average per Partnership, total earnings | $13,021 | | $11,418 | |
| 8. | Average per Partner, total earnings | $3,513 | | $3,553 | |
| 9. | Operating Income | $3,343,131 | | $1,906,560 | |
|  | Operating Costs | | | | |
| 10. | Cost of sales & operations | $2,043,105 | 61.1% | $437,995 | 23.0% |
| 11. | Salaries and wages | $160,215 | 4.8% | $137,397 | 7.2% |
| 12. | Rent paid | $51,001 | 1.5% | $54,998 | 2.9% |
| 13. | Interest paid | $95,949 | 2.9% | $88,776 | 4.7% |
| 14. | Taxes paid | $46,178 | 1.4% | $47,316 | 2.5% |
| 15. | Bad debts | $867 | 0.0% | $1,009 | 0.1% |
| 16. | Repairs | $91,724 | 2.7% | $88,303 | 4.6% |
| 17. | Depreciation | $187,645 | 5.6% | $293,295 | 15.4% |
| 18. | Depletion | $0 | n.a. | $0 | n.a. |
| 19. | Pension & profit sharing plans | $1,325 | 0.0% | $875 | 0.1% |
| 20. | Employee benefits programs | $12,180 | 0.4% | $9,670 | 0.5% |
| 21. | Other deductions | $431,625 | 12.9% | $525,788 | 27.6% |
| 22. | Total operating costs | $3,121,814 | 93.4% | $1,685,582 | 88.4% |
|  | Operating Income and Distribution | | | | |
| 23. | Operating Income | $3,343,131 | 100.0% | $1,906,560 | 100.0% |
| 24. | Less: Cost of sales and operations | $2,043,105 | 61.1% | $437,995 | 23.0% |
| 25. | Gross operating profit | $1,300,026 | 38.9% | $1,468,565 | 77.0% |
| 26. | Additional operating costs | $1,078,709 | 32.3% | $1,247,587 | 65.4% |
| 27. | Net operating profit | $221,317 | 6.6% | $220,978 | 11.6% |
| 28. | Less: Guaranteed payments to partners | $73,982 | | $62,854 | |
| 29. | Distribution to partners | $147,335 | | $158,124 | |
| 30. | Other charges | $30,480 | | $10,010 | |
| 31. | Net change partners' capital | $116,855 | | $148,114 | |
|  | Selected Ratios | | | | |
| 32. | Coverage ratio: times interest earned | 1.3 | | 1.5 | |
| 33. | Inventory turnover (times) | n.a. | | 71.3 | |
| 34. | Days' sales in inventory | n.a. | | 7.3 | |
| 35. | Average age of inventory (days) | n.a. | | 5.1 | |
| 36. | Return on assets, net inc., less def | 7.5% | | 9.2% | |
| 37. | Return on assets, gross operating profit | 83.2% | | 91.2% | |
| 38. | Return on assets, net operating profit | 14.2% | | 13.7% | |

*Page 47*

Table 1: Partnerships With and Without Net Income:  OTHER TRANSPORTATION (069,070,074,075,076)

Dollar values in thousands, except averages

|  |  | 1984 |  | 1985 |  |
|---|---|---|---|---|---|
| 1. | Number of Partnerships | 3,803 | | 4,414 | |
| 2. | Number of Partners | 21,412 | | 19,973 | |
| 3. | Total Assets | $4,823,305 | | $5,322,474 | |
| 4. | Average total assets per Partnership | $1,268,290 | | $1,205,816 | |
| 5. | Average total assets per Partner | $225,262 | | $266,483 | |
| 6. | Net Income, less Deficit | $228,742 | | $276,422 | |
| 7. | Average per Partnership, total earnings | $60,150 | | $62,632 | |
| 8. | Average per Partner, total earnings | $10,683 | | $13,842 | |
| 9. | Operating Income | $3,757,651 | | $4,229,031 | |
|  | Operating Costs | | | | |
| 10. | Cost of sales & operations | $1,995,062 | 53.1% | $2,138,367 | 50.6% |
| 11. | Salaries and wages | $84,997 | 2.3% | $136,137 | 3.2% |
| 12. | Rent paid | $17,593 | 0.5% | $28,448 | 0.7% |
| 13. | Interest paid | $280,340 | 7.5% | $296,062 | 7.0% |
| 14. | Taxes paid | $26,530 | 0.7% | $42,557 | 1.0% |
| 15. | Bad debts | $3,938 | 0.1% | $2,317 | 0.1% |
| 16. | Repairs | $28,082 | 0.8% | $52,474 | 1.2% |
| 17. | Depreciation | $448,906 | 12.0% | $533,584 | 12.6% |
| 18. | Depletion | $0 | n.a. | $0 | n.a. |
| 19. | Pension & profit sharing plans | $1,214 | 0.0% | $7,446 | 0.2% |
| 20. | Employee benefits programs | $1,675 | 0.0% | $4,129 | 0.1% |
| 21. | Other deductions | $594,876 | 15.8% | $612,112 | 14.5% |
| 22. | Total operating costs | $3,483,214 | 92.7% | $3,853,635 | 91.1% |
|  | Operating Income and Distribution | | | | |
| 23. | Operating Income | $3,757,651 | 100.0% | $4,229,031 | 100.0% |
| 24. | Less:  Cost of sales and operations | $1,995,062 | 53.1% | $2,138,367 | 50.6% |
| 25. | Gross operating profit | $1,762,589 | 46.9% | $2,090,664 | 49.4% |
| 26. | Additional operating costs | $1,488,152 | 39.6% | $1,715,268 | 40.6% |
| 27. | Net operating profit | $274,437 | 7.3% | $375,396 | 8.9% |
| 28. | Less:  Guaranteed payments to partners | $7,466 | | $36,554 | |
| 29. | Distribution to partners | $266,971 | | $338,842 | |
| 30. | Other charges | $38,229 | | $62,422 | |
| 31. | Net change partners' capital | $228,742 | | $276,420 | |
|  | Selected Ratios | | | | |
| 32. | Coverage ratio:  times interest earned | (0.0) | | 0.3 | |
| 33. | Inventory turnover (times) | n.a. | | 165.8 | |
| 34. | Days' sales in inventory | n.a. | | 2.3 | |
| 35. | Average age of inventory (days) | n.a. | | 2.2 | |
| 36. | Return on assets, net inc., less def | 4.7% | | 5.2% | |
| 37. | Return on assets, gross operating profit | 36.5% | | 39.3% | |
| 38. | Return on assets, net operating profit | 5.7% | | 7.1% | |

*Page 48*

Table 1: Partnerships With and Without Net Income:  COMMUNICATION, ELECTRIC, GAS AND SANITARY SERVICES (080,081,082)

Dollar values in thousands, except averages

| | 1984 | | 1985 | |
|---|---|---|---|---|
| 1. Number of Partnerships | 6,795 | | 7,564 | |
| 2. Number of Partners | 87,393 | | 124,603 | |
| | | | | |
| 3. Total Assets | $14,723,908 | | $19,534,865 | |
| 4. Average total assets per Partnership | $2,166,874 | | $2,582,610 | |
| 5. Average total assets per Partner | $168,479 | | $156,777 | |
| | | | | |
| 6. Net Income, less Deficit | ($2,352,630) | | ($3,491,010) | |
| 7. Average per Partnership, total earnings | ($346,227) | | ($461,522) | |
| 8. Average per Partner, total earnings | ($26,920) | | ($28,017) | |
| | | | | |
| 9. Operating Income | $4,224,121 | | $5,611,928 | |
| Operating Costs | | | | |
| 10. Cost of sales & operations | $1,534,125 | 36.3% | $1,714,538 | 30.6% |
| 11. Salaries and wages | $442,619 | 10.5% | $526,309 | 9.4% |
| 12. Rent paid | $121,299 | 2.9% | $159,919 | 2.9% |
| 13. Interest paid | $877,327 | 20.8% | $923,670 | 16.5% |
| 14. Taxes paid | $110,937 | 2.6% | $147,695 | 2.6% |
| 15. Bad debts | $39,231 | 0.9% | $85,363 | 1.5% |
| 16. Repairs | $31,234 | 0.7% | $71,008 | 1.3% |
| 17. Depreciation | $1,274,323 | 30.2% | $1,804,355 | 32.2% |
| 18. Depletion | $3,848 | 0.1% | $0 | n.a. |
| 19. Pension & profit sharing plans | $0 | n.a. | $6,885 | 0.1% |
| 20. Employee benefits programs | $26,195 | 0.6% | $25,716 | 0.5% |
| 21. Other deductions | $1,935,411 | 45.8% | $3,310,682 | 59.0% |
| 22. Total operating costs | $6,396,555 | 151.4% | $8,776,143 | 156.4% |
| | | | | |
| Operating Income and Distribution | | | | |
| 23. Operating Income | $4,224,121 | 100.0% | $5,611,928 | 100.0% |
| 24. Less: Cost of sales and operations | $1,534,125 | 36.3% | $1,714,538 | 30.6% |
| 25. Gross operating profit | $2,689,996 | 63.7% | $3,897,390 | 69.5% |
| 26. Additional operating costs | $4,862,430 | 115.1% | $7,061,605 | 125.8% |
| 27. Net operating profit | ($2,172,434) | (51.4%) | ($3,164,215) | (56.4%) |
| 28. Less: Guaranteed payments to partners | $20,855 | | $57,767 | |
| 29. Distribution to partners | ($2,193,289) | | ($3,221,982) | |
| 30. Other charges | $190,581 | | $269,032 | |
| 31. Net change partners' capital | ($2,383,870) | | ($3,491,014) | |
| | | | | |
| Selected Ratios | | | | |
| 32. Coverage ratio:  times interest earned | (3.5) | | (4.4) | |
| 33. Inventory turnover (times) | n.a. | | 31.2 | |
| 34. Days' sales in inventory | n.a. | | 11.8 | |
| 35. Average age of inventory (days) | n.a. | | 11.7 | |
| 36. Return on assets, net inc., less def | (16.0%) | | (17.9%) | |
| 37. Return on assets, gross operating profit | 18.3% | | 20.0% | |
| 38. Return on assets, net operating profit | (14.8%) | | (16.2%) | |

Table 1: Partnerships With and Without Net Income:  083.  WHOLESALE AND RETAIL TRADE

Dollar values in thousands, except averages

| | | 1984 | | 1985 | |
|---|---|---|---|---|---|
| 1. | Number of Partnerships | 184,841 | | 200,532 | |
| 2. | Number of Partners | 443,712 | | 492,511 | |
| | | | | | |
| 3. | Total Assets | $21,222,015 | | $20,568,181 | |
| 4. | Average total assets per Partnership | $114,812 | | $102,568 | |
| 5. | Average total assets per Partner | $47,828 | | $41,762 | |
| | | | | | |
| 6. | Net Income, less Deficit | $1,666,476 | | $1,976,685 | |
| 7. | Average per Partnership, total earnings | $9,020 | | $9,862 | |
| 8. | Average per Partner, total earnings | $3,758 | | $4,015 | |
| | | | | | |
| 9. | Operating Income | $73,373,547 | | $70,095,779 | |
| | Operating Costs | | | | |
| 10. | Cost of sales & operations | $56,135,446 | 76.5% | $50,880,944 | 72.6% |
| 11. | Salaries and wages | $4,195,391 | 5.7% | $4,700,929 | 6.7% |
| 12. | Rent paid | $1,555,041 | 2.1% | $1,616,405 | 2.3% |
| 13. | Interest paid | $913,839 | 1.3% | $838,254 | 1.2% |
| 14. | Taxes paid | $883,974 | 1.2% | $993,650 | 1.4% |
| 15. | Bad debts | $97,612 | 0.1% | $110,385 | 0.2% |
| 16. | Repairs | $327,448 | 0.5% | $365,825 | 0.5% |
| 17. | Depreciation | $1,038,977 | 1.4% | $1,130,463 | 1.6% |
| 18. | Depletion | $5,938 | 0.0% | $3,798 | 0.0% |
| 19. | Pension & profit sharing plans | $33,964 | 0.1% | $35,694 | 0.1% |
| 20. | Employee benefits programs | $84,400 | 0.1% | $77,797 | 0.1% |
| 21. | Other deductions | $5,548,418 | 7.6% | $6,321,086 | 9.0% |
| 22. | Total operating costs | $70,825,702 | 96.5% | $67,079,074 | 95.7% |
| | | | | | |
| | Operating Income and Distribution | | | | |
| 23. | Operating Income | $73,373,547 | 100.0% | $70,095,779 | 100.0% |
| 24. | Less: Cost of sales and operations | $56,135,446 | 76.5% | $50,880,944 | 72.6% |
| 25. | Gross operating profit | $17,238,101 | 23.5% | $19,214,835 | 27.4% |
| 26. | Additional operating costs | $14,690,256 | 20.0% | $16,198,130 | 23.1% |
| 27. | Net operating profit | $2,547,845 | 3.5% | $3,016,705 | 4.3% |
| 28. | Less: Guaranteed payments to partners | $777,739 | | $938,473 | |
| 29. | Distribution to partners | $1,770,106 | | $2,078,232 | |
| 30. | Other charges | $108,884 | | $105,391 | |
| 31. | Net change partners' capital | $1,661,222 | | $1,972,841 | |
| | | | | | |
| | Selected Ratios | | | | |
| 32. | Coverage ratio: times interest earned | 1.8 | | 2.6 | |
| 33. | Inventory turnover (times) | 9.5 | | 8.2 | |
| 34. | Days' sales in inventory | 40.5 | | 47.1 | |
| 35. | Average age of inventory (days) | 38.5 | | 44.6 | |
| 36. | Return on assets, net inc., less def | 7.9% | | 9.6% | |
| 37. | Return on assets, gross operating profit | 81.2% | | 93.4% | |
| 38. | Return on assets, net operating profit | 12.0% | | 14.7% | |

*Page 50*

Table 1: Partnerships With and Without Net Income: 084. WHOLESALE TRADE

Dollar values in thousands, except averages

| | | 1984 | | 1985 | |
|---|---|---|---|---|---|
| 1. | Number of Partnerships | 21,359 | | 26,796 | |
| 2. | Number of Partners | 56,782 | | 72,486 | |
| 3. | Total Assets | $7,775,074 | | $7,024,498 | |
| 4. | Average total assets per Partnership | $364,019 | | $262,147 | |
| 5. | Average total assets per Partner | $136,929 | | $96,908 | |
| 6. | Net Income, less Deficit | $371,099 | | $467,394 | |
| 7. | Average per Partnership, total earnings | $17,385 | | $17,450 | |
| 8. | Average per Partner, total earnings | $6,539 | | $6,451 | |
| 9. | Operating Income | $28,580,398 | | $23,882,056 | |
| | Operating Costs | | | | |
| 10. | Cost of sales & operations | $24,923,035 | 87.2% | $19,990,747 | 83.7% |
| 11. | Salaries and wages | $725,474 | 2.5% | $747,416 | 3.1% |
| 12. | Rent paid | $146,291 | 0.5% | $141,962 | 0.6% |
| 13. | Interest paid | $359,969 | 1.3% | $271,789 | 1.1% |
| 14. | Taxes paid | $135,505 | 0.5% | $131,681 | 0.6% |
| 15. | Bad debts | $47,134 | 0.2% | $51,690 | 0.2% |
| 16. | Repairs | $78,369 | 0.3% | $78,931 | 0.3% |
| 17. | Depreciation | $240,019 | 0.8% | $208,761 | 0.9% |
| 18. | Depletion | $4,575 | 0.0% | $2,939 | 0.0% |
| 19. | Pension & profit sharing plans | $16,816 | 0.1% | $13,089 | 0.1% |
| 20. | Employee benefits programs | $31,743 | 0.1% | $23,863 | 0.1% |
| 21. | Other deductions | $1,235,130 | 4.3% | $1,519,465 | 6.4% |
| 22. | Total operating costs | $27,944,160 | 97.8% | $23,182,387 | 97.1% |
| | Operating Income and Distribution | | | | |
| 23. | Operating Income | $28,580,398 | 100.0% | $23,882,056 | 100.0% |
| 24. | Less: Cost of sales and operations | $24,923,035 | 87.2% | $19,990,747 | 83.7% |
| 25. | Gross operating profit | $3,657,363 | 12.8% | $3,891,309 | 16.3% |
| 26. | Additional operating costs | $3,021,125 | 10.6% | $3,191,640 | 13.4% |
| 27. | Net operating profit | $636,238 | 2.2% | $699,669 | 2.9% |
| 28. | Less: Guaranteed payments to partners | $224,577 | | $203,863 | |
| 29. | Distribution to partners | $411,661 | | $495,806 | |
| 30. | Other charges | $40,661 | | $28,467 | |
| 31. | Net change partners' capital | $371,000 | | $467,339 | |
| | Selected Ratios | | | | |
| 32. | Coverage ratio: times interest earned | 0.8 | | 1.6 | |
| 33. | Inventory turnover (times) | 13.8 | | 12.3 | |
| 34. | Days' sales in inventory | 27.6 | | 30.7 | |
| 35. | Average age of inventory (days) | 26.5 | | 29.8 | |
| 36. | Return on assets, net inc., less def | 4.8% | | 6.7% | |
| 37. | Return on assets, gross operating profit | 47.0% | | 55.4% | |
| 38. | Return on assets, net operating profit | 8.2% | | 1.0% | |

Table 1: Partnerships With and Without Net Income:  100.  RETAIL TRADE

Dollar values in thousands, except averages

|  |  | 1984 |  | 1985 |  |
|---|---|---|---|---|---|
| 1. | Number of Partnerships | 163,473 |  | 172,725 |  |
| 2. | Number of Partners | 386,907 |  | 418,002 |  |
| 3. | Total Assets | $13,434,830 |  | $13,543,683 |  |
| 4. | Average total assets per Partnership | $82,184 |  | $78,412 |  |
| 5. | Average total assets per Partner | $34,724 |  | $32,401 |  |
| 6. | Net Income, less Deficit | $1,294,922 |  | $1,509,191 |  |
| 7. | Average per Partnership, total earnings | $7,925 |  | $8,742 |  |
| 8. | Average per Partner, total earnings | $3,348 |  | $3,612 |  |
| 9. | Operating Income | $44,760,051 |  | $46,152,001 |  |
|  | Operating Costs |  |  |  |  |
| 10. | Cost of sales & operations | $31,183,888 | 69.7% | $30,832,740 | 66.8% |
| 11. | Salaries and wages | $3,468,333 | 7.8% | $3,953,199 | 8.6% |
| 12. | Rent paid | $1,408,686 | 3.2% | $1,473,760 | 3.2% |
| 13. | Interest paid | $553,832 | 1.2% | $566,465 | 1.2% |
| 14. | Taxes paid | $748,274 | 1.7% | $861,904 | 1.9% |
| 15. | Bad debts | $50,435 | 0.1% | $58,695 | 0.1% |
| 16. | Repairs | $248,924 | 0.6% | $286,875 | 0.6% |
| 17. | Depreciation | $798,610 | 1.8% | $921,702 | 2.0% |
| 18. | Depletion | $1,363 | n.a. | $860 | n.a. |
| 19. | Pension & profit sharing plans | $17,147 | 0.0% | $22,605 | 0.1% |
| 20. | Employee benefits programs | $52,605 | 0.1% | $53,934 | 0.1% |
| 21. | Other deductions | $4,312,014 | 9.6% | $4,798,537 | 10.4% |
| 22. | Total operating costs | $42,849,265 | 95.7% | $43,835,066 | 95.0% |
|  | Operating Income and Distribution |  |  |  |  |
| 23. | Operating Income | $44,760,051 | 100.0% | $46,152,001 | 100.0% |
| 24. | Less:  Cost of sales and operations | $31,183,888 | 69.7% | $30,832,740 | 66.8% |
| 25. | Gross operating profit | $13,576,163 | 30.3% | $15,319,261 | 33.2% |
| 26. | Additional operating costs | $11,665,377 | 26.1% | $13,002,326 | 28.2% |
| 27. | Net operating profit | $1,910,786 | 4.3% | $2,316,935 | 5.0% |
| 28. | Less:  Guaranteed payments to partners | $553,089 |  | $734,610 |  |
| 29. | Distribution to partners | $1,357,697 |  | $1,582,325 |  |
| 30. | Other charges | $67,929 |  | $76,924 |  |
| 31. | Net change partners' capital | $1,289,768 |  | $1,505,401 |  |
|  | Selected Ratios |  |  |  |  |
| 32. | Coverage ratio:  times interest earned | 2.5 |  | 3.1 |  |
| 33. | Inventory turnover (times) | 7.6 |  | 6.7 |  |
| 34. | Days' sales in inventory | 50.9 |  | 57.8 |  |
| 35. | Average age of inventory (days) | 48.0 |  | 54.3 |  |
| 36. | Return on assets, net inc., less def | 9.6% |  | 11.1% |  |
| 37. | Return on assets, gross operating profit | 101.1% |  | 113.1% |  |
| 38. | Return on assets, net operating profit | 14.2% |  | 17.1% |  |

Table 1: Partnerships With and Without Net Income:  101.  BUILDING MATERIALS, PAINT, HARDWARE, GARDEN SUPPLY, AND MOBILE HOME DEALER

Dollar values in thousands, except averages

|  |  | 1984 |  | 1985 |  |
|---|---|---|---|---|---|
| 1. | Number of Partnerships | 7,992 |  | 8,567 |  |
| 2. | Number of Partners | 18,927 |  | 20,836 |  |
| 3. | Total Assets | $1,965,093 |  | $1,155,860 |  |
| 4. | Average total assets per Partnership | $245,883 |  | $134,920 |  |
| 5. | Average total assets per Partner | $103,825 |  | $55,474 |  |
| 6. | Net Income, less Deficit | $156,633 |  | $92,298 |  |
| 7. | Average per Partnership, total earnings | $19,606 |  | $10,783 |  |
| 8. | Average per Partner, total earnings | $8,279 |  | $4,433 |  |
| 9. | Operating Income | $2,496,016 |  | $3,042,189 |  |
|  | Operating Costs |  |  |  |  |
| 10. | Cost of sales & operations | $1,662,313 | 66.6% | $2,128,188 | 70.0% |
| 11. | Salaries and wages | $176,080 | 7.1% | $226,100 | 7.4% |
| 12. | Rent paid | $38,766 | 1.6% | $43,237 | 1.4% |
| 13. | Interest paid | $46,144 | 1.9% | $47,682 | 1.6% |
| 14. | Taxes paid | $42,941 | 1.7% | $51,371 | 1.7% |
| 15. | Bad debts | $7,128 | 0.3% | $8,272 | 0.3% |
| 16. | Repairs | $11,676 | 0.5% | $27,104 | 0.9% |
| 17. | Depreciation | $38,970 | 1.6% | $53,065 | 1.7% |
| 18. | Depletion | $0 | n.a. | $0 | n.a. |
| 19. | Pension & profit sharing plans | $1,801 | 0.1% | $2,308 | 0.1% |
| 20. | Employee benefits programs | $9,339 | 0.4% | $3,526 | 0.1% |
| 21. | Other deductions | $244,236 | 9.8% | $278,587 | 9.2% |
| 22. | Total operating costs | $2,279,447 | 91.3% | $2,869,474 | 94.3% |
|  | Operating Income and Distribution |  |  |  |  |
| 23. | Operating Income | $2,496,016 | 100.0% | $3,042,189 | 100.0% |
| 24. | Less: Cost of sales and operations | $1,662,313 | 66.6% | $2,128,188 | 70.0% |
| 25. | Gross operating profit | $833,703 | 33.4% | $914,001 | 30.0% |
| 26. | Additional operating costs | $617,134 | 24.7% | $741,286 | 24.4% |
| 27. | Net operating profit | $216,569 | 8.7% | $172,715 | 5.7% |
| 28. | Less: Guaranteed payments to partners | $54,335 |  | $77,009 |  |
| 29. | Distribution to partners | $162,234 |  | $95,706 |  |
| 30. | Other charges | $5,654 |  | $3,443 |  |
| 31. | Net change partners' capital | $156,580 |  | $92,263 |  |
|  | Selected Ratios |  |  |  |  |
| 32. | Coverage ratio:  times interest earned | 3.7 |  | 2.6 |  |
| 33. | Inventory turnover (times) | 4.2 |  | 3.9 |  |
| 34. | Days' sales in inventory | 89.9 |  | 96.1 |  |
| 35. | Average age of inventory (days) | 86.3 |  | 93.2 |  |
| 36. | Return on assets, net inc., less def | 8.0% |  | 8.0% |  |
| 37. | Return on assets, gross operating profit | 42.4% |  | 79.1% |  |
| 38. | Return on assets, net operating profit | 11.0% |  | 14.9% |  |

*Page 53*

Table 1: Partnerships With and Without Net Income: 107. GENERAL MERCHANDISE STORES

Dollar values in thousands, except averages

| | 1984 | | 1985 | |
|---|---|---|---|---|
| 1. Number of Partnerships | 4,937 | | 5,669 | |
| 2. Number of Partners | 10,574 | | 12,038 | |
| 3. Total Assets | $395,985 | | $501,138 | |
| 4. Average total assets per Partnership | $80,208 | | $88,400 | |
| 5. Average total assets per Partner | $37,449 | | $41,630 | |
| 6. Net Income, less Deficit | $5,757 | | $40,662 | |
| 7. Average per Partnership, total earnings | $1,171 | | $7,177 | |
| 8. Average per Partner, total earnings | $547 | | $3,380 | |
| 9. Operating Income | $856,617 | | $1,417,448 | |
| Operating Costs | | | | |
| 10. Cost of sales & operations | $587,322 | 68.6% | $962,065 | 67.9% |
| 11. Salaries and wages | $76,718 | 9.0% | $103,707 | 7.3% |
| 12. Rent paid | $32,100 | 3.8% | $52,295 | 3.7% |
| 13. Interest paid | $10,634 | 1.2% | $12,529 | 0.9% |
| 14. Taxes paid | $15,126 | 1.8% | $28,144 | 2.0% |
| 15. Bad debts | $917 | 0.1% | $1,579 | 0.1% |
| 16. Repairs | $1,999 | 0.2% | $3,228 | 0.2% |
| 17. Depreciation | $19,620 | 2.3% | $28,377 | 2.0% |
| 18. Depletion | $0 | n.a. | $0 | n.a. |
| 19. Pension & profit sharing plans | $764 | 0.1% | $679 | 0.1% |
| 20. Employee benefits programs | $635 | 0.1% | $1,121 | 0.1% |
| 21. Other deductions | $78,219 | 9.1% | $154,636 | 10.9% |
| 22. Total operating costs | $824,113 | 96.2% | $1,348,421 | 95.1% |
| Operating Income and Distribution | | | | |
| 23. Operating Income | $856,617 | 100.0% | $1,417,448 | 100.0% |
| 24. Less: Cost of sales and operations | $587,322 | 68.6% | $962,065 | 67.9% |
| 25. Gross operating profit | $269,295 | 31.4% | $455,383 | 32.1% |
| 26. Additional operating costs | $236,791 | 27.6% | $386,356 | 27.3% |
| 27. Net operating profit | $32,504 | 3.8% | $69,027 | 4.9% |
| 28. Less: Guaranteed payments to partners | $23,129 | | $25,071 | |
| 29. Distribution to partners | $9,375 | | $43,956 | |
| 30. Other charges | $3,677 | | $3,356 | |
| 31. Net change partners' capital | $5,698 | | $40,600 | |
| Selected Ratios | | | | |
| 32. Coverage ratio: times interest earned | 2.1 | | 4.5 | |
| 33. Inventory turnover (times) | 5.0 | | 5.2 | |
| 34. Days' sales in inventory | 79.4 | | 80.5 | |
| 35. Average age of inventory (days) | 72.7 | | 70.5 | |
| 36. Return on assets, net inc., less def | 1.5% | | 8.1% | |
| 37. Return on assets, gross operating profit | 68.0% | | 90.9% | |
| 38. Return on assets, net operating profit | 8.2% | | 13.8% | |

*Page 54*

Table 1: Partnerships With and Without Net Income:  110.  FOOD STORES

Dollar values in thousands, except averages

| | 1984 | | 1985 | |
|---|---|---|---|---|
| 1.  Number of Partnerships | 23,657 | | 18,802 | |
| 2.  Number of Partners | 51,787 | | 41,327 | |
| | | | | |
| 3.  Total Assets | $1,387,041 | | $1,216,342 | |
| 4.     Average total assets per Partnership | $58,631 | | $64,692 | |
| 5.     Average total assets per Partner | $26,784 | | $29,432 | |
| | | | | |
| 6.  Net Income, less Deficit | $274,030 | | $189,411 | |
| 7.     Average per Partnership, total earnings | $11,585 | | $10,079 | |
| 8.     Average per Partner, total earnings | $5,292 | | $4,586 | |
| | | | | |
| 9.  Operating Income | $8,874,040 | | $8,108,464 | |
| Operating Costs | | | | |
| 10.    Cost of sales & operations | $6,964,358 | 78.5% | $6,249,965 | 77.1% |
| 11.    Salaries and wages | $517,360 | 5.8% | $499,525 | 6.2% |
| 12.    Rent paid | $144,522 | 1.6% | $152,171 | 1.9% |
| 13.    Interest paid | $54,636 | 0.6% | $60,005 | 0.7% |
| 14.    Taxes paid | $103,586 | 1.2% | $102,460 | 1.3% |
| 15.    Bad debts | $9,588 | 0.1% | $9,820 | 0.1% |
| 16.    Repairs | $33,412 | 0.4% | $40,157 | 0.5% |
| 17.    Depreciation | $108,867 | 1.2% | $112,440 | 1.4% |
| 18.    Depletion | $202 | n.a. | $860 | 0.0% |
| 19.    Pension & profit sharing plans | $6,857 | 0.1% | $3,476 | 0.0% |
| 20.    Employee benefits programs | $8,930 | 0.1% | $11,454 | 0.1% |
| 21.    Other deductions | $605,344 | 6.8% | $575,704 | 7.1% |
| 22.    Total operating costs | $8,559,891 | 96.5% | $7,818,707 | 96.4% |
| | | | | |
| Operating Income and Distribution | | | | |
| 23.    Operating Income | $8,874,040 | 100.0% | $8,108,464 | 100.0% |
| 24.       Less: Cost of sales and operations | $6,964,358 | 78.5% | $6,249,965 | 77.1% |
| 25.    Gross operating profit | $1,909,682 | 21.5% | $1,858,499 | 22.9% |
| 26.       Additional operating costs | $1,595,533 | 18.0% | $1,568,742 | 19.4% |
| 27.    Net operating profit | $314,149 | 3.5% | $289,757 | 3.6% |
| 28.       Less: Guaranteed payments to partners | $38,798 | | $96,880 | |
| 29.    Distribution to partners | $275,351 | | $192,877 | |
| 30.    Other charges | $3,550 | | $4,136 | |
| 31.    Net change partners' capital | $271,801 | | $188,741 | |
| | | | | |
| Selected Ratios | | | | |
| 32.    Coverage ratio:  times interest earned | 4.8 | | 3.8 | |
| 33.    Inventory turnover (times) | 14.3 | | 14.5 | |
| 34.    Days' sales in inventory | 27.2 | | 25.5 | |
| 35.    Average age of inventory (days) | 25.5 | | 25.1 | |
| 36.    Return on assets, net inc., less def | 19.8% | | 15.6% | |
| 37.    Return on assets, gross operating profit | 137.7% | | 152.8% | |
| 38.    Return on assets, net operating profit | 22.7% | | 23.8% | |

Table 1: Partnerships With and Without Net Income: 111.   GROCERY STORES

Dollar values in thousands, except averages

|  |  | 1984 |  | 1985 |  |
|---|---|---|---|---|---|
| 1. | Number of Partnerships | 11,674 |  | 11,299 |  |
| 2. | Number of Partners | 25,461 |  | 24,175 |  |
| 3. | Total Assets | $903,871 |  | $930,223 |  |
| 4. | Average total assets per Partnership | $77,426 |  | $82,328 |  |
| 5. | Average total assets per Partner | $35,500 |  | $38,479 |  |
| 6. | Net Income, less Deficit | $143,159 |  | $156,579 |  |
| 7. | Average per Partnership, total earnings | $12,265 |  | $13,861 |  |
| 8. | Average per Partner, total earnings | $5,624 |  | $6,478 |  |
| 9. | Operating Income | $6,163,775 |  | $6,120,109 |  |
|  | Operating Costs |  |  |  |  |
| 10. | Cost of sales & operations | $5,004,176 | 81.2% | $4,849,282 | 79.2% |
| 11. | Salaries and wages | $364,847 | 5.9% | $375,413 | 6.1% |
| 12. | Rent paid | $69,479 | 1.1% | $70,861 | 1.2% |
| 13. | Interest paid | $37,757 | 0.6% | $42,461 | 0.7% |
| 14. | Taxes paid | $63,421 | 1.0% | $72,874 | 1.2% |
| 15. | Bad debts | $8,286 | 0.1% | $9,592 | 0.2% |
| 16. | Repairs | $22,411 | 0.4% | $29,561 | 0.5% |
| 17. | Depreciation | $63,838 | 1.0% | $78,252 | 1.3% |
| 18. | Depletion | $169 | n.a. | $823 | 0.0% |
| 19. | Pension & profit sharing plans | $6,673 | 0.1% | $3,301 | 0.1% |
| 20. | Employee benefits programs | $7,691 | 0.1% | $10,341 | 0.2% |
| 21. | Other deductions | $342,292 | 5.6% | $381,888 | 6.2% |
| 22. | Total operating costs | $5,993,225 | 97.2% | $5,925,273 | 96.8% |
|  | Operating Income and Distribution |  |  |  |  |
| 23. | Operating Income | $6,163,775 | 100.0% | $6,120,109 | 100.0% |
| 24. | Less: Cost of sales and operations | $5,004,176 | 81.2% | $4,849,282 | 79.2% |
| 25. | Gross operating profit | $1,159,599 | 18.8% | $1,270,827 | 20.8% |
| 26. | Additional operating costs | $989,049 | 16.1% | $1,075,991 | 17.6% |
| 27. | Net operating profit | $170,550 | 2.8% | $194,836 | 3.2% |
| 28. | Less: Guaranteed payments to partners | $26,383 |  | $35,025 |  |
| 29. | Distribution to partners | $144,167 |  | $159,811 |  |
| 30. | Other charges | $3,193 |  | $3,856 |  |
| 31. | Net change partners' capital | $140,974 |  | $155,955 |  |
|  | Selected Ratios |  |  |  |  |
| 32. | Coverage ratio: times interest earned | 3.5 |  | 3.6 |  |
| 33. | Inventory turnover (times) | 13.6 |  | 13.4 |  |
| 34. | Days' sales in inventory | 27.6 |  | 27.9 |  |
| 35. | Average age of inventory (days) | 26.8 |  | 27.2 |  |
| 36. | Return on assets, net inc., less def | 15.8% |  | 16.8% |  |
| 37. | Return on assets, gross operating profit | 128.3% |  | 136.6% |  |
| 38. | Return on assets, net operating profit | 18.9% |  | 21.0% |  |

Table 1: Partnerships With and Without Net Income:  OTHER FOOD STORES (112,113,114,115,116,117)

Dollar values in thousands, except averages

| | | 1984 | | 1985 | |
|---|---|---|---|---|---|
| 1. | Number of Partnerships | 11,982 | | 7,503 | |
| 2. | Number of Partners | 26,327 | | 17,152 | |
| | | | | | |
| 3. | Total Assets | $483,170 | | $286,119 | |
| 4. | Average total assets per Partnership | $40,325 | | $38,134 | |
| 5. | Average total assets per Partner | $18,353 | | $16,681 | |
| | | | | | |
| 6. | Net Income, less Deficit | $130,871 | | $32,833 | |
| 7. | Average per Partnership, total earnings | $10,923 | | $4,384 | |
| 8. | Average per Partner, total earnings | $4,971 | | $1,918 | |
| | | | | | |
| 9. | Operating Income | $2,710,265 | | $1,988,355 | |
| | Operating Costs | | | | |
| 10. | Cost of sales & operations | $1,960,183 | 72.3% | $1,400,682 | 70.4% |
| 11. | Salaries and wages | $152,512 | 5.6% | $124,113 | 6.2% |
| 12. | Rent paid | $75,042 | 2.8% | $81,310 | 4.1% |
| 13. | Interest paid | $16,879 | 0.6% | $17,544 | 0.9% |
| 14. | Taxes paid | $40,165 | 1.5% | $29,586 | 1.5% |
| 15. | Bad debts | $1,301 | 0.1% | $229 | 0.0% |
| 16. | Repairs | $11,001 | 0.4% | $10,596 | 0.5% |
| 17. | Depreciation | $45,031 | 1.7% | $34,188 | 1.7% |
| 18. | Depletion | $33 | n.a. | $37 | n.a. |
| 19. | Pension & profit sharing plans | $184 | 0.0% | $176 | 0.0% |
| 20. | Employee benefits programs | $1,239 | 0.1% | $1,113 | 0.1% |
| 21. | Other deductions | $263,052 | 9.7% | $193,814 | 9.8% |
| 22. | Total operating costs | $2,566,667 | 94.7% | $1,893,434 | 95.2% |
| | | | | | |
| | Operating Income and Distribution | | | | |
| 23. | Operating Income | $2,710,265 | 100.0% | $1,988,355 | 100.0% |
| 24. | Less: Cost of sales and operations | $1,960,183 | 72.3% | $1,400,682 | 70.4% |
| 25. | Gross operating profit | $750,082 | 27.7% | $587,673 | 29.6% |
| 26. | Additional operating costs | $606,484 | 22.4% | $492,752 | 24.8% |
| 27. | Net operating profit | $143,598 | 5.3% | $94,921 | 4.8% |
| 28. | Less: Guaranteed payments to partners | $12,415 | | $61,854 | |
| 29. | Distribution to partners | $131,183 | | $33,067 | |
| 30. | Other charges | $357 | | $280 | |
| 31. | Net change partners' capital | $130,826 | | $32,787 | |
| | | | | | |
| | Selected Ratios | | | | |
| 32. | Coverage ratio: times interest earned | 7.5 | | 4.4 | |
| 33. | Inventory turnover (times) | 16.5 | | 20.5 | |
| 34. | Days' sales in inventory | 26.4 | | 17.2 | |
| 35. | Average age of inventory (days) | 22.1 | | 17.8 | |
| 36. | Return on assets, net inc., less def | 27.1% | | 11.5% | |
| 37. | Return on assets, gross operating profit | 155.2% | | 205.4% | |
| 38. | Return on assets, net operating profit | 29.7% | | 33.2% | |

Table 1: Partnerships With and Without Net Income: 118. AUTOMOTIVE DEALERS AND SERVICE STATIONS

Dollar values in thousands, except averages

| | 1984 | | 1985 | |
|---|---|---|---|---|
| 1. Number of Partnerships | 14,080 | | 17,305 | |
| 2. Number of Partners | 33,155 | | 41,192 | |
| 3. Total Assets | $2,452,932 | | $2,184,034 | |
| 4. Average total assets per Partnership | $174,214 | | $126,208 | |
| 5. Average total assets per Partner | $73,984 | | $53,021 | |
| 6. Net Income, less Deficit | $251,547 | | $275,483 | |
| 7. Average per Partnership, total earnings | $17,875 | | $15,927 | |
| 8. Average per Partner, total earnings | $7,591 | | $6,691 | |
| 9. Operating Income | $11,587,706 | | $10,602,768 | |
| Operating Costs | | | | |
| 10. Cost of sales & operations | $9,723,441 | 83.9% | $8,749,965 | 82.5% |
| 11. Salaries and wages | $433,043 | 3.7% | $429,445 | 4.1% |
| 12. Rent paid | $135,327 | 1.2% | $129,640 | 1.2% |
| 13. Interest paid | $108,165 | 0.9% | $90,661 | 0.9% |
| 14. Taxes paid | $93,558 | 0.8% | $103,247 | 0.10% |
| 15. Bad debts | $9,856 | 0.1% | $7,570 | 0.1% |
| 16. Repairs | $35,943 | 0.3% | $33,206 | 0.3% |
| 17. Depreciation | $102,569 | 0.9% | $96,185 | 0.9% |
| 18. Depletion | $690 | 0.0% | $0 | n.a. |
| 19. Pension & profit sharing plans | $1,118 | 0.0% | $1,634 | 0.0% |
| 20. Employee benefits programs | $12,880 | 0.1% | $8,512 | 0.1% |
| 21. Other deductions | $518,295 | 4.5% | $540,038 | 5.1% |
| 22. Total operating costs | $11,175,550 | 96.4% | $10,190,347 | 96.1% |
| Operating Income and Distribution | | | | |
| 23. Operating Income | $11,587,706 | 100.0% | $10,602,768 | 100.0% |
| 24. Less: Cost of sales and operations | $9,723,441 | 83.9% | $8,749,965 | 82.5% |
| 25. Gross operating profit | $1,864,265 | 16.1% | $1,852,803 | 17.5% |
| 26. Additional operating costs | $1,452,109 | 12.5% | $1,440,382 | 13.6% |
| 27. Net operating profit | $412,156 | 3.6% | $412,421 | 3.9% |
| 28. Less: Guaranteed payments to partners | $132,512 | | $131,373 | |
| 29. Distribution to partners | $279,644 | | $281,048 | |
| 30. Other charges | $28,762 | | $5,808 | |
| 31. Net change partners' capital | $250,882 | | $275,240 | |
| Selected Ratios | | | | |
| 32. Coverage ratio: times interest earned | 2.8 | | 3.6 | |
| 33. Inventory turnover (times) | 10.2 | | 9.4 | |
| 34. Days' sales in inventory | 35.9 | | 41.2 | |
| 35. Average age of inventory (days) | 35.8 | | 38.9 | |
| 36. Return on assets, net inc., less def | 10.3% | | 12.6% | |
| 37. Return on assets, gross operating profit | 76.0% | | 84.8% | |
| 38. Return on assets, net operating profit | 16.8% | | 18.9% | |

Table 1: Partnerships With and Without Net Income: MOTOR VEHICLE DEALERS (119,120)

Dollar values in thousands, except averages

| | | 1984 | | 1985 | |
|---|---|---|---|---|---|
| 1. | Number of Partnerships | 3,982 | | 4,920 | |
| 2. | Number of Partners | 8,964 | | 12,256 | |
| 3. | Total Assets | $657,992 | | $934,953 | |
| 4. | Average total assets per Partnership | $165,242 | | $190,031 | |
| 5. | Average total assets per Partner | $73,404 | | $76,285 | |
| 6. | Net Income, less Deficit | $117,925 | | $126,703 | |
| 7. | Average per Partnership, total earnings | $29,621 | | $25,758 | |
| 8. | Average per Partner, total earnings | $13,158 | | $10,340 | |
| 9. | Operating Income | $3,298,085 | | $3,856,766 | |
| | Operating Costs | | | | |
| 10. | Cost of sales & operations | $2,806,631 | 85.1% | $3,274,460 | 84.9% |
| 11. | Salaries and wages | $110,131 | 3.3% | $137,968 | 3.6% |
| 12. | Rent paid | $20,046 | 0.6% | $26,169 | 0.7% |
| 13. | Interest paid | $34,892 | 1.1% | $34,654 | 0.9% |
| 14. | Taxes paid | $20,721 | 0.6% | $26,214 | 0.7% |
| 15. | Bad debts | $3,042 | 0.1% | $3,514 | 0.1% |
| 16. | Repairs | $13,081 | 0.4% | $14,301 | 0.4% |
| 17. | Depreciation | $14,953 | 0.5% | $20,755 | 0.5% |
| 18. | Depletion | $44 | n.a. | $0 | n.a. |
| 19. | Pension & profit sharing plans | $496 | 0.0% | $946 | 0.0% |
| 20. | Employee benefits programs | $5,228 | 0.2% | $6,054 | 0.2% |
| 21. | Other deductions | $125,119 | 3.8% | $159,033 | 4.1% |
| 22. | Total operating costs | $3,154,515 | 95.7% | $3,704,083 | 96.0% |
| | Operating Income and Distribution | | | | |
| 23. | Operating Income | $3,298,085 | 100.0% | $3,856,766 | 100.0% |
| 24. | Less: Cost of sales and operations | $2,806,631 | 85.1% | $3,274,460 | 84.9% |
| 25. | Gross operating profit | $491,454 | 14.9% | $582,306 | 15.1% |
| 26. | Additional operating costs | $347,884 | 10.6% | $429,623 | 11.1% |
| 27. | Net operating profit | $143,570 | 4.4% | $152,683 | 4.0% |
| 28. | Less: Guaranteed payments to partners | $25,372 | | $24,487 | |
| 29. | Distribution to partners | $118,198 | | $128,196 | |
| 30. | Other charges | $403 | | $1,508 | |
| 31. | Net change partners' capital | $117,795 | | $126,688 | |
| | Selected Ratios | | | | |
| 32. | Coverage ratio: times interest earned | 3.1 | | 3.4 | |
| 33. | Inventory turnover (times) | 7.9 | | 7.6 | |
| 34. | Days' sales in inventory | 50.8 | | 53.3 | |
| 35. | Average age of inventory (days) | 46.0 | | 47.9 | |
| 36. | Return on assets, net inc., less def | 17.9% | | 13.6% | |
| 37. | Return on assets, gross operating profit | 74.7% | | 62.3% | |
| 38. | Return on assets, net operating profit | 21.8% | | 16.3% | |

Table 1: Partnerships With and Without Net Income:  122.  GASOLINE SERVICE STATIONS

Dollar values in thousands, except averages

|  |  | 1984 |  | 1985 |  |
|---|---|---|---|---|---|
| 1. | Number of Partnerships | 6,059 | | 6,486 | |
| 2. | Number of Partners | 13,525 | | 14,193 | |
| 3. | Total Assets | $987,948 | | $591,308 | |
| 4. | Average total assets per Partnership | $163,055 | | $91,167 | |
| 5. | Average total assets per Partner | $73,046 | | $41,662 | |
| 6. | Net Income, less Deficit | $78,974 | | $122,815 | |
| 7. | Average per Partnership, total earnings | $13,042 | | $18,942 | |
| 8. | Average per Partner, total earnings | $5,843 | | $8,656 | |
| 9. | Operating Income | $6,463,107 | | $5,091,773 | |
|  | Operating Costs | | | | |
| 10. | Cost of sales & operations | $5,723,188 | 88.6% | $4,333,698 | 85.1% |
| 11. | Salaries and wages | $167,102 | 2.6% | $171,125 | 3.4% |
| 12. | Rent paid | $76,088 | 1.2% | $68,697 | 1.4% |
| 13. | Interest paid | $39,451 | 0.6% | $25,485 | 0.5% |
| 14. | Taxes paid | $52,897 | 0.8% | $54,851 | 1.1% |
| 15. | Bad debts | $4,262 | 0.1% | $2,099 | 0.0% |
| 16. | Repairs | $14,520 | 0.2% | $12,973 | 0.3% |
| 17. | Depreciation | $47,101 | 0.7% | $48,250 | 0.10% |
| 18. | Depletion | $646 | 0.0% | $0 | n.a. |
| 19. | Pension & profit sharing plans | $209 | n.a. | $125 | n.a. |
| 20. | Employee benefits programs | $2,899 | 0.0% | $353 | 0.0% |
| 21. | Other deductions | $202,481 | 3.1% | $207,346 | 4.1% |
| 22. | Total operating costs | $6,330,865 | 98.0% | $4,925,086 | 96.7% |
|  | Operating Income and Distribution | | | | |
| 23. | Operating Income | $6,463,107 | 100.0% | $5,091,773 | 100.0% |
| 24. | Less:  Cost of sales and operations | $5,723,188 | 88.6% | $4,333,698 | 85.1% |
| 25. | Gross operating profit | $739,919 | 11.5% | $758,075 | 14.9% |
| 26. | Additional operating costs | $607,677 | 9.4% | $591,388 | 11.6% |
| 27. | Net operating profit | $132,242 | 2.1% | $166,687 | 3.3% |
| 28. | Less:  Guaranteed payments to partners | $50,037 | | $40,457 | |
| 29. | Distribution to partners | $82,205 | | $126,230 | |
| 30. | Other charges | $3,252 | | $3,499 | |
| 31. | Net change partners' capital | $78,953 | | $122,731 | |
|  | Selected Ratios | | | | |
| 32. | Coverage ratio:  times interest earned | 2.4 | | 5.5 | |
| 33. | Inventory turnover (times) | 21.1 | | 34.8 | |
| 34. | Days' sales in inventory | 13.7 | | 10.8 | |
| 35. | Average age of inventory (days) | 17.3 | | 10.5 | |
| 36. | Return on assets, net inc., less def | 8.0% | | 20.8% | |
| 37. | Return on assets, gross operating profit | 74.9% | | 128.2% | |
| 38. | Return on assets, net operating profit | 13.4% | | 28.2% | |

*Page 60*

Table 1: Partnerships With and Without Net Income:  OTHER AUTOMOTIVE DEALERS (121,123,124,125,126)

Dollar values in thousands, except averages

|  |  | 1984 |  | 1985 |  |
|---|---|---|---|---|---|
| 1. | Number of Partnerships | 4,068 | | 5,899 | |
| 2. | Number of Partners | 10,667 | | 14,744 | |
| 3. | Total Assets | $806,992 | | $657,774 | |
| 4. | Average total assets per Partnership | $198,376 | | $111,506 | |
| 5. | Average total assets per Partner | $75,653 | | $44,613 | |
| 6. | Net Income, less Deficit | $54,647 | | $25,964 | |
| 7. | Average per Partnership, total earnings | $13,447 | | $4,413 | |
| 8. | Average per Partner, total earnings | $5,128 | | $1,765 | |
| 9. | Operating Income | $1,826,514 | | $1,654,228 | |
| | Operating Costs | | | | |
| 10. | Cost of sales & operations | $1,193,622 | 65.4% | $1,141,807 | 69.0% |
| 11. | Salaries and wages | $155,811 | 8.5% | $120,350 | 7.3% |
| 12. | Rent paid | $39,193 | 2.2% | $34,774 | 2.1% |
| 13. | Interest paid | $33,822 | 1.9% | $30,521 | 1.9% |
| 14. | Taxes paid | $19,940 | 1.1% | $22,182 | 1.3% |
| 15. | Bad debts | $2,552 | 0.1% | $1,957 | 0.1% |
| 16. | Repairs | $8,343 | 0.5% | $5,932 | 0.4% |
| 17. | Depreciation | $40,515 | 2.2% | $27,180 | 1.6% |
| 18. | Depletion | $0 | n.a. | $0 | n.a. |
| 19. | Pension & profit sharing plans | $413 | 0.0% | $563 | 0.0% |
| 20. | Employee benefits programs | $4,752 | 0.3% | $2,105 | 0.1% |
| 21. | Other deductions | $190,694 | 10.4% | $173,663 | 10.5% |
| 22. | Total operating costs | $1,690,170 | 92.5% | $1,561,180 | 94.4% |
| | Operating Income and Distribution | | | | |
| 23. | Operating Income | $1,826,514 | 100.0% | $1,654,228 | 100.0% |
| 24. | Less:  Cost of sales and operations | $1,193,622 | 65.4% | $1,141,807 | 69.0% |
| 25. | Gross operating profit | $632,892 | 34.7% | $512,421 | 31.0% |
| 26. | Additional operating costs | $496,548 | 27.2% | $419,373 | 25.4% |
| 27. | Net operating profit | $136,344 | 7.5% | $93,048 | 5.6% |
| 28. | Less:  Guaranteed payments to partners | $57,103 | | $66,429 | |
| 29. | Distribution to partners | $79,241 | | $26,619 | |
| 30. | Other charges | $25,107 | | $800 | |
| 31. | Net change partners' capital | $54,134 | | $25,819 | |
| | Selected Ratios | | | | |
| 32. | Coverage ratio:  times interest earned | 3.0 | | 2.1 | |
| 33. | Inventory turnover (times) | 3.6 | | 3.0 | |
| 34. | Days' sales in inventory | 107.4 | | 121.9 | |
| 35. | Average age of inventory (days) | 100.2 | | 120.9 | |
| 36. | Return on assets, net inc., less def | 6.8% | | 4.0% | |
| 37. | Return on assets, gross operating profit | 78.4% | | 77.9% | |
| 38. | Return on assets, net operating profit | 16.9% | | 14.2% | |

*Page 61*

Table 1: Partnerships With and Without Net Income:  127.  APPAREL AND ACCESSORY STORES

Dollar values in thousands, except averages

|  |  | 1984 |  | 1985 |  |
|---|---|---|---|---|---|
| 1. | Number of Partnerships | 12,268 |  | 12,575 |  |
| 2. | Number of Partners | 29,319 |  | 29,381 |  |
| 3. | Total Assets | $807,707 |  | $0 |  |
| 4. | Average total assets per Partnership | $65,839 |  | $0 |  |
| 5. | Average total assets per Partner | $27,549 |  | $0 |  |
| 6. | Net Income, less Deficit | $7,365 |  | $46,837 |  |
| 7. | Average per Partnership, total earnings | $603 |  | $3,728 |  |
| 8. | Average per Partner, total earnings | $252 |  | $1,596 |  |
| 9. | Operating Income | $1,765,784 |  | $1,773,124 |  |
|  | Operating Costs |  |  |  |  |
| 10. | Cost of sales & operations | $1,098,751 | 62.2% | $1,090,798 | 61.5% |
| 11. | Salaries and wages | $173,104 | 9.8% | $154,314 | 8.7% |
| 12. | Rent paid | $132,666 | 7.5% | $106,039 | 6.0% |
| 13. | Interest paid | $17,184 | 0.10% | $16,089 | 0.9% |
| 14. | Taxes paid | $38,195 | 2.2% | $47,145 | 2.7% |
| 15. | Bad debts | $944 | 0.1% | $1,598 | 0.1% |
| 16. | Repairs | $9,239 | 0.5% | $8,292 | 0.5% |
| 17. | Depreciation | $29,867 | 1.7% | $26,950 | 1.5% |
| 18. | Depletion | $0 | n.a. | $0 | n.a. |
| 19. | Pension & profit sharing plans | $320 | 0.0% | $967 | 0.1% |
| 20. | Employee benefits programs | $1,376 | 0.1% | $5,976 | 0.3% |
| 21. | Other deductions | $222,828 | 12.6% | $217,125 | 12.3% |
| 22. | Total operating costs | $1,724,474 | 97.7% | $1,675,293 | 94.5% |
|  | Operating Income and Distribution |  |  |  |  |
| 23. | Operating Income | $1,765,784 | 100.0% | $1,773,124 | 100.0% |
| 24. | Less: Cost of sales and operations | $1,098,751 | 62.2% | $1,090,798 | 61.5% |
| 25. | Gross operating profit | $667,033 | 37.8% | $682,326 | 38.5% |
| 26. | Additional operating costs | $625,723 | 35.4% | $584,495 | 33.0% |
| 27. | Net operating profit | $41,310 | 2.3% | $97,831 | 5.5% |
| 28. | Less: Guaranteed payments to partners | $32,614 |  | $47,744 |  |
| 29. | Distribution to partners | $8,696 |  | $50,087 |  |
| 30. | Other charges | $1,331 |  | $3,250 |  |
| 31. | Net change partners' capital | $7,365 |  | $46,837 |  |
|  | Selected Ratios |  |  |  |  |
| 32. | Coverage ratio: times interest earned | 1.4 |  | 5.1 |  |
| 33. | Inventory turnover (times) | 2.7 |  | 2.3 |  |
| 34. | Days' sales in inventory | 152.0 |  | 167.7 |  |
| 35. | Average age of inventory (days) | 137.0 |  | 156.1 |  |
| 36. | Return on assets, net inc., less def | 0.9% |  | n.a. |  |
| 37. | Return on assets, gross operating profit | 82.6% |  | n.a. |  |
| 38. | Return on assets, net operating profit | 5.1% |  | n.a. |  |

Table 1: Partnerships With and Without Net Income:   136.   FURNITURE AND HOME FURNISHINGS STORES

Dollar values in thousands, except averages

|  |  | 1984 | | 1985 | |
|---|---|---|---|---|---|
| 1. | Number of Partnerships | 10,056 | | 10,807 | |
| 2. | Number of Partners | 21,925 | | 25,531 | |
| | | | | | |
| 3. | Total Assets | $794,871 | | $993,778 | |
| 4. | Average total assets per Partnership | $79,044 | | $91,957 | |
| 5. | Average total assets per Partner | $36,254 | | $38,924 | |
| | | | | | |
| 6. | Net Income, less Deficit | $151,633 | | $172,942 | |
| 7. | Average per Partnership, total earnings | $15,081 | | $16,007 | |
| 8. | Average per Partner, total earnings | $6,917 | | $6,776 | |
| | | | | | |
| 9. | Operating Income | $2,146,440 | | $2,543,401 | |
| | Operating Costs | | | | |
| 10. | Cost of sales & operations | $1,416,801 | 66.0% | $1,600,612 | 62.9% |
| 11. | Salaries and wages | $129,956 | 6.1% | $168,202 | 6.6% |
| 12. | Rent paid | $78,095 | 3.6% | $79,149 | 3.1% |
| 13. | Interest paid | $22,505 | 1.1% | $28,846 | 1.1% |
| 14. | Taxes paid | $30,237 | 1.4% | $39,247 | 1.5% |
| 15. | Bad debts | $3,887 | 0.2% | $5,674 | 0.2% |
| 16. | Repairs | $6,729 | 0.3% | $10,536 | 0.4% |
| 17. | Depreciation | $24,523 | 1.1% | $34,278 | 1.4% |
| 18. | Depletion | $0 | n.a. | $0 | n.a. |
| 19. | Pension & profit sharing plans | $365 | 0.0% | $7,778 | 0.3% |
| 20. | Employee benefits programs | $893 | 0.0% | $2,235 | 0.1% |
| 21. | Other deductions | $254,748 | 11.9% | $342,590 | 13.5% |
| 22. | Total operating costs | $1,968,842 | 91.7% | $2,319,175 | 91.2% |
| | | | | | |
| | Operating Income and Distribution | | | | |
| 23. | Operating Income | $2,146,440 | 100.0% | $2,543,401 | 100.0% |
| 24. | Less:  Cost of sales and operations | $1,416,801 | 66.0% | $1,600,612 | 62.9% |
| 25. | Gross operating profit | $729,639 | 34.0% | $942,789 | 37.1% |
| 26. | Additional operating costs | $552,041 | 25.7% | $718,563 | 28.3% |
| 27. | Net operating profit | $177,598 | 8.3% | $224,226 | 8.8% |
| 28. | Less:  Guaranteed payments to partners | $25,038 | | $50,161 | |
| 29. | Distribution to partners | $152,560 | | $174,065 | |
| 30. | Other charges | $1,030 | | $1,151 | |
| 31. | Net change partners' capital | $151,530 | | $172,914 | |
| | | | | | |
| | Selected Ratios | | | | |
| 32. | Coverage ratio:  times interest earned | 6.9 | | 6.8 | |
| 33. | Inventory turnover (times) | 4.1 | | 3.8 | |
| 34. | Days' sales in inventory | 104.3 | | 105.5 | |
| 35. | Average age of inventory (days) | 88.9 | | 96.9 | |
| 36. | Return on assets, net inc., less def | 19.1% | | 17.4% | |
| 37. | Return on assets, gross operating profit | 91.8% | | 94.9% | |
| 38. | Return on assets, net operating profit | 22.3% | | 22.6% | |

*Page 63*

Table 1: Partnerships With and Without Net Income:  145.  EATING PLACES

Dollar values in thousands, except averages

|  |  | 1984 |  | 1985 |  |
|---|---|---|---|---|---|
| 1. | Number of Partnerships | 31,539 |  | 32,787 |  |
| 2. | Number of Partners | 88,894 |  | 92,362 |  |
|  |  |  |  |  |  |
| 3. | Total Assets | $2,707,639 |  | $0 |  |
| 4. | Average total assets per Partnership | $85,851 |  | $0 |  |
| 5. | Average total assets per Partner | $30,459 |  | $0 |  |
|  |  |  |  |  |  |
| 6. | Net Income, less Deficit | $180,893 |  | $343,561 |  |
| 7. | Average per Partnership, total earnings | $5,738 |  | $10,482 |  |
| 8. | Average per Partner, total earnings | $2,036 |  | $3,721 |  |
|  |  |  |  |  |  |
| 9. | Operating Income | $8,383,081 |  | $8,892,511 |  |
|  | Operating Costs |  |  |  |  |
| 10. | Cost of sales & operations | $3,844,633 | 45.9% | $3,820,772 | 43.0% |
| 11. | Salaries and wages | $1,351,628 | 16.1% | $1,594,093 | 17.9% |
| 12. | Rent paid | $559,021 | 6.7% | $553,053 | 6.2% |
| 13. | Interest paid | $168,247 | 2.0% | $146,084 | 1.6% |
| 14. | Taxes paid | $271,087 | 3.2% | $295,912 | 3.3% |
| 15. | Bad debts | $1,385 | 0.0% | $3,168 | 0.0% |
| 16. | Repairs | $104,429 | 1.3% | $103,652 | 1.2% |
| 17. | Depreciation | $292,545 | 3.5% | $310,127 | 3.5% |
| 18. | Depletion | $0 | n.a. | $0 | n.a. |
| 19. | Pension & profit sharing plans | $1,072 | 0.0% | $1,172 | 0.0% |
| 20. | Employee benefits programs | $9,403 | 0.1% | $10,271 | 0.1% |
| 21. | Other deductions | $1,487,537 | 17.7% | $1,544,177 | 17.4% |
| 22. | Total operating costs | $8,092,340 | 96.5% | $8,384,270 | 94.3% |
|  |  |  |  |  |  |
| | Operating Income and Distribution |  |  |  |  |
| 23. | Operating Income | $8,383,081 | 100.0% | $8,892,511 | 100.0% |
| 24. | Less:  Cost of sales and operations | $3,844,633 | 45.9% | $3,820,772 | 43.0% |
| 25. | Gross operating profit | $4,538,448 | 54.1% | $5,071,739 | 57.0% |
| 26. | Additional operating costs | $4,247,707 | 50.7% | $4,563,498 | 51.3% |
| 27. | Net operating profit | $290,741 | 3.5% | $508,241 | 5.7% |
| 28. | Less:  Guaranteed payments to partners | $92,536 |  | $124,661 |  |
| 29. | Distribution to partners | $198,205 |  | $383,580 |  |
| 30. | Other charges | $18,665 |  | $41,809 |  |
| 31. | Net change partners' capital | $179,540 |  | $341,771 |  |
|  |  |  |  |  |  |
| | Selected Ratios |  |  |  |  |
| 32. | Coverage ratio:  times interest earned | 0.7 |  | 2.5 |  |
| 33. | Inventory turnover (times) | 29.8 |  | 28.2 |  |
| 34. | Days' sales in inventory | 12.9 |  | 13.3 |  |
| 35. | Average age of inventory (days) | 12.2 |  | 12.9 |  |
| 36. | Return on assets, net inc., less def | 6.7% |  | n.a. |  |
| 37. | Return on assets, gross operating profit | 167.6% |  | n.a. |  |
| 38. | Return on assets, net operating profit | 10.7% |  | n.a. |  |

Table 1: Partnerships With and Without Net Income:  146.  DRINKING PLACES

Dollar values in thousands, except averages

|  |  | 1984 |  | 1985 |  |
|---|---|---|---|---|---|
| 1. | Number of Partnerships | 3,591 | | 4,778 | |
| 2. | Number of Partners | 7,631 | | 10,055 | |
| 3. | Total Assets | $160,629 | | $233,381 | |
| 4. | Average total assets per Partnership | $44,731 | | $48,845 | |
| 5. | Average total assets per Partner | $21,050 | | $23,210 | |
| 6. | Net Income, less Deficit | ($999) | | $60,540 | |
| 7. | Average per Partnership, total earnings | ($277) | | $12,672 | |
| 8. | Average per Partner, total earnings | ($130) | | $6,021 | |
| 9. | Operating Income | $287,313 | | $714,287 | |
|  | Operating Costs | | | | |
| 10. | Cost of sales & operations | $144,543 | 50.3% | $332,757 | 46.6% |
| 11. | Salaries and wages | $22,143 | 7.7% | $87,324 | 12.2% |
| 12. | Rent paid | $15,660 | 5.5% | $30,340 | 4.3% |
| 13. | Interest paid | $10,874 | 3.8% | $8,442 | 1.2% |
| 14. | Taxes paid | $15,110 | 5.3% | $29,798 | 4.2% |
| 15. | Bad debts | $40 | 0.0% | $12 | n.a. |
| 16. | Repairs | $5,390 | 1.9% | $12,063 | 1.7% |
| 17. | Depreciation | $19,218 | 6.7% | $32,486 | 4.6% |
| 18. | Depletion | $0 | n.a. | $0 | n.a. |
| 19. | Pension & profit sharing plans | $0 | n.a. | $0 | n.a. |
| 20. | Employee benefits programs | $173 | 0.1% | $1,081 | 0.2% |
| 21. | Other deductions | $47,587 | 16.6% | $112,910 | 15.8% |
| 22. | Total operating costs | $280,742 | 97.7% | $647,250 | 90.6% |
|  | Operating Income and Distribution | | | | |
| 23. | Operating Income | $287,313 | 100.0% | $714,287 | 100.0% |
| 24. | Less: Cost of sales and operations | $144,543 | 50.3% | $332,757 | 46.6% |
| 25. | Gross operating profit | $142,770 | 49.7% | $381,530 | 53.4% |
| 26. | Additional operating costs | $136,199 | 47.4% | $314,493 | 44.0% |
| 27. | Net operating profit | $6,571 | 2.3% | $67,037 | 9.4% |
| 28. | Less: Guaranteed payments to partners | $5,225 | | $4,723 | |
| 29. | Distribution to partners | $1,346 | | $62,314 | |
| 30. | Other charges | $2,349 | | $1,810 | |
| 31. | Net change partners' capital | ($1,003) | | $60,504 | |
|  | Selected Ratios | | | | |
| 32. | Coverage ratio: times interest earned | (0.4) | | 6.9 | |
| 33. | Inventory turnover (times) | 31.0 | | 16.6 | |
| 34. | Days' sales in inventory | 12.6 | | 22.9 | |
| 35. | Average age of inventory (days) | 11.8 | | 22.0 | |
| 36. | Return on assets, net inc., less def | (0.6%) | | 25.9% | |
| 37. | Return on assets, gross operating profit | 88.9% | | 163.5% | |
| 38. | Return on assets, net operating profit | 4.1% | | 28.7% | |

Table 1: Partnerships With and Without Net Income:  149.  LIQUOR STORES

Dollar values in thousands, except averages

|  | 1984 | | 1985 | |
|---|---|---|---|---|
| 1.  Number of Partnerships | 3,167 | | 3,024 | |
| 2.  Number of Partners | 7,176 | | 6,728 | |
| 3.  Total Assets | $394,940 | | $299,838 | |
| 4.    Average total assets per Partnership | $124,705 | | $99,153 | |
| 5.    Average total assets per Partner | $55,036 | | $44,566 | |
| 6.  Net Income, less Deficit | $48,952 | | $35,953 | |
| 7.    Average per Partnership, total earnings | $15,459 | | $11,892 | |
| 8.    Average per Partner, total earnings | $6,823 | | $5,345 | |
| 9.  Operating Income | $1,539,106 | | $1,100,109 | |
|     Operating Costs | | | | |
| 10.    Cost of sales & operations | $1,211,429 | 78.7% | $870,878 | 79.2% |
| 11.    Salaries and wages | $88,369 | 5.7% | $45,106 | 4.1% |
| 12.    Rent paid | $21,085 | 1.4% | $21,935 | 2.0% |
| 13.    Interest paid | $18,621 | 1.2% | $13,175 | 1.2% |
| 14.    Taxes paid | $26,078 | 1.7% | $24,748 | 2.3% |
| 15.    Bad debts | $1,668 | 0.1% | $249 | 0.0% |
| 16.    Repairs | $6,213 | 0.4% | $5,817 | 0.5% |
| 17.    Depreciation | $26,911 | 1.8% | $14,153 | 1.3% |
| 18.    Depletion | $0 | n.a. | $0 | n.a. |
| 19.    Pension & profit sharing plans | $0 | n.a. | $0 | n.a. |
| 20.    Employee benefits programs | $130 | 0.0% | $183 | 0.0% |
| 21.    Other deductions | $81,816 | 5.3% | $60,971 | 5.5% |
| 22.    Total operating costs | $1,482,320 | 96.3% | $1,057,215 | 96.1% |
| Operating Income and Distribution | | | | |
| 23.    Operating Income | $1,539,106 | 100.0% | $1,100,109 | 100.0% |
| 24.      Less:  Cost of sales and operations | $1,211,429 | 78.7% | $870,878 | 79.2% |
| 25.    Gross operating profit | $327,677 | 21.3% | $229,231 | 20.8% |
| 26.      Additional operating costs | $270,891 | 17.6% | $186,337 | 16.9% |
| 27.    Net operating profit | $56,786 | 3.7% | $42,894 | 3.9% |
| 28.      Less:  Guaranteed payments to partners | $7,828 | | $6,895 | |
| 29.    Distribution to partners | $48,958 | | $35,999 | |
| 30.    Other charges | $6 | | $46 | |
| 31.    Net change partners' capital | $48,952 | | $35,953 | |
| Selected Ratios | | | | |
| 32.    Coverage ratio:  times interest earned | 2.1 | | 2.3 | |
| 33.    Inventory turnover (times) | 7.2 | | 6.0 | |
| 34.    Days' sales in inventory | 51.1 | | 61.1 | |
| 35.    Average age of inventory (days) | 51.0 | | 60.8 | |
| 36.    Return on assets, net inc., less def | 12.4% | | 12.0% | |
| 37.    Return on assets, gross operating profit | 83.0% | | 76.5% | |
| 38.    Return on assets, net operating profit | 14.4% | | 14.3% | |

Table 1: Partnerships With and Without Net Income:  OTHER RETAIL STORES (148,150 TO 164,167,168,169,170)

Dollar values in thousands, except averages

|  |  | 1984 |  | 1985 |  |
|---|---|---|---|---|---|
| 1. | Number of Partnerships | 52,186 |  | 58,412 |  |
| 2. | Number of Partners | 117,518 |  | 138,552 |  |
| 3. | Total Assets | $2,367,994 |  | $3,236,526 |  |
| 4. | Average total assets per Partnership | $45,376 |  | $55,409 |  |
| 5. | Average total assets per Partner | $20,150 |  | $23,360 |  |
| 6. | Net Income, less Deficit | $219,111 |  | $251,504 |  |
| 7. | Average per Partnership, total earnings | $4,201 |  | $4,309 |  |
| 8. | Average per Partner, total earnings | $1,866 |  | $1,816 |  |
| 9. | Operating Income | $6,823,948 |  | $7,957,701 |  |
|  | Operating Costs |  |  |  |  |
| 10. | Cost of sales & operations | $4,530,295 | 66.4% | $5,026,742 | 63.2% |
| 11. | Salaries and wages | $499,933 | 7.3% | $645,383 | 8.1% |
| 12. | Rent paid | $251,445 | 3.7% | $305,902 | 3.8% |
| 13. | Interest paid | $96,821 | 1.4% | $142,951 | 1.8% |
| 14. | Taxes paid | $112,355 | 1.7% | $139,832 | 1.8% |
| 15. | Bad debts | $15,022 | 0.2% | $20,754 | 0.3% |
| 16. | Repairs | $33,895 | 0.5% | $42,820 | 0.5% |
| 17. | Depreciation | $135,522 | 2.0% | $213,640 | 2.7% |
| 18. | Depletion | $470 | 0.0% | $0 | n.a. |
| 19. | Pension & profit sharing plans | $4,850 | 0.1% | $4,591 | 0.1% |
| 20. | Employee benefits programs | $8,847 | 0.1% | $9,575 | 0.1% |
| 21. | Other deductions | $771,405 | 11.3% | $971,798 | 12.2% |
| 22. | Total operating costs | $6,461,547 | 94.7% | $7,524,915 | 94.6% |

Operating Income and Distribution

|  |  | 1984 |  | 1985 |  |
|---|---|---|---|---|---|
| 23. | Operating Income | $6,823,948 | 100.0% | $7,957,701 | 100.0% |
| 24. | Less:  Cost of sales and operations | $4,530,295 | 66.4% | $5,026,742 | 63.2% |
| 25. | Gross operating profit | $2,293,653 | 33.6% | $2,930,959 | 36.8% |
| 26. | Additional operating costs | $1,931,252 | 28.3% | $2,498,173 | 31.4% |
| 27. | Net operating profit | $362,401 | 5.3% | $432,786 | 5.4% |
| 28. | Less:  Guaranteed payments to partners | $141,074 |  | $170,091 |  |
| 29. | Distribution to partners | $221,327 |  | $262,695 |  |
| 30. | Other charges | $2,904 |  | $12,118 |  |
| 31. | Net change partners' capital | $218,423 |  | $250,577 |  |

Selected Ratios

|  |  | 1984 | 1985 |
|---|---|---|---|
| 32. | Coverage ratio:  times interest earned | 2.7 | 2.0 |
| 33. | Inventory turnover (times) | 4.1 | 3.9 |
| 34. | Days' sales in inventory | 93.5 | 103.1 |
| 35. | Average age of inventory (days) | 88.2 | 94.8 |
| 36. | Return on assets, net inc., less def | 9.3% | 7.8% |
| 37. | Return on assets, gross operating profit | 96.9% | 90.6% |
| 38. | Return on assets, net operating profit | 15.3% | 13.4% |

Table 1: Partnerships With and Without Net Income:  172.  FINANCE, INSURANCE, AND REAL  ESTATE

Dollar values in thousands, except averages

| | 1984 | | 1985 | |
|---|---|---|---|---|
| 1.  Number of Partnerships | 790,902 | | 843,867 | |
| 2.  Number of Partners | 7,408,313 | | 7,754,557 | |
| | | | | |
| 3.  Total Assets | $770,457,317 | | $979,786,543 | |
| 4.  Average total assets per Partnership | $974,150 | | $1,161,067 | |
| 5.  Average total assets per Partner | $103,999 | | $126,350 | |
| | | | | |
| 6.  Net Income, less Deficit | ($19,243,718) | | ($25,928,668) | |
| 7.  Average per Partnership, total earnings | ($24,330) | | ($30,724) | |
| 8.  Average per Partner, total earnings | ($2,597) | | ($3,343) | |
| | | | | |
| 9.  Total Receipts | $54,902,201 | | $45,873,102 | |
| Operating Costs | | | | |
| 10.  Cost of sales & operations | $38,507,475 | 70.1% | $28,284,922 | 61.7% |
| 11.  Salaries and wages | $2,590,101 | 4.7% | $3,703,094 | 8.1% |
| 12.  Rent paid | $735,671 | 1.3% | $805,432 | 1.8% |
| 13.  Interest paid | $15,487,083 | 28.2% | $17,772,393 | 38.7% |
| 14.  Taxes paid | $1,859,838 | 3.4% | $2,187,992 | 4.8% |
| 15.  Bad debts | $194,731 | 0.4% | $232,559 | 0.5% |
| 16.  Repairs | $470,394 | 0.9% | $460,933 | 1.0% |
| 17.  Depreciation | $5,180,942 | 9.4% | $5,961,683 | 13.0% |
| 18.  Depletion | $1,918 | n.a. | $10,542 | 0.0% |
| 19.  Pension & profit sharing plans | $45,035 | 0.1% | $113,262 | 0.3% |
| 20.  Employee benefits programs | $71,725 | 0.1% | $120,440 | 0.3% |
| 21.  Other deductions | $13,366,407 | 24.4% | $14,826,952 | 32.3% |
| 22.  Total operating costs | $78,512,419 | 143.0% | $74,481,938 | 162.4% |
| | | | | |
| Operating Income and Distribution | | | | |
| 23.  Total Receipts | $54,902,201 | 100.0% | $45,873,102 | 100.0% |
| 24.  Less:  Cost of sales and operations | $38,507,475 | 70.1% | $28,284,922 | 61.7% |
| 25.  Gross operating profit | $16,394,726 | 29.9% | $17,588,180 | 38.3% |
| 26.  Additional operating costs | $40,004,944 | 72.9% | $46,197,016 | 100.7% |
| 27.  Net operating profit | ($23,610,218) | (43.0%) | ($28,608,836) | (62.4%) |
| 28.  Less:  Guaranteed payments to partners | $1,392,157 | | $1,557,468 | |
| 29.  Distribution to partners | ($25,002,375) | | ($30,166,304) | |
| 30.  Other charges | $33,702,676 | | $42,199,651 | |
| 31.  Net change partners' capital | ($58,705,051) | | ($72,365,955) | |
| | | | | |
| Selected Ratios | | | | |
| 32.  Coverage ratio:  times interest earned | (2.5) | | (2.6) | |
| 33.  Inventory turnover (times) | n.a. | | n.a. | |
| 34.  Days' sales in inventory | n.a. | | n.a. | |
| 35.  Average age of inventory (days) | n.a. | | n.a. | |
| 36.  Return on assets, net inc., less def | (2.5%) | | (2.7%) | |
| 37.  Return on assets, gross operating profit | 2.1% | | 1.8% | |
| 38.  Return on assets, net operating profit | (3.1%) | | (2.9%) | |

Table 1: Partnerships With and Without Net Income:  173.  FINANCE

Dollar values in thousands, except averages

|  |  | 1984 |  | 1985 |  |
|---|---|---|---|---|---|
| 1. | Number of Partnerships | 144,175 |  | 141,481 |  |
| 2. | Number of Partners | 2,163,044 |  | 1,733,011 |  |
| 3. | Total Assets | $168,934,031 |  | $252,087,705 |  |
| 4. | Average total assets per Partnership | $1,171,729 |  | $1,781,778 |  |
| 5. | Average total assets per Partner | $78,100 |  | $145,462 |  |
| 6. | Net Income, less Deficit | $1,359,929 |  | $3,462,095 |  |
| 7. | Average per Partnership, total earnings | $9,435 |  | $24,474 |  |
| 8. | Average per Partner, total earnings | $629 |  | $1,998 |  |
| 9. | Total Receipts | $26,170,236 |  | $15,244,569 |  |
|  | Operating Costs |  |  |  |  |
| 10. | Cost of sales & operations | $22,016,952 | 84.1% | $10,163,521 | 66.7% |
| 11. | Salaries and wages | $1,157,532 | 4.4% | $1,677,763 | 11.0% |
| 12. | Rent paid | $198,099 | 0.8% | $174,211 | 1.1% |
| 13. | Interest paid | $5,097,467 | 19.5% | $5,676,961 | 37.2% |
| 14. | Taxes paid | $286,617 | 1.1% | $345,857 | 2.3% |
| 15. | Bad debts | $80,009 | 0.3% | $51,736 | 0.3% |
| 16. | Repairs | $33,994 | 0.1% | $51,604 | 0.3% |
| 17. | Depreciation | $586,568 | 2.2% | $576,757 | 3.8% |
| 18. | Depletion | $464 | n.a. | $511 | n.a. |
| 19. | Pension & profit sharing plans | $28,232 | 0.1% | $93,835 | 0.6% |
| 20. | Employee benefits programs | $33,629 | 0.1% | $40,958 | 0.3% |
| 21. | Other deductions | $3,732,363 | 14.3% | $3,698,846 | 24.3% |
| 22. | Total operating costs | $33,252,121 | 127.1% | $22,553,128 | 147.9% |
|  | Operating Income and Distribution |  |  |  |  |
| 23. | Total Receipts | $26,170,236 | 100.0% | $15,244,569 | 100.0% |
| 24. | Less: Cost of sales and operations | $22,016,952 | 84.1% | $10,163,521 | 66.7% |
| 25. | Gross operating profit | $4,153,284 | 15.9% | $5,081,048 | 33.3% |
| 26. | Additional operating costs | $11,235,169 | 42.9% | $12,389,607 | 81.3% |
| 27. | Net operating profit | ($7,081,885) | (27.1%) | ($7,308,559) | (47.9%) |
| 28. | Less: Guaranteed payments to partners | $419,345 |  | $553,798 |  |
| 29. | Distribution to partners | ($7,501,230) |  | ($7,862,357) |  |
| 30. | Other charges | $2,495,437 |  | $3,062,306 |  |
| 31. | Net change partners' capital | ($9,996,667) |  | ($10,924,663) |  |
|  | Selected Ratios |  |  |  |  |
| 32. | Coverage ratio: times interest earned | (2.4) |  | (2.3) |  |
| 33. | Inventory turnover (times) | n.a. |  | n.a. |  |
| 34. | Days' sales in inventory | n.a. |  | n.a. |  |
| 35. | Average age of inventory (days) | n.a. |  | n.a. |  |
| 36. | Return on assets, net inc., less def | 0.8% |  | 1.4% |  |
| 37. | Return on assets, gross operating profit | 2.5% |  | 2.0% |  |
| 38. | Return on assets, net operating profit | (4.2%) |  | (2.9%) |  |

Table 1: Partnerships With and Without Net Income:  BANKING AND CREDIT AGENCIES OTHER THAN BANKS (174,175)

Dollar values in thousands, except averages

| | 1984 | | 1985 | |
|---|---|---|---|---|
| 1. Number of Partnerships | 3,708 | | 4,066 | |
| 2. Number of Partners | 252,898 | | 40,391 | |
| | | | | |
| 3. Total Assets | $17,281,211 | | $6,385,594 | |
| 4. Average total assets per Partnership | $4,660,521 | | $1,570,485 | |
| 5. Average total assets per Partner | $68,333 | | $158,094 | |
| | | | | |
| 6. Net Income, less Deficit | $577,292 | | $120,065 | |
| 7. Average per Partnership, total earnings | $155,692 | | $29,531 | |
| 8. Average per Partner, total earnings | $2,283 | | $2,973 | |
| | | | | |
| 9. Total Receipts | $732,280 | | $632,300 | |
| Operating Costs | | | | |
| 10. Cost of sales & operations | $600,043 | 81.9% | $462,042 | 73.1% |
| 11. Salaries and wages | $74,659 | 10.2% | $71,296 | 11.3% |
| 12. Rent paid | $11,722 | 1.6% | $12,018 | 1.9% |
| 13. Interest paid | $212,081 | 29.0% | $389,031 | 61.5% |
| 14. Taxes paid | $5,908 | 0.8% | $3,696 | 0.6% |
| 15. Bad debts | $6,929 | 0.10% | $14,749 | 2.3% |
| 16. Repairs | $1,105 | 0.2% | $2,311 | 0.4% |
| 17. Depreciation | $10,952 | 1.5% | $10,385 | 1.6% |
| 18. Depletion | $0 | n.a. | $0 | n.a. |
| 19. Pension & profit sharing plans | $2,602 | 0.4% | $1,676 | 0.3% |
| 20. Employee benefits programs | $2,706 | 0.4% | $3,094 | 0.5% |
| 21. Other deductions | $108,072 | 14.8% | $97,652 | 15.4% |
| 22. Total operating costs | $1,036,796 | 141.6% | $1,068,045 | 168.9% |
| | | | | |
| Operating Income and Distribution | | | | |
| 23. Total Receipts | $732,280 | 100.0% | $632,300 | 100.0% |
| 24. Less: Cost of sales and operations | $600,043 | 81.9% | $462,042 | 73.1% |
| 25. Gross operating profit | $132,237 | 18.1% | $170,258 | 26.9% |
| 26. Additional operating costs | $436,753 | 59.6% | $606,003 | 95.8% |
| 27. Net operating profit | ($304,516) | (41.6%) | ($435,745) | (68.9%) |
| 28. Less: Guaranteed payments to partners | $13,397 | | $6,301 | |
| 29. Distribution to partners | ($317,913) | | ($442,046) | |
| 30. Other charges | $11,183 | | $7,906 | |
| 31. Net change partners' capital | ($329,096) | | ($449,952) | |
| | | | | |
| Selected Ratios | | | | |
| 32. Coverage ratio: times interest earned | (2.4) | | (2.1) | |
| 33. Inventory turnover (times) | n.a. | | n.a. | |
| 34. Days' sales in inventory | n.a. | | n.a. | |
| 35. Average age of inventory (days) | n.a. | | n.a. | |
| 36. Return on assets, net inc., less def | 3.3% | | 1.9% | |
| 37. Return on assets, gross operating profit | 0.8% | | 2.7% | |
| 38. Return on assets, net operating profit | (1.8%) | | (6.8%) | |

Table 1: Partnerships With and Without Net Income:   176.   SECURITY AND COMMODITY BROKERS AND SERVICES

Dollar values in thousands, except averages

|  |  | 1984 |  | 1985 |  |
|---|---|---|---|---|---|
| 1. | Number of Partnerships | 5,906 | | 2,398 | |
| 2. | Number of Partners | 98,369 | | 104,582 | |
| 3. | Total Assets | $54,851,976 | | $79,912,690 | |
| 4. | Average total assets per Partnership | $9,287,500 | | $33,324,725 | |
| 5. | Average total assets per Partner | $557,614 | | $764,115 | |
| 6. | Net Income, less Deficit | ($90,981) | | $1,338,746 | |
| 7. | Average per Partnership, total earnings | ($15,365) | | $558,372 | |
| 8. | Average per Partner, total earnings | ($923) | | $12,803 | |
| 9. | Total Receipts | $22,699,407 | | $11,158,778 | |
|  | Operating Costs | | | | |
| 10. | Cost of sales & operations | $20,284,623 | 89.4% | $7,963,459 | 71.4% |
| 11. | Salaries and wages | $888,598 | 3.9% | $1,092,593 | 9.8% |
| 12. | Rent paid | $148,237 | 0.7% | $93,252 | 0.8% |
| 13. | Interest paid | $3,273,752 | 14.4% | $2,457,175 | 22.0% |
| 14. | Taxes paid | $77,463 | 0.3% | $93,092 | 0.8% |
| 15. | Bad debts | $13,935 | 0.1% | $6,854 | 0.1% |
| 16. | Repairs | $7,378 | 0.0% | $6,092 | 0.1% |
| 17. | Depreciation | $30,855 | 0.1% | $37,342 | 0.3% |
| 18. | Depletion | $166 | n.a. | $131 | n.a. |
| 19. | Pension & profit sharing plans | $24,558 | 0.1% | $25,789 | 0.2% |
| 20. | Employee benefits programs | $22,570 | 0.1% | $27,901 | 0.3% |
| 21. | Other deductions | $1,610,605 | 7.1% | $1,675,925 | 15.0% |
| 22. | Total operating costs | $26,382,893 | 116.2% | $13,479,629 | 120.8% |
|  | **Operating Income and Distribution** | | | | |
| 23. | Total Receipts | $22,699,407 | 100.0% | $11,158,778 | 100.0% |
| 24. | Less: Cost of sales and operations | $20,284,623 | 89.4% | $7,963,459 | 71.4% |
| 25. | Gross operating profit | $2,414,784 | 10.6% | $3,195,319 | 28.6% |
| 26. | Additional operating costs | $6,098,270 | 26.9% | $5,516,170 | 49.4% |
| 27. | Net operating profit | ($3,683,486) | (16.2%) | ($2,320,851) | (20.8%) |
| 28. | Less: Guaranteed payments to partners | $236,070 | | $230,627 | |
| 29. | Distribution to partners | ($3,919,556) | | ($2,551,478) | |
| 30. | Other charges | $302,834 | | $137,279 | |
| 31. | Net change partners' capital | ($4,222,390) | | ($2,688,757) | |
|  | **Selected Ratios** | | | | |
| 32. | Coverage ratio: times interest earned | (2.1) | | (1.9) | |
| 33. | Inventory turnover (times) | n.a. | | n.a. | |
| 34. | Days' sales in inventory | n.a. | | n.a. | |
| 35. | Average age of inventory (days) | n.a. | | n.a. | |
| 36. | Return on assets, net inc., less def | (0.2%) | | 1.7% | |
| 37. | Return on assets, gross operating profit | 4.4% | | 4.0% | |
| 38. | Return on assets, net operating profit | (6.7%) | | (2.9%) | |

*Page 71*

Table 1: Partnerships With and Without Net Income:  180.  HOLDING AND INVESTMENT COMPANIES

Dollar values in thousands, except averages

| | 1984 | | 1985 | |
|---|---|---|---|---|
| 1.  Number of Partnerships | 134,562 | | 135,017 | |
| 2.  Number of Partners | 1,811,777 | | 1,588,028 | |
| | | | | |
| 3.  Total Assets | $96,800,843 | | $165,789,422 | |
| 4.  Average total assets per Partnership | $719,377 | | $1,227,915 | |
| 5.  Average total assets per Partner | $53,429 | | $104,400 | |
| | | | | |
| 6.  Net Income, less Deficit | $873,618 | | $2,003,283 | |
| 7.  Average per Partnership, total earnings | $6,494 | | $14,840 | |
| 8.  Average per Partner, total earnings | $482 | | $1,262 | |
| | | | | |
| 9.  Total Receipts | $2,738,548 | | $3,453,490 | |
| Operating Costs | | | | |
| 10.  Cost of sales & operations | $1,132,286 | 41.4% | $1,738,020 | 50.3% |
| 11.  Salaries and wages | $194,275 | 7.1% | $513,874 | 14.9% |
| 12.  Rent paid | $38,140 | 1.4% | $68,942 | 2.0% |
| 13.  Interest paid | $1,611,634 | 58.9% | $2,830,755 | 82.0% |
| 14.  Taxes paid | $203,246 | 7.4% | $249,069 | 7.2% |
| 15.  Bad debts | $59,145 | 2.2% | $30,133 | 0.9% |
| 16.  Repairs | $25,511 | 0.9% | $43,202 | 1.3% |
| 17.  Depreciation | $546,764 | 20.0% | $529,040 | 15.3% |
| 18.  Depletion | $299 | 0.0% | $380 | 0.0% |
| 19.  Pension & profit sharing plans | $1,072 | 0.0% | $66,370 | 1.9% |
| 20.  Employee benefits programs | $8,353 | 0.3% | $9,963 | 0.3% |
| 21.  Other deductions | $2,013,686 | 73.5% | $1,925,256 | 55.8% |
| 22.  Total operating costs | $5,834,436 | 213.1% | $8,005,453 | 231.8% |
| | | | | |
| Operating Income and Distribution | | | | |
| 23.  Total Receipts | $2,738,548 | 100.0% | $3,453,490 | 100.0% |
| 24.  Less:  Cost of sales and operations | $1,132,286 | 41.4% | $1,738,020 | 50.3% |
| 25.  Gross operating profit | $1,606,262 | 58.7% | $1,715,470 | 49.7% |
| 26.  Additional operating costs | $4,702,150 | 171.7% | $6,267,433 | 181.5% |
| 27.  Net operating profit | ($3,095,888) | (113.1%) | ($4,551,963) | (131.8%) |
| 28.  Less:  Guaranteed payments to partners | $169,878 | | $316,870 | |
| 29.  Distribution to partners | ($3,265,766) | | ($4,868,833) | |
| 30.  Other charges | $2,179,417 | | $2,917,122 | |
| 31.  Net change partners' capital | ($5,445,183) | | ($7,785,955) | |
| | | | | |
| Selected Ratios | | | | |
| 32.  Coverage ratio:  times interest earned | (2.9) | | (2.6) | |
| 33.  Inventory turnover (times) | n.a. | | n.a. | |
| 34.  Days' sales in inventory | n.a. | | n.a. | |
| 35.  Average age of inventory (days) | n.a. | | n.a. | |
| 36.  Return on assets, net inc., less def | 0.9% | | 1.2% | |
| 37.  Return on assets, gross operating profit | 1.7% | | 1.0% | |
| 38.  Return on assets, net operating profit | (3.2%) | | (2.8%) | |

*Page 72*

Table 1: Partnerships With and Without Net Income:  184.  INSURANCE AGENTS, BROKERS, AND SERVICES

Dollar values in thousands, except averages

| | 1984 | | 1985 | |
|---|---|---|---|---|
| 1. Number of Partnerships | 9,808 | | 8,360 | |
| 2. Number of Partners | 114,077 | | 29,060 | |
| | | | | |
| 3. Total Assets | $3,098,157 | | $3,356,758 | |
| 4. Average total assets per Partnership | $315,881 | | $401,526 | |
| 5. Average total assets per Partner | $27,158 | | $115,511 | |
| | | | | |
| 6. Net Income, less Deficit | $600,341 | | $367,804 | |
| 7. Average per Partnership, total earnings | $61,217 | | $44,005 | |
| 8. Average per Partner, total earnings | $5,263 | | $12,659 | |
| | | | | |
| 9. Total Receipts | $2,720,885 | | $2,019,801 | |
| Operating Costs | | | | |
| 10. Cost of sales & operations | $403,175 | 14.8% | $284,695 | 14.1% |
| 11. Salaries and wages | $216,082 | 7.9% | $254,055 | 12.6% |
| 12. Rent paid | $33,314 | 1.2% | $42,775 | 2.1% |
| 13. Interest paid | $34,675 | 1.3% | $38,266 | 1.9% |
| 14. Taxes paid | $33,619 | 1.2% | $35,370 | 1.8% |
| 15. Bad debts | $39,127 | 1.4% | $32,618 | 1.6% |
| 16. Repairs | $3,250 | 0.1% | $6,025 | 0.3% |
| 17. Depreciation | $24,097 | 0.9% | $38,796 | 1.9% |
| 18. Depletion | $0 | n.a. | $0 | n.a. |
| 19. Pension & profit sharing plans | $6,318 | 0.2% | $5,270 | 0.3% |
| 20. Employee benefits programs | $5,091 | 0.2% | $3,696 | 0.2% |
| 21. Other deductions | $1,620,910 | 59.6% | $1,727,336 | 85.5% |
| 22. Total operating costs | $2,419,820 | 88.9% | $2,469,013 | 122.2% |
| | | | | |
| Operating Income and Distribution | | | | |
| 23. Total Receipts | $2,720,885 | 100.0% | $2,019,801 | 100.0% |
| 24. Less: Cost of sales and operations | $403,175 | 14.8% | $284,695 | 14.1% |
| 25. Gross operating profit | $2,317,710 | 85.2% | $1,735,106 | 85.9% |
| 26. Additional operating costs | $2,016,645 | 74.1% | $2,184,318 | 108.2% |
| 27. Net operating profit | $301,065 | 11.1% | ($449,212) | (22.2%) |
| 28. Less: Guaranteed payments to partners | $78,559 | | $73,841 | |
| 29. Distribution to partners | $222,506 | | ($523,053) | |
| 30. Other charges | $18,773 | | $21,266 | |
| 31. Net change partners' capital | $203,733 | | ($544,319) | |
| | | | | |
| Selected Ratios | | | | |
| 32. Coverage ratio: times interest earned | 7.7 | | (12.7) | |
| 33. Inventory turnover (times) | n.a. | | n.a. | |
| 34. Days' sales in inventory | n.a. | | n.a. | |
| 35. Average age of inventory (days) | n.a. | | n.a. | |
| 36. Return on assets, net inc., less def | 19.4% | | 11.0% | |
| 37. Return on assets, gross operating profit | 74.8% | | 51.7% | |
| 38. Return on assets, net operating profit | 9.7% | | (13.4%) | |

Table 1: Partnerships With and Without Net Income: 185. REAL ESTATE

Dollar values in thousands, except averages

|  |  | 1984 |  | 1985 |  |
|---|---|---|---|---|---|
| 1. | Number of Partnerships | 636,920 | | 694,027 | |
| 2. | Number of Partners | 5,131,192 | | 5,992,476 | |
| 3. | Total Assets | $598,425,129 | | $724,342,079 | |
| 4. | Average total assets per Partnership | $939,561 | | $1,043,680 | |
| 5. | Average total assets per Partner | $116,625 | | $120,875 | |
| 6. | Net Income, less Deficit | ($21,203,988) | | ($29,758,568) | |
| 7. | Average per Partnership, total earnings | ($33,290) | | ($42,877) | |
| 8. | Average per Partner, total earnings | ($4,132) | | ($4,966) | |
| 9. | Total Receipts | $26,011,081 | | $28,608,732 | |
|  | Operating Costs | | | | |
| 10. | Cost of sales & operations | $16,087,348 | 61.9% | $17,836,706 | 62.4% |
| 11. | Salaries and wages | $1,216,487 | 4.7% | $1,771,275 | 6.2% |
| 12. | Rent paid | $504,258 | 1.9% | $588,446 | 2.1% |
| 13. | Interest paid | $10,354,941 | 39.8% | $12,057,165 | 42.2% |
| 14. | Taxes paid | $1,539,602 | 5.9% | $1,806,764 | 6.3% |
| 15. | Bad debts | $75,596 | 0.3% | $148,205 | 0.5% |
| 16. | Repairs | $433,150 | 1.7% | $403,303 | 1.4% |
| 17. | Depreciation | $4,568,277 | 17.6% | $5,346,121 | 18.7% |
| 18. | Depletion | $1,454 | 0.0% | $10,031 | 0.0% |
| 19. | Pension & profit sharing plans | $10,485 | 0.0% | $14,156 | 0.1% |
| 20. | Employee benefits programs | $33,005 | 0.1% | $75,786 | 0.3% |
| 21. | Other deductions | $8,013,134 | 30.8% | $9,400,785 | 32.9% |
| 22. | Total operating costs | $42,838,479 | 164.7% | $49,459,799 | 172.9% |
| | Operating Income and Distribution | | | | |
| 23. | Total Receipts | $26,011,081 | 100.0% | $28,608,732 | 100.0% |
| 24. | Less: Cost of sales and operations | $16,087,348 | 61.9% | $17,836,706 | 62.4% |
| 25. | Gross operating profit | $9,923,733 | 38.2% | $10,772,026 | 37.7% |
| 26. | Additional operating costs | $26,751,131 | 102.9% | $31,623,093 | 110.5% |
| 27. | Net operating profit | ($16,827,398) | (64.7%) | ($20,851,067) | (72.9%) |
| 28. | Less: Guaranteed payments to partners | $894,253 | | $929,829 | |
| 29. | Distribution to partners | ($17,721,651) | | ($21,780,896) | |
| 30. | Other charges | $31,190,465 | | $39,116,079 | |
| 31. | Net change partners' capital | ($48,912,116) | | ($60,896,975) | |
| | Selected Ratios | | | | |
| 32. | Coverage ratio: times interest earned | (2.6) | | (2.7) | |
| 33. | Inventory turnover (times) | n.a. | | n.a. | |
| 34. | Days' sales in inventory | n.a. | | n.a. | |
| 35. | Average age of inventory (days) | n.a. | | n.a. | |
| 36. | Return on assets, net inc., less def | (3.5%) | | (4.1%) | |
| 37. | Return on assets, gross operating profit | 1.7% | | 1.5% | |
| 38. | Return on assets, net operating profit | (2.8%) | | (2.9%) | |

*Page 74*

Table 1: Partnerships With and Without Net Income: 186. OPERATORS AND LESSORS OF BUILDINGS

Dollar values in thousands, except averages

|  |  | 1984 | | 1985 | |
|---|---|---|---|---|---|
| 1. | Number of Partnerships | 536,216 | | 582,487 | |
| 2. | Number of Partners | 4,510,523 | | 5,185,721 | |
| 3. | Total Assets | $508,026,692 | | $610,701,790 | |
| 4. | Average total assets per Partnership | $947,429 | | $1,048,438 | |
| 5. | Average total assets per Partner | $112,631 | | $117,766 | |
| 6. | Net Income, less Deficit | ($18,885,837) | | ($26,204,238) | |
| 7. | Average per Partnership, total earnings | ($35,219) | | ($44,986) | |
| 8. | Average per Partner, total earnings | ($4,187) | | ($5,053) | |
| 9. | Total Receipts | $8,010,782 | | $8,986,289 | |
|  | Operating Costs | | | | |
| 10. | Cost of sales & operations | $3,401,992 | 42.5% | $3,880,724 | 43.2% |
| 11. | Salaries and wages | $696,509 | 8.7% | $1,064,168 | 11.8% |
| 12. | Rent paid | $373,254 | 4.7% | $362,503 | 4.0% |
| 13. | Interest paid | $7,050,216 | 88.0% | $8,348,764 | 92.9% |
| 14. | Taxes paid | $1,120,793 | 14.0% | $1,373,908 | 15.3% |
| 15. | Bad debts | $50,791 | 0.6% | $104,094 | 1.2% |
| 16. | Repairs | $322,597 | 4.0% | $313,357 | 3.5% |
| 17. | Depreciation | $3,984,966 | 49.8% | $4,573,779 | 50.9% |
| 18. | Depletion | $977 | 0.0% | $7,132 | 0.1% |
| 19. | Pension & profit sharing plans | $5,062 | 0.1% | $9,000 | 0.1% |
| 20. | Employee benefits programs | $23,138 | 0.3% | $49,376 | 0.6% |
| 21. | Other deductions | $4,845,300 | 60.5% | $5,632,454 | 62.7% |
| 22. | Total operating costs | $21,876,004 | 273.1% | $25,720,034 | 286.2% |
|  | Operating Income and Distribution | | | | |
| 23. | Total Receipts | $8,010,782 | 100.0% | $8,986,289 | 100.0% |
| 24. | Less: Cost of sales and operations | $3,401,992 | 42.5% | $3,880,724 | 43.2% |
| 25. | Gross operating profit | $4,608,790 | 57.5% | $5,105,565 | 56.8% |
| 26. | Additional operating costs | $18,474,012 | 230.6% | $21,839,310 | 243.0% |
| 27. | Net operating profit | ($13,865,222) | (173.1%) | ($16,733,745) | (186.2%) |
| 28. | Less: Guaranteed payments to partners | $611,115 | | $701,846 | |
| 29. | Distribution to partners | ($14,476,337) | | ($17,435,591) | |
| 30. | Other charges | $28,259,400 | | $35,627,718 | |
| 31. | Net change partners' capital | ($42,735,737) | | ($53,063,309) | |
|  | Selected Ratios | | | | |
| 32. | Coverage ratio: times interest earned | (3.0) | | (3.0) | |
| 33. | Inventory turnover (times) | n.a. | | n.a. | |
| 34. | Days' sales in inventory | n.a. | | n.a. | |
| 35. | Average age of inventory (days) | n.a. | | n.a. | |
| 36. | Return on assets, net inc., less def | (3.7%) | | (4.3%) | |
| 37. | Return on assets, gross operating profit | 0.9% | | 0.8% | |
| 38. | Return on assets, net operating profit | (2.7%) | | (2.7%) | |

*Page 75*

Table 1: Partnerships With and Without Net Income:  187.  LESSORS, OTHER THAN BUILDINGS

Dollar values in thousands, except averages

|  |  | 1984 |  | 1985 |  |
|---|---|---|---|---|---|
| 1. | Number of Partnerships | 32,558 | | 37,589 | |
| 2. | Number of Partners | 214,681 | | 253,820 | |
| 3. | Total Assets | $12,948,716 | | $14,408,993 | |
| 4. | Average total assets per Partnership | $397,712 | | $383,330 | |
| 5. | Average total assets per Partner | $60,316 | | $56,769 | |
| 6. | Net Income, less Deficit | ($505,372) | | ($615,982) | |
| 7. | Average per Partnership, total earnings | ($15,522) | | ($16,387) | |
| 8. | Average per Partner, total earnings | ($2,354) | | ($2,427) | |
| 9. | Total Receipts | $227,656 | | $326,234 | |
| | Operating Costs | | | | |
| 10. | Cost of sales & operations | $84,462 | 37.1% | $96,346 | 29.5% |
| 11. | Salaries and wages | $28,910 | 12.7% | $37,367 | 11.5% |
| 12. | Rent paid | $5,291 | 2.3% | $6,218 | 1.9% |
| 13. | Interest paid | $179,002 | 78.6% | $271,419 | 83.2% |
| 14. | Taxes paid | $30,535 | 13.4% | $40,275 | 12.4% |
| 15. | Bad debts | $117 | 0.1% | $3,895 | 1.2% |
| 16. | Repairs | $34,746 | 15.3% | $19,248 | 5.9% |
| 17. | Depreciation | $159,390 | 70.0% | $225,067 | 69.0% |
| 18. | Depletion | $174 | 0.1% | $2,713 | 0.8% |
| 19. | Pension & profit sharing plans | $2,210 | 0.10% | $2,591 | 0.8% |
| 20. | Employee benefits programs | $2,022 | 0.9% | $1,976 | 0.6% |
| 21. | Other deductions | $134,455 | 59.1% | $166,993 | 51.2% |
| 22. | Total operating costs | $661,315 | 290.5% | $874,108 | 267.9% |
| | Operating Income and Distribution | | | | |
| 23. | Total Receipts | $227,656 | 100.0% | $326,234 | 100.0% |
| 24. | Less:  Cost of sales and operations | $84,462 | 37.1% | $96,346 | 29.5% |
| 25. | Gross operating profit | $143,194 | 62.9% | $229,888 | 70.5% |
| 26. | Additional operating costs | $576,853 | 253.4% | $777,762 | 238.4% |
| 27. | Net operating profit | ($433,659) | (190.5%) | ($547,874) | (167.9%) |
| 28. | Less:  Guaranteed payments to partners | $5,368 | | $8,439 | |
| 29. | Distribution to partners | ($439,027) | | ($556,313) | |
| 30. | Other charges | $803,958 | | $931,363 | |
| 31. | Net change partners' capital | ($1,242,985) | | ($1,487,676) | |
| | Selected Ratios | | | | |
| 32. | Coverage ratio:  times interest earned | (3.4) | | (3.0) | |
| 33. | Inventory turnover (times) | n.a. | | n.a. | |
| 34. | Days' sales in inventory | n.a. | | n.a. | |
| 35. | Average age of inventory (days) | n.a. | | n.a. | |
| 36. | Return on assets, net inc., less def | (3.9%) | | (4.3%) | |
| 37. | Return on assets, gross operating profit | 1.1% | | 1.6% | |
| 38. | Return on assets, net operating profit | (3.4%) | | (3.8%) | |

*Page 76*

Table 1: Partnerships With and Without Net Income:  188.  REAL ESTATE AGENTS, BROKERS, AND MANAGERS

Dollar values in thousands, except averages

|  |  | 1984 |  | 1985 |  |
|---|---|---|---|---|---|
| 1. | Number of Partnerships | 18,049 | | 17,707 | |
| 2. | Number of Partners | 168,403 | | 166,541 | |
| 3. | Total Assets | $9,015,244 | | $10,364,584 | |
| 4. | Average total assets per Partnership | $499,487 | | $585,338 | |
| 5. | Average total assets per Partner | $53,534 | | $62,234 | |
| 6. | Net Income, less Deficit | ($221,749) | | ($347,198) | |
| 7. | Average per Partnership, total earnings | ($12,278) | | ($19,606) | |
| 8. | Average per Partner, total earnings | ($1,316) | | ($2,085) | |
| 9. | Total Receipts | $2,123,896 | | $2,046,049 | |
|  | Operating Costs | | | | |
| 10. | Cost of sales & operations | $581,840 | 27.4% | $545,113 | 26.6% |
| 11. | Salaries and wages | $208,936 | 9.8% | $325,661 | 15.9% |
| 12. | Rent paid | $61,603 | 2.9% | $119,531 | 5.8% |
| 13. | Interest paid | $324,876 | 15.3% | $358,554 | 17.5% |
| 14. | Taxes paid | $65,114 | 3.1% | $64,215 | 3.1% |
| 15. | Bad debts | $1,856 | 0.1% | $3,795 | 0.2% |
| 16. | Repairs | $36,362 | 1.7% | $25,231 | 1.2% |
| 17. | Depreciation | $153,728 | 7.2% | $152,532 | 7.5% |
| 18. | Depletion | $0 | n.a. | $12 | n.a. |
| 19. | Pension & profit sharing plans | $1,409 | 0.1% | $1,069 | 0.1% |
| 20. | Employee benefits programs | $1,154 | 0.1% | $12,075 | 0.6% |
| 21. | Other deductions | $802,139 | 37.8% | $994,244 | 48.6% |
| 22. | Total operating costs | $2,239,093 | 105.4% | $2,602,130 | 127.2% |
|  | Operating Income and Distribution | | | | |
| 23. | Total Receipts | $2,123,896 | 100.0% | $2,046,049 | 100.0% |
| 24. | Less: Cost of sales and operations | $581,840 | 27.4% | $545,113 | 26.6% |
| 25. | Gross operating profit | $1,542,056 | 72.6% | $1,500,936 | 73.4% |
| 26. | Additional operating costs | $1,657,253 | 78.0% | $2,057,017 | 100.5% |
| 27. | Net operating profit | ($115,197) | (5.4%) | ($556,081) | (27.2%) |
| 28. | Less: Guaranteed payments to partners | $140,573 | | $36,768 | |
| 29. | Distribution to partners | ($255,770) | | ($592,849) | |
| 30. | Other charges | $465,027 | | $565,456 | |
| 31. | Net change partners' capital | ($720,797) | | ($1,158,305) | |
|  | Selected Ratios | | | | |
| 32. | Coverage ratio: times interest earned | (1.4) | | (2.6) | |
| 33. | Inventory turnover (times) | n.a. | | n.a. | |
| 34. | Days' sales in inventory | n.a. | | n.a. | |
| 35. | Average age of inventory (days) | n.a. | | n.a. | |
| 36. | Return on assets, net inc., less def | (2.5%) | | (3.4%) | |
| 37. | Return on assets, gross operating profit | 17.1% | | 14.5% | |
| 38. | Return on assets, net operating profit | (1.3%) | | (5.4%) | |

*Page 77*

Table 1: Partnerships With and Without Net Income:  OTHER REAL ESTATE (189,190,191,192)

Dollar values in thousands, except averages

|    |                                              | 1984 | | 1985 | |
|----|----------------------------------------------|------|--|------|--|
| 1. | Number of Partnerships                       | 50,096 | | 56,244 | |
| 2. | Number of Partners                           | 267,585 | | 386,393 | |
| 3. | Total Assets                                 | $68,434,478 | | $88,866,711 | |
| 4. | Average total assets per Partnership         | $1,366,067 | | $1,580,021 | |
| 5. | Average total assets per Partner             | $255,749 | | $229,990 | |
| 6. | Net Income, less Deficit                     | ($1,591,031) | | ($2,591,151) | |
| 7. | Average per Partnership, total earnings      | ($31,757) | | ($46,067) | |
| 8. | Average per Partner, total earnings          | ($5,945) | | ($6,706) | |
| 9. | Total Receipts                               | $15,648,747 | | $17,250,160 | |
|    | Operating Costs                              |      | |      | |
| 10. | Cost of sales & operations                  | $12,019,054 | 76.8% | $13,314,522 | 77.2% |
| 11. | Salaries and wages                          | $282,134 | 1.8% | $344,080 | 2.0% |
| 12. | Rent paid                                   | $64,110 | 0.4% | $100,193 | 0.6% |
| 13. | Interest paid                               | $2,800,848 | 17.9% | $3,078,439 | 17.9% |
| 14. | Taxes paid                                  | $323,161 | 2.1% | $328,366 | 1.9% |
| 15. | Bad debts                                   | $22,833 | 0.2% | $36,422 | 0.2% |
| 16. | Repairs                                     | $39,445 | 0.3% | $45,467 | 0.3% |
| 17. | Depreciation                                | $270,188 | 1.7% | $394,743 | 2.3% |
| 18. | Depletion                                   | $303 | n.a. | $174 | n.a. |
| 19. | Pension & profit sharing plans              | $1,803 | 0.0% | $1,497 | 0.0% |
| 20. | Employee benefits programs                  | $6,690 | 0.0% | $12,359 | 0.1% |
| 21. | Other deductions                            | $2,231,241 | 14.3% | $2,607,082 | 15.1% |
| 22. | Total operating costs                       | $18,062,065 | 115.4% | $20,263,526 | 117.5% |
|    | Operating Income and Distribution            |      | |      | |
| 23. | Total Receipts                              | $15,648,747 | 100.0% | $17,250,160 | 100.0% |
| 24. | Less:  Cost of sales and operations         | $12,019,054 | 76.8% | $13,314,522 | 77.2% |
| 25. | Gross operating profit                      | $3,629,693 | 23.2% | $3,935,638 | 22.8% |
| 26. | Additional operating costs                  | $6,043,011 | 38.6% | $6,949,004 | 40.3% |
| 27. | Net operating profit                        | ($2,413,318) | (15.4%) | ($3,013,366) | (17.5%) |
| 28. | Less:  Guaranteed payments to partners      | $137,197 | | $182,775 | |
| 29. | Distribution to partners                    | ($2,550,515) | | ($3,196,141) | |
| 30. | Other charges                               | $1,662,081 | | $1,991,543 | |
| 31. | Net change partners' capital                | ($4,212,596) | | ($5,187,684) | |
|    | Selected Ratios                              |      | |      | |
| 32. | Coverage ratio:  times interest earned      | (1.9) | | (2.0) | |
| 33. | Inventory turnover (times)                  | n.a. | | n.a. | |
| 34. | Days' sales in inventory                    | n.a. | | n.a. | |
| 35. | Average age of inventory (days)             | n.a. | | n.a. | |
| 36. | Return on assets, net inc., less def        | (2.3%) | | (2.9%) | |
| 37. | Return on assets, gross operating profit    | 5.3% | | 4.4% | |
| 38. | Return on assets, net operating profit      | (3.5%) | | (3.4%) | |

*Page 78*

Table 1: Partnerships With and Without Net Income:  193.  SERVICES

Dollar values in thousands, except averages

| | | 1984 | | 1985 | |
|---|---|---|---|---|---|
| 1. | Number of Partnerships | 331,103 | | 341,295 | |
| 2. | Number of Partners | 1,577,704 | | 1,713,060 | |
| | | | | | |
| 3. | Total Assets | $87,984,078 | | $106,596,624 | |
| 4. | Average total assets per Partnership | $265,730 | | $312,330 | |
| 5. | Average total assets per Partner | $55,767 | | $62,226 | |
| | | | | | |
| 6. | Net Income, less Deficit | $15,583,256 | | $16,541,329 | |
| 7. | Average per Partnership, total earnings | $47,074 | | $48,478 | |
| 8. | Average per Partner, total earnings | $9,879 | | $9,658 | |
| | | | | | |
| 9. | Operating Income | $97,822,373 | | $112,742,962 | |
| | Operating Costs | | | | |
| 10. | Cost of sales & operations | $16,818,253 | 17.2% | $19,258,556 | 17.1% |
| 11. | Salaries and wages | $18,307,874 | 18.7% | $21,404,764 | 19.0% |
| 12. | Rent paid | $4,332,236 | 4.4% | $5,103,106 | 4.5% |
| 13. | Interest paid | $4,817,213 | 4.9% | $5,887,018 | 5.2% |
| 14. | Taxes paid | $2,583,201 | 2.6% | $2,992,718 | 2.7% |
| 15. | Bad debts | $216,556 | 0.2% | $235,404 | 0.2% |
| 16. | Repairs | $873,290 | 0.9% | $921,292 | 0.8% |
| 17. | Depreciation | $6,645,519 | 6.8% | $7,565,877 | 6.7% |
| 18. | Depletion | $9,838 | 0.0% | $9,036 | 0.0% |
| 19. | Pension & profit sharing plans | $376,184 | 0.4% | $465,798 | 0.4% |
| 20. | Employee benefits programs | $566,989 | 0.6% | $618,512 | 0.6% |
| 21. | Other deductions | $21,978,091 | 22.5% | $25,478,082 | 22.6% |
| 22. | Total operating costs | $77,538,388 | 79.3% | $89,947,557 | 79.8% |
| | | | | | |
| | Operating Income and Distribution | | | | |
| 23. | Operating Income | $97,822,373 | 100.0% | $112,742,962 | 100.0% |
| 24. | Less:  Cost of sales and operations | $16,818,253 | 17.2% | $19,258,556 | 17.1% |
| 25. | Gross operating profit | $81,004,120 | 82.8% | $93,484,406 | 82.9% |
| 26. | Additional operating costs | $60,720,135 | 62.1% | $70,689,001 | 62.7% |
| 27. | Net operating profit | $20,283,985 | 20.7% | $22,795,405 | 20.2% |
| 28. | Less:  Guaranteed payments to partners | $2,998,483 | | $4,074,008 | |
| 29. | Distribution to partners | $17,285,502 | | $18,721,397 | |
| 30. | Other charges | $1,715,390 | | $2,187,462 | |
| 31. | Net change partners' capital | $15,570,112 | | $16,533,935 | |
| | | | | | |
| | Selected Ratios | | | | |
| 32. | Coverage ratio:  times interest earned | 3.2 | | 2.9 | |
| 33. | Inventory turnover (times) | n.a. | | n.a. | |
| 34. | Days' sales in inventory | n.a. | | n.a. | |
| 35. | Average age of inventory (days) | n.a. | | n.a. | |
| 36. | Return on assets, net inc., less def | 17.7% | | 15.5% | |
| 37. | Return on assets, gross operating profit | 92.1% | | 87.7% | |
| 38. | Return on assets, net operating profit | 23.1% | | 21.4% | |

Table 1: Partnerships With and Without Net Income:  194.  HOTELS AND OTHER LODGING PLACES

Dollar values in thousands, except averages

|  |  | 1984 |  | 1985 |  |
|---|---|---|---|---|---|
| 1. | Number of Partnerships | 18,917 | | 21,794 | |
| 2. | Number of Partners | 241,166 | | 189,576 | |
| 3. | Total Assets | $33,129,585 | | $44,547,559 | |
| 4. | Average total assets per Partnership | $1,751,313 | | $2,044,029 | |
| 5. | Average total assets per Partner | $137,373 | | $234,985 | |
| 6. | Net Income, less Deficit | ($2,109,805) | | ($3,383,463) | |
| 7. | Average per Partnership, total earnings | ($111,525) | | ($155,242) | |
| 8. | Average per Partner, total earnings | ($8,748) | | ($17,847) | |
| 9. | Operating Income | $15,188,701 | | $18,310,017 | |
|  | Operating Costs | | | | |
| 10. | Cost of sales & operations | $5,510,319 | 36.3% | $6,811,549 | 37.2% |
| 11. | Salaries and wages | $1,859,107 | 12.2% | $2,146,100 | 11.7% |
| 12. | Rent paid | $246,138 | 1.6% | $263,368 | 1.4% |
| 13. | Interest paid | $2,463,792 | 16.2% | $3,205,772 | 17.5% |
| 14. | Taxes paid | $636,313 | 4.2% | $824,752 | 4.5% |
| 15. | Bad debts | $33,312 | 0.2% | $36,908 | 0.2% |
| 16. | Repairs | $314,750 | 2.1% | $354,750 | 1.9% |
| 17. | Depreciation | $1,822,946 | 12.0% | $2,403,880 | 13.1% |
| 18. | Depletion | $2,431 | 0.0% | $288 | n.a. |
| 19. | Pension & profit sharing plans | $6,623 | 0.0% | $9,219 | 0.1% |
| 20. | Employee benefits programs | $113,012 | 0.7% | $113,184 | 0.6% |
| 21. | Other deductions | $3,870,211 | 25.5% | $4,787,136 | 26.1% |
| 22. | Total operating costs | $16,881,643 | 111.2% | $20,961,343 | 114.5% |
|  | Operating Income and Distribution | | | | |
| 23. | Operating Income | $15,188,701 | 100.0% | $18,310,017 | 100.0% |
| 24. | Less: Cost of sales and operations | $5,510,319 | 36.3% | $6,811,549 | 37.2% |
| 25. | Gross operating profit | $9,678,382 | 63.7% | $11,498,468 | 62.8% |
| 26. | Additional operating costs | $11,371,324 | 74.9% | $14,149,794 | 77.3% |
| 27. | Net operating profit | ($1,692,942) | (11.2%) | ($2,651,326) | (14.5%) |
| 28. | Less: Guaranteed payments to partners | $90,669 | | $116,418 | |
| 29. | Distribution to partners | ($1,783,611) | | ($2,767,744) | |
| 30. | Other charges | $328,883 | | $620,156 | |
| 31. | Net change partners' capital | ($2,112,494) | | ($3,387,900) | |
|  | Selected Ratios | | | | |
| 32. | Coverage ratio:  times interest earned | (1.7) | | (1.8) | |
| 33. | Inventory turnover (times) | n.a. | | n.a. | |
| 34. | Days' sales in inventory | n.a. | | n.a. | |
| 35. | Average age of inventory (days) | n.a. | | n.a. | |
| 36. | Return on assets, net inc., less def | (6.4%) | | (7.6%) | |
| 37. | Return on assets, gross operating profit | 29.2% | | 25.8% | |
| 38. | Return on assets, net operating profit | (5.1%) | | (6.0%) | |

*Page 80*

Table 1: Partnerships With and Without Net Income:  196.  MOTELS, MOTOR HOTELS, AND COURTS

Dollar values in thousands, except averages

| | 1984 | | 1985 | |
|---|---|---|---|---|
| 1. Number of Partnerships | 9,995 | | 9,954 | |
| 2. Number of Partners | 156,598 | | 70,494 | |
| 3. Total Assets | $9,283,527 | | $11,640,068 | |
| 4. Average total assets per Partnership | $928,817 | | $1,169,386 | |
| 5. Average total assets per Partner | $59,283 | | $165,121 | |
| 6. Net Income, less Deficit | ($271,855) | | ($470,144) | |
| 7. Average per Partnership, total earnings | ($27,196) | | ($47,226) | |
| 8. Average per Partner, total earnings | ($1,736) | | ($6,669) | |
| 9. Operating Income | $4,235,605 | | $4,845,298 | |
| Operating Costs | | | | |
| 10. Cost of sales & operations | $717,931 | 17.0% | $903,258 | 18.6% |
| 11. Salaries and wages | $609,110 | 14.4% | $702,529 | 14.5% |
| 12. Rent paid | $78,640 | 1.9% | $77,481 | 1.6% |
| 13. Interest paid | $744,949 | 17.6% | $876,320 | 18.1% |
| 14. Taxes paid | $201,538 | 4.8% | $239,593 | 4.9% |
| 15. Bad debts | $8,013 | 0.2% | $9,862 | 0.2% |
| 16. Repairs | $128,642 | 3.0% | $129,687 | 2.7% |
| 17. Depreciation | $614,750 | 14.5% | $744,025 | 15.4% |
| 18. Depletion | $0 | n.a. | $288 | 0.0% |
| 19. Pension & profit sharing plans | $1,105 | 0.0% | $1,061 | 0.0% |
| 20. Employee benefits programs | $14,920 | 0.4% | $17,531 | 0.4% |
| 21. Other deductions | $1,305,282 | 30.8% | $1,502,244 | 31.0% |
| 22. Total operating costs | $4,425,413 | 104.5% | $5,204,894 | 107.4% |
| Operating Income and Distribution | | | | |
| 23. Operating Income | $4,235,605 | 100.0% | $4,845,298 | 100.0% |
| 24. Less: Cost of sales and operations | $717,931 | 17.0% | $903,258 | 18.6% |
| 25. Gross operating profit | $3,517,674 | 83.1% | $3,942,040 | 81.4% |
| 26. Additional operating costs | $3,707,482 | 87.5% | $4,301,636 | 88.8% |
| 27. Net operating profit | ($189,808) | (4.5%) | ($359,596) | (7.4%) |
| 28. Less: Guaranteed payments to partners | $33,336 | | $53,920 | |
| 29. Distribution to partners | ($223,144) | | ($413,516) | |
| 30. Other charges | $49,244 | | $57,642 | |
| 31. Net change partners' capital | ($272,388) | | ($471,158) | |
| Selected Ratios | | | | |
| 32. Coverage ratio: times interest earned | (1.3) | | (1.4) | |
| 33. Inventory turnover (times) | n.a. | | n.a. | |
| 34. Days' sales in inventory | n.a. | | n.a. | |
| 35. Average age of inventory (days) | n.a. | | n.a. | |
| 36. Return on assets, net inc., less def | (2.9%) | | (4.0%) | |
| 37. Return on assets, gross operating profit | 37.9% | | 33.9% | |
| 38. Return on assets, net operating profit | (2.0%) | | (3.1%) | |

*Page 81*

Table 1: Partnerships With and Without Net Income:  OTHER LODGING PLACES (195,197,198,199,200)

Dollar values in thousands, except averages

|     |                                            | 1984 |       | 1985 |       |
| --- | ------------------------------------------ | ---- | ----- | ---- | ----- |
| 1.  | Number of Partnerships                     | 8,922 | | 11,840 | |
| 2.  | Number of Partners                         | 84,567 | | 119,082 | |
| 3.  | Total Assets                               | $23,846,058 | | $32,907,491 | |
| 4.  | Average total assets per Partnership       | $2,672,726 | | $2,779,349 | |
| 5.  | Average total assets per Partner           | $281,978 | | $276,343 | |
| 6.  | Net Income, less Deficit                   | ($1,837,950) | | ($2,913,319) | |
| 7.  | Average per Partnership, total earnings    | ($205,996) | | ($246,052) | |
| 8.  | Average per Partner, total earnings        | ($21,733) | | ($24,464) | |
| 9.  | Operating Income                           | $10,953,096 | | $13,464,719 | |
|     | Operating Costs                            | | | | |
| 10. | Cost of sales & operations                 | $4,792,388 | 43.8% | $5,908,291 | 43.9% |
| 11. | Salaries and wages                         | $1,249,997 | 11.4% | $1,443,570 | 10.7% |
| 12. | Rent paid                                  | $167,498 | 1.5% | $185,887 | 1.4% |
| 13. | Interest paid                              | $1,718,843 | 15.7% | $2,329,452 | 17.3% |
| 14. | Taxes paid                                 | $434,775 | 4.0% | $585,159 | 4.4% |
| 15. | Bad debts                                  | $25,299 | 0.2% | $27,045 | 0.2% |
| 16. | Repairs                                    | $186,108 | 1.7% | $225,053 | 1.7% |
| 17. | Depreciation                               | $1,208,197 | 11.0% | $1,659,885 | 12.3% |
| 18. | Depletion                                  | $2,431 | 0.0% | $0 | n.a. |
| 19. | Pension & profit sharing plans             | $5,518 | 0.1% | $8,158 | 0.1% |
| 20. | Employee benefits programs                 | $98,092 | 0.9% | $95,653 | 0.7% |
| 21. | Other deductions                           | $2,564,929 | 23.4% | $3,284,874 | 24.4% |
| 22. | Total operating costs                      | $12,456,231 | 113.7% | $15,756,449 | 117.0% |
|     | **Operating Income and Distribution**      | | | | |
| 23. | Operating Income                           | $10,953,096 | 100.0% | $13,464,719 | 100.0% |
| 24. | Less:  Cost of sales and operations        | $4,792,388 | 43.8% | $5,908,291 | 43.9% |
| 25. | Gross operating profit                     | $6,160,708 | 56.3% | $7,556,428 | 56.1% |
| 26. | Additional operating costs                 | $7,663,843 | 70.0% | $9,848,158 | 73.1% |
| 27. | Net operating profit                       | ($1,503,135) | (13.7%) | ($2,291,730) | (17.0%) |
| 28. | Less:  Guaranteed payments to partners     | $57,332 | | $62,497 | |
| 29. | Distribution to partners                   | ($1,560,467) | | ($2,354,227) | |
| 30. | Other charges                              | $279,639 | | $562,514 | |
| 31. | Net change partners' capital               | ($1,840,106) | | ($2,916,741) | |
|     | **Selected Ratios**                        | | | | |
| 32. | Coverage ratio:  times interest earned     | (1.9) | | (2.0) | |
| 33. | Inventory turnover (times)                 | n.a. | | n.a. | |
| 34. | Days' sales in inventory                   | n.a. | | n.a. | |
| 35. | Average age of inventory (days)            | n.a. | | n.a. | |
| 36. | Return on assets, net inc., less def       | (7.7%) | | (8.9%) | |
| 37. | Return on assets, gross operating profit   | 25.8% | | 23.0% | |
| 38. | Return on assets, net operating profit     | (6.3%) | | (7.0%) | |

*Page 82*

Table 1: Partnerships With and Without Net Income:  201.  PERSONAL SERVICES

Dollar values in thousands, except averages

| | | 1984 | | 1985 | |
|---|---|---|---|---|---|
| 1. | Number of Partnerships | 33,282 | | 34,967 | |
| 2. | Number of Partners | 79,816 | | 86,106 | |
| 3. | Total Assets | $867,678 | | $1,194,960 | |
| 4. | Average total assets per Partnership | $26,070 | | $34,174 | |
| 5. | Average total assets per Partner | $10,871 | | $13,878 | |
| 6. | Net Income, less Deficit | $214,290 | | $261,075 | |
| 7. | Average per Partnership, total earnings | $6,442 | | $7,469 | |
| 8. | Average per Partner, total earnings | $2,686 | | $3,033 | |
| 9. | Operating Income | $2,300,988 | | $2,564,222 | |
| | Operating Costs | | | | |
| 10. | Cost of sales & operations | $446,966 | 19.4% | $537,694 | 21.0% |
| 11. | Salaries and wages | $388,158 | 16.9% | $366,088 | 14.3% |
| 12. | Rent paid | $158,315 | 6.9% | $290,477 | 11.3% |
| 13. | Interest paid | $47,501 | 2.1% | $59,478 | 2.3% |
| 14. | Taxes paid | $54,629 | 2.4% | $73,764 | 2.9% |
| 15. | Bad debts | $3,775 | 0.2% | $3,204 | 0.1% |
| 16. | Repairs | $35,295 | 1.5% | $47,670 | 1.9% |
| 17. | Depreciation | $152,157 | 6.6% | $177,301 | 6.9% |
| 18. | Depletion | $0 | n.a. | $54 | n.a. |
| 19. | Pension & profit sharing plans | $470 | 0.0% | $1,063 | 0.0% |
| 20. | Employee benefits programs | $3,515 | 0.2% | $3,420 | 0.1% |
| 21. | Other deductions | $684,074 | 29.7% | $649,896 | 25.3% |
| 22. | Total operating costs | $1,974,856 | 85.8% | $2,210,183 | 86.2% |
| | Operating Income and Distribution | | | | |
| 23. | Operating Income | $2,300,988 | 100.0% | $2,564,222 | 100.0% |
| 24. | Less:  Cost of sales and operations | $446,966 | 19.4% | $537,694 | 21.0% |
| 25. | Gross operating profit | $1,854,022 | 80.6% | $2,026,528 | 79.0% |
| 26. | Additional operating costs | $1,527,890 | 66.4% | $1,672,489 | 65.2% |
| 27. | Net operating profit | $326,132 | 14.2% | $354,039 | 13.8% |
| 28. | Less:  Guaranteed payments to partners | $103,513 | | $88,220 | |
| 29. | Distribution to partners | $222,619 | | $265,819 | |
| 30. | Other charges | $8,330 | | $4,818 | |
| 31. | Net change partners' capital | $214,289 | | $261,001 | |
| | Selected Ratios | | | | |
| 32. | Coverage ratio:  times interest earned | 5.9 | | 5.0 | |
| 33. | Inventory turnover (times) | n.a. | | n.a. | |
| 34. | Days' sales in inventory | n.a. | | n.a. | |
| 35. | Average age of inventory (days) | n.a. | | n.a. | |
| 36. | Return on assets, net inc., less def | 24.7% | | 21.9% | |
| 37. | Return on assets, gross operating profit | 213.7% | | 169.6% | |
| 38. | Return on assets, net operating profit | 37.6% | | 29.6% | |

*Page 83*

Table 1: Partnerships With and Without Net Income: LAUNDRIES, DRY CLEANING, AND GARMENT SERVICES (202,203)

Dollar values in thousands, except averages

| | | 1984 | | 1985 | |
|---|---|---|---|---|---|
| 1. | Number of Partnerships | 6,940 | | 8,854 | |
| 2. | Number of Partners | 15,170 | | 20,296 | |
| 3. | Total Assets | $227,191 | | $347,652 | |
| 4. | Average total assets per Partnership | $32,736 | | $39,265 | |
| 5. | Average total assets per Partner | $14,976 | | $17,129 | |
| 6. | Net Income, less Deficit | $52,679 | | $38,870 | |
| 7. | Average per Partnership, total earnings | $7,593 | | $4,391 | |
| 8. | Average per Partner, total earnings | $3,474 | | $1,915 | |
| 9. | Operating Income | $658,199 | | $747,706 | |
| | Operating Costs | | | | |
| 10. | Cost of sales & operations | $80,656 | 12.3% | $122,248 | 16.4% |
| 11. | Salaries and wages | $119,907 | 18.2% | $124,061 | 16.6% |
| 12. | Rent paid | $49,437 | 7.5% | $91,776 | 12.3% |
| 13. | Interest paid | $16,841 | 2.6% | $21,791 | 2.9% |
| 14. | Taxes paid | $17,054 | 2.6% | $29,292 | 3.9% |
| 15. | Bad debts | $123 | 0.0% | $596 | 0.1% |
| 16. | Repairs | $18,669 | 2.8% | $20,692 | 2.8% |
| 17. | Depreciation | $54,877 | 8.3% | $84,347 | 11.3% |
| 18. | Depletion | $0 | n.a. | $0 | n.a. |
| 19. | Pension & profit sharing plans | $0 | n.a. | $453 | 0.1% |
| 20. | Employee benefits programs | $1,471 | 0.2% | $905 | 0.1% |
| 21. | Other deductions | $230,836 | 35.1% | $206,007 | 27.6% |
| 22. | Total operating costs | $589,872 | 89.6% | $702,242 | 93.9% |
| | Operating Income and Distribution | | | | |
| 23. | Operating Income | $658,199 | 100.0% | $747,706 | 100.0% |
| 24. | Less: Cost of sales and operations | $80,656 | 12.3% | $122,248 | 16.4% |
| 25. | Gross operating profit | $577,543 | 87.8% | $625,458 | 83.7% |
| 26. | Additional operating costs | $509,216 | 77.4% | $579,994 | 77.6% |
| 27. | Net operating profit | $68,327 | 10.4% | $45,464 | 6.1% |
| 28. | Less: Guaranteed payments to partners | $15,183 | | $5,972 | |
| 29. | Distribution to partners | $53,144 | | $39,492 | |
| 30. | Other charges | $466 | | $696 | |
| 31. | Net change partners' capital | $52,678 | | $38,796 | |
| | Selected Ratios | | | | |
| 32. | Coverage ratio: times interest earned | 3.1 | | 1.1 | |
| 33. | Inventory turnover (times) | n.a. | | n.a. | |
| 34. | Days' sales in inventory | n.a. | | n.a. | |
| 35. | Average age of inventory (days) | n.a. | | n.a. | |
| 36. | Return on assets, net inc., less def | 23.2% | | 11.2% | |
| 37. | Return on assets, gross operating profit | n.a. | | 179.9% | |
| 38. | Return on assets, net operating profit | 30.1% | | 13.1% | |

*Page 84*

Table 1: Partnerships With and Without Net Income:  206.  BEAUTY SHOPS

Dollar values in thousands, except averages

| | 1984 | | 1985 | |
|---|---|---|---|---|
| 1. Number of Partnerships | 10,200 | | 9,357 | |
| 2. Number of Partners | 23,702 | | 20,486 | |
| | | | | |
| 3. Total Assets | $85,696 | | $343,352 | |
| 4. Average total assets per Partnership | $8,402 | | $36,695 | |
| 5. Average total assets per Partner | $3,616 | | $16,760 | |
| | | | | |
| 6. Net Income, less Deficit | ($5,523) | | $16,261 | |
| 7. Average per Partnership, total earnings | ($537) | | $1,742 | |
| 8. Average per Partner, total earnings | ($231) | | $796 | |
| | | | | |
| 9. Operating Income | $338,901 | | $533,840 | |
| Operating Costs | | | | |
| 10. Cost of sales & operations | $58,822 | 17.4% | $154,559 | 29.0% |
| 11. Salaries and wages | $57,442 | 17.0% | $98,083 | 18.4% |
| 12. Rent paid | $46,357 | 13.7% | $78,886 | 14.8% |
| 13. Interest paid | $12,884 | 3.8% | $10,560 | 2.0% |
| 14. Taxes paid | $13,723 | 4.1% | $14,060 | 2.6% |
| 15. Bad debts | $40 | 0.0% | $65 | 0.0% |
| 16. Repairs | $3,920 | 1.2% | $6,232 | 1.2% |
| 17. Depreciation | $21,318 | 6.3% | $19,948 | 3.7% |
| 18. Depletion | $0 | n.a. | $0 | n.a. |
| 19. Pension & profit sharing plans | $0 | n.a. | $0 | n.a. |
| 20. Employee benefits programs | $0 | n.a. | $300 | 0.1% |
| 21. Other deductions | $81,338 | 24.0% | $98,376 | 18.4% |
| 22. Total operating costs | $295,844 | 87.3% | $481,069 | 90.1% |
| | | | | |
| Operating Income and Distribution | | | | |
| 23. Operating Income | $338,901 | 100.0% | $533,840 | 100.0% |
| 24. Less: Cost of sales and operations | $58,822 | 17.4% | $154,559 | 29.0% |
| 25. Gross operating profit | $280,079 | 82.6% | $379,281 | 71.1% |
| 26. Additional operating costs | $237,022 | 69.9% | $326,510 | 61.2% |
| 27. Net operating profit | $43,057 | 12.7% | $52,771 | 9.9% |
| 28. Less: Guaranteed payments to partners | $48,396 | | $36,493 | |
| 29. Distribution to partners | ($5,339) | | $16,278 | |
| 30. Other charges | $184 | | $17 | |
| 31. Net change partners' capital | ($5,523) | | $16,261 | |
| | | | | |
| Selected Ratios | | | | |
| 32. Coverage ratio: times interest earned | 2.3 | | 4.0 | |
| 33. Inventory turnover (times) | n.a. | | n.a. | |
| 34. Days' sales in inventory | n.a. | | n.a. | |
| 35. Average age of inventory (days) | n.a. | | n.a. | |
| 36. Return on assets, net inc., less def | (6.4%) | | 4.7% | |
| 37. Return on assets, gross operating profit | n.a. | | 110.5% | |
| 38. Return on assets, net operating profit | 50.2% | | 15.4% | |

*Page 85*

Table 1: Partnerships With and Without Net Income:  207.  BARBER SHOPS

Dollar values in thousands, except averages

|  |  | 1984 |  | 1985 |  |
|---|---|---|---|---|---|
| 1. | Number of Partnerships | 3,528 |  | 4,234 |  |
| 2. | Number of Partners | 9,086 |  | 13,813 |  |
| 3. | Total Assets | $10,854 |  | $21,472 |  |
| 4. | Average total assets per Partnership | $3,077 |  | $5,071 |  |
| 5. | Average total assets per Partner | $1,195 |  | $1,554 |  |
| 6. | Net Income, less Deficit | $31,743 |  | $116,458 |  |
| 7. | Average per Partnership, total earnings | $8,997 |  | $27,506 |  |
| 8. | Average per Partner, total earnings | $3,494 |  | $8,431 |  |
| 9. | Operating Income | $306,775 |  | $280,882 |  |
|  | Operating Costs |  |  |  |  |
| 10. | Cost of sales & operations | $37,413 | 12.2% | $76,414 | 27.2% |
| 11. | Salaries and wages | $104,670 | 34.1% | $0 | n.a. |
| 12. | Rent paid | $15,882 | 5.2% | $26,578 | 9.5% |
| 13. | Interest paid | $0 | n.a. | $2,621 | 0.9% |
| 14. | Taxes paid | $3,756 | 1.2% | $8,369 | 3.0% |
| 15. | Bad debts | $0 | n.a. | $0 | n.a. |
| 16. | Repairs | $0 | n.a. | $394 | 0.1% |
| 17. | Depreciation | $5,232 | 1.7% | $7,574 | 2.7% |
| 18. | Depletion | $0 | n.a. | $0 | n.a. |
| 19. | Pension & profit sharing plans | $0 | n.a. | $0 | n.a. |
| 20. | Employee benefits programs | $0 | n.a. | $0 | n.a. |
| 21. | Other deductions | $108,080 | 35.2% | $41,450 | 14.8% |
| 22. | Total operating costs | $275,033 | 89.7% | $163,400 | 58.2% |
|  | Operating Income and Distribution |  |  |  |  |
| 23. | Operating Income | $306,775 | 100.0% | $280,882 | 100.0% |
| 24. | Less:  Cost of sales and operations | $37,413 | 12.2% | $76,414 | 27.2% |
| 25. | Gross operating profit | $269,362 | 87.8% | $204,468 | 72.8% |
| 26. | Additional operating costs | $237,620 | 77.5% | $86,986 | 31.0% |
| 27. | Net operating profit | $31,742 | 10.4% | $117,482 | 41.8% |
| 28. | Less:  Guaranteed payments to partners | $0 |  | $1,024 |  |
| 29. | Distribution to partners | $31,742 |  | $116,458 |  |
| 30. | Other charges | $0 |  | $0 |  |
| 31. | Net change partners' capital | $31,742 |  | $116,458 |  |
|  | Selected Ratios |  |  |  |  |
| 32. | Coverage ratio:  times interest earned | n.a. |  | 43.8 |  |
| 33. | Inventory turnover (times) | n.a. |  | n.a. |  |
| 34. | Days' sales in inventory | n.a. |  | n.a. |  |
| 35. | Average age of inventory (days) | n.a. |  | n.a. |  |
| 36. | Return on assets, net inc., less def | n.a. |  | n.a. |  |
| 37. | Return on assets, gross operating profit | n.a. |  | n.a. |  |
| 38. | Return on assets, net operating profit | n.a. |  | n.a. |  |

*Page 86*

Table 1: Partnerships With and Without Net Income:  OTHER PERSONAL SERVICES (205,208,209,210)

Dollar values in thousands, except averages

|  |  | 1984 |  | 1985 |  |
|---|---|---|---|---|---|
| 1. | Number of Partnerships | 12,614 | | 12,522 | |
| 2. | Number of Partners | 31,858 | | 31,510 | |
| 3. | Total Assets | $543,937 | | $482,483 | |
| 4. | Average total assets per Partnership | $43,122 | | $38,531 | |
| 5. | Average total assets per Partner | $17,074 | | $15,312 | |
| 6. | Net Income, less Deficit | $135,391 | | $89,486 | |
| 7. | Average per Partnership, total earnings | $10,737 | | $7,150 | |
| 8. | Average per Partner, total earnings | $4,251 | | $2,841 | |
| 9. | Operating Income | $997,113 | | $1,001,794 | |
|  | Operating Costs | | | | |
| 10. | Cost of sales & operations | $270,075 | 27.1% | $184,473 | 18.4% |
| 11. | Salaries and wages | $106,139 | 10.6% | $143,944 | 14.4% |
| 12. | Rent paid | $46,640 | 4.7% | $93,236 | 9.3% |
| 13. | Interest paid | $17,777 | 1.8% | $24,506 | 2.5% |
| 14. | Taxes paid | $20,096 | 2.0% | $22,043 | 2.2% |
| 15. | Bad debts | $3,612 | 0.4% | $2,543 | 0.3% |
| 16. | Repairs | $12,706 | 1.3% | $20,352 | 2.0% |
| 17. | Depreciation | $70,728 | 7.1% | $65,431 | 6.5% |
| 18. | Depletion | $0 | n.a. | $54 | 0.0% |
| 19. | Pension & profit sharing plans | $470 | 0.1% | $610 | 0.1% |
| 20. | Employee benefits programs | $2,044 | 0.2% | $2,215 | 0.2% |
| 21. | Other deductions | $263,820 | 26.5% | $304,053 | 30.4% |
| 22. | Total operating costs | $814,107 | 81.7% | $863,460 | 86.2% |
|  | Operating Income and Distribution | | | | |
| 23. | Operating Income | $997,113 | 100.0% | $1,001,794 | 100.0% |
| 24. | Less: Cost of sales and operations | $270,075 | 27.1% | $184,473 | 18.4% |
| 25. | Gross operating profit | $727,038 | 72.9% | $817,321 | 81.6% |
| 26. | Additional operating costs | $544,032 | 54.6% | $678,987 | 67.8% |
| 27. | Net operating profit | $183,006 | 18.4% | $138,334 | 13.8% |
| 28. | Less: Guaranteed payments to partners | $39,934 | | $44,741 | |
| 29. | Distribution to partners | $143,072 | | $93,593 | |
| 30. | Other charges | $7,681 | | $4,106 | |
| 31. | Net change partners' capital | $135,391 | | $89,487 | |
|  | Selected Ratios | | | | |
| 32. | Coverage ratio:  times interest earned | 9.3 | | 4.6 | |
| 33. | Inventory turnover (times) | n.a. | | n.a. | |
| 34. | Days' sales in inventory | n.a. | | n.a. | |
| 35. | Average age of inventory (days) | n.a. | | n.a. | |
| 36. | Return on assets, net inc., less def | 24.9% | | 18.6% | |
| 37. | Return on assets, gross operating profit | 133.7% | | 169.4% | |
| 38. | Return on assets, net operating profit | 33.6% | | 28.7% | |

Table 1: Partnerships With and Without Net Income:  211.  BUSINESS SERVICES

Dollar values in thousands, except averages

| | | 1984 | | 1985 | |
|---|---|---|---|---|---|
| 1. | Number of Partnerships | 80,189 | | 81,289 | |
| 2. | Number of Partners | 451,534 | | 564,856 | |
| 3. | Total Assets | $21,454,480 | | $25,041,323 | |
| 4. | Average total assets per Partnership | $267,549 | | $308,053 | |
| 5. | Average total assets per Partner | $47,515 | | $44,332 | |
| 6. | Net Income, less Deficit | $296,751 | | $274,212 | |
| 7. | Average per Partnership, total earnings | $3,703 | | $3,376 | |
| 8. | Average per Partner, total earnings | $658 | | $486 | |
| 9. | Operating Income | $9,956,057 | | $11,137,829 | |
| | Operating Costs | | | | |
| 10. | Cost of sales & operations | $2,245,430 | 22.6% | $2,512,612 | 22.6% |
| 11. | Salaries and wages | $796,371 | 8.0% | $902,216 | 8.1% |
| 12. | Rent paid | $495,219 | 5.0% | $509,382 | 4.6% |
| 13. | Interest paid | $869,171 | 8.7% | $963,978 | 8.7% |
| 14. | Taxes paid | $135,198 | 1.4% | $141,309 | 1.3% |
| 15. | Bad debts | $71,398 | 0.7% | $98,541 | 0.9% |
| 16. | Repairs | $148,116 | 1.5% | $96,951 | 0.9% |
| 17. | Depreciation | $1,596,169 | 16.0% | $1,705,585 | 15.3% |
| 18. | Depletion | $2,464 | 0.0% | $614 | 0.0% |
| 19. | Pension & profit sharing plans | $14,180 | 0.1% | $17,629 | 0.2% |
| 20. | Employee benefits programs | $12,359 | 0.1% | $24,924 | 0.2% |
| 21. | Other deductions | $2,095,333 | 21.1% | $2,548,789 | 22.9% |
| 22. | Total operating costs | $8,485,789 | 85.2% | $9,522,850 | 85.5% |
| | Operating Income and Distribution | | | | |
| 23. | Operating Income | $9,956,057 | 100.0% | $11,137,829 | 100.0% |
| 24. | Less: Cost of sales and operations | $2,245,430 | 22.6% | $2,512,612 | 22.6% |
| 25. | Gross operating profit | $7,710,627 | 77.5% | $8,625,217 | 77.4% |
| 26. | Additional operating costs | $6,240,359 | 62.7% | $7,010,238 | 62.9% |
| 27. | Net operating profit | $1,470,268 | 14.8% | $1,614,979 | 14.5% |
| 28. | Less: Guaranteed payments to partners | $213,954 | | $210,242 | |
| 29. | Distribution to partners | $1,256,314 | | $1,404,737 | |
| 30. | Other charges | $963,944 | | $1,130,845 | |
| 31. | Net change partners' capital | $292,370 | | $273,892 | |
| | Selected Ratios | | | | |
| 32. | Coverage ratio: times interest earned | 0.7 | | 0.7 | |
| 33. | Inventory turnover (times) | n.a. | | n.a. | |
| 34. | Days' sales in inventory | n.a. | | n.a. | |
| 35. | Average age of inventory (days) | n.a. | | n.a. | |
| 36. | Return on assets, net inc., less def | 1.4% | | 1.1% | |
| 37. | Return on assets, gross operating profit | 35.9% | | 34.4% | |
| 38. | Return on assets, net operating profit | 6.9% | | 6.5% | |

*Page 88*

Table 1: Partnerships With and Without Net Income:  218.  AUTOMOTIVE REPAIR SERVICES

Dollar values in thousands, except averages

|  | | 1984 | | 1985 | |
|---|---|---|---|---|---|
| 1. | Number of Partnerships | 35,396 | | 30,188 | |
| 2. | Number of Partners | 76,991 | | 67,760 | |
| 3. | Total Assets | $1,851,550 | | $1,634,041 | |
| 4. | Average total assets per Partnership | $52,310 | | $54,129 | |
| 5. | Average total assets per Partner | $24,049 | | $24,115 | |
| 6. | Net Income, less Deficit | $350,080 | | $399,607 | |
| 7. | Average per Partnership, total earnings | $9,894 | | $13,241 | |
| 8. | Average per Partner, total earnings | $4,549 | | $5,899 | |
| 9. | Operating Income | $3,913,505 | | $4,269,509 | |
| | Operating Costs | | | | |
| 10. | Cost of sales & operations | $1,962,105 | 50.1% | $2,252,815 | 52.8% |
| 11. | Salaries and wages | $308,539 | 7.9% | $318,938 | 7.5% |
| 12. | Rent paid | $174,382 | 4.5% | $151,372 | 3.6% |
| 13. | Interest paid | $119,028 | 3.0% | $131,169 | 3.1% |
| 14. | Taxes paid | $75,057 | 1.9% | $74,827 | 1.8% |
| 15. | Bad debts | $7,727 | 0.2% | $6,579 | 0.2% |
| 16. | Repairs | $28,829 | 0.7% | $26,238 | 0.6% |
| 17. | Depreciation | $206,001 | 5.3% | $235,772 | 5.5% |
| 18. | Depletion | $0 | n.a. | $1 | n.a. |
| 19. | Pension & profit sharing plans | $76 | n.a. | $49 | n.a. |
| 20. | Employee benefits programs | $6,728 | 0.2% | $12,143 | 0.3% |
| 21. | Other deductions | $519,124 | 13.3% | $554,558 | 13.0% |
| 22. | Total operating costs | $3,409,902 | 87.1% | $3,764,461 | 88.2% |
| | Operating Income and Distribution | | | | |
| 23. | Operating Income | $3,913,505 | 100.0% | $4,269,509 | 100.0% |
| 24. | Less: Cost of sales and operations | $1,962,105 | 50.1% | $2,252,815 | 52.8% |
| 25. | Gross operating profit | $1,951,400 | 49.9% | $2,016,694 | 47.2% |
| 26. | Additional operating costs | $1,447,797 | 37.0% | $1,511,646 | 35.4% |
| 27. | Net operating profit | $503,603 | 12.9% | $505,048 | 11.8% |
| 28. | Less: Guaranteed payments to partners | $119,770 | | $101,276 | |
| 29. | Distribution to partners | $383,833 | | $403,772 | |
| 30. | Other charges | $36,059 | | $4,164 | |
| 31. | Net change partners' capital | $347,774 | | $399,608 | |
| | Selected Ratios | | | | |
| 32. | Coverage ratio: times interest earned | 3.2 | | 2.9 | |
| 33. | Inventory turnover (times) | n.a. | | n.a. | |
| 34. | Days' sales in inventory | n.a. | | n.a. | |
| 35. | Average age of inventory (days) | n.a. | | n.a. | |
| 36. | Return on assets, net inc., less def | 18.9% | | 24.5% | |
| 37. | Return on assets, gross operating profit | 105.4% | | 123.4% | |
| 38. | Return on assets, net operating profit | 27.2% | | 30.9% | |

*Page 89*

Table 1: Partnerships With and Without Net Income:  AUTOMOBILE REPAIR SHOPS, TOTAL (219,220,221,222,223)

Dollar values in thousands, except averages

| | 1984 | | 1985 | |
|---|---|---|---|---|
| 1. Number of Partnerships | 25,707 | | 20,561 | |
| 2. Number of Partners | 55,462 | | 45,051 | |
| 3. Total Assets | $822,042 | | $513,923 | |
| 4.   Average total assets per Partnership | $31,977 | | $24,995 | |
| 5.   Average total assets per Partner | $14,822 | | $11,408 | |
| 6. Net Income, less Deficit | $317,260 | | $338,210 | |
| 7.   Average per Partnership, total earnings | $12,345 | | $16,452 | |
| 8.   Average per Partner, total earnings | $5,722 | | $7,509 | |
| 9. Operating Income | $2,755,762 | | $2,981,279 | |
| Operating Costs | | | | |
| 10.   Cost of sales & operations | $1,481,284 | 53.8% | $1,664,471 | 55.8% |
| 11.   Salaries and wages | $218,109 | 7.9% | $242,173 | 8.1% |
| 12.   Rent paid | $122,309 | 4.4% | $113,447 | 3.8% |
| 13.   Interest paid | $36,478 | 1.3% | $35,499 | 1.2% |
| 14.   Taxes paid | $48,354 | 1.8% | $54,917 | 1.8% |
| 15.   Bad debts | $6,048 | 0.2% | $4,354 | 0.2% |
| 16.   Repairs | $13,356 | 0.5% | $10,594 | 0.4% |
| 17.   Depreciation | $63,716 | 2.3% | $54,759 | 1.8% |
| 18.   Depletion | $0 | n.a. | $0 | n.a. |
| 19.   Pension & profit sharing plans | $0 | n.a. | $0 | n.a. |
| 20.   Employee benefits programs | $4,857 | 0.2% | $10,977 | 0.4% |
| 21.   Other deductions | $360,505 | 13.1% | $383,228 | 12.9% |
| 22.   Total operating costs | $2,357,322 | 85.5% | $2,574,419 | 86.4% |
| Operating Income and Distribution | | | | |
| 23.   Operating Income | $2,755,762 | 100.0% | $2,981,279 | 100.0% |
| 24.     Less:  Cost of sales and operations | $1,481,284 | 53.8% | $1,664,471 | 55.8% |
| 25.   Gross operating profit | $1,274,478 | 46.3% | $1,316,808 | 44.2% |
| 26.     Additional operating costs | $876,038 | 31.8% | $909,948 | 30.5% |
| 27.   Net operating profit | $398,440 | 14.5% | $406,860 | 13.7% |
| 28.     Less:  Guaranteed payments to partners | $80,613 | | $66,970 | |
| 29.   Distribution to partners | $317,827 | | $339,890 | |
| 30.   Other charges | $2,873 | | $1,680 | |
| 31.   Net change partners' capital | $314,954 | | $338,210 | |
| Selected Ratios | | | | |
| 32.   Coverage ratio:  times interest earned | 9.9 | | 10.5 | |
| 33.   Inventory turnover (times) | n.a. | | n.a. | |
| 34.   Days' sales in inventory | n.a. | | n.a. | |
| 35.   Average age of inventory (days) | n.a. | | n.a. | |
| 36.   Return on assets, net inc., less def | 38.6% | | 65.8% | |
| 37.   Return on assets, gross operating profit | 155.0% | | n.a. | |
| 38.   Return on assets, net operating profit | 48.5% | | 79.2% | |

Table 1: Partnerships With and Without Net Income:  222.  GENERAL AUTOMOTIVE REPAIR SHOPS

Dollar values in thousands, except averages

|    |                                              | 1984        |        | 1985        |        |
|----|----------------------------------------------|-------------|--------|-------------|--------|
| 1. | Number of Partnerships                       | 14,738      |        | 9,949       |        |
| 2. | Number of Partners                           | 32,581      |        | 23,509      |        |
| 3. | Total Assets                                 | $426,517    |        | $302,365    |        |
| 4. | Average total assets per Partnership         | $28,940     |        | $30,392     |        |
| 5. | Average total assets per Partner             | $13,091     |        | $12,862     |        |
| 6. | Net Income, less Deficit                     | $148,678    |        | $157,236    |        |
| 7. | Average per Partnership, total earnings      | $10,091     |        | $15,809     |        |
| 8. | Average per Partner, total earnings          | $4,564      |        | $6,690      |        |
| 9. | Operating Income                             | $1,406,842  |        | $1,554,297  |        |
|    | Operating Costs                              |             |        |             |        |
| 10.| Cost of sales & operations                   | $798,872    | 56.8%  | $848,553    | 54.6%  |
| 11.| Salaries and wages                           | $78,900     | 5.6%   | $120,235    | 7.7%   |
| 12.| Rent paid                                    | $79,716     | 5.7%   | $66,956     | 4.3%   |
| 13.| Interest paid                                | $17,093     | 1.2%   | $17,237     | 1.1%   |
| 14.| Taxes paid                                   | $20,571     | 1.5%   | $27,198     | 1.8%   |
| 15.| Bad debts                                    | $4,218      | 0.3%   | $3,316      | 0.2%   |
| 16.| Repairs                                      | $8,094      | 0.6%   | $4,259      | 0.3%   |
| 17.| Depreciation                                 | $36,942     | 2.6%   | $26,303     | 1.7%   |
| 18.| Depletion                                    | $0          | n.a.   | $0          | n.a.   |
| 19.| Pension & profit sharing plans               | $0          | n.a.   | $0          | n.a.   |
| 20.| Employee benefits programs                   | $2,068      | 0.2%   | $8,838      | 0.6%   |
| 21.| Other deductions                             | $174,774    | 12.4%  | $226,312    | 14.6%  |
| 22.| Total operating costs                        | $1,223,554  | 87.0%  | $1,349,207  | 86.8%  |
|    | Operating Income and Distribution            |             |        |             |        |
| 23.| Operating Income                             | $1,406,842  | 100.0% | $1,554,297  | 100.0% |
| 24.| Less: Cost of sales and operations           | $798,872    | 56.8%  | $848,553    | 54.6%  |
| 25.| Gross operating profit                       | $607,970    | 43.2%  | $705,744    | 45.4%  |
| 26.| Additional operating costs                   | $424,682    | 30.2%  | $500,654    | 32.2%  |
| 27.| Net operating profit                         | $183,288    | 13.0%  | $205,090    | 13.2%  |
| 28.| Less: Guaranteed payments to partners        | $36,715     |        | $46,174     |        |
| 29.| Distribution to partners                     | $146,573    |        | $158,916    |        |
| 30.| Other charges                                | $201        |        | $1,680      |        |
| 31.| Net change partners' capital                 | $146,372    |        | $157,236    |        |
|    | Selected Ratios                              |             |        |             |        |
| 32.| Coverage ratio: times interest earned        | 9.7         |        | 10.9        |        |
| 33.| Inventory turnover (times)                   | n.a.        |        | n.a.        |        |
| 34.| Days' sales in inventory                     | n.a.        |        | n.a.        |        |
| 35.| Average age of inventory (days)              | n.a.        |        | n.a.        |        |
| 36.| Return on assets, net inc., less def         | 34.9%       |        | 52.0%       |        |
| 37.| Return on assets, gross operating profit     | 142.5%      |        | 233.4%      |        |
| 38.| Return on assets, net operating profit       | 43.0%       |        | 67.8%       |        |

Table 1: Partnerships With and Without Net Income:  OTHER AUTOMOBILE REPAIR (221,223)

Dollar values in thousands, except averages

|  |  | 1984 | | 1985 | |
|---|---|---|---|---|---|
| 1. | Number of Partnerships | 10,969 | | 10,612 | |
| 2. | Number of Partners | 22,881 | | 21,542 | |
| 3. | Total Assets | $395,525 | | $211,558 | |
| 4. | Average total assets per Partnership | $36,058 | | $19,936 | |
| 5. | Average total assets per Partner | $17,286 | | $9,821 | |
| 6. | Net Income, less Deficit | $168,581 | | $180,974 | |
| 7. | Average per Partnership, total earnings | $15,373 | | $17,056 | |
| 8. | Average per Partner, total earnings | $7,370 | | $8,402 | |
| 9. | Operating Income | $1,348,920 | | $1,426,982 | |
|  | Operating Costs | | | | |
| 10. | Cost of sales & operations | $682,411 | 50.6% | $815,918 | 57.2% |
| 11. | Salaries and wages | $139,209 | 10.3% | $121,938 | 8.6% |
| 12. | Rent paid | $42,593 | 3.2% | $46,491 | 3.3% |
| 13. | Interest paid | $19,385 | 1.4% | $18,261 | 1.3% |
| 14. | Taxes paid | $27,783 | 2.1% | $27,720 | 1.9% |
| 15. | Bad debts | $1,830 | 0.1% | $1,037 | 0.1% |
| 16. | Repairs | $5,262 | 0.4% | $6,335 | 0.4% |
| 17. | Depreciation | $26,776 | 2.0% | $28,456 | 2.0% |
| 18. | Depletion | $0 | n.a. | $0 | n.a. |
| 19. | Pension & profit sharing plans | $0 | n.a. | $0 | n.a. |
| 20. | Employee benefits programs | $2,789 | 0.2% | $2,139 | 0.2% |
| 21. | Other deductions | $185,731 | 13.8% | $156,917 | 11.0% |
| 22. | Total operating costs | $1,133,769 | 84.1% | $1,225,212 | 85.9% |
|  | Operating Income and Distribution | | | | |
| 23. | Operating Income | $1,348,920 | 100.0% | $1,426,982 | 100.0% |
| 24. | Less:  Cost of sales and operations | $682,411 | 50.6% | $815,918 | 57.2% |
| 25. | Gross operating profit | $666,509 | 49.4% | $611,064 | 42.8% |
| 26. | Additional operating costs | $451,358 | 33.5% | $409,294 | 28.7% |
| 27. | Net operating profit | $215,151 | 16.0% | $201,770 | 14.1% |
| 28. | Less:  Guaranteed payments to partners | $43,898 | | $20,796 | |
| 29. | Distribution to partners | $171,253 | | $180,974 | |
| 30. | Other charges | $2,671 | | $0 | |
| 31. | Net change partners' capital | $168,582 | | $180,974 | |
|  | Selected Ratios | | | | |
| 32. | Coverage ratio:  times interest earned | 10.1 | | 10.1 | |
| 33. | Inventory turnover (times) | n.a. | | n.a. | |
| 34. | Days' sales in inventory | n.a. | | n.a. | |
| 35. | Average age of inventory (days) | n.a. | | n.a. | |
| 36. | Return on assets, net inc., less def | 42.6% | | 85.5% | |
| 37. | Return on assets, gross operating profit | 168.5% | | n.a. | |
| 38. | Return on assets, net operating profit | 54.4% | | 95.4% | |

*Page 92*

Table 1: Partnerships With and Without Net Income:  AUTOMOBILE PARKING AND OTHER SERVICES (219,220,224)

Dollar values in thousands, except averages

|  |  | 1984 | | 1985 | |
|---|---|---|---|---|---|
| 1. | Number of Partnerships | 9,690 | | 9,627 | |
| 2. | Number of Partners | 21,529 | | 22,709 | |
| 3. | Total Assets | $1,029,508 | | $1,120,118 | |
| 4. | Average total assets per Partnership | $106,244 | | $116,352 | |
| 5. | Average total assets per Partner | $47,820 | | $49,325 | |
| 6. | Net Income, less Deficit | $32,820 | | $61,398 | |
| 7. | Average per Partnership, total earnings | $3,391 | | $6,381 | |
| 8. | Average per Partner, total earnings | $1,526 | | $2,705 | |
| 9. | Operating Income | $1,157,744 | | $1,288,230 | |
|  | Operating Costs | | | | |
| 10. | Cost of sales & operations | $480,822 | 41.5% | $588,344 | 45.7% |
| 11. | Salaries and wages | $90,430 | 7.8% | $76,764 | 6.0% |
| 12. | Rent paid | $52,073 | 4.5% | $37,925 | 2.9% |
| 13. | Interest paid | $82,550 | 7.1% | $95,671 | 7.4% |
| 14. | Taxes paid | $26,703 | 2.3% | $19,910 | 1.6% |
| 15. | Bad debts | $1,679 | 0.2% | $2,225 | 0.2% |
| 16. | Repairs | $15,474 | 1.3% | $15,644 | 1.2% |
| 17. | Depreciation | $142,281 | 12.3% | $181,012 | 14.1% |
| 18. | Depletion | $0 | n.a. | $1 | n.a. |
| 19. | Pension & profit sharing plans | $76 | 0.0% | $49 | n.a. |
| 20. | Employee benefits programs | $1,872 | 0.2% | $1,166 | 0.1% |
| 21. | Other deductions | $158,619 | 13.7% | $171,330 | 13.3% |
| 22. | Total operating costs | $1,052,579 | 90.9% | $1,190,041 | 92.4% |
|  | **Operating Income and Distribution** | | | | |
| 23. | Operating Income | $1,157,744 | 100.0% | $1,288,230 | 100.0% |
| 24. | Less: Cost of sales and operations | $480,822 | 41.5% | $588,344 | 45.7% |
| 25. | Gross operating profit | $676,922 | 58.5% | $699,886 | 54.3% |
| 26. | Additional operating costs | $571,757 | 49.4% | $601,697 | 46.7% |
| 27. | Net operating profit | $105,165 | 9.1% | $98,189 | 7.6% |
| 28. | Less: Guaranteed payments to partners | $39,157 | | $34,307 | |
| 29. | Distribution to partners | $66,008 | | $63,882 | |
| 30. | Other charges | $33,187 | | $2,484 | |
| 31. | Net change partners' capital | $32,821 | | $61,398 | |
|  | **Selected Ratios** | | | | |
| 32. | Coverage ratio:  times interest earned | 0.3 | | 0.0 | |
| 33. | Inventory turnover (times) | n.a. | | n.a. | |
| 34. | Days' sales in inventory | n.a. | | n.a. | |
| 35. | Average age of inventory (days) | n.a. | | n.a. | |
| 36. | Return on assets, net inc., less def | 3.2% | | 5.5% | |
| 37. | Return on assets, gross operating profit | 65.8% | | 62.5% | |
| 38. | Return on assets, net operating profit | 10.2% | | 8.8% | |

Table 1: Partnerships With and Without Net Income: 225. MISCELLANEOUS REPAIR SERVICES

Dollar values in thousands, except averages

|  |  | 1984 |  | 1985 |  |
|---|---|---|---|---|---|
| 1. | Number of Partnerships | 11,300 |  | 7,778 |  |
| 2. | Number of Partners | 25,155 |  | 15,879 |  |
| 3. | Total Assets | $345,559 |  | $217,083 |  |
| 4. | Average total assets per Partnership | $30,580 |  | $27,910 |  |
| 5. | Average total assets per Partner | $13,737 |  | $13,671 |  |
| 6. | Net Income, less Deficit | $146,779 |  | $103,215 |  |
| 7. | Average per Partnership, total earnings | $12,992 |  | $13,275 |  |
| 8. | Average per Partner, total earnings | $5,836 |  | $6,502 |  |
| 9. | Operating Income | $1,058,121 |  | $995,426 |  |
|  | Operating Costs |  |  |  |  |
| 10. | Cost of sales & operations | $547,993 | 51.8% | $536,664 | 53.9% |
| 11. | Salaries and wages | $47,852 | 4.5% | $46,719 | 4.7% |
| 12. | Rent paid | $23,451 | 2.2% | $17,134 | 1.7% |
| 13. | Interest paid | $19,690 | 1.9% | $16,517 | 1.7% |
| 14. | Taxes paid | $14,431 | 1.4% | $16,647 | 1.7% |
| 15. | Bad debts | $1,411 | 0.1% | $1,195 | 0.1% |
| 16. | Repairs | $4,067 | 0.4% | $5,885 | 0.6% |
| 17. | Depreciation | $59,708 | 5.6% | $59,776 | 6.0% |
| 18. | Depletion | $0 | n.a. | $0 | n.a. |
| 19. | Pension & profit sharing plans | $77 | 0.0% | $29 | n.a. |
| 20. | Employee benefits programs | $232 | 0.0% | $155 | 0.0% |
| 21. | Other deductions | $167,395 | 15.8% | $156,747 | 15.8% |
| 22. | Total operating costs | $886,307 | 83.8% | $857,468 | 86.1% |
|  | Operating Income and Distribution |  |  |  |  |
| 23. | Operating Income | $1,058,121 | 100.0% | $995,426 | 100.0% |
| 24. | Less:  Cost of sales and operations | $547,993 | 51.8% | $536,664 | 53.9% |
| 25. | Gross operating profit | $510,128 | 48.2% | $458,762 | 46.1% |
| 26. | Additional operating costs | $338,314 | 32.0% | $320,804 | 32.2% |
| 27. | Net operating profit | $171,814 | 16.2% | $137,958 | 13.9% |
| 28. | Less:  Guaranteed payments to partners | $25,025 |  | $34,695 |  |
| 29. | Distribution to partners | $146,789 |  | $103,263 |  |
| 30. | Other charges | $10 |  | $48 |  |
| 31. | Net change partners' capital | $146,779 |  | $103,215 |  |
|  | Selected Ratios |  |  |  |  |
| 32. | Coverage ratio:  times interest earned | 7.7 |  | 7.4 |  |
| 33. | Inventory turnover (times) | n.a. |  | n.a. |  |
| 34. | Days' sales in inventory | n.a. |  | n.a. |  |
| 35. | Average age of inventory (days) | n.a. |  | n.a. |  |
| 36. | Return on assets, net inc., less def | 42.5% |  | 47.6% |  |
| 37. | Return on assets, gross operating profit | 147.6% |  | 211.3% |  |
| 38. | Return on assets, net operating profit | 49.7% |  | 63.6% |  |

Table 1: Partnerships With and Without Net Income:  AMUSEMENT AND RECREATION SERVICES, INCLUDING MOTION PICTURES (230,233)

Dollar values in thousands, except averages

| | | 1984 | | 1985 | |
|---|---|---|---|---|---|
| 1. | Number of Partnerships | 31,832 | | 29,545 | |
| 2. | Number of Partners | 193,392 | | 193,432 | |
| 3. | Total Assets | $10,293,588 | | $12,259,147 | |
| 4. | Average total assets per Partnership | $323,372 | | $414,931 | |
| 5. | Average total assets per Partner | $53,227 | | $63,377 | |
| 6. | Net Income, less Deficit | ($833,558) | | ($391,809) | |
| 7. | Average per Partnership, total earnings | ($26,181) | | ($13,256) | |
| 8. | Average per Partner, total earnings | ($4,309) | | ($2,025) | |
| 9. | Operating Income | $8,316,328 | | $9,509,716 | |
| | Operating Costs | | | | |
| 10. | Cost of sales & operations | $2,139,205 | 25.7% | $2,814,769 | 29.6% |
| 11. | Salaries and wages | $1,056,083 | 12.7% | $1,246,745 | 13.1% |
| 12. | Rent paid | $220,800 | 2.7% | $211,718 | 2.2% |
| 13. | Interest paid | $500,704 | 6.0% | $572,122 | 6.0% |
| 14. | Taxes paid | $174,138 | 2.1% | $169,664 | 1.8% |
| 15. | Bad debts | $27,009 | 0.3% | $24,791 | 0.3% |
| 16. | Repairs | $74,956 | 0.9% | $85,160 | 0.9% |
| 17. | Depreciation | $1,407,462 | 16.9% | $1,168,399 | 12.3% |
| 18. | Depletion | $2,210 | 0.0% | $99 | n.a. |
| 19. | Pension & profit sharing plans | $21,374 | 0.3% | $21,655 | 0.2% |
| 20. | Employee benefits programs | $19,667 | 0.2% | $28,149 | 0.3% |
| 21. | Other deductions | $3,153,722 | 37.9% | $3,187,186 | 33.5% |
| 22. | Total operating costs | $8,797,506 | 105.8% | $9,530,844 | 100.2% |
| | Operating Income and Distribution | | | | |
| 23. | Operating Income | $8,316,328 | 100.0% | $9,509,716 | 100.0% |
| 24. | Less:  Cost of sales and operations | $2,139,205 | 25.7% | $2,814,769 | 29.6% |
| 25. | Gross operating profit | $6,177,123 | 74.3% | $6,694,947 | 70.4% |
| 26. | Additional operating costs | $6,658,301 | 80.1% | $6,716,075 | 70.6% |
| 27. | Net operating profit | ($481,178) | (5.8%) | ($21,128) | (0.2%) |
| 28. | Less:  Guaranteed payments to partners | $159,652 | | $174,243 | |
| 29. | Distribution to partners | ($640,830) | | ($195,371) | |
| 30. | Other charges | $192,904 | | $196,824 | |
| 31. | Net change partners' capital | ($833,734) | | ($392,195) | |
| | Selected Ratios | | | | |
| 32. | Coverage ratio:  times interest earned | (2.0) | | (1.0) | |
| 33. | Inventory turnover (times) | n.a. | | n.a. | |
| 34. | Days' sales in inventory | n.a. | | n.a. | |
| 35. | Average age of inventory (days) | n.a. | | n.a. | |
| 36. | Return on assets, net inc., less def | (8.1%) | | (3.2%) | |
| 37. | Return on assets, gross operating profit | 60.0% | | 54.6% | |
| 38. | Return on assets, net operating profit | (4.7%) | | (0.2%) | |

Table 1: Partnerships With and Without Net Income:  240.  MEDICAL AND HEALTH SERVICES

Dollar values in thousands, except averages

| | | 1984 | | 1985 | |
|---|---|---|---|---|---|
| 1. | Number of Partnerships | 30,160 | | 36,557 | |
| 2. | Number of Partners | 130,874 | | 203,837 | |
| | | | | | |
| 3. | Total Assets | $5,991,946 | | $7,454,810 | |
| 4. | Average total assets per Partnership | $198,672 | | $203,923 | |
| 5. | Average total assets per Partner | $45,784 | | $36,572 | |
| | | | | | |
| 6. | Net Income, less Deficit | $4,639,983 | | $4,413,387 | |
| 7. | Average per Partnership, total earnings | $153,859 | | $120,752 | |
| 8. | Average per Partner, total earnings | $35,457 | | $21,656 | |
| | | | | | |
| 9. | Operating Income | $14,646,090 | | $16,927,551 | |
| | Operating Costs | | | | |
| 10. | Cost of sales & operations | $1,042,148 | 7.1% | $1,281,805 | 7.6% |
| 11. | Salaries and wages | $2,771,148 | 18.9% | $3,315,423 | 19.6% |
| 12. | Rent paid | $622,317 | 4.3% | $742,852 | 4.4% |
| 13. | Interest paid | $612,796 | 4.2% | $440,328 | 2.6% |
| 14. | Taxes paid | $315,158 | 2.2% | $381,754 | 2.3% |
| 15. | Bad debts | $22,140 | 0.2% | $24,545 | 0.2% |
| 16. | Repairs | $74,706 | 0.5% | $78,953 | 0.5% |
| 17. | Depreciation | $29,675 | 0.2% | $475,856 | 2.8% |
| 18. | Depletion | $2,206 | 0.0% | $0 | n.a. |
| 19. | Pension & profit sharing plans | $82,277 | 0.6% | $91,177 | 0.5% |
| 20. | Employee benefits programs | $131,665 | 0.9% | $147,015 | 0.9% |
| 21. | Other deductions | $3,855,606 | 26.3% | $4,526,847 | 26.7% |
| 22. | Total operating costs | $9,562,429 | 65.3% | $11,507,676 | 68.0% |
| | | | | | |
| | Operating Income and Distribution | | | | |
| 23. | Operating Income | $14,646,090 | 100.0% | $16,927,551 | 100.0% |
| 24. | Less: Cost of sales and operations | $1,042,148 | 7.1% | $1,281,805 | 7.6% |
| 25. | Gross operating profit | $13,603,942 | 92.9% | $15,645,746 | 92.4% |
| 26. | Additional operating costs | $8,520,281 | 58.2% | $10,225,871 | 60.4% |
| 27. | Net operating profit | $5,083,661 | 34.7% | $5,419,875 | 32.0% |
| 28. | Less: Guaranteed payments to partners | $416,461 | | $958,378 | |
| 29. | Distribution to partners | $4,667,200 | | $4,461,497 | |
| 30. | Other charges | $27,804 | | $49,231 | |
| 31. | Net change partners' capital | $4,639,396 | | $4,412,266 | |
| | | | | | |
| | Selected Ratios | | | | |
| 32. | Coverage ratio:  times interest earned | 7.3 | | 11.3 | |
| 33. | Inventory turnover (times) | n.a. | | n.a. | |
| 34. | Days' sales in inventory | n.a. | | n.a. | |
| 35. | Average age of inventory (days) | n.a. | | n.a. | |
| 36. | Return on assets, net inc., less def | 77.4% | | 59.2% | |
| 37. | Return on assets, gross operating profit | 227.0% | | 209.9% | |
| 38. | Return on assets, net operating profit | 84.8% | | 72.7% | |

Table 1: Partnerships With and Without Net Income:  241.  OFFICES OF PHYSICIANS

Dollar values in thousands, except averages

|  |  | 1984 |  | 1985 |  |
|---|---|---|---|---|---|
| 1. | Number of Partnerships | 10,062 |  | 9,759 |  |
| 2. | Number of Partners | 37,340 |  | 39,397 |  |
| 3. | Total Assets | $988,987 |  | $895,741 |  |
| 4. | Average total assets per Partnership | $98,289 |  | $91,786 |  |
| 5. | Average total assets per Partner | $26,486 |  | $22,736 |  |
| 6. | Net Income, less Deficit | $3,194,786 |  | $2,933,788 |  |
| 7. | Average per Partnership, total earnings | $317,532 |  | $300,691 |  |
| 8. | Average per Partner, total earnings | $85,565 |  | $74,484 |  |
| 9. | Operating Income | $7,117,554 |  | $7,371,668 |  |
|  | Operating Costs |  |  |  |  |
| 10. | Cost of sales & operations | $53,703 | 0.8% | $132,033 | 1.8% |
| 11. | Salaries and wages | $1,279,870 | 18.0% | $1,266,451 | 17.2% |
| 12. | Rent paid | $344,105 | 4.8% | $337,673 | 4.6% |
| 13. | Interest paid | $34,946 | 0.5% | $38,865 | 0.5% |
| 14. | Taxes paid | $106,333 | 1.5% | $102,918 | 1.4% |
| 15. | Bad debts | $9,027 | 0.1% | $6,569 | 0.1% |
| 16. | Repairs | $25,792 | 0.4% | $24,288 | 0.3% |
| 17. | Depreciation | $66,938 | 0.9% | $87,760 | 1.2% |
| 18. | Depletion | $0 | n.a. | $0 | n.a. |
| 19. | Pension & profit sharing plans | $66,655 | 0.9% | $72,004 | 0.10% |
| 20. | Employee benefits programs | $84,814 | 1.2% | $74,713 | 1.0% |
| 21. | Other deductions | $1,632,306 | 22.9% | $1,633,890 | 22.2% |
| 22. | Total operating costs | $3,704,513 | 52.1% | $3,777,185 | 51.2% |
|  | Operating Income and Distribution |  |  |  |  |
| 23. | Operating Income | $7,117,554 | 100.0% | $7,371,668 | 100.0% |
| 24. | Less:  Cost of sales and operations | $53,703 | 0.8% | $132,033 | 1.8% |
| 25. | Gross operating profit | $7,063,851 | 99.3% | $7,239,635 | 98.2% |
| 26. | Additional operating costs | $3,650,810 | 51.3% | $3,645,152 | 49.5% |
| 27. | Net operating profit | $3,413,041 | 48.0% | $3,594,483 | 48.8% |
| 28. | Less:  Guaranteed payments to partners | $217,905 |  | $659,469 |  |
| 29. | Distribution to partners | $3,195,136 |  | $2,935,014 |  |
| 30. | Other charges | $374 |  | $1,247 |  |
| 31. | Net change partners' capital | $3,194,762 |  | $2,933,767 |  |
|  | Selected Ratios |  |  |  |  |
| 32. | Coverage ratio:  times interest earned | 96.7 |  | 91.5 |  |
| 33. | Inventory turnover (times) | n.a. |  | n.a. |  |
| 34. | Days' sales in inventory | n.a. |  | n.a. |  |
| 35. | Average age of inventory (days) | n.a. |  | n.a. |  |
| 36. | Return on assets, net inc., less def | n.a. |  | n.a. |  |
| 37. | Return on assets, gross operating profit | n.a. |  | n.a. |  |
| 38. | Return on assets, net operating profit | n.a. |  | n.a. |  |

*Page 97*

Table 1: Partnerships With and Without Net Income:  OTHER MEDICAL AND HEALTH SERVICES (242 TO 251)

Dollar values in thousands, except averages

|     |                                            | 1984 | | 1985 | |
| --- | ------------------------------------------ | ----------- | ------ | ----------- | ------ |
| 1.  | Number of Partnerships                     | 20,098      |        | 26,798      |        |
| 2.  | Number of Partners                         | 93,534      |        | 164,440     |        |
| 3.  | Total Assets                               | $5,002,959  |        | $6,559,069  |        |
| 4.  | Average total assets per Partnership       | $248,928    |        | $244,760    |        |
| 5.  | Average total assets per Partner           | $53,488     |        | $39,887     |        |
| 6.  | Net Income, less Deficit                   | $1,445,196  |        | $1,479,599  |        |
| 7.  | Average per Partnership, total earnings    | $71,917     |        | $55,224     |        |
| 8.  | Average per Partner, total earnings        | $15,453     |        | $9,000      |        |
| 9.  | Operating Income                           | $7,528,536  |        | $9,555,883  |        |
|     | Operating Costs                            |             |        |             |        |
| 10. | Cost of sales & operations                 | $988,446    | 13.1%  | $1,149,772  | 12.0%  |
| 11. | Salaries and wages                         | $1,491,278  | 19.8%  | $2,048,971  | 21.4%  |
| 12. | Rent paid                                  | $278,212    | 3.7%   | $405,179    | 4.2%   |
| 13. | Interest paid                              | $277,850    | 3.7%   | $401,463    | 4.2%   |
| 14. | Taxes paid                                 | $208,825    | 2.8%   | $278,836    | 2.9%   |
| 15. | Bad debts                                  | $13,113     | 0.2%   | $17,976     | 0.2%   |
| 16. | Repairs                                    | $48,913     | 0.7%   | $54,665     | 0.6%   |
| 17. | Depreciation                               | $262,737    | 3.5%   | $388,096    | 4.1%   |
| 18. | Depletion                                  | $2,206      | 0.0%   | $0          | n.a.   |
| 19. | Pension & profit sharing plans             | $15,621     | 0.2%   | $19,173     | 0.2%   |
| 20. | Employee benefits programs                 | $46,852     | 0.6%   | $72,302     | 0.8%   |
| 21. | Other deductions                           | $2,223,300  | 29.5%  | $2,892,957  | 30.3%  |
| 22. | Total operating costs                      | $5,857,916  | 77.8%  | $7,730,491  | 80.9%  |
|     | Operating Income and Distribution          |             |        |             |        |
| 23. | Operating Income                           | $7,528,536  | 100.0% | $9,555,883  | 100.0% |
| 24. | Less:  Cost of sales and operations        | $988,446    | 13.1%  | $1,149,772  | 12.0%  |
| 25. | Gross operating profit                     | $6,540,090  | 86.9%  | $8,406,111  | 88.0%  |
| 26. | Additional operating costs                 | $4,869,470  | 64.7%  | $6,580,719  | 68.9%  |
| 27. | Net operating profit                       | $1,670,620  | 22.2%  | $1,825,392  | 19.1%  |
| 28. | Less:  Guaranteed payments to partners     | $198,556    |        | $298,909    |        |
| 29. | Distribution to partners                   | $1,472,064  |        | $1,526,483  |        |
| 30. | Other charges                              | $27,430     |        | $47,985     |        |
| 31. | Net change partners' capital               | $1,444,634  |        | $1,478,498  |        |
|     | Selected Ratios                            |             |        |             |        |
| 32. | Coverage ratio:  times interest earned     | 5.0         |        | 3.6         |        |
| 33. | Inventory turnover (times)                 | n.a.        |        | n.a.        |        |
| 34. | Days' sales in inventory                   | n.a.        |        | n.a.        |        |
| 35. | Average age of inventory (days)            | n.a.        |        | n.a.        |        |
| 36. | Return on assets, net inc., less def       | 28.9%       |        | 22.6%       |        |
| 37. | Return on assets, gross operating profit   | 130.7%      |        | 128.2%      |        |
| 38. | Return on assets, net operating profit     | 33.4%       |        | 27.8%       |        |

*Page 98*

Table 1: Partnerships With and Without Net Income:  252.  LEGAL SERVICES

Dollar values in thousands, except averages

| | 1984 | | 1985 | |
|---|---|---|---|---|
| 1.  Number of Partnerships | 25,152 | | 30,795 | |
| 2.  Number of Partners | 121,066 | | 132,861 | |
| | | | | |
| 3.  Total Assets | $5,218,289 | | $6,109,263 | |
| 4.    Average total assets per Partnership | $207,470 | | $198,385 | |
| 5.    Average total assets per Partner | $43,103 | | $45,982 | |
| | | | | |
| 6.  Net Income, less Deficit | $10,006,130 | | $10,654,560 | |
| 7.    Average per Partnership, total earnings | $397,852 | | $346,007 | |
| 8.    Average per Partner, total earnings | $82,655 | | $80,199 | |
| | | | | |
| 9.  Operating Income | $24,265,190 | | $26,950,118 | |
| Operating Costs | | | | |
| 10.    Cost of sales & operations | $236,101 | 0.10% | $271,627 | 1.0% |
| 11.    Salaries and wages | $6,082,280 | 25.1% | $6,866,222 | 25.5% |
| 12.    Rent paid | $1,599,442 | 6.6% | $1,884,783 | 7.0% |
| 13.    Interest paid | $184,177 | 0.8% | $207,523 | 0.8% |
| 14.    Taxes paid | $634,875 | 2.6% | $705,496 | 2.6% |
| 15.    Bad debts | $17,548 | 0.1% | $19,707 | 0.1% |
| 16.    Repairs | $102,068 | 0.4% | $130,514 | 0.5% |
| 17.    Depreciation | $540,724 | 2.2% | $645,331 | 2.4% |
| 18.    Depletion | $205 | n.a. | $7,616 | 0.0% |
| 19.    Pension & profit sharing plans | $159,877 | 0.7% | $195,516 | 0.7% |
| 20.    Employee benefits programs | $149,428 | 0.6% | $170,378 | 0.6% |
| 21.    Other deductions | $3,891,032 | 16.0% | $4,411,144 | 16.4% |
| 22.    Total operating costs | $13,600,667 | 56.1% | $15,516,652 | 57.6% |
| | | | | |
| Operating Income and Distribution | | | | |
| 23.    Operating Income | $24,265,190 | 100.0% | $26,950,118 | 100.0% |
| 24.      Less:  Cost of sales and operations | $236,101 | 0.10% | $271,627 | 1.0% |
| 25.    Gross operating profit | $24,029,089 | 99.0% | $26,678,491 | 99.0% |
| 26.      Additional operating costs | $13,364,566 | 55.1% | $15,245,025 | 56.6% |
| 27.    Net operating profit | $10,664,523 | 44.0% | $11,433,466 | 42.4% |
| 28.      Less:  Guaranteed payments to partners | $638,068 | | $724,164 | |
| 29.    Distribution to partners | $10,026,455 | | $10,709,302 | |
| 30.    Other charges | $23,236 | | $55,537 | |
| 31.    Net change partners' capital | $10,003,219 | | $10,653,765 | |
| | | | | |
| Selected Ratios | | | | |
| 32.    Coverage ratio:  times interest earned | 56.9 | | 54.1 | |
| 33.    Inventory turnover (times) | n.a. | | n.a. | |
| 34.    Days' sales in inventory | n.a. | | n.a. | |
| 35.    Average age of inventory (days) | n.a. | | n.a. | |
| 36.    Return on assets, net inc., less def | 191.8% | | 174.4% | |
| 37.    Return on assets, gross operating profit | n.a. | | n.a. | |
| 38.    Return on assets, net operating profit | 204.4% | | 187.2% | |

Table 1: Partnerships With and Without Net Income:  255.  ENGINEERING AND ARCHITECTURAL SERVICES

Dollar values in thousands, except averages

| | 1984 | | 1985 | |
|---|---|---|---|---|
| 1.  Number of Partnerships | 6,704 | | 10,922 | |
| 2.  Number of Partners | 18,166 | | 28,253 | |
| 3.  Total Assets | $799,987 | | $680,036 | |
| 4.    Average total assets per Partnership | $119,330 | | $62,263 | |
| 5.    Average total assets per Partner | $44,038 | | $24,070 | |
| 6.  Net Income, less Deficit | $337,863 | | $456,343 | |
| 7.    Average per Partnership, total earnings | $50,430 | | $41,808 | |
| 8.    Average per Partner, total earnings | $18,611 | | $16,162 | |
| 9.  Operating Income | $3,271,429 | | $3,982,373 | |
| Operating Costs | | | | |
| 10.   Cost of sales & operations | $975,248 | 29.8% | $1,044,106 | 26.2% |
| 11.   Salaries and wages | $701,042 | 21.4% | $861,821 | 21.6% |
| 12.   Rent paid | $115,079 | 3.5% | $145,103 | 3.6% |
| 13.   Interest paid | $31,802 | 0.10% | $26,107 | 0.7% |
| 14.   Taxes paid | $75,984 | 2.3% | $89,807 | 2.3% |
| 15.   Bad debts | $7,388 | 0.2% | $2,137 | 0.1% |
| 16.   Repairs | $8,609 | 0.3% | $11,148 | 0.3% |
| 17.   Depreciation | $51,878 | 1.6% | $79,396 | 2.0% |
| 18.   Depletion | $322 | 0.0% | $0 | n.a. |
| 19.   Pension & profit sharing plans | $18,740 | 0.6% | $19,233 | 0.5% |
| 20.   Employee benefits programs | $23,812 | 0.7% | $29,263 | 0.7% |
| 21.   Other deductions | $699,573 | 21.4% | $915,949 | 23.0% |
| 22.   Total operating costs | $2,709,484 | 82.8% | $3,224,080 | 81.0% |
| Operating Income and Distribution | | | | |
| 23.   Operating Income | $3,271,429 | 100.0% | $3,982,373 | 100.0% |
| 24.     Less: Cost of sales and operations | $975,248 | 29.8% | $1,044,106 | 26.2% |
| 25.   Gross operating profit | $2,296,181 | 70.2% | $2,938,267 | 73.8% |
| 26.     Additional operating costs | $1,734,236 | 53.0% | $2,179,974 | 54.7% |
| 27.   Net operating profit | $561,945 | 17.2% | $758,293 | 19.0% |
| 28.     Less:  Guaranteed payments to partners | $217,438 | | $280,087 | |
| 29.   Distribution to partners | $344,507 | | $478,206 | |
| 30.   Other charges | $6,651 | | $21,873 | |
| 31.   Net change partners' capital | $337,856 | | $456,333 | |
| Selected Ratios | | | | |
| 32.   Coverage ratio:  times interest earned | 16.7 | | 28.1 | |
| 33.   Inventory turnover (times) | n.a. | | n.a. | |
| 34.   Days' sales in inventory | n.a. | | n.a. | |
| 35.   Average age of inventory (days) | n.a. | | n.a. | |
| 36.   Return on assets, net inc., less def | 42.2% | | 67.1% | |
| 37.   Return on assets, gross operating profit | n.a. | | n.a. | |
| 38.   Return on assets, net operating profit | 70.2% | | 111.5% | |

Table 1: Partnerships With and Without Net Income:  256.  ACCOUNTING, AUDITING, AND BOOKKEEPING SERVICES

Dollar values in thousands, except averages

|  |  | 1984 |  | 1985 |  |
|---|---|---|---|---|---|
| 1. | Number of Partnerships | 14,253 |  | 18,131 |  |
| 2. | Number of Partners | 55,293 |  | 70,958 |  |
| 3. | Total Assets | $2,501,793 |  | $2,684,676 |  |
| 4. | Average total assets per Partnership | $175,527 |  | $148,071 |  |
| 5. | Average total assets per Partner | $45,246 |  | $37,835 |  |
| 6. | Net Income, less Deficit | $2,309,180 |  | $2,845,985 |  |
| 7. | Average per Partnership, total earnings | $162,072 |  | $157,036 |  |
| 8. | Average per Partner, total earnings | $41,778 |  | $40,125 |  |
| 9. | Operating Income | $10,481,371 |  | $14,185,219 |  |
|  | Operating Costs |  |  |  |  |
| 10. | Cost of sales & operations | $155,187 | 1.5% | $153,145 | 1.1% |
| 11. | Salaries and wages | $3,735,830 | 35.6% | $5,016,604 | 35.4% |
| 12. | Rent paid | $570,234 | 5.4% | $806,914 | 5.7% |
| 13. | Interest paid | $104,900 | 1.0% | $120,779 | 0.9% |
| 14. | Taxes paid | $345,293 | 3.3% | $460,696 | 3.3% |
| 15. | Bad debts | $19,843 | 0.2% | $15,836 | 0.1% |
| 16. | Repairs | $48,413 | 0.5% | $63,118 | 0.4% |
| 17. | Depreciation | $226,562 | 2.2% | $326,257 | 2.3% |
| 18. | Depletion | $0 | n.a. | $363 | n.a. |
| 19. | Pension & profit sharing plans | $69,398 | 0.7% | $104,436 | 0.7% |
| 20. | Employee benefits programs | $75,676 | 0.7% | $78,716 | 0.6% |
| 21. | Other deductions | $1,983,324 | 18.9% | $2,948,159 | 20.8% |
| 22. | Total operating costs | $7,334,748 | 70.0% | $10,095,272 | 71.2% |
|  | Operating Income and Distribution |  |  |  |  |
| 23. | Operating Income | $10,481,371 | 100.0% | $14,185,219 | 100.0% |
| 24. | Less: Cost of sales and operations | $155,187 | 1.5% | $153,145 | 1.1% |
| 25. | Gross operating profit | $10,326,184 | 98.5% | $14,032,074 | 98.9% |
| 26. | Additional operating costs | $7,179,561 | 68.5% | $9,942,127 | 70.1% |
| 27. | Net operating profit | $3,146,623 | 30.0% | $4,089,947 | 28.8% |
| 28. | Less: Guaranteed payments to partners | $826,569 |  | $1,235,786 |  |
| 29. | Distribution to partners | $2,320,054 |  | $2,854,161 |  |
| 30. | Other charges | $10,962 |  | $8,426 |  |
| 31. | Net change partners' capital | $2,309,092 |  | $2,845,735 |  |
|  | Selected Ratios |  |  |  |  |
| 32. | Coverage ratio: times interest earned | 29.0 |  | 32.9 |  |
| 33. | Inventory turnover (times) | n.a. |  | n.a. |  |
| 34. | Days' sales in inventory | n.a. |  | n.a. |  |
| 35. | Average age of inventory (days) | n.a. |  | n.a. |  |
| 36. | Return on assets, net inc., less def | 92.3% |  | 106.0% |  |
| 37. | Return on assets, gross operating profit | n.a. |  | n.a. |  |
| 38. | Return on assets, net operating profit | 125.8% |  | 152.3% |  |

Table 1: Partnerships With and Without Net Income: 257. CERTIFIED PUBLIC ACCOUNTANTS

Dollar values in thousands, except averages

|  | 1984 | | 1985 | |
|---|---|---|---|---|
| 1. Number of Partnerships | 8,233 | | 11,034 | |
| 2. Number of Partners | 39,319 | | 53,251 | |
| 3. Total Assets | $2,218,028 | | $2,388,117 | |
| 4. Average total assets per Partnership | $269,407 | | $216,433 | |
| 5. Average total assets per Partner | $56,411 | | $44,846 | |
| 6. Net Income, less Deficit | $2,204,732 | | $2,709,165 | |
| 7. Average per Partnership, total earnings | $267,882 | | $245,632 | |
| 8. Average per Partner, total earnings | $56,092 | | $50,897 | |
| 9. Operating Income | $9,830,956 | | $13,381,480 | |
| Operating Costs | | | | |
| 10. Cost of sales & operations | $141,863 | 1.4% | $130,316 | 0.10% |
| 11. Salaries and wages | $3,545,257 | 36.1% | $4,800,313 | 35.9% |
| 12. Rent paid | $534,947 | 5.4% | $759,719 | 5.7% |
| 13. Interest paid | $98,520 | 1.0% | $104,100 | 0.8% |
| 14. Taxes paid | $324,764 | 3.3% | $436,851 | 3.3% |
| 15. Bad debts | $19,690 | 0.2% | $15,835 | 0.1% |
| 16. Repairs | $43,326 | 0.4% | $53,908 | 0.4% |
| 17. Depreciation | $204,981 | 2.1% | $299,174 | 2.2% |
| 18. Depletion | $0 | n.a. | $363 | n.a. |
| 19. Pension & profit sharing plans | $68,635 | 0.7% | $103,346 | 0.8% |
| 20. Employee benefits programs | $73,211 | 0.7% | $75,433 | 0.6% |
| 21. Other deductions | $1,821,084 | 18.5% | $2,750,847 | 20.6% |
| 22. Total operating costs | $6,876,366 | 70.0% | $9,530,454 | 71.2% |
| Operating Income and Distribution | | | | |
| 23. Operating Income | $9,830,956 | 100.0% | $13,381,480 | 100.0% |
| 24. Less: Cost of sales and operations | $141,863 | 1.4% | $130,316 | 0.10% |
| 25. Gross operating profit | $9,689,093 | 98.6% | $13,251,164 | 99.0% |
| 26. Additional operating costs | $6,734,503 | 68.5% | $9,400,138 | 70.3% |
| 27. Net operating profit | $2,954,590 | 30.1% | $3,851,026 | 28.8% |
| 28. Less: Guaranteed payments to partners | $741,637 | | $1,135,016 | |
| 29. Distribution to partners | $2,212,953 | | $2,716,010 | |
| 30. Other charges | $8,309 | | $7,094 | |
| 31. Net change partners' capital | $2,204,644 | | $2,708,916 | |
| Selected Ratios | | | | |
| 32. Coverage ratio: times interest earned | 29.0 | | 36.0 | |
| 33. Inventory turnover (times) | n.a. | | n.a. | |
| 34. Days' sales in inventory | n.a. | | n.a. | |
| 35. Average age of inventory (days) | n.a. | | n.a. | |
| 36. Return on assets, net inc., less def | 99.4% | | 113.4% | |
| 37. Return on assets, gross operating profit | n.a. | | n.a. | |
| 38. Return on assets, net operating profit | 133.2% | | 161.3% | |

Table 1: Partnerships With and Without Net Income:  258.  OTHER ACCOUNTING, AUDITING, AND BOOKKEEPING SERVICES

Dollar values in thousands, except averages

|     |                                              | 1984      |        | 1985      |        |
|-----|----------------------------------------------|-----------|--------|-----------|--------|
| 1.  | Number of Partnerships                       | 6,020     |        | 7,097     |        |
| 2.  | Number of Partners                           | 15,974    |        | 17,707    |        |
| 3.  | Total Assets                                 | $283,765  |        | $296,559  |        |
| 4.  | Average total assets per Partnership         | $47,137   |        | $41,787   |        |
| 5.  | Average total assets per Partner             | $17,764   |        | $16,748   |        |
| 6.  | Net Income, less Deficit                     | $104,448  |        | $136,819  |        |
| 7.  | Average per Partnership, total earnings      | $17,364   |        | $19,293   |        |
| 8.  | Average per Partner, total earnings          | $6,544    |        | $7,733    |        |
| 9.  | Operating Income                             | $650,415  |        | $803,739  |        |
|     | Operating Costs                              |           |        |           |        |
| 10. | Cost of sales & operations                   | $13,324   | 2.1%   | $22,828   | 2.8%   |
| 11. | Salaries and wages                           | $190,574  | 29.3%  | $216,291  | 26.9%  |
| 12. | Rent paid                                    | $35,287   | 5.4%   | $47,195   | 5.9%   |
| 13. | Interest paid                                | $6,380    | 0.10%  | $16,678   | 2.1%   |
| 14. | Taxes paid                                   | $20,529   | 3.2%   | $23,845   | 3.0%   |
| 15. | Bad debts                                    | $153      | 0.0%   | $2        | n.a.   |
| 16. | Repairs                                      | $5,088    | 0.8%   | $9,210    | 1.2%   |
| 17. | Depreciation                                 | $21,581   | 3.3%   | $27,083   | 3.4%   |
| 18. | Depletion                                    | $0        | n.a.   | $0        | n.a.   |
| 19. | Pension & profit sharing plans               | $762      | 0.1%   | $1,093    | 0.1%   |
| 20. | Employee benefits programs                   | $2,465    | 0.4%   | $3,283    | 0.4%   |
| 21. | Other deductions                             | $162,240  | 24.9%  | $197,310  | 24.6%  |
| 22. | Total operating costs                        | $458,383  | 70.5%  | $564,818  | 70.3%  |
|     | Operating Income and Distribution            |           |        |           |        |
| 23. | Operating Income                             | $650,415  | 100.0% | $803,739  | 100.0% |
| 24. | Less:  Cost of sales and operations          | $13,324   | 2.1%   | $22,828   | 2.8%   |
| 25. | Gross operating profit                       | $637,091  | 98.0%  | $780,911  | 97.2%  |
| 26. | Additional operating costs                   | $445,059  | 68.4%  | $541,990  | 67.4%  |
| 27. | Net operating profit                         | $192,032  | 29.5%  | $238,921  | 29.7%  |
| 28. | Less:  Guaranteed payments to partners       | $84,932   |        | $100,770  |        |
| 29. | Distribution to partners                     | $107,100  |        | $138,151  |        |
| 30. | Other charges                                | $2,652    |        | $1,332    |        |
| 31. | Net change partners' capital                 | $104,448  |        | $136,819  |        |
|     | Selected Ratios                              |           |        |           |        |
| 32. | Coverage ratio:  times interest earned       | 29.1      |        | 13.3      |        |
| 33. | Inventory turnover (times)                   | n.a.      |        | n.a.      |        |
| 34. | Days' sales in inventory                     | n.a.      |        | n.a.      |        |
| 35. | Average age of inventory (days)              | n.a.      |        | n.a.      |        |
| 36. | Return on assets, net inc., less def         | 36.8%     |        | 46.1%     |        |
| 37. | Return on assets, gross operating profit     | 224.5%    |        | n.a.      |        |
| 38. | Return on assets, net operating profit       | 67.7%     |        | 80.6%     |        |

Table 1: Partnerships With and Without Net Income:  OTHER SERVICES (253,259)

Dollar values in thousands, except averages

| | 1984 | | 1985 | |
|---|---|---|---|---|
| 1.  Number of Partnerships | 43,916 | | 39,329 | |
| 2.  Number of Partners | 184,250 | | 159,542 | |
| | | | | |
| 3.  Total Assets | $5,529,623 | | $4,773,726 | |
| 4.    Average total assets per Partnership | $125,914 | | $121,379 | |
| 5.    Average total assets per Partner | $30,012 | | $29,921 | |
| | | | | |
| 6.  Net Income, less Deficit | $225,564 | | $908,217 | |
| 7.    Average per Partnership, total earnings | $5,141 | | $23,097 | |
| 8.    Average per Partner, total earnings | $1,225 | | $5,694 | |
| | | | | |
| 9.  Operating Income | $4,424,592 | | $3,910,983 | |
| Operating Costs | | | | |
| 10.    Cost of sales & operations | $1,557,551 | 35.2% | $1,041,770 | 26.6% |
| 11.    Salaries and wages | $561,461 | 12.7% | $317,891 | 8.1% |
| 12.    Rent paid | $106,860 | 2.4% | $80,003 | 2.1% |
| 13.    Interest paid | $163,650 | 3.7% | $143,246 | 3.7% |
| 14.    Taxes paid | $122,125 | 2.8% | $54,003 | 1.4% |
| 15.    Bad debts | $5,004 | 0.1% | $1,961 | 0.1% |
| 16.    Repairs | $33,482 | 0.8% | $20,904 | 0.5% |
| 17.    Depreciation | $249,544 | 5.6% | $288,324 | 7.4% |
| 18.    Depletion | $0 | n.a. | $0 | n.a. |
| 19.    Pension & profit sharing plans | $3,092 | 0.1% | $5,792 | 0.2% |
| 20.    Employee benefits programs | $30,893 | 0.7% | $11,165 | 0.3% |
| 21.    Other deductions | $1,058,697 | 23.9% | $791,668 | 20.2% |
| 22.    Total operating costs | $3,892,359 | 88.0% | $2,756,727 | 70.5% |
| | | | | |
| Operating Income and Distribution | | | | |
| 23.    Operating Income | $4,424,592 | 100.0% | $3,910,983 | 100.0% |
| 24.        Less:  Cost of sales and operations | $1,557,551 | 35.2% | $1,041,770 | 26.6% |
| 25.    Gross operating profit | $2,867,041 | 64.8% | $2,869,213 | 73.4% |
| 26.        Additional operating costs | $2,334,808 | 52.8% | $1,714,957 | 43.9% |
| 27.    Net operating profit | $532,233 | 12.0% | $1,154,256 | 29.5% |
| 28.        Less:  Guaranteed payments to partners | $187,364 | | $150,499 | |
| 29.    Distribution to partners | $344,869 | | $1,003,757 | |
| 30.    Other charges | $119,305 | | $95,540 | |
| 31.    Net change partners' capital | $225,564 | | $908,217 | |
| | | | | |
| Selected Ratios | | | | |
| 32.    Coverage ratio:  times interest earned | 2.3 | | 7.1 | |
| 33.    Inventory turnover (times) | n.a. | | n.a. | |
| 34.    Days' sales in inventory | n.a. | | n.a. | |
| 35.    Average age of inventory (days) | n.a. | | n.a. | |
| 36.    Return on assets, net inc., less def | 4.1% | | 19.0% | |
| 37.    Return on assets, gross operating profit | 51.9% | | 60.1% | |
| 38.    Return on assets, net operating profit | 9.6% | | 24.2% | |

# TABLE 2
## Partnerships with Net Income

Table 2: Partnerships With Net Income:  001.  ALL INDUSTRIES

Dollar values in thousands, except averages

|  |  | 1984 |  | 1985 |  |
|---|---|---|---|---|---|
| 1. | Number of Partnerships | 844,738 |  | 875,846 |  |
| 2. | Number of Partners | 6,503,366 |  | 6,644,942 |  |
| 3. | Total Assets | $400,421,162 |  | $493,550,274 |  |
| 4. | Average total assets per Partnership | $474,018 |  | $563,513 |  |
| 5. | Average total assets per Partner | $61,571 |  | $74,275 |  |
| 6. | Net Income | $69,696,922 |  | $77,044,693 |  |
| 7. | Average per Partnership, total earnings | $82,511 |  | $87,971 |  |
| 8. | Average per Partner, total earnings | $10,718 |  | $11,595 |  |
| 9. | Operating Income | $258,326,889 |  | $265,309,862 |  |
|  | Operating Costs |  |  |  |  |
| 10. | Cost of sales & operations | $104,964,326 | 40.6% | $93,657,333 | 35.3% |
| 11. | Salaries and wages | $21,352,660 | 8.3% | $24,793,006 | 9.3% |
| 12. | Rent paid | $5,176,220 | 2.0% | $5,808,600 | 2.2% |
| 13. | Interest paid | $8,365,130 | 3.2% | $9,082,223 | 3.4% |
| 14. | Taxes paid | $4,057,822 | 1.6% | $4,552,830 | 1.7% |
| 15. | Bad debts | $301,628 | 0.1% | $322,746 | 0.1% |
| 16. | Repairs | $1,290,767 | 0.5% | $1,403,977 | 0.5% |
| 17. | Depreciation | $6,590,729 | 2.6% | $7,537,960 | 2.8% |
| 18. | Depletion | $192,824 | 0.1% | $217,843 | 0.1% |
| 19. | Pension & profit sharing plans | $464,054 | 0.2% | $635,396 | 0.2% |
| 20. | Employee benefits programs | $603,825 | 0.2% | $645,073 | 0.2% |
| 21. | Other deductions | $30,394,977 | 11.8% | $34,321,169 | 12.9% |
| 22. | Total operating costs | $183,773,214 | 71.1% | $182,987,970 | 69.0% |
|  | Operating Income and Distribution |  |  |  |  |
| 23. | Operating Income | $258,326,889 | 100.0% | $265,309,862 | 100.0% |
| 24. | Less: Cost of sales and operations | $104,964,326 | 40.6% | $93,657,333 | 35.3% |
| 25. | Gross operating profit | $153,362,563 | 59.4% | $171,652,529 | 64.7% |
| 26. | Additional operating costs | $78,808,888 | 30.5% | $89,330,637 | 33.7% |
| 27. | Net operating profit | $74,553,675 | 28.9% | $82,321,892 | 31.0% |
| 28. | Less: Guaranteed payments to partners | $3,482,555 |  | $4,005,864 |  |
| 29. | Distribution to partners | $71,071,120 |  | $78,316,028 |  |
| 30. | Other charges | $1,392,450 |  | $1,281,151 |  |
| 31. | Net change partners' capital | $69,678,670 |  | $77,034,877 |  |
|  | Selected Ratios |  |  |  |  |
| 32. | Coverage ratio: times interest earned | 7.9 |  | 8.1 |  |
| 33. | Inventory turnover (times) | 7.2 |  | 6.9 |  |
| 34. | Days' sales in inventory | 42.6 |  | 52.5 |  |
| 35. | Average age of inventory (days) | 50.5 |  | 52.8 |  |
| 36. | Return on assets, net income | 17.4% |  | 15.6% |  |
| 37. | Return on assets, gross operating profit | 38.3% |  | 34.8% |  |
| 38. | Return on assets, net operating profit | 18.6% |  | 16.7% |  |

Table 2: Partnerships With Net Income:  002.  AGRICULTURE, FORESTRY, AND FISHING

Dollar values in thousands, except averages

|  |  | 1984 |  | 1985 |  |
|---|---|---|---|---|---|
| 1. | Number of Partnerships | 72,835 |  | 76,204 |  |
| 2. | Number of Partners | 230,866 |  | 297,953 |  |
| 3. | Total Assets | $9,688,783 |  | $9,875,797 |  |
| 4. | Average total assets per Partnership | $133,024 |  | $129,597 |  |
| 5. | Average total assets per Partner | $41,967 |  | $33,145 |  |
| 6. | Net Income | $2,478,151 |  | $2,796,816 |  |
| 7. | Average per Partnership, total earnings | $34,025 |  | $36,703 |  |
| 8. | Average per Partner, total earnings | $10,734 |  | $9,387 |  |
| 9. | Total Receipts | $4,003,756 |  | $4,108,355 |  |
|  | Operating Costs |  |  |  |  |
| 10. | Cost of sales & operations | $2,296,649 | 57.4% | $2,132,956 | 51.9% |
| 11. | Salaries and wages | $216,707 | 5.4% | $263,053 | 6.4% |
| 12. | Rent paid | $35,011 | 0.9% | $40,552 | 0.10% |
| 13. | Interest paid | $92,730 | 2.3% | $101,543 | 2.5% |
| 14. | Taxes paid | $48,712 | 1.2% | $48,822 | 1.2% |
| 15. | Bad debts | $2,045 | 0.1% | $3,050 | 0.1% |
| 16. | Repairs | $76,611 | 1.9% | $98,113 | 2.4% |
| 17. | Depreciation | $141,457 | 3.5% | $154,898 | 3.8% |
| 18. | Depletion | $6,032 | 0.2% | $27,179 | 0.7% |
| 19. | Pension & profit sharing plans | $5,672 | 0.1% | $1,401 | 0.0% |
| 20. | Employee benefits programs | $3,235 | 0.1% | $1,335 | 0.0% |
| 21. | Other deductions | $579,336 | 14.5% | $669,948 | 16.3% |
| 22. | Total operating costs | $3,504,208 | 87.5% | $3,542,892 | 86.2% |
|  | Operating Income and Distribution |  |  |  |  |
| 23. | Total Receipts | $4,003,756 | 100.0% | $4,108,355 | 100.0% |
| 24. | Less:  Cost of sales and operations | $2,296,649 | 57.4% | $2,132,956 | 51.9% |
| 25. | Gross operating profit | $1,707,107 | 42.6% | $1,975,399 | 48.1% |
| 26. | Additional operating costs | $1,207,559 | 30.2% | $1,409,936 | 34.3% |
| 27. | Net operating profit | $499,548 | 12.5% | $565,463 | 13.8% |
| 28. | Less:  Guaranteed payments to partners | $76,669 |  | $133,689 |  |
| 29. | Distribution to partners | $422,879 |  | $431,774 |  |
| 30. | Other charges | $72,477 |  | $105,728 |  |
| 31. | Net change partners' capital | $350,402 |  | $326,046 |  |
|  | Selected Ratios |  |  |  |  |
| 32. | Coverage ratio:  times interest earned | 4.4 |  | 4.6 |  |
| 33. | Inventory turnover (times) | 9.7 |  | 9.9 |  |
| 34. | Days' sales in inventory | 31.1 |  | 39.8 |  |
| 35. | Average age of inventory (days) | 37.7 |  | 36.8 |  |
| 36. | Return on assets, net income | 25.6% |  | 28.3% |  |
| 37. | Return on assets, gross operating profit | 17.6% |  | 20.0% |  |
| 38. | Return on assets, net operating profit | 5.2% |  | 5.7% |  |

Table 2: Partnerships With Net Income:   003.   FARMS

Dollar values in thousands, except averages

|  | 1984 | | 1985 | |
|---|---|---|---|---|
| 1.  Number of Partnerships | 58,788 | | 59,543 | |
| 2.  Number of Partners | 197,598 | | 256,988 | |
| 3.  Total Assets | $8,449,528 | | $8,431,588 | |
| 4.    Average total assets per Partnership | $143,729 | | $141,605 | |
| 5.    Average total assets per Partner | $42,761 | | $32,809 | |
| 6.  Net Income | $2,038,860 | | $2,339,960 | |
| 7.    Average per Partnership, total earnings | $34,683 | | $39,300 | |
| 8.    Average per Partner, total earnings | $10,319 | | $9,106 | |
| 9.  Total Receipts | $2,239,529 | | $2,033,891 | |
| Operating Costs | | | | |
| 10.    Cost of sales & operations | $1,572,853 | 70.2% | $1,266,859 | 62.3% |
| 11.    Salaries and wages | $83,753 | 3.7% | $93,324 | 4.6% |
| 12.    Rent paid | $19,737 | 0.9% | $17,311 | 0.9% |
| 13.    Interest paid | $64,966 | 2.9% | $59,232 | 2.9% |
| 14.    Taxes paid | $23,993 | 1.1% | $24,798 | 1.2% |
| 15.    Bad debts | $1,435 | 0.1% | $798 | 0.0% |
| 16.    Repairs | $22,897 | 1.0% | $35,950 | 1.8% |
| 17.    Depreciation | $51,444 | 2.3% | $69,817 | 3.4% |
| 18.    Depletion | $30 | n.a. | $20 | n.a. |
| 19.    Pension & profit sharing plans | $3,544 | 0.2% | $600 | 0.0% |
| 20.    Employee benefits programs | $2,367 | 0.1% | $893 | 0.0% |
| 21.    Other deductions | $259,347 | 11.6% | $292,688 | 14.4% |
| 22.    Total operating costs | $2,106,377 | 94.1% | $1,862,296 | 91.6% |
| Operating Income and Distribution | | | | |
| 23.    Total Receipts | $2,239,529 | 100.0% | $2,033,891 | 100.0% |
| 24.      Less: Cost of sales and operations | $1,572,853 | 70.2% | $1,266,859 | 62.3% |
| 25.    Gross operating profit | $666,676 | 29.8% | $767,032 | 37.7% |
| 26.      Additional operating costs | $533,524 | 23.8% | $595,437 | 29.3% |
| 27.    Net operating profit | $133,152 | 6.0% | $171,595 | 8.4% |
| 28.      Less: Guaranteed payments to partners | $61,309 | | $80,481 | |
| 29.    Distribution to partners | $71,843 | | $91,114 | |
| 30.    Other charges | $68,591 | | $86,520 | |
| 31.    Net change partners' capital | $3,252 | | $4,594 | |
| Selected Ratios | | | | |
| 32.    Coverage ratio:  times interest earned | 1.1 | | 1.9 | |
| 33.    Inventory turnover (times) | 7.5 | | 6.7 | |
| 34.    Days' sales in inventory | 41.9 | | 58.9 | |
| 35.    Average age of inventory (days) | 48.5 | | 54.7 | |
| 36.    Return on assets, net income | 24.1% | | 27.8% | |
| 37.    Return on assets, gross operating profit | 7.9% | | 9.1% | |
| 38.    Return on assets, net operating profit | 1.6% | | 2.0% | |

Table 2: Partnerships With Net Income:  004.  FIELD CROPS

Dollar values in thousands, except averages

|  |  | 1984 |  | 1985 |  |
|---|---|---|---|---|---|
| 1. | Number of Partnerships | 27,575 |  | 29,560 |  |
| 2. | Number of Partners | 102,359 |  | 110,352 |  |
| 3. | Total Assets | $4,003,538 |  | $4,051,638 |  |
| 4. | Average total assets per Partnership | $145,187 |  | $137,065 |  |
| 5. | Average total assets per Partner | $39,113 |  | $36,716 |  |
| 6. | Net Income | $1,023,547 |  | $1,120,850 |  |
| 7. | Average per Partnership, total earnings | $37,120 |  | $37,920 |  |
| 8. | Average per Partner, total earnings | $1,000 |  | $10,158 |  |
| 9. | Total Receipts | $537,157 |  | $789,896 |  |
|  | Operating Costs |  |  |  |  |
| 10. | Cost of sales & operations | $282,280 | 52.6% | $410,465 | 52.0% |
| 11. | Salaries and wages | $42,676 | 7.9% | $51,409 | 6.5% |
| 12. | Rent paid | $8,915 | 1.7% | $10,569 | 1.3% |
| 13. | Interest paid | $15,994 | 3.0% | $27,066 | 3.4% |
| 14. | Taxes paid | $15,663 | 2.9% | $17,406 | 2.2% |
| 15. | Bad debts | $781 | 0.2% | $415 | 0.1% |
| 16. | Repairs | $14,704 | 2.7% | $22,939 | 2.9% |
| 17. | Depreciation | $25,392 | 4.7% | $42,870 | 5.4% |
| 18. | Depletion | $0 | n.a. | $0 | n.a. |
| 19. | Pension & profit sharing plans | $2,536 | 0.5% | $0 | n.a. |
| 20. | Employee benefits programs | $1,816 | 0.3% | $146 | 0.0% |
| 21. | Other deductions | $81,545 | 15.2% | $141,303 | 17.9% |
| 22. | Total operating costs | $492,304 | 91.7% | $724,588 | 91.7% |
|  | Operating Income and Distribution |  |  |  |  |
| 23. | Total Receipts | $537,157 | 100.0% | $789,896 | 100.0% |
| 24. | Less: Cost of sales and operations | $282,280 | 52.6% | $410,465 | 52.0% |
| 25. | Gross operating profit | $254,877 | 47.5% | $379,431 | 48.0% |
| 26. | Additional operating costs | $210,024 | 39.1% | $314,123 | 39.8% |
| 27. | Net operating profit | $44,853 | 8.4% | $65,308 | 8.3% |
| 28. | Less: Guaranteed payments to partners | $33,825 |  | $50,350 |  |
| 29. | Distribution to partners | $11,028 |  | $14,958 |  |
| 30. | Other charges | $12,089 |  | $37,582 |  |
| 31. | Net change partners' capital | ($1,061) |  | ($22,624) |  |
|  | Selected Ratios |  |  |  |  |
| 32. | Coverage ratio:  times interest earned | 1.8 |  | 1.4 |  |
| 33. | Inventory turnover (times) | 2.3 |  | 3.5 |  |
| 34. | Days' sales in inventory | 146.3 |  | 115.1 |  |
| 35. | Average age of inventory (days) | 159.7 |  | 104.0 |  |
| 36. | Return on assets, net income | 25.6% |  | 27.7% |  |
| 37. | Return on assets, gross operating profit | 6.4% |  | 9.4% |  |
| 38. | Return on assets, net operating profit | 1.1% |  | 1.6% |  |

Table 2: Partnerships With Net Income:  005.  VEGETABLE AND MELON

Dollar values in thousands, except averages

|  |  | 1984 |  | 1985 |  |
|---|---|---|---|---|---|
| 1. | Number of Partnerships | 1,597 | | 2,260 | |
| 2. | Number of Partners | 4,331 | | 5,324 | |
| 3. | Total Assets | $326,605 | | $318,406 | |
| 4. | Average total assets per Partnership | $204,512 | | $140,888 | |
| 5. | Average total assets per Partner | $75,411 | | $59,806 | |
| 6. | Net Income | $182,323 | | $110,542 | |
| 7. | Average per Partnership, total earnings | $114,167 | | $48,913 | |
| 8. | Average per Partner, total earnings | $42,097 | | $20,763 | |
| 9. | Total Receipts | $55,856 | | $44,188 | |
|  | Operating Costs | | | | |
| 10. | Cost of sales & operations | $44,557 | 79.8% | $31,953 | 72.3% |
| 11. | Salaries and wages | $2,640 | 4.7% | $4,551 | 10.3% |
| 12. | Rent paid | $40 | 0.1% | $0 | n.a. |
| 13. | Interest paid | $379 | 0.7% | $1,773 | 4.0% |
| 14. | Taxes paid | $475 | 0.9% | $561 | 1.3% |
| 15. | Bad debts | $0 | n.a. | $0 | n.a. |
| 16. | Repairs | $546 | 0.10% | $213 | 0.5% |
| 17. | Depreciation | ($725) | (1.3%) | $620 | 1.4% |
| 18. | Depletion | $0 | n.a. | $0 | n.a. |
| 19. | Pension & profit sharing plans | $0 | n.a. | $0 | n.a. |
| 20. | Employee benefits programs | $130 | 0.2% | $227 | 0.5% |
| 21. | Other deductions | $3,070 | 5.5% | $4,403 | 1.0% |
| 22. | Total operating costs | $51,121 | 91.5% | $44,301 | 100.3% |
|  | Operating Income and Distribution | | | | |
| 23. | Total Receipts | $55,856 | 100.0% | $44,188 | 100.0% |
| 24. | Less: Cost of sales and operations | $44,557 | 79.8% | $31,953 | 72.3% |
| 25. | Gross operating profit | $11,299 | 20.2% | $12,235 | 27.7% |
| 26. | Additional operating costs | $6,564 | 11.8% | $12,348 | 27.9% |
| 27. | Net operating profit | $4,735 | 8.5% | ($113) | (0.3%) |
| 28. | Less: Guaranteed payments to partners | $1,110 | | $1,718 | |
| 29. | Distribution to partners | $3,625 | | ($1,831) | |
| 30. | Other charges | $6,043 | | $3,922 | |
| 31. | Net change partners' capital | ($2,418) | | ($5,753) | |
|  | Selected Ratios | | | | |
| 32. | Coverage ratio:  times interest earned | 11.5 | | (1.1) | |
| 33. | Inventory turnover (times) | 27.5 | | 3.7 | |
| 34. | Days' sales in inventory | 21.7 | | 110.9 | |
| 35. | Average age of inventory (days) | 13.3 | | 99.2 | |
| 36. | Return on assets, net income | 55.8% | | 34.7% | |
| 37. | Return on assets, gross operating profit | 3.5% | | 3.8% | |
| 38. | Return on assets, net operating profit | 1.5% | | (0.0%) | |

*Page 109*

Table 2: Partnerships With Net Income:  006.  FRUIT AND TREE NUT

Dollar values in thousands, except averages

|  |  | 1984 |  | 1985 |  |
|---|---|---|---|---|---|
| 1. | Number of Partnerships | 3,677 | | 2,906 | |
| 2. | Number of Partners | 30,678 | | 44,935 | |
| 3. | Total Assets | $1,471,202 | | $1,559,741 | |
| 4. | Average total assets per Partnership | $400,109 | | $536,731 | |
| 5. | Average total assets per Partner | $47,956 | | $34,711 | |
| 6. | Net Income | $150,974 | | $201,534 | |
| 7. | Average per Partnership, total earnings | $41,059 | | $69,353 | |
| 8. | Average per Partner, total earnings | $4,921 | | $4,485 | |
| 9. | Total Receipts | $117,998 | | $154,550 | |
|  | Operating Costs | | | | |
| 10. | Cost of sales & operations | $61,585 | 52.2% | $87,219 | 56.4% |
| 11. | Salaries and wages | $4,796 | 4.1% | $6,770 | 4.4% |
| 12. | Rent paid | $1,600 | 1.4% | $342 | 0.2% |
| 13. | Interest paid | $10,668 | 9.0% | $9,957 | 6.4% |
| 14. | Taxes paid | $2,504 | 2.1% | $3,172 | 2.1% |
| 15. | Bad debts | $92 | 0.1% | $18 | 0.0% |
| 16. | Repairs | $2,004 | 1.7% | $2,961 | 1.9% |
| 17. | Depreciation | $4,580 | 3.9% | $4,389 | 2.8% |
| 18. | Depletion | $0 | n.a. | $0 | n.a. |
| 19. | Pension & profit sharing plans | $429 | 0.4% | $76 | 0.1% |
| 20. | Employee benefits programs | $53 | 0.0% | $27 | 0.0% |
| 21. | Other deductions | $27,421 | 23.2% | $30,316 | 19.6% |
| 22. | Total operating costs | $115,732 | 98.1% | $145,253 | 94.0% |
| | Operating Income and Distribution | | | | |
| 23. | Total Receipts | $117,998 | 100.0% | $154,550 | 100.0% |
| 24. | Less: Cost of sales and operations | $61,585 | 52.2% | $87,219 | 56.4% |
| 25. | Gross operating profit | $56,413 | 47.8% | $67,331 | 43.6% |
| 26. | Additional operating costs | $54,147 | 45.9% | $58,034 | 37.6% |
| 27. | Net operating profit | $2,266 | 1.9% | $9,297 | 6.0% |
| 28. | Less: Guaranteed payments to partners | $1,142 | | $4,871 | |
| 29. | Distribution to partners | $1,124 | | $4,426 | |
| 30. | Other charges | $6,415 | | $15,878 | |
| 31. | Net change partners' capital | ($5,291) | | ($11,452) | |
| | Selected Ratios | | | | |
| 32. | Coverage ratio: times interest earned | (0.8) | | (0.1) | |
| 33. | Inventory turnover (times) | 6.1 | | 8.8 | |
| 34. | Days' sales in inventory | 58.8 | | 42.3 | |
| 35. | Average age of inventory (days) | 59.5 | | 41.3 | |
| 36. | Return on assets, net income | 10.3% | | 12.9% | |
| 37. | Return on assets, gross operating profit | 3.8% | | 4.3% | |
| 38. | Return on assets, net operating profit | 0.2% | | 0.6% | |

Table 2: Partnerships With Net Income:  008.  BEEF CATTLE FEEDLOTS

Dollar values in thousands, except averages

|     |                                            | 1984 |      | 1985 |      |
|-----|--------------------------------------------|------|------|------|------|
| 1.  | Number of Partnerships                     | 1,148 | | 653 | |
| 2.  | Number of Partners                         | 3,413 | | 40,025 | |
| 3.  | Total Assets                               | $373,643 | | $272,895 | |
| 4.  | Average total assets per Partnership       | $325,473 | | $417,910 | |
| 5.  | Average total assets per Partner           | $109,476 | | $6,818 | |
| 6.  | Net Income                                 | $29,244 | | $172,928 | |
| 7.  | Average per Partnership, total earnings    | $25,475 | | $264,822 | |
| 8.  | Average per Partner, total earnings        | $8,569 | | $4,321 | |
| 9.  | Total Receipts                             | $179,943 | | $201,043 | |
|     | Operating Costs                            | | | | |
| 10. | Cost of sales & operations                 | $140,144 | 77.9% | $168,917 | 84.0% |
| 11. | Salaries and wages                         | $8,224 | 4.6% | $4,821 | 2.4% |
| 12. | Rent paid                                  | $611 | 0.3% | $829 | 0.4% |
| 13. | Interest paid                              | $3,015 | 1.7% | $6,853 | 3.4% |
| 14. | Taxes paid                                 | $515 | 0.3% | $541 | 0.3% |
| 15. | Bad debts                                  | $0 | n.a. | $241 | 0.1% |
| 16. | Repairs                                    | $1,067 | 0.6% | $1,137 | 0.6% |
| 17. | Depreciation                               | $2,922 | 1.6% | $1,482 | 0.7% |
| 18. | Depletion                                  | $0 | n.a. | $20 | 0.0% |
| 19. | Pension & profit sharing plans             | $29 | 0.0% | $75 | 0.0% |
| 20. | Employee benefits programs                 | $84 | 0.1% | $152 | 0.1% |
| 21. | Other deductions                           | $18,875 | 10.5% | $14,159 | 7.0% |
| 22. | Total operating costs                      | $175,486 | 97.5% | $199,227 | 99.1% |
|     | Operating Income and Distribution          | | | | |
| 23. | Total Receipts                             | $179,943 | 100.0% | $201,043 | 100.0% |
| 24. | Less:  Cost of sales and operations        | $140,144 | 77.9% | $168,917 | 84.0% |
| 25. | Gross operating profit                     | $39,799 | 22.1% | $32,126 | 16.0% |
| 26. | Additional operating costs                 | $35,342 | 19.6% | $30,310 | 15.1% |
| 27. | Net operating profit                       | $4,457 | 2.5% | $1,816 | 0.9% |
| 28. | Less:  Guaranteed payments to partners     | $1,722 | | $706 | |
| 29. | Distribution to partners                   | $2,735 | | $1,110 | |
| 30. | Other charges                              | $919 | | $1,268 | |
| 31. | Net change partners' capital               | $1,816 | | ($158) | |
|     | Selected Ratios                            | | | | |
| 32. | Coverage ratio:  times interest earned     | 0.5 | | (0.7) | |
| 33. | Inventory turnover (times)                 | 9.7 | | 6.0 | |
| 34. | Days' sales in inventory                   | 35.9 | | 71.3 | |
| 35. | Average age of inventory (days)            | 37.8 | | 61.0 | |
| 36. | Return on assets, net income               | 7.8% | | 63.4% | |
| 37. | Return on assets, gross operating profit   | 10.7% | | 11.8% | |
| 38. | Return on assets, net operating profit     | 1.2% | | 0.7% | |

Table 2: Partnerships With Net Income:  009.  BEEF CATTLE, EXCEPT FEEDLOTS

Dollar values in thousands, except averages

| | | 1984 | | 1985 | |
|---|---|---|---|---|---|
| 1. | Number of Partnerships | 8,809 | | 5,325 | |
| 2. | Number of Partners | 21,780 | | 11,811 | |
| | | | | | |
| 3. | Total Assets | $797,992 | | $722,442 | |
| 4. | Average total assets per Partnership | $90,588 | | $135,670 | |
| 5. | Average total assets per Partner | $36,639 | | $61,167 | |
| | | | | | |
| 6. | Net Income | $212,244 | | $74,584 | |
| 7. | Average per Partnership, total earnings | $24,094 | | $14,007 | |
| 8. | Average per Partner, total earnings | $9,745 | | $6,315 | |
| | | | | | |
| 9. | Total Receipts | $398,396 | | $148,263 | |
| | Operating Costs | | | | |
| 10. | Cost of sales & operations | $344,308 | 86.4% | $93,457 | 63.0% |
| 11. | Salaries and wages | $2,056 | 0.5% | $1,434 | 0.10% |
| 12. | Rent paid | $2,051 | 0.5% | $226 | 0.2% |
| 13. | Interest paid | $12,848 | 3.2% | $5,244 | 3.5% |
| 14. | Taxes paid | $480 | 0.1% | $989 | 0.7% |
| 15. | Bad debts | $420 | 0.1% | $12 | 0.0% |
| 16. | Repairs | $221 | 0.1% | $4,468 | 3.0% |
| 17. | Depreciation | $1,248 | 0.3% | $6,394 | 4.3% |
| 18. | Depletion | $16 | n.a. | $0 | n.a. |
| 19. | Pension & profit sharing plans | $0 | n.a. | $0 | n.a. |
| 20. | Employee benefits programs | $0 | n.a. | $28 | 0.0% |
| 21. | Other deductions | $41,253 | 10.4% | $27,007 | 18.2% |
| 22. | Total operating costs | $404,901 | 101.6% | $139,259 | 93.9% |
| | | | | | |
| | Operating Income and Distribution | | | | |
| 23. | Total Receipts | $398,396 | 100.0% | $148,263 | 100.0% |
| 24. | Less:  Cost of sales and operations | $344,308 | 86.4% | $93,457 | 63.0% |
| 25. | Gross operating profit | $54,088 | 13.6% | $54,806 | 37.0% |
| 26. | Additional operating costs | $60,593 | 15.2% | $45,802 | 30.9% |
| 27. | Net operating profit | ($6,505) | (1.6%) | $9,004 | 6.1% |
| 28. | Less:  Guaranteed payments to partners | $178 | | $2,878 | |
| 29. | Distribution to partners | ($6,683) | | $6,126 | |
| 30. | Other charges | $32,582 | | $10,469 | |
| 31. | Net change partners' capital | ($39,265) | | ($4,343) | |
| | | | | | |
| | Selected Ratios | | | | |
| 32. | Coverage ratio:  times interest earned | (1.5) | | 0.7 | |
| 33. | Inventory turnover (times) | 29.7 | | 30.2 | |
| 34. | Days' sales in inventory | 8.7 | | 13.3 | |
| 35. | Average age of inventory (days) | 12.3 | | 12.1 | |
| 36. | Return on assets, net income | 26.6% | | 10.3% | |
| 37. | Return on assets, gross operating profit | 6.8% | | 7.6% | |
| 38. | Return on assets, net operating profit | (0.8%) | | 1.3% | |

*Page 112*

Table 2: Partnerships With Net Income:  010.  HOGS, SHEEP, AND GOATS

Dollar values in thousands, except averages

|  |  | 1984 | | 1985 | |
|---|---|---|---|---|---|
| 1. | Number of Partnerships | 3,624 | | 2,999 | |
| 2. | Number of Partners | 7,767 | | 6,135 | |
| 3. | Total Assets | $59,798 | | $82,114 | |
| 4. | Average total assets per Partnership | $16,501 | | $27,380 | |
| 5. | Average total assets per Partner | $7,699 | | $13,385 | |
| 6. | Net Income | $45,002 | | $120,216 | |
| 7. | Average per Partnership, total earnings | $12,419 | | $40,085 | |
| 8. | Average per Partner, total earnings | $5,795 | | $19,595 | |
| 9. | Total Receipts | $133,170 | | $127,266 | |
|  | Operating Costs |  | |  | |
| 10. | Cost of sales & operations | $125,198 | 94.0% | $83,206 | 65.4% |
| 11. | Salaries and wages | $199 | 0.2% | $221 | 0.2% |
| 12. | Rent paid | $0 | n.a. | $1 | n.a. |
| 13. | Interest paid | $2,073 | 1.6% | $14 | 0.0% |
| 14. | Taxes paid | $15 | 0.0% | $18 | 0.0% |
| 15. | Bad debts | $0 | n.a. | $0 | n.a. |
| 16. | Repairs | $16 | 0.0% | $19 | 0.0% |
| 17. | Depreciation | $43 | 0.0% | $124 | 0.1% |
| 18. | Depletion | $0 | n.a. | $0 | n.a. |
| 19. | Pension & profit sharing plans | $0 | n.a. | $0 | n.a. |
| 20. | Employee benefits programs | $0 | n.a. | $7 | 0.0% |
| 21. | Other deductions | $4,090 | 3.1% | $626 | 0.5% |
| 22. | Total operating costs | $131,634 | 98.9% | $84,236 | 66.2% |
|  | Operating Income and Distribution |  | |  | |
| 23. | Total Receipts | $133,170 | 100.0% | $127,266 | 100.0% |
| 24. | Less: Cost of sales and operations | $125,198 | 94.0% | $83,206 | 65.4% |
| 25. | Gross operating profit | $7,972 | 6.0% | $44,060 | 34.6% |
| 26. | Additional operating costs | $6,436 | 4.8% | $1,030 | 0.8% |
| 27. | Net operating profit | $1,536 | 1.2% | $43,030 | 33.8% |
| 28. | Less: Guaranteed payments to partners | $5,725 | | $0 | |
| 29. | Distribution to partners | ($4,189) | | $43,030 | |
| 30. | Other charges | $0 | | $489 | |
| 31. | Net change partners' capital | ($4,189) | | $42,541 | |
|  | Selected Ratios |  | |  | |
| 32. | Coverage ratio: times interest earned | (0.3) | | 3,072 | |
| 33. | Inventory turnover (times) | 77.0 | | 11,886 | |
| 34. | Days' sales in inventory | 0.1 | | 0.1 | |
| 35. | Average age of inventory (days) | 4.7 | | 0.0 | |
| 36. | Return on assets, net income | 75.3% | | 146.4% | |
| 37. | Return on assets, gross operating profit | 13.3% | | 53.7% | |
| 38. | Return on assets, net operating profit | 2.6% | | 52.4% | |

Table 2: Partnerships With Net Income:  011.  DAIRY FARMS

Dollar values in thousands, except averages

| | 1984 | | 1985 | |
|---|---|---|---|---|
| 1.  Number of Partnerships | 8,129 | | 11,214 | |
| 2.  Number of Partners | 17,700 | | 27,095 | |
| | | | | |
| 3.  Total Assets | $758,383 | | $838,874 | |
| 4.    Average total assets per Partnership | $93,294 | | $74,806 | |
| 5.    Average total assets per Partner | $42,847 | | $30,960 | |
| | | | | |
| 6.  Net Income | $227,359 | | $395,888 | |
| 7.    Average per Partnership, total earnings | $27,970 | | $35,304 | |
| 8.    Average per Partner, total earnings | $12,846 | | $14,612 | |
| | | | | |
| 9.  Total Receipts | $319,407 | | $153,655 | |
| Operating Costs | | | | |
| 10.   Cost of sales & operations | $224,336 | 70.2% | $85,721 | 55.8% |
| 11.   Salaries and wages | $3,627 | 1.1% | $10,830 | 7.1% |
| 12.   Rent paid | $4,236 | 1.3% | $3,808 | 2.5% |
| 13.   Interest paid | $8,019 | 2.5% | $4,698 | 3.1% |
| 14.   Taxes paid | $1,943 | 0.6% | $471 | 0.3% |
| 15.   Bad debts | $86 | 0.0% | $12 | 0.0% |
| 16.   Repairs | $1,543 | 0.5% | $1,502 | 0.10% |
| 17.   Depreciation | $3,962 | 1.2% | $9,071 | 5.9% |
| 18.   Depletion | $0 | n.a. | $0 | n.a. |
| 19.   Pension & profit sharing plans | $184 | 0.1% | $0 | n.a. |
| 20.   Employee benefits programs | $0 | n.a. | $0 | n.a. |
| 21.   Other deductions | $10,657 | 3.3% | $23,523 | 15.3% |
| 22.   Total operating costs | $258,593 | 81.0% | $139,636 | 90.9% |
| | | | | |
| Operating Income and Distribution | | | | |
| 23.   Total Receipts | $319,407 | 100.0% | $153,655 | 100.0% |
| 24.     Less:  Cost of sales and operations | $224,336 | 70.2% | $85,721 | 55.8% |
| 25.   Gross operating profit | $95,071 | 29.8% | $67,934 | 44.2% |
| 26.     Additional operating costs | $34,257 | 10.7% | $53,915 | 35.1% |
| 27.   Net operating profit | $60,814 | 19.0% | $14,019 | 9.1% |
| 28.     Less:  Guaranteed payments to partners | $10,033 | | $10,674 | |
| 29.   Distribution to partners | $50,781 | | $3,345 | |
| 30.   Other charges | $11,596 | | $16,460 | |
| 31.   Net change partners' capital | $39,185 | | ($13,115) | |
| | | | | |
| Selected Ratios | | | | |
| 32.   Coverage ratio:  times interest earned | 6.6 | | 2.0 | |
| 33.   Inventory turnover (times) | 7.8 | | 19.9 | |
| 34.   Days' sales in inventory | 8.3 | | 19.1 | |
| 35.   Average age of inventory (days) | 46.5 | | 18.3 | |
| 36.   Return on assets, net income | 30.0% | | 47.2% | |
| 37.   Return on assets, gross operating profit | 12.5% | | 8.1% | |
| 38.   Return on assets, net operating profit | 8.0% | | 1.7% | |

*Page 114*

Table 2: Partnerships With Net Income:  012.  POULTRY AND EGGS

Dollar values in thousands, except averages

|  | 1984 | | 1985 | |
|---|---|---|---|---|
| 1. Number of Partnerships | 641 | | 549 | |
| 2. Number of Partners | 1,554 | | 1,347 | |
| 3. Total Assets | $391,777 | | $355,498 | |
| 4. Average total assets per Partnership | $611,197 | | $647,537 | |
| 5. Average total assets per Partner | $252,109 | | $263,918 | |
| 6. Net Income | $52,052 | | $55,630 | |
| 7. Average per Partnership, total earnings | $81,209 | | $101,336 | |
| 8. Average per Partner, total earnings | $33,497 | | $41,302 | |
| 9. Total Receipts | $300,063 | | $213,208 | |
| Operating Costs | | | | |
| 10. Cost of sales & operations | $205,790 | 68.6% | $147,885 | 69.4% |
| 11. Salaries and wages | $8,616 | 2.9% | $4,863 | 2.3% |
| 12. Rent paid | $455 | 0.2% | $200 | 0.1% |
| 13. Interest paid | $3,480 | 1.2% | $1,176 | 0.6% |
| 14. Taxes paid | $1,041 | 0.4% | $674 | 0.3% |
| 15. Bad debts | $2 | n.a. | $45 | 0.0% |
| 16. Repairs | $1,939 | 0.7% | $1,468 | 0.7% |
| 17. Depreciation | $7,082 | 2.4% | $2,709 | 1.3% |
| 18. Depletion | $0 | n.a. | $0 | n.a. |
| 19. Pension & profit sharing plans | $122 | 0.0% | $132 | 0.1% |
| 20. Employee benefits programs | $153 | 0.1% | $224 | 0.1% |
| 21. Other deductions | $49,180 | 16.4% | $36,021 | 16.9% |
| 22. Total operating costs | $277,860 | 92.6% | $195,397 | 91.7% |
| Operating Income and Distribution | | | | |
| 23. Total Receipts | $300,063 | 100.0% | $213,208 | 100.0% |
| 24. Less: Cost of sales and operations | $205,790 | 68.6% | $147,885 | 69.4% |
| 25. Gross operating profit | $94,273 | 31.4% | $65,323 | 30.6% |
| 26. Additional operating costs | $72,070 | 24.0% | $47,512 | 22.3% |
| 27. Net operating profit | $22,203 | 7.4% | $17,811 | 8.4% |
| 28. Less: Guaranteed payments to partners | $2,839 | | $3,728 | |
| 29. Distribution to partners | $19,364 | | $14,083 | |
| 30. Other charges | $0 | | $1 | |
| 31. Net change partners' capital | $19,364 | | $14,082 | |
| Selected Ratios | | | | |
| 32. Coverage ratio: times interest earned | 5.4 | | 14.2 | |
| 33. Inventory turnover (times) | 63.9 | | 36.7 | |
| 34. Days' sales in inventory | 7.7 | | 10.7 | |
| 35. Average age of inventory (days) | 5.7 | | 1.0 | |
| 36. Return on assets, net income | 13.3% | | 15.7% | |
| 37. Return on assets, gross operating profit | 24.1% | | 18.4% | |
| 38. Return on assets, net operating profit | 5.7% | | 5.0% | |

*Page 115*

Table 2: Partnerships With Net Income:  GENERAL LIVESTOCK, INCLUDING ANIMAL SPECIALTY (013,014)

Dollar values in thousands, except averages

|     |                                            | 1984       |        | 1985       |        |
|-----|--------------------------------------------|------------|--------|------------|--------|
| 1.  | Number of Partnerships                     | 1,588      |        | 1,471      |        |
| 2.  | Number of Partners                         | 3,495      |        | 4,722      |        |
| 3.  | Total Assets                               | $200,509   |        | $186,522   |        |
| 4.  | Average total assets per Partnership       | $126,265   |        | $126,799   |        |
| 5.  | Average total assets per Partner           | $57,370    |        | $39,501    |        |
| 6.  | Net Income                                 | $61,930    |        | $58,814    |        |
| 7.  | Average per Partnership, total earnings    | $39,001    |        | $39,985    |        |
| 8.  | Average per Partner, total earnings        | $17,721    |        | $12,456    |        |
| 9.  | Total Receipts                             | $140,746   |        | $158,119   |        |
|     | Operating Costs                            |            |        |            |        |
| 10. | Cost of sales & operations                 | $119,891   | 85.2%  | $139,063   | 88.0%  |
| 11. | Salaries and wages                         | $4,983     | 3.5%   | $3,023     | 1.9%   |
| 12. | Rent paid                                  | $945       | 0.7%   | $441       | 0.3%   |
| 13. | Interest paid                              | $2,665     | 1.9%   | $534       | 0.3%   |
| 14. | Taxes paid                                 | $650       | 0.5%   | $306       | 0.2%   |
| 15. | Bad debts                                  | $37        | 0.0%   | $44        | 0.0%   |
| 16. | Repairs                                    | $593       | 0.4%   | $478       | 0.3%   |
| 17. | Depreciation                               | $3,418     | 2.4%   | $957       | 0.6%   |
| 18. | Depletion                                  | $14        | 0.0%   | $0         | n.a.   |
| 19. | Pension & profit sharing plans             | $221       | 0.2%   | $289       | 0.2%   |
| 20. | Employee benefits programs                 | $131       | 0.1%   | $82        | 0.1%   |
| 21. | Other deductions                           | $10,026    | 7.1%   | $5,882     | 3.7%   |
| 22. | Total operating costs                      | $143,574   | 102.0% | $151,099   | 95.6%  |

Operating Income and Distribution

|     |                                            | 1984       |        | 1985       |        |
|-----|--------------------------------------------|------------|--------|------------|--------|
| 23. | Total Receipts                             | $140,746   | 100.0% | $158,119   | 100.0% |
| 24. | Less:  Cost of sales and operations        | $119,891   | 85.2%  | $139,063   | 88.0%  |
| 25. | Gross operating profit                     | $20,855    | 14.8%  | $19,056    | 12.1%  |
| 26. | Additional operating costs                 | $23,683    | 16.8%  | $12,036    | 7.6%   |
| 27. | Net operating profit                       | ($2,828)   | (2.0%) | $7,020     | 4.4%   |
| 28. | Less:  Guaranteed payments to partners     | $3,818     |        | $3,806     |        |
| 29. | Distribution to partners                   | ($6,646)   |        | $3,214     |        |
| 30. | Other charges                              | $348       |        | $451       |        |
| 31. | Net change partners' capital               | ($6,994)   |        | $2,763     |        |

Selected Ratios

|     |                                            | 1984       | 1985   |
|-----|--------------------------------------------|------------|--------|
| 32. | Coverage ratio:  times interest earned     | (2.1)      | 12.2   |
| 33. | Inventory turnover (times)                 | 8.8        | 9.7    |
| 34. | Days' sales in inventory                   | 68.9       | 25.1   |
| 35. | Average age of inventory (days)            | 41.4       | 37.5   |
| 36. | Return on assets, net income               | 30.9%      | 31.5%  |
| 37. | Return on assets, gross operating profit   | 10.4%      | 10.2%  |
| 38. | Return on assets, net operating profit     | (1.4%)     | 3.8%   |

Table 2: Partnerships With Net Income:  OTHER FARMS (007,015)

Dollar values in thousands, except averages

| | | 1984 | | 1985 | |
|---|---|---|---|---|---|
| 1. | Number of Partnerships | 2,002 | | 2,606 | |
| 2. | Number of Partners | 4,520 | | 5,241 | |
| | | | | | |
| 3. | Total Assets | $66,081 | | $43,459 | |
| 4. | Average total assets per Partnership | $33,007 | | $16,677 | |
| 5. | Average total assets per Partner | $14,620 | | $8,292 | |
| | | | | | |
| 6. | Net Income | $54,186 | | $28,974 | |
| 7. | Average per Partnership, total earnings | $27,066 | | $11,119 | |
| 8. | Average per Partner, total earnings | $11,988 | | $5,529 | |
| | | | | | |
| 9. | Total Receipts | $56,792 | | $43,703 | |
| | Operating Costs | | | | |
| 10. | Cost of sales & operations | $24,764 | 43.6% | $18,975 | 43.4% |
| 11. | Salaries and wages | $5,935 | 10.5% | $5,401 | 12.4% |
| 12. | Rent paid | $884 | 1.6% | $895 | 2.1% |
| 13. | Interest paid | $5,826 | 10.3% | $1,918 | 4.4% |
| 14. | Taxes paid | $708 | 1.3% | $660 | 1.5% |
| 15. | Bad debts | $17 | 0.0% | $11 | 0.0% |
| 16. | Repairs | $264 | 0.5% | $764 | 1.8% |
| 17. | Depreciation | $2,117 | 3.7% | $1,201 | 2.8% |
| 18. | Depletion | $0 | n.a. | $0 | n.a. |
| 19. | Pension & profit sharing plans | $24 | 0.0% | $28 | 0.1% |
| 20. | Employee benefits programs | $0 | n.a. | $0 | n.a. |
| 21. | Other deductions | $13,232 | 23.3% | $9,444 | 21.6% |
| 22. | Total operating costs | $53,771 | 94.7% | $39,297 | 89.9% |
| | | | | | |
| | Operating Income and Distribution | | | | |
| 23. | Total Receipts | $56,792 | 100.0% | $43,703 | 100.0% |
| 24. | Less:  Cost of sales and operations | $24,764 | 43.6% | $18,975 | 43.4% |
| 25. | Gross operating profit | $32,028 | 56.4% | $24,728 | 56.6% |
| 26. | Additional operating costs | $29,007 | 51.1% | $20,322 | 46.5% |
| 27. | Net operating profit | $3,021 | 5.3% | $4,406 | 10.1% |
| 28. | Less:  Guaranteed payments to partners | $918 | | $1,752 | |
| 29. | Distribution to partners | $2,103 | | $2,654 | |
| 30. | Other charges | $0 | | $0 | |
| 31. | Net change partners' capital | $2,103 | | $2,654 | |
| | | | | | |
| | Selected Ratios | | | | |
| 32. | Coverage ratio:  times interest earned | (0.5) | | 1.3 | |
| 33. | Inventory turnover (times) | 48.2 | | 43.2 | |
| 34. | Days' sales in inventory | 8.6 | | 7.2 | |
| 35. | Average age of inventory (days) | 7.6 | | 8.4 | |
| 36. | Return on assets, net income | 82.0% | | 66.7% | |
| 37. | Return on assets, gross operating profit | 48.5% | | 56.9% | |
| 38. | Return on assets, net operating profit | 4.6% | | 10.1% | |

Table 2: Partnerships With Net Income:  AGRICULTURAL SERVICES, FORESTRY AND FISHING (016,022,023)

Dollar values in thousands, except averages

|  |  | 1984 |  | 1985 |  |
|---|---|---|---|---|---|
| 1. | Number of Partnerships | 14,047 | | 16,661 | |
| 2. | Number of Partners | 33,268 | | 40,966 | |
| 3. | Total Assets | $1,239,255 | | $1,444,208 | |
| 4. | Average total assets per Partnership | $88,222 | | $86,682 | |
| 5. | Average total assets per Partner | $37,251 | | $35,254 | |
| 6. | Net Income | $439,291 | | $456,855 | |
| 7. | Average per Partnership, total earnings | $31,274 | | $27,424 | |
| 8. | Average per Partner, total earnings | $13,205 | | $11,153 | |
| 9. | Total Receipts | $1,764,227 | | $2,074,464 | |
| | Operating Costs | | | | |
| 10. | Cost of sales & operations | $723,795 | 41.0% | $866,096 | 41.8% |
| 11. | Salaries and wages | $132,954 | 7.5% | $169,728 | 8.2% |
| 12. | Rent paid | $15,274 | 0.9% | $23,241 | 1.1% |
| 13. | Interest paid | $27,765 | 1.6% | $42,312 | 2.0% |
| 14. | Taxes paid | $24,718 | 1.4% | $24,024 | 1.2% |
| 15. | Bad debts | $610 | 0.0% | $2,252 | 0.1% |
| 16. | Repairs | $53,713 | 3.0% | $62,163 | 3.0% |
| 17. | Depreciation | $90,014 | 5.1% | $85,081 | 4.1% |
| 18. | Depletion | $6,002 | 0.3% | $27,159 | 1.3% |
| 19. | Pension & profit sharing plans | $2,129 | 0.1% | $801 | 0.0% |
| 20. | Employee benefits programs | $867 | 0.1% | $442 | 0.0% |
| 21. | Other deductions | $319,989 | 18.1% | $377,261 | 18.2% |
| 22. | Total operating costs | $1,397,830 | 79.2% | $1,680,597 | 81.0% |
| | Operating Income and Distribution | | | | |
| 23. | Total Receipts | $1,764,227 | 100.0% | $2,074,464 | 100.0% |
| 24. | Less: Cost of sales and operations | $723,795 | 41.0% | $866,096 | 41.8% |
| 25. | Gross operating profit | $1,040,432 | 59.0% | $1,208,368 | 58.3% |
| 26. | Additional operating costs | $674,035 | 38.2% | $814,501 | 39.3% |
| 27. | Net operating profit | $366,397 | 20.8% | $393,867 | 19.0% |
| 28. | Less: Guaranteed payments to partners | $15,360 | | $53,208 | |
| 29. | Distribution to partners | $351,037 | | $340,659 | |
| 30. | Other charges | $3,887 | | $19,208 | |
| 31. | Net change partners' capital | $347,150 | | $321,451 | |
| | Selected Ratios | | | | |
| 32. | Coverage ratio:  times interest earned | 12.2 | | 8.3 | |
| 33. | Inventory turnover (times) | 25.7 | | 34.3 | |
| 34. | Days' sales in inventory | 7.7 | | 12.0 | |
| 35. | Average age of inventory (days) | 14.2 | | 10.6 | |
| 36. | Return on assets, net income | 35.5% | | 31.6% | |
| 37. | Return on assets, gross operating profit | 84.0% | | 83.7% | |
| 38. | Return on assets, net operating profit | 29.6% | | 27.3% | |

Table 2: Partnerships With Net Income:  026.  MINING

Dollar values in thousands, except averages

|  |  | 1984 |  | 1985 |  |
|---|---|---|---|---|---|
| 1. | Number of Partnerships | 30,606 |  | 32,585 |  |
| 2. | Number of Partners | 1,359,138 |  | 1,514,585 |  |
| 3. | Total Assets | $24,208,151 |  | $41,645,913 |  |
| 4. | Average total assets per Partnership | $790,961 |  | $1,278,070 |  |
| 5. | Average total assets per Partner | $17,811 |  | $27,497 |  |
| 6. | Net Income | $7,857,115 |  | $7,884,137 |  |
| 7. | Average per Partnership, total earnings | $256,721 |  | $241,957 |  |
| 8. | Average per Partner, total earnings | $5,781 |  | $5,206 |  |
| 9. | Operating Income | $17,792,218 |  | $18,788,982 |  |
|  | Operating Costs |  |  |  |  |
| 10. | Cost of sales & operations | $4,019,098 | 22.6% | $4,477,229 | 23.8% |
| 11. | Salaries and wages | $259,973 | 1.5% | $188,063 | 1.0% |
| 12. | Rent paid | $127,754 | 0.7% | $62,348 | 0.3% |
| 13. | Interest paid | $422,292 | 2.4% | $304,813 | 1.6% |
| 14. | Taxes paid | $486,771 | 2.7% | $571,531 | 3.0% |
| 15. | Bad debts | $18,169 | 0.1% | $21,405 | 0.1% |
| 16. | Repairs | $57,375 | 0.3% | $44,908 | 0.2% |
| 17. | Depreciation | $1,137,548 | 6.4% | $1,334,642 | 7.1% |
| 18. | Depletion | $173,930 | 0.10% | $165,325 | 0.9% |
| 19. | Pension & profit sharing plans | $15,185 | 0.1% | $14,353 | 0.1% |
| 20. | Employee benefits programs | $9,869 | 0.1% | $10,002 | 0.1% |
| 21. | Other deductions | $2,950,893 | 16.6% | $3,605,380 | 19.2% |
| 22. | Total operating costs | $9,678,860 | 54.4% | $10,799,999 | 57.5% |
|  | Operating Income and Distribution |  |  |  |  |
| 23. | Operating Income | $17,792,218 | 100.0% | $18,788,982 | 100.0% |
| 24. | Less: Cost of sales and operations | $4,019,098 | 22.6% | $4,477,229 | 23.8% |
| 25. | Gross operating profit | $13,773,120 | 77.4% | $14,311,753 | 76.2% |
| 26. | Additional operating costs | $5,659,762 | 31.8% | $6,322,770 | 33.7% |
| 27. | Net operating profit | $8,113,358 | 45.6% | $7,988,983 | 42.5% |
| 28. | Less: Guaranteed payments to partners | $81,208 |  | $47,957 |  |
| 29. | Distribution to partners | $8,032,150 |  | $7,941,026 |  |
| 30. | Other charges | $175,038 |  | $56,889 |  |
| 31. | Net change partners' capital | $7,857,112 |  | $7,884,137 |  |
|  | Selected Ratios |  |  |  |  |
| 32. | Coverage ratio: times interest earned | 18.2 |  | 25.2 |  |
| 33. | Inventory turnover (times) | 16.7 |  | 29.4 |  |
| 34. | Days' sales in inventory | 22.3 |  | 12.4 |  |
| 35. | Average age of inventory (days) | 21.8 |  | 12.4 |  |
| 36. | Return on assets, net income | 32.5% |  | 18.9% |  |
| 37. | Return on assets, gross operating profit | 56.9% |  | 34.4% |  |
| 38. | Return on assets, net operating profit | 33.5% |  | 19.2% |  |

Table 2: Partnerships With Net Income: 029. OIL AND GAS EXTRACTION

Dollar values in thousands, except averages

|  | | 1984 | | 1985 | |
|---|---|---|---|---|---|
| 1. | Number of Partnerships | 26,813 | | 30,005 | |
| 2. | Number of Partners | 1,320,479 | | 1,477,779 | |
| 3. | Total Assets | $21,583,632 | | $38,013,038 | |
| 4. | Average total assets per Partnership | $804,969 | | $1,266,890 | |
| 5. | Average total assets per Partner | $16,345 | | $25,723 | |
| 6. | Net Income | $7,348,703 | | $7,280,664 | |
| 7. | Average per Partnership, total earnings | $274,075 | | $242,650 | |
| 8. | Average per Partner, total earnings | $5,565 | | $4,927 | |
| 9. | Operating Income | $14,575,138 | | $15,370,905 | |
|  | Operating Costs | | | | |
| 10. | Cost of sales & operations | $2,430,629 | 16.7% | $2,769,245 | 18.0% |
| 11. | Salaries and wages | $84,259 | 0.6% | $88,548 | 0.6% |
| 12. | Rent paid | $92,980 | 0.6% | $46,437 | 0.3% |
| 13. | Interest paid | $378,255 | 2.6% | $273,545 | 1.8% |
| 14. | Taxes paid | $376,965 | 2.6% | $477,553 | 3.1% |
| 15. | Bad debts | $16,591 | 0.1% | $6,306 | 0.0% |
| 16. | Repairs | $27,162 | 0.2% | $28,736 | 0.2% |
| 17. | Depreciation | $992,284 | 6.8% | $1,146,454 | 7.5% |
| 18. | Depletion | $2,307 | 0.0% | $2,159 | 0.0% |
| 19. | Pension & profit sharing plans | $3,896 | 0.0% | $2,626 | 0.0% |
| 20. | Employee benefits programs | $2,149 | 0.0% | $3,366 | 0.0% |
| 21. | Other deductions | $2,573,666 | 17.7% | $3,167,143 | 20.6% |
| 22. | Total operating costs | $6,981,146 | 47.9% | $8,012,118 | 52.1% |
|  | Operating Income and Distribution | | | | |
| 23. | Operating Income | $14,575,138 | 100.0% | $15,370,905 | 100.0% |
| 24. | Less: Cost of sales and operations | $2,430,629 | 16.7% | $2,769,245 | 18.0% |
| 25. | Gross operating profit | $12,144,509 | 83.3% | $12,601,660 | 82.0% |
| 26. | Additional operating costs | $4,550,517 | 31.2% | $5,242,873 | 34.1% |
| 27. | Net operating profit | $7,593,992 | 52.1% | $7,358,787 | 47.9% |
| 28. | Less: Guaranteed payments to partners | $72,637 | | $44,247 | |
| 29. | Distribution to partners | $7,521,355 | | $7,314,540 | |
| 30. | Other charges | $172,655 | | $33,876 | |
| 31. | Net change partners' capital | $7,348,700 | | $7,280,664 | |
|  | Selected Ratios | | | | |
| 32. | Coverage ratio: times interest earned | 19.1 | | 25.9 | |
| 33. | Inventory turnover (times) | 20.0 | | 170.8 | |
| 34. | Days' sales in inventory | 18.0 | | 1.8 | |
| 35. | Average age of inventory (days) | 18.3 | | 2.1 | |
| 36. | Return on assets, net income | 34.1% | | 19.2% | |
| 37. | Return on assets, gross operating profit | 56.3% | | 33.2% | |
| 38. | Return on assets, net operating profit | 35.2% | | 19.4% | |

*Page 120*

Table 2: Partnerships With Net Income:  OTHER MINING (027,028,030)

Dollar values in thousands, except averages

|  |  | 1984 |  | 1985 |  |
|---|---|---|---|---|---|
| 1. | Number of Partnerships | 3,794 | | 2,580 | |
| 2. | Number of Partners | 38,659 | | 36,805 | |
| 3. | Total Assets | $2,624,520 | | $3,632,875 | |
| 4. | Average total assets per Partnership | $691,755 | | $1,408,091 | |
| 5. | Average total assets per Partner | $67,889 | | $98,706 | |
| 6. | Net Income | $508,411 | | $603,473 | |
| 7. | Average per Partnership, total earnings | $134,006 | | $233,906 | |
| 8. | Average per Partner, total earnings | $13,151 | | $16,397 | |
| 9. | Operating Income | $3,217,080 | | $3,418,077 | |
|  | Operating Costs | | | | |
| 10. | Cost of sales & operations | $1,588,469 | 49.4% | $1,707,984 | 50.0% |
| 11. | Salaries and wages | $175,714 | 5.5% | $99,515 | 2.9% |
| 12. | Rent paid | $34,774 | 1.1% | $15,912 | 0.5% |
| 13. | Interest paid | $44,037 | 1.4% | $31,268 | 0.9% |
| 14. | Taxes paid | $109,806 | 3.4% | $93,978 | 2.8% |
| 15. | Bad debts | $1,579 | 0.1% | $15,100 | 0.4% |
| 16. | Repairs | $30,213 | 0.9% | $16,172 | 0.5% |
| 17. | Depreciation | $145,263 | 4.5% | $188,188 | 5.5% |
| 18. | Depletion | $171,622 | 5.3% | $163,166 | 4.8% |
| 19. | Pension & profit sharing plans | $11,289 | 0.4% | $11,727 | 0.3% |
| 20. | Employee benefits programs | $7,720 | 0.2% | $6,636 | 0.2% |
| 21. | Other deductions | $377,227 | 11.7% | $438,234 | 12.8% |
| 22. | Total operating costs | $2,697,713 | 83.9% | $2,787,880 | 81.6% |
| | Operating Income and Distribution | | | | |
| 23. | Operating Income | $3,217,080 | 100.0% | $3,418,077 | 100.0% |
| 24. | Less:  Cost of sales and operations | $1,588,469 | 49.4% | $1,707,984 | 50.0% |
| 25. | Gross operating profit | $1,628,611 | 50.6% | $1,710,093 | 50.0% |
| 26. | Additional operating costs | $1,109,244 | 34.5% | $1,079,896 | 31.6% |
| 27. | Net operating profit | $519,367 | 16.1% | $630,197 | 18.4% |
| 28. | Less:  Guaranteed payments to partners | $8,572 | | $3,710 | |
| 29. | Distribution to partners | $510,795 | | $626,487 | |
| 30. | Other charges | $2,383 | | $23,014 | |
| 31. | Net change partners' capital | $508,412 | | $603,473 | |
| | Selected Ratios | | | | |
| 32. | Coverage ratio:  times interest earned | 10.8 | | 19.2 | |
| 33. | Inventory turnover (times) | 13.4 | | 12.5 | |
| 34. | Days' sales in inventory | 28.8 | | 29.7 | |
| 35. | Average age of inventory (days) | 27.3 | | 29.1 | |
| 36. | Return on assets, net income | 19.4% | | 16.6% | |
| 37. | Return on assets, gross operating profit | 62.1% | | 47.1% | |
| 38. | Return on assets, net operating profit | 19.8% | | 17.4% | |

*Page 121*

Table 2: Partnerships With Net Income:  031.  CONSTRUCTION

Dollar values in thousands, except averages

| | | 1984 | | 1985 | |
|---|---|---|---|---|---|
| 1. | Number of Partnerships | 46,921 | | 40,885 | |
| 2. | Number of Partners | 110,082 | | 95,382 | |
| | | | | | |
| 3. | Total Assets | $7,807,779 | | $9,081,760 | |
| 4. | Average total assets per Partnership | $166,403 | | $222,129 | |
| 5. | Average total assets per Partner | $70,927 | | $95,215 | |
| | | | | | |
| 6. | Net Income | $2,966,387 | | $2,742,982 | |
| 7. | Average per Partnership, total earnings | $63,224 | | $67,093 | |
| 8. | Average per Partner, total earnings | $26,949 | | $28,759 | |
| | | | | | |
| 9. | Operating Income | $19,419,157 | | $17,564,462 | |
| | Operating Costs | | | | |
| 10. | Cost of sales & operations | $13,745,488 | 70.8% | $12,146,235 | 69.2% |
| 11. | Salaries and wages | $625,952 | 3.2% | $573,279 | 3.3% |
| 12. | Rent paid | $69,546 | 0.4% | $95,153 | 0.5% |
| 13. | Interest paid | $171,805 | 0.9% | $175,180 | 1.0% |
| 14. | Taxes paid | $155,340 | 0.8% | $162,920 | 0.9% |
| 15. | Bad debts | $7,945 | 0.0% | $12,094 | 0.1% |
| 16. | Repairs | $65,688 | 0.3% | $105,880 | 0.6% |
| 17. | Depreciation | $234,860 | 1.2% | $236,684 | 1.4% |
| 18. | Depletion | $745 | n.a. | $356 | n.a. |
| 19. | Pension & profit sharing plans | $6,272 | 0.0% | $8,115 | 0.1% |
| 20. | Employee benefits programs | $8,485 | 0.0% | $11,316 | 0.1% |
| 21. | Other deductions | $1,188,287 | 6.1% | $1,143,185 | 6.5% |
| 22. | Total operating costs | $16,281,505 | 83.8% | $14,671,287 | 83.5% |
| | | | | | |
| | Operating Income and Distribution | | | | |
| 23. | Operating Income | $19,419,157 | 100.0% | $17,564,462 | 100.0% |
| 24. | Less: Cost of sales and operations | $13,745,488 | 70.8% | $12,146,235 | 69.2% |
| 25. | Gross operating profit | $5,673,669 | 29.2% | $5,418,227 | 30.9% |
| 26. | Additional operating costs | $2,536,017 | 13.1% | $2,525,052 | 14.4% |
| 27. | Net operating profit | $3,137,652 | 16.2% | $2,893,175 | 16.5% |
| 28. | Less: Guaranteed payments to partners | $158,202 | | $128,767 | |
| 29. | Distribution to partners | $2,979,450 | | $2,764,408 | |
| 30. | Other charges | $14,156 | | $22,316 | |
| 31. | Net change partners' capital | $2,965,294 | | $2,742,092 | |
| | | | | | |
| | Selected Ratios | | | | |
| 32. | Coverage ratio: times interest earned | 17.3 | | 15.5 | |
| 33. | Inventory turnover (times) | 8.8 | | 5.7 | |
| 34. | Days' sales in inventory | 36.8 | | 68.1 | |
| 35. | Average age of inventory (days) | 41.5 | | 63.7 | |
| 36. | Return on assets, net income | 38.0% | | 30.2% | |
| 37. | Return on assets, gross operating profit | 72.7% | | 59.7% | |
| 38. | Return on assets, net operating profit | 40.2% | | 31.9% | |

Table 2: Partnerships With Net Income:  GENERAL CONTRACTORS, TOTAL (032,035)

Dollar values in thousands, except averages

| | 1984 | | 1985 | |
|---|---|---|---|---|
| 1. Number of Partnerships | 15,428 | | 12,225 | |
| 2. Number of Partners | 40,431 | | 28,329 | |
| | | | | |
| 3. Total Assets | $6,358,493 | | $7,421,549 | |
| 4. Average total assets per Partnership | $412,140 | | $607,080 | |
| 5. Average total assets per Partner | $157,268 | | $261,977 | |
| | | | | |
| 6. Net Income | $1,707,116 | | $1,581,483 | |
| 7. Average per Partnership, total earnings | $110,657 | | $129,368 | |
| 8. Average per Partner, total earnings | $42,225 | | $55,827 | |
| | | | | |
| 9. Operating Income | $13,151,784 | | $11,186,760 | |
| Operating Costs | | | | |
| 10. Cost of sales & operations | $10,288,076 | 78.2% | $8,507,156 | 76.1% |
| 11. Salaries and wages | $217,837 | 1.7% | $183,237 | 1.6% |
| 12. Rent paid | $25,516 | 0.2% | $35,796 | 0.3% |
| 13. Interest paid | $121,787 | 0.9% | $128,140 | 1.2% |
| 14. Taxes paid | $85,420 | 0.7% | $48,020 | 0.4% |
| 15. Bad debts | $4,093 | 0.0% | $5,803 | 0.1% |
| 16. Repairs | $24,774 | 0.2% | $63,926 | 0.6% |
| 17. Depreciation | $76,224 | 0.6% | $90,266 | 0.8% |
| 18. Depletion | $455 | n.a. | $87 | n.a. |
| 19. Pension & profit sharing plans | $2,942 | 0.0% | $3,035 | 0.0% |
| 20. Employee benefits programs | $4,952 | 0.0% | $3,559 | 0.0% |
| 21. Other deductions | $487,010 | 3.7% | $485,555 | 4.3% |
| 22. Total operating costs | $11,339,442 | 86.2% | $9,554,593 | 85.4% |
| | | | | |
| Operating Income and Distribution | | | | |
| 23. Operating Income | $13,151,784 | 100.0% | $11,186,760 | 100.0% |
| 24. Less: Cost of sales and operations | $10,288,076 | 78.2% | $8,507,156 | 76.1% |
| 25. Gross operating profit | $2,863,708 | 21.8% | $2,679,604 | 24.0% |
| 26. Additional operating costs | $1,051,366 | 8.0% | $1,047,437 | 9.4% |
| 27. Net operating profit | $1,812,342 | 13.8% | $1,632,167 | 14.6% |
| 28. Less: Guaranteed payments to partners | $92,410 | | $37,189 | |
| 29. Distribution to partners | $1,719,932 | | $1,594,978 | |
| 30. Other charges | $13,173 | | $13,508 | |
| 31. Net change partners' capital | $1,706,759 | | $1,581,470 | |
| | | | | |
| Selected Ratios | | | | |
| 32. Coverage ratio: times interest earned | 13.9 | | 11.7 | |
| 33. Inventory turnover (times) | 7.8 | | 4.4 | |
| 34. Days' sales in inventory | 39.8 | | 88.4 | |
| 35. Average age of inventory (days) | 47.1 | | 83.0 | |
| 36. Return on assets, net income | 26.9% | | 21.3% | |
| 37. Return on assets, gross operating profit | 45.0% | | 36.1% | |
| 38. Return on assets, net operating profit | 28.5% | | 22.0% | |

*Page 123*

Table 2: Partnerships With Net Income: 038. SPECIAL TRADE CONTRACTORS

Dollar values in thousands, except averages

| | | 1984 | | 1985 | |
|---|---|---|---|---|---|
| 1. | Number of Partnerships | 31,461 | | 28,660 | |
| 2. | Number of Partners | 69,557 | | 67,053 | |
| | | | | | |
| 3. | Total Assets | $1,449,116 | | $1,660,210 | |
| 4. | Average total assets per Partnership | $46,061 | | $57,928 | |
| 5. | Average total assets per Partner | $20,834 | | $24,760 | |
| | | | | | |
| 6. | Net Income | $1,233,078 | | $1,161,499 | |
| 7. | Average per Partnership, total earnings | $39,196 | | $40,530 | |
| 8. | Average per Partner, total earnings | $17,729 | | $17,323 | |
| | | | | | |
| 9. | Operating Income | $6,229,858 | | $6,377,702 | |
| | Operating Costs | | | | |
| 10. | Cost of sales & operations | $3,457,412 | 55.5% | $3,639,078 | 57.1% |
| 11. | Salaries and wages | $408,116 | 6.6% | $390,042 | 6.1% |
| 12. | Rent paid | $44,030 | 0.7% | $59,357 | 0.9% |
| 13. | Interest paid | $50,018 | 0.8% | $47,040 | 0.7% |
| 14. | Taxes paid | $69,920 | 1.1% | $114,900 | 1.8% |
| 15. | Bad debts | $3,851 | 0.1% | $6,290 | 0.1% |
| 16. | Repairs | $40,914 | 0.7% | $41,953 | 0.7% |
| 17. | Depreciation | $158,637 | 2.6% | $146,418 | 2.3% |
| 18. | Depletion | $290 | n.a. | $269 | n.a. |
| 19. | Pension & profit sharing plans | $3,330 | 0.1% | $5,080 | 0.1% |
| 20. | Employee benefits programs | $3,532 | 0.1% | $7,757 | 0.1% |
| 21. | Other deductions | $689,954 | 11.1% | $657,632 | 10.3% |
| 22. | Total operating costs | $4,930,739 | 79.2% | $5,116,692 | 80.2% |
| | | | | | |
| | Operating Income and Distribution | | | | |
| 23. | Operating Income | $6,229,858 | 100.0% | $6,377,702 | 100.0% |
| 24. | Less: Cost of sales and operations | $3,457,412 | 55.5% | $3,639,078 | 57.1% |
| 25. | Gross operating profit | $2,772,446 | 44.5% | $2,738,624 | 42.9% |
| 26. | Additional operating costs | $1,473,327 | 23.7% | $1,477,614 | 23.2% |
| 27. | Net operating profit | $1,299,119 | 20.9% | $1,261,010 | 19.8% |
| 28. | Less: Guaranteed payments to partners | $65,792 | | $91,577 | |
| 29. | Distribution to partners | $1,233,327 | | $1,169,433 | |
| 30. | Other charges | $983 | | $8,810 | |
| 31. | Net change partners' capital | $1,232,344 | | $1,160,623 | |
| | | | | | |
| | Selected Ratios | | | | |
| 32. | Coverage ratio: times interest earned | 25.0 | | 25.8 | |
| 33. | Inventory turnover (times) | 14.7 | | 19.5 | |
| 34. | Days' sales in inventory | 27.8 | | 20.8 | |
| 35. | Average age of inventory (days) | 24.9 | | 18.7 | |
| 36. | Return on assets, net income | 85.1% | | 70.0% | |
| 37. | Return on assets, gross operating profit | 191.3% | | 165.0% | |
| 38. | Return on assets, net operating profit | 89.7% | | 76.0% | |

*Page 124*

Table 2: Partnerships With Net Income:  039.  PLUMBING, HEATING, AND AIR CONDITIONING

Dollar values in thousands, except averages

|  |  | 1984 |  | 1985 |  |
|---|---|---|---|---|---|
| 1. | Number of Partnerships | 3,587 | | 3,099 | |
| 2. | Number of Partners | 9,704 | | 6,949 | |
| 3. | Total Assets | $268,818 | | $279,072 | |
| 4. | Average total assets per Partnership | $74,942 | | $90,052 | |
| 5. | Average total assets per Partner | $27,702 | | $40,160 | |
| 6. | Net Income | $263,268 | | $212,834 | |
| 7. | Average per Partnership, total earnings | $73,396 | | $68,679 | |
| 8. | Average per Partner, total earnings | $27,130 | | $30,628 | |
| 9. | Operating Income | $1,121,590 | | $1,328,349 | |
|  | Operating Costs | | | | |
| 10. | Cost of sales & operations | $641,800 | 57.2% | $890,598 | 67.1% |
| 11. | Salaries and wages | $34,683 | 3.1% | $58,217 | 4.4% |
| 12. | Rent paid | $13,799 | 1.2% | $19,278 | 1.5% |
| 13. | Interest paid | $4,159 | 0.4% | $7,783 | 0.6% |
| 14. | Taxes paid | $9,320 | 0.8% | $25,938 | 2.0% |
| 15. | Bad debts | $1,585 | 0.1% | $291 | 0.0% |
| 16. | Repairs | $3,742 | 0.3% | $3,872 | 0.3% |
| 17. | Depreciation | $31,441 | 2.8% | $18,801 | 1.4% |
| 18. | Depletion | $0 | n.a. | $0 | n.a. |
| 19. | Pension & profit sharing plans | $0 | n.a. | $158 | 0.0% |
| 20. | Employee benefits programs | $379 | 0.0% | $1,961 | 0.2% |
| 21. | Other deductions | $113,762 | 10.1% | $86,758 | 6.5% |
| 22. | Total operating costs | $854,670 | 76.2% | $1,114,280 | 83.9% |
|  | Operating Income and Distribution | | | | |
| 23. | Operating Income | $1,121,590 | 100.0% | $1,328,349 | 100.0% |
| 24. | Less:  Cost of sales and operations | $641,800 | 57.2% | $890,598 | 67.1% |
| 25. | Gross operating profit | $479,790 | 42.8% | $437,751 | 33.0% |
| 26. | Additional operating costs | $212,870 | 19.0% | $223,682 | 16.8% |
| 27. | Net operating profit | $266,920 | 23.8% | $214,069 | 16.1% |
| 28. | Less:  Guaranteed payments to partners | $3,466 | | $1,755 | |
| 29. | Distribution to partners | $263,454 | | $212,314 | |
| 30. | Other charges | $186 | | $104 | |
| 31. | Net change partners' capital | $263,268 | | $212,210 | |
|  | Selected Ratios | | | | |
| 32. | Coverage ratio:  times interest earned | 63.2 | | 26.5 | |
| 33. | Inventory turnover (times) | 14.5 | | 9.7 | |
| 34. | Days' sales in inventory | 33.3 | | 44.5 | |
| 35. | Average age of inventory (days) | 25.2 | | 37.6 | |
| 36. | Return on assets, net income | 97.9% | | 76.3% | |
| 37. | Return on assets, gross operating profit | 178.5% | | 156.9% | |
| 38. | Return on assets, net operating profit | 99.3% | | 76.7% | |

Table 2: Partnerships With Net Income:  040.  PAINTING, PAPER HANGING AND DECORATING

Dollar values in thousands, except averages

|  |  | 1984 |  | 1985 |  |
|---|---|---|---|---|---|
| 1. | Number of Partnerships | 4,298 | | 5,446 | |
| 2. | Number of Partners | 9,092 | | 13,426 | |
| 3. | Total Assets | $87,285 | | $37,992 | |
| 4. | Average total assets per Partnership | $20,308 | | $6,976 | |
| 5. | Average total assets per Partner | $9,600 | | $2,830 | |
| 6. | Net Income | $186,834 | | $176,838 | |
| 7. | Average per Partnership, total earnings | $43,470 | | $32,471 | |
| 8. | Average per Partner, total earnings | $20,549 | | $13,171 | |
| 9. | Operating Income | $433,195 | | $569,357 | |
|  | Operating Costs | | | | |
| 10. | Cost of sales & operations | $134,357 | 31.0% | $204,739 | 36.0% |
| 11. | Salaries and wages | $27,804 | 6.4% | $81,742 | 14.4% |
| 12. | Rent paid | $1,063 | 0.3% | $2,615 | 0.5% |
| 13. | Interest paid | $1,294 | 0.3% | $638 | 0.1% |
| 14. | Taxes paid | $6,550 | 1.5% | $9,225 | 1.6% |
| 15. | Bad debts | $0 | n.a. | $28 | n.a. |
| 16. | Repairs | $707 | 0.2% | $759 | 0.1% |
| 17. | Depreciation | $8,192 | 1.9% | $10,000 | 1.8% |
| 18. | Depletion | $0 | n.a. | $0 | n.a. |
| 19. | Pension & profit sharing plans | $0 | n.a. | $1,772 | 0.3% |
| 20. | Employee benefits programs | $0 | n.a. | $0 | n.a. |
| 21. | Other deductions | $66,342 | 15.3% | $79,910 | 14.0% |
| 22. | Total operating costs | $246,309 | 56.9% | $391,428 | 68.8% |
|  | Operating Income and Distribution | | | | |
| 23. | Operating Income | $433,195 | 100.0% | $569,357 | 100.0% |
| 24. | Less:  Cost of sales and operations | $134,357 | 31.0% | $204,739 | 36.0% |
| 25. | Gross operating profit | $298,838 | 69.0% | $364,618 | 64.0% |
| 26. | Additional operating costs | $111,952 | 25.8% | $186,689 | 32.8% |
| 27. | Net operating profit | $186,886 | 43.1% | $177,929 | 31.3% |
| 28. | Less:  Guaranteed payments to partners | $0 | | $1,074 | |
| 29. | Distribution to partners | $186,886 | | $176,855 | |
| 30. | Other charges | $52 | | $16 | |
| 31. | Net change partners' capital | $186,834 | | $176,839 | |
|  | Selected Ratios | | | | |
| 32. | Coverage ratio:  times interest earned | 143.4 | | 277.9 | |
| 33. | Inventory turnover (times) | n.a. | | n.a. | |
| 34. | Days' sales in inventory | n.a. | | n.a. | |
| 35. | Average age of inventory (days) | n.a. | | n.a. | |
| 36. | Return on assets, net income | 214.1% | | n.a. | |
| 37. | Return on assets, gross operating profit | n.a. | | n.a. | |
| 38. | Return on assets, net operating profit | 214.1% | | n.a. | |

Table 2: Partnerships With Net Income:  042.  MASONRY, STONE WORK, TILE SETTING, AND PLASTERING

Dollar values in thousands, except averages

|  |  | 1984 |  | 1985 |  |
|---|---|---|---|---|---|
| 1. | Number of Partnerships | 3,949 | | 1,732 | |
| 2. | Number of Partners | 8,572 | | 3,906 | |
| 3. | Total Assets | $48,782 | | $57,004 | |
| 4. | Average total assets per Partnership | $12,353 | | $32,912 | |
| 5. | Average total assets per Partner | $5,691 | | $14,594 | |
| 6. | Net Income | $86,475 | | $59,136 | |
| 7. | Average per Partnership, total earnings | $21,902 | | $34,152 | |
| 8. | Average per Partner, total earnings | $10,090 | | $15,144 | |
| 9. | Operating Income | $700,690 | | $442,209 | |
|  | Operating Costs | | | | |
| 10. | Cost of sales & operations | $336,015 | 48.0% | $218,800 | 49.5% |
| 11. | Salaries and wages | $130,979 | 18.7% | $48,190 | 10.9% |
| 12. | Rent paid | $5,815 | 0.8% | $9,032 | 2.0% |
| 13. | Interest paid | $5,319 | 0.8% | $2,416 | 0.6% |
| 14. | Taxes paid | $6,508 | 0.9% | $7,065 | 1.6% |
| 15. | Bad debts | $753 | 0.1% | $670 | 0.2% |
| 16. | Repairs | $16,535 | 2.4% | $14,969 | 3.4% |
| 17. | Depreciation | $9,105 | 1.3% | $8,033 | 1.8% |
| 18. | Depletion | $263 | 0.0% | $235 | 0.1% |
| 19. | Pension & profit sharing plans | $1,914 | 0.3% | $1,340 | 0.3% |
| 20. | Employee benefits programs | $2,146 | 0.3% | $1,715 | 0.4% |
| 21. | Other deductions | $83,070 | 11.9% | $55,498 | 12.6% |
| 22. | Total operating costs | $598,422 | 85.4% | $367,963 | 83.2% |
|  | Operating Income and Distribution | | | | |
| 23. | Operating Income | $700,690 | 100.0% | $442,209 | 100.0% |
| 24. | Less: Cost of sales and operations | $336,015 | 48.0% | $218,800 | 49.5% |
| 25. | Gross operating profit | $364,675 | 52.1% | $223,409 | 50.5% |
| 26. | Additional operating costs | $262,407 | 37.5% | $149,163 | 33.7% |
| 27. | Net operating profit | $102,268 | 14.6% | $74,246 | 16.8% |
| 28. | Less: Guaranteed payments to partners | $15,782 | | $15,110 | |
| 29. | Distribution to partners | $86,486 | | $59,136 | |
| 30. | Other charges | $11 | | $0 | |
| 31. | Net change partners' capital | $86,475 | | $59,136 | |
|  | Selected Ratios | | | | |
| 32. | Coverage ratio: times interest earned | 18.2 | | 29.7 | |
| 33. | Inventory turnover (times) | 74.1 | | 11.3 | |
| 34. | Days' sales in inventory | 5.3 | | 57.7 | |
| 35. | Average age of inventory (days) | 4.9 | | 32.3 | |
| 36. | Return on assets, net income | 177.3% | | 103.7% | |
| 37. | Return on assets, gross operating profit | n.a. | | n.a. | |
| 38. | Return on assets, net operating profit | 209.6% | | 130.3% | |

Table 2: Partnerships With Net Income:  CONTRACTORS NOT ELSEWHERE CLASSIFIED (041,043,044,046,047)

Dollar values in thousands, except averages

|  |  | 1984 |  | 1985 |  |
|---|---|---|---|---|---|
| 1. | Number of Partnerships | 19,628 |  | 18,384 |  |
| 2. | Number of Partners | 42,189 |  | 42,772 |  |
| 3. | Total Assets | $1,044,232 |  | $1,286,143 |  |
| 4. | Average total assets per Partnership | $53,201 |  | $69,960 |  |
| 5. | Average total assets per Partner | $24,751 |  | $30,070 |  |
| 6. | Net Income | $696,502 |  | $712,690 |  |
| 7. | Average per Partnership, total earnings | $35,487 |  | $38,771 |  |
| 8. | Average per Partner, total earnings | $16,510 |  | $16,664 |  |
| 9. | Operating Income | $3,974,383 |  | $4,037,788 |  |
|  | Operating Costs |  |  |  |  |
| 10. | Cost of sales & operations | $2,345,240 | 59.0% | $2,324,941 | 57.6% |
| 11. | Salaries and wages | $214,650 | 5.4% | $201,893 | 5.0% |
| 12. | Rent paid | $23,353 | 0.6% | $28,433 | 0.7% |
| 13. | Interest paid | $39,426 | 0.10% | $36,204 | 0.9% |
| 14. | Taxes paid | $47,542 | 1.2% | $72,673 | 1.8% |
| 15. | Bad debts | $1,514 | 0.0% | $5,301 | 0.1% |
| 16. | Repairs | $19,930 | 0.5% | $22,352 | 0.6% |
| 17. | Depreciation | $109,719 | 2.8% | $109,584 | 2.7% |
| 18. | Depletion | $27 | n.a. | $34 | n.a. |
| 19. | Pension & profit sharing plans | $1,415 | 0.0% | $1,810 | 0.0% |
| 20. | Employee benefits programs | $1,007 | 0.0% | $4,081 | 0.1% |
| 21. | Other deductions | $426,780 | 10.7% | $435,467 | 10.8% |
| 22. | Total operating costs | $3,231,338 | 81.3% | $3,243,024 | 80.3% |
|  | Operating Income and Distribution |  |  |  |  |
| 23. | Operating Income | $3,974,383 | 100.0% | $4,037,788 | 100.0% |
| 24. | Less:  Cost of sales and operations | $2,345,240 | 59.0% | $2,324,941 | 57.6% |
| 25. | Gross operating profit | $1,629,143 | 41.0% | $1,712,847 | 42.4% |
| 26. | Additional operating costs | $886,098 | 22.3% | $918,083 | 22.7% |
| 27. | Net operating profit | $743,045 | 18.7% | $794,764 | 19.7% |
| 28. | Less:  Guaranteed payments to partners | $46,544 |  | $73,637 |  |
| 29. | Distribution to partners | $696,501 |  | $721,127 |  |
| 30. | Other charges | $734 |  | $8,688 |  |
| 31. | Net change partners' capital | $695,767 |  | $712,439 |  |
|  | Selected Ratios |  |  |  |  |
| 32. | Coverage ratio:  times interest earned | 17.9 |  | 21.0 |  |
| 33. | Inventory turnover (times) | 12.6 |  | 30.9 |  |
| 34. | Days' sales in inventory | 31.1 |  | 1.0 |  |
| 35. | Average age of inventory (days) | 29.0 |  | 11.8 |  |
| 36. | Return on assets, net income | 66.7% |  | 55.4% |  |
| 37. | Return on assets, gross operating profit | 156.0% |  | 133.2% |  |
| 38. | Return on assets, net operating profit | 71.2% |  | 61.8% |  |

Table 2: Partnerships With Net Income: 049.  MANUFACTURING

Dollar values in thousands, except averages

|  |  | 1984 |  | 1985 |  |
|---|---|---|---|---|---|
| 1. | Number of Partnerships | 14,943 |  | 12,193 |  |
| 2. | Number of Partners | 37,144 |  | 33,404 |  |
| 3. | Total Assets | $5,521,206 |  | $7,673,207 |  |
| 4. | Average total assets per Partnership | $369,484 |  | $629,312 |  |
| 5. | Average total assets per Partner | $148,643 |  | $229,709 |  |
| 6. | Net Income | $1,165,440 |  | $1,228,381 |  |
| 7. | Average per Partnership, total earnings | $77,997 |  | $100,753 |  |
| 8. | Average per Partner, total earnings | $31,378 |  | $36,777 |  |
| 9. | Operating Income | $10,350,644 |  | $13,686,013 |  |
|  | Operating Costs |  |  |  |  |
| 10. | Cost of sales & operations | $6,914,599 | 66.8% | $9,136,317 | 66.8% |
| 11. | Salaries and wages | $556,105 | 5.4% | $838,477 | 6.1% |
| 12. | Rent paid | $84,718 | 0.8% | $118,281 | 0.9% |
| 13. | Interest paid | $168,527 | 1.6% | $232,217 | 1.7% |
| 14. | Taxes paid | $115,032 | 1.1% | $151,411 | 1.1% |
| 15. | Bad debts | $19,533 | 0.2% | $23,888 | 0.2% |
| 16. | Repairs | $83,702 | 0.8% | $79,090 | 0.6% |
| 17. | Depreciation | $211,161 | 2.0% | $272,907 | 2.0% |
| 18. | Depletion | $4,273 | 0.0% | $5,716 | 0.0% |
| 19. | Pension & profit sharing plans | $12,168 | 0.1% | $32,052 | 0.2% |
| 20. | Employee benefits programs | $32,787 | 0.3% | $50,149 | 0.4% |
| 21. | Other deductions | $914,510 | 8.8% | $1,409,132 | 10.3% |
| 22. | Total operating costs | $9,117,929 | 88.1% | $12,351,423 | 90.3% |

Operating Income and Distribution

|  |  | 1984 |  | 1985 |  |
|---|---|---|---|---|---|
| 23. | Operating Income | $10,350,644 | 100.0% | $13,686,013 | 100.0% |
| 24. | Less:  Cost of sales and operations | $6,914,599 | 66.8% | $9,136,317 | 66.8% |
| 25. | Gross operating profit | $3,436,045 | 33.2% | $4,549,696 | 33.2% |
| 26. | Additional operating costs | $2,203,330 | 21.3% | $3,215,106 | 23.5% |
| 27. | Net operating profit | $1,232,715 | 11.9% | $1,334,590 | 9.8% |
| 28. | Less:  Guaranteed payments to partners | $64,167 |  | $101,082 |  |
| 29. | Distribution to partners | $1,168,548 |  | $1,233,508 |  |
| 30. | Other charges | $3,922 |  | $6,913 |  |
| 31. | Net change partners' capital | $1,164,626 |  | $1,226,595 |  |

Selected Ratios

|  |  | 1984 | 1985 |
|---|---|---|---|
| 32. | Coverage ratio:  times interest earned | 6.3 | 4.8 |
| 33. | Inventory turnover (times) | 8.8 | 6.9 |
| 34. | Days' sales in inventory | 47.0 | 55.5 |
| 35. | Average age of inventory (days) | 41.3 | 52.7 |
| 36. | Return on assets, net income | 21.1% | 16.0% |
| 37. | Return on assets, gross operating profit | 62.2% | 59.3% |
| 38. | Return on assets, net operating profit | 22.3% | 17.4% |

Table 2: Partnerships With Net Income:  054.  LUMBER AND WOOD PRODUCTS, EXCEPT FURNITURE

Dollar values in thousands, except averages

|  |  | 1984 |  | 1985 |  |
|---|---|---|---|---|---|
| 1. | Number of Partnerships | 1,638 |  | 1,081 |  |
| 2. | Number of Partners | 4,512 |  | 3,069 |  |
| 3. | Total Assets | $433,053 |  | $432,590 |  |
| 4. | Average total assets per Partnership | $264,379 |  | $400,176 |  |
| 5. | Average total assets per Partner | $95,978 |  | $140,955 |  |
| 6. | Net Income | $73,457 |  | $75,328 |  |
| 7. | Average per Partnership, total earnings | $44,853 |  | $69,696 |  |
| 8. | Average per Partner, total earnings | $16,283 |  | $24,549 |  |
| 9. | Operating Income | $913,736 |  | $1,003,783 |  |
|  | Operating Costs |  |  |  |  |
| 10. | Cost of sales & operations | $613,290 | 67.1% | $724,313 | 72.2% |
| 11. | Salaries and wages | $43,179 | 4.7% | $48,173 | 4.8% |
| 12. | Rent paid | $6,271 | 0.7% | $10,915 | 1.1% |
| 13. | Interest paid | $17,707 | 1.9% | $19,533 | 2.0% |
| 14. | Taxes paid | $9,533 | 1.0% | $7,918 | 0.8% |
| 15. | Bad debts | $2,405 | 0.3% | $712 | 0.1% |
| 16. | Repairs | $29,074 | 3.2% | $15,239 | 1.5% |
| 17. | Depreciation | $26,403 | 2.9% | $24,040 | 2.4% |
| 18. | Depletion | $0 | n.a. | $973 | 0.1% |
| 19. | Pension & profit sharing plans | $499 | 0.1% | $780 | 0.1% |
| 20. | Employee benefits programs | $1,295 | 0.1% | $564 | 0.1% |
| 21. | Other deductions | $77,063 | 8.4% | $60,523 | 6.0% |
| 22. | Total operating costs | $826,894 | 90.5% | $913,710 | 91.0% |
|  | Operating Income and Distribution |  |  |  |  |
| 23. | Operating Income | $913,736 | 100.0% | $1,003,783 | 100.0% |
| 24. | Less:  Cost of sales and operations | $613,290 | 67.1% | $724,313 | 72.2% |
| 25. | Gross operating profit | $300,446 | 32.9% | $279,470 | 27.8% |
| 26. | Additional operating costs | $213,604 | 23.4% | $189,397 | 18.9% |
| 27. | Net operating profit | $86,842 | 9.5% | $90,073 | 9.0% |
| 28. | Less:  Guaranteed payments to partners | $11,967 |  | $13,718 |  |
| 29. | Distribution to partners | $74,875 |  | $76,355 |  |
| 30. | Other charges | $1,594 |  | $1,054 |  |
| 31. | Net change partners' capital | $73,281 |  | $75,301 |  |
|  | Selected Ratios |  |  |  |  |
| 32. | Coverage ratio:  times interest earned | 3.9 |  | 3.6 |  |
| 33. | Inventory turnover (times) | 1.0 |  | 11.9 |  |
| 34. | Days' sales in inventory | 41.7 |  | 34.1 |  |
| 35. | Average age of inventory (days) | 36.6 |  | 30.6 |  |
| 36. | Return on assets, net income | 17.0% |  | 17.4% |  |
| 37. | Return on assets, gross operating profit | 69.4% |  | 64.6% |  |
| 38. | Return on assets, net operating profit | 20.1% |  | 20.8% |  |

Table 2: Partnerships With Net Income:  056.  PRINTING, PUBLISHING, AND ALLIED INDUSTRIES

Dollar values in thousands, except averages

|  |  | 1984 |  | 1985 |  |
|---|---|---|---|---|---|
| 1. | Number of Partnerships | 2,941 | | 1,698 | |
| 2. | Number of Partners | 7,059 | | 5,306 | |
| 3. | Total Assets | $721,306 | | $1,071,139 | |
| 4. | Average total assets per Partnership | $245,259 | | $630,824 | |
| 5. | Average total assets per Partner | $102,182 | | $201,873 | |
| 6. | Net Income | $212,446 | | $277,436 | |
| 7. | Average per Partnership, total earnings | $72,241 | | $163,409 | |
| 8. | Average per Partner, total earnings | $30,098 | | $52,293 | |
| 9. | Operating Income | $1,175,702 | | $1,838,380 | |
|  | Operating Costs | | | | |
| 10. | Cost of sales & operations | $553,062 | 47.0% | $685,378 | 37.3% |
| 11. | Salaries and wages | $138,597 | 11.8% | $284,601 | 15.5% |
| 12. | Rent paid | $15,987 | 1.4% | $20,511 | 1.1% |
| 13. | Interest paid | $18,644 | 1.6% | $23,005 | 1.3% |
| 14. | Taxes paid | $22,058 | 1.9% | $39,532 | 2.2% |
| 15. | Bad debts | $3,694 | 0.3% | $7,327 | 0.4% |
| 16. | Repairs | $4,500 | 0.4% | $8,503 | 0.5% |
| 17. | Depreciation | $30,303 | 2.6% | $38,677 | 2.1% |
| 18. | Depletion | $0 | n.a. | $0 | n.a. |
| 19. | Pension & profit sharing plans | $3,475 | 0.3% | $6,845 | 0.4% |
| 20. | Employee benefits programs | $5,648 | 0.5% | $17,045 | 0.9% |
| 21. | Other deductions | $152,180 | 12.9% | $395,340 | 21.5% |
| 22. | Total operating costs | $948,586 | 80.7% | $1,527,412 | 83.1% |
|  | Operating Income and Distribution | | | | |
| 23. | Operating Income | $1,175,702 | 100.0% | $1,838,380 | 100.0% |
| 24. | Less: Cost of sales and operations | $553,062 | 47.0% | $685,378 | 37.3% |
| 25. | Gross operating profit | $622,640 | 53.0% | $1,153,002 | 62.7% |
| 26. | Additional operating costs | $395,524 | 33.6% | $842,034 | 45.8% |
| 27. | Net operating profit | $227,116 | 19.3% | $310,968 | 16.9% |
| 28. | Less: Guaranteed payments to partners | $15,152 | | $32,164 | |
| 29. | Distribution to partners | $211,964 | | $278,804 | |
| 30. | Other charges | $36 | | $2,016 | |
| 31. | Net change partners' capital | $211,928 | | $276,788 | |
|  | Selected Ratios | | | | |
| 32. | Coverage ratio:  times interest earned | 11.2 | | 12.5 | |
| 33. | Inventory turnover (times) | 19.7 | | 9.1 | |
| 34. | Days' sales in inventory | 20.1 | | 45.8 | |
| 35. | Average age of inventory (days) | 18.5 | | 40.3 | |
| 36. | Return on assets, net income | 29.5% | | 25.9% | |
| 37. | Return on assets, gross operating profit | 86.3% | | 107.6% | |
| 38. | Return on assets, net operating profit | 31.5% | | 29.0% | |

Table 2: Partnerships With Net Income:  062.  MACHINERY, EXCEPT ELECTRICAL

Dollar values in thousands, except averages

|  | 1984 | | 1985 | |
|---|---|---|---|---|
| 1. Number of Partnerships | 493 | | 260 | |
| 2. Number of Partners | 1,017 | | 576 | |
| 3. Total Assets | $192,920 | | $172,355 | |
| 4. Average total assets per Partnership | $391,318 | | $662,904 | |
| 5. Average total assets per Partner | $189,695 | | $299,227 | |
| 6. Net Income | $51,331 | | $31,233 | |
| 7. Average per Partnership, total earnings | $104,120 | | $120,175 | |
| 8. Average per Partner, total earnings | $50,473 | | $54,246 | |
| 9. Operating Income | $217,678 | | $337,331 | |
| Operating Costs | | | | |
| 10. Cost of sales & operations | $134,053 | 61.6% | $242,464 | 71.9% |
| 11. Salaries and wages | $3,799 | 1.8% | $8,776 | 2.6% |
| 12. Rent paid | $303 | 0.1% | $3,831 | 1.1% |
| 13. Interest paid | $9,924 | 4.6% | $1,248 | 0.4% |
| 14. Taxes paid | $595 | 0.3% | $3,539 | 1.1% |
| 15. Bad debts | $14 | 0.0% | $1,107 | 0.3% |
| 16. Repairs | $249 | 0.1% | $1,270 | 0.4% |
| 17. Depreciation | $4,234 | 2.0% | $6,570 | 2.0% |
| 18. Depletion | $0 | n.a. | $0 | n.a. |
| 19. Pension & profit sharing plans | $214 | 0.1% | $973 | 0.3% |
| 20. Employee benefits programs | $0 | n.a. | $1,701 | 0.5% |
| 21. Other deductions | $12,714 | 5.8% | $22,168 | 6.6% |
| 22. Total operating costs | $166,099 | 76.3% | $293,647 | 87.1% |
| Operating Income and Distribution | | | | |
| 23. Operating Income | $217,678 | 100.0% | $337,331 | 100.0% |
| 24. Less: Cost of sales and operations | $134,053 | 61.6% | $242,464 | 71.9% |
| 25. Gross operating profit | $83,625 | 38.4% | $94,867 | 28.1% |
| 26. Additional operating costs | $32,046 | 14.7% | $51,183 | 15.2% |
| 27. Net operating profit | $51,579 | 23.7% | $43,684 | 13.0% |
| 28. Less: Guaranteed payments to partners | $249 | | $12,451 | |
| 29. Distribution to partners | $51,330 | | $31,233 | |
| 30. Other charges | $0 | | $0 | |
| 31. Net change partners' capital | $51,330 | | $31,233 | |
| Selected Ratios | | | | |
| 32. Coverage ratio: times interest earned | 4.2 | | 34.0 | |
| 33. Inventory turnover (times) | 4.9 | | 7.4 | |
| 34. Days' sales in inventory | 70.9 | | 99.4 | |
| 35. Average age of inventory (days) | 75.3 | | 49.7 | |
| 36. Return on assets, net income | 26.6% | | 18.1% | |
| 37. Return on assets, gross operating profit | 43.4% | | 55.0% | |
| 38. Return on assets, net operating profit | 26.7% | | 25.4% | |

Table 2: Partnerships With Net Income:  OTHER MANUFACTURING INDUSTRIES (050,053,055,057-061,063,064,065,066)

Dollar values in thousands, except averages

| | 1984 | | 1985 | |
|---|---|---|---|---|
| 1. Number of Partnerships | 9,870 | | 9,153 | |
| 2. Number of Partners | 24,557 | | 24,453 | |
| | | | | |
| 3. Total Assets | $4,173,926 | | $5,997,124 | |
| 4. Average total assets per Partnership | $422,890 | | $655,209 | |
| 5. Average total assets per Partner | $169,969 | | $245,251 | |
| | | | | |
| 6. Net Income | $828,207 | | $844,385 | |
| 7. Average per Partnership, total earnings | $83,915 | | $92,257 | |
| 8. Average per Partner, total earnings | $33,727 | | $34,533 | |
| | | | | |
| 9. Operating Income | $8,043,447 | | $10,506,519 | |
| Operating Costs | | | | |
| 10. Cost of sales & operations | $5,614,195 | 69.8% | $7,484,161 | 71.2% |
| 11. Salaries and wages | $370,531 | 4.6% | $496,927 | 4.7% |
| 12. Rent paid | $62,157 | 0.8% | $83,024 | 0.8% |
| 13. Interest paid | $122,253 | 1.5% | $188,425 | 1.8% |
| 14. Taxes paid | $82,845 | 1.0% | $100,421 | 0.10% |
| 15. Bad debts | $13,420 | 0.2% | $14,743 | 0.1% |
| 16. Repairs | $49,879 | 0.6% | $54,079 | 0.5% |
| 17. Depreciation | $150,216 | 1.9% | $203,619 | 1.9% |
| 18. Depletion | $4,273 | 0.1% | $4,743 | 0.1% |
| 19. Pension & profit sharing plans | $7,980 | 0.1% | $23,455 | 0.2% |
| 20. Employee benefits programs | $25,844 | 0.3% | $30,830 | 0.3% |
| 21. Other deductions | $672,554 | 8.4% | $931,117 | 8.9% |
| 22. Total operating costs | $7,176,347 | 89.2% | $9,616,655 | 91.5% |
| | | | | |
| Operating Income and Distribution | | | | |
| 23. Operating Income | $8,043,447 | 100.0% | $10,506,519 | 100.0% |
| 24. Less: Cost of sales and operations | $5,614,195 | 69.8% | $7,484,161 | 71.2% |
| 25. Gross operating profit | $2,429,252 | 30.2% | $3,022,358 | 28.8% |
| 26. Additional operating costs | $1,562,152 | 19.4% | $2,132,494 | 20.3% |
| 27. Net operating profit | $867,100 | 10.8% | $889,864 | 8.5% |
| 28. Less: Guaranteed payments to partners | $36,800 | | $42,749 | |
| 29. Distribution to partners | $830,300 | | $847,115 | |
| 30. Other charges | $2,293 | | $3,842 | |
| 31. Net change partners' capital | $828,007 | | $843,273 | |
| | | | | |
| Selected Ratios | | | | |
| 32. Coverage ratio: times interest earned | 6.1 | | 3.7 | |
| 33. Inventory turnover (times) | 8.4 | | 6.8 | |
| 34. Days' sales in inventory | 49.6 | | 57.0 | |
| 35. Average age of inventory (days) | 43.3 | | 53.9 | |
| 36. Return on assets, net income | 19.8% | | 14.1% | |
| 37. Return on assets, gross operating profit | 58.2% | | 50.4% | |
| 38. Return on assets, net operating profit | 20.8% | | 14.8% | |

Table 2: Partnerships With Net Income:  067.  TRANSPORTATION, COMMUNICATION ELECTRIC, GAS, AND SANITARY SERVICES

Dollar values in thousands, except averages

| | 1984 | | 1985 | |
|---|---|---|---|---|
| 1.  Number of Partnerships | 13,553 | | 14,744 | |
| 2.  Number of Partners | 42,949 | | 45,423 | |
| | | | | |
| 3.  Total Assets | $5,200,772 | | $5,857,966 | |
| 4.   Average total assets per Partnership | $383,736 | | $397,312 | |
| 5.   Average total assets per Partner | $121,092 | | $128,965 | |
| | | | | |
| 6.  Net Income | $1,280,499 | | $1,360,425 | |
| 7.   Average per Partnership, total earnings | $94,486 | | $92,276 | |
| 8.   Average per Partner, total earnings | $29,816 | | $29,952 | |
| | | | | |
| 9.  Operating Income | $7,804,033 | | $6,388,561 | |
| Operating Costs | | | | |
| 10.   Cost of sales & operations | $4,283,095 | 54.9% | $2,474,475 | 38.7% |
| 11.   Salaries and wages | $284,279 | 3.6% | $260,834 | 4.1% |
| 12.   Rent paid | $61,047 | 0.8% | $77,570 | 1.2% |
| 13.   Interest paid | $215,598 | 2.8% | $223,481 | 3.5% |
| 14.   Taxes paid | $79,414 | 1.0% | $75,811 | 1.2% |
| 15.   Bad debts | $9,332 | 0.1% | $8,986 | 0.1% |
| 16.   Repairs | $116,377 | 1.5% | $104,112 | 1.6% |
| 17.   Depreciation | $414,316 | 5.3% | $545,578 | 8.5% |
| 18.   Depletion | $0 | n.a. | $0 | n.a. |
| 19.   Pension & profit sharing plans | $2,533 | 0.0% | $7,845 | 0.1% |
| 20.   Employee benefits programs | $16,552 | 0.2% | $5,569 | 0.1% |
| 21.   Other deductions | $961,862 | 12.3% | $1,154,072 | 18.1% |
| 22.   Total operating costs | $6,444,406 | 82.6% | $4,938,493 | 77.3% |
| | | | | |
| Operating Income and Distribution | | | | |
| 23.   Operating Income | $7,804,033 | 100.0% | $6,388,561 | 100.0% |
| 24.    Less:  Cost of sales and operations | $4,283,095 | 54.9% | $2,474,475 | 38.7% |
| 25.   Gross operating profit | $3,520,938 | 45.1% | $3,914,086 | 61.3% |
| 26.    Additional operating costs | $2,161,311 | 27.7% | $2,464,018 | 38.6% |
| 27.   Net operating profit | $1,359,627 | 17.4% | $1,450,068 | 22.7% |
| 28.    Less:  Guaranteed payments to partners | $73,060 | | $86,901 | |
| 29.   Distribution to partners | $1,286,567 | | $1,363,167 | |
| 30.   Other charges | $6,068 | | $2,902 | |
| 31.   Net change partners' capital | $1,280,499 | | $1,360,265 | |
| | | | | |
| Selected Ratios | | | | |
| 32.   Coverage ratio:  times interest earned | 5.3 | | 5.5 | |
| 33.   Inventory turnover (times) | n.a. | | n.a. | |
| 34.   Days' sales in inventory | n.a. | | n.a. | |
| 35.   Average age of inventory (days) | n.a. | | n.a. | |
| 36.   Return on assets, net income | 24.6% | | 23.2% | |
| 37.   Return on assets, gross operating profit | 67.7% | | 66.8% | |
| 38.   Return on assets, net operating profit | 26.1% | | 24.8% | |

Table 2: Partnerships With Net Income:  TRANSPORTATION, TOTAL (068,071,074,075,076)

Dollar values in thousands, except averages

| | | 1984 | | 1985 | |
|---|---|---|---|---|---|
| 1. | Number of Partnerships | 10,169 | | 10,445 | |
| 2. | Number of Partners | 34,040 | | 26,087 | |
| | | | | | |
| 3. | Total Assets | $3,026,465 | | $3,287,940 | |
| 4. | Average total assets per Partnership | $297,617 | | $314,786 | |
| 5. | Average total assets per Partner | $88,909 | | $126,037 | |
| | | | | | |
| 6. | Net Income | $972,883 | | $998,164 | |
| 7. | Average per Partnership, total earnings | $95,678 | | $95,569 | |
| 8. | Average per Partner, total earnings | $28,582 | | $38,265 | |
| | | | | | |
| 9. | Operating Income | $5,982,628 | | $4,340,849 | |
| | Operating Costs | | | | |
| 10. | Cost of sales & operations | $3,481,438 | 58.2% | $1,715,945 | 39.5% |
| 11. | Salaries and wages | $180,101 | 3.0% | $150,255 | 3.5% |
| 12. | Rent paid | $46,149 | 0.8% | $57,960 | 1.3% |
| 13. | Interest paid | $122,560 | 2.1% | $139,170 | 3.2% |
| 14. | Taxes paid | $55,449 | 0.9% | $49,796 | 1.2% |
| 15. | Bad debts | $2,475 | 0.0% | $1,203 | 0.0% |
| 16. | Repairs | $102,349 | 1.7% | $88,047 | 2.0% |
| 17. | Depreciation | $265,713 | 4.4% | $371,336 | 8.6% |
| 18. | Depletion | $0 | n.a. | $0 | n.a. |
| 19. | Pension & profit sharing plans | $1,879 | 0.0% | $7,536 | 0.2% |
| 20. | Employee benefits programs | $11,156 | 0.2% | $1,682 | 0.0% |
| 21. | Other deductions | $673,145 | 11.3% | $706,397 | 16.3% |
| 22. | Total operating costs | $4,942,414 | 82.6% | $3,289,487 | 75.8% |
| | | | | | |
| | Operating Income and Distribution | | | | |
| 23. | Operating Income | $5,982,628 | 100.0% | $4,340,849 | 100.0% |
| 24. | Less:  Cost of sales and operations | $3,481,438 | 58.2% | $1,715,945 | 39.5% |
| 25. | Gross operating profit | $2,501,190 | 41.8% | $2,624,904 | 60.5% |
| 26. | Additional operating costs | $1,460,976 | 24.4% | $1,573,542 | 36.3% |
| 27. | Net operating profit | $1,040,214 | 17.4% | $1,051,362 | 24.2% |
| 28. | Less:  Guaranteed payments to partners | $62,831 | | $53,208 | |
| 29. | Distribution to partners | $977,383 | | $998,154 | |
| 30. | Other charges | $4,500 | | $149 | |
| 31. | Net change partners' capital | $972,883 | | $998,005 | |
| | | | | | |
| | Selected Ratios | | | | |
| 32. | Coverage ratio:  times interest earned | 7.5 | | 6.6 | |
| 33. | Inventory turnover (times) | n.a. | | n.a. | |
| 34. | Days' sales in inventory | n.a. | | n.a. | |
| 35. | Average age of inventory (days) | n.a. | | n.a. | |
| 36. | Return on assets, net income | 32.2% | | 30.4% | |
| 37. | Return on assets, gross operating profit | 82.6% | | 79.8% | |
| 38. | Return on assets, net operating profit | 34.4% | | 32.0% | |

Table 2: Partnerships With Net Income:  071.  TRUCKING AND WAREHOUSING

Dollar values in thousands, except averages

|  |  | 1984 |  | 1985 |  |
|---|---|---|---|---|---|
| 1. | Number of Partnerships | 8,390 | | 8,028 | |
| 2. | Number of Partners | 27,545 | | 19,085 | |
| 3. | Total Assets | $1,075,166 | | $985,662 | |
| 4. | Average total assets per Partnership | $128,149 | | $122,778 | |
| 5. | Average total assets per Partner | $39,033 | | $51,646 | |
| 6. | Net Income | $183,689 | | $194,280 | |
| 7. | Average per Partnership, total earnings | $21,901 | | $24,203 | |
| 8. | Average per Partner, total earnings | $6,671 | | $10,181 | |
| 9. | Operating Income | $3,075,912 | | $1,352,626 | |
| | Operating Costs | | | | |
| 10. | Cost of sales & operations | $1,951,828 | 63.5% | $315,346 | 23.3% |
| 11. | Salaries and wages | $136,935 | 4.5% | $79,020 | 5.8% |
| 12. | Rent paid | $36,200 | 1.2% | $45,980 | 3.4% |
| 13. | Interest paid | $58,820 | 1.9% | $56,758 | 4.2% |
| 14. | Taxes paid | $38,750 | 1.3% | $28,889 | 2.1% |
| 15. | Bad debts | $528 | 0.0% | $166 | 0.0% |
| 16. | Repairs | $86,825 | 2.8% | $66,485 | 4.9% |
| 17. | Depreciation | $143,238 | 4.7% | $209,992 | 15.5% |
| 18. | Depletion | $0 | n.a. | $0 | n.a. |
| 19. | Pension & profit sharing plans | $1,325 | 0.0% | $487 | 0.0% |
| 20. | Employee benefits programs | $10,480 | 0.3% | $486 | 0.0% |
| 21. | Other deductions | $367,717 | 12.0% | $336,239 | 24.9% |
| 22. | Total operating costs | $2,832,646 | 92.1% | $1,140,008 | 84.3% |
| | Operating Income and Distribution | | | | |
| 23. | Operating Income | $3,075,912 | 100.0% | $1,352,626 | 100.0% |
| 24. | Less:  Cost of sales and operations | $1,951,828 | 63.5% | $315,346 | 23.3% |
| 25. | Gross operating profit | $1,124,084 | 36.5% | $1,037,280 | 76.7% |
| 26. | Additional operating costs | $880,818 | 28.6% | $824,662 | 61.0% |
| 27. | Net operating profit | $243,266 | 7.9% | $212,618 | 15.7% |
| 28. | Less:  Guaranteed payments to partners | $57,334 | | $18,498 | |
| 29. | Distribution to partners | $185,932 | | $194,120 | |
| 30. | Other charges | $2,243 | | $0 | |
| 31. | Net change partners' capital | $183,689 | | $194,120 | |
| | Selected Ratios | | | | |
| 32. | Coverage ratio:  times interest earned | 3.1 | | 2.8 | |
| 33. | Inventory turnover (times) | n.a. | | 511.1 | |
| 34. | Days' sales in inventory | n.a. | | 0.7 | |
| 35. | Average age of inventory (days) | n.a. | | 0.7 | |
| 36. | Return on assets, net income | 17.1% | | 19.7% | |
| 37. | Return on assets, gross operating profit | 104.6% | | 105.2% | |
| 38. | Return on assets, net operating profit | 22.6% | | 21.6% | |

*Page 136*

**Table 2: Partnerships With Net Income: OTHER TRANSPORTATION (069,070,074,075,076)**

Dollar values in thousands, except averages

| | | 1984 | | 1985 | |
|---|---|---|---|---|---|
| 1. | Number of Partnerships | 1,778 | | 2,417 | |
| 2. | Number of Partners | 6,495 | | 7,002 | |
| 3. | Total Assets | $1,951,300 | | $2,302,278 | |
| 4. | Average total assets per Partnership | $1,097,469 | | $952,535 | |
| 5. | Average total assets per Partner | $300,431 | | $328,803 | |
| 6. | Net Income | $789,195 | | $803,884 | |
| 7. | Average per Partnership, total earnings | $443,870 | | $332,610 | |
| 8. | Average per Partner, total earnings | $121,509 | | $114,813 | |
| 9. | Operating Income | $2,906,716 | | $2,988,223 | |
| | Operating Costs | | | | |
| 10. | Cost of sales & operations | $1,529,611 | 52.6% | $1,400,599 | 46.9% |
| 11. | Salaries and wages | $43,166 | 1.5% | $71,235 | 2.4% |
| 12. | Rent paid | $9,948 | 0.3% | $11,981 | 0.4% |
| 13. | Interest paid | $63,741 | 2.2% | $82,412 | 2.8% |
| 14. | Taxes paid | $16,699 | 0.6% | $20,907 | 0.7% |
| 15. | Bad debts | $1,947 | 0.1% | $1,037 | 0.0% |
| 16. | Repairs | $15,524 | 0.5% | $21,562 | 0.7% |
| 17. | Depreciation | $122,474 | 4.2% | $161,344 | 5.4% |
| 18. | Depletion | $0 | n.a. | $0 | n.a. |
| 19. | Pension & profit sharing plans | $554 | 0.0% | $7,049 | 0.2% |
| 20. | Employee benefits programs | $676 | 0.0% | $1,196 | 0.0% |
| 21. | Other deductions | $305,428 | 10.5% | $370,158 | 12.4% |
| 22. | Total operating costs | $2,109,768 | 72.6% | $2,149,480 | 71.9% |
| | Operating Income and Distribution | | | | |
| 23. | Operating Income | $2,906,716 | 100.0% | $2,988,223 | 100.0% |
| 24. | Less: Cost of sales and operations | $1,529,611 | 52.6% | $1,400,599 | 46.9% |
| 25. | Gross operating profit | $1,377,105 | 47.4% | $1,587,624 | 53.1% |
| 26. | Additional operating costs | $580,157 | 20.0% | $748,881 | 25.1% |
| 27. | Net operating profit | $796,948 | 27.4% | $838,743 | 28.1% |
| 28. | Less: Guaranteed payments to partners | $5,497 | | $34,710 | |
| 29. | Distribution to partners | $791,451 | | $804,033 | |
| 30. | Other charges | $2,257 | | $149 | |
| 31. | Net change partners' capital | $789,194 | | $803,884 | |
| | Selected Ratios | | | | |
| 32. | Coverage ratio: times interest earned | 11.5 | | 9.2 | |
| 33. | Inventory turnover (times) | n.a. | | 173.6 | |
| 34. | Days' sales in inventory | n.a. | | 2.2 | |
| 35. | Average age of inventory (days) | n.a. | | 2.1 | |
| 36. | Return on assets, net income | 40.4% | | 34.9% | |
| 37. | Return on assets, gross operating profit | 70.6% | | 69.0% | |
| 38. | Return on assets, net operating profit | 40.8% | | 36.4% | |

Table 2: Partnerships With Net Income:  COMMUNICATION, ELECTRIC, GAS AND SANITARY SERVICES (080,081,082)

Dollar values in thousands, except averages

| | | 1984 | | 1985 | |
|---|---|---|---|---|---|
| 1. | Number of Partnerships | 3,384 | | 4,299 | |
| 2. | Number of Partners | 8,909 | | 19,336 | |
| | | | | | |
| 3. | Total Assets | $2,174,307 | | $2,570,026 | |
| 4. | Average total assets per Partnership | $642,526 | | $597,819 | |
| 5. | Average total assets per Partner | $244,057 | | $132,914 | |
| | | | | | |
| 6. | Net Income | $307,616 | | $362,261 | |
| 7. | Average per Partnership, total earnings | $90,906 | | $84,274 | |
| 8. | Average per Partner, total earnings | $34,530 | | $18,737 | |
| | | | | | |
| 9. | Operating Income | $1,821,404 | | $2,047,712 | |
| | Operating Costs | | | | |
| 10. | Cost of sales & operations | $801,657 | 44.0% | $758,530 | 37.0% |
| 11. | Salaries and wages | $104,178 | 5.7% | $110,579 | 5.4% |
| 12. | Rent paid | $14,898 | 0.8% | $19,610 | 0.10% |
| 13. | Interest paid | $93,038 | 5.1% | $84,311 | 4.1% |
| 14. | Taxes paid | $23,965 | 1.3% | $26,015 | 1.3% |
| 15. | Bad debts | $6,857 | 0.4% | $7,783 | 0.4% |
| 16. | Repairs | $14,028 | 0.8% | $16,066 | 0.8% |
| 17. | Depreciation | $148,602 | 8.2% | $174,242 | 8.5% |
| 18. | Depletion | $0 | n.a. | $0 | n.a. |
| 19. | Pension & profit sharing plans | $654 | 0.0% | $309 | 0.0% |
| 20. | Employee benefits programs | $5,396 | 0.3% | $3,887 | 0.2% |
| 21. | Other deductions | $288,717 | 15.9% | $447,673 | 21.9% |
| 22. | Total operating costs | $1,501,991 | 82.5% | $1,649,005 | 80.5% |
| | | | | | |
| | Operating Income and Distribution | | | | |
| 23. | Operating Income | $1,821,404 | 100.0% | $2,047,712 | 100.0% |
| 24. | Less:  Cost of sales and operations | $801,657 | 44.0% | $758,530 | 37.0% |
| 25. | Gross operating profit | $1,019,747 | 56.0% | $1,289,182 | 63.0% |
| 26. | Additional operating costs | $700,334 | 38.5% | $890,475 | 43.5% |
| 27. | Net operating profit | $319,413 | 17.5% | $398,707 | 19.5% |
| 28. | Less:  Guaranteed payments to partners | $10,230 | | $33,693 | |
| 29. | Distribution to partners | $309,183 | | $365,014 | |
| 30. | Other charges | $1,568 | | $2,753 | |
| 31. | Net change partners' capital | $307,615 | | $362,261 | |
| | | | | | |
| | Selected Ratios | | | | |
| 32. | Coverage ratio:  times interest earned | 2.4 | | 3.7 | |
| 33. | Inventory turnover (times) | n.a. | | 63.1 | |
| 34. | Days' sales in inventory | n.a. | | 5.8 | |
| 35. | Average age of inventory (days) | n.a. | | 5.8 | |
| 36. | Return on assets, net income | 14.2% | | 14.1% | |
| 37. | Return on assets, gross operating profit | 46.9% | | 50.2% | |
| 38. | Return on assets, net operating profit | 14.7% | | 15.5% | |

Table 2: Partnerships With Net Income:  083.  WHOLESALE AND RETAIL TRADE

Dollar values in thousands, except averages

|  |  | 1984 |  | 1985 |  |
|---|---|---|---|---|---|
| 1. | Number of Partnerships | 97,879 |  | 113,172 |  |
| 2. | Number of Partners | 231,710 |  | 273,802 |  |
| 3. | Total Assets | $12,412,133 |  | $11,769,980 |  |
| 4. | Average total assets per Partnership | $126,811 |  | $104,001 |  |
| 5. | Average total assets per Partner | $53,568 |  | $42,987 |  |
| 6. | Net Income | $3,238,481 |  | $3,466,952 |  |
| 7. | Average per Partnership, total earnings | $33,092 |  | $30,638 |  |
| 8. | Average per Partner, total earnings | $13,979 |  | $12,664 |  |
| 9. | Operating Income | $47,823,585 |  | $47,461,234 |  |
|  | Operating Costs |  |  |  |  |
| 10. | Cost of sales & operations | $34,631,489 | 72.4% | $33,086,227 | 69.7% |
| 11. | Salaries and wages | $2,975,232 | 6.2% | $3,202,001 | 6.8% |
| 12. | Rent paid | $889,229 | 1.9% | $1,042,650 | 2.2% |
| 13. | Interest paid | $401,485 | 0.8% | $388,746 | 0.8% |
| 14. | Taxes paid | $591,813 | 1.2% | $682,793 | 1.4% |
| 15. | Bad debts | $57,502 | 0.1% | $60,336 | 0.1% |
| 16. | Repairs | $198,299 | 0.4% | $252,879 | 0.5% |
| 17. | Depreciation | $530,720 | 1.1% | $559,380 | 1.2% |
| 18. | Depletion | $5,724 | 0.0% | $2,551 | 0.0% |
| 19. | Pension & profit sharing plans | $24,616 | 0.1% | $31,699 | 0.1% |
| 20. | Employee benefits programs | $64,502 | 0.1% | $50,589 | 0.1% |
| 21. | Other deductions | $3,672,656 | 7.7% | $4,149,601 | 8.7% |
| 22. | Total operating costs | $44,048,161 | 92.1% | $43,512,288 | 91.7% |
|  | Operating Income and Distribution |  |  |  |  |
| 23. | Operating Income | $47,823,585 | 100.0% | $47,461,234 | 100.0% |
| 24. | Less: Cost of sales and operations | $34,631,489 | 72.4% | $33,086,227 | 69.7% |
| 25. | Gross operating profit | $13,192,096 | 27.6% | $14,375,007 | 30.3% |
| 26. | Additional operating costs | $9,416,672 | 19.7% | $10,426,061 | 22.0% |
| 27. | Net operating profit | $3,775,424 | 7.9% | $3,948,946 | 8.3% |
| 28. | Less: Guaranteed payments to partners | $527,136 |  | $465,589 |  |
| 29. | Distribution to partners | $3,248,288 |  | $3,483,357 |  |
| 30. | Other charges | $14,701 |  | $19,241 |  |
| 31. | Net change partners' capital | $3,233,587 |  | $3,464,116 |  |
|  | Selected Ratios |  |  |  |  |
| 32. | Coverage ratio: times interest earned | 8.4 |  | 9.2 |  |
| 33. | Inventory turnover (times) | 9.1 |  | 8.5 |  |
| 34. | Days' sales in inventory | 42.8 |  | 45.5 |  |
| 35. | Average age of inventory (days) | 40.3 |  | 42.9 |  |
| 36. | Return on assets, net income | 26.1% |  | 29.5% |  |
| 37. | Return on assets, gross operating profit | 106.3% |  | 122.1% |  |
| 38. | Return on assets, net operating profit | 30.4% |  | 33.6% |  |

*Page 139*

Table 2: Partnerships With Net Income:  084.  WHOLESALE TRADE

Dollar values in thousands, except averages

|  |  | 1984 |  | 1985 |  |
|---|---|---|---|---|---|
| 1. | Number of Partnerships | 14,731 | | 18,082 | |
| 2. | Number of Partners | 34,896 | | 45,746 | |
| 3. | Total Assets | $4,359,868 | | $3,711,114 | |
| 4. | Average total assets per Partnership | $295,966 | | $205,238 | |
| 5. | Average total assets per Partner | $124,939 | | $81,124 | |
| 6. | Net Income | $839,618 | | $857,136 | |
| 7. | Average per Partnership, total earnings | $57,008 | | $47,408 | |
| 8. | Average per Partner, total earnings | $24,066 | | $18,739 | |
| 9. | Operating Income | $14,752,918 | | $14,065,531 | |
|  | Operating Costs |  | | | |
| 10. | Cost of sales & operations | $11,819,790 | 80.1% | $10,996,113 | 78.2% |
| 11. | Salaries and wages | $504,300 | 3.4% | $534,287 | 3.8% |
| 12. | Rent paid | $100,420 | 0.7% | $102,775 | 0.7% |
| 13. | Interest paid | $137,033 | 0.9% | $101,161 | 0.7% |
| 14. | Taxes paid | $94,570 | 0.6% | $101,566 | 0.7% |
| 15. | Bad debts | $21,495 | 0.2% | $23,185 | 0.2% |
| 16. | Repairs | $41,724 | 0.3% | $63,378 | 0.5% |
| 17. | Depreciation | $99,099 | 0.7% | $94,519 | 0.7% |
| 18. | Depletion | $4,575 | 0.0% | $2,514 | 0.0% |
| 19. | Pension & profit sharing plans | $13,538 | 0.1% | $10,973 | 0.1% |
| 20. | Employee benefits programs | $23,438 | 0.2% | $14,900 | 0.1% |
| 21. | Other deductions | $874,057 | 5.9% | $1,052,044 | 7.5% |
| 22. | Total operating costs | $13,734,067 | 93.1% | $13,097,458 | 93.1% |
|  | Operating Income and Distribution |  | | | |
| 23. | Operating Income | $14,752,918 | 100.0% | $14,065,531 | 100.0% |
| 24. | Less:  Cost of sales and operations | $11,819,790 | 80.1% | $10,996,113 | 78.2% |
| 25. | Gross operating profit | $2,933,128 | 19.9% | $3,069,418 | 21.8% |
| 26. | Additional operating costs | $1,914,277 | 13.0% | $2,101,345 | 14.9% |
| 27. | Net operating profit | $1,018,851 | 6.9% | $968,073 | 6.9% |
| 28. | Less:  Guaranteed payments to partners | $172,821 | | $102,957 | |
| 29. | Distribution to partners | $846,030 | | $865,116 | |
| 30. | Other charges | $6,440 | | $8,024 | |
| 31. | Net change partners' capital | $839,590 | | $857,092 | |
|  | Selected Ratios |  | | | |
| 32. | Coverage ratio:  times interest earned | 6.4 | | 8.6 | |
| 33. | Inventory turnover (times) | 12.8 | | 11.9 | |
| 34. | Days' sales in inventory | 31.7 | | 32.5 | |
| 35. | Average age of inventory (days) | 28.6 | | 30.7 | |
| 36. | Return on assets, net income | 19.3% | | 23.1% | |
| 37. | Return on assets, gross operating profit | 67.3% | | 82.7% | |
| 38. | Return on assets, net operating profit | 23.4% | | 26.1% | |

Table 2: Partnerships With Net Income:  100.  RETAIL TRADE

Dollar values in thousands, except averages

|  | 1984 | | 1985 | |
|---|---|---|---|---|
| 1.  Number of Partnerships | 83,141 | | 94,585 | |
| 2.  Number of Partners | 196,795 | | 227,044 | |
| 3.  Total Assets | $8,040,801 | | $8,058,866 | |
| 4.    Average total assets per Partnership | $96,713 | | $85,202 | |
| 5.    Average total assets per Partner | $40,859 | | $35,495 | |
| 6.  Net Income | $2,398,115 | | $2,607,636 | |
| 7.    Average per Partnership, total earnings | $28,848 | | $27,573 | |
| 8.    Average per Partner, total earnings | $12,188 | | $11,487 | |
| 9.  Operating Income | $33,037,569 | | $33,336,868 | |
| Operating Costs | | | | |
| 10.   Cost of sales & operations | $22,783,176 | 69.0% | $22,034,915 | 66.1% |
| 11.   Salaries and wages | $2,469,348 | 7.5% | $2,667,714 | 8.0% |
| 12.   Rent paid | $788,745 | 2.4% | $939,876 | 2.8% |
| 13.   Interest paid | $264,414 | 0.8% | $287,586 | 0.9% |
| 14.   Taxes paid | $497,049 | 1.5% | $581,210 | 1.7% |
| 15.   Bad debts | $35,963 | 0.1% | $37,151 | 0.1% |
| 16.   Repairs | $156,420 | 0.5% | $189,482 | 0.6% |
| 17.   Depreciation | $431,271 | 1.3% | $464,861 | 1.4% |
| 18.   Depletion | $1,149 | n.a. | $37 | n.a. |
| 19.   Pension & profit sharing plans | $11,078 | 0.0% | $20,726 | 0.1% |
| 20.   Employee benefits programs | $41,012 | 0.1% | $35,690 | 0.1% |
| 21.   Other deductions | $2,797,326 | 8.5% | $3,096,132 | 9.3% |
| 22.   Total operating costs | $30,281,817 | 91.7% | $30,358,173 | 91.1% |
| Operating Income and Distribution | | | | |
| 23.   Operating Income | $33,037,569 | 100.0% | $33,336,868 | 100.0% |
| 24.     Less:  Cost of sales and operations | $22,783,176 | 69.0% | $22,034,915 | 66.1% |
| 25.   Gross operating profit | $10,254,393 | 31.0% | $11,301,953 | 33.9% |
| 26.     Additional operating costs | $7,498,641 | 22.7% | $8,323,258 | 25.0% |
| 27.   Net operating profit | $2,755,752 | 8.3% | $2,978,695 | 8.9% |
| 28.     Less:  Guaranteed payments to partners | $354,242 | | $362,633 | |
| 29.   Distribution to partners | $2,401,510 | | $2,616,062 | |
| 30.   Other charges | $8,261 | | $11,219 | |
| 31.   Net change partners' capital | $2,393,249 | | $2,604,843 | |
| Selected Ratios | | | | |
| 32.   Coverage ratio:  times interest earned | 9.4 | | 9.4 | |
| 33.   Inventory turnover (times) | 7.9 | | 7.4 | |
| 34.   Days' sales in inventory | 48.6 | | 52.1 | |
| 35.   Average age of inventory (days) | 46.3 | | 49.1 | |
| 36.   Return on assets, net income | 29.8% | | 32.4% | |
| 37.   Return on assets, gross operating profit | 127.5% | | 140.2% | |
| 38.   Return on assets, net operating profit | 34.3% | | 37.0% | |

*Page 141*

Table 2: Partnerships With Net Income:  101.  BUILDING MATERIALS, PAINT, HARDWARE, GARDEN SUPPLY, AND MOBILE HOME DEALERS

Dollar values in thousands, except averages

|  |  | 1984 |  | 1985 |  |
|---|---|---|---|---|---|
| 1. | Number of Partnerships | 2,918 |  | 3,911 |  |
| 2. | Number of Partners | 7,606 |  | 9,358 |  |
| 3. | Total Assets | $818,446 |  | $714,942 |  |
| 4. | Average total assets per Partnership | $280,482 |  | $182,803 |  |
| 5. | Average total assets per Partner | $107,605 |  | $76,399 |  |
| 6. | Net Income | $208,625 |  | $159,409 |  |
| 7. | Average per Partnership, total earnings | $71,509 |  | $40,769 |  |
| 8. | Average per Partner, total earnings | $27,434 |  | $17,039 |  |
| 9. | Operating Income | $2,096,543 |  | $1,974,843 |  |
|  | Operating Costs |  |  |  |  |
| 10. | Cost of sales & operations | $1,400,597 | 66.8% | $1,343,477 | 68.0% |
| 11. | Salaries and wages | $133,953 | 6.4% | $146,367 | 7.4% |
| 12. | Rent paid | $26,313 | 1.3% | $25,181 | 1.3% |
| 13. | Interest paid | $23,707 | 1.1% | $19,272 | 0.10% |
| 14. | Taxes paid | $32,559 | 1.6% | $31,887 | 1.6% |
| 15. | Bad debts | $5,986 | 0.3% | $5,168 | 0.3% |
| 16. | Repairs | $7,656 | 0.4% | $11,661 | 0.6% |
| 17. | Depreciation | $20,860 | 0.10% | $21,636 | 1.1% |
| 18. | Depletion | $0 | n.a. | $0 | n.a. |
| 19. | Pension & profit sharing plans | $1,772 | 0.1% | $2,269 | 0.1% |
| 20. | Employee benefits programs | $9,208 | 0.4% | $3,230 | 0.2% |
| 21. | Other deductions | $186,874 | 8.9% | $165,157 | 8.4% |
| 22. | Total operating costs | $1,849,516 | 88.2% | $1,775,339 | 89.9% |
|  | Operating Income and Distribution |  |  |  |  |
| 23. | Operating Income | $2,096,543 | 100.0% | $1,974,843 | 100.0% |
| 24. | Less:  Cost of sales and operations | $1,400,597 | 66.8% | $1,343,477 | 68.0% |
| 25. | Gross operating profit | $695,946 | 33.2% | $631,366 | 32.0% |
| 26. | Additional operating costs | $448,919 | 21.4% | $431,862 | 21.9% |
| 27. | Net operating profit | $247,027 | 11.8% | $199,504 | 10.1% |
| 28. | Less:  Guaranteed payments to partners | $38,427 |  | $38,017 |  |
| 29. | Distribution to partners | $208,600 |  | $161,487 |  |
| 30. | Other charges | $6 |  | $2,112 |  |
| 31. | Net change partners' capital | $208,594 |  | $159,375 |  |
|  | Selected Ratios |  |  |  |  |
| 32. | Coverage ratio:  times interest earned | 9.4 |  | 9.4 |  |
| 33. | Inventory turnover (times) | 4.7 |  | 4.6 |  |
| 34. | Days' sales in inventory | 80.8 |  | 81.4 |  |
| 35. | Average age of inventory (days) | 78.3 |  | 79.1 |  |
| 36. | Return on assets, net income | 25.5% |  | 22.3% |  |
| 37. | Return on assets, gross operating profit | 85.0% |  | 88.3% |  |
| 38. | Return on assets, net operating profit | 30.2% |  | 27.9% |  |

Table 2: Partnerships With Net Income:  107.  GENERAL MERCHANDISE STORES

Dollar values in thousands, except averages

| | | 1984 | | 1985 | |
|---|---|---|---|---|---|
| 1. | Number of Partnerships | 1,739 | | 3,336 | |
| 2. | Number of Partners | 4,068 | | 7,188 | |
| 3. | Total Assets | $134,846 | | $306,922 | |
| 4. | Average total assets per Partnership | $77,542 | | $92,003 | |
| 5. | Average total assets per Partner | $33,148 | | $42,699 | |
| 6. | Net Income | $55,889 | | $64,883 | |
| 7. | Average per Partnership, total earnings | $32,144 | | $19,451 | |
| 8. | Average per Partner, total earnings | $13,741 | | $9,027 | |
| 9. | Operating Income | $534,676 | | $1,073,173 | |
| | Operating Costs | | | | |
| 10. | Cost of sales & operations | $370,751 | 69.3% | $739,015 | 68.9% |
| 11. | Salaries and wages | $35,549 | 6.7% | $64,515 | 6.0% |
| 12. | Rent paid | $15,532 | 2.9% | $29,723 | 2.8% |
| 13. | Interest paid | $2,079 | 0.4% | $10,115 | 0.9% |
| 14. | Taxes paid | $4,857 | 0.9% | $14,650 | 1.4% |
| 15. | Bad debts | $809 | 0.2% | $606 | 0.1% |
| 16. | Repairs | $1,321 | 0.3% | $2,681 | 0.3% |
| 17. | Depreciation | $2,908 | 0.5% | $11,708 | 1.1% |
| 18. | Depletion | $0 | n.a. | $0 | n.a. |
| 19. | Pension & profit sharing plans | $764 | 0.1% | $679 | 0.1% |
| 20. | Employee benefits programs | $422 | 0.1% | $741 | 0.1% |
| 21. | Other deductions | $34,777 | 6.5% | $127,490 | 11.9% |
| 22. | Total operating costs | $469,828 | 87.9% | $1,001,984 | 93.4% |
| | Operating Income and Distribution | | | | |
| 23. | Operating Income | $534,676 | 100.0% | $1,073,173 | 100.0% |
| 24. | Less: Cost of sales and operations | $370,751 | 69.3% | $739,015 | 68.9% |
| 25. | Gross operating profit | $163,925 | 30.7% | $334,158 | 31.1% |
| 26. | Additional operating costs | $99,077 | 18.5% | $262,969 | 24.5% |
| 27. | Net operating profit | $64,848 | 12.1% | $71,189 | 6.6% |
| 28. | Less: Guaranteed payments to partners | $9,018 | | $6,367 | |
| 29. | Distribution to partners | $55,830 | | $64,822 | |
| 30. | Other charges | $0 | | $0 | |
| 31. | Net change partners' capital | $55,830 | | $64,822 | |
| | Selected Ratios | | | | |
| 32. | Coverage ratio: times interest earned | 30.2 | | 6.0 | |
| 33. | Inventory turnover (times) | 4.9 | | 7.2 | |
| 34. | Days' sales in inventory | 78.0 | | 60.1 | |
| 35. | Average age of inventory (days) | 74.2 | | 51.1 | |
| 36. | Return on assets, net income | 41.5% | | 21.1% | |
| 37. | Return on assets, gross operating profit | 121.6% | | 108.9% | |
| 38. | Return on assets, net operating profit | 48.1% | | 23.2% | |

*Page 143*

Table 2: Partnerships With Net Income:   110.   FOOD STORES

Dollar values in thousands, except averages

|  |  | 1984 |  | 1985 |  |
|---|---|---|---|---|---|
| 1. | Number of Partnerships | 16,213 |  | 13,591 |  |
| 2. | Number of Partners | 35,389 |  | 28,796 |  |
| 3. | Total Assets | $960,445 |  | $725,107 |  |
| 4. | Average total assets per Partnership | $59,239 |  | $53,352 |  |
| 5. | Average total assets per Partner | $27,140 |  | $25,181 |  |
| 6. | Net Income | $373,226 |  | $292,759 |  |
| 7. | Average per Partnership, total earnings | $23,022 |  | $21,543 |  |
| 8. | Average per Partner, total earnings | $10,547 |  | $10,168 |  |
| 9. | Operating Income | $7,168,536 |  | $5,662,600 |  |
|  | Operating Costs |  |  |  |  |
| 10. | Cost of sales & operations | $5,573,173 | 77.7% | $4,312,156 | 76.2% |
| 11. | Salaries and wages | $407,045 | 5.7% | $323,593 | 5.7% |
| 12. | Rent paid | $104,453 | 1.5% | $106,935 | 1.9% |
| 13. | Interest paid | $28,561 | 0.4% | $33,871 | 0.6% |
| 14. | Taxes paid | $75,240 | 1.1% | $69,132 | 1.2% |
| 15. | Bad debts | $5,325 | 0.1% | $5,928 | 0.1% |
| 16. | Repairs | $21,351 | 0.3% | $24,848 | 0.4% |
| 17. | Depreciation | $69,633 | 0.10% | $68,234 | 1.2% |
| 18. | Depletion | $33 | n.a. | $37 | n.a. |
| 19. | Pension & profit sharing plans | $1,246 | 0.0% | $2,640 | 0.1% |
| 20. | Employee benefits programs | $6,118 | 0.1% | $7,440 | 0.1% |
| 21. | Other deductions | $473,395 | 6.6% | $377,999 | 6.7% |
| 22. | Total operating costs | $6,767,758 | 94.4% | $5,332,865 | 94.2% |
|  | Operating Income and Distribution |  |  |  |  |
| 23. | Operating Income | $7,168,536 | 100.0% | $5,662,600 | 100.0% |
| 24. | Less:  Cost of sales and operations | $5,573,173 | 77.7% | $4,312,156 | 76.2% |
| 25. | Gross operating profit | $1,595,363 | 22.3% | $1,350,444 | 23.9% |
| 26. | Additional operating costs | $1,194,585 | 16.7% | $1,020,709 | 18.0% |
| 27. | Net operating profit | $400,778 | 5.6% | $329,735 | 5.8% |
| 28. | Less:  Guaranteed payments to partners | $28,310 |  | $34,052 |  |
| 29. | Distribution to partners | $372,468 |  | $295,683 |  |
| 30. | Other charges | $1,427 |  | $2,975 |  |
| 31. | Net change partners' capital | $371,041 |  | $292,708 |  |
|  | Selected Ratios |  |  |  |  |
| 32. | Coverage ratio:  times interest earned | 13.0 |  | 8.7 |  |
| 33. | Inventory turnover (times) | 17.1 |  | 14.9 |  |
| 34. | Days' sales in inventory | 22.4 |  | 24.6 |  |
| 35. | Average age of inventory (days) | 21.4 |  | 24.5 |  |
| 36. | Return on assets, net income | 38.9% |  | 40.4% |  |
| 37. | Return on assets, gross operating profit | 166.1% |  | 186.2% |  |
| 38. | Return on assets, net operating profit | 41.7% |  | 45.5% |  |

*Page 144*

Table 2: Partnerships With Net Income:  111.  GROCERY STORES

Dollar values in thousands, except averages

|  | | 1984 | | 1985 | |
|---|---|---|---|---|---|
| 1. | Number of Partnerships | 7,930 | | 8,759 | |
| 2. | Number of Partners | 17,344 | | 18,752 | |
| | | | | | |
| 3. | Total Assets | $683,103 | | $620,826 | |
| 4. | Average total assets per Partnership | $86,142 | | $70,879 | |
| 5. | Average total assets per Partner | $39,386 | | $33,107 | |
| | | | | | |
| 6. | Net Income | $193,019 | | $223,775 | |
| 7. | Average per Partnership, total earnings | $24,343 | | $25,550 | |
| 8. | Average per Partner, total earnings | $11,130 | | $11,934 | |
| | | | | | |
| 9. | Operating Income | $5,088,218 | | $4,237,200 | |
| | Operating Costs | | | | |
| 10. | Cost of sales & operations | $4,100,469 | 80.6% | $3,296,054 | 77.8% |
| 11. | Salaries and wages | $301,994 | 5.9% | $234,145 | 5.5% |
| 12. | Rent paid | $58,263 | 1.2% | $50,980 | 1.2% |
| 13. | Interest paid | $22,427 | 0.4% | $27,449 | 0.7% |
| 14. | Taxes paid | $49,320 | 0.10% | $46,933 | 1.1% |
| 15. | Bad debts | $5,104 | 0.1% | $5,732 | 0.1% |
| 16. | Repairs | $15,132 | 0.3% | $17,188 | 0.4% |
| 17. | Depreciation | $45,861 | 0.9% | $52,332 | 1.2% |
| 18. | Depletion | $0 | n.a. | $0 | n.a. |
| 19. | Pension & profit sharing plans | $1,174 | 0.0% | $2,531 | 0.1% |
| 20. | Employee benefits programs | $5,017 | 0.1% | $6,364 | 0.2% |
| 21. | Other deductions | $269,991 | 5.3% | $252,790 | 6.0% |
| 22. | Total operating costs | $4,876,937 | 95.9% | $3,992,549 | 94.2% |
| | | | | | |
| | Operating Income and Distribution | | | | |
| 23. | Operating Income | $5,088,218 | 100.0% | $4,237,200 | 100.0% |
| 24. | Less:  Cost of sales and operations | $4,100,469 | 80.6% | $3,296,054 | 77.8% |
| 25. | Gross operating profit | $987,749 | 19.4% | $941,146 | 22.2% |
| 26. | Additional operating costs | $776,468 | 15.3% | $696,495 | 16.4% |
| 27. | Net operating profit | $211,281 | 4.2% | $244,651 | 5.8% |
| 28. | Less:  Guaranteed payments to partners | $19,367 | | $18,059 | |
| 29. | Distribution to partners | $191,914 | | $226,592 | |
| 30. | Other charges | $1,080 | | $2,868 | |
| 31. | Net change partners' capital | $190,834 | | $223,724 | |
| | | | | | |
| | Selected Ratios | | | | |
| 32. | Coverage ratio:  times interest earned | 8.4 | | 7.9 | |
| 33. | Inventory turnover (times) | 14.9 | | 13.7 | |
| 34. | Days' sales in inventory | 25.4 | | 27.1 | |
| 35. | Average age of inventory (days) | 24.4 | | 26.7 | |
| 36. | Return on assets, net income | 28.3% | | 36.0% | |
| 37. | Return on assets, gross operating profit | 144.6% | | 151.6% | |
| 38. | Return on assets, net operating profit | 30.9% | | 39.4% | |

Table 2: Partnerships With Net Income:  OTHER FOOD STORES (112,113,114,115,116,117)

Dollar values in thousands, except averages

|  |  | 1984 | | 1985 | |
|---|---|---|---|---|---|
| 1. | Number of Partnerships | 8,282 | | 4,832 | |
| 2. | Number of Partners | 18,045 | | 10,044 | |
| | | | | | |
| 3. | Total Assets | $277,341 | | $104,280 | |
| 4. | Average total assets per Partnership | $33,487 | | $21,581 | |
| 5. | Average total assets per Partner | $15,369 | | $10,382 | |
| | | | | | |
| 6. | Net Income | $180,206 | | $68,985 | |
| 7. | Average per Partnership, total earnings | $21,760 | | $14,280 | |
| 8. | Average per Partner, total earnings | $9,987 | | $6,870 | |
| | | | | | |
| 9. | Operating Income | $2,080,318 | | $1,425,400 | |
| | Operating Costs | | | | |
| 10. | Cost of sales & operations | $1,472,704 | 70.8% | $1,016,101 | 71.3% |
| 11. | Salaries and wages | $105,051 | 5.1% | $89,447 | 6.3% |
| 12. | Rent paid | $46,190 | 2.2% | $55,955 | 3.9% |
| 13. | Interest paid | $6,133 | 0.3% | $6,423 | 0.5% |
| 14. | Taxes paid | $25,921 | 1.3% | $22,199 | 1.6% |
| 15. | Bad debts | $221 | 0.0% | $196 | 0.0% |
| 16. | Repairs | $6,219 | 0.3% | $7,659 | 0.5% |
| 17. | Depreciation | $23,771 | 1.1% | $15,902 | 1.1% |
| 18. | Depletion | $33 | n.a. | $37 | n.a. |
| 19. | Pension & profit sharing plans | $72 | n.a. | $110 | 0.0% |
| 20. | Employee benefits programs | $1,102 | 0.1% | $1,076 | 0.1% |
| 21. | Other deductions | $203,404 | 9.8% | $125,210 | 8.8% |
| 22. | Total operating costs | $1,890,821 | 90.9% | $1,340,316 | 94.0% |
| | | | | | |
| | Operating Income and Distribution | | | | |
| 23. | Operating Income | $2,080,318 | 100.0% | $1,425,400 | 100.0% |
| 24. | Less:  Cost of sales and operations | $1,472,704 | 70.8% | $1,016,101 | 71.3% |
| 25. | Gross operating profit | $607,614 | 29.2% | $409,299 | 28.7% |
| 26. | Additional operating costs | $418,117 | 20.1% | $324,215 | 22.8% |
| 27. | Net operating profit | $189,497 | 9.1% | $85,084 | 6.0% |
| 28. | Less:  Guaranteed payments to partners | $8,943 | | $15,993 | |
| 29. | Distribution to partners | $180,554 | | $69,091 | |
| 30. | Other charges | $347 | | $107 | |
| 31. | Net change partners' capital | $180,207 | | $68,984 | |
| | | | | | |
| | Selected Ratios | | | | |
| 32. | Coverage ratio:  times interest earned | 29.9 | | 12.3 | |
| 33. | Inventory turnover (times) | 28.2 | | 21.1 | |
| 34. | Days' sales in inventory | 14.1 | | 16.3 | |
| 35. | Average age of inventory (days) | 12.9 | | 17.3 | |
| 36. | Return on assets, net income | 65.0% | | 66.2% | |
| 37. | Return on assets, gross operating profit | 219.1% | | n.a. | |
| 38. | Return on assets, net operating profit | 68.3% | | 81.6% | |

Table 2: Partnerships With Net Income: 118. AUTOMOTIVE DEALERS AND SERVICE STATIONS

Dollar values in thousands, except averages

|  |  | 1984 |  | 1985 |  |
|---|---|---|---|---|---|
| 1. | Number of Partnerships | 9,783 | | 9,494 | |
| 2. | Number of Partners | 23,391 | | 21,865 | |
| 3. | Total Assets | $1,519,639 | | $1,337,036 | |
| 4. | Average total assets per Partnership | $155,335 | | $140,830 | |
| 5. | Average total assets per Partner | $64,967 | | $61,150 | |
| 6. | Net Income | $382,947 | | $376,289 | |
| 7. | Average per Partnership, total earnings | $39,153 | | $39,640 | |
| 8. | Average per Partner, total earnings | $16,375 | | $17,212 | |
| 9. | Operating Income | $8,424,303 | | $7,907,617 | |
| | Operating Costs | | | | |
| 10. | Cost of sales & operations | $6,895,441 | 81.9% | $6,537,008 | 82.7% |
| 11. | Salaries and wages | $348,015 | 4.1% | $291,476 | 3.7% |
| 12. | Rent paid | $95,380 | 1.1% | $84,363 | 1.1% |
| 13. | Interest paid | $64,041 | 0.8% | $53,061 | 0.7% |
| 14. | Taxes paid | $71,468 | 0.9% | $64,544 | 0.8% |
| 15. | Bad debts | $7,242 | 0.1% | $4,837 | 0.1% |
| 16. | Repairs | $25,923 | 0.3% | $27,735 | 0.4% |
| 17. | Depreciation | $59,595 | 0.7% | $57,922 | 0.7% |
| 18. | Depletion | $646 | 0.0% | $0 | n.a. |
| 19. | Pension & profit sharing plans | $1,077 | 0.0% | $1,258 | 0.0% |
| 20. | Employee benefits programs | $9,584 | 0.1% | $6,506 | 0.1% |
| 21. | Other deductions | $374,177 | 4.4% | $348,867 | 4.4% |
| 22. | Total operating costs | $7,953,254 | 94.4% | $7,477,821 | 94.6% |
| | Operating Income and Distribution | | | | |
| 23. | Operating Income | $8,424,303 | 100.0% | $7,907,617 | 100.0% |
| 24. | Less: Cost of sales and operations | $6,895,441 | 81.9% | $6,537,008 | 82.7% |
| 25. | Gross operating profit | $1,528,862 | 18.2% | $1,370,609 | 17.3% |
| 26. | Additional operating costs | $1,057,813 | 12.6% | $940,813 | 11.9% |
| 27. | Net operating profit | $471,049 | 5.6% | $429,796 | 5.4% |
| 28. | Less: Guaranteed payments to partners | $87,095 | | $53,506 | |
| 29. | Distribution to partners | $383,954 | | $376,290 | |
| 30. | Other charges | $1,672 | | $245 | |
| 31. | Net change partners' capital | $382,282 | | $376,045 | |
| | Selected Ratios | | | | |
| 32. | Coverage ratio: times interest earned | 6.4 | | 7.1 | |
| 33. | Inventory turnover (times) | 9.9 | | 11.0 | |
| 34. | Days' sales in inventory | 37.2 | | 35.1 | |
| 35. | Average age of inventory (days) | 36.8 | | 33.2 | |
| 36. | Return on assets, net income | 25.2% | | 28.1% | |
| 37. | Return on assets, gross operating profit | 100.6% | | 102.5% | |
| 38. | Return on assets, net operating profit | 31.0% | | 32.2% | |

Table 2: Partnerships With Net Income:  MOTOR VEHICLE DEALERS (119,120)

Dollar values in thousands, except averages

| | | 1984 | | 1985 | |
|---|---|---|---|---|---|
| 1. | Number of Partnerships | 2,643 | | 2,545 | |
| 2. | Number of Partners | 6,217 | | 5,954 | |
| 3. | Total Assets | $578,126 | | $617,368 | |
| 4. | Average total assets per Partnership | $218,739 | | $242,581 | |
| 5. | Average total assets per Partner | $92,991 | | $103,690 | |
| 6. | Net Income | $137,596 | | $153,831 | |
| 7. | Average per Partnership, total earnings | $52,066 | | $60,449 | |
| 8. | Average per Partner, total earnings | $22,135 | | $25,839 | |
| 9. | Operating Income | $2,901,946 | | $3,088,025 | |
| | Operating Costs | | | | |
| 10. | Cost of sales & operations | $2,451,388 | 84.5% | $2,611,319 | 84.6% |
| 11. | Salaries and wages | $99,376 | 3.4% | $106,292 | 3.4% |
| 12. | Rent paid | $17,385 | 0.6% | $18,593 | 0.6% |
| 13. | Interest paid | $26,090 | 0.9% | $22,458 | 0.7% |
| 14. | Taxes paid | $18,708 | 0.6% | $19,749 | 0.6% |
| 15. | Bad debts | $2,178 | 0.1% | $2,516 | 0.1% |
| 16. | Repairs | $12,521 | 0.4% | $13,093 | 0.4% |
| 17. | Depreciation | $13,207 | 0.5% | $12,787 | 0.4% |
| 18. | Depletion | $0 | n.a. | $0 | n.a. |
| 19. | Pension & profit sharing plans | $496 | 0.0% | $768 | 0.0% |
| 20. | Employee benefits programs | $4,697 | 0.2% | $4,671 | 0.2% |
| 21. | Other deductions | $102,694 | 3.5% | $109,551 | 3.6% |
| 22. | Total operating costs | $2,748,871 | 94.7% | $2,921,812 | 94.6% |
| | Operating Income and Distribution | | | | |
| 23. | Operating Income | $2,901,946 | 100.0% | $3,088,025 | 100.0% |
| 24. | Less:  Cost of sales and operations | $2,451,388 | 84.5% | $2,611,319 | 84.6% |
| 25. | Gross operating profit | $450,558 | 15.5% | $476,706 | 15.4% |
| 26. | Additional operating costs | $297,483 | 10.3% | $310,493 | 10.1% |
| 27. | Net operating profit | $153,075 | 5.3% | $166,213 | 5.4% |
| 28. | Less:  Guaranteed payments to partners | $15,219 | | $12,272 | |
| 29. | Distribution to partners | $137,856 | | $153,941 | |
| 30. | Other charges | $391 | | $125 | |
| 31. | Net change partners' capital | $137,465 | | $153,816 | |
| | Selected Ratios | | | | |
| 32. | Coverage ratio:  times interest earned | 4.9 | | 6.4 | |
| 33. | Inventory turnover (times) | 8.7 | | 8.0 | |
| 34. | Days' sales in inventory | 46.9 | | 48.5 | |
| 35. | Average age of inventory (days) | 42.1 | | 45.4 | |
| 36. | Return on assets, net income | 23.8% | | 24.9% | |
| 37. | Return on assets, gross operating profit | 77.9% | | 77.2% | |
| 38. | Return on assets, net operating profit | 26.5% | | 26.9% | |

Table 2: Partnerships With Net Income:  122.  GASOLINE SERVICE STATIONS

Dollar values in thousands, except averages

|  |  | 1984 | | 1985 | |
|---|---|---|---|---|---|
| 1. | Number of Partnerships | 4,212 | | 4,395 | |
| 2. | Number of Partners | 9,325 | | 9,740 | |
| 3. | Total Assets | $488,670 | | $443,946 | |
| 4. | Average total assets per Partnership | $116,019 | | $101,012 | |
| 5. | Average total assets per Partner | $52,404 | | $45,580 | |
| 6. | Net Income | $136,764 | | $160,419 | |
| 7. | Average per Partnership, total earnings | $32,476 | | $36,505 | |
| 8. | Average per Partner, total earnings | $14,669 | | $16,472 | |
| 9. | Operating Income | $3,947,168 | | $3,833,370 | |
|  | Operating Costs | | | | |
| 10. | Cost of sales & operations | $3,401,549 | 86.2% | $3,243,725 | 84.6% |
| 11. | Salaries and wages | $114,499 | 2.9% | $130,352 | 3.4% |
| 12. | Rent paid | $44,408 | 1.1% | $45,169 | 1.2% |
| 13. | Interest paid | $21,681 | 0.6% | $15,714 | 0.4% |
| 14. | Taxes paid | $36,649 | 0.9% | $33,158 | 0.9% |
| 15. | Bad debts | $3,184 | 0.1% | $1,444 | 0.0% |
| 16. | Repairs | $9,928 | 0.3% | $10,128 | 0.3% |
| 17. | Depreciation | $31,948 | 0.8% | $32,246 | 0.8% |
| 18. | Depletion | $646 | 0.0% | $0 | n.a. |
| 19. | Pension & profit sharing plans | $168 | n.a. | $65 | n.a. |
| 20. | Employee benefits programs | $933 | 0.0% | $274 | 0.0% |
| 21. | Other deductions | $118,704 | 3.0% | $138,353 | 3.6% |
| 22. | Total operating costs | $3,784,318 | 95.9% | $3,650,712 | 95.2% |
| | Operating Income and Distribution | | | | |
| 23. | Operating Income | $3,947,168 | 100.0% | $3,833,370 | 100.0% |
| 24. | Less: Cost of sales and operations | $3,401,549 | 86.2% | $3,243,725 | 84.6% |
| 25. | Gross operating profit | $545,619 | 13.8% | $589,645 | 15.4% |
| 26. | Additional operating costs | $382,769 | 9.7% | $406,987 | 10.6% |
| 27. | Net operating profit | $162,850 | 4.1% | $182,658 | 4.8% |
| 28. | Less: Guaranteed payments to partners | $25,432 | | $22,272 | |
| 29. | Distribution to partners | $137,418 | | $160,386 | |
| 30. | Other charges | $675 | | $50 | |
| 31. | Net change partners' capital | $136,743 | | $160,336 | |
| | Selected Ratios | | | | |
| 32. | Coverage ratio: times interest earned | 6.5 | | 10.6 | |
| 33. | Inventory turnover (times) | 21.1 | | 33.1 | |
| 34. | Days' sales in inventory | 12.2 | | 11.5 | |
| 35. | Average age of inventory (days) | 17.3 | | 11.0 | |
| 36. | Return on assets, net income | 28.0% | | 36.1% | |
| 37. | Return on assets, gross operating profit | 111.7% | | 132.8% | |
| 38. | Return on assets, net operating profit | 33.3% | | 41.1% | |

Table 2: Partnerships With Net Income:  OTHER AUTOMOTIVE DEALERS (121,123,124,125,126)

Dollar values in thousands, except averages

|  |  | 1984 |  | 1985 |  |
|---|---|---|---|---|---|
| 1. | Number of Partnerships | 2,928 |  | 2,555 |  |
| 2. | Number of Partners | 7,848 |  | 6,170 |  |
| 3. | Total Assets | $452,843 |  | $275,722 |  |
| 4. | Average total assets per Partnership | $154,659 |  | $107,915 |  |
| 5. | Average total assets per Partner | $57,702 |  | $44,688 |  |
| 6. | Net Income | $108,587 |  | $62,038 |  |
| 7. | Average per Partnership, total earnings | $37,102 |  | $24,288 |  |
| 8. | Average per Partner, total earnings | $13,842 |  | $10,058 |  |
| 9. | Operating Income | $1,575,189 |  | $986,223 |  |
|  | Operating Costs |  |  |  |  |
| 10. | Cost of sales & operations | $1,042,504 | 66.2% | $681,965 | 69.2% |
| 11. | Salaries and wages | $134,140 | 8.5% | $54,831 | 5.6% |
| 12. | Rent paid | $33,587 | 2.1% | $20,601 | 2.1% |
| 13. | Interest paid | $16,271 | 1.0% | $14,888 | 1.5% |
| 14. | Taxes paid | $16,110 | 1.0% | $11,638 | 1.2% |
| 15. | Bad debts | $1,879 | 0.1% | $877 | 0.1% |
| 16. | Repairs | $3,473 | 0.2% | $4,514 | 0.5% |
| 17. | Depreciation | $14,439 | 0.9% | $12,890 | 1.3% |
| 18. | Depletion | $0 | n.a. | $0 | n.a. |
| 19. | Pension & profit sharing plans | $413 | 0.0% | $426 | 0.0% |
| 20. | Employee benefits programs | $3,955 | 0.3% | $1,561 | 0.2% |
| 21. | Other deductions | $152,780 | 9.7% | $100,960 | 10.2% |
| 22. | Total operating costs | $1,420,064 | 90.2% | $905,297 | 91.8% |
|  | Operating Income and Distribution |  |  |  |  |
| 23. | Operating Income | $1,575,189 | 100.0% | $986,223 | 100.0% |
| 24. | Less:  Cost of sales and operations | $1,042,504 | 66.2% | $681,965 | 69.2% |
| 25. | Gross operating profit | $532,685 | 33.8% | $304,258 | 30.9% |
| 26. | Additional operating costs | $377,560 | 24.0% | $223,332 | 22.7% |
| 27. | Net operating profit | $155,125 | 9.9% | $80,926 | 8.2% |
| 28. | Less:  Guaranteed payments to partners | $46,444 |  | $18,962 |  |
| 29. | Distribution to partners | $108,681 |  | $61,964 |  |
| 30. | Other charges | $607 |  | $71 |  |
| 31. | Net change partners' capital | $108,074 |  | $61,893 |  |
|  | Selected Ratios |  |  |  |  |
| 32. | Coverage ratio:  times interest earned | 8.5 |  | 4.4 |  |
| 33. | Inventory turnover (times) | 4.2 |  | 4.0 |  |
| 34. | Days' sales in inventory | 95.9 |  | 96.2 |  |
| 35. | Average age of inventory (days) | 87.9 |  | 92.3 |  |
| 36. | Return on assets, net income | 24.0% |  | 22.5% |  |
| 37. | Return on assets, gross operating profit | 117.6% |  | 110.4% |  |
| 38. | Return on assets, net operating profit | 34.3% |  | 29.4% |  |

*Page 150*

Table 2: Partnerships With Net Income:  127.  APPAREL AND ACCESSORY STORES

Dollar values in thousands, except averages

| | | 1984 | | 1985 | |
|---|---|---|---|---|---|
| 1. | Number of Partnerships | 7,348 | | 6,159 | |
| 2. | Number of Partners | 15,183 | | 14,203 | |
| | | | | | |
| 3. | Total Assets | $572,282 | | $518,224 | |
| 4. | Average total assets per Partnership | $77,883 | | $84,141 | |
| 5. | Average total assets per Partner | $37,692 | | $36,487 | |
| | | | | | |
| 6. | Net Income | $79,820 | | $99,919 | |
| 7. | Average per Partnership, total earnings | $10,864 | | $16,229 | |
| 8. | Average per Partner, total earnings | $5,258 | | $7,038 | |
| | | | | | |
| 9. | Operating Income | $1,346,071 | | $1,239,039 | |
| | Operating Costs | | | | |
| 10. | Cost of sales & operations | $831,642 | 61.8% | $751,321 | 60.6% |
| 11. | Salaries and wages | $136,184 | 10.1% | $109,549 | 8.8% |
| 12. | Rent paid | $76,973 | 5.7% | $51,748 | 4.2% |
| 13. | Interest paid | $11,021 | 0.8% | $6,705 | 0.5% |
| 14. | Taxes paid | $28,646 | 2.1% | $29,381 | 2.4% |
| 15. | Bad debts | $746 | 0.1% | $1,066 | 0.1% |
| 16. | Repairs | $6,924 | 0.5% | $4,986 | 0.4% |
| 17. | Depreciation | $23,027 | 1.7% | $12,963 | 1.1% |
| 18. | Depletion | $0 | n.a. | $0 | n.a. |
| 19. | Pension & profit sharing plans | $320 | 0.0% | $684 | 0.1% |
| 20. | Employee benefits programs | $1,264 | 0.1% | $895 | 0.1% |
| 21. | Other deductions | $138,389 | 10.3% | $133,993 | 10.8% |
| 22. | Total operating costs | $1,255,136 | 93.2% | $1,103,291 | 89.0% |
| | | | | | |
| | Operating Income and Distribution | | | | |
| 23. | Operating Income | $1,346,071 | 100.0% | $1,239,039 | 100.0% |
| 24. | Less:  Cost of sales and operations | $831,642 | 61.8% | $751,321 | 60.6% |
| 25. | Gross operating profit | $514,429 | 38.2% | $487,718 | 39.4% |
| 26. | Additional operating costs | $423,494 | 31.5% | $351,970 | 28.4% |
| 27. | Net operating profit | $90,935 | 6.8% | $135,748 | 11.0% |
| 28. | Less:  Guaranteed payments to partners | $10,891 | | $35,457 | |
| 29. | Distribution to partners | $80,044 | | $100,291 | |
| 30. | Other charges | $224 | | $372 | |
| 31. | Net change partners' capital | $79,820 | | $99,919 | |
| | | | | | |
| | Selected Ratios | | | | |
| 32. | Coverage ratio:  times interest earned | 7.3 | | 19.3 | |
| 33. | Inventory turnover (times) | 2.7 | | 2.4 | |
| 34. | Days' sales in inventory | 143.2 | | 160.6 | |
| 35. | Average age of inventory (days) | 133.6 | | 153.0 | |
| 36. | Return on assets, net income | 14.0% | | 19.3% | |
| 37. | Return on assets, gross operating profit | 89.9% | | 94.1% | |
| 38. | Return on assets, net operating profit | 15.9% | | 26.2% | |

Table 2: Partnerships With Net Income:  136.  FURNITURE AND HOME FURNISHINGS STORES

Dollar values in thousands, except averages

| | 1984 | | 1985 | |
|---|---|---|---|---|
| 1.  Number of Partnerships | 5,503 | | 7,593 | |
| 2.  Number of Partners | 11,813 | | 18,590 | |
| | | | | |
| 3.  Total Assets | $695,253 | | $702,178 | |
| 4.  Average total assets per Partnership | $126,341 | | $92,477 | |
| 5.  Average total assets per Partner | $58,855 | | $37,772 | |
| | | | | |
| 6.  Net Income | $189,110 | | $202,659 | |
| 7.  Average per Partnership, total earnings | $34,369 | | $26,693 | |
| 8.  Average per Partner, total earnings | $16,011 | | $10,902 | |
| | | | | |
| 9.  Operating Income | $1,680,839 | | $1,985,216 | |
| Operating Costs | | | | |
| 10.  Cost of sales & operations | $1,096,592 | 65.2% | $1,224,277 | 61.7% |
| 11.  Salaries and wages | $98,634 | 5.9% | $128,044 | 6.5% |
| 12.  Rent paid | $41,091 | 2.4% | $54,462 | 2.7% |
| 13.  Interest paid | $13,248 | 0.8% | $19,039 | 0.10% |
| 14.  Taxes paid | $25,172 | 1.5% | $33,061 | 1.7% |
| 15.  Bad debts | $3,056 | 0.2% | $4,578 | 0.2% |
| 16.  Repairs | $4,491 | 0.3% | $7,317 | 0.4% |
| 17.  Depreciation | $18,067 | 1.1% | $25,681 | 1.3% |
| 18.  Depletion | $0 | n.a. | $0 | n.a. |
| 19.  Pension & profit sharing plans | $365 | 0.0% | $7,738 | 0.4% |
| 20.  Employee benefits programs | $414 | 0.0% | $1,597 | 0.1% |
| 21.  Other deductions | $166,015 | 9.9% | $258,320 | 13.0% |
| 22.  Total operating costs | $1,467,248 | 87.3% | $1,764,142 | 88.9% |
| | | | | |
| Operating Income and Distribution | | | | |
| 23.  Operating Income | $1,680,839 | 100.0% | $1,985,216 | 100.0% |
| 24.  Less: Cost of sales and operations | $1,096,592 | 65.2% | $1,224,277 | 61.7% |
| 25.  Gross operating profit | $584,247 | 34.8% | $760,939 | 38.3% |
| 26.  Additional operating costs | $370,656 | 22.1% | $539,865 | 27.2% |
| 27.  Net operating profit | $213,591 | 12.7% | $221,074 | 11.1% |
| 28.  Less: Guaranteed payments to partners | $23,555 | | $18,007 | |
| 29.  Distribution to partners | $190,036 | | $203,067 | |
| 30.  Other charges | $1,030 | | $436 | |
| 31.  Net change partners' capital | $189,006 | | $202,631 | |
| | | | | |
| Selected Ratios | | | | |
| 32.  Coverage ratio: times interest earned | 15.1 | | 10.6 | |
| 33.  Inventory turnover (times) | 4.1 | | 4.1 | |
| 34.  Days' sales in inventory | 101.7 | | 95.7 | |
| 35.  Average age of inventory (days) | 90.0 | | 89.3 | |
| 36.  Return on assets, net income | 27.2% | | 28.9% | |
| 37.  Return on assets, gross operating profit | 84.0% | | 108.4% | |
| 38.  Return on assets, net operating profit | 30.7% | | 31.5% | |

Table 2: Partnerships With Net Income: 145. EATING PLACES

Dollar values in thousands, except averages

| | | 1984 | | 1985 | |
|---|---|---|---|---|---|
| 1. | Number of Partnerships | 15,308 | | 20,125 | |
| 2. | Number of Partners | 43,904 | | 54,257 | |
| 3. | Total Assets | $1,460,725 | | $1,600,344 | |
| 4. | Average total assets per Partnership | $95,422 | | $79,520 | |
| 5. | Average total assets per Partner | $33,271 | | $29,496 | |
| 6. | Net Income | $547,523 | | $718,052 | |
| 7. | Average per Partnership, total earnings | $35,770 | | $35,684 | |
| 8. | Average per Partner, total earnings | $12,472 | | $13,236 | |
| 9. | Operating Income | $5,152,354 | | $6,424,077 | |
| | Operating Costs | | | | |
| 10. | Cost of sales & operations | $2,236,623 | 43.4% | $2,744,407 | 42.7% |
| 11. | Salaries and wages | $809,751 | 15.7% | $1,044,714 | 16.3% |
| 12. | Rent paid | $288,122 | 5.6% | $357,304 | 5.6% |
| 13. | Interest paid | $55,056 | 1.1% | $64,489 | 1.0% |
| 14. | Taxes paid | $159,376 | 3.1% | $211,840 | 3.3% |
| 15. | Bad debts | $492 | 0.0% | $1,510 | 0.0% |
| 16. | Repairs | $57,135 | 1.1% | $68,229 | 1.1% |
| 17. | Depreciation | $131,597 | 2.6% | $138,936 | 2.2% |
| 18. | Depletion | $0 | n.a. | $0 | n.a. |
| 19. | Pension & profit sharing plans | $1,046 | 0.0% | $919 | 0.0% |
| 20. | Employee benefits programs | $5,428 | 0.1% | $6,111 | 0.1% |
| 21. | Other deductions | $808,021 | 15.7% | $969,149 | 15.1% |
| 22. | Total operating costs | $4,553,778 | 88.4% | $5,609,031 | 87.3% |
| | Operating Income and Distribution | | | | |
| 23. | Operating Income | $5,152,354 | 100.0% | $6,424,077 | 100.0% |
| 24. | Less: Cost of sales and operations | $2,236,623 | 43.4% | $2,744,407 | 42.7% |
| 25. | Gross operating profit | $2,915,731 | 56.6% | $3,679,670 | 57.3% |
| 26. | Additional operating costs | $2,317,155 | 45.0% | $2,864,624 | 44.6% |
| 27. | Net operating profit | $598,576 | 11.6% | $815,046 | 12.7% |
| 28. | Less: Guaranteed payments to partners | $50,267 | | $95,446 | |
| 29. | Distribution to partners | $548,309 | | $719,600 | |
| 30. | Other charges | $1,917 | | $2,972 | |
| 31. | Net change partners' capital | $546,392 | | $716,628 | |
| | Selected Ratios | | | | |
| 32. | Coverage ratio: times interest earned | 9.9 | | 11.6 | |
| 33. | Inventory turnover (times) | 26.2 | | 28.8 | |
| 34. | Days' sales in inventory | 14.4 | | 12.8 | |
| 35. | Average age of inventory (days) | 14.0 | | 12.7 | |
| 36. | Return on assets, net income | 37.5% | | 44.9% | |
| 37. | Return on assets, gross operating profit | 199.6% | | 229.9% | |
| 38. | Return on assets, net operating profit | 41.0% | | 50.9% | |

*Page 153*

Table 2: Partnerships With Net Income: 146.  DRINKING PLACES

Dollar values in thousands, except averages

| | 1984 | | 1985 | |
|---|---|---|---|---|
| 1. Number of Partnerships | 3,101 | | 3,141 | |
| 2. Number of Partners | 6,413 | | 6,448 | |
| | | | | |
| 3. Total Assets | $36,365 | | $89,339 | |
| 4. Average total assets per Partnership | $11,727 | | $28,443 | |
| 5. Average total assets per Partner | $5,671 | | $13,855 | |
| | | | | |
| 6. Net Income | $15,200 | | $79,515 | |
| 7. Average per Partnership, total earnings | $4,902 | | $25,316 | |
| 8. Average per Partner, total earnings | $2,370 | | $12,332 | |
| | | | | |
| 9. Operating Income | $181,818 | | $541,755 | |
| Operating Costs | | | | |
| 10. Cost of sales & operations | $85,336 | 46.9% | $269,599 | 49.8% |
| 11. Salaries and wages | $14,412 | 7.9% | $46,363 | 8.6% |
| 12. Rent paid | $10,048 | 5.5% | $21,783 | 4.0% |
| 13. Interest paid | $4,169 | 2.3% | $5,439 | 1.0% |
| 14. Taxes paid | $11,037 | 6.1% | $22,538 | 4.2% |
| 15. Bad debts | $3 | n.a. | $2 | n.a. |
| 16. Repairs | $3,165 | 1.7% | $7,845 | 1.5% |
| 17. Depreciation | $6,366 | 3.5% | $17,829 | 3.3% |
| 18. Depletion | $0 | n.a. | $0 | n.a. |
| 19. Pension & profit sharing plans | $0 | n.a. | $0 | n.a. |
| 20. Employee benefits programs | $0 | n.a. | $1,001 | 0.2% |
| 21. Other deductions | $28,897 | 15.9% | $65,943 | 12.2% |
| 22. Total operating costs | $163,437 | 89.9% | $458,379 | 84.6% |
| | | | | |
| Operating Income and Distribution | | | | |
| 23. Operating Income | $181,818 | 100.0% | $541,755 | 100.0% |
| 24. Less: Cost of sales and operations | $85,336 | 46.9% | $269,599 | 49.8% |
| 25. Gross operating profit | $96,482 | 53.1% | $272,156 | 50.2% |
| 26. Additional operating costs | $78,101 | 43.0% | $188,780 | 34.9% |
| 27. Net operating profit | $18,381 | 10.1% | $83,376 | 15.4% |
| 28. Less: Guaranteed payments to partners | $1,672 | | $2,112 | |
| 29. Distribution to partners | $16,709 | | $81,264 | |
| 30. Other charges | $1,513 | | $1,785 | |
| 31. Net change partners' capital | $15,196 | | $79,479 | |
| | | | | |
| Selected Ratios | | | | |
| 32. Coverage ratio: times interest earned | 3.4 | | 14.3 | |
| 33. Inventory turnover (times) | 33.8 | | 15.4 | |
| 34. Days' sales in inventory | 12.1 | | 24.5 | |
| 35. Average age of inventory (days) | 10.8 | | 23.7 | |
| 36. Return on assets, net income | 41.8% | | 89.0% | |
| 37. Return on assets, gross operating profit | n.a. | | n.a. | |
| 38. Return on assets, net operating profit | 50.6% | | 93.3% | |

Table 2: Partnerships With Net Income:   149.   LIQUOR STORES

Dollar values in thousands, except averages

|  |  | 1984 | | 1985 | |
|---|---|---|---|---|---|
| 1. | Number of Partnerships | 2,183 | | 1,193 | |
| 2. | Number of Partners | 4,919 | | 2,896 | |
| 3. | Total Assets | $297,404 | | $214,021 | |
| 4. | Average total assets per Partnership | $136,236 | | $179,397 | |
| 5. | Average total assets per Partner | $60,460 | | $73,902 | |
| 6. | Net Income | $64,661 | | $48,302 | |
| 7. | Average per Partnership, total earnings | $29,622 | | $40,491 | |
| 8. | Average per Partner, total earnings | $13,146 | | $16,680 | |
| 9. | Operating Income | $1,201,959 | | $773,771 | |
|  | Operating Costs | | | | |
| 10. | Cost of sales & operations | $947,822 | 78.9% | $599,573 | 77.5% |
| 11. | Salaries and wages | $67,360 | 5.6% | $28,368 | 3.7% |
| 12. | Rent paid | $11,128 | 0.9% | $15,819 | 2.0% |
| 13. | Interest paid | $10,395 | 0.9% | $11,666 | 1.5% |
| 14. | Taxes paid | $16,757 | 1.4% | $12,590 | 1.6% |
| 15. | Bad debts | $542 | 0.1% | $221 | 0.0% |
| 16. | Repairs | $5,248 | 0.4% | $4,384 | 0.6% |
| 17. | Depreciation | $18,119 | 1.5% | $11,484 | 1.5% |
| 18. | Depletion | $0 | n.a. | $0 | n.a. |
| 19. | Pension & profit sharing plans | $0 | n.a. | $0 | n.a. |
| 20. | Employee benefits programs | $130 | 0.0% | $183 | 0.0% |
| 21. | Other deductions | $55,838 | 4.7% | $37,364 | 4.8% |
| 22. | Total operating costs | $1,133,339 | 94.3% | $721,652 | 93.3% |
|  | Operating Income and Distribution | | | | |
| 23. | Operating Income | $1,201,959 | 100.0% | $773,771 | 100.0% |
| 24. | Less: Cost of sales and operations | $947,822 | 78.9% | $599,573 | 77.5% |
| 25. | Gross operating profit | $254,137 | 21.1% | $174,198 | 22.5% |
| 26. | Additional operating costs | $185,517 | 15.4% | $122,079 | 15.8% |
| 27. | Net operating profit | $68,620 | 5.7% | $52,119 | 6.7% |
| 28. | Less: Guaranteed payments to partners | $3,954 | | $3,770 | |
| 29. | Distribution to partners | $64,666 | | $48,349 | |
| 30. | Other charges | $6 | | $46 | |
| 31. | Net change partners' capital | $64,660 | | $48,303 | |
|  | Selected Ratios | | | | |
| 32. | Coverage ratio: times interest earned | 5.6 | | 3.5 | |
| 33. | Inventory turnover (times) | 8.6 | | 6.9 | |
| 34. | Days' sales in inventory | 41.7 | | 58.9 | |
| 35. | Average age of inventory (days) | 42.6 | | 53.1 | |
| 36. | Return on assets, net income | 21.7% | | 22.6% | |
| 37. | Return on assets, gross operating profit | 85.5% | | 81.4% | |
| 38. | Return on assets, net operating profit | 23.1% | | 24.4% | |

*Page 155*

Table 2: Partnerships With Net Income:  OTHER RETAIL STORES (148,150 TO 164,167,168,169,170)

Dollar values in thousands, except averages

| | | 1984 | | 1985 | |
|---|---|---|---|---|---|
| 1. | Number of Partnerships | 19,047 | | 26,042 | |
| 2. | Number of Partners | 44,108 | | 63,442 | |
| 3. | Total Assets | $1,545,396 | | $1,850,753 | |
| 4. | Average total assets per Partnership | $81,136 | | $71,068 | |
| 5. | Average total assets per Partner | $35,037 | | $29,172 | |
| 6. | Net Income | $481,114 | | $565,848 | |
| 7. | Average per Partnership, total earnings | $25,265 | | $21,731 | |
| 8. | Average per Partner, total earnings | $10,910 | | $8,920 | |
| 9. | Operating Income | $5,250,469 | | $5,754,778 | |
| | Operating Costs | | | | |
| 10. | Cost of sales & operations | $3,345,198 | 63.7% | $3,514,082 | 61.1% |
| 11. | Salaries and wages | $418,447 | 8.0% | $484,725 | 8.4% |
| 12. | Rent paid | $119,706 | 2.3% | $192,558 | 3.4% |
| 13. | Interest paid | $52,138 | 0.10% | $63,929 | 1.1% |
| 14. | Taxes paid | $71,937 | 1.4% | $91,585 | 1.6% |
| 15. | Bad debts | $11,763 | 0.2% | $13,235 | 0.2% |
| 16. | Repairs | $23,207 | 0.4% | $29,797 | 0.5% |
| 17. | Depreciation | $81,094 | 1.5% | $98,468 | 1.7% |
| 18. | Depletion | $470 | 0.0% | $0 | n.a. |
| 19. | Pension & profit sharing plans | $4,488 | 0.1% | $4,538 | 0.1% |
| 20. | Employee benefits programs | $8,442 | 0.2% | $7,986 | 0.1% |
| 21. | Other deductions | $530,944 | 10.1% | $611,863 | 10.6% |
| 22. | Total operating costs | $4,668,521 | 88.9% | $5,113,680 | 88.9% |
| | Operating Income and Distribution | | | | |
| 23. | Operating Income | $5,250,469 | 100.0% | $5,754,778 | 100.0% |
| 24. | Less: Cost of sales and operations | $3,345,198 | 63.7% | $3,514,082 | 61.1% |
| 25. | Gross operating profit | $1,905,271 | 36.3% | $2,240,696 | 38.9% |
| 26. | Additional operating costs | $1,323,323 | 25.2% | $1,599,598 | 27.8% |
| 27. | Net operating profit | $581,948 | 11.1% | $641,098 | 11.1% |
| 28. | Less: Guaranteed payments to partners | $101,054 | | $75,889 | |
| 29. | Distribution to partners | $480,894 | | $565,209 | |
| 30. | Other charges | $467 | | $275 | |
| 31. | Net change partners' capital | $480,427 | | $564,934 | |
| | Selected Ratios | | | | |
| 32. | Coverage ratio:  times interest earned | 10.2 | | 9.0 | |
| 33. | Inventory turnover (times) | 4.7 | | 4.0 | |
| 34. | Days' sales in inventory | 83.7 | | 98.0 | |
| 35. | Average age of inventory (days) | 78.4 | | 90.4 | |
| 36. | Return on assets, net income | 31.1% | | 30.6% | |
| 37. | Return on assets, gross operating profit | 123.3% | | 121.1% | |
| 38. | Return on assets, net operating profit | 37.7% | | 34.6% | |

Table 2: Partnerships With Net Income:  172.  FINANCE, INSURANCE, AND REAL ESTATE

Dollar values in thousands, except averages

| | | 1984 | | 1985 | |
|---|---|---|---|---|---|
| 1. | Number of Partnerships | 349,777 | | 369,113 | |
| 2. | Number of Partners | 3,599,939 | | 3,459,656 | |
| | | | | | |
| 3. | Total Assets | $299,690,708 | | $367,511,700 | |
| 4. | Average total assets per Partnership | $856,805 | | $995,662 | |
| 5. | Average total assets per Partner | $83,249 | | $106,228 | |
| | | | | | |
| 6. | Net Income | $25,646,379 | | $30,382,765 | |
| 7. | Average per Partnership, total earnings | $73,324 | | $82,315 | |
| 8. | Average per Partner, total earnings | $7,124 | | $8,782 | |
| | | | | | |
| 9. | Total Receipts | $39,247,900 | | $30,236,525 | |
| | Operating Costs | | | | |
| 10. | Cost of sales & operations | $27,895,951 | 71.1% | $18,182,990 | 60.1% |
| 11. | Salaries and wages | $1,542,229 | 3.9% | $1,995,687 | 6.6% |
| 12. | Rent paid | $413,848 | 1.1% | $341,287 | 1.1% |
| 13. | Interest paid | $5,497,567 | 14.0% | $6,123,536 | 20.3% |
| 14. | Taxes paid | $722,186 | 1.8% | $733,515 | 2.4% |
| 15. | Bad debts | $43,104 | 0.1% | $59,535 | 0.2% |
| 16. | Repairs | $157,774 | 0.4% | $162,944 | 0.5% |
| 17. | Depreciation | $1,390,999 | 3.5% | $1,488,383 | 4.9% |
| 18. | Depletion | $1,183 | n.a. | $7,780 | 0.0% |
| 19. | Pension & profit sharing plans | $37,050 | 0.1% | $98,980 | 0.3% |
| 20. | Employee benefits programs | $42,652 | 0.1% | $58,352 | 0.2% |
| 21. | Other deductions | $5,318,845 | 13.6% | $5,814,776 | 19.2% |
| 22. | Total operating costs | $43,063,835 | 109.7% | $35,068,471 | 116.0% |
| | | | | | |
| | Operating Income and Distribution | | | | |
| 23. | Total Receipts | $39,247,900 | 100.0% | $30,236,525 | 100.0% |
| 24. | Less: Cost of sales and operations | $27,895,951 | 71.1% | $18,182,990 | 60.1% |
| 25. | Gross operating profit | $11,351,949 | 28.9% | $12,053,535 | 39.9% |
| 26. | Additional operating costs | $15,167,884 | 38.7% | $16,885,481 | 55.8% |
| 27. | Net operating profit | ($3,815,935) | (9.7%) | ($4,831,946) | (16.0%) |
| 28. | Less: Guaranteed payments to partners | $542,643 | | $609,639 | |
| 29. | Distribution to partners | ($4,358,578) | | ($5,441,585) | |
| 30. | Other charges | $982,015 | | $943,531 | |
| 31. | Net change partners' capital | ($5,340,593) | | ($6,385,116) | |
| | | | | | |
| | Selected Ratios | | | | |
| 32. | Coverage ratio: times interest earned | (1.7) | | (1.8) | |
| 33. | Inventory turnover (times) | n.a. | | n.a. | |
| 34. | Days' sales in inventory | n.a. | | n.a. | |
| 35. | Average age of inventory (days) | n.a. | | n.a. | |
| 36. | Return on assets, net income | 8.6% | | 8.3% | |
| 37. | Return on assets, gross operating profit | 3.8% | | 3.3% | |
| 38. | Return on assets, net operating profit | (1.3%) | | (1.3%) | |

*Page 157*

Table 2: Partnerships With Net Income:  173.  FINANCE

Dollar values in thousands, except averages

| | | 1984 | | 1985 | |
|---|---|---|---|---|---|
| 1. | Number of Partnerships | 81,296 | | 80,203 | |
| 2. | Number of Partners | 1,568,510 | | 1,078,105 | |
| 3. | Total Assets | $103,179,987 | | $141,238,586 | |
| 4. | Average total assets per Partnership | $1,269,189 | | $1,761,014 | |
| 5. | Average total assets per Partner | $65,782 | | $131,006 | |
| 6. | Net Income | $6,413,803 | | $8,809,057 | |
| 7. | Average per Partnership, total earnings | $78,897 | | $109,838 | |
| 8. | Average per Partner, total earnings | $4,089 | | $8,171 | |
| 9. | Total Receipts | $21,228,618 | | $11,955,096 | |
| | Operating Costs | | | | |
| 10. | Cost of sales & operations | $18,056,840 | 85.1% | $7,771,015 | 65.0% |
| 11. | Salaries and wages | $830,092 | 3.9% | $1,190,426 | 1.0% |
| 12. | Rent paid | $145,346 | 0.7% | $114,046 | 0.10% |
| 13. | Interest paid | $3,145,298 | 14.8% | $3,697,419 | 30.9% |
| 14. | Taxes paid | $145,067 | 0.7% | $169,148 | 1.4% |
| 15. | Bad debts | $23,368 | 0.1% | $24,106 | 0.2% |
| 16. | Repairs | $13,639 | 0.1% | $36,380 | 0.3% |
| 17. | Depreciation | $273,768 | 1.3% | $268,391 | 2.2% |
| 18. | Depletion | $439 | n.a. | $511 | n.a. |
| 19. | Pension & profit sharing plans | $23,993 | 0.1% | $87,631 | 0.7% |
| 20. | Employee benefits programs | $23,445 | 0.1% | $26,977 | 0.2% |
| 21. | Other deductions | $1,297,635 | 6.1% | $1,686,337 | 14.1% |
| 22. | Total operating costs | $23,979,099 | 113.0% | $15,072,905 | 126.1% |
| | Operating Income and Distribution | | | | |
| 23. | Total Receipts | $21,228,618 | 100.0% | $11,955,096 | 100.0% |
| 24. | Less: Cost of sales and operations | $18,056,840 | 85.1% | $7,771,015 | 65.0% |
| 25. | Gross operating profit | $3,171,778 | 14.9% | $4,184,081 | 35.0% |
| 26. | Additional operating costs | $5,922,259 | 27.9% | $7,301,890 | 61.1% |
| 27. | Net operating profit | ($2,750,481) | (13.0%) | ($3,117,809) | (26.1%) |
| 28. | Less: Guaranteed payments to partners | $219,584 | | $289,717 | |
| 29. | Distribution to partners | ($2,970,065) | | ($3,407,526) | |
| 30. | Other charges | $102,705 | | $120,430 | |
| 31. | Net change partners' capital | ($3,072,770) | | ($3,527,956) | |
| | Selected Ratios | | | | |
| 32. | Coverage ratio: times interest earned | (1.9) | | (1.8) | |
| 33. | Inventory turnover (times) | n.a. | | n.a. | |
| 34. | Days' sales in inventory | n.a. | | n.a. | |
| 35. | Average age of inventory (days) | n.a. | | n.a. | |
| 36. | Return on assets, net income | 6.2% | | 6.2% | |
| 37. | Return on assets, gross operating profit | 3.1% | | 3.0% | |
| 38. | Return on assets, net operating profit | (2.7%) | | (2.2%) | |

Table 2: Partnerships With Net Income:  BANKING AND CREDIT AGENCIES OTHER THAN BANKS (174,175)

Dollar values in thousands, except averages

|  |  | 1984 |  | 1985 |  |
| --- | --- | --- | --- | --- | --- |
| 1. | Number of Partnerships | 2,472 |  | 3,873 |  |
| 2. | Number of Partners | 246,665 |  | 38,579 |  |
| 3. | Total Assets | $16,711,361 |  | $3,403,789 |  |
| 4. | Average total assets per Partnership | $6,760,259 |  | $878,851 |  |
| 5. | Average total assets per Partner | $67,749 |  | $88,229 |  |
| 6. | Net Income | $650,711 |  | $155,182 |  |
| 7. | Average per Partnership, total earnings | $263,234 |  | $40,069 |  |
| 8. | Average per Partner, total earnings | $2,638 |  | $4,023 |  |
| 9. | Total Receipts | $587,165 |  | $489,439 |  |
|  | Operating Costs |  |  |  |  |
| 10. | Cost of sales & operations | $446,599 | 76.1% | $323,205 | 66.0% |
| 11. | Salaries and wages | $60,710 | 10.3% | $64,567 | 13.2% |
| 12. | Rent paid | $7,750 | 1.3% | $9,597 | 2.0% |
| 13. | Interest paid | $193,365 | 32.9% | $140,397 | 28.7% |
| 14. | Taxes paid | $4,244 | 0.7% | $2,788 | 0.6% |
| 15. | Bad debts | $3,577 | 0.6% | $6,486 | 1.3% |
| 16. | Repairs | $903 | 0.2% | $1,758 | 0.4% |
| 17. | Depreciation | $6,758 | 1.2% | $5,130 | 1.1% |
| 18. | Depletion | $0 | n.a. | $0 | n.a. |
| 19. | Pension & profit sharing plans | $1,069 | 0.2% | $1,650 | 0.3% |
| 20. | Employee benefits programs | $2,600 | 0.4% | $2,950 | 0.6% |
| 21. | Other deductions | $62,309 | 10.6% | $82,910 | 16.9% |
| 22. | Total operating costs | $789,901 | 134.5% | $641,533 | 131.1% |
|  | Operating Income and Distribution |  |  |  |  |
| 23. | Total Receipts | $587,165 | 100.0% | $489,439 | 100.0% |
| 24. | Less:  Cost of sales and operations | $446,599 | 76.1% | $323,205 | 66.0% |
| 25. | Gross operating profit | $140,566 | 23.9% | $166,234 | 34.0% |
| 26. | Additional operating costs | $343,302 | 58.5% | $318,328 | 65.0% |
| 27. | Net operating profit | ($202,736) | (34.5%) | ($152,094) | (31.1%) |
| 28. | Less:  Guaranteed payments to partners | $4,326 |  | $5,541 |  |
| 29. | Distribution to partners | ($207,062) |  | ($157,635) |  |
| 30. | Other charges | $95 |  | $658 |  |
| 31. | Net change partners' capital | ($207,157) |  | ($158,293) |  |
|  | Selected Ratios |  |  |  |  |
| 32. | Coverage ratio:  times interest earned | (2.1) |  | (2.1) |  |
| 33. | Inventory turnover (times) | n.a. |  | n.a. |  |
| 34. | Days' sales in inventory | n.a. |  | n.a. |  |
| 35. | Average age of inventory (days) | n.a. |  | n.a. |  |
| 36. | Return on assets, net income | 3.9% |  | 4.6% |  |
| 37. | Return on assets, gross operating profit | 0.8% |  | 4.9% |  |
| 38. | Return on assets, net operating profit | (1.2%) |  | (4.5%) |  |

Table 2: Partnerships With Net Income:  176.  SECURITY AND COMMODITY BROKERS AND SERVICES

Dollar values in thousands, except averages

|  |  | 1984 |  | 1985 |  |
|---|---|---|---|---|---|
| 1. | Number of Partnerships | 1,933 |  | 1,589 |  |
| 2. | Number of Partners | 36,572 |  | 93,236 |  |
| 3. | Total Assets | $29,513,944 |  | $46,649,091 |  |
| 4. | Average total assets per Partnership | $15,268,466 |  | $29,357,515 |  |
| 5. | Average total assets per Partner | $807,009 |  | $500,333 |  |
| 6. | Net Income | $1,184,823 |  | $2,093,442 |  |
| 7. | Average per Partnership, total earnings | $613,032 |  | $1,317,556 |  |
| 8. | Average per Partner, total earnings | $32,402 |  | $22,455 |  |
| 9. | Total Receipts | $19,058,216 |  | $9,818,444 |  |
|  | Operating Costs |  |  |  |  |
| 10. | Cost of sales & operations | $17,098,180 | 89.7% | $7,024,670 | 71.6% |
| 11. | Salaries and wages | $702,601 | 3.7% | $735,801 | 7.5% |
| 12. | Rent paid | $124,847 | 0.7% | $64,288 | 0.7% |
| 13. | Interest paid | $2,350,377 | 12.3% | $1,727,123 | 17.6% |
| 14. | Taxes paid | $57,354 | 0.3% | $63,778 | 0.7% |
| 15. | Bad debts | $4,306 | 0.0% | $3,596 | 0.0% |
| 16. | Repairs | $6,163 | 0.0% | $4,716 | 0.1% |
| 17. | Depreciation | $21,220 | 0.1% | $23,091 | 0.2% |
| 18. | Depletion | $166 | n.a. | $131 | n.a. |
| 19. | Pension & profit sharing plans | $22,246 | 0.1% | $20,272 | 0.2% |
| 20. | Employee benefits programs | $19,656 | 0.1% | $21,987 | 0.2% |
| 21. | Other deductions | $731,553 | 3.8% | $898,137 | 9.2% |
| 22. | Total operating costs | $21,138,820 | 110.9% | $10,587,590 | 107.8% |
|  | Operating Income and Distribution |  |  |  |  |
| 23. | Total Receipts | $19,058,216 | 100.0% | $9,818,444 | 100.0% |
| 24. | Less:  Cost of sales and operations | $17,098,180 | 89.7% | $7,024,670 | 71.6% |
| 25. | Gross operating profit | $1,960,036 | 10.3% | $2,793,774 | 28.5% |
| 26. | Additional operating costs | $4,040,640 | 21.2% | $3,562,920 | 36.3% |
| 27. | Net operating profit | ($2,080,604) | (10.9%) | ($769,146) | (7.8%) |
| 28. | Less:  Guaranteed payments to partners | $166,882 |  | $153,705 |  |
| 29. | Distribution to partners | ($2,247,486) |  | ($922,851) |  |
| 30. | Other charges | $18,064 |  | $20,382 |  |
| 31. | Net change partners' capital | ($2,265,550) |  | ($943,233) |  |
|  | Selected Ratios |  |  |  |  |
| 32. | Coverage ratio:  times interest earned | (1.9) |  | (1.5) |  |
| 33. | Inventory turnover (times) | n.a. |  | n.a. |  |
| 34. | Days' sales in inventory | n.a. |  | n.a. |  |
| 35. | Average age of inventory (days) | n.a. |  | n.a. |  |
| 36. | Return on assets, net income | 4.0% |  | 4.5% |  |
| 37. | Return on assets, gross operating profit | 6.6% |  | 6.0% |  |
| 38. | Return on assets, net operating profit | (7.1%) |  | (1.7%) |  |

Table 2: Partnerships With Net Income: 180. HOLDING AND INVESTMENT COMPANIES

Dollar values in thousands, except averages

| | | 1984 | | 1985 | |
|---|---|---|---|---|---|
| 1. | Number of Partnerships | 76,891 | | 74,741 | |
| 2. | Number of Partners | 1,285,274 | | 946,290 | |
| | | | | | |
| 3. | Total Assets | $56,954,683 | | $91,185,707 | |
| 4. | Average total assets per Partnership | $740,720 | | $1,220,023 | |
| 5. | Average total assets per Partner | $44,313 | | $96,361 | |
| | | | | | |
| 6. | Net Income | $4,578,269 | | $6,560,433 | |
| 7. | Average per Partnership, total earnings | $59,543 | | $87,777 | |
| 8. | Average per Partner, total earnings | $3,562 | | $6,933 | |
| | | | | | |
| 9. | Total Receipts | $1,583,237 | | $1,647,212 | |
| | Operating Costs | | | | |
| 10. | Cost of sales & operations | $512,062 | 32.3% | $423,140 | 25.7% |
| 11. | Salaries and wages | $66,782 | 4.2% | $390,058 | 23.7% |
| 12. | Rent paid | $12,749 | 0.8% | $40,162 | 2.4% |
| 13. | Interest paid | $601,557 | 38.0% | $1,829,899 | 111.1% |
| 14. | Taxes paid | $83,470 | 5.3% | $102,581 | 6.2% |
| 15. | Bad debts | $15,485 | 0.10% | $14,024 | 0.9% |
| 16. | Repairs | $6,574 | 0.4% | $29,906 | 1.8% |
| 17. | Depreciation | $245,785 | 15.5% | $240,170 | 14.6% |
| 18. | Depletion | $273 | 0.0% | $380 | 0.0% |
| 19. | Pension & profit sharing plans | $677 | 0.0% | $65,709 | 4.0% |
| 20. | Employee benefits programs | $1,189 | 0.1% | $2,040 | 0.1% |
| 21. | Other deductions | $503,774 | 31.8% | $705,287 | 42.8% |
| 22. | Total operating costs | $2,050,377 | 129.5% | $3,843,779 | 233.4% |
| | | | | | |
| | Operating Income and Distribution | | | | |
| 23. | Total Receipts | $1,583,237 | 100.0% | $1,647,212 | 100.0% |
| 24. | Less: Cost of sales and operations | $512,062 | 32.3% | $423,140 | 25.7% |
| 25. | Gross operating profit | $1,071,175 | 67.7% | $1,224,072 | 74.3% |
| 26. | Additional operating costs | $1,538,315 | 97.2% | $3,420,639 | 207.7% |
| 27. | Net operating profit | ($467,140) | (29.5%) | ($2,196,567) | (133.4%) |
| 28. | Less: Guaranteed payments to partners | $48,376 | | $130,472 | |
| 29. | Distribution to partners | ($515,516) | | ($2,327,039) | |
| 30. | Other charges | $84,546 | | $99,392 | |
| 31. | Net change partners' capital | ($600,062) | | ($2,426,431) | |
| | | | | | |
| | Selected Ratios | | | | |
| 32. | Coverage ratio: times interest earned | (1.8) | | (2.2) | |
| 33. | Inventory turnover (times) | n.a. | | n.a. | |
| 34. | Days' sales in inventory | n.a. | | n.a. | |
| 35. | Average age of inventory (days) | n.a. | | n.a. | |
| 36. | Return on assets, net income | 8.0% | | 7.2% | |
| 37. | Return on assets, gross operating profit | 1.9% | | 1.3% | |
| 38. | Return on assets, net operating profit | (0.8%) | | (2.4%) | |

*Page 161*

Table 2: Partnerships With Net Income:  184.  INSURANCE AGENTS, BROKERS, AND SERVICES

Dollar values in thousands, except averages

|  |  | 1984 |  | 1985 |  |
|---|---|---|---|---|---|
| 1. | Number of Partnerships | 6,959 | | 3,998 | |
| 2. | Number of Partners | 44,239 | | 17,316 | |
| 3. | Total Assets | $2,583,195 | | $2,812,482 | |
| 4. | Average total assets per Partnership | $371,202 | | $703,472 | |
| 5. | Average total assets per Partner | $58,392 | | $162,421 | |
| 6. | Net Income | $684,586 | | $566,367 | |
| 7. | Average per Partnership, total earnings | $98,384 | | $141,677 | |
| 8. | Average per Partner, total earnings | $15,476 | | $32,711 | |
| 9. | Total Receipts | $2,500,237 | | $1,532,368 | |
|  | Operating Costs | | | | |
| 10. | Cost of sales & operations | $320,456 | 12.8% | $163,135 | 10.7% |
| 11. | Salaries and wages | $196,151 | 7.9% | $223,227 | 14.6% |
| 12. | Rent paid | $30,555 | 1.2% | $30,866 | 2.0% |
| 13. | Interest paid | $27,198 | 1.1% | $24,581 | 1.6% |
| 14. | Taxes paid | $29,937 | 1.2% | $30,349 | 2.0% |
| 15. | Bad debts | $2,800 | 0.1% | $9,116 | 0.6% |
| 16. | Repairs | $3,065 | 0.1% | $4,226 | 0.3% |
| 17. | Depreciation | $20,500 | 0.8% | $18,078 | 1.2% |
| 18. | Depletion | $0 | n.a. | $0 | n.a. |
| 19. | Pension & profit sharing plans | $6,312 | 0.3% | $5,183 | 0.3% |
| 20. | Employee benefits programs | $4,623 | 0.2% | $3,334 | 0.2% |
| 21. | Other deductions | $1,438,214 | 57.5% | $1,276,844 | 83.3% |
| 22. | Total operating costs | $2,079,973 | 83.2% | $1,789,050 | 116.8% |
|  | Operating Income and Distribution | | | | |
| 23. | Total Receipts | $2,500,237 | 100.0% | $1,532,368 | 100.0% |
| 24. | Less:  Cost of sales and operations | $320,456 | 12.8% | $163,135 | 10.7% |
| 25. | Gross operating profit | $2,179,781 | 87.2% | $1,369,233 | 89.4% |
| 26. | Additional operating costs | $1,759,517 | 70.4% | $1,625,915 | 106.1% |
| 27. | Net operating profit | $420,264 | 16.8% | ($256,682) | (16.8%) |
| 28. | Less:  Guaranteed payments to partners | $71,396 | | $56,598 | |
| 29. | Distribution to partners | $348,868 | | ($313,280) | |
| 30. | Other charges | $7,182 | | $10,959 | |
| 31. | Net change partners' capital | $341,686 | | ($324,239) | |
|  | Selected Ratios | | | | |
| 32. | Coverage ratio:  times interest earned | 14.5 | | (11.4) | |
| 33. | Inventory turnover (times) | n.a. | | n.a. | |
| 34. | Days' sales in inventory | n.a. | | n.a. | |
| 35. | Average age of inventory (days) | n.a. | | n.a. | |
| 36. | Return on assets, net income | 26.5% | | 20.1% | |
| 37. | Return on assets, gross operating profit | 84.4% | | 48.7% | |
| 38. | Return on assets, net operating profit | 16.3% | | (9.1%) | |

**Table 2: Partnerships With Net Income:** 185. REAL ESTATE

Dollar values in thousands, except averages

| | | 1984 | | 1985 | |
|---|---|---|---|---|---|
| 1. | Number of Partnerships | 261,522 | | 284,911 | |
| 2. | Number of Partners | 1,987,189 | | 2,364,235 | |
| | | | | | |
| 3. | Total Assets | $193,927,526 | | $223,460,633 | |
| 4. | Average total assets per Partnership | $741,534 | | $784,317 | |
| 5. | Average total assets per Partner | $97,589 | | $94,517 | |
| | | | | | |
| 6. | Net Income | $18,547,990 | | $21,007,341 | |
| 7. | Average per Partnership, total earnings | $70,924 | | $73,734 | |
| 8. | Average per Partner, total earnings | $9,334 | | $8,886 | |
| | | | | | |
| 9. | Total Receipts | $15,519,044 | | $16,749,062 | |
| | Operating Costs | | | | |
| 10. | Cost of sales & operations | $9,518,654 | 61.3% | $10,248,840 | 61.2% |
| 11. | Salaries and wages | $515,987 | 3.3% | $582,035 | 3.5% |
| 12. | Rent paid | $237,947 | 1.5% | $196,375 | 1.2% |
| 13. | Interest paid | $2,325,070 | 15.0% | $2,401,535 | 14.3% |
| 14. | Taxes paid | $547,182 | 3.5% | $534,019 | 3.2% |
| 15. | Bad debts | $16,936 | 0.1% | $26,313 | 0.2% |
| 16. | Repairs | $141,070 | 0.9% | $122,340 | 0.7% |
| 17. | Depreciation | $1,096,728 | 7.1% | $1,201,915 | 7.2% |
| 18. | Depletion | $744 | n.a. | $7,270 | 0.0% |
| 19. | Pension & profit sharing plans | $6,746 | 0.0% | $6,165 | 0.0% |
| 20. | Employee benefits programs | $14,584 | 0.1% | $28,042 | 0.2% |
| 21. | Other deductions | $2,582,997 | 16.6% | $2,851,591 | 17.0% |
| 22. | Total operating costs | $17,004,761 | 109.6% | $18,206,517 | 108.7% |
| | | | | | |
| | Operating Income and Distribution | | | | |
| 23. | Total Receipts | $15,519,044 | 100.0% | $16,749,062 | 100.0% |
| 24. | Less: Cost of sales and operations | $9,518,654 | 61.3% | $10,248,840 | 61.2% |
| 25. | Gross operating profit | $6,000,390 | 38.7% | $6,500,222 | 38.8% |
| 26. | Additional operating costs | $7,486,107 | 48.2% | $7,957,677 | 47.5% |
| 27. | Net operating profit | ($1,485,717) | (9.6%) | ($1,457,455) | (8.7%) |
| 28. | Less: Guaranteed payments to partners | $251,664 | | $263,324 | |
| 29. | Distribution to partners | ($1,737,381) | | ($1,720,779) | |
| 30. | Other charges | $872,129 | | $812,141 | |
| 31. | Net change partners' capital | ($2,609,510) | | ($2,532,920) | |
| | | | | | |
| | Selected Ratios | | | | |
| 32. | Coverage ratio: times interest earned | (1.6) | | (1.6) | |
| 33. | Inventory turnover (times) | n.a. | | n.a. | |
| 34. | Days' sales in inventory | n.a. | | n.a. | |
| 35. | Average age of inventory (days) | n.a. | | n.a. | |
| 36. | Return on assets, net income | 9.6% | | 9.4% | |
| 37. | Return on assets, gross operating profit | 3.1% | | 2.9% | |
| 38. | Return on assets, net operating profit | (0.8%) | | (0.7%) | |

Table 2: Partnerships With Net Income:   186.   OPERATORS AND LESSORS OF BUILDINGS

Dollar values in thousands, except averages

|  |  | 1984 |  | 1985 |  |
|---|---|---|---|---|---|
| 1. | Number of Partnerships | 221,716 |  | 236,714 |  |
| 2. | Number of Partners | 1,758,213 |  | 2,000,024 |  |
| 3. | Total Assets | $166,291,617 |  | $189,847,924 |  |
| 4. | Average total assets per Partnership | $750,021 |  | $802,014 |  |
| 5. | Average total assets per Partner | $94,580 |  | $94,923 |  |
| 6. | Net Income | $14,696,416 |  | $17,000,587 |  |
| 7. | Average per Partnership, total earnings | $66,286 |  | $71,820 |  |
| 8. | Average per Partner, total earnings | $8,359 |  | $8,500 |  |
| 9. | Total Receipts | $3,904,302 |  | $4,331,133 |  |
|  | Operating Costs |  |  |  |  |
| 10. | Cost of sales & operations | $1,795,016 | 46.0% | $2,103,596 | 48.6% |
| 11. | Salaries and wages | $272,039 | 7.0% | $251,641 | 5.8% |
| 12. | Rent paid | $183,486 | 4.7% | $96,274 | 2.2% |
| 13. | Interest paid | $1,523,362 | 39.0% | $1,625,347 | 37.5% |
| 14. | Taxes paid | $414,008 | 10.6% | $399,851 | 9.2% |
| 15. | Bad debts | $13,266 | 0.3% | $14,512 | 0.3% |
| 16. | Repairs | $107,569 | 2.8% | $95,659 | 2.2% |
| 17. | Depreciation | $973,217 | 24.9% | $1,071,787 | 24.8% |
| 18. | Depletion | $330 | 0.0% | $4,535 | 0.1% |
| 19. | Pension & profit sharing plans | $2,308 | 0.1% | $2,889 | 0.1% |
| 20. | Employee benefits programs | $9,081 | 0.2% | $10,814 | 0.3% |
| 21. | Other deductions | $1,375,964 | 35.2% | $1,397,162 | 32.3% |
| 22. | Total operating costs | $6,669,677 | 170.8% | $7,074,132 | 163.3% |
|  | Operating Income and Distribution |  |  |  |  |
| 23. | Total Receipts | $3,904,302 | 100.0% | $4,331,133 | 100.0% |
| 24. | Less: Cost of sales and operations | $1,795,016 | 46.0% | $2,103,596 | 48.6% |
| 25. | Gross operating profit | $2,109,286 | 54.0% | $2,227,537 | 51.4% |
| 26. | Additional operating costs | $4,874,661 | 124.9% | $4,970,536 | 114.8% |
| 27. | Net operating profit | ($2,765,375) | (70.8%) | ($2,742,999) | (63.3%) |
| 28. | Less: Guaranteed payments to partners | $158,029 |  | $176,935 |  |
| 29. | Distribution to partners | ($2,923,404) |  | ($2,919,934) |  |
| 30. | Other charges | $766,371 |  | $695,717 |  |
| 31. | Net change partners' capital | ($3,689,775) |  | ($3,615,651) |  |
|  | Selected Ratios |  |  |  |  |
| 32. | Coverage ratio: times interest earned | (2.8) |  | (2.7) |  |
| 33. | Inventory turnover (times) | n.a. |  | n.a. |  |
| 34. | Days' sales in inventory | n.a. |  | n.a. |  |
| 35. | Average age of inventory (days) | n.a. |  | n.a. |  |
| 36. | Return on assets, net income | 8.8% |  | 9.0% |  |
| 37. | Return on assets, gross operating profit | 1.3% |  | 1.2% |  |
| 38. | Return on assets, net operating profit | (1.7%) |  | (1.4%) |  |

Table 2: Partnerships With Net Income:  187.  LESSORS, OTHER THAN BUILDINGS

Dollar values in thousands, except averages

| | | 1984 | | 1985 | |
|---|---|---|---|---|---|
| 1. | Number of Partnerships | 14,912 | | 18,083 | |
| 2. | Number of Partners | 103,984 | | 123,203 | |
| | | | | | |
| 3. | Total Assets | $4,086,440 | | $5,599,584 | |
| 4. | Average total assets per Partnership | $274,037 | | $309,660 | |
| 5. | Average total assets per Partner | $39,299 | | $45,450 | |
| | | | | | |
| 6. | Net Income | $562,541 | | $620,152 | |
| 7. | Average per Partnership, total earnings | $37,724 | | $34,295 | |
| 8. | Average per Partner, total earnings | $5,410 | | $5,034 | |
| | | | | | |
| 9. | Total Receipts | $105,457 | | $163,429 | |
| | Operating Costs | | | | |
| 10. | Cost of sales & operations | $18,823 | 17.9% | $32,384 | 19.8% |
| 11. | Salaries and wages | $22,672 | 21.5% | $27,581 | 16.9% |
| 12. | Rent paid | $3,877 | 3.7% | $5,386 | 3.3% |
| 13. | Interest paid | $29,349 | 27.8% | $51,118 | 31.3% |
| 14. | Taxes paid | $8,197 | 7.8% | $14,381 | 8.8% |
| 15. | Bad debts | $17 | 0.0% | $2,090 | 1.3% |
| 16. | Repairs | $1,927 | 1.8% | $3,986 | 2.4% |
| 17. | Depreciation | $24,118 | 22.9% | $42,292 | 25.9% |
| 18. | Depletion | $174 | 0.2% | $2,708 | 1.7% |
| 19. | Pension & profit sharing plans | $2,210 | 2.1% | $2,591 | 1.6% |
| 20. | Employee benefits programs | $1,579 | 1.5% | $1,854 | 1.1% |
| 21. | Other deductions | $18,342 | 17.4% | $39,094 | 23.9% |
| 22. | Total operating costs | $131,286 | 124.5% | $225,465 | 138.0% |
| | | | | | |
| | Operating Income and Distribution | | | | |
| 23. | Total Receipts | $105,457 | 100.0% | $163,429 | 100.0% |
| 24. | Less: Cost of sales and operations | $18,823 | 17.9% | $32,384 | 19.8% |
| 25. | Gross operating profit | $86,634 | 82.2% | $131,045 | 80.2% |
| 26. | Additional operating costs | $112,463 | 106.6% | $193,081 | 118.1% |
| 27. | Net operating profit | ($25,829) | (24.5%) | ($62,036) | (38.0%) |
| 28. | Less: Guaranteed payments to partners | $2,786 | | $6,395 | |
| 29. | Distribution to partners | ($28,615) | | ($68,431) | |
| 30. | Other charges | $1,848 | | $9,724 | |
| 31. | Net change partners' capital | ($30,463) | | ($78,155) | |
| | | | | | |
| | Selected Ratios | | | | |
| 32. | Coverage ratio:  times interest earned | (1.9) | | (2.2) | |
| 33. | Inventory turnover (times) | n.a. | | n.a. | |
| 34. | Days' sales in inventory | n.a. | | n.a. | |
| 35. | Average age of inventory (days) | n.a. | | n.a. | |
| 36. | Return on assets, net income | 13.8% | | 11.1% | |
| 37. | Return on assets, gross operating profit | 2.1% | | 2.3% | |
| 38. | Return on assets, net operating profit | (0.6%) | | (1.1%) | |

Table 2: Partnerships With Net Income:  188.  REAL ESTATE AGENTS, BROKERS, AND MANAGERS

Dollar values in thousands, except averages

|     |                                        | 1984        |        | 1985        |         |
|-----|----------------------------------------|-------------|--------|-------------|---------|
| 1.  | Number of Partnerships                 | 5,803       |        | 8,864       |         |
| 2.  | Number of Partners                     | 31,798      |        | 68,630      |         |
| 3.  | Total Assets                           | $3,511,559  |        | $3,964,430  |         |
| 4.  | Average total assets per Partnership   | $605,128    |        | $447,251    |         |
| 5.  | Average total assets per Partner       | $110,433    |        | $57,765     |         |
| 6.  | Net Income                             | $432,887    |        | $494,884    |         |
| 7.  | Average per Partnership, total earnings| $74,605     |        | $55,833     |         |
| 8.  | Average per Partner, total earnings    | $13,615     |        | $7,211      |         |
| 9.  | Total Receipts                         | $1,282,817  |        | $1,200,775  |         |
|     | Operating Costs                        |             |        |             |         |
| 10. | Cost of sales & operations             | $362,976    | 28.3%  | $337,573    | 28.1%   |
| 11. | Salaries and wages                     | $116,532    | 9.1%   | $175,283    | 14.6%   |
| 12. | Rent paid                              | $34,596     | 2.7%   | $74,057     | 6.2%    |
| 13. | Interest paid                          | $82,229     | 6.4%   | $87,267     | 7.3%    |
| 14. | Taxes paid                             | $30,649     | 2.4%   | $24,991     | 2.1%    |
| 15. | Bad debts                              | $589        | 0.1%   | $2,063      | 0.2%    |
| 16. | Repairs                                | $16,891     | 1.3%   | $7,372      | 0.6%    |
| 17. | Depreciation                           | $42,852     | 3.3%   | $36,738     | 3.1%    |
| 18. | Depletion                              | $0          | n.a.   | $12         | n.a.    |
| 19. | Pension & profit sharing plans         | $1,088      | 0.1%   | $653        | 0.1%    |
| 20. | Employee benefits programs             | $444        | 0.0%   | $10,040     | 0.8%    |
| 21. | Other deductions                       | $370,554    | 28.9%  | $504,746    | 42.0%   |
| 22. | Total operating costs                  | $1,059,476  | 82.6%  | $1,260,795  | 105.0%  |
|     | Operating Income and Distribution      |             |        |             |         |
| 23. | Total Receipts                         | $1,282,817  | 100.0% | $1,200,775  | 100.0%  |
| 24. | Less:  Cost of sales and operations    | $362,976    | 28.3%  | $337,573    | 28.1%   |
| 25. | Gross operating profit                 | $919,841    | 71.7%  | $863,202    | 71.9%   |
| 26. | Additional operating costs             | $696,500    | 54.3%  | $923,222    | 76.9%   |
| 27. | Net operating profit                   | $223,341    | 17.4%  | ($60,020)   | (5.0%)  |
| 28. | Less:  Guaranteed payments to partners | $45,959     |        | $22,777     |         |
| 29. | Distribution to partners               | $177,382    |        | ($82,797)   |         |
| 30. | Other charges                          | $16,053     |        | $12,937     |         |
| 31. | Net change partners' capital           | $161,329    |        | ($95,734)   |         |
|     | Selected Ratios                        |             |        |             |         |
| 32. | Coverage ratio:  times interest earned | 1.7         |        | (1.7)       |         |
| 33. | Inventory turnover (times)             | n.a.        |        | n.a.        |         |
| 34. | Days' sales in inventory               | n.a.        |        | n.a.        |         |
| 35. | Average age of inventory (days)        | n.a.        |        | n.a.        |         |
| 36. | Return on assets, net income           | 12.3%       |        | 12.5%       |         |
| 37. | Return on assets, gross operating profit| 26.2%      |        | 21.8%       |         |
| 38. | Return on assets, net operating profit | 6.4%        |        | (1.5%)      |         |

Table 2: Partnerships With Net Income:  OTHER REAL ESTATE (189,190,191,192)

Dollar values in thousands, except averages

|  |  | 1984 |  | 1985 |  |
|---|---|---|---|---|---|
| 1. | Number of Partnerships | 19,091 | | 21,250 | |
| 2. | Number of Partners | 93,194 | | 172,376 | |
| 3. | Total Assets | $20,037,910 | | $24,048,694 | |
| 4. | Average total assets per Partnership | $1,049,600 | | $1,131,703 | |
| 5. | Average total assets per Partner | $215,013 | | $139,513 | |
| 6. | Net Income | $2,856,146 | | $2,891,717 | |
| 7. | Average per Partnership, total earnings | $149,609 | | $136,083 | |
| 8. | Average per Partner, total earnings | $30,648 | | $16,776 | |
| 9. | Total Receipts | $10,226,468 | | $11,053,725 | |
|  | Operating Costs | | | | |
| 10. | Cost of sales & operations | $7,341,839 | 71.8% | $7,775,286 | 70.3% |
| 11. | Salaries and wages | $104,745 | 1.0% | $127,529 | 1.2% |
| 12. | Rent paid | $15,988 | 0.2% | $20,659 | 0.2% |
| 13. | Interest paid | $690,131 | 6.8% | $637,804 | 5.8% |
| 14. | Taxes paid | $94,327 | 0.9% | $94,795 | 0.9% |
| 15. | Bad debts | $3,065 | 0.0% | $7,648 | 0.1% |
| 16. | Repairs | $14,683 | 0.1% | $15,324 | 0.1% |
| 17. | Depreciation | $56,539 | 0.6% | $51,098 | 0.5% |
| 18. | Depletion | $240 | n.a. | $15 | n.a. |
| 19. | Pension & profit sharing plans | $1,140 | 0.0% | $31 | n.a. |
| 20. | Employee benefits programs | $3,481 | 0.0% | $5,333 | 0.1% |
| 21. | Other deductions | $818,136 | 8.0% | $910,591 | 8.2% |
| 22. | Total operating costs | $9,144,322 | 89.4% | $9,646,125 | 87.3% |
|  | Operating Income and Distribution | | | | |
| 23. | Total Receipts | $10,226,468 | 100.0% | $11,053,725 | 100.0% |
| 24. | Less: Cost of sales and operations | $7,341,839 | 71.8% | $7,775,286 | 70.3% |
| 25. | Gross operating profit | $2,884,629 | 28.2% | $3,278,439 | 29.7% |
| 26. | Additional operating costs | $1,802,483 | 17.6% | $1,870,839 | 16.9% |
| 27. | Net operating profit | $1,082,146 | 10.6% | $1,407,600 | 12.7% |
| 28. | Less: Guaranteed payments to partners | $44,889 | | $57,218 | |
| 29. | Distribution to partners | $1,037,257 | | $1,350,382 | |
| 30. | Other charges | $87,858 | | $93,762 | |
| 31. | Net change partners' capital | $949,399 | | $1,256,620 | |
|  | Selected Ratios | | | | |
| 32. | Coverage ratio: times interest earned | 0.6 | | 1.2 | |
| 33. | Inventory turnover (times) | n.a. | | n.a. | |
| 34. | Days' sales in inventory | n.a. | | n.a. | |
| 35. | Average age of inventory (days) | n.a. | | n.a. | |
| 36. | Return on assets, net income | 14.3% | | 12.0% | |
| 37. | Return on assets, gross operating profit | 14.4% | | 13.6% | |
| 38. | Return on assets, net operating profit | 5.4% | | 5.9% | |

Table 2: Partnerships With Net Income:  193.  SERVICES

Dollar values in thousands, except averages

| | 1984 | | 1985 | |
|---|---|---|---|---|
| 1. Number of Partnerships | 204,282 | | 207,341 | |
| 2. Number of Partners | 843,410 | | 886,670 | |
| | | | | |
| 3. Total Assets | $34,749,015 | | $39,281,378 | |
| 4. Average total assets per Partnership | $170,103 | | $189,453 | |
| 5. Average total assets per Partner | $41,201 | | $44,302 | |
| | | | | |
| 6. Net Income | $24,800,274 | | $26,941,589 | |
| 7. Average per Partnership, total earnings | $121,412 | | $129,950 | |
| 8. Average per Partner, total earnings | $29,407 | | $30,388 | |
| | | | | |
| 9. Operating Income | $77,349,648 | | $86,528,967 | |
| Operating Costs | | | | |
| 10. Cost of sales & operations | $10,285,719 | 13.3% | $11,305,613 | 13.1% |
| 11. Salaries and wages | $14,868,604 | 19.2% | $17,404,582 | 20.1% |
| 12. Rent paid | $3,478,299 | 4.5% | $4,005,801 | 4.6% |
| 13. Interest paid | $1,376,474 | 1.8% | $1,511,247 | 1.8% |
| 14. Taxes paid | $1,849,891 | 2.4% | $2,112,773 | 2.4% |
| 15. Bad debts | $142,964 | 0.2% | $131,501 | 0.2% |
| 16. Repairs | $519,478 | 0.7% | $549,657 | 0.6% |
| 17. Depreciation | $2,492,869 | 3.2% | $2,897,478 | 3.4% |
| 18. Depletion | $937 | n.a. | $8,936 | 0.0% |
| 19. Pension & profit sharing plans | $360,336 | 0.5% | $440,400 | 0.5% |
| 20. Employee benefits programs | $423,038 | 0.6% | $457,395 | 0.5% |
| 21. Other deductions | $14,673,397 | 19.0% | $16,208,462 | 18.7% |
| 22. Total operating costs | $50,482,997 | 65.3% | $57,037,178 | 65.9% |
| | | | | |
| Operating Income and Distribution | | | | |
| 23. Operating Income | $77,349,648 | 100.0% | $86,528,967 | 100.0% |
| 24. Less: Cost of sales and operations | $10,285,719 | 13.3% | $11,305,613 | 13.1% |
| 25. Gross operating profit | $67,063,929 | 86.7% | $75,223,354 | 86.9% |
| 26. Additional operating costs | $40,197,278 | 52.0% | $45,731,565 | 52.9% |
| 27. Net operating profit | $26,866,651 | 34.7% | $29,491,789 | 34.1% |
| 28. Less: Guaranteed payments to partners | $1,955,958 | | $2,431,791 | |
| 29. Distribution to partners | $24,910,693 | | $27,059,998 | |
| 30. Other charges | $121,410 | | $121,741 | |
| 31. Net change partners' capital | $24,789,283 | | $26,938,257 | |
| | | | | |
| Selected Ratios | | | | |
| 32. Coverage ratio:  times interest earned | 18.5 | | 18.5 | |
| 33. Inventory turnover (times) | n.a. | | n.a. | |
| 34. Days' sales in inventory | n.a. | | n.a. | |
| 35. Average age of inventory (days) | n.a. | | n.a. | |
| 36. Return on assets, net income | 71.4% | | 68.6% | |
| 37. Return on assets, gross operating profit | 193.0% | | 191.5% | |
| 38. Return on assets, net operating profit | 77.3% | | 75.1% | |

Table 2: Partnerships With Net Income:  194.  HOTELS AND OTHER LODGING PLACES

Dollar values in thousands, except averages

|  |  | 1984 |  | 1985 |  |
|---|---|---|---|---|---|
| 1. | Number of Partnerships | 8,831 |  | 7,863 |  |
| 2. | Number of Partners | 99,558 |  | 47,797 |  |
| 3. | Total Assets | $7,012,517 |  | $8,239,038 |  |
| 4. | Average total assets per Partnership | $794,080 |  | $1,047,824 |  |
| 5. | Average total assets per Partner | $70,437 |  | $172,376 |  |
| 6. | Net Income | $817,886 |  | $854,783 |  |
| 7. | Average per Partnership, total earnings | $92,620 |  | $108,716 |  |
| 8. | Average per Partner, total earnings | $8,216 |  | $17,885 |  |
| 9. | Operating Income | $6,529,310 |  | $6,538,196 |  |
|  | Operating Costs |  |  |  |  |
| 10. | Cost of sales & operations | $2,442,921 | 37.4% | $2,351,505 | 36.0% |
| 11. | Salaries and wages | $628,485 | 9.6% | $651,781 | 1.0% |
| 12. | Rent paid | $88,101 | 1.4% | $96,765 | 1.5% |
| 13. | Interest paid | $373,254 | 5.7% | $384,868 | 5.9% |
| 14. | Taxes paid | $246,518 | 3.8% | $279,187 | 4.3% |
| 15. | Bad debts | $8,171 | 0.1% | $8,980 | 0.1% |
| 16. | Repairs | $133,435 | 2.0% | $129,784 | 2.0% |
| 17. | Depreciation | $352,864 | 5.4% | $375,965 | 5.8% |
| 18. | Depletion | $0 | n.a. | $288 | n.a. |
| 19. | Pension & profit sharing plans | $4,139 | 0.1% | $4,682 | 0.1% |
| 20. | Employee benefits programs | $29,957 | 0.5% | $30,277 | 0.5% |
| 21. | Other deductions | $1,357,094 | 20.8% | $1,313,508 | 20.1% |
| 22. | Total operating costs | $5,665,679 | 86.8% | $5,628,623 | 86.1% |
|  | Operating Income and Distribution |  |  |  |  |
| 23. | Operating Income | $6,529,310 | 100.0% | $6,538,196 | 100.0% |
| 24. | Less:  Cost of sales and operations | $2,442,921 | 37.4% | $2,351,505 | 36.0% |
| 25. | Gross operating profit | $4,086,389 | 62.6% | $4,186,691 | 64.0% |
| 26. | Additional operating costs | $3,222,758 | 49.4% | $3,277,118 | 50.1% |
| 27. | Net operating profit | $863,631 | 13.2% | $909,573 | 13.9% |
| 28. | Less:  Guaranteed payments to partners | $39,402 |  | $49,294 |  |
| 29. | Distribution to partners | $824,229 |  | $860,279 |  |
| 30. | Other charges | $7,082 |  | $6,528 |  |
| 31. | Net change partners' capital | $817,147 |  | $853,751 |  |
|  | Selected Ratios |  |  |  |  |
| 32. | Coverage ratio:  times interest earned | 1.3 |  | 1.4 |  |
| 33. | Inventory turnover (times) | n.a. |  | n.a. |  |
| 34. | Days' sales in inventory | n.a. |  | n.a. |  |
| 35. | Average age of inventory (days) | n.a. |  | n.a. |  |
| 36. | Return on assets, net income | 11.7% |  | 10.4% |  |
| 37. | Return on assets, gross operating profit | 58.3% |  | 50.8% |  |
| 38. | Return on assets, net operating profit | 12.3% |  | 11.0% |  |

*Page 169*

Table 2: Partnerships With Net Income: 196.  MOTELS, MOTOR HOTELS, AND COURTS

Dollar values in thousands, except averages

|  |  | 1984 |  | 1985 |  |
|---|---|---|---|---|---|
| 1. | Number of Partnerships | 4,925 |  | 3,139 |  |
| 2. | Number of Partners | 76,852 |  | 22,582 |  |
| 3. | Total Assets | $2,777,579 |  | $3,693,752 |  |
| 4. | Average total assets per Partnership | $563,975 |  | $1,176,729 |  |
| 5. | Average total assets per Partner | $36,142 |  | $163,571 |  |
| 6. | Net Income | $339,449 |  | $355,154 |  |
| 7. | Average per Partnership, total earnings | $68,927 |  | $113,153 |  |
| 8. | Average per Partner, total earnings | $4,417 |  | $15,729 |  |
| 9. | Operating Income | $2,009,781 |  | $2,024,781 |  |
|  | Operating Costs |  |  |  |  |
| 10. | Cost of sales & operations | $259,322 | 12.9% | $275,080 | 13.6% |
| 11. | Salaries and wages | $261,351 | 13.0% | $258,630 | 12.8% |
| 12. | Rent paid | $44,265 | 2.2% | $39,673 | 2.0% |
| 13. | Interest paid | $176,815 | 8.8% | $193,811 | 9.6% |
| 14. | Taxes paid | $90,326 | 4.5% | $91,041 | 4.5% |
| 15. | Bad debts | $2,712 | 0.1% | $2,259 | 0.1% |
| 16. | Repairs | $65,715 | 3.3% | $55,564 | 2.7% |
| 17. | Depreciation | $187,586 | 9.3% | $191,810 | 9.5% |
| 18. | Depletion | $0 | n.a. | $288 | 0.0% |
| 19. | Pension & profit sharing plans | $580 | 0.0% | $645 | 0.0% |
| 20. | Employee benefits programs | $7,664 | 0.4% | $7,603 | 0.4% |
| 21. | Other deductions | $557,084 | 27.7% | $516,800 | 25.5% |
| 22. | Total operating costs | $1,653,685 | 82.3% | $1,633,826 | 80.7% |
|  | Operating Income and Distribution |  |  |  |  |
| 23. | Operating Income | $2,009,781 | 100.0% | $2,024,781 | 100.0% |
| 24. | Less:  Cost of sales and operations | $259,322 | 12.9% | $275,080 | 13.6% |
| 25. | Gross operating profit | $1,750,459 | 87.1% | $1,749,701 | 86.4% |
| 26. | Additional operating costs | $1,394,363 | 69.4% | $1,358,746 | 67.1% |
| 27. | Net operating profit | $356,096 | 17.7% | $390,955 | 19.3% |
| 28. | Less:  Guaranteed payments to partners | $15,321 |  | $32,877 |  |
| 29. | Distribution to partners | $340,775 |  | $358,078 |  |
| 30. | Other charges | $1,590 |  | $3,546 |  |
| 31. | Net change partners' capital | $339,185 |  | $354,532 |  |
|  | Selected Ratios |  |  |  |  |
| 32. | Coverage ratio:  times interest earned | 1.0 |  | 1.0 |  |
| 33. | Inventory turnover (times) | n.a. |  | n.a. |  |
| 34. | Days' sales in inventory | n.a. |  | n.a. |  |
| 35. | Average age of inventory (days) | n.a. |  | n.a. |  |
| 36. | Return on assets, net income | 12.2% |  | 9.6% |  |
| 37. | Return on assets, gross operating profit | 63.0% |  | 47.4% |  |
| 38. | Return on assets, net operating profit | 12.8% |  | 10.6% |  |

Table 2: Partnerships With Net Income:  OTHER LODGING PLACES (195,197,198,199,200)

Dollar values in thousands, except averages

|  | | 1984 | | 1985 | |
|---|---|---|---|---|---|
| 1. | Number of Partnerships | 3,906 | | 4,724 | |
| 2. | Number of Partners | 22,706 | | 25,214 | |
| 3. | Total Assets | $4,234,938 | | $4,545,286 | |
| 4. | Average total assets per Partnership | $1,084,214 | | $962,169 | |
| 5. | Average total assets per Partner | $186,512 | | $180,268 | |
| 6. | Net Income | $478,437 | | $499,629 | |
| 7. | Average per Partnership, total earnings | $122,494 | | $105,767 | |
| 8. | Average per Partner, total earnings | $21,072 | | $19,816 | |
| 9. | Operating Income | $4,519,529 | | $4,513,415 | |
|  | Operating Costs | | | | |
| 10. | Cost of sales & operations | $2,183,599 | 48.3% | $2,076,425 | 46.0% |
| 11. | Salaries and wages | $367,135 | 8.1% | $393,151 | 8.7% |
| 12. | Rent paid | $43,836 | 0.10% | $57,092 | 1.3% |
| 13. | Interest paid | $196,440 | 4.4% | $191,057 | 4.2% |
| 14. | Taxes paid | $156,192 | 3.5% | $188,146 | 4.2% |
| 15. | Bad debts | $5,460 | 0.1% | $6,721 | 0.2% |
| 16. | Repairs | $67,720 | 1.5% | $74,220 | 1.6% |
| 17. | Depreciation | $165,275 | 3.7% | $184,156 | 4.1% |
| 18. | Depletion | $0 | n.a. | $0 | n.a. |
| 19. | Pension & profit sharing plans | $3,559 | 0.1% | $4,037 | 0.1% |
| 20. | Employee benefits programs | $22,293 | 0.5% | $22,674 | 0.5% |
| 21. | Other deductions | $800,010 | 17.7% | $796,707 | 17.7% |
| 22. | Total operating costs | $4,011,994 | 88.8% | $3,994,797 | 88.5% |
|  | Operating Income and Distribution | | | | |
| 23. | Operating Income | $4,519,529 | 100.0% | $4,513,415 | 100.0% |
| 24. | Less:  Cost of sales and operations | $2,183,599 | 48.3% | $2,076,425 | 46.0% |
| 25. | Gross operating profit | $2,335,930 | 51.7% | $2,436,990 | 54.0% |
| 26. | Additional operating costs | $1,828,395 | 40.5% | $1,918,372 | 42.5% |
| 27. | Net operating profit | $507,535 | 11.2% | $518,618 | 11.5% |
| 28. | Less:  Guaranteed payments to partners | $24,081 | | $16,417 | |
| 29. | Distribution to partners | $483,454 | | $502,201 | |
| 30. | Other charges | $5,492 | | $2,983 | |
| 31. | Net change partners' capital | $477,962 | | $499,218 | |
|  | Selected Ratios | | | | |
| 32. | Coverage ratio:  times interest earned | 1.6 | | 1.7 | |
| 33. | Inventory turnover (times) | n.a. | | n.a. | |
| 34. | Days' sales in inventory | n.a. | | n.a. | |
| 35. | Average age of inventory (days) | n.a. | | n.a. | |
| 36. | Return on assets, net income | 11.3% | | 11.0% | |
| 37. | Return on assets, gross operating profit | 55.2% | | 53.6% | |
| 38. | Return on assets, net operating profit | 12.0% | | 11.4% | |

Table 2: Partnerships With Net Income:  201.  PERSONAL SERVICES

Dollar values in thousands, except averages

|  |  | 1984 |  | 1985 |  |
|---|---|---|---|---|---|
| 1. | Number of Partnerships | 23,512 |  | 23,116 |  |
| 2. | Number of Partners | 57,124 |  | 54,875 |  |
| 3. | Total Assets | $458,489 |  | $731,517 |  |
| 4. | Average total assets per Partnership | $19,500 |  | $31,645 |  |
| 5. | Average total assets per Partner | $8,026 |  | $13,331 |  |
| 6. | Net Income | $358,422 |  | $436,093 |  |
| 7. | Average per Partnership, total earnings | $15,247 |  | $18,868 |  |
| 8. | Average per Partner, total earnings | $6,275 |  | $7,948 |  |
| 9. | Operating Income | $1,574,605 |  | $1,745,200 |  |
|  | Operating Costs |  |  |  |  |
| 10. | Cost of sales & operations | $323,602 | 20.6% | $343,690 | 19.7% |
| 11. | Salaries and wages | $153,438 | 9.7% | $159,157 | 9.1% |
| 12. | Rent paid | $85,423 | 5.4% | $132,100 | 7.6% |
| 13. | Interest paid | $18,683 | 1.2% | $27,007 | 1.6% |
| 14. | Taxes paid | $31,819 | 2.0% | $41,993 | 2.4% |
| 15. | Bad debts | $1,981 | 0.1% | $2,970 | 0.2% |
| 16. | Repairs | $23,872 | 1.5% | $28,903 | 1.7% |
| 17. | Depreciation | $84,377 | 5.4% | $91,693 | 5.3% |
| 18. | Depletion | $0 | n.a. | $54 | n.a. |
| 19. | Pension & profit sharing plans | $499 | 0.0% | $1,063 | 0.1% |
| 20. | Employee benefits programs | $2,379 | 0.2% | $3,222 | 0.2% |
| 21. | Other deductions | $433,731 | 27.6% | $413,439 | 23.7% |
| 22. | Total operating costs | $1,159,804 | 73.7% | $1,245,365 | 71.4% |
|  | Operating Income and Distribution |  |  |  |  |
| 23. | Operating Income | $1,574,605 | 100.0% | $1,745,200 | 100.0% |
| 24. | Less:  Cost of sales and operations | $323,602 | 20.6% | $343,690 | 19.7% |
| 25. | Gross operating profit | $1,251,003 | 79.5% | $1,401,510 | 80.3% |
| 26. | Additional operating costs | $836,202 | 53.1% | $901,675 | 51.7% |
| 27. | Net operating profit | $414,801 | 26.3% | $499,835 | 28.6% |
| 28. | Less:  Guaranteed payments to partners | $54,176 |  | $62,529 |  |
| 29. | Distribution to partners | $360,625 |  | $437,306 |  |
| 30. | Other charges | $2,203 |  | $1,287 |  |
| 31. | Net change partners' capital | $358,422 |  | $436,019 |  |
|  | Selected Ratios |  |  |  |  |
| 32. | Coverage ratio:  times interest earned | 21.2 |  | 17.5 |  |
| 33. | Inventory turnover (times) | n.a. |  | n.a. |  |
| 34. | Days' sales in inventory | n.a. |  | n.a. |  |
| 35. | Average age of inventory (days) | n.a. |  | n.a. |  |
| 36. | Return on assets, net income | 78.2% |  | 59.6% |  |
| 37. | Return on assets, gross operating profit | n.a. |  | 191.6% |  |
| 38. | Return on assets, net operating profit | 90.5% |  | 68.3% |  |

*Page 172*

Table 2: Partnerships With Net Income:  LAUNDRIES, DRY CLEANING, AND GARMENT SERVICES (202,203)

Dollar values in thousands, except averages

| | | 1984 | | 1985 | |
|---|---|---|---|---|---|
| 1. | Number of Partnerships | 6,379 | | 5,529 | |
| 2. | Number of Partners | 13,881 | | 12,312 | |
| 3. | Total Assets | $134,660 | | $134,979 | |
| 4. | Average total assets per Partnership | $21,110 | | $24,413 | |
| 5. | Average total assets per Partner | $9,701 | | $10,963 | |
| 6. | Net Income | $66,653 | | $78,700 | |
| 7. | Average per Partnership, total earnings | $10,451 | | $14,235 | |
| 8. | Average per Partner, total earnings | $4,803 | | $6,392 | |
| 9. | Operating Income | $520,344 | | $496,110 | |
| | Operating Costs | | | | |
| 10. | Cost of sales & operations | $41,773 | 8.0% | $62,745 | 12.7% |
| 11. | Salaries and wages | $90,302 | 17.4% | $68,158 | 13.7% |
| 12. | Rent paid | $43,182 | 8.3% | $60,006 | 12.1% |
| 13. | Interest paid | $10,292 | 2.0% | $8,003 | 1.6% |
| 14. | Taxes paid | $14,828 | 2.9% | $16,693 | 3.4% |
| 15. | Bad debts | $103 | 0.0% | $459 | 0.1% |
| 16. | Repairs | $13,583 | 2.6% | $10,686 | 2.2% |
| 17. | Depreciation | $36,473 | 7.0% | $41,407 | 8.4% |
| 18. | Depletion | $0 | n.a. | $0 | n.a. |
| 19. | Pension & profit sharing plans | $0 | n.a. | $453 | 0.1% |
| 20. | Employee benefits programs | $1,410 | 0.3% | $708 | 0.1% |
| 21. | Other deductions | $186,799 | 35.9% | $143,767 | 29.0% |
| 22. | Total operating costs | $438,745 | 84.3% | $413,159 | 83.3% |
| | Operating Income and Distribution | | | | |
| 23. | Operating Income | $520,344 | 100.0% | $496,110 | 100.0% |
| 24. | Less:  Cost of sales and operations | $41,773 | 8.0% | $62,745 | 12.7% |
| 25. | Gross operating profit | $478,571 | 92.0% | $433,365 | 87.4% |
| 26. | Additional operating costs | $396,972 | 76.3% | $350,414 | 70.6% |
| 27. | Net operating profit | $81,599 | 15.7% | $82,951 | 16.7% |
| 28. | Less:  Guaranteed payments to partners | $14,946 | | $4,291 | |
| 29. | Distribution to partners | $66,653 | | $78,660 | |
| 30. | Other charges | $0 | | $35 | |
| 31. | Net change partners' capital | $66,653 | | $78,625 | |
| | Selected Ratios | | | | |
| 32. | Coverage ratio:  times interest earned | 6.9 | | 9.4 | |
| 33. | Inventory turnover (times) | n.a. | | n.a. | |
| 34. | Days' sales in inventory | n.a. | | n.a. | |
| 35. | Average age of inventory (days) | n.a. | | n.a. | |
| 36. | Return on assets, net income | 49.5% | | 58.3% | |
| 37. | Return on assets, gross operating profit | n.a. | | n.a. | |
| 38. | Return on assets, net operating profit | 60.6% | | 61.5% | |

Table 2: Partnerships With Net Income:  206.  BEAUTY SHOPS

Dollar values in thousands, except averages

| | 1984 | | 1985 | |
|---|---|---|---|---|
| 1.  Number of Partnerships | 4,019 | | 5,345 | |
| 2.  Number of Partners | 9,130 | | 11,261 | |
| | | | | |
| 3.  Total Assets | $18,625 | | $266,514 | |
| 4.   Average total assets per Partnership | $4,634 | | $49,862 | |
| 5.   Average total assets per Partner | $2,040 | | $23,667 | |
| | | | | |
| 6.  Net Income | $39,265 | | $56,039 | |
| 7.   Average per Partnership, total earnings | $9,770 | | $10,487 | |
| 8.   Average per Partner, total earnings | $4,301 | | $4,978 | |
| | | | | |
| 9.  Operating Income | $96,696 | | $205,855 | |
| Operating Costs | | | | |
| 10.   Cost of sales & operations | $12,860 | 13.3% | $54,847 | 26.6% |
| 11.   Salaries and wages | $3,301 | 3.4% | $17,067 | 8.3% |
| 12.   Rent paid | $11,617 | 12.0% | $28,425 | 13.8% |
| 13.   Interest paid | $311 | 0.3% | $1,871 | 0.9% |
| 14.   Taxes paid | $1,121 | 1.2% | $2,735 | 1.3% |
| 15.   Bad debts | $0 | n.a. | $65 | 0.0% |
| 16.   Repairs | $328 | 0.3% | $648 | 0.3% |
| 17.   Depreciation | $3,259 | 3.4% | $5,729 | 2.8% |
| 18.   Depletion | $0 | n.a. | $0 | n.a. |
| 19.   Pension & profit sharing plans | $0 | n.a. | $0 | n.a. |
| 20.   Employee benefits programs | $0 | n.a. | $300 | 0.2% |
| 21.   Other deductions | $24,634 | 25.5% | $24,916 | 12.1% |
| 22.   Total operating costs | $57,431 | 59.4% | $136,603 | 66.4% |
| | | | | |
| Operating Income and Distribution | | | | |
| 23.   Operating Income | $96,696 | 100.0% | $205,855 | 100.0% |
| 24.    Less:  Cost of sales and operations | $12,860 | 13.3% | $54,847 | 26.6% |
| 25.   Gross operating profit | $83,836 | 86.7% | $151,008 | 73.4% |
| 26.    Additional operating costs | $44,571 | 46.1% | $81,756 | 39.7% |
| 27.   Net operating profit | $39,265 | 40.6% | $69,252 | 33.6% |
| 28.    Less:  Guaranteed payments to partners | $0 | | $13,213 | |
| 29.   Distribution to partners | $39,265 | | $56,039 | |
| 30.   Other charges | $0 | | $0 | |
| 31.   Net change partners' capital | $39,265 | | $56,039 | |
| | | | | |
| Selected Ratios | | | | |
| 32.   Coverage ratio:  times interest earned | 125.3 | | 36.0 | |
| 33.   Inventory turnover (times) | n.a. | | n.a. | |
| 34.   Days' sales in inventory | n.a. | | n.a. | |
| 35.   Average age of inventory (days) | n.a. | | n.a. | |
| 36.   Return on assets, net income | 210.8% | | 21.0% | |
| 37.   Return on assets, gross operating profit | n.a. | | 56.7% | |
| 38.   Return on assets, net operating profit | 210.8% | | 26.0% | |

Table 2: Partnerships With Net Income: 207. BARBER SHOPS

Dollar values in thousands, except averages

| | | 1984 | | 1985 | |
|---|---|---|---|---|---|
| 1. | Number of Partnerships | 2,514 | | 4,234 | |
| 2. | Number of Partners | 7,057 | | 13,813 | |
| | | | | | |
| 3. | Total Assets | $10,854 | | $21,472 | |
| 4. | Average total assets per Partnership | $4,317 | | $5,071 | |
| 5. | Average total assets per Partner | $1,538 | | $1,554 | |
| | | | | | |
| 6. | Net Income | $38,082 | | $116,458 | |
| 7. | Average per Partnership, total earnings | $15,148 | | $27,506 | |
| 8. | Average per Partner, total earnings | $5,396 | | $8,431 | |
| | | | | | |
| 9. | Operating Income | $117,288 | | $280,882 | |
| | Operating Costs | | | | |
| 10. | Cost of sales & operations | $37,413 | 31.9% | $76,414 | 27.2% |
| 11. | Salaries and wages | $0 | n.a. | $0 | n.a. |
| 12. | Rent paid | $15,882 | 13.5% | $26,578 | 9.5% |
| 13. | Interest paid | $0 | n.a. | $2,621 | 0.9% |
| 14. | Taxes paid | $3,756 | 3.2% | $8,369 | 3.0% |
| 15. | Bad debts | $0 | n.a. | $0 | n.a. |
| 16. | Repairs | $0 | n.a. | $394 | 0.1% |
| 17. | Depreciation | $3,846 | 3.3% | $7,574 | 2.7% |
| 18. | Depletion | $0 | n.a. | $0 | n.a. |
| 19. | Pension & profit sharing plans | $0 | n.a. | $0 | n.a. |
| 20. | Employee benefits programs | $0 | n.a. | $0 | n.a. |
| 21. | Other deductions | $18,310 | 15.6% | $41,460 | 14.8% |
| 22. | Total operating costs | $79,207 | 67.5% | $163,410 | 58.2% |
| | | | | | |
| | Operating Income and Distribution | | | | |
| 23. | Operating Income | $117,288 | 100.0% | $280,882 | 100.0% |
| 24. | Less: Cost of sales and operations | $37,413 | 31.9% | $76,414 | 27.2% |
| 25. | Gross operating profit | $79,875 | 68.1% | $204,468 | 72.8% |
| 26. | Additional operating costs | $41,794 | 35.6% | $86,996 | 31.0% |
| 27. | Net operating profit | $38,081 | 32.5% | $117,472 | 41.8% |
| 28. | Less: Guaranteed payments to partners | $0 | | $1,014 | |
| 29. | Distribution to partners | $38,081 | | $116,458 | |
| 30. | Other charges | $0 | | $0 | |
| 31. | Net change partners' capital | $38,081 | | $116,458 | |
| | | | | | |
| | Selected Ratios | | | | |
| 32. | Coverage ratio: times interest earned | n.a. | | 43.8 | |
| 33. | Inventory turnover (times) | n.a. | | n.a. | |
| 34. | Days' sales in inventory | n.a. | | n.a. | |
| 35. | Average age of inventory (days) | n.a. | | n.a. | |
| 36. | Return on assets, net income | n.a. | | n.a. | |
| 37. | Return on assets, gross operating profit | n.a. | | n.a. | |
| 38. | Return on assets, net operating profit | n.a. | | n.a. | |

Table 2: Partnerships With Net Income: OTHER PERSONAL SERVICES (205,208,209,210)

Dollar values in thousands, except averages

| | 1984 | | 1985 | |
|---|---|---|---|---|
| 1.  Number of Partnerships | 10,600 | | 8,007 | |
| 2.  Number of Partners | 27,057 | | 17,489 | |
| | | | | |
| 3.  Total Assets | $294,350 | | $299,552 | |
| 4.     Average total assets per Partnership | $27,769 | | $37,411 | |
| 5.     Average total assets per Partner | $10,879 | | $17,128 | |
| | | | | |
| 6.  Net Income | $214,422 | | $184,897 | |
| 7.     Average per Partnership, total earnings | $20,232 | | $23,097 | |
| 8.     Average per Partner, total earnings | $7,926 | | $10,575 | |
| | | | | |
| 9.  Operating Income | $840,277 | | $762,353 | |
|     Operating Costs | | | | |
| 10.    Cost of sales & operations | $231,556 | 27.6% | $149,684 | 19.6% |
| 11.    Salaries and wages | $59,835 | 7.1% | $73,932 | 9.7% |
| 12.    Rent paid | $14,743 | 1.8% | $17,091 | 2.2% |
| 13.    Interest paid | $8,080 | 0.10% | $14,511 | 1.9% |
| 14.    Taxes paid | $12,114 | 1.4% | $14,196 | 1.9% |
| 15.    Bad debts | $1,878 | 0.2% | $2,447 | 0.3% |
| 16.    Repairs | $9,961 | 1.2% | $17,175 | 2.3% |
| 17.    Depreciation | $41,123 | 4.9% | $36,983 | 4.9% |
| 18.    Depletion | $0 | n.a. | $54 | 0.0% |
| 19.    Pension & profit sharing plans | $449 | 0.1% | $610 | 0.1% |
| 20.    Employee benefits programs | $696 | 0.1% | $2,215 | 0.3% |
| 21.    Other deductions | $203,987 | 24.3% | $203,292 | 26.7% |
| 22.    Total operating costs | $584,422 | 69.6% | $532,190 | 69.8% |
| | | | | |
| Operating Income and Distribution | | | | |
| 23.    Operating Income | $840,277 | 100.0% | $762,353 | 100.0% |
| 24.       Less: Cost of sales and operations | $231,556 | 27.6% | $149,684 | 19.6% |
| 25.    Gross operating profit | $608,721 | 72.4% | $612,669 | 80.4% |
| 26.       Additional operating costs | $352,866 | 42.0% | $382,506 | 50.2% |
| 27.    Net operating profit | $255,855 | 30.5% | $230,163 | 30.2% |
| 28.       Less: Guaranteed payments to partners | $39,229 | | $44,012 | |
| 29.    Distribution to partners | $216,626 | | $186,151 | |
| 30.    Other charges | $2,203 | | $1,254 | |
| 31.    Net change partners' capital | $214,423 | | $184,897 | |
| | | | | |
| Selected Ratios | | | | |
| 32.    Coverage ratio: times interest earned | 30.7 | | 14.9 | |
| 33.    Inventory turnover (times) | n.a. | | n.a. | |
| 34.    Days' sales in inventory | n.a. | | n.a. | |
| 35.    Average age of inventory (days) | n.a. | | n.a. | |
| 36.    Return on assets, net income | 72.9% | | 61.7% | |
| 37.    Return on assets, gross operating profit | 206.8% | | 204.5% | |
| 38.    Return on assets, net operating profit | 86.9% | | 76.8% | |

*Page 176*

Table 2: Partnerships With Net Income:  211.  BUSINESS SERVICES

Dollar values in thousands, except averages

|  | 1984 | | 1985 | |
|---|---|---|---|---|
| 1. Number of Partnerships | 45,159 | | 41,642 | |
| 2. Number of Partners | 234,183 | | 317,851 | |
| 3. Total Assets | $8,948,134 | | $10,171,257 | |
| 4.   Average total assets per Partnership | $198,147 | | $244,255 | |
| 5.   Average total assets per Partner | $38,210 | | $32,000 | |
| 6. Net Income | $2,581,576 | | $2,893,085 | |
| 7.   Average per Partnership, total earnings | $57,168 | | $69,478 | |
| 8.   Average per Partner, total earnings | $11,024 | | $9,102 | |
| 9. Operating Income | $7,391,276 | | $8,117,451 | |
| Operating Costs | | | | |
| 10.   Cost of sales & operations | $1,482,120 | 20.1% | $1,724,934 | 21.3% |
| 11.   Salaries and wages | $595,897 | 8.1% | $625,164 | 7.7% |
| 12.   Rent paid | $277,995 | 3.8% | $197,492 | 2.4% |
| 13.   Interest paid | $261,696 | 3.5% | $277,542 | 3.4% |
| 14.   Taxes paid | $99,896 | 1.4% | $99,071 | 1.2% |
| 15.   Bad debts | $62,298 | 0.8% | $54,673 | 0.7% |
| 16.   Repairs | $65,389 | 0.9% | $49,785 | 0.6% |
| 17.   Depreciation | $520,940 | 7.1% | $640,033 | 7.9% |
| 18.   Depletion | $410 | 0.0% | $614 | 0.0% |
| 19.   Pension & profit sharing plans | $12,656 | 0.2% | $15,332 | 0.2% |
| 20.   Employee benefits programs | $9,245 | 0.1% | $13,357 | 0.2% |
| 21.   Other deductions | $1,302,353 | 17.6% | $1,360,171 | 16.8% |
| 22.   Total operating costs | $4,695,275 | 63.5% | $5,058,488 | 62.3% |
| Operating Income and Distribution | | | | |
| 23.   Operating Income | $7,391,276 | 100.0% | $8,117,451 | 100.0% |
| 24.     Less: Cost of sales and operations | $1,482,120 | 20.1% | $1,724,934 | 21.3% |
| 25.   Gross operating profit | $5,909,156 | 80.0% | $6,392,517 | 78.8% |
| 26.     Additional operating costs | $3,213,155 | 43.5% | $3,333,554 | 41.1% |
| 27.   Net operating profit | $2,696,001 | 36.5% | $3,058,963 | 37.7% |
| 28.     Less: Guaranteed payments to partners | $79,296 | | $133,435 | |
| 29.   Distribution to partners | $2,616,705 | | $2,925,528 | |
| 30.   Other charges | $39,509 | | $32,763 | |
| 31.   Net change partners' capital | $2,577,196 | | $2,892,765 | |
| Selected Ratios | | | | |
| 32.   Coverage ratio: times interest earned | 9.3 | | 10.0 | |
| 33.   Inventory turnover (times) | n.a. | | n.a. | |
| 34.   Days' sales in inventory | n.a. | | n.a. | |
| 35.   Average age of inventory (days) | n.a. | | n.a. | |
| 36.   Return on assets, net income | 28.9% | | 28.4% | |
| 37.   Return on assets, gross operating profit | 66.0% | | 62.9% | |
| 38.   Return on assets, net operating profit | 30.1% | | 30.1% | |

*Page 177*

Table 2: Partnerships With Net Income:  218.  AUTOMOTIVE REPAIR SERVICES

Dollar values in thousands, except averages

|  | | 1984 | | 1985 | |
|---|---|---|---|---|---|
| 1. | Number of Partnerships | 24,117 | | 20,675 | |
| 2. | Number of Partners | 52,687 | | 46,827 | |
| | | | | | |
| 3. | Total Assets | $1,124,741 | | $916,869 | |
| 4. | Average total assets per Partnership | $46,637 | | $44,347 | |
| 5. | Average total assets per Partner | $21,348 | | $19,580 | |
| | | | | | |
| 6. | Net Income | $488,026 | | $536,394 | |
| 7. | Average per Partnership, total earnings | $20,238 | | $25,946 | |
| 8. | Average per Partner, total earnings | $9,264 | | $11,455 | |
| | | | | | |
| 9. | Operating Income | $2,774,231 | | $3,464,331 | |
| | Operating Costs | | | | |
| 10. | Cost of sales & operations | $1,317,856 | 47.5% | $1,846,843 | 53.3% |
| 11. | Salaries and wages | $223,172 | 8.0% | $281,927 | 8.1% |
| 12. | Rent paid | $120,975 | 4.4% | $113,882 | 3.3% |
| 13. | Interest paid | $44,189 | 1.6% | $55,620 | 1.6% |
| 14. | Taxes paid | $56,077 | 2.0% | $57,207 | 1.7% |
| 15. | Bad debts | $2,726 | 0.1% | $5,415 | 0.2% |
| 16. | Repairs | $19,446 | 0.7% | $18,059 | 0.5% |
| 17. | Depreciation | $89,081 | 3.2% | $105,486 | 3.0% |
| 18. | Depletion | $0 | n.a. | $0 | n.a. |
| 19. | Pension & profit sharing plans | $76 | n.a. | $27 | n.a. |
| 20. | Employee benefits programs | $5,417 | 0.2% | $11,308 | 0.3% |
| 21. | Other deductions | $355,578 | 12.8% | $397,057 | 11.5% |
| 22. | Total operating costs | $2,236,899 | 80.6% | $2,892,831 | 83.5% |
| | | | | | |
| | Operating Income and Distribution | | | | |
| 23. | Operating Income | $2,774,231 | 100.0% | $3,464,331 | 100.0% |
| 24. | Less:  Cost of sales and operations | $1,317,856 | 47.5% | $1,846,843 | 53.3% |
| 25. | Gross operating profit | $1,456,375 | 52.5% | $1,617,488 | 46.7% |
| 26. | Additional operating costs | $919,043 | 33.1% | $1,045,988 | 30.2% |
| 27. | Net operating profit | $537,332 | 19.4% | $571,500 | 16.5% |
| 28. | Less:  Guaranteed payments to partners | $51,484 | | $31,601 | |
| 29. | Distribution to partners | $485,848 | | $539,899 | |
| 30. | Other charges | $127 | | $3,505 | |
| 31. | Net change partners' capital | $485,721 | | $536,394 | |
| | | | | | |
| | Selected Ratios | | | | |
| 32. | Coverage ratio:  times interest earned | 11.2 | | 9.3 | |
| 33. | Inventory turnover (times) | n.a. | | n.a. | |
| 34. | Days' sales in inventory | n.a. | | n.a. | |
| 35. | Average age of inventory (days) | n.a. | | n.a. | |
| 36. | Return on assets, net income | 43.4% | | 58.5% | |
| 37. | Return on assets, gross operating profit | 129.5% | | 176.4% | |
| 38. | Return on assets, net operating profit | 47.8% | | 62.3% | |

Table 2: Partnerships With Net Income:  AUTOMOBILE REPAIR SHOPS, TOTAL (219,220,221,222,223)

Dollar values in thousands, except averages

| | 1984 | | 1985 | |
|---|---|---|---|---|
| 1. Number of Partnerships | 18,625 | | 14,864 | |
| 2. Number of Partners | 40,573 | | 33,554 | |
| | | | | |
| 3. Total Assets | $610,666 | | $377,463 | |
| 4. Average total assets per Partnership | $32,787 | | $25,394 | |
| 5. Average total assets per Partner | $15,051 | | $11,249 | |
| | | | | |
| 6. Net Income | $363,021 | | $393,603 | |
| 7. Average per Partnership, total earnings | $19,493 | | $26,482 | |
| 8. Average per Partner, total earnings | $8,948 | | $11,731 | |
| | | | | |
| 9. Operating Income | $1,954,427 | | $2,520,917 | |
| Operating Costs | | | | |
| 10. Cost of sales & operations | $892,479 | 45.7% | $1,319,168 | 52.3% |
| 11. Salaries and wages | $171,029 | 8.8% | $238,048 | 9.4% |
| 12. Rent paid | $92,028 | 4.7% | $89,784 | 3.6% |
| 13. Interest paid | $19,145 | 0.10% | $24,289 | 0.10% |
| 14. Taxes paid | $39,513 | 2.0% | $45,182 | 1.8% |
| 15. Bad debts | $2,494 | 0.1% | $3,811 | 0.2% |
| 16. Repairs | $10,003 | 0.5% | $7,867 | 0.3% |
| 17. Depreciation | $45,173 | 2.3% | $43,632 | 1.7% |
| 18. Depletion | $0 | n.a. | $0 | n.a. |
| 19. Pension & profit sharing plans | $0 | n.a. | $0 | n.a. |
| 20. Employee benefits programs | $4,857 | 0.3% | $10,901 | 0.4% |
| 21. Other deductions | $274,591 | 14.1% | $315,008 | 12.5% |
| 22. Total operating costs | $1,553,618 | 79.5% | $2,097,690 | 83.2% |
| | | | | |
| Operating Income and Distribution | | | | |
| 23. Operating Income | $1,954,427 | 100.0% | $2,520,917 | 100.0% |
| 24. Less: Cost of sales and operations | $892,479 | 45.7% | $1,319,168 | 52.3% |
| 25. Gross operating profit | $1,061,948 | 54.3% | $1,201,749 | 47.7% |
| 26. Additional operating costs | $661,139 | 33.8% | $778,522 | 30.9% |
| 27. Net operating profit | $400,809 | 20.5% | $423,227 | 16.8% |
| 28. Less: Guaranteed payments to partners | $40,029 | | $27,944 | |
| 29. Distribution to partners | $360,780 | | $395,283 | |
| 30. Other charges | $65 | | $1,680 | |
| 31. Net change partners' capital | $360,715 | | $393,603 | |
| | | | | |
| Selected Ratios | | | | |
| 32. Coverage ratio: times interest earned | 19.9 | | 16.4 | |
| 33. Inventory turnover (times) | n.a. | | n.a. | |
| 34. Days' sales in inventory | n.a. | | n.a. | |
| 35. Average age of inventory (days) | n.a. | | n.a. | |
| 36. Return on assets, net income | 59.5% | | 104.3% | |
| 37. Return on assets, gross operating profit | 173.9% | | n.a. | |
| 38. Return on assets, net operating profit | 65.6% | | 112.1% | |

Table 2: Partnerships With Net Income:  222.  GENERAL AUTOMOTIVE REPAIR SHOPS

Dollar values in thousands, except averages

|  |  | 1984 |  | 1985 |  |
|---|---|---|---|---|---|
| 1. | Number of Partnerships | 10,899 | | 8,689 | |
| 2. | Number of Partners | 24,904 | | 20,989 | |
| 3. | Total Assets | $383,395 | | $206,919 | |
| 4. | Average total assets per Partnership | $35,177 | | $23,814 | |
| 5. | Average total assets per Partner | $15,395 | | $9,858 | |
| 6. | Net Income | $167,365 | | $189,778 | |
| 7. | Average per Partnership, total earnings | $15,356 | | $21,844 | |
| 8. | Average per Partner, total earnings | $6,721 | | $9,043 | |
| 9. | Operating Income | $815,131 | | $1,392,318 | |
|  | Operating Costs | | | | |
| 10. | Cost of sales & operations | $371,610 | 45.6% | $727,825 | 52.3% |
| 11. | Salaries and wages | $41,788 | 5.1% | $120,235 | 8.6% |
| 12. | Rent paid | $56,654 | 7.0% | $58,970 | 4.2% |
| 13. | Interest paid | $9,446 | 1.2% | $11,580 | 0.8% |
| 14. | Taxes paid | $15,253 | 1.9% | $23,877 | 1.7% |
| 15. | Bad debts | $1,002 | 0.1% | $3,145 | 0.2% |
| 16. | Repairs | $5,741 | 0.7% | $3,153 | 0.2% |
| 17. | Depreciation | $25,941 | 3.2% | $23,618 | 1.7% |
| 18. | Depletion | $0 | n.a. | $0 | n.a. |
| 19. | Pension & profit sharing plans | $0 | n.a. | $0 | n.a. |
| 20. | Employee benefits programs | $2,068 | 0.3% | $8,762 | 0.6% |
| 21. | Other deductions | $113,058 | 13.9% | $193,040 | 13.9% |
| 22. | Total operating costs | $644,867 | 79.1% | $1,174,205 | 84.3% |
|  | Operating Income and Distribution | | | | |
| 23. | Operating Income | $815,131 | 100.0% | $1,392,318 | 100.0% |
| 24. | Less: Cost of sales and operations | $371,610 | 45.6% | $727,825 | 52.3% |
| 25. | Gross operating profit | $443,521 | 54.4% | $664,493 | 47.7% |
| 26. | Additional operating costs | $273,257 | 33.5% | $446,380 | 32.1% |
| 27. | Net operating profit | $170,264 | 20.9% | $218,113 | 15.7% |
| 28. | Less: Guaranteed payments to partners | $5,176 | | $26,654 | |
| 29. | Distribution to partners | $165,088 | | $191,459 | |
| 30. | Other charges | $29 | | $1,680 | |
| 31. | Net change partners' capital | $165,059 | | $189,779 | |
|  | Selected Ratios | | | | |
| 32. | Coverage ratio: times interest earned | 17.0 | | 17.8 | |
| 33. | Inventory turnover (times) | n.a. | | n.a. | |
| 34. | Days' sales in inventory | n.a. | | n.a. | |
| 35. | Average age of inventory (days) | n.a. | | n.a. | |
| 36. | Return on assets, net income | 43.7% | | 91.7% | |
| 37. | Return on assets, gross operating profit | 115.7% | | n.a. | |
| 38. | Return on assets, net operating profit | 44.4% | | 105.4% | |

*Page 180*

Table 2: Partnerships With Net Income:  OTHER AUTOMOBILE REPAIR (221,223)

Dollar values in thousands, except averages

|  | | 1984 | | 1985 | |
|---|---|---|---|---|---|
| 1. | Number of Partnerships | 7,725 | | 6,176 | |
| 2. | Number of Partners | 15,670 | | 12,565 | |
| 3. | Total Assets | $227,271 | | $170,544 | |
| 4. | Average total assets per Partnership | $29,420 | | $27,614 | |
| 5. | Average total assets per Partner | $14,504 | | $13,573 | |
| 6. | Net Income | $195,656 | | $203,825 | |
| 7. | Average per Partnership, total earnings | $25,332 | | $33,003 | |
| 8. | Average per Partner, total earnings | $12,488 | | $16,222 | |
| 9. | Operating Income | $1,139,296 | | $1,128,600 | |
|  | Operating Costs | | | | |
| 10. | Cost of sales & operations | $520,869 | 45.7% | $591,342 | 52.4% |
| 11. | Salaries and wages | $129,241 | 11.3% | $117,813 | 10.4% |
| 12. | Rent paid | $35,374 | 3.1% | $30,814 | 2.7% |
| 13. | Interest paid | $9,699 | 0.9% | $12,709 | 1.1% |
| 14. | Taxes paid | $24,259 | 2.1% | $21,304 | 1.9% |
| 15. | Bad debts | $1,492 | 0.1% | $666 | 0.1% |
| 16. | Repairs | $4,262 | 0.4% | $4,715 | 0.4% |
| 17. | Depreciation | $19,233 | 1.7% | $20,015 | 1.8% |
| 18. | Depletion | $0 | n.a. | $0 | n.a. |
| 19. | Pension & profit sharing plans | $0 | n.a. | $0 | n.a. |
| 20. | Employee benefits programs | $2,789 | 0.2% | $2,139 | 0.2% |
| 21. | Other deductions | $161,533 | 14.2% | $121,967 | 10.8% |
| 22. | Total operating costs | $908,751 | 79.8% | $923,484 | 81.8% |
|  | Operating Income and Distribution | | | | |
| 23. | Operating Income | $1,139,296 | 100.0% | $1,128,600 | 100.0% |
| 24. | Less:  Cost of sales and operations | $520,869 | 45.7% | $591,342 | 52.4% |
| 25. | Gross operating profit | $618,427 | 54.3% | $537,258 | 47.6% |
| 26. | Additional operating costs | $387,882 | 34.1% | $332,142 | 29.4% |
| 27. | Net operating profit | $230,545 | 20.2% | $205,116 | 18.2% |
| 28. | Less:  Guaranteed payments to partners | $34,853 | | $1,291 | |
| 29. | Distribution to partners | $195,692 | | $203,825 | |
| 30. | Other charges | $36 | | $0 | |
| 31. | Net change partners' capital | $195,656 | | $203,825 | |
|  | Selected Ratios | | | | |
| 32. | Coverage ratio:  times interest earned | 22.8 | | 15.1 | |
| 33. | Inventory turnover (times) | n.a. | | n.a. | |
| 34. | Days' sales in inventory | n.a. | | n.a. | |
| 35. | Average age of inventory (days) | n.a. | | n.a. | |
| 36. | Return on assets, net income | 86.1% | | 119.5% | |
| 37. | Return on assets, gross operating profit | n.a. | | n.a. | |
| 38. | Return on assets, net operating profit | 101.4% | | 120.3% | |

Table 2: Partnerships With Net Income:  AUTOMOBILE PARKING AND OTHER SERVICES (219,220,224)

Dollar values in thousands, except averages

|  |  | 1984 |  | 1985 |  |
|---|---|---|---|---|---|
| 1. | Number of Partnerships | 5,492 | | 5,810 | |
| 2. | Number of Partners | 12,114 | | 13,273 | |
| 3. | Total Assets | $514,076 | | $539,406 | |
| 4. | Average total assets per Partnership | $93,605 | | $92,841 | |
| 5. | Average total assets per Partner | $42,437 | | $40,639 | |
| 6. | Net Income | $125,005 | | $142,791 | |
| 7. | Average per Partnership, total earnings | $22,763 | | $24,577 | |
| 8. | Average per Partner, total earnings | $10,320 | | $10,758 | |
| 9. | Operating Income | $819,804 | | $943,414 | |
|  | Operating Costs | | | | |
| 10. | Cost of sales & operations | $425,377 | 51.9% | $527,675 | 55.9% |
| 11. | Salaries and wages | $52,143 | 6.4% | $43,879 | 4.7% |
| 12. | Rent paid | $28,947 | 3.5% | $24,098 | 2.6% |
| 13. | Interest paid | $25,044 | 3.1% | $31,330 | 3.3% |
| 14. | Taxes paid | $16,564 | 2.0% | $12,026 | 1.3% |
| 15. | Bad debts | $232 | 0.0% | $1,605 | 0.2% |
| 16. | Repairs | $9,443 | 1.2% | $10,191 | 1.1% |
| 17. | Depreciation | $43,909 | 5.4% | $61,854 | 6.6% |
| 18. | Depletion | $0 | n.a. | $0 | n.a. |
| 19. | Pension & profit sharing plans | $76 | 0.0% | $27 | n.a. |
| 20. | Employee benefits programs | $560 | 0.1% | $406 | 0.0% |
| 21. | Other deductions | $80,987 | 9.9% | $82,050 | 8.7% |
| 22. | Total operating costs | $683,282 | 83.4% | $795,141 | 84.3% |
|  | Operating Income and Distribution | | | | |
| 23. | Operating Income | $819,804 | 100.0% | $943,414 | 100.0% |
| 24. | Less: Cost of sales and operations | $425,377 | 51.9% | $527,675 | 55.9% |
| 25. | Gross operating profit | $394,427 | 48.1% | $415,739 | 44.1% |
| 26. | Additional operating costs | $257,905 | 31.5% | $267,466 | 28.4% |
| 27. | Net operating profit | $136,522 | 16.7% | $148,273 | 15.7% |
| 28. | Less: Guaranteed payments to partners | $11,455 | | $3,657 | |
| 29. | Distribution to partners | $125,067 | | $144,616 | |
| 30. | Other charges | $62 | | $1,825 | |
| 31. | Net change partners' capital | $125,005 | | $142,791 | |
|  | Selected Ratios | | | | |
| 32. | Coverage ratio:  times interest earned | 4.5 | | 3.7 | |
| 33. | Inventory turnover (times) | n.a. | | n.a. | |
| 34. | Days' sales in inventory | n.a. | | n.a. | |
| 35. | Average age of inventory (days) | n.a. | | n.a. | |
| 36. | Return on assets, net income | 24.3% | | 26.5% | |
| 37. | Return on assets, gross operating profit | 76.7% | | 77.1% | |
| 38. | Return on assets, net operating profit | 26.6% | | 27.5% | |

Table 2: Partnerships With Net Income:  225.  MISCELLANEOUS REPAIR SERVICES

Dollar values in thousands, except averages

|  |  | 1984 |  | 1985 |  |
|---|---|---|---|---|---|
| 1. | Number of Partnerships | 9,155 |  | 5,335 |  |
| 2. | Number of Partners | 18,318 |  | 10,888 |  |
| 3. | Total Assets | $159,652 |  | $171,409 |  |
| 4. | Average total assets per Partnership | $17,439 |  | $32,129 |  |
| 5. | Average total assets per Partner | $8,716 |  | $15,743 |  |
| 6. | Net Income | $177,111 |  | $117,670 |  |
| 7. | Average per Partnership, total earnings | $19,349 |  | $22,059 |  |
| 8. | Average per Partner, total earnings | $9,670 |  | $10,809 |  |
| 9. | Operating Income | $1,000,486 |  | $826,218 |  |
|  | Operating Costs |  |  |  |  |
| 10. | Cost of sales & operations | $517,728 | 51.8% | $447,230 | 54.1% |
| 11. | Salaries and wages | $46,432 | 4.6% | $38,404 | 4.7% |
| 12. | Rent paid | $18,099 | 1.8% | $15,525 | 1.9% |
| 13. | Interest paid | $12,806 | 1.3% | $10,779 | 1.3% |
| 14. | Taxes paid | $14,044 | 1.4% | $14,803 | 1.8% |
| 15. | Bad debts | $1,205 | 0.1% | $1,195 | 0.1% |
| 16. | Repairs | $3,659 | 0.4% | $4,309 | 0.5% |
| 17. | Depreciation | $36,807 | 3.7% | $44,779 | 5.4% |
| 18. | Depletion | $0 | n.a. | $0 | n.a. |
| 19. | Pension & profit sharing plans | $77 | 0.0% | $29 | n.a. |
| 20. | Employee benefits programs | $16 | n.a. | $155 | 0.0% |
| 21. | Other deductions | $147,602 | 14.8% | $118,376 | 14.3% |
| 22. | Total operating costs | $798,475 | 79.8% | $695,584 | 84.2% |
|  | Operating Income and Distribution |  |  |  |  |
| 23. | Operating Income | $1,000,486 | 100.0% | $826,218 | 100.0% |
| 24. | Less:  Cost of sales and operations | $517,728 | 51.8% | $447,230 | 54.1% |
| 25. | Gross operating profit | $482,758 | 48.3% | $378,988 | 45.9% |
| 26. | Additional operating costs | $280,747 | 28.1% | $248,354 | 30.1% |
| 27. | Net operating profit | $202,011 | 20.2% | $130,634 | 15.8% |
| 28. | Less:  Guaranteed payments to partners | $24,900 |  | $12,916 |  |
| 29. | Distribution to partners | $177,111 |  | $117,718 |  |
| 30. | Other charges | $0 |  | $48 |  |
| 31. | Net change partners' capital | $177,111 |  | $117,670 |  |
|  | Selected Ratios |  |  |  |  |
| 32. | Coverage ratio:  times interest earned | 14.8 |  | 11.1 |  |
| 33. | Inventory turnover (times) | n.a. |  | n.a. |  |
| 34. | Days' sales in inventory | n.a. |  | n.a. |  |
| 35. | Average age of inventory (days) | n.a. |  | n.a. |  |
| 36. | Return on assets, net income | 110.9% |  | 68.7% |  |
| 37. | Return on assets, gross operating profit | n.a. |  | 221.1% |  |
| 38. | Return on assets, net operating profit | 126.5% |  | 76.2% |  |

Table 2: Partnerships With Net Income:  AMUSEMENT AND RECREATION SERVICES, INCLUDING MOTION PICTURES (230,233)

Dollar values in thousands, except averages

| | 1984 | | 1985 | |
|---|---|---|---|---|
| 1. Number of Partnerships | 10,130 | | 9,280 | |
| 2. Number of Partners | 60,985 | | 48,039 | |
| | | | | |
| 3. Total Assets | $3,821,220 | | $4,630,369 | |
| 4.   Average total assets per Partnership | $377,218 | | $498,962 | |
| 5.   Average total assets per Partner | $62,658 | | $96,388 | |
| | | | | |
| 6. Net Income | $1,098,605 | | $1,231,564 | |
| 7.   Average per Partnership, total earnings | $108,457 | | $132,722 | |
| 8.   Average per Partner, total earnings | $18,015 | | $25,639 | |
| | | | | |
| 9. Operating Income | $5,239,466 | | $5,751,904 | |
| Operating Costs | | | | |
| 10.   Cost of sales & operations | $1,224,815 | 23.4% | $1,619,435 | 28.2% |
| 11.   Salaries and wages | $535,269 | 10.2% | $621,259 | 10.8% |
| 12.   Rent paid | $107,308 | 2.1% | $100,881 | 1.8% |
| 13.   Interest paid | $158,585 | 3.0% | $197,130 | 3.4% |
| 14.   Taxes paid | $91,524 | 1.8% | $89,546 | 1.6% |
| 15.   Bad debts | $6,441 | 0.1% | $7,687 | 0.1% |
| 16.   Repairs | $38,688 | 0.7% | $45,576 | 0.8% |
| 17.   Depreciation | $334,024 | 6.4% | $320,028 | 5.6% |
| 18.   Depletion | $0 | n.a. | $0 | n.a. |
| 19.   Pension & profit sharing plans | $13,066 | 0.3% | $9,762 | 0.2% |
| 20.   Employee benefits programs | $9,523 | 0.2% | $11,108 | 0.2% |
| 21.   Other deductions | $1,524,094 | 29.1% | $1,373,656 | 23.9% |
| 22.   Total operating costs | $4,043,340 | 77.2% | $4,396,087 | 76.4% |
| | | | | |
| Operating Income and Distribution | | | | |
| 23.   Operating Income | $5,239,466 | 100.0% | $5,751,904 | 100.0% |
| 24.     Less: Cost of sales and operations | $1,224,815 | 23.4% | $1,619,435 | 28.2% |
| 25.   Gross operating profit | $4,014,651 | 76.6% | $4,132,469 | 71.9% |
| 26.     Additional operating costs | $2,818,525 | 53.8% | $2,776,652 | 48.3% |
| 27.   Net operating profit | $1,196,126 | 22.8% | $1,355,817 | 23.6% |
| 28.     Less: Guaranteed payments to partners | $63,450 | | $97,880 | |
| 29.   Distribution to partners | $1,132,676 | | $1,257,937 | |
| 30.   Other charges | $34,074 | | $26,392 | |
| 31.   Net change partners' capital | $1,098,602 | | $1,231,545 | |
| | | | | |
| Selected Ratios | | | | |
| 32.   Coverage ratio:  times interest earned | 6.5 | | 5.9 | |
| 33.   Inventory turnover (times) | n.a. | | n.a. | |
| 34.   Days' sales in inventory | n.a. | | n.a. | |
| 35.   Average age of inventory (days) | n.a. | | n.a. | |
| 36.   Return on assets, net income | 28.8% | | 26.6% | |
| 37.   Return on assets, gross operating profit | 105.1% | | 89.3% | |
| 38.   Return on assets, net operating profit | 31.3% | | 29.3% | |

Table 2: Partnerships With Net Income:   240.   MEDICAL AND HEALTH SERVICES

Dollar values in thousands, except averages

|  |  | 1984 |  | 1985 |  |
|---|---|---|---|---|---|
| 1. | Number of Partnerships | 23,654 | | 25,949 | |
| 2. | Number of Partners | 86,840 | | 92,890 | |
| 3. | Total Assets | $2,936,711 | | $3,438,842 | |
| 4. | Average total assets per Partnership | $124,153 | | $132,523 | |
| 5. | Average total assets per Partner | $33,817 | | $37,021 | |
| 6. | Net Income | $5,222,888 | | $5,225,417 | |
| 7. | Average per Partnership, total earnings | $220,815 | | $201,386 | |
| 8. | Average per Partner, total earnings | $60,147 | | $56,258 | |
| 9. | Operating Income | $12,890,260 | | $13,806,998 | |
|  | Operating Costs | | | | |
| 10. | Cost of sales & operations | $810,518 | 6.3% | $907,059 | 6.6% |
| 11. | Salaries and wages | $2,298,034 | 17.8% | $2,538,328 | 18.4% |
| 12. | Rent paid | $517,281 | 4.0% | $593,225 | 4.3% |
| 13. | Interest paid | $158,045 | 1.2% | $167,419 | 1.2% |
| 14. | Taxes paid | $251,710 | 2.0% | $280,429 | 2.0% |
| 15. | Bad debts | $17,275 | 0.1% | $13,050 | 0.1% |
| 16. | Repairs | $59,823 | 0.5% | $61,989 | 0.5% |
| 17. | Depreciation | $229,271 | 1.8% | $274,600 | 2.0% |
| 18. | Depletion | $0 | n.a. | $0 | n.a. |
| 19. | Pension & profit sharing plans | $81,324 | 0.6% | $88,267 | 0.6% |
| 20. | Employee benefits programs | $117,538 | 0.9% | $111,717 | 0.8% |
| 21. | Other deductions | $2,847,432 | 22.1% | $3,195,494 | 23.1% |
| 22. | Total operating costs | $7,388,809 | 57.3% | $8,232,452 | 59.6% |
|  | Operating Income and Distribution | | | | |
| 23. | Operating Income | $12,890,260 | 100.0% | $13,806,998 | 100.0% |
| 24. | Less: Cost of sales and operations | $810,518 | 6.3% | $907,059 | 6.6% |
| 25. | Gross operating profit | $12,079,742 | 93.7% | $12,899,939 | 93.4% |
| 26. | Additional operating costs | $6,578,291 | 51.0% | $7,325,393 | 53.1% |
| 27. | Net operating profit | $5,501,451 | 42.7% | $5,574,546 | 40.4% |
| 28. | Less: Guaranteed payments to partners | $275,744 | | $345,200 | |
| 29. | Distribution to partners | $5,225,707 | | $5,229,346 | |
| 30. | Other charges | $3,377 | | $4,804 | |
| 31. | Net change partners' capital | $5,222,330 | | $5,224,542 | |
|  | Selected Ratios | | | | |
| 32. | Coverage ratio: times interest earned | 33.8 | | 32.3 | |
| 33. | Inventory turnover (times) | n.a. | | n.a. | |
| 34. | Days' sales in inventory | n.a. | | n.a. | |
| 35. | Average age of inventory (days) | n.a. | | n.a. | |
| 36. | Return on assets, net income | 177.9% | | 152.0% | |
| 37. | Return on assets, gross operating profit | n.a. | | n.a. | |
| 38. | Return on assets, net operating profit | 187.3% | | 162.1% | |

*Page 185*

Table 2: Partnerships With Net Income: 241. OFFICES OF PHYSICIANS

Dollar values in thousands, except averages

|  |  | 1984 | | 1985 | |
|---|---|---|---|---|---|
| 1. | Number of Partnerships | 9,671 | | 8,329 | |
| 2. | Number of Partners | 36,211 | | 34,799 | |
| 3. | Total Assets | $728,135 | | $756,312 | |
| 4. | Average total assets per Partnership | $75,291 | | $90,805 | |
| 5. | Average total assets per Partner | $20,108 | | $21,734 | |
| 6. | Net Income | $3,201,877 | | $2,948,408 | |
| 7. | Average per Partnership, total earnings | $331,101 | | $354,019 | |
| 8. | Average per Partner, total earnings | $88,428 | | $84,733 | |
| 9. | Operating Income | $6,841,596 | | $6,670,455 | |
|  | Operating Costs | | | | |
| 10. | Cost of sales & operations | $53,265 | 0.8% | $128,177 | 1.9% |
| 11. | Salaries and wages | $1,255,115 | 18.4% | $1,226,040 | 18.4% |
| 12. | Rent paid | $335,379 | 4.9% | $322,834 | 4.8% |
| 13. | Interest paid | $32,805 | 0.5% | $29,460 | 0.4% |
| 14. | Taxes paid | $104,099 | 1.5% | $99,419 | 1.5% |
| 15. | Bad debts | $9,027 | 0.1% | $6,224 | 0.1% |
| 16. | Repairs | $25,365 | 0.4% | $23,838 | 0.4% |
| 17. | Depreciation | $64,424 | 0.9% | $65,652 | 0.10% |
| 18. | Depletion | $0 | n.a. | $0 | n.a. |
| 19. | Pension & profit sharing plans | $66,572 | 0.10% | $70,619 | 1.1% |
| 20. | Employee benefits programs | $84,239 | 1.2% | $73,954 | 1.1% |
| 21. | Other deductions | $1,412,017 | 20.6% | $1,460,748 | 21.9% |
| 22. | Total operating costs | $3,442,331 | 50.3% | $3,506,986 | 52.6% |
| | Operating Income and Distribution | | | | |
| 23. | Operating Income | $6,841,596 | 100.0% | $6,670,455 | 100.0% |
| 24. | Less: Cost of sales and operations | $53,265 | 0.8% | $128,177 | 1.9% |
| 25. | Gross operating profit | $6,788,331 | 99.2% | $6,542,278 | 98.1% |
| 26. | Additional operating costs | $3,389,066 | 49.5% | $3,378,809 | 50.7% |
| 27. | Net operating profit | $3,399,265 | 49.7% | $3,163,469 | 47.4% |
| 28. | Less: Guaranteed payments to partners | $197,038 | | $214,081 | |
| 29. | Distribution to partners | $3,202,227 | | $2,949,388 | |
| 30. | Other charges | $374 | | $1,002 | |
| 31. | Net change partners' capital | $3,201,853 | | $2,948,386 | |
| | Selected Ratios | | | | |
| 32. | Coverage ratio: times interest earned | 102.6 | | 106.4 | |
| 33. | Inventory turnover (times) | n.a. | | n.a. | |
| 34. | Days' sales in inventory | n.a. | | n.a. | |
| 35. | Average age of inventory (days) | n.a. | | n.a. | |
| 36. | Return on assets, net income | n.a. | | n.a. | |
| 37. | Return on assets, gross operating profit | n.a. | | n.a. | |
| 38. | Return on assets, net operating profit | n.a. | | n.a. | |

*Page 186*

**Table 2: Partnerships With Net Income: OTHER MEDICAL AND HEALTH SERVICES (242 TO 251)**

Dollar values in thousands, except averages

| | | 1984 | | 1985 | |
|---|---|---|---|---|---|
| 1. | Number of Partnerships | 13,983 | | 17,620 | |
| 2. | Number of Partners | 50,630 | | 58,090 | |
| | | | | | |
| 3. | Total Assets | $2,208,577 | | $2,682,530 | |
| 4. | Average total assets per Partnership | $157,947 | | $152,243 | |
| 5. | Average total assets per Partner | $43,622 | | $46,179 | |
| | | | | | |
| 6. | Net Income | $2,021,011 | | $2,277,009 | |
| 7. | Average per Partnership, total earnings | $144,539 | | $129,236 | |
| 8. | Average per Partner, total earnings | $39,919 | | $39,200 | |
| | | | | | |
| 9. | Operating Income | $6,048,665 | | $7,136,543 | |
| | Operating Costs | | | | |
| 10. | Cost of sales & operations | $575,253 | 9.5% | $778,882 | 10.9% |
| 11. | Salaries and wages | $1,042,921 | 17.2% | $1,312,287 | 18.4% |
| 12. | Rent paid | $181,903 | 3.0% | $270,391 | 3.8% |
| 13. | Interest paid | $125,239 | 2.1% | $137,960 | 1.9% |
| 14. | Taxes paid | $147,611 | 2.4% | $181,010 | 2.5% |
| 15. | Bad debts | $8,248 | 0.1% | $6,826 | 0.1% |
| 16. | Repairs | $34,458 | 0.6% | $38,151 | 0.5% |
| 17. | Depreciation | $346,844 | 5.7% | $208,948 | 2.9% |
| 18. | Depletion | $0 | n.a. | $0 | n.a. |
| 19. | Pension & profit sharing plans | $14,752 | 0.2% | $17,648 | 0.3% |
| 20. | Employee benefits programs | $33,299 | 0.6% | $37,764 | 0.5% |
| 21. | Other deductions | $1,435,415 | 23.7% | $1,734,745 | 24.3% |
| 22. | Total operating costs | $3,946,476 | 65.3% | $4,725,467 | 66.2% |
| | | | | | |
| | Operating Income and Distribution | | | | |
| 23. | Operating Income | $6,048,665 | 100.0% | $7,136,543 | 100.0% |
| 24. | Less: Cost of sales and operations | $575,253 | 9.5% | $778,882 | 10.9% |
| 25. | Gross operating profit | $5,473,412 | 90.5% | $6,357,661 | 89.1% |
| 26. | Additional operating costs | $3,371,223 | 55.7% | $3,946,585 | 55.3% |
| 27. | Net operating profit | $2,102,189 | 34.8% | $2,411,076 | 33.8% |
| 28. | Less: Guaranteed payments to partners | $78,706 | | $131,119 | |
| 29. | Distribution to partners | $2,023,483 | | $2,279,957 | |
| 30. | Other charges | $3,004 | | $3,802 | |
| 31. | Net change partners' capital | $2,020,479 | | $2,276,155 | |
| | | | | | |
| | Selected Ratios | | | | |
| 32. | Coverage ratio: times interest earned | 15.8 | | 16.5 | |
| 33. | Inventory turnover (times) | n.a. | | n.a. | |
| 34. | Days' sales in inventory | n.a. | | n.a. | |
| 35. | Average age of inventory (days) | n.a. | | n.a. | |
| 36. | Return on assets, net income | 91.5% | | 84.9% | |
| 37. | Return on assets, gross operating profit | 247.8% | | 237.0% | |
| 38. | Return on assets, net operating profit | 95.2% | | 89.9% | |

Table 2: Partnerships With Net Income:  252.  LEGAL SERVICES

Dollar values in thousands, except averages

| | | 1984 | | 1985 | |
|---|---|---|---|---|---|
| 1. | Number of Partnerships | 24,074 | | 28,735 | |
| 2. | Number of Partners | 112,752 | | 123,589 | |
| 3. | Total Assets | $5,119,359 | | $5,944,733 | |
| 4. | Average total assets per Partnership | $212,651 | | $206,881 | |
| 5. | Average total assets per Partner | $45,404 | | $48,101 | |
| 6. | Net Income | $10,056,899 | | $10,737,805 | |
| 7. | Average per Partnership, total earnings | $417,770 | | $373,705 | |
| 8. | Average per Partner, total earnings | $89,199 | | $86,888 | |
| 9. | Operating Income | $23,750,822 | | $26,439,744 | |
| | Operating Costs | | | | |
| 10. | Cost of sales & operations | $210,007 | 0.9% | $238,037 | 0.9% |
| 11. | Salaries and wages | $5,930,273 | 25.0% | $6,715,279 | 25.4% |
| 12. | Rent paid | $1,553,320 | 6.5% | $1,831,564 | 6.9% |
| 13. | Interest paid | $177,376 | 0.8% | $203,275 | 0.8% |
| 14. | Taxes paid | $622,336 | 2.6% | $690,791 | 2.6% |
| 15. | Bad debts | $17,548 | 0.1% | $19,567 | 0.1% |
| 16. | Repairs | $101,245 | 0.4% | $129,023 | 0.5% |
| 17. | Depreciation | $526,185 | 2.2% | $628,068 | 2.4% |
| 18. | Depletion | $205 | n.a. | $7,616 | 0.0% |
| 19. | Pension & profit sharing plans | $158,469 | 0.7% | $194,687 | 0.7% |
| 20. | Employee benefits programs | $148,709 | 0.6% | $167,190 | 0.6% |
| 21. | Other deductions | $3,738,242 | 15.7% | $4,241,548 | 16.0% |
| 22. | Total operating costs | $13,186,825 | 55.5% | $15,067,440 | 57.0% |
| | Operating Income and Distribution | | | | |
| 23. | Operating Income | $23,750,822 | 100.0% | $26,439,744 | 100.0% |
| 24. | Less:  Cost of sales and operations | $210,007 | 0.9% | $238,037 | 0.9% |
| 25. | Gross operating profit | $23,540,815 | 99.1% | $26,201,707 | 99.1% |
| 26. | Additional operating costs | $12,976,818 | 54.6% | $14,829,403 | 56.1% |
| 27. | Net operating profit | $10,563,997 | 44.5% | $11,372,304 | 43.0% |
| 28. | Less:  Guaranteed payments to partners | $488,038 | | $602,903 | |
| 29. | Distribution to partners | $10,075,959 | | $10,769,401 | |
| 30. | Other charges | $21,970 | | $32,392 | |
| 31. | Net change partners' capital | $10,053,989 | | $10,737,009 | |
| | Selected Ratios | | | | |
| 32. | Coverage ratio:  times interest earned | 58.6 | | 55.0 | |
| 33. | Inventory turnover (times) | n.a. | | n.a. | |
| 34. | Days' sales in inventory | n.a. | | n.a. | |
| 35. | Average age of inventory (days) | n.a. | | n.a. | |
| 36. | Return on assets, net income | 196.5% | | 180.6% | |
| 37. | Return on assets, gross operating profit | n.a. | | n.a. | |
| 38. | Return on assets, net operating profit | 206.4% | | 191.3% | |

*Page 188*

Table 2: Partnerships With Net Income:  255.  ENGINEERING AND ARCHITECTURAL SERVICES

Dollar values in thousands, except averages

| | | 1984 | | 1985 | |
|---|---|---|---|---|---|
| 1. | Number of Partnerships | 3,717 | | 7,351 | |
| 2. | Number of Partners | 8,970 | | 18,567 | |
| | | | | | |
| 3. | Total Assets | $420,969 | | $469,929 | |
| 4. | Average total assets per Partnership | $113,255 | | $63,927 | |
| 5. | Average total assets per Partner | $46,931 | | $25,310 | |
| | | | | | |
| 6. | Net Income | $408,510 | | $523,278 | |
| 7. | Average per Partnership, total earnings | $109,927 | | $71,205 | |
| 8. | Average per Partner, total earnings | $45,552 | | $28,191 | |
| | | | | | |
| 9. | Operating Income | $2,695,120 | | $3,302,330 | |
| | Operating Costs | | | | |
| 10. | Cost of sales & operations | $709,727 | 26.3% | $911,996 | 27.6% |
| 11. | Salaries and wages | $636,300 | 23.6% | $703,558 | 21.3% |
| 12. | Rent paid | $96,651 | 3.6% | $118,005 | 3.6% |
| 13. | Interest paid | $15,823 | 0.6% | $19,360 | 0.6% |
| 14. | Taxes paid | $68,948 | 2.6% | $76,863 | 2.3% |
| 15. | Bad debts | $2,102 | 0.1% | $1,368 | 0.0% |
| 16. | Repairs | $7,344 | 0.3% | $9,984 | 0.3% |
| 17. | Depreciation | $37,491 | 1.4% | $64,045 | 1.9% |
| 18. | Depletion | $322 | 0.0% | $0 | n.a. |
| 19. | Pension & profit sharing plans | $18,318 | 0.7% | $19,230 | 0.6% |
| 20. | Employee benefits programs | $20,249 | 0.8% | $27,484 | 0.8% |
| 21. | Other deductions | $584,884 | 21.7% | $674,323 | 20.4% |
| 22. | Total operating costs | $2,198,166 | 81.6% | $2,626,226 | 79.5% |
| | | | | | |
| | Operating Income and Distribution | | | | |
| 23. | Operating Income | $2,695,120 | 100.0% | $3,302,330 | 100.0% |
| 24. | Less:  Cost of sales and operations | $709,727 | 26.3% | $911,996 | 27.6% |
| 25. | Gross operating profit | $1,985,393 | 73.7% | $2,390,334 | 72.4% |
| 26. | Additional operating costs | $1,488,439 | 55.2% | $1,714,230 | 51.9% |
| 27. | Net operating profit | $496,954 | 18.4% | $676,104 | 20.5% |
| 28. | Less:  Guaranteed payments to partners | $87,733 | | $150,229 | |
| 29. | Distribution to partners | $409,221 | | $525,875 | |
| 30. | Other charges | $718 | | $2,607 | |
| 31. | Net change partners' capital | $408,503 | | $523,268 | |
| | | | | | |
| | Selected Ratios | | | | |
| 32. | Coverage ratio:  times interest earned | 30.4 | | 33.9 | |
| 33. | Inventory turnover (times) | n.a. | | n.a. | |
| 34. | Days' sales in inventory | n.a. | | n.a. | |
| 35. | Average age of inventory (days) | n.a. | | n.a. | |
| 36. | Return on assets, net income | 97.0% | | 111.4% | |
| 37. | Return on assets, gross operating profit | n.a. | | n.a. | |
| 38. | Return on assets, net operating profit | 118.1% | | 143.9% | |

Table 2: Partnerships With Net Income:  256.  ACCOUNTING, AUDITING, AND BOOKKEEPING SERVICES

Dollar values in thousands, except averages

|  |  | 1984 |  | 1985 |  |
|---|---|---|---|---|---|
| 1. | Number of Partnerships | 10,815 |  | 13,097 |  |
| 2. | Number of Partners | 47,299 |  | 55,494 |  |
| 3. | Total Assets | $2,216,723 |  | $2,448,358 |  |
| 4. | Average total assets per Partnership | $204,967 |  | $186,940 |  |
| 5. | Average total assets per Partner | $46,866 |  | $44,119 |  |
| 6. | Net Income | $2,349,895 |  | $2,970,468 |  |
| 7. | Average per Partnership, total earnings | $217,347 |  | $226,873 |  |
| 8. | Average per Partner, total earnings | $49,697 |  | $53,544 |  |
| 9. | Operating Income | $10,108,025 |  | $13,291,888 |  |
|  | Operating Costs |  |  |  |  |
| 10. | Cost of sales & operations | $133,662 | 1.3% | $145,023 | 1.1% |
| 11. | Salaries and wages | $3,615,173 | 35.8% | $4,793,377 | 36.1% |
| 12. | Rent paid | $543,670 | 5.4% | $746,171 | 5.6% |
| 13. | Interest paid | $90,239 | 0.9% | $104,287 | 0.8% |
| 14. | Taxes paid | $334,740 | 3.3% | $437,729 | 3.3% |
| 15. | Bad debts | $19,680 | 0.2% | $15,836 | 0.1% |
| 16. | Repairs | $45,794 | 0.5% | $60,438 | 0.5% |
| 17. | Depreciation | $216,815 | 2.1% | $298,597 | 2.3% |
| 18. | Depletion | $0 | n.a. | $363 | n.a. |
| 19. | Pension & profit sharing plans | $69,228 | 0.7% | $102,391 | 0.8% |
| 20. | Employee benefits programs | $75,244 | 0.7% | $71,184 | 0.5% |
| 21. | Other deductions | $1,892,453 | 18.7% | $2,647,198 | 19.9% |
| 22. | Total operating costs | $7,036,786 | 69.6% | $9,422,800 | 70.9% |
| Operating Income and Distribution |  |  |  |  |  |
| 23. | Operating Income | $10,108,025 | 100.0% | $13,291,888 | 100.0% |
| 24. | Less:  Cost of sales and operations | $133,662 | 1.3% | $145,023 | 1.1% |
| 25. | Gross operating profit | $9,974,363 | 98.7% | $13,146,865 | 98.9% |
| 26. | Additional operating costs | $6,903,124 | 68.3% | $9,277,777 | 69.8% |
| 27. | Net operating profit | $3,071,239 | 30.4% | $3,869,088 | 29.1% |
| 28. | Less:  Guaranteed payments to partners | $711,722 |  | $890,483 |  |
| 29. | Distribution to partners | $2,359,517 |  | $2,978,605 |  |
| 30. | Other charges | $9,710 |  | $8,343 |  |
| 31. | Net change partners' capital | $2,349,807 |  | $2,970,262 |  |
| Selected Ratios |  |  |  |  |  |
| 32. | Coverage ratio:  times interest earned | 33.0 |  | 36.1 |  |
| 33. | Inventory turnover (times) | n.a. |  | n.a. |  |
| 34. | Days' sales in inventory | n.a. |  | n.a. |  |
| 35. | Average age of inventory (days) | n.a. |  | n.a. |  |
| 36. | Return on assets, net income | 106.0% |  | 121.3% |  |
| 37. | Return on assets, gross operating profit | n.a. |  | n.a. |  |
| 38. | Return on assets, net operating profit | 138.6% |  | 158.0% |  |

Table 2: Partnerships With Net Income:  257.  CERTIFIED PUBLIC ACCOUNTANTS

Dollar values in thousands, except averages

|  |  | 1984 |  | 1985 |  |
|---|---|---|---|---|---|
| 1. | Number of Partnerships | 7,056 | | 9,491 | |
| 2. | Number of Partners | 36,601 | | 44,872 | |
| 3. | Total Assets | $2,071,932 | | $2,279,928 | |
| 4. | Average total assets per Partnership | $293,641 | | $240,220 | |
| 5. | Average total assets per Partner | $56,609 | | $50,810 | |
| 6. | Net Income | $2,223,639 | | $2,800,951 | |
| 7. | Average per Partnership, total earnings | $315,236 | | $295,205 | |
| 8. | Average per Partner, total earnings | $60,772 | | $62,440 | |
| 9. | Operating Income | $9,550,867 | | $12,600,682 | |
|  | Operating Costs | | | | |
| 10. | Cost of sales & operations | $120,339 | 1.3% | $122,194 | 0.10% |
| 11. | Salaries and wages | $3,449,570 | 36.1% | $4,600,067 | 36.5% |
| 12. | Rent paid | $515,360 | 5.4% | $708,171 | 5.6% |
| 13. | Interest paid | $85,511 | 0.9% | $94,045 | 0.8% |
| 14. | Taxes paid | $316,453 | 3.3% | $416,089 | 3.3% |
| 15. | Bad debts | $19,662 | 0.2% | $15,835 | 0.1% |
| 16. | Repairs | $41,360 | 0.4% | $52,219 | 0.4% |
| 17. | Depreciation | $197,547 | 2.1% | $276,798 | 2.2% |
| 18. | Depletion | $0 | n.a. | $363 | n.a. |
| 19. | Pension & profit sharing plans | $68,465 | 0.7% | $101,300 | 0.8% |
| 20. | Employee benefits programs | $72,779 | 0.8% | $68,420 | 0.5% |
| 21. | Other deductions | $1,762,863 | 18.5% | $2,497,361 | 19.8% |
| 22. | Total operating costs | $6,649,997 | 69.6% | $8,953,068 | 71.1% |
|  | Operating Income and Distribution | | | | |
| 23. | Operating Income | $9,550,867 | 100.0% | $12,600,682 | 100.0% |
| 24. | Less:  Cost of sales and operations | $120,339 | 1.3% | $122,194 | 0.10% |
| 25. | Gross operating profit | $9,430,528 | 98.7% | $12,478,488 | 99.0% |
| 26. | Additional operating costs | $6,529,658 | 68.4% | $8,830,874 | 70.1% |
| 27. | Net operating profit | $2,900,870 | 30.4% | $3,647,614 | 29.0% |
| 28. | Less:  Guaranteed payments to partners | $669,028 | | $839,857 | |
| 29. | Distribution to partners | $2,231,842 | | $2,807,757 | |
| 30. | Other charges | $8,291 | | $7,011 | |
| 31. | Net change partners' capital | $2,223,551 | | $2,800,746 | |
|  | Selected Ratios | | | | |
| 32. | Coverage ratio:  times interest earned | 32.9 | | 37.8 | |
| 33. | Inventory turnover (times) | n.a. | | n.a. | |
| 34. | Days' sales in inventory | n.a. | | n.a. | |
| 35. | Average age of inventory (days) | n.a. | | n.a. | |
| 36. | Return on assets, net income | 107.3% | | 122.9% | |
| 37. | Return on assets, gross operating profit | n.a. | | n.a. | |
| 38. | Return on assets, net operating profit | 140.0% | | 160.0% | |

Table 2: Partnerships With Net Income:  258.  OTHER ACCOUNTING, AUDITING, AND BOOKKEEPING SERVICES

Dollar values in thousands, except averages

| | 1984 | | 1985 | |
|---|---|---|---|---|
| 1. Number of Partnerships | 3,759 | | 3,606 | |
| 2. Number of Partners | 10,698 | | 10,622 | |
| | | | | |
| 3. Total Assets | $144,791 | | $168,430 | |
| 4. Average total assets per Partnership | $38,518 | | $46,708 | |
| 5. Average total assets per Partner | $13,534 | | $15,857 | |
| | | | | |
| 6. Net Income | $126,256 | | $169,517 | |
| 7. Average per Partnership, total earnings | $33,599 | | $47,024 | |
| 8. Average per Partner, total earnings | $11,806 | | $15,964 | |
| | | | | |
| 9. Operating Income | $557,158 | | $691,207 | |
| Operating Costs | | | | |
| 10. Cost of sales & operations | $13,324 | 2.4% | $22,828 | 3.3% |
| 11. Salaries and wages | $165,603 | 29.7% | $193,310 | 28.0% |
| 12. Rent paid | $28,310 | 5.1% | $38,000 | 5.5% |
| 13. Interest paid | $4,728 | 0.9% | $10,242 | 1.5% |
| 14. Taxes paid | $18,286 | 3.3% | $21,641 | 3.1% |
| 15. Bad debts | $18 | n.a. | $2 | n.a. |
| 16. Repairs | $4,434 | 0.8% | $8,219 | 1.2% |
| 17. Depreciation | $19,272 | 3.5% | $21,799 | 3.2% |
| 18. Depletion | $0 | n.a. | $0 | n.a. |
| 19. Pension & profit sharing plans | $762 | 0.1% | $1,091 | 0.2% |
| 20. Employee benefits programs | $2,465 | 0.4% | $2,764 | 0.4% |
| 21. Other deductions | $129,589 | 23.3% | $149,837 | 21.7% |
| 22. Total operating costs | $386,791 | 69.4% | $469,733 | 68.0% |
| | | | | |
| Operating Income and Distribution | | | | |
| 23. Operating Income | $557,158 | 100.0% | $691,207 | 100.0% |
| 24. Less: Cost of sales and operations | $13,324 | 2.4% | $22,828 | 3.3% |
| 25. Gross operating profit | $543,834 | 97.6% | $668,379 | 96.7% |
| 26. Additional operating costs | $373,467 | 67.0% | $446,905 | 64.7% |
| 27. Net operating profit | $170,367 | 30.6% | $221,474 | 32.0% |
| 28. Less: Guaranteed payments to partners | $42,694 | | $50,625 | |
| 29. Distribution to partners | $127,673 | | $170,849 | |
| 30. Other charges | $1,417 | | $1,332 | |
| 31. Net change partners' capital | $126,256 | | $169,517 | |
| | | | | |
| Selected Ratios | | | | |
| 32. Coverage ratio: times interest earned | 35.0 | | 20.6 | |
| 33. Inventory turnover (times) | n.a. | | n.a. | |
| 34. Days' sales in inventory | n.a. | | n.a. | |
| 35. Average age of inventory (days) | n.a. | | n.a. | |
| 36. Return on assets, net income | 87.2% | | 100.7% | |
| 37. Return on assets, gross operating profit | n.a. | | n.a. | |
| 38. Return on assets, net operating profit | 117.7% | | 131.5% | |

*Page 192*

Table 2: Partnerships With Net Income:  OTHER SERVICES (253,259)

Dollar values in thousands, except averages

| | | 1984 | | 1985 | |
|---|---|---|---|---|---|
| 1. | Number of Partnerships | 21,119 | | 24,298 | |
| 2. | Number of Partners | 64,695 | | 69,856 | |
| | | | | | |
| 3. | Total Assets | $2,530,502 | | $2,119,057 | |
| 4. | Average total assets per Partnership | $119,821 | | $87,211 | |
| 5. | Average total assets per Partner | $39,114 | | $30,335 | |
| | | | | | |
| 6. | Net Income | $1,240,455 | | $1,415,032 | |
| 7. | Average per Partnership, total earnings | $58,740 | | $58,239 | |
| 8. | Average per Partner, total earnings | $19,175 | | $20,257 | |
| | | | | | |
| 9. | Operating Income | $3,396,047 | | $3,244,706 | |
| | Operating Costs | | | | |
| 10. | Cost of sales & operations | $1,112,764 | 32.8% | $769,861 | 23.7% |
| 11. | Salaries and wages | $206,129 | 6.1% | $276,349 | 8.5% |
| 12. | Rent paid | $69,476 | 2.1% | $60,190 | 1.9% |
| 13. | Interest paid | $65,778 | 1.9% | $63,961 | 2.0% |
| 14. | Taxes paid | $32,279 | 0.10% | $45,153 | 1.4% |
| 15. | Bad debts | $3,537 | 0.1% | $759 | 0.0% |
| 16. | Repairs | $20,784 | 0.6% | $11,807 | 0.4% |
| 17. | Depreciation | $64,965 | 1.9% | $54,184 | 1.7% |
| 18. | Depletion | $0 | n.a. | $0 | n.a. |
| 19. | Pension & profit sharing plans | $2,534 | 0.1% | $4,931 | 0.2% |
| 20. | Employee benefits programs | $4,761 | 0.1% | $10,393 | 0.3% |
| 21. | Other deductions | $489,935 | 14.4% | $473,691 | 14.6% |
| 22. | Total operating costs | $2,072,942 | 61.0% | $1,771,279 | 54.6% |
| | | | | | |
| | Operating Income and Distribution | | | | |
| 23. | Operating Income | $3,396,047 | 100.0% | $3,244,706 | 100.0% |
| 24. | Less:  Cost of sales and operations | $1,112,764 | 32.8% | $769,861 | 23.7% |
| 25. | Gross operating profit | $2,283,283 | 67.2% | $2,474,845 | 76.3% |
| 26. | Additional operating costs | $960,178 | 28.3% | $1,001,418 | 30.9% |
| 27. | Net operating profit | $1,323,105 | 39.0% | $1,473,427 | 45.4% |
| 28. | Less:  Guaranteed payments to partners | $80,014 | | $55,323 | |
| 29. | Distribution to partners | $1,243,091 | | $1,418,104 | |
| 30. | Other charges | $2,637 | | $3,072 | |
| 31. | Net change partners' capital | $1,240,454 | | $1,415,032 | |
| | | | | | |
| | Selected Ratios | | | | |
| 32. | Coverage ratio:  times interest earned | 19.1 | | 22.0 | |
| 33. | Inventory turnover (times) | n.a. | | n.a. | |
| 34. | Days' sales in inventory | n.a. | | n.a. | |
| 35. | Average age of inventory (days) | n.a. | | n.a. | |
| 36. | Return on assets, net income | 49.0% | | 66.8% | |
| 37. | Return on assets, gross operating profit | 90.2% | | 116.8% | |
| 38. | Return on assets, net operating profit | 52.3% | | 69.5% | |

*Page 193*

# TABLE 3

## Historical Summary
## of Partnerships

## TABLE 3

### 001: ALL INDUSTRIES, WITH AND WITHOUT NET INCOME

| | 1976 | 1977 | 1978 | 1979 | 1980 | 1981 | 1982 | 1983 | 1984 | 1985 |
|---|---|---|---|---|---|---|---|---|---|---|
| 1. Number of Partnerships | 1,096,441 | 1,153,398 | 1,234,157 | 1,299,593 | 1,379,654 | 1,460,502 | 1,514,212 | 1,541,539 | 1,643,581 | 1,713,603 |
| 2. Number of Partners | 5,370,236 | 6,079,860 | 6,121,455 | 6,954,767 | 8,419,899 | 9,095,165 | 9,764,667 | 10,589,338 | 12,426,721 | 13,244,824 |
| **Selected Financial Statistics** | | | | | | | | | | |
| (Items 3 to 9 inclusive in 000's of dollars) | | | | | | | | | | |
| 3. Operating Income | 157,572,880 | 176,548,047 | 214,856,305 | 253,000,742 | 285,967,243 | 262,497,878 | 284,037,048 | 278,347,015 | 318,342,380 | 302,733,374 |
| 4. Depreciation | 11,086,857 | 12,334,740 | 14,519,760 | 17,662,667 | 21,576,190 | n.a. | n.a. | n.a. | 46,939,395 | 53,650,790 |
| 5. Taxes Paid | 6,395,919 | 6,914,357 | 7,364,870 | 8,328,583 | 9,553,145 | 5,040,336 | 5,288,971 | 5,909,545 | 6,673,186 | 7,745,756 |
| 6. Interest Paid | 12,346,003 | 13,455,385 | 16,022,804 | 21,275,551 | 28,362,386 | 19,586,018 | 21,517,044 | 22,364,264 | 25,437,588 | 28,674,933 |
| 7. Payroll Deductions | 18,933,893 | 19,964,455 | 22,252,594 | 26,092,084 | 29,332,070 | 27,696,916 | 30,373,162 | n.a. | 36,348,857 | 42,729,310 |
| 8. Payments to Partners | 2,948,646 | 2,966,695 | 3,500,460 | 4,109,882 | 4,746,253 | 5,212,661 | 5,350,678 | 5,838,956 | 7,517,503 | 7,694,236 |
| 9. Net Income, less Deficit | 10,422,811 | 13,264,168 | 14,446,809 | 15,205,908 | 8,248,656 | 273,489 | 731,458 | 261,004 | (3,500,024) | (8,883,674) |
| **Selected Average Financial Statistics** | | | | | | | | | | |
| (Items 10 to 13 inclusive in $) | | | | | | | | | | |
| 10. Av. Payment Partnership | 2,689 | 2,572 | 2,836 | 3,162 | 3,440 | 3,569 | 3,534 | 3,788 | 4,574 | 4,490 |
| 11. Av. Payment Partner | 549 | 488 | 572 | 591 | 564 | 573 | 548 | 551 | 605 | 581 |
| 12. Av. Income Partnership | 9,506 | 11,500 | 11,706 | 11,701 | 5,979 | 187 | 483 | 169 | (2,130) | (5,184) |
| 13. Av. Income Partner | 1,941 | 2,182 | 2,360 | 2,186 | 980 | 30 | 75 | 25 | (282) | (671) |
| **Selected Financial Statistics as Percent of Op. Income** | | | | | | | | | | |
| 14. Depreciation / Op. Income (%) | 7.0 | 7.0 | 6.8 | 7.0 | 7.5 | n.a. | n.a. | n.a. | 14.7 | 17.7 |
| 15. Interest / Op. Income (%) | 7.8 | 7.6 | 7.5 | 8.4 | 9.9 | 7.5 | 7.6 | 8.0 | 8.0 | 9.5 |
| 16. Payroll / Op. Income (%) | 12.0 | 11.3 | 10.4 | 10.3 | 10.3 | 10.6 | 10.7 | n.a. | 11.4 | 14.1 |
| **Selected Index Numbers (1976 = 100)** | | | | | | | | | | |
| 17. Partnerships | 100.0 | 105.2 | 112.6 | 118.5 | 125.8 | 133.2 | 138.1 | 140.6 | 149.9 | 156.3 |
| 18. Partners | 100.0 | 113.2 | 114.0 | 129.5 | 156.8 | 169.4 | 181.8 | 197.2 | 231.4 | 246.6 |
| 19. Operating Income | 100.0 | 112.0 | 136.4 | 160.6 | 181.5 | 166.6 | 180.3 | 176.6 | 202.0 | 192.1 |
| 20. Payments to Partners | 100.0 | 100.6 | 118.7 | 139.4 | 161.0 | 176.8 | 181.5 | 198.0 | 254.9 | 260.9 |
| **Selected Financial Statistics (Constant $, 1976 = 100)** | | | | | | | | | | |
| 21. Operating Income | 100.0 | 108.7 | 120.8 | 127.9 | 135.8 | 121.3 | 132.6 | 127.4 | 141.0 | 140.4 |
| 22. Payments to Partners | 100.0 | 94.5 | 103.6 | 109.3 | 111.2 | 110.7 | 107.0 | 113.1 | 139.7 | 138.1 |
| 23. Av. Payment, Partnership | 100.0 | 89.8 | 92.0 | 92.2 | 88.4 | 83.1 | 77.5 | 80.5 | 93.2 | 88.4 |
| 24. Av. Payment, Partner | 100.0 | 83.5 | 91.0 | 84.5 | 71.1 | 65.2 | 59.0 | 57.4 | 60.2 | 55.9 |

TABLE 3

002: AGRICULTURE, FORESTRY, AND FISHING, WITH AND WITHOUT NET INCOME

| | 1976 | 1977 | 1978 | 1979 | 1980 | 1981 | 1982 | 1983 | 1984 | 1985 |
|---|---|---|---|---|---|---|---|---|---|---|
| 1. Number of Partnerships | 121,337 | 121,042 | 126,938 | 124,825 | 126,224 | 124,973 | 132,997 | 136,603 | 139,306 | 135,909 |
| 2. Number of Partners | 342,934 | 353,897 | 380,363 | 375,386 | 380,982 | 405,594 | 449,872 | 466,132 | 494,392 | 584,789 |
| **Selected Financial Statistics** (Items 3 to 9 inclusive in 000's of dollars) | | | | | | | | | | |
| 3. Operating Income | 12,909,758 | 13,537,056 | 18,044,938 | 20,809,259 | 21,610,584 | 4,993,144 | 5,003,741 | 5,948,575 | 5,885,672 | 6,528,606 |
| 4. Depreciation | 1,102,523 | 1,145,865 | 1,354,772 | 1,548,171 | 1,821,456 | n.a. | n.a. | n.a. | 2,380,076 | 2,652,655 |
| 5. Taxes Paid | 332,804 | 348,261 | 348,628 | 376,444 | 409,233 | 69,427 | 64,551 | 89,055 | 88,031 | 101,883 |
| 6. Interest Paid | 730,058 | 827,930 | 1,037,438 | 1,285,845 | 1,738,249 | 341,580 | 407,974 | 356,011 | 363,290 | 369,296 |
| 7. Payroll Deductions | 1,123,911 | 1,167,557 | 1,254,671 | 1,551,281 | 1,652,665 | 434,029 | 481,023 | n.a. | 556,635 | 784,240 |
| 8. Payments to Partners | 144,602 | 161,272 | 234,470 | 238,050 | 262,900 | 310,131 | 281,789 | 307,763 | 254,850 | 327,549 |
| 9. Net Income, less Deficit | 1,014,820 | 791,386 | 1,234,872 | 1,061,398 | 471,548 | 70,361 | 70,103 | 14,484 | (749,030) | (1,049,433) |
| **Selected Average Financial Statistics** (Items 10 to 13 inclusive in $) | | | | | | | | | | |
| 10. Av. Payment Partnership | 1,192 | 1,332 | 1,847 | 1,907 | 2,083 | 2,482 | 2,119 | 2,253 | 1,829 | 2,410 |
| 11. Av. Payment Partner | 422 | 456 | 616 | 634 | 690 | 765 | 626 | 660 | 515 | 560 |
| 12. Av. Income Partnership | 8,364 | 6,538 | 9,728 | 8,503 | 3,736 | 563 | 527 | 106 | (5,377) | (7,722) |
| 13. Av. Income Partner | 2,959 | 2,236 | 3,247 | 2,827 | 1,238 | 173 | 156 | 31 | (1,515) | (1,795) |
| **Selected Financial Statistics as Percent of Op. Income** | | | | | | | | | | |
| 14. Depreciation / Op. Income (%) | 8.5 | 8.5 | 7.5 | 7.4 | 8.4 | n.a. | n.a. | n.a. | 40.4 | 40.6 |
| 15. Interest / Op. Income (%) | 5.7 | 6.1 | 5.8 | 6.2 | 8.0 | 6.8 | 8.2 | 6.0 | 6.2 | 5.7 |
| 16. Payroll / Op. Income (%) | 8.7 | 8.6 | 7.0 | 7.5 | 7.7 | 8.7 | 9.6 | n.a. | 9.5 | 12.0 |
| **Selected Index Numbers (1976 = 100)** | | | | | | | | | | |
| 17. Partnerships | 100.0 | 99.8 | 104.6 | 102.9 | 104.0 | 103.0 | 109.6 | 112.6 | 114.8 | 112.0 |
| 18. Partners | 100.0 | 103.2 | 110.9 | 109.5 | 111.1 | 118.3 | 131.2 | 135.9 | 144.2 | 170.5 |
| 19. Operating Income | 100.0 | 104.9 | 139.8 | 161.2 | 167.4 | 38.7 | 38.8 | 46.1 | 45.6 | 50.6 |
| 20. Payments to Partners | 100.0 | 111.5 | 162.1 | 164.6 | 181.8 | 214.5 | 194.9 | 212.8 | 176.2 | 226.5 |
| **Selected Financial Statistics (Constant $, 1976 = 100)** | | | | | | | | | | |
| 21. Operating Income | 100.0 | 101.7 | 123.9 | 128.4 | 125.3 | 28.2 | 28.5 | 33.2 | 31.8 | 37.0 |
| 22. Payments to Partners | 100.0 | 104.8 | 141.5 | 129.1 | 125.6 | 134.2 | 114.9 | 121.6 | 96.6 | 119.9 |
| 23. Av. Payment, Partnership | 100.0 | 105.0 | 135.2 | 125.5 | 120.7 | 130.3 | 104.9 | 108.0 | 84.1 | 107.0 |
| 24. Av. Payment, Partner | 100.0 | 101.5 | 127.4 | 118.1 | 113.2 | 113.6 | 87.7 | 89.4 | 67.1 | 70.4 |

TABLE 3

003: FARMS, WITH AND WITHOUT NET INCOME

| | 1976 | 1977 | 1978 | 1979 | 1980 | 1981 | 1982 | 1983 | 1984 | 1985 |
|---|---|---|---|---|---|---|---|---|---|---|
| 1 Number of Partnerships | 106,653 | 105,679 | 109,538 | 108,327 | 108,094 | 108,199 | 112,388 | 110,965 | 112,817 | 109,544 |
| 2 Number of Partners | 305,960 | 315,596 | 333,661 | 324,147 | 330,749 | 346,911 | 377,829 | 365,895 | 389,673 | 490,873 |
| **Selected Financial Statistics** | | | | | | | | | | |
| (Items 3 to 9 inclusive in 000's of dollars) | | | | | | | | | | |
| 3. Operating Income | 11,560,523 | 11,724,851 | 15,961,328 | 18,559,302 | 19,173,526 | 2,574,407 | 2,510,481 | 2,729,130 | 3,113,091 | 3,344,233 |
| 4. Depreciation | 1,010,018 | 1,036,358 | 1,237,848 | 1,400,462 | 1,626,626 | n.a. | n.a. | n.a. | 2,019,052 | 2,270,500 |
| 5. Taxes Paid | 301,453 | 308,206 | 309,844 | 332,977 | 364,313 | 35,057 | 37,725 | 51,031 | 40,128 | 44,962 |
| 6. Interest Paid | 695,124 | 770,338 | 975,654 | 1,205,231 | 1,611,661 | 189,012 | 244,827 | 193,419 | 194,734 | 207,233 |
| 7. Payroll Deductions | 922,108 | 932,287 | 1,026,168 | 1,248,176 | 1,359,667 | 175,788 | 190,093 | n.a. | 222,319 | 264,414 |
| 8. Payments to Partners | 111,270 | 113,813 | 171,240 | 175,700 | 204,531 | 253,402 | 219,787 | 237,397 | 199,687 | 250,952 |
| 9. Net Income, less Deficit | 891,986 | 599,614 | 1,080,377 | 924,208 | 426,353 | 63,479 | 59,903 | 10,321 | (606,945) | (854,370) |
| **Selected Average Financial Statistics** | | | | | | | | | | |
| (Items 10 to 13 inclusive in $) | | | | | | | | | | |
| 10. Av. Payment Partnership | 1,043 | 1,077 | 1,563 | 1,622 | 1,892 | 2,342 | 1,956 | 2,139 | 1,770 | 2,291 |
| 11. Av. Payment Partner | 364 | 361 | 513 | 542 | 618 | 730 | 582 | 649 | 512 | 511 |
| 12. Av. Income Partnership | 8,363 | 5,674 | 9,863 | 8,532 | 3,944 | 587 | 533 | 93 | (5,380) | (7,799) |
| 13. Av. Income Partner | 2,915 | 1,900 | 3,238 | 2,851 | 1,289 | 183 | 159 | 28 | (1,558) | (1,741) |
| **Selected Financial Statistics as Percent of Op. Income** | | | | | | | | | | |
| 14. Depreciation / Op. Income (%) | 8.7 | 8.8 | 7.8 | 7.6 | 8.5 | n.a. | n.a. | n.a. | 64.9 | 67.9 |
| 15. Interest / Op. Income (%) | 6.0 | 6.6 | 6.1 | 6.5 | 8.4 | 7.3 | 9.8 | 7.1 | 6.3 | 6.2 |
| 16. Payroll / Op. Income (%) | 8.0 | 8.0 | 6.4 | 6.7 | 7.1 | 6.8 | 7.6 | n.a. | 7.1 | 7.9 |
| **Selected Index Numbers (1976 = 100)** | | | | | | | | | | |
| 17. Partnerships | 100.0 | 99.1 | 102.7 | 101.6 | 101.4 | 101.4 | 105.4 | 104.0 | 105.8 | 102.7 |
| 18. Partners | 100.0 | 103.1 | 109.1 | 105.9 | 108.1 | 113.4 | 123.5 | 119.6 | 127.4 | 160.4 |
| 19. Operating Income | 100.0 | 101.4 | 138.1 | 160.5 | 165.9 | 22.3 | 21.7 | 23.6 | 26.9 | 28.9 |
| 20. Payments to Partners | 100.0 | 102.3 | 153.9 | 157.9 | 183.8 | 227.7 | 197.5 | 213.4 | 179.5 | 225.5 |
| **Selected Financial Statistics (Constant $, 1976 = 100)** | | | | | | | | | | |
| 21. Operating Income | 100.0 | 98.4 | 122.4 | 127.9 | 124.1 | 16.2 | 16.0 | 17.0 | 18.8 | 21.1 |
| 22. Payments to Partners | 100.0 | 96.1 | 134.3 | 123.8 | 127.0 | 142.5 | 116.5 | 121.9 | 98.4 | 119.3 |
| 23. Av. Payment, Partnership | 100.0 | 96.9 | 130.7 | 121.9 | 125.3 | 140.5 | 110.6 | 117.2 | 93.0 | 116.2 |
| 24. Av. Payment, Partner | 100.0 | 93.3 | 123.3 | 116.7 | 117.2 | 125.6 | 94.2 | 101.7 | 77.4 | 74.5 |

TABLE 3

004: FIELD CROPS, WITH AND WITHOUT NET INCOME

| | 1976 | 1977 | 1978 | 1979 | 1980 | 1981 | 1982 | 1983 | 1984 | 1985 |
|---|---|---|---|---|---|---|---|---|---|---|
| 1. Number of Partnerships | 42,681 | 42,151 | 42,545 | 39,452 | 41,888 | 44,573 | 47,193 | 48,097 | 41,997 | 44,982 |
| 2. Number of Partners | 119,663 | 120,228 | 128,840 | 116,337 | 123,527 | 140,919 | 148,991 | 170,174 | 156,679 | 159,343 |
| **Selected Financial Statistics** (Items 3 to 9 inclusive in 000's of dollars) | | | | | | | | | | |
| 3. Operating Income | 4,344,571 | 4,112,696 | 5,130,961 | 4,808,118 | 6,648,618 | 667,928 | 606,245 | 821,676 | 891,685 | 1,345,465 |
| 4. Depreciation | 471,555 | 465,605 | 539,806 | 536,666 | 692,031 | n.a. | n.a. | n.a. | 628,488 | 800,348 |
| 5. Taxes Paid | 122,775 | 120,863 | 127,225 | 115,786 | 143,991 | 10,030 | 14,458 | 22,349 | 22,115 | 27,675 |
| 6. Interest Paid | 302,449 | 300,069 | 383,732 | 401,596 | 614,203 | 53,925 | 93,255 | 65,267 | 46,850 | 69,015 |
| 7. Payroll Deductions | 352,880 | 329,141 | 398,574 | 362,413 | 458,008 | 44,301 | 67,433 | n.a. | 119,244 | 153,198 |
| 8. Payments to Partners | 45,745 | 45,183 | 82,142 | 71,659 | 68,812 | 103,079 | 94,277 | 100,863 | 70,339 | 129,980 |
| 9. Net Income, less Deficit | 718,423 | 429,057 | 481,331 | 458,191 | 469,790 | 1,360 | 12,193 | 670,455 | 392,779 | 381,496 |
| **Selected Average Financial Statistics** (Items 10 to 13 inclusive in $) | | | | | | | | | | |
| 10. Av. Payment Partnership | 1,072 | 1,072 | 1,931 | 1,816 | 1,643 | 2,313 | 1,998 | 2,097 | 1,675 | 2,890 |
| 11. Av. Payment Partner | 382 | 376 | 638 | 616 | 557 | 731 | 633 | 593 | 449 | 816 |
| 12. Av. Income Partnership | 16,832 | 10,179 | 11,313 | 11,614 | 11,215 | 31 | 258 | 13,940 | 9,353 | 8,481 |
| 13. Av. Income Partner | 6,004 | 3,569 | 3,736 | 3,938 | 3,803 | 10 | 82 | 3,940 | 2,507 | 2,394 |
| **Selected Financial Statistics as Percent of Op. Income** | | | | | | | | | | |
| 14. Depreciation / Op. Income (%) | 10.9 | 11.3 | 10.5 | 11.2 | 10.4 | n.a. | n.a. | n.a. | 70.5 | 59.5 |
| 15. Interest / Op. Income (%) | 7.0 | 7.3 | 7.5 | 8.4 | 9.2 | 8.1 | 15.4 | 7.9 | 5.3 | 5.1 |
| 16. Payroll / Op. Income (%) | 8.1 | 8.0 | 7.8 | 7.5 | 6.9 | 6.6 | 11.1 | n.a. | 13.4 | 11.4 |
| **Selected Index Numbers** (1976 = 100) | | | | | | | | | | |
| 17. Partnerships | 100.0 | 98.8 | 99.7 | 92.4 | 98.1 | 104.4 | 110.6 | 112.7 | 98.4 | 105.4 |
| 18. Partners | 100.0 | 100.5 | 107.7 | 97.2 | 103.2 | 117.8 | 124.5 | 142.2 | 130.9 | 133.2 |
| 19. Operating Income | 100.0 | 94.7 | 118.1 | 110.7 | 153.0 | 15.4 | 14.0 | 18.9 | 20.5 | 31.0 |
| 20. Payments to Partners | 100.0 | 98.8 | 179.6 | 156.6 | 150.4 | 225.3 | 206.1 | 220.5 | 153.8 | 284.1 |
| **Selected Financial Statistics** (Constant $, 1976 = 100) | | | | | | | | | | |
| 21. Operating Income | 100.0 | 91.8 | 104.7 | 88.2 | 114.5 | 11.2 | 10.3 | 13.6 | 14.3 | 22.6 |
| 22. Payments to Partners | 100.0 | 92.8 | 156.7 | 122.9 | 103.9 | 141.0 | 121.5 | 126.0 | 84.3 | 150.4 |
| 23. Av. Payment, Partnership | 100.0 | 94.0 | 157.2 | 132.8 | 105.9 | 135.1 | 109.9 | 111.8 | 85.6 | 142.7 |
| 24. Av. Payment, Partner | 100.0 | 92.3 | 145.8 | 126.2 | 100.8 | 119.5 | 97.7 | 88.8 | 64.2 | 112.8 |

## TABLE 3

## 005:  VEGETABLE AND MELON, WITH AND WITHOUT NET INCOME

| | 1976 | 1977 | 1978 | 1979 | 1980 | 1981 | 1982 | 1983 | 1984 | 1985 |
|---|---|---|---|---|---|---|---|---|---|---|
| 1. Number of Partnerships | 3,745 | 3,009 | 2,618 | 3,475 | 1,970 | 2,191 | 2,609 | 2,214 | 1,968 | 2,497 |
| 2. Number of Partners | 11,450 | 8,469 | 8,292 | 8,561 | 4,763 | 7,009 | 8,247 | 7,005 | 5,385 | 6,204 |
| **Selected Financial Statistics** | | | | | | | | | | |
| **(Items 3 to 9 inclusive in 000's of dollars)** | | | | | | | | | | |
| 3. Operating Income | 632,410 | 615,949 | 770,052 | 1,277,367 | 703,468 | 110,139 | 65,616 | 224,638 | 71,548 | 52,861 |
| 4. Depreciation | 40,289 | 40,057 | 45,800 | 81,907 | 39,578 | n.a. | n.a. | n.a. | 63,894 | 68,534 |
| 5. Taxes Paid | 22,236 | 20,674 | 20,564 | 35,470 | 21,036 | 985 | 382 | 1,276 | 738 | 591 |
| 6. Interest Paid | 20,689 | 25,127 | 22,675 | 51,189 | 35,334 | 7,757 | 2,043 | 15,214 | 1,905 | 3,118 |
| 7. Payroll Deductions | 108,561 | 146,778 | 125,333 | 228,089 | 145,984 | 7,702 | 5,877 | n.a. | 7,853 | 11,586 |
| 8. Payments to Partners | 6,455 | 5,842 | 6,327 | 6,664 | 7,048 | 11,907 | 6,222 | 6,506 | 4,856 | 4,752 |
| 9. Net Income, less Deficit | 56,470 | 71,596 | 101,597 | 82,507 | 29,986 | 22,389 | 8,394 | 10,329 | 163,432 | (13,118) |
| **Selected Average Financial Statistics** | | | | | | | | | | |
| **(Items 10 to 13 inclusive in $)** | | | | | | | | | | |
| 10. Av. Payment Partnership | 1,724 | 1,942 | 2,417 | 1,918 | 3,578 | 5,435 | 2,385 | 2,939 | 2,467 | 1,903 |
| 11. Av. Payment Partner | 564 | 690 | 763 | 778 | 1,480 | 1,699 | 754 | 929 | 902 | 766 |
| 12. Av. Income Partnership | 15,079 | 23,794 | 38,807 | 23,743 | 15,221 | 10,219 | 3,217 | 4,665 | 83,045 | (5,254) |
| 13. Av. Income Partner | 4,932 | 8,454 | 12,252 | 9,638 | 6,296 | 3,194 | 1,018 | 1,475 | 30,349 | (2,114) |
| **Selected Financial Statistics as Percent of Op. Income** | | | | | | | | | | |
| 14. Depreciation / Op. Income (%) | 6.4 | 6.5 | 6.0 | 6.4 | 5.6 | n.a. | n.a. | n.a. | 89.3 | 129.7 |
| 15. Interest / Op. Income (%) | 3.3 | 4.1 | 2.9 | 4.0 | 5.0 | 7.0 | 3.1 | 6.8 | 2.7 | 5.9 |
| 16. Payroll / Op. Income (%) | 17.2 | 23.8 | 16.3 | 17.9 | 20.8 | 7.0 | 9.0 | n.a. | 11.0 | 21.9 |
| **Selected Index Numbers (1976 = 100)** | | | | | | | | | | |
| 17. Partnerships | 100.0 | 80.3 | 69.9 | 92.8 | 52.6 | 58.5 | 69.7 | 59.1 | 52.6 | 66.7 |
| 18. Partners | 100.0 | 74.0 | 72.4 | 74.8 | 41.6 | 61.2 | 72.0 | 61.2 | 47.0 | 54.2 |
| 19. Operating Income | 100.0 | 97.4 | 121.8 | 202.0 | 111.2 | 17.4 | 10.4 | 35.5 | 11.3 | 8.4 |
| 20. Payments to Partners | 100.0 | 90.5 | 98.0 | 103.2 | 109.2 | 184.5 | 96.4 | 100.8 | 75.2 | 73.6 |
| **Selected Financial Statistics (Constant $, 1976 = 100)** | | | | | | | | | | |
| 21. Operating Income | 100.0 | 94.5 | 107.9 | 160.9 | 83.2 | 12.7 | 7.6 | 25.6 | 7.9 | 6.1 |
| 22. Payments to Partners | 100.0 | 85.0 | 85.5 | 81.0 | 75.4 | 115.5 | 56.8 | 57.6 | 41.2 | 39.0 |
| 23. Av. Payment, Partnership | 100.0 | 105.8 | 122.4 | 87.2 | 143.4 | 197.3 | 81.6 | 97.4 | 78.4 | 58.5 |
| 24. Av. Payment, Partner | 100.0 | 114.9 | 118.0 | 108.3 | 181.5 | 188.7 | 78.9 | 94.1 | 87.7 | 72.0 |

TABLE 3

006:  FRUIT AND TREE NUT, WITH AND WITHOUT NET INCOME

| | 1976 | 1977 | 1978 | 1979 | 1980 | 1981 | 1982 | 1983 | 1984 | 1985 |
|---|---|---|---|---|---|---|---|---|---|---|
| 1. Number of Partnerships | 9,714 | 8,523 | 9,566 | 10,845 | 9,742 | 10,774 | 10,161 | 12,091 | 11,379 | 10,409 |
| 2. Number of Partners | 41,409 | 45,520 | 45,616 | 51,676 | 50,791 | 56,558 | 62,779 | 56,978 | 76,204 | 94,126 |
| **Selected Financial Statistics** (Items 3 to 9 inclusive in 000's of dollars) | | | | | | | | | | |
| 3. Operating Income | 792,298 | 877,182 | 994,976 | 1,308,000 | 1,321,727 | 245,365 | 283,043 | 223,664 | 213,040 | 212,007 |
| 4. Depreciation | 74,299 | 85,657 | 95,983 | 121,387 | 126,409 | n.a. | n.a. | n.a. | 274,796 | 299,836 |
| 5. Taxes Paid | 51,405 | 54,033 | 41,817 | 46,919 | 48,062 | 7,214 | 6,502 | 5,883 | 6,856 | 6,604 |
| 6. Interest Paid | 75,863 | 116,034 | 124,998 | 154,307 | 185,104 | 49,763 | 53,088 | 23,504 | 38,372 | 51,597 |
| 7. Payroll Deductions | 173,179 | 173,947 | 157,054 | 231,032 | 253,403 | 36,489 | 38,207 | n.a. | 30,894 | 24,678 |
| 8. Payments to Partners | 11,101 | 17,257 | 16,211 | 18,622 | 22,545 | 29,850 | 23,917 | 17,555 | 25,727 | 16,185 |
| 9. Net Income, less Deficit | 233 | 5,323 | 1,095 | 60,697 | 5,440 | 18,073 | 13,697 | 26,333 | (369,356) | (385,425) |
| **Selected Average Financial Statistics** (Items 10 to 13 inclusive in $) | | | | | | | | | | |
| 10. Av. Payment Partnership | 1,143 | 2,025 | 1,695 | 1,717 | 2,314 | 2,771 | 2,354 | 1,452 | 2,261 | 1,555 |
| 11. Av. Payment Partner | 268 | 379 | 355 | 360 | 444 | 528 | 381 | 308 | 338 | 172 |
| 12. Av. Income Partnership | 24 | 625 | 114 | 5,597 | 558 | 1,677 | 1,348 | 2,178 | (32,459) | (37,028) |
| 13. Av. Income Partner | 6 | 117 | 24 | 1,175 | 107 | 320 | 218 | 462 | (4,847) | (4,095) |
| **Selected Financial Statistics as Percent of Op. Income** | | | | | | | | | | |
| 14. Depreciation / Op. Income (%) | 9.4 | 9.8 | 9.7 | 9.3 | 9.6 | n.a. | n.a. | n.a. | 129.0 | 141.4 |
| 15. Interest / Op. Income (%) | 9.6 | 13.2 | 12.6 | 11.8 | 14.0 | 20.3 | 18.8 | 10.5 | 18.0 | 24.3 |
| 16. Payroll / Op. Income (%) | 21.9 | 19.8 | 15.8 | 17.7 | 19.2 | 14.9 | 13.5 | n.a. | 14.5 | 11.6 |
| **Selected Index Numbers** (1976 = 100) | | | | | | | | | | |
| 17. Partnerships | 100.0 | 87.7 | 98.5 | 111.6 | 100.3 | 110.9 | 104.6 | 124.5 | 117.1 | 107.2 |
| 18. Partners | 100.0 | 109.9 | 110.2 | 124.8 | 122.7 | 136.6 | 151.6 | 137.6 | 184.0 | 227.3 |
| 19. Operating Income | 100.0 | 110.7 | 125.6 | 165.1 | 166.8 | 31.0 | 35.7 | 28.2 | 26.9 | 26.8 |
| 20. Payments to Partners | 100.0 | 155.5 | 146.0 | 167.8 | 203.1 | 268.9 | 215.4 | 158.1 | 231.8 | 145.8 |
| **Selected Financial Statistics** (Constant $, 1976 = 100) | | | | | | | | | | |
| 21. Operating Income | 100.0 | 107.4 | 111.3 | 131.5 | 124.8 | 22.5 | 26.3 | 20.4 | 18.8 | 19.6 |
| 22. Payments to Partners | 100.0 | 146.0 | 127.4 | 131.6 | 140.3 | 168.3 | 127.1 | 90.4 | 127.0 | 77.2 |
| 23. Av. Payment, Partnership | 100.0 | 166.5 | 129.4 | 117.9 | 139.9 | 151.7 | 121.4 | 72.7 | 108.5 | 72.1 |
| 24. Av. Payment, Partner | 100.0 | 132.9 | 115.8 | 105.6 | 114.5 | 123.4 | 84.0 | 65.5 | 69.3 | 33.7 |

## TABLE 3

## 008: BEEF CATTLE FEEDLOTS, WITH AND WITHOUT NET INCOME

| | 1976 | 1977 | 1978 | 1979 | 1980 | 1981 | 1982 | 1983 | 1984 | 1985 |
|---|---|---|---|---|---|---|---|---|---|---|
| 1. Number of Partnerships | 778 | 1,338 | 1,202 | 2,004 | 1,412 | 2,032 | 1,343 | 2,414 | 1,646 | 1,813 |
| 2. Number of Partners | 5,941 | 4,163 | 3,751 | 7,120 | 4,858 | 12,952 | 8,508 | 8,103 | 6,286 | 82,004 |

### Selected Financial Statistics
(Items 3 to 9 inclusive in 000's of dollars)

| | 1976 | 1977 | 1978 | 1979 | 1980 | 1981 | 1982 | 1983 | 1984 | 1985 |
|---|---|---|---|---|---|---|---|---|---|---|
| 3. Operating Income | 214,068 | 478,167 | 719,656 | 1,176,655 | 938,289 | 198,328 | 296,960 | 244,129 | 266,690 | 288,162 |
| 4. Depreciation | 6,565 | 9,413 | 15,511 | 23,267 | 23,399 | n.a. | n.a. | n.a. | 26,652 | 22,012 |
| 5. Taxes Paid | 1,284 | 3,006 | 4,028 | 5,448 | 4,865 | 471 | 709 | 855 | 521 | 674 |
| 6. Interest Paid | 6,717 | 13,871 | 24,379 | 37,933 | 40,106 | 5,288 | 9,199 | 5,038 | 3,687 | 7,678 |
| 7. Payroll Deductions | 3,378 | 11,207 | 22,060 | 19,936 | 17,055 | 4,221 | 7,936 | n.a. | 9,467 | 7,251 |
| 8. Payments to Partners | 1,634 | 1,586 | 2,448 | 3,251 | 2,810 | 1,649 | 4,026 | 5,383 | 1,722 | 1,192 |
| 9. Net Income, less Deficit | 595 | 12,681 | 51,685 | 21,021 | 2,786 | 7,299 | 24,987 | 4,729 | (826) | 119,944 |

### Selected Average Financial Statistics
(Items 10 to 13 inclusive in $)

| | 1976 | 1977 | 1978 | 1979 | 1980 | 1981 | 1982 | 1983 | 1984 | 1985 |
|---|---|---|---|---|---|---|---|---|---|---|
| 10. Av. Payment Partnership | 2,100 | 1,185 | 2,037 | 1,622 | 1,990 | 812 | 2,998 | 2,230 | 1,046 | 657 |
| 11. Av. Payment Partner | 275 | 381 | 653 | 457 | 578 | 127 | 473 | 664 | 274 | 15 |
| 12. Av. Income Partnership | 765 | 9,478 | 42,999 | 10,490 | 1,973 | 3,592 | 18,605 | 1,959 | (502) | 66,158 |
| 13. Av. Income Partner | 100 | 3,046 | 13,779 | 2,952 | 573 | 564 | 2,937 | 584 | (131) | 1,463 |

### Selected Financial Statistics as Percent of Op. Income

| | 1976 | 1977 | 1978 | 1979 | 1980 | 1981 | 1982 | 1983 | 1984 | 1985 |
|---|---|---|---|---|---|---|---|---|---|---|
| 14. Depreciation / Op. Income (%) | 3.1 | 2.0 | 2.2 | 2.0 | 2.5 | n.a. | n.a. | n.a. | 1.0 | 7.6 |
| 15. Interest / Op. Income (%) | 3.1 | 2.9 | 3.4 | 3.2 | 4.3 | 2.7 | 3.1 | 2.1 | 1.4 | 2.7 |
| 16. Payroll / Op. Income (%) | 1.6 | 2.3 | 3.1 | 1.7 | 1.8 | 2.1 | 2.7 | n.a. | 3.6 | 2.5 |

### Selected Index Numbers (1976 = 100)

| | 1976 | 1977 | 1978 | 1979 | 1980 | 1981 | 1982 | 1983 | 1984 | 1985 |
|---|---|---|---|---|---|---|---|---|---|---|
| 17. Partnerships | 100.0 | 172.0 | 154.5 | 257.6 | 181.5 | 261.2 | 172.6 | 310.3 | 211.6 | 233.0 |
| 18. Partners | 100.0 | 70.1 | 63.1 | 119.8 | 81.8 | 218.0 | 143.2 | 136.4 | 105.8 | 1,380 |
| 19. Operating Income | 100.0 | 223.4 | 336.2 | 549.7 | 438.3 | 92.6 | 138.7 | 114.0 | 124.6 | 134.6 |
| 20. Payments to Partners | 100.0 | 97.1 | 149.8 | 199.0 | 172.0 | 100.9 | 246.4 | 329.4 | 105.4 | 72.9 |

### Selected Financial Statistics (Constant $, 1976 = 100)

| | 1976 | 1977 | 1978 | 1979 | 1980 | 1981 | 1982 | 1983 | 1984 | 1985 |
|---|---|---|---|---|---|---|---|---|---|---|
| 21. Operating Income | 100.0 | 216.6 | 297.9 | 438.0 | 328.0 | 67.5 | 102.0 | 82.2 | 86.9 | 98.4 |
| 22. Payments to Partners | 100.0 | 91.2 | 130.7 | 156.0 | 118.8 | 63.2 | 145.3 | 188.2 | 57.8 | 38.6 |
| 23. Av. Payment, Partnership | 100.0 | 53.0 | 84.6 | 60.6 | 65.4 | 24.2 | 84.2 | 60.6 | 27.3 | 16.6 |
| 24. Av. Payment, Partner | 100.0 | 130.2 | 207.1 | 130.2 | 145.1 | 29.1 | 101.7 | 138.2 | 54.6 | 3.1 |

TABLE 3

009: BEEF CATTLE, EXCEPT FEEDLOTS, WITH AND WITHOUT NET INCOME

| | 1976 | 1977 | 1978 | 1979 | 1980 | 1981 | 1982 | 1983 | 1984 | 1985 |
|---|---|---|---|---|---|---|---|---|---|---|
| 1. Number of Partnerships | 24,481 | 24,472 | 25,653 | 23,247 | 22,159 | 17,004 | 19,074 | 18,852 | 19,845 | 15,925 |
| 2. Number of Partners | 64,183 | 70,041 | 68,393 | 65,413 | 60,764 | 43,233 | 54,978 | 50,267 | 55,878 | 60,947 |
| **Selected Financial Statistics** (Items 3 to 9 inclusive in 000's of dollars) | | | | | | | | | | |
| 3. Operating Income | 2,570,212 | 2,552,341 | 4,569,868 | 5,130,282 | 3,996,261 | 449,564 | 376,353 | 400,244 | 535,249 | 545,091 |
| 4. Depreciation | 184,945 | 172,781 | 219,463 | 231,428 | 248,224 | n.a. | n.a. | n.a. | 199,889 | 287,527 |
| 5. Taxes Paid | 44,946 | 45,038 | 52,359 | 51,357 | 54,058 | 5,036 | 3,260 | 12,236 | 2,874 | 2,854 |
| 6. Interest Paid | 164,186 | 181,896 | 229,433 | 283,680 | 358,750 | 37,627 | 36,077 | 42,554 | 44,389 | 35,824 |
| 7. Payroll Deductions | 99,349 | 84,711 | 111,072 | 111,598 | 145,021 | 17,799 | 16,389 | n.a. | 8,120 | 10,839 |
| 8. Payments to Partners | 12,163 | 16,949 | 22,565 | 26,285 | 37,673 | 34,518 | 22,803 | 29,759 | 30,386 | 37,591 |
| 9. Net Income, less Deficit | 10,328 | 12,611 | 156,459 | 68,876 | 14,786 | 35,692 | 32,396 | 34,430 | (344,282) | (841,298) |
| **Selected Average Financial Statistics** (Items 10 to 13 inclusive in $) | | | | | | | | | | |
| 10. Av. Payment Partnership | 497 | 693 | 880 | 1,131 | 1,700 | 2,030 | 1,196 | 1,579 | 1,531 | 2,361 |
| 11. Av. Payment Partner | 190 | 242 | 330 | 402 | 620 | 798 | 415 | 592 | 544 | 617 |
| 12. Av. Income Partnership | 422 | 515 | 6,099 | 2,963 | 667 | 2,099 | 1,698 | 1,826 | (17,349) | (52,829) |
| 13. Av. Income Partner | 161 | 180 | 2,288 | 1,053 | 243 | 826 | 589 | 685 | (6,161) | (13,804) |
| **Selected Financial Statistics as Percent of Op. Income** | | | | | | | | | | |
| 14. Depreciation / Op. Income (%) | 7.2 | 6.8 | 4.8 | 4.5 | 6.2 | n.a. | n.a. | n.a. | 37.4 | 52.8 |
| 15. Interest / Op. Income (%) | 6.4 | 7.1 | 5.0 | 5.5 | 9.0 | 8.4 | 9.6 | 10.6 | 8.3 | 6.6 |
| 16. Payroll / Op. Income (%) | 3.9 | 3.3 | 2.4 | 2.2 | 3.6 | 4.0 | 4.4 | n.a. | 1.5 | 2.0 |
| **Selected Index Numbers (1976 = 100)** | | | | | | | | | | |
| 17. Partnerships | 100.0 | 100.0 | 104.8 | 95.0 | 90.5 | 69.5 | 77.9 | 77.0 | 81.1 | 65.1 |
| 18. Partners | 100.0 | 109.1 | 106.6 | 101.9 | 94.7 | 67.4 | 85.7 | 78.3 | 87.1 | 95.0 |
| 19. Operating Income | 100.0 | 99.3 | 177.8 | 199.6 | 155.5 | 17.5 | 14.6 | 15.6 | 20.8 | 21.2 |
| 20. Payments to Partners | 100.0 | 139.3 | 185.5 | 216.1 | 309.7 | 283.8 | 187.5 | 244.7 | 249.8 | 309.1 |
| **Selected Financial Statistics (Constant $, 1976 = 100)** | | | | | | | | | | |
| 21. Operating Income | 100.0 | 96.3 | 157.6 | 159.0 | 116.3 | 12.7 | 10.8 | 11.2 | 14.5 | 15.5 |
| 22. Payments to Partners | 100.0 | 130.9 | 161.9 | 169.5 | 214.0 | 177.6 | 110.6 | 139.8 | 136.9 | 163.5 |
| 23. Av. Payment, Partnership | 100.0 | 131.1 | 154.4 | 178.4 | 236.4 | 255.7 | 142.1 | 181.5 | 168.8 | 251.5 |
| 24. Av. Payment, Partner | 100.0 | 119.7 | 152.1 | 166.4 | 225.8 | 263.6 | 129.6 | 178.1 | 157.4 | 171.8 |

TABLE 3

010: HOGS, SHEEP, AND GOATS, WITH AND WITHOUT NET INCOME

| | 1976 | 1977 | 1978 | 1979 | 1980 | 1981 | 1982 | 1983 | 1984 | 1985 |
|---|---|---|---|---|---|---|---|---|---|---|
| 1. Number of Partnerships | 5,584 | 5,877 | 6,586 | 6,125 | 6,162 | 4,883 | 3,922 | 3,593 | 5,714 | 4,179 |
| 2. Number of Partners | 13,122 | 14,464 | 15,782 | 15,003 | 16,156 | 14,245 | 13,987 | 12,304 | 13,509 | 11,763 |
| **Selected Financial Statistics** (Items 3 to 9 inclusive in 000's of dollars) | | | | | | | | | | |
| 3. Operating Income | 498,368 | 560,458 | 817,230 | 876,484 | 990,390 | 185,197 | 164,033 | 37,295 | 187,610 | 169,560 |
| 4. Depreciation | 37,776 | 45,594 | 65,221 | 71,862 | 76,115 | n.a. | n.a. | n.a. | 59,540 | 37,449 |
| 5. Taxes Paid | 6,288 | 6,773 | 12,162 | 11,133 | 12,148 | 794 | 537 | 545 | 118 | 359 |
| 6. Interest Paid | 15,989 | 25,351 | 29,207 | 47,677 | 59,179 | 4,937 | 4,694 | 3,399 | 4,106 | 1,326 |
| 7. Payroll Deductions | 12,209 | 10,287 | 38,343 | 28,454 | 60,482 | 3,668 | 2,104 | n.a. | 346 | 796 |
| 8. Payments to Partners | 1,924 | 2,783 | 8,444 | 3,918 | 5,759 | 8,656 | 1,708 | 197 | 6,023 | 7,078 |
| 9. Net Income, less Deficit | 46,879 | 59,887 | 81,067 | 13,072 | 4,534 | 12,826 | 521 | 3,264 | (16,480) | 62,132 |
| **Selected Average Financial Statistics** (Items 10 to 13 inclusive in $) | | | | | | | | | | |
| 10. Av. Payment Partnership | 345 | 474 | 1,282 | 640 | 935 | 1,773 | 435 | 55 | 1,054 | 1,694 |
| 11. Av. Payment Partner | 147 | 192 | 535 | 261 | 356 | 608 | 122 | 16 | 446 | 602 |
| 12. Av. Income Partnership | 8,395 | 10,190 | 12,309 | 2,134 | 736 | 2,627 | 133 | 908 | (2,884) | 14,868 |
| 13. Av. Income Partner | 3,573 | 4,140 | 5,137 | 871 | 281 | 900 | 37 | 265 | (1,220) | 5,282 |
| **Selected Financial Statistics as Percent of Op. Income** | | | | | | | | | | |
| 14. Depreciation / Op. Income (%) | 7.6 | 8.1 | 8.0 | 8.2 | 7.7 | n.a. | n.a. | n.a. | 31.7 | 22.1 |
| 15. Interest / Op. Income (%) | 3.2 | 4.5 | 3.6 | 5.4 | 6.0 | 2.7 | 2.9 | 9.1 | 2.2 | 0.8 |
| 16. Payroll / Op. Income (%) | 2.5 | 1.8 | 4.7 | 3.3 | 6.1 | 2.0 | 1.3 | n.a. | 0.2 | 0.5 |
| **Selected Index Numbers (1976 = 100)** | | | | | | | | | | |
| 17. Partnerships | 100.0 | 105.2 | 117.9 | 109.7 | 110.4 | 87.4 | 70.2 | 64.3 | 102.3 | 74.8 |
| 18. Partners | 100.0 | 110.2 | 120.3 | 114.3 | 123.1 | 108.6 | 106.6 | 93.8 | 102.9 | 89.6 |
| 19. Operating Income | 100.0 | 112.5 | 164.0 | 175.9 | 198.7 | 37.2 | 32.9 | 7.5 | 37.6 | 34.0 |
| 20. Payments to Partners | 100.0 | 144.6 | 438.9 | 203.6 | 299.3 | 449.9 | 88.8 | 10.2 | 313.0 | 367.9 |
| **Selected Financial Statistics (Constant $, 1976 = 100)** | | | | | | | | | | |
| 21. Operating Income | 100.0 | 109.1 | 145.3 | 140.1 | 148.7 | 27.1 | 24.2 | 5.4 | 26.3 | 24.9 |
| 22. Payments to Partners | 100.0 | 135.9 | 383.0 | 159.7 | 206.8 | 281.6 | 52.4 | 5.9 | 171.6 | 194.7 |
| 23. Av. Payment, Partnership | 100.0 | 129.2 | 324.6 | 145.5 | 187.5 | 322.1 | 74.2 | 8.9 | 167.8 | 260.3 |
| 24. Av. Payment, Partner | 100.0 | 123.3 | 318.6 | 139.5 | 167.4 | 259.3 | 48.8 | 5.8 | 166.3 | 217.5 |

TABLE 3

011: DAIRY FARMS, WITH AND WITHOUT NET INCOME

| | 1976 | 1977 | 1978 | 1979 | 1980 | 1981 | 1982 | 1983 | 1984 | 1985 |
|---|---|---|---|---|---|---|---|---|---|---|
| 1. Number of Partnerships | 13,947 | 14,481 | 15,036 | 16,575 | 17,460 | 15,687 | 16,539 | 15,863 | 18,328 | 17,940 |
| 2. Number of Partners | 33,198 | 35,019 | 45,240 | 40,145 | 48,391 | 40,247 | 40,774 | 39,309 | 42,257 | 43,195 |
| **Selected Financial Statistics** (Items 3 to 9 inclusive in 000's of dollars) | | | | | | | | | | |
| 3. Operating Income | 1,758,603 | 1,769,788 | 2,165,416 | 2,724,259 | 3,355,153 | 179,641 | 151,557 | 188,590 | 336,130 | 184,769 |
| 4. Depreciation | 161,438 | 180,902 | 217,347 | 269,948 | 326,326 | n.a. | n.a. | n.a. | 519,592 | 524,181 |
| 5. Taxes Paid | 37,685 | 42,356 | 39,840 | 46,325 | 57,522 | 2,310 | 1,609 | 1,881 | 2,290 | 1,078 |
| 6. Interest Paid | 90,599 | 90,549 | 136,532 | 181,144 | 241,668 | 5,365 | 6,490 | 9,497 | 9,424 | 8,650 |
| 7. Payroll Deductions | 94,780 | 98,249 | 110,879 | 152,201 | 177,580 | 17,955 | 12,641 | n.a. | 8,914 | 21,471 |
| 8. Payments to Partners | 19,723 | 15,373 | 25,092 | 32,738 | 45,213 | 52,287 | 55,387 | 59,574 | 43,405 | 42,825 |
| 9. Net Income, less Deficit | 198,954 | 216,825 | 213,166 | 260,317 | 244,159 | 121,336 | 72,834 | 2,456 | (84,740) | 222,785 |
| **Selected Average Financial Statistics** (Items 10 to 13 inclusive in $) | | | | | | | | | | |
| 10. Av. Payment Partnership | 1,414 | 1,062 | 1,669 | 1,975 | 2,590 | 3,333 | 3,349 | 3,756 | 2,368 | 2,387 |
| 11. Av. Payment Partner | 594 | 439 | 555 | 815 | 934 | 1,299 | 1,358 | 1,516 | 1,027 | 991 |
| 12. Av. Income Partnership | 14,265 | 14,973 | 14,177 | 15,705 | 13,984 | 7,735 | 4,404 | 155 | (4,624) | 12,418 |
| 13. Av. Income Partner | 5,993 | 6,192 | 4,712 | 6,484 | 5,046 | 3,015 | 1,786 | 62 | (2,005) | 5,158 |
| **Selected Financial Statistics as Percent of Op. Income** | | | | | | | | | | |
| 14. Depreciation / Op. Income (%) | 9.2 | 10.2 | 10.0 | 9.9 | 9.7 | n.a. | n.a. | n.a. | 154.6 | 283.7 |
| 15. Interest / Op. Income (%) | 5.2 | 5.1 | 6.3 | 6.7 | 7.2 | 3.0 | 4.3 | 5.0 | 2.8 | 4.7 |
| 16. Payroll / Op. Income (%) | 5.4 | 5.6 | 5.1 | 5.6 | 5.3 | 1.0 | 8.3 | n.a. | 2.7 | 11.6 |
| **Selected Index Numbers** (1976 = 100) | | | | | | | | | | |
| 17. Partnerships | 100.0 | 103.8 | 107.8 | 118.8 | 125.2 | 112.5 | 118.6 | 113.7 | 131.4 | 128.6 |
| 18. Partners | 100.0 | 105.5 | 136.3 | 120.9 | 145.8 | 121.2 | 122.8 | 118.4 | 127.3 | 130.1 |
| 19. Operating Income | 100.0 | 100.6 | 123.1 | 154.9 | 190.8 | 10.2 | 8.6 | 10.7 | 19.1 | 10.5 |
| 20. Payments to Partners | 100.0 | 77.9 | 127.2 | 166.0 | 229.2 | 265.1 | 280.8 | 302.1 | 220.1 | 217.1 |
| **Selected Financial Statistics** (Constant $, 1976 = 100) | | | | | | | | | | |
| 21. Operating Income | 100.0 | 97.6 | 109.1 | 123.4 | 142.8 | 7.4 | 6.3 | 7.7 | 13.3 | 7.7 |
| 22. Payments to Partners | 100.0 | 73.2 | 111.0 | 130.2 | 158.4 | 165.9 | 165.6 | 172.6 | 120.6 | 114.9 |
| 23. Av. Payment, Partnership | 100.0 | 70.5 | 103.0 | 109.5 | 126.5 | 147.6 | 139.6 | 151.8 | 91.8 | 89.3 |
| 24. Av. Payment, Partner | 100.0 | 69.5 | 81.5 | 107.6 | 108.5 | 136.9 | 134.9 | 145.8 | 94.7 | 88.4 |

*Page 203*

TABLE 3

012: POULTRY AND EGGS, WITH AND WITHOUT NET INCOME

| | 1976 | 1977 | 1978 | 1979 | 1980 | 1981 | 1982 | 1983 | 1984 | 1985 |
|---|---|---|---|---|---|---|---|---|---|---|
| 1. Number of Partnerships | 1,763 | 1,507 | 1,047 | 1,200 | 1,113 | 1,000 | 1,108 | 695 | 978 | 732 |
| 2. Number of Partners | 4,277 | 4,768 | 2,659 | 3,237 | 2,701 | 3,512 | 2,909 | 2,067 | 2,552 | 1,951 |
| **Selected Financial Statistics** | | | | | | | | | | |
| **(Items 3 to 9 inclusive in 000's of dollars)** | | | | | | | | | | |
| 3. Operating Income | 466,034 | 540,780 | 477,458 | 621,035 | 562,842 | 264,609 | 227,121 | 306,055 | 324,627 | 266,575 |
| 4. Depreciation | 15,103 | 22,581 | 14,228 | 22,258 | 33,048 | n.a. | n.a. | n.a. | 55,018 | 11,002 |
| 5. Taxes Paid | 5,862 | 8,110 | 3,180 | 4,896 | 6,041 | 1,018 | 1,141 | 1,197 | 1,168 | 1,164 |
| 6. Interest Paid | 7,185 | 11,378 | 10,784 | 16,742 | 27,235 | 5,128 | 6,451 | 9,828 | 7,065 | 3,936 |
| 7. Payroll Deductions | 24,442 | 37,558 | 22,448 | 31,082 | 28,425 | 10,398 | 8,777 | n.a. | 9,397 | 8,861 |
| 8. Payments to Partners | 1,471 | 2,679 | 2,300 | 4,848 | 6,453 | 3,295 | 2,662 | 1,435 | 2,909 | 3,780 |
| 9. Net Income, less Deficit | 3,164 | 6,262 | 17,712 | 744 | 4,515 | 2,443 | 2,517 | 3,794 | 7,156 | 23,955 |
| **Selected Average Financial Statistics** | | | | | | | | | | |
| **(Items 10 to 13 inclusive in $)** | | | | | | | | | | |
| 10. Av. Payment Partnership | 834 | 1,778 | 2,197 | 4,040 | 5,798 | 3,295 | 2,403 | 2,065 | 2,974 | 5,164 |
| 11. Av. Payment Partner | 344 | 562 | 865 | 1,498 | 2,389 | 938 | 915 | 694 | 1,140 | 1,937 |
| 12. Av. Income Partnership | 1,795 | 4,155 | 16,917 | 620 | 4,057 | 2,443 | 2,272 | 5,459 | 7,317 | 32,725 |
| 13. Av. Income Partner | 740 | 1,313 | 6,661 | 230 | 1,672 | 696 | 865 | 1,836 | 2,804 | 12,278 |
| **Selected Financial Statistics as Percent of Op. Income** | | | | | | | | | | |
| 14. Depreciation / Op. Income (%) | 3.2 | 4.2 | 3.0 | 3.6 | 5.9 | n.a. | n.a. | n.a. | 17.0 | 4.1 |
| 15. Interest / Op. Income (%) | 1.5 | 2.1 | 2.3 | 2.7 | 4.8 | 1.9 | 2.8 | 3.2 | 2.2 | 1.5 |
| 16. Payroll / Op. Income (%) | 5.2 | 7.0 | 4.7 | 5.0 | 5.1 | 3.9 | 3.9 | n.a. | 2.9 | 3.3 |
| **Selected Index Numbers (1976 = 100)** | | | | | | | | | | |
| 17. Partnerships | 100.0 | 85.5 | 59.4 | 68.1 | 63.1 | 56.7 | 62.8 | 39.4 | 55.5 | 41.5 |
| 18. Partners | 100.0 | 111.5 | 62.2 | 75.7 | 63.2 | 82.1 | 68.0 | 48.3 | 59.7 | 45.6 |
| 19. Operating Income | 100.0 | 116.0 | 102.5 | 133.3 | 120.8 | 56.8 | 48.7 | 65.7 | 69.7 | 57.2 |
| 20. Payments to Partners | 100.0 | 182.1 | 156.4 | 329.6 | 438.7 | 224.0 | 181.0 | 97.6 | 197.8 | 257.0 |
| **Selected Financial Statistics (Constant $, 1976 = 100)** | | | | | | | | | | |
| 21. Operating Income | 100.0 | 112.5 | 90.8 | 106.2 | 90.4 | 41.3 | 35.9 | 47.4 | 48.6 | 41.8 |
| 22. Payments to Partners | 100.0 | 171.1 | 136.4 | 258.5 | 303.1 | 140.2 | 106.7 | 55.7 | 108.4 | 136.0 |
| 23. Av. Payment, Partnership | 100.0 | 200.3 | 229.7 | 379.7 | 480.0 | 247.3 | 169.8 | 141.4 | 195.4 | 327.6 |
| 24. Av. Payment, Partner | 100.0 | 153.7 | 219.6 | 341.6 | 479.9 | 170.5 | 156.7 | 115.5 | 181.4 | 297.9 |

TABLE 3

GENERAL LIVESTOCK, INCLUDING ANIMAL SPECIALTY (013,014), WITH AND WITHOUT NET INCOME

| | 1976 | 1977 | 1978 | 1979 | 1980 | 1981 | 1982 | 1983 | 1984 | 1985 |
|---|---|---|---|---|---|---|---|---|---|---|
| 1. Number of Partnerships | 1,814 | 1,887 | 3,428 | 2,843 | 3,417 | 6,604 | 7,104 | 5,301 | 6,418 | 7,479 |
| 2. Number of Partners | 5,733 | 4,617 | 8,949 | 6,924 | 8,961 | 18,850 | 25,144 | 14,916 | 20,607 | 22,105 |
| **Selected Financial Statistics** (Items 3 to 9 inclusive in 000's of dollars) | | | | | | | | | | |
| 3. Operating Income | 93,467 | 37,967 | 121,283 | 295,433 | 329,006 | 176,647 | 290,206 | 173,239 | 200,974 | 199,812 |
| 4. Depreciation | 8,334 | 5,579 | 13,615 | 17,103 | 39,022 | n.a. | n.a. | n.a. | 145,048 | 148,659 |
| 5. Taxes Paid | 1,968 | 1,404 | 2,575 | 3,914 | 4,719 | 3,375 | 5,501 | 1,332 | 1,534 | 1,194 |
| 6. Interest Paid | 6,081 | 2,343 | 7,089 | 12,834 | 29,539 | 17,250 | 31,715 | 12,761 | 19,273 | 9,713 |
| 7. Payroll Deductions | 7,386 | 2,430 | 6,853 | 20,259 | 17,606 | 16,591 | 19,423 | n.a. | 11,479 | 8,988 |
| 8. Payments to Partners | 1,556 | 1,615 | 2,813 | 3,796 | 3,181 | 3,520 | 7,014 | 9,115 | 7,268 | 5,670 |
| 9. Net Income, less Deficit | 4,786 | 1,631 | 8,100 | 1,207 | 5,121 | 11,572 | 14,532 | 8,407 | (319,447) | (365,778) |
| **Selected Average Financial Statistics** (Items 10 to 13 inclusive in $) | | | | | | | | | | |
| 10. Av. Payment Partnership | 858 | 856 | 821 | 1,335 | 931 | 533 | 987 | 1,719 | 1,132 | 758 |
| 11. Av. Payment Partner | 271 | 350 | 314 | 548 | 355 | 187 | 279 | 611 | 353 | 257 |
| 12. Av. Income Partnership | 2,638 | 864 | 2,363 | 425 | 1,499 | 1,752 | 2,046 | 1,586 | (49,774) | (48,907) |
| 13. Av. Income Partner | 835 | 353 | 905 | 174 | 571 | 614 | 578 | 564 | (15,502) | (16,547) |
| **Selected Financial Statistics as Percent of Op. Income** | | | | | | | | | | |
| 14. Depreciation / Op. Income (%) | 8.9 | 14.7 | 11.2 | 5.8 | 11.9 | n.a. | n.a. | n.a. | 72.2 | 74.4 |
| 15. Interest / Op. Income (%) | 6.5 | 6.2 | 5.9 | 4.3 | 9.0 | 9.8 | 10.9 | 7.4 | 9.6 | 4.9 |
| 16. Payroll / Op. Income (%) | 7.9 | 6.4 | 5.7 | 6.9 | 5.4 | 9.4 | 6.7 | n.a. | 5.7 | 4.5 |
| **Selected Index Numbers (1976 = 100)** | | | | | | | | | | |
| 17. Partnerships | 100.0 | 104.0 | 189.0 | 156.7 | 188.4 | 364.1 | 391.6 | 292.2 | 353.8 | 412.3 |
| 18. Partners | 100.0 | 80.5 | 156.1 | 120.8 | 156.3 | 328.8 | 438.6 | 260.2 | 359.4 | 385.6 |
| 19. Operating Income | 100.0 | 40.6 | 129.8 | 316.1 | 352.0 | 189.0 | 310.5 | 185.3 | 215.0 | 213.8 |
| 20. Payments to Partners | 100.0 | 103.8 | 180.8 | 244.0 | 204.4 | 226.2 | 450.8 | 585.8 | 467.1 | 364.4 |
| **Selected Financial Statistics (Constant $, 1976 = 100)** | | | | | | | | | | |
| 21. Operating Income | 100.0 | 39.4 | 115.0 | 251.8 | 263.4 | 137.6 | 228.4 | 133.7 | 150.0 | 156.3 |
| 22. Payments to Partners | 100.0 | 97.5 | 157.7 | 191.3 | 141.2 | 141.6 | 265.8 | 334.7 | 256.0 | 192.8 |
| 23. Av. Payment, Partnership | 100.0 | 93.8 | 83.5 | 122.0 | 74.9 | 39.0 | 67.8 | 114.5 | 72.4 | 46.7 |
| 24. Av. Payment, Partner | 100.0 | 121.2 | 101.1 | 158.3 | 90.5 | 43.3 | 60.9 | 128.8 | 71.0 | 50.3 |

TABLE 3

OTHER FARMS (007,015), WITH AND WITHOUT NET INCOME

| | 1976 | 1977 | 1978 | 1979 | 1980 | 1981 | 1982 | 1983 | 1984 | 1985 |
|---|---|---|---|---|---|---|---|---|---|---|
| 1. Number of Partnerships | 2,146 | 2,434 | 1,857 | 2,561 | 2,971 | 3,450 | 3,337 | 1,845 | 4,544 | 3,590 |
| 2. Number of Partners | 6,984 | 8,307 | 6,139 | 9,731 | 9,835 | 9,385 | 11,513 | 4,771 | 10,316 | 9,236 |
| **Selected Financial Statistics** | | | | | | | | | | |
| **(Items 3 to 9 inclusive in 000's of dollars)** | | | | | | | | | | |
| 3. Operating Income | 190,492 | 179,523 | 194,428 | 341,667 | 327,772 | 96,990 | 49,348 | 109,602 | 85,538 | 79,932 |
| 4. Depreciation | 9,714 | 8,189 | 10,874 | 32,691 | 22,474 | n.a. | n.a. | n.a. | 46,134 | 42,406 |
| 5. Taxes Paid | 7,004 | 5,949 | 6,094 | 11,730 | 11,869 | 3,826 | 3,625 | 3,475 | 1,914 | 2,768 |
| 6. Interest Paid | 5,366 | 3,720 | 6,823 | 18,042 | 20,542 | 1,974 | 1,815 | 6,357 | 19,663 | 16,377 |
| 7. Payroll Deductions | 45,944 | 37,979 | 33,550 | 62,606 | 56,103 | 16,664 | 11,306 | n.a. | 16,604 | 16,926 |
| 8. Payments to Partners | 9,498 | 4,546 | 2,896 | 3,919 | 5,037 | 4,641 | 1,771 | 7,010 | 4,544 | 1,900 |
| 9. Net Income, less Deficit | 2,610 | 103 | 6,605 | 4,165 | 6,490 | 23,342 | 12,094 | 9,463 | (35,178) | (59,064) |
| **Selected Average Financial Statistics** | | | | | | | | | | |
| **(Items 10 to 13 inclusive in $)** | | | | | | | | | | |
| 10. Av. Payment Partnership | 4,426 | 1,868 | 1,560 | 1,530 | 1,695 | 1,345 | 531 | 3,799 | 1,000 | 529 |
| 11. Av. Payment Partner | 1,360 | 547 | 472 | 403 | 512 | 495 | 154 | 1,469 | 440 | 206 |
| 12. Av. Income Partnership | 1,216 | 42 | 3,557 | 1,626 | 2,184 | 6,766 | 3,624 | 5,129 | (7,742) | (16,452) |
| 13. Av. Income Partner | 374 | 12 | 1,076 | 428 | 660 | 2,487 | 1,050 | 1,983 | (3,410) | (6,395) |
| **Selected Financial Statistics as Percent of Op. Income** | | | | | | | | | | |
| 14. Depreciation / Op. Income (%) | 5.1 | 4.6 | 5.6 | 9.6 | 6.9 | n.a. | n.a. | n.a. | 53.9 | 53.1 |
| 15. Interest / Op. Income (%) | 2.8 | 2.1 | 3.5 | 5.3 | 6.3 | 2.0 | 3.7 | 5.8 | 23.0 | 20.5 |
| 16. Payroll / Op. Income (%) | 24.1 | 21.2 | 17.3 | 18.3 | 17.1 | 17.2 | 22.9 | n.a. | 19.4 | 21.2 |
| **Selected Index Numbers (1976 = 100)** | | | | | | | | | | |
| 17. Partnerships | 100.0 | 113.4 | 86.5 | 119.3 | 138.4 | 160.8 | 155.5 | 86.0 | 211.7 | 167.3 |
| 18. Partners | 100.0 | 118.9 | 87.9 | 139.3 | 140.8 | 134.4 | 164.8 | 68.3 | 147.7 | 132.2 |
| 19. Operating Income | 100.0 | 94.2 | 102.1 | 179.4 | 172.1 | 50.9 | 25.9 | 57.5 | 44.9 | 42.0 |
| 20. Payments to Partners | 100.0 | 47.9 | 30.5 | 41.3 | 53.0 | 48.9 | 18.6 | 73.8 | 47.8 | 20.0 |
| **Selected Financial Statistics (Constant $, 1976 = 100)** | | | | | | | | | | |
| 21. Operating Income | 100.0 | 91.4 | 90.5 | 142.9 | 128.8 | 37.1 | 19.1 | 41.5 | 31.3 | 30.7 |
| 22. Payments to Partners | 100.0 | 45.0 | 26.6 | 32.4 | 36.6 | 30.6 | 11.0 | 42.2 | 26.2 | 10.6 |
| 23. Av. Payment, Partnership | 100.0 | 39.6 | 30.7 | 27.1 | 26.5 | 19.0 | 7.1 | 49.0 | 12.4 | 6.3 |
| 24. Av. Payment, Partner | 100.0 | 37.7 | 30.3 | 23.2 | 26.0 | 22.8 | 6.6 | 61.7 | 17.7 | 8.0 |

TABLE 3

AGRICULTURAL SERVICES, FORESTRY AND FISHING (016,022,023), WITH AND WITHOUT NET INCOME

| | 1976 | 1977 | 1978 | 1979 | 1980 | 1981 | 1982 | 1983 | 1984 | 1985 |
|---|---|---|---|---|---|---|---|---|---|---|
| 1. Number of Partnerships | 14,684 | 15,363 | 17,400 | 16,498 | 18,131 | 16,775 | 20,609 | 25,639 | 26,489 | 26,365 |
| 2. Number of Partners | 36,974 | 38,301 | 46,702 | 51,239 | 50,233 | 58,684 | 72,044 | 100,237 | 104,718 | 93,917 |
| **Selected Financial Statistics** (Items 3 to 9 inclusive in 000's of dollars) | | | | | | | | | | |
| 3. Operating Income | 1,349,235 | 1,812,205 | 2,083,610 | 2,249,958 | 2,437,057 | 2,418,736 | 2,493,261 | 3,219,445 | 2,772,581 | 3,184,373 |
| 4. Depreciation | 92,505 | 109,507 | 116,923 | 147,709 | 194,830 | n.a. | n.a. | n.a. | 361,024 | 382,155 |
| 5. Taxes Paid | 31,351 | 40,055 | 38,785 | 43,467 | 44,921 | 34,370 | 26,826 | 38,025 | 47,903 | 56,922 |
| 6. Interest Paid | 34,934 | 57,592 | 61,783 | 80,614 | 126,589 | 152,567 | 163,147 | 162,593 | 168,556 | 162,062 |
| 7. Payroll Deductions | 201,803 | 235,270 | 228,504 | 303,106 | 292,999 | 258,241 | 290,930 | n.a. | 334,316 | 519,826 |
| 8. Payments to Partners | 33,332 | 47,459 | 63,230 | 62,349 | 58,369 | 56,729 | 62,002 | 70,365 | 55,163 | 76,597 |
| 9. Net Income, less Deficit | 122,834 | 191,772 | 154,495 | 146,477 | 60,794 | 16,713 | 52,259 | 4,162 | (142,084) | (195,065) |
| **Selected Average Financial Statistics** (Items 10 to 13 inclusive in $) | | | | | | | | | | |
| 10. Av. Payment Partnership | 2,270 | 3,089 | 3,634 | 3,779 | 3,219 | 3,382 | 3,008 | 2,744 | 2,082 | 2,905 |
| 11. Av. Payment Partner | 901 | 1,239 | 1,354 | 1,217 | 1,162 | 967 | 861 | 702 | 527 | 816 |
| 12. Av. Income Partnership | 8,365 | 12,483 | 8,879 | 8,878 | 3,353 | 996 | 2,536 | 162 | (5,364) | (7,399) |
| 13. Av. Income Partner | 3,322 | 5,007 | 3,308 | 2,859 | 1,210 | 285 | 725 | 42 | (1,357) | (2,077) |
| **Selected Financial Statistics as Percent of Op. Income** | | | | | | | | | | |
| 14. Depreciation / Op. Income (%) | 6.9 | 6.0 | 5.6 | 6.6 | 8.0 | n.a. | n.a. | n.a. | 13.0 | 12.0 |
| 15. Interest / Op. Income (%) | 2.6 | 3.2 | 3.0 | 3.6 | 5.2 | 6.3 | 6.5 | 5.1 | 6.1 | 5.1 |
| 16. Payroll / Op. Income (%) | 15.0 | 13.0 | 11.0 | 13.5 | 12.0 | 10.7 | 11.7 | n.a. | 12.1 | 16.3 |
| **Selected Index Numbers (1976 = 100)** | | | | | | | | | | |
| 17. Partnerships | 100.0 | 104.6 | 118.5 | 112.4 | 123.5 | 114.2 | 140.4 | 174.6 | 180.4 | 179.5 |
| 18. Partners | 100.0 | 103.6 | 126.3 | 138.6 | 135.9 | 158.7 | 194.9 | 271.1 | 283.2 | 254.0 |
| 19. Operating Income | 100.0 | 134.3 | 154.4 | 166.8 | 180.6 | 179.3 | 184.8 | 238.6 | 205.5 | 236.0 |
| 20. Payments to Partners | 100.0 | 142.4 | 189.7 | 187.1 | 175.1 | 170.2 | 186.0 | 211.1 | 165.5 | 229.8 |
| **Selected Financial Statistics (Constant $, 1976 = 100)** | | | | | | | | | | |
| 21. Operating Income | 100.0 | 126.2 | 134.7 | 130.8 | 124.8 | 112.2 | 109.0 | 136.3 | 112.6 | 124.9 |
| 22. Payments to Partners | 100.0 | 133.8 | 165.5 | 146.7 | 121.0 | 106.5 | 109.7 | 120.6 | 90.7 | 121.6 |
| 23. Av. Payment, Partnership | 100.0 | 127.8 | 139.7 | 130.5 | 97.9 | 93.3 | 78.1 | 69.1 | 50.2 | 67.8 |
| 24. Av. Payment, Partner | 100.0 | 129.2 | 131.1 | 105.9 | 89.1 | 67.1 | 56.4 | 44.4 | 32.0 | 47.8 |

TABLE 3

026: MINING, WITH AND WITHOUT NET INCOME

| | 1976 | 1977 | 1978 | 1979 | 1980 | 1981 | 1982 | 1983 | 1984 | 1985 |
|---|---|---|---|---|---|---|---|---|---|---|
| 1. Number of Partnerships | 17,812 | 21,966 | 23,629 | 28,069 | 35,076 | 51,368 | 55,766 | 59,596 | 56,548 | 62,363 |
| 2. Number of Partners | 360,777 | 388,273 | 468,566 | 689,445 | 721,879 | 1,475,289 | 1,574,375 | 2,083,107 | 2,007,460 | 2,207,066 |
| **Selected Financial Statistics** | | | | | | | | | | |
| (Items 3 to 9 inclusive in 000's of dollars) | | | | | | | | | | |
| 3. Operating Income | 5,258,499 | 5,866,303 | 6,563,203 | 9,721,011 | 13,200,978 | 15,329,327 | 17,563,468 | 17,077,101 | 18,637,767 | 19,922,394 |
| 4. Depreciation | 448,917 | 541,930 | 653,150 | 895,340 | 1,276,019 | n.a. | n.a. | n.a. | 3,238,631 | 3,774,129 |
| 5. Taxes Paid | 170,760 | 220,926 | 250,814 | 373,545 | 654,870 | 601,396 | 655,182 | 737,806 | 626,753 | 742,756 |
| 6. Interest Paid | 122,965 | 189,142 | 274,975 | 490,097 | 697,799 | 973,541 | 1,441,765 | 1,347,854 | 1,446,686 | 1,197,096 |
| 7. Payroll Deductions | 348,479 | 420,459 | 460,634 | 618,472 | 845,102 | 810,083 | 1,049,637 | n.a. | 985,781 | 1,001,923 |
| 8. Payments to Partners | 34,142 | 45,305 | 45,174 | 82,010 | 113,427 | 159,781 | 243,849 | 272,678 | 132,832 | 96,651 |
| 9. Net Income, less Deficit | 4,692 | 55,017 | 285,724 | 250,823 | 420,833 | 1,010,909 | 882,982 | 410,976 | 69,112 | 1,481,701 |
| **Selected Average Financial Statistics** | | | | | | | | | | |
| (Items 10 to 13 inclusive in $) | | | | | | | | | | |
| 10. Av. Payment Partnership | 1,917 | 2,063 | 1,912 | 2,922 | 3,234 | 3,111 | 4,373 | 4,575 | 2,349 | 1,550 |
| 11. Av. Payment Partner | 95 | 117 | 96 | 119 | 157 | 108 | 155 | 131 | 66 | 44 |
| 12. Av. Income Partnership | 263 | 2,505 | 12,092 | 8,936 | 11,998 | 19,680 | 15,834 | 6,896 | 1,222 | 23,759 |
| 13. Av. Income Partner | 13 | 142 | 610 | 364 | 583 | 685 | 561 | 197 | 34 | 671 |
| **Selected Financial Statistics as Percent of Op. Income** | | | | | | | | | | |
| 14. Depreciation / Op. Income (%) | 8.5 | 9.2 | 1.0 | 9.2 | 9.7 | n.a. | n.a. | n.a. | 17.4 | 18.9 |
| 15. Interest / Op. Income (%) | 2.3 | 3.2 | 4.2 | 5.0 | 5.3 | 6.4 | 8.2 | 7.9 | 7.8 | 6.0 |
| 16. Payroll / Op. Income (%) | 6.6 | 7.2 | 7.0 | 6.4 | 6.4 | 5.3 | 6.0 | n.a. | 5.3 | 5.0 |
| **Selected Index Numbers (1976 = 100)** | | | | | | | | | | |
| 17. Partnerships | 100.0 | 123.3 | 132.7 | 157.6 | 196.9 | 288.4 | 313.1 | 334.6 | 317.5 | 350.1 |
| 18. Partners | 100.0 | 107.6 | 129.9 | 191.1 | 200.1 | 408.9 | 436.4 | 577.4 | 556.4 | 611.8 |
| 19. Operating Income | 100.0 | 111.6 | 124.8 | 184.9 | 251.0 | 291.5 | 334.0 | 324.8 | 354.4 | 378.9 |
| 20. Payments to Partners | 100.0 | 132.7 | 132.3 | 240.2 | 332.2 | 468.0 | 714.2 | 798.7 | 389.1 | 283.1 |
| **Selected Financial Statistics (Constant $, 1976 = 100)** | | | | | | | | | | |
| 21. Operating Income | 100.0 | 112.2 | 114.0 | 139.6 | 178.7 | 209.4 | 268.1 | 247.5 | 254.5 | 289.9 |
| 22. Payments to Partners | 100.0 | 124.7 | 115.5 | 188.4 | 229.5 | 292.9 | 421.2 | 456.3 | 213.2 | 149.8 |
| 23. Av. Payment, Partnership | 100.0 | 101.1 | 87.1 | 119.5 | 116.5 | 101.6 | 134.6 | 136.4 | 67.2 | 42.8 |
| 24. Av. Payment, Partner | 100.0 | 115.3 | 88.3 | 99.1 | 115.3 | 72.1 | 97.3 | 79.3 | 37.8 | 25.2 |

TABLE 3

029:  OIL AND GAS EXTRACTION, WITH AND WITHOUT NET INCOME

| | 1976 | 1977 | 1978 | 1979 | 1980 | 1981 | 1982 | 1983 | 1984 | 1985 |
|---|---|---|---|---|---|---|---|---|---|---|
| 1. Number of Partnerships | 14,671 | 18,259 | 20,076 | 24,052 | 31,405 | 47,107 | 50,837 | 56,172 | 50,980 | 55,816 |
| 2. Number of Partners | 343,234 | 358,881 | 446,264 | 636,793 | 686,431 | 1,441,161 | 1,512,328 | 1,987,935 | 1,883,264 | 2,130,764 |
| **Selected Financial Statistics** (Items 3 to 9 inclusive in 000's of dollars) | | | | | | | | | | |
| 3. Operating Income | 3,499,036 | 3,703,552 | 4,058,644 | 6,049,862 | 9,252,091 | 11,009,438 | 13,717,073 | 13,225,667 | 14,177,318 | 15,577,355 |
| 4. Depreciation | 249,318 | 332,098 | 401,435 | 553,779 | 869,425 | n.a. | n.a. | n.a. | 2,525,663 | 3,100,080 |
| 5. Taxes Paid | 99,302 | 125,144 | 131,968 | 81,288 | 453,352 | 438,271 | 504,678 | 595,306 | 471,390 | 590,405 |
| 6. Interest Paid | 86,749 | 97,224 | 134,637 | 300,245 | 475,063 | 712,013 | 1,183,312 | 1,079,898 | 1,151,108 | 904,948 |
| 7. Payroll Deductions | 141,855 | 158,367 | 163,190 | 221,343 | 386,772 | 358,485 | 560,777 | n.a. | 362,321 | 402,206 |
| 8. Payments to Partners | 18,595 | 25,982 | 22,876 | 60,223 | 91,458 | 132,545 | 186,093 | 260,968 | 116,652 | 84,367 |
| 9. Net Income, less Deficit | 619,339 | 26,752 | 241,577 | 171,156 | 369,385 | 938,647 | 772,741 | 354,585 | 787,343 | 2,272,782 |
| **Selected Average Financial Statistics** (Items 10 to 13 inclusive in $) | | | | | | | | | | |
| 10. Av. Payment Partnership | 1,267 | 1,423 | 1,139 | 2,504 | 2,912 | 2,814 | 3,661 | 4,646 | 2,288 | 1,512 |
| 11. Av. Payment Partner | 54 | 72 | 51 | 95 | 133 | 92 | 123 | 131 | 62 | 40 |
| 12. Av. Income Partnership | 42,215 | 1,465 | 12,033 | 7,116 | 11,762 | 19,926 | 15,200 | 6,312 | 15,444 | 40,719 |
| 13. Av. Income Partner | 1,804 | 75 | 541 | 269 | 538 | 651 | 511 | 178 | 418 | 1,067 |
| **Selected Financial Statistics as Percent of Op. Income** | | | | | | | | | | |
| 14. Depreciation / Op. Income (%) | 7.1 | 9.0 | 9.9 | 9.2 | 9.4 | n.a. | n.a. | n.a. | 17.8 | 19.9 |
| 15. Interest / Op. Income (%) | 2.5 | 2.6 | 3.3 | 5.0 | 5.1 | 6.5 | 8.6 | 8.2 | 8.1 | 5.8 |
| 16. Payroll / Op. Income (%) | 4.1 | 4.3 | 4.0 | 3.7 | 4.2 | 3.3 | 4.1 | n.a. | 2.6 | 2.6 |
| **Selected Index Numbers (1976 = 100)** | | | | | | | | | | |
| 17. Partnerships | 100.0 | 124.5 | 136.8 | 163.9 | 214.1 | 321.1 | 346.5 | 382.9 | 347.5 | 380.5 |
| 18. Partners | 100.0 | 104.6 | 130.0 | 185.5 | 200.0 | 419.9 | 440.6 | 579.2 | 548.7 | 620.8 |
| 19. Operating Income | 100.0 | 105.8 | 116.0 | 172.9 | 264.4 | 314.6 | 392.0 | 378.0 | 405.2 | 445.2 |
| 20. Payments to Partners | 100.0 | 139.7 | 123.0 | 323.9 | 491.8 | 712.8 | 1,000 | 1,403 | 627.3 | 453.7 |
| **Selected Financial Statistics (Constant $, 1976 = 100)** | | | | | | | | | | |
| 21. Operating Income | 100.0 | 106.5 | 106.0 | 130.6 | 188.3 | 226.0 | 314.6 | 288.1 | 291.0 | 340.7 |
| 22. Payments to Partners | 100.0 | 131.3 | 107.3 | 254.0 | 339.8 | 446.2 | 590.2 | 801.9 | 343.8 | 240.1 |
| 23. Av. Payment, Partnership | 100.0 | 105.5 | 78.4 | 155.0 | 158.7 | 139.0 | 170.3 | 209.4 | 98.9 | 63.1 |
| 24. Av. Payment, Partner | 100.0 | 125.9 | 81.8 | 138.5 | 169.9 | 107.0 | 135.3 | 138.5 | 62.9 | 37.8 |

## TABLE 3

### OTHER MINING (027,028,030), WITH AND WITHOUT NET INCOME

| | 1976 | 1977 | 1978 | 1979 | 1980 | 1981 | 1982 | 1983 | 1984 | 1985 |
|---|---|---|---|---|---|---|---|---|---|---|
| 1. Number of Partnerships | 3,141 | 3,707 | 3,553 | 4,017 | 3,671 | 4,260 | 4,929 | 3,423 | 5,568 | 6,548 |
| 2. Number of Partners | 17,543 | 29,392 | 22,302 | 52,652 | 35,448 | 34,128 | 62,047 | 95,173 | 124,196 | 76,302 |
| **Selected Financial Statistics** (Items 3 to 9 inclusive in 000's of dollars) | | | | | | | | | | |
| 3. Operating Income | 1,759,463 | 2,162,751 | 2,504,560 | 3,671,148 | 3,948,887 | 4,319,888 | 3,846,395 | 3,851,434 | 4,460,449 | 4,345,039 |
| 4. Depreciation | 199,599 | 209,832 | 251,715 | 341,561 | 406,594 | n.a. | n.a. | n.a. | 712,967 | 674,049 |
| 5. Taxes Paid | 71,458 | 95,782 | 118,847 | 192,258 | 201,518 | 163,124 | 150,505 | 142,500 | 155,363 | 152,351 |
| 6. Interest Paid | 36,216 | 91,918 | 140,338 | 189,852 | 222,737 | 261,527 | 258,453 | 267,955 | 295,579 | 292,149 |
| 7. Payroll Deductions | 206,624 | 262,092 | 297,445 | 397,129 | 458,330 | 451,598 | 488,859 | n.a. | 623,461 | 599,716 |
| 8. Payments to Partners | 15,547 | 19,323 | 22,298 | 21,787 | 21,968 | 27,236 | 57,757 | 11,710 | 5,568 | 6,548 |
| 9. Net Income, less Deficit | 115,593 | 40,530 | 44,145 | 133,747 | 51,447 | 72,262 | 110,240 | 56,389 | (718,230) | (791,082) |
| **Selected Average Financial Statistics** (Items 10 to 13 inclusive in $) | | | | | | | | | | |
| 10. Av. Payment Partnership | 4,950 | 5,213 | 6,276 | 5,424 | 5,984 | 6,393 | 11,718 | 3,421 | 1,000 | 1,000 |
| 11. Av. Payment Partner | 886 | 657 | 1,000 | 414 | 620 | 798 | 931 | 123 | 45 | 86 |
| 12. Av. Income Partnership | 36,801 | 10,933 | 12,425 | 33,295 | 14,014 | 16,963 | 22,366 | 16,474 | (128,992) | (120,813) |
| 13. Av. Income Partner | 6,589 | 1,379 | 1,979 | 2,540 | 1,451 | 2,117 | 1,777 | 592 | (5,783) | (10,368) |
| **Selected Financial Statistics as Percent of Op. Income** | | | | | | | | | | |
| 14. Depreciation / Op. Income (%) | 11.3 | 9.7 | 10.1 | 9.3 | 10.3 | n.a. | n.a. | n.a. | 16.0 | 15.5 |
| 15. Interest / Op. Income (%) | 2.1 | 4.3 | 5.6 | 5.2 | 5.6 | 6.1 | 6.7 | 7.0 | 6.6 | 6.7 |
| 16. Payroll / Op. Income (%) | 11.7 | 12.1 | 11.9 | 10.8 | 11.6 | 10.5 | 12.7 | n.a. | 14.0 | 13.8 |
| **Selected Index Numbers (1976 = 100)** | | | | | | | | | | |
| 17. Partnerships | 100.0 | 118.0 | 113.1 | 127.9 | 116.9 | 135.6 | 156.9 | 109.0 | 177.3 | 208.5 |
| 18. Partners | 100.0 | 167.5 | 127.1 | 300.1 | 202.1 | 194.5 | 353.7 | 542.5 | 708.0 | 434.9 |
| 19. Operating Income | 100.0 | 122.9 | 142.3 | 208.7 | 224.4 | 245.5 | 218.6 | 218.9 | 253.5 | 247.0 |
| 20. Payments to Partners | 100.0 | 124.3 | 143.4 | 140.1 | 141.3 | 175.2 | 371.5 | 75.3 | 35.8 | 42.1 |
| **Selected Financial Statistics (Constant $, 1976 = 100)** | | | | | | | | | | |
| 21. Operating Income | 100.0 | 123.6 | 130.0 | 157.6 | 159.8 | 176.4 | 175.5 | 166.9 | 182.1 | 189.0 |
| 22. Payments to Partners | 100.0 | 116.8 | 125.1 | 109.9 | 97.6 | 109.7 | 219.1 | 43.0 | 19.6 | 22.3 |
| 23. Av. Payment, Partnership | 100.0 | 98.9 | 110.6 | 85.9 | 83.5 | 80.8 | 139.6 | 39.5 | 11.1 | 10.7 |
| 24. Av. Payment, Partner | 100.0 | 69.6 | 98.5 | 36.6 | 48.3 | 56.4 | 61.9 | 7.9 | 2.7 | 5.2 |

TABLE 3

031: CONSTRUCTION, WITH AND WITHOUT NET INCOME

| | 1976 | 1977 | 1978 | 1979 | 1980 | 1981 | 1982 | 1983 | 1984 | 1985 |
|---|---|---|---|---|---|---|---|---|---|---|
| 1. Number of Partnerships | 60,390 | 69,217 | 78,032 | 75,275 | 66,590 | 69,856 | 65,762 | 63,592 | 64,607 | 56,665 |
| 2. Number of Partners | 138,409 | 156,429 | 177,685 | 168,549 | 160,212 | 165,054 | 151,859 | 148,768 | 173,273 | 134,034 |
| **Selected Financial Statistics** (Items 3 to 9 inclusive in 000's of dollars) | | | | | | | | | | |
| 3. Operating Income | 13,106,707 | 14,230,085 | 16,052,651 | 19,733,317 | 18,407,210 | 16,553,667 | 18,051,601 | 21,623,001 | 23,198,439 | 21,476,357 |
| 4. Depreciation | 243,890 | 295,548 | 280,532 | 334,917 | 357,997 | n.a. | n.a. | n.a. | 556,881 | 536,547 |
| 5. Taxes Paid | 197,418 | 202,347 | 233,000 | 267,601 | 225,106 | 155,316 | 147,279 | 158,995 | 223,235 | 215,055 |
| 6. Interest Paid | 194,424 | 207,049 | 239,671 | 343,927 | 486,454 | 473,191 | 556,820 | 434,914 | 475,227 | 372,977 |
| 7. Payroll Deductions | 2,458,217 | 2,062,519 | 2,122,451 | 2,500,562 | 2,208,230 | 1,914,083 | 2,674,091 | n.a. | 2,613,680 | 2,838,156 |
| 8. Payments to Partners | 255,688 | 270,743 | 372,836 | 386,039 | 341,987 | 326,982 | 310,385 | 286,144 | 405,140 | 370,549 |
| 9. Net Income, less Deficit | 1,139,001 | 1,458,221 | 1,770,242 | 2,126,987 | 1,560,093 | 1,209,222 | 1,419,497 | 2,167,975 | 2,193,322 | 2,207,401 |
| **Selected Average Financial Statistics** (Items 10 to 13 inclusive in $) | | | | | | | | | | |
| 10. Av. Payment Partnership | 4,234 | 3,912 | 4,778 | 5,128 | 5,136 | 4,681 | 4,720 | 4,500 | 6,271 | 6,539 |
| 11. Av. Payment Partner | 1,847 | 1,731 | 2,098 | 2,290 | 2,135 | 1,981 | 2,044 | 1,923 | 2,338 | 2,765 |
| 12. Av. Income Partnership | 18,861 | 21,067 | 22,686 | 28,256 | 23,428 | 17,310 | 21,585 | 34,092 | 33,949 | 38,955 |
| 13. Av. Income Partner | 8,229 | 9,322 | 9,963 | 12,619 | 9,738 | 7,326 | 9,347 | 14,573 | 12,658 | 16,469 |
| **Selected Financial Statistics as Percent of Op. Income** | | | | | | | | | | |
| 14. Depreciation / Op. Income (%) | 1.9 | 2.1 | 1.8 | 1.7 | 1.9 | n.a. | n.a. | n.a. | 2.4 | 2.5 |
| 15. Interest / Op. Income (%) | 1.5 | 1.5 | 1.5 | 1.7 | 2.6 | 2.9 | 3.1 | 2.0 | 2.1 | 1.7 |
| 16. Payroll / Op. Income (%) | 18.8 | 14.5 | 13.2 | 12.7 | 12.0 | 11.6 | 14.8 | n.a. | 11.3 | 13.2 |
| **Selected Index Numbers (1976 = 100)** | | | | | | | | | | |
| 17. Partnerships | 100.0 | 114.6 | 129.2 | 124.6 | 110.3 | 115.7 | 108.9 | 105.3 | 107.0 | 93.8 |
| 18. Partners | 100.0 | 113.0 | 128.4 | 121.8 | 115.8 | 119.3 | 109.7 | 107.5 | 125.2 | 96.8 |
| 19. Operating Income | 100.0 | 108.6 | 122.5 | 150.6 | 140.4 | 126.3 | 137.7 | 165.0 | 177.0 | 163.9 |
| 20. Payments to Partners | 100.0 | 105.9 | 145.8 | 151.0 | 133.8 | 127.9 | 121.4 | 111.9 | 158.5 | 144.9 |
| **Selected Financial Statistics (Constant $, 1976 = 100)** | | | | | | | | | | |
| 21. Operating Income | 100.0 | 102.0 | 106.9 | 118.1 | 97.0 | 79.1 | 81.2 | 94.3 | 97.0 | 86.7 |
| 22. Payments to Partners | 100.0 | 99.5 | 127.2 | 118.4 | 92.4 | 80.0 | 71.6 | 63.9 | 86.8 | 76.7 |
| 23. Av. Payment, Partnership | 100.0 | 86.8 | 98.5 | 95.0 | 83.8 | 69.2 | 65.8 | 60.7 | 81.2 | 81.7 |
| 24. Av. Payment, Partner | 100.0 | 88.0 | 99.1 | 97.2 | 79.8 | 67.1 | 65.3 | 59.4 | 69.4 | 79.2 |

*Page 211*

TABLE 3

GENERAL CONTRACTORS, TOTAL (032,035), WITH AND WITHOUT NET INCOME

| | 1976 | 1977 | 1978 | 1979 | 1980 | 1981 | 1982 | 1983 | 1984 | 1985 |
|---|---|---|---|---|---|---|---|---|---|---|
| 1. Number of Partnerships | 21,947 | 27,021 | 31,647 | 30,326 | 28,110 | 27,558 | 25,594 | 26,723 | 25,574 | 20,999 |
| 2. Number of Partners | 54,160 | 63,899 | 76,180 | 72,729 | 70,944 | 68,896 | 63,102 | 65,915 | 65,095 | 50,928 |
| **Selected Financial Statistics (Items 3 to 9 inclusive in 000's of dollars)** | | | | | | | | | | |
| 3. Operating Income | 9,276,993 | 9,733,021 | 10,457,131 | 14,065,407 | 13,081,552 | 10,513,390 | 12,054,126 | 15,613,000 | 15,746,593 | 13,482,530 |
| 4. Depreciation | 152,654 | 191,059 | 136,175 | 179,050 | 180,150 | n.a. | n.a. | n.a. | 261,928 | 235,255 |
| 5. Taxes Paid | 117,378 | 111,066 | 111,787 | 143,000 | 118,188 | 73,042 | 71,887 | 89,788 | 116,253 | 80,478 |
| 6. Interest Paid | 171,833 | 177,988 | 196,951 | 292,859 | 417,689 | 373,237 | 430,986 | 357,884 | 372,544 | 265,564 |
| 7. Payroll Deductions | 1,720,792 | 1,192,739 | 1,063,105 | 1,432,360 | 1,274,231 | 976,232 | 1,454,905 | n.a. | 1,543,078 | 1,457,476 |
| 8. Payments to Partners | 92,077 | 103,378 | 143,151 | 173,043 | 137,481 | 112,501 | 77,603 | 137,467 | 249,972 | 20,999 |
| 9. Net Income, less Deficit | 613,676 | 829,216 | 902,886 | 1,314,702 | 854,497 | 512,345 | 758,089 | 1,720,864 | 1,113,145 | 1,213,941 |
| **Selected Average Financial Statistics (Items 10 to 13 inclusive in $)** | | | | | | | | | | |
| 10. Av. Payment Partnership | 4,195 | 3,826 | 4,523 | 5,706 | 4,891 | 4,082 | 3,032 | 5,144 | 9,774 | 1,000 |
| 11. Av. Payment Partner | 1,700 | 1,618 | 1,879 | 2,379 | 1,938 | 1,633 | 1,230 | 2,086 | 3,840 | 412 |
| 12. Av. Income Partnership | 27,962 | 30,688 | 28,530 | 43,352 | 30,398 | 18,592 | 29,620 | 64,396 | 43,526 | 57,809 |
| 13. Av. Income Partner | 11,331 | 12,977 | 11,852 | 18,077 | 12,045 | 7,436 | 12,014 | 26,107 | 17,100 | 23,836 |
| **Selected Financial Statistics as Percent of Op. Income** | | | | | | | | | | |
| 14. Depreciation / Op. Income (%) | 1.7 | 2.0 | 1.3 | 1.3 | 1.4 | n.a. | n.a. | n.a. | 1.7 | 1.7 |
| 15. Interest / Op. Income (%) | 1.9 | 1.8 | 1.9 | 2.1 | 3.2 | 3.6 | 3.6 | 2.3 | 2.4 | 2.0 |
| 16. Payroll / Op. Income (%) | 18.6 | 12.3 | 10.2 | 10.2 | 9.7 | 9.3 | 12.1 | n.a. | 9.8 | 10.8 |
| **Selected Index Numbers (1976 = 100)** | | | | | | | | | | |
| 17. Partnerships | 100.0 | 123.1 | 144.2 | 138.2 | 128.1 | 125.6 | 116.6 | 121.8 | 116.5 | 95.7 |
| 18. Partners | 100.0 | 118.0 | 140.7 | 134.3 | 131.0 | 127.2 | 116.5 | 121.7 | 120.2 | 94.0 |
| 19. Operating Income | 100.0 | 104.9 | 112.7 | 151.6 | 141.0 | 113.3 | 129.9 | 168.3 | 169.7 | 145.3 |
| 20. Payments to Partners | 100.0 | 112.3 | 155.5 | 187.9 | 149.3 | 122.2 | 84.3 | 149.3 | 271.5 | 22.8 |
| **Selected Financial Statistics (Constant $, 1976 = 100)** | | | | | | | | | | |
| 21. Operating Income | 100.0 | 98.6 | 98.4 | 118.9 | 97.4 | 70.9 | 76.6 | 96.2 | 93.0 | 76.9 |
| 22. Payments to Partners | 100.0 | 105.5 | 135.7 | 147.4 | 103.2 | 76.5 | 49.7 | 85.3 | 148.8 | 12.1 |
| 23. Av. Payment, Partnership | 100.0 | 85.7 | 94.1 | 106.7 | 80.5 | 60.9 | 42.6 | 70.1 | 127.7 | 12.6 |
| 24. Av. Payment, Partner | 100.0 | 89.4 | 96.5 | 109.7 | 78.7 | 60.1 | 42.6 | 70.1 | 123.8 | 12.8 |

TABLE 3

038: SPECIAL TRADE CONTRACTORS, WITH AND WITHOUT NET INCOME

| | 1976 | 1977 | 1978 | 1979 | 1980 | 1981 | 1982 | 1983 | 1984 | 1985 |
|---|---|---|---|---|---|---|---|---|---|---|
| 1. Number of Partnerships | 38,395 | 42,116 | 46,121 | 44,948 | 38,188 | 41,611 | 40,001 | 35,883 | 39,001 | 35,666 |
| 2. Number of Partners | 84,153 | 92,322 | 100,963 | 95,818 | 82,562 | 94,785 | 88,423 | 79,899 | 108,083 | 83,106 |
| **Selected Financial Statistics** (Items 3 to 9 inclusive in 000's of dollars) | | | | | | | | | | |
| 3. Operating Income | 3,822,764 | 4,491,685 | 5,583,546 | 5,593,106 | 5,311,359 | 5,977,220 | 5,987,347 | 6,004,577 | 7,414,330 | 7,993,828 |
| 4. Depreciation | 91,039 | 104,489 | 143,776 | 155,858 | 176,516 | n.a. | n.a. | n.a. | 294,953 | 301,292 |
| 5. Taxes Paid | 79,891 | 91,074 | 120,359 | 120,878 | 106,837 | 82,053 | 75,366 | 69,207 | 106,982 | 134,576 |
| 6. Interest Paid | 22,530 | 28,566 | 42,562 | 51,069 | 68,765 | 98,035 | 125,762 | 77,022 | 102,683 | 107,413 |
| 7. Payroll Deductions | 735,841 | 867,218 | 1,056,994 | 1,031,701 | 933,998 | 932,675 | 1,216,962 | n.a. | 1,070,602 | 1,380,680 |
| 8. Payments to Partners | 163,611 | 167,365 | 229,685 | 212,995 | 204,507 | 214,481 | 232,782 | 148,677 | 155,167 | 173,756 |
| 9. Net Income, less Deficit | 523,547 | 627,154 | 865,338 | 808,350 | 696,557 | 694,133 | 659,788 | 695,546 | 1,053,985 | 993,460 |
| **Selected Average Financial Statistics** (Items 10 to 13 inclusive in $) | | | | | | | | | | |
| 10. Av. Payment Partnership | 4,261 | 3,974 | 4,980 | 4,739 | 5,355 | 5,154 | 5,819 | 4,143 | 3,979 | 4,872 |
| 11. Av. Payment Partner | 1,944 | 1,813 | 2,275 | 2,223 | 2,477 | 2,263 | 2,633 | 1,861 | 1,436 | 2,091 |
| 12. Av. Income Partnership | 13,636 | 14,891 | 18,762 | 17,984 | 18,240 | 16,681 | 16,494 | 19,384 | 27,025 | 27,855 |
| 13. Av. Income Partner | 6,221 | 6,793 | 8,571 | 8,436 | 8,437 | 7,323 | 7,462 | 8,705 | 9,752 | 11,954 |
| **Selected Financial Statistics as Percent of Op. Income** | | | | | | | | | | |
| 14. Depreciation / Op. Income (%) | 2.4 | 2.3 | 2.6 | 2.8 | 3.3 | n.a. | n.a. | n.a. | 4.0 | 3.8 |
| 15. Interest / Op. Income (%) | 0.6 | 0.6 | 0.8 | 0.9 | 1.3 | 1.6 | 2.1 | 1.3 | 1.4 | 1.3 |
| 16. Payroll / Op. Income (%) | 19.3 | 19.3 | 18.9 | 18.5 | 17.6 | 15.6 | 20.3 | n.a. | 14.4 | 17.3 |
| **Selected Index Numbers** (1976 = 100) | | | | | | | | | | |
| 17. Partnerships | 100.0 | 109.7 | 120.1 | 117.1 | 99.5 | 108.4 | 104.2 | 93.5 | 101.6 | 92.9 |
| 18. Partners | 100.0 | 109.7 | 120.0 | 113.9 | 98.1 | 112.6 | 105.1 | 94.9 | 128.4 | 98.8 |
| 19. Operating Income | 100.0 | 117.5 | 146.1 | 146.3 | 138.9 | 156.4 | 156.6 | 157.1 | 194.0 | 209.1 |
| 20. Payments to Partners | 100.0 | 102.3 | 140.4 | 130.2 | 125.0 | 131.1 | 142.3 | 90.9 | 94.8 | 106.2 |
| **Selected Financial Statistics** (Constant $, 1976 = 100) | | | | | | | | | | |
| 21. Operating Income | 100.0 | 110.4 | 127.4 | 114.7 | 96.0 | 97.9 | 92.4 | 89.7 | 106.3 | 110.7 |
| 22. Payments to Partners | 100.0 | 96.1 | 122.5 | 102.1 | 86.4 | 82.1 | 83.9 | 51.9 | 52.0 | 56.2 |
| 23. Av. Payment, Partnership | 100.0 | 87.6 | 102.0 | 87.2 | 86.8 | 75.7 | 80.5 | 55.5 | 51.2 | 60.5 |
| 24. Av. Payment, Partner | 100.0 | 87.6 | 102.1 | 89.7 | 88.0 | 72.9 | 79.9 | 54.7 | 40.5 | 56.9 |

*Page 213*

TABLE 3

039: PLUMBING, HEATING, AND AIR CONDITIONING, WITH AND WITHOUT NET INCOME

| | 1976 | 1977 | 1978 | 1979 | 1980 | 1981 | 1982 | 1983 | 1984 | 1985 |
|---|---|---|---|---|---|---|---|---|---|---|
| 1. Number of Partnerships | 4,941 | 5,567 | 5,583 | 6,017 | 4,479 | 5,584 | 6,279 | 5,527 | 4,252 | 3,762 |
| 2. Number of Partners | 11,039 | 13,070 | 11,924 | 13,092 | 9,557 | 11,878 | 12,640 | 12,254 | 11,279 | 8,281 |
| **Selected Financial Statistics** (Items 3 to 9 inclusive in 000's of dollars) | | | | | | | | | | |
| 3. Operating Income | 633,810 | 843,289 | 895,654 | 946,541 | 790,389 | 847,279 | 942,135 | 1,015,518 | 1,214,737 | 1,393,351 |
| 4. Depreciation | 8,599 | 13,374 | 16,162 | 17,868 | 13,639 | n.a. | n.a. | n.a. | 39,192 | 24,517 |
| 5. Taxes Paid | 10,895 | 17,490 | 19,462 | 17,813 | 12,618 | 11,039 | 10,255 | 12,009 | 13,013 | 28,808 |
| 6. Interest Paid | 2,861 | 4,529 | 5,563 | 8,270 | 8,658 | 6,334 | 8,239 | 9,992 | 6,759 | 10,216 |
| 7. Payroll Deductions | 96,667 | 133,185 | 132,177 | 115,378 | 103,124 | 97,067 | 110,543 | n.a. | 114,378 | 226,329 |
| 8. Payments to Partners | 16,510 | 22,116 | 40,773 | 36,608 | 44,807 | 37,204 | 23,725 | 7,186 | 7,686 | 8,540 |
| 9. Net Income, less Deficit | 68,711 | 98,455 | 104,367 | 111,513 | 71,265 | 82,749 | 141,614 | 123,860 | 252,801 | 207,239 |
| **Selected Average Financial Statistics** (Items 10 to 13 inclusive in $) | | | | | | | | | | |
| 10. Av. Payment Partnership | 3,341 | 3,973 | 7,303 | 6,084 | 10,004 | 6,663 | 3,778 | 1,300 | 1,808 | 2,270 |
| 11. Av. Payment Partner | 1,496 | 1,692 | 3,419 | 2,796 | 4,688 | 3,132 | 1,877 | 586 | 681 | 1,031 |
| 12. Av. Income Partnership | 13,906 | 17,685 | 18,694 | 18,533 | 15,911 | 14,819 | 22,554 | 22,410 | 59,455 | 55,087 |
| 13. Av. Income Partner | 6,224 | 7,533 | 8,753 | 8,518 | 7,457 | 6,967 | 11,204 | 10,108 | 22,413 | 25,026 |
| **Selected Financial Statistics as Percent of Op. Income** | | | | | | | | | | |
| 14. Depreciation / Op. Income (%) | 1.4 | 1.6 | 1.8 | 1.9 | 1.7 | n.a. | n.a. | n.a. | 3.2 | 1.8 |
| 15. Interest / Op. Income (%) | 0.5 | 0.5 | 0.6 | 0.9 | 1.1 | 0.8 | 0.9 | 0.10 | 0.6 | 0.7 |
| 16. Payroll / Op. Income (%) | 15.3 | 15.8 | 14.8 | 12.2 | 13.1 | 11.5 | 11.7 | n.a. | 9.4 | 16.2 |
| **Selected Index Numbers (1976 = 100)** | | | | | | | | | | |
| 17. Partnerships | 100.0 | 112.7 | 113.0 | 121.8 | 90.6 | 113.0 | 127.1 | 111.9 | 86.1 | 76.1 |
| 18. Partners | 100.0 | 118.4 | 108.0 | 118.6 | 86.6 | 107.6 | 114.5 | 111.0 | 102.2 | 75.0 |
| 19. Operating Income | 100.0 | 133.1 | 141.3 | 149.3 | 124.7 | 133.7 | 148.6 | 160.2 | 191.7 | 219.8 |
| 20. Payments to Partners | 100.0 | 134.0 | 247.0 | 221.7 | 271.4 | 225.3 | 143.7 | 43.5 | 46.6 | 51.7 |
| **Selected Financial Statistics (Constant $, 1976 = 100)** | | | | | | | | | | |
| 21. Operating Income | 100.0 | 125.0 | 123.3 | 117.1 | 86.2 | 83.7 | 87.7 | 91.5 | 105.0 | 116.3 |
| 22. Payments to Partners | 100.0 | 125.8 | 215.5 | 173.9 | 187.5 | 141.0 | 84.7 | 24.9 | 25.5 | 27.4 |
| 23. Av. Payment, Partnership | 100.0 | 111.7 | 190.7 | 142.8 | 206.8 | 124.8 | 66.7 | 22.2 | 29.6 | 36.0 |
| 24. Av. Payment, Partner | 100.0 | 106.2 | 199.5 | 146.6 | 216.6 | 131.1 | 74.0 | 22.3 | 25.0 | 36.5 |

## TABLE 3

### 040: PAINTING, PAPER HANGING AND DECORATING, WITH AND WITHOUT NET INCOME

| | 1976 | 1977 | 1978 | 1979 | 1980 | 1981 | 1982 | 1983 | 1984 | 1985 |
|---|---|---|---|---|---|---|---|---|---|---|
| 1. Number of Partnerships | 5,260 | 4,830 | 5,081 | 3,889 | 3,895 | 6,151 | 4,383 | 5,007 | 6,345 | 6,515 |
| 2. Number of Partners | 11,380 | 10,178 | 11,059 | 8,538 | 8,308 | 13,617 | 9,594 | 10,414 | 14,156 | 15,564 |
| **Selected Financial Statistics** (Items 3 to 9 inclusive in 000's of dollars) | | | | | | | | | | |
| 3. Operating Income | 294,685 | 269,576 | 396,675 | 316,154 | 259,104 | 337,186 | 336,617 | 538,702 | 573,770 | 772,851 |
| 4. Depreciation | 4,924 | 4,456 | 8,002 | 6,736 | 6,611 | n.a. | n.a. | n.a. | 10,063 | 33,483 |
| 5. Taxes Paid | 6,150 | 6,726 | 11,600 | 8,424 | 4,613 | 5,711 | 5,769 | 6,668 | 15,952 | 14,505 |
| 6. Interest Paid | 1,397 | 1,109 | 2,696 | 2,568 | 2,139 | 2,754 | 1,316 | 1,471 | 2,108 | 4,061 |
| 7. Payroll Deductions | 65,024 | 63,501 | 99,012 | 94,882 | 49,233 | 50,571 | 61,411 | n.a. | 90,484 | 187,429 |
| 8. Payments to Partners | 19,336 | 10,721 | 15,482 | 19,036 | 17,888 | 36,105 | 51,662 | 40,163 | 25,211 | 1,074 |
| 9. Net Income, less Deficit | 62,042 | 68,054 | 100,023 | 61,896 | 56,150 | 77,394 | 37,980 | 78,734 | 181,855 | 170,053 |
| **Selected Average Financial Statistics** (Items 10 to 13 inclusive in $) | | | | | | | | | | |
| 10. Av. Payment Partnership | 3,676 | 2,220 | 3,047 | 4,895 | 4,593 | 5,870 | 11,787 | 8,021 | 3,973 | 165 |
| 11. Av. Payment Partner | 1,699 | 1,053 | 1,400 | 2,230 | 2,153 | 2,651 | 5,385 | 3,857 | 1,781 | 69 |
| 12. Av. Income Partnership | 11,795 | 14,090 | 19,686 | 15,916 | 14,416 | 12,582 | 8,665 | 15,725 | 28,661 | 26,102 |
| 13. Av. Income Partner | 5,452 | 6,686 | 9,044 | 7,249 | 6,759 | 5,684 | 3,959 | 7,560 | 12,846 | 10,926 |
| **Selected Financial Statistics as Percent of Op. Income** | | | | | | | | | | |
| 14. Depreciation / Op. Income (%) | 1.7 | 1.7 | 2.0 | 2.1 | 2.6 | n.a. | n.a. | n.a. | 1.8 | 4.3 |
| 15. Interest / Op. Income (%) | 0.5 | 0.4 | 0.7 | 0.8 | 0.8 | 0.8 | 0.4 | 0.3 | 0.4 | 0.5 |
| 16. Payroll / Op. Income (%) | 22.1 | 23.6 | 25.0 | 30.0 | 19.0 | 15.0 | 18.2 | n.a. | 15.8 | 24.3 |
| **Selected Index Numbers** (1976 = 100) | | | | | | | | | | |
| 17. Partnerships | 100.0 | 91.8 | 96.6 | 73.9 | 74.0 | 116.9 | 83.3 | 95.2 | 120.6 | 123.9 |
| 18. Partners | 100.0 | 89.4 | 97.2 | 75.0 | 73.0 | 119.7 | 84.3 | 91.5 | 124.4 | 136.8 |
| 19. Operating Income | 100.0 | 91.5 | 134.6 | 107.3 | 87.9 | 114.4 | 114.2 | 182.8 | 194.7 | 262.3 |
| 20. Payments to Partners | 100.0 | 55.4 | 80.1 | 98.4 | 92.5 | 186.7 | 267.2 | 207.7 | 130.4 | 5.6 |
| **Selected Financial Statistics** (Constant $, 1976 = 100) | | | | | | | | | | |
| 21. Operating Income | 100.0 | 85.9 | 117.5 | 84.1 | 60.7 | 71.6 | 67.4 | 104.5 | 106.7 | 138.8 |
| 22. Payments to Partners | 100.0 | 52.1 | 69.9 | 77.2 | 63.9 | 116.9 | 157.6 | 118.7 | 71.5 | 2.9 |
| 23. Av. Payment, Partnership | 100.0 | 56.7 | 72.3 | 104.5 | 86.3 | 100.0 | 189.1 | 124.7 | 59.2 | 2.4 |
| 24. Av. Payment, Partner | 100.0 | 58.2 | 71.8 | 103.0 | 87.5 | 97.6 | 186.9 | 129.7 | 57.4 | 2.1 |

## TABLE 3

### 042: MASONRY, STONE WORK, TILE SETTING, AND PLASTERING, WITH AND WITHOUT NET INCOME

| | 1976 | 1977 | 1978 | 1979 | 1980 | 1981 | 1982 | 1983 | 1984 | 1985 |
|---|---|---|---|---|---|---|---|---|---|---|
| 1. Number of Partnerships | 5,194 | 7,082 | 6,156 | 6,020 | 6,034 | 4,513 | 3,492 | 1,390 | 4,199 | 2,218 |
| 2. Number of Partners | 10,945 | 15,337 | 13,505 | 12,663 | 13,359 | 11,045 | 7,516 | 3,678 | 9,072 | 5,012 |
| **Selected Financial Statistics** (Items 3 to 9 inclusive in 000's of dollars) | | | | | | | | | | |
| 3. Operating Income | 433,165 | 583,838 | 759,232 | 736,956 | 742,629 | 608,815 | 637,980 | 467,548 | 796,947 | 671,074 |
| 4. Depreciation | 8,114 | 10,593 | 12,172 | 14,156 | 19,276 | n.a. | n.a. | n.a. | 16,703 | 14,497 |
| 5. Taxes Paid | 10,501 | 14,184 | 20,075 | 21,812 | 19,128 | 13,985 | 14,280 | 16,027 | 12,407 | 9,590 |
| 6. Interest Paid | 1,633 | 2,559 | 3,792 | 2,973 | 5,716 | 3,231 | 6,364 | 8,911 | 12,204 | 6,434 |
| 7. Payroll Deductions | 108,758 | 153,806 | 207,630 | 212,581 | 197,315 | 172,463 | 181,969 | n.a. | 227,500 | 176,163 |
| 8. Payments to Partners | 18,468 | 23,578 | 25,545 | 23,736 | 22,885 | 25,412 | 18,174 | 11,334 | 25,431 | 48,301 |
| 9. Net Income, less Deficit | 74,599 | 121,825 | 151,303 | 126,709 | 114,699 | 120,892 | 105,586 | 22,286 | 80,023 | 50,404 |
| **Selected Average Financial Statistics** (Items 10 to 13 inclusive in $) | | | | | | | | | | |
| 10. Av. Payment Partnership | 3,556 | 3,329 | 4,150 | 3,943 | 3,793 | 5,631 | 5,204 | 8,154 | 6,056 | 21,777 |
| 11. Av. Payment Partner | 1,687 | 1,537 | 1,892 | 1,874 | 1,713 | 2,301 | 2,418 | 3,082 | 2,803 | 9,637 |
| 12. Av. Income Partnership | 14,363 | 17,202 | 24,578 | 21,048 | 19,009 | 26,788 | 30,237 | 16,033 | 19,058 | 22,725 |
| 13. Av. Income Partner | 6,816 | 7,943 | 11,203 | 10,006 | 8,586 | 10,945 | 14,048 | 6,059 | 8,821 | 10,057 |
| **Selected Financial Statistics as Percent of Op. Income** | | | | | | | | | | |
| 14. Depreciation / Op. Income (%) | 1.9 | 1.8 | 1.6 | 1.9 | 2.6 | n.a. | n.a. | n.a. | 2.1 | 2.2 |
| 15. Interest / Op. Income (%) | 0.4 | 0.4 | 0.5 | 0.4 | 0.8 | 0.5 | 1.0 | 1.9 | 1.5 | 0.10 |
| 16. Payroll / Op. Income (%) | 25.1 | 26.3 | 27.4 | 28.9 | 26.6 | 28.3 | 28.5 | n.a. | 28.6 | 26.3 |
| **Selected Index Numbers (1976 = 100)** | | | | | | | | | | |
| 17. Partnerships | 100.0 | 136.3 | 118.5 | 115.9 | 116.2 | 86.9 | 67.2 | 26.8 | 80.8 | 42.7 |
| 18. Partners | 100.0 | 140.1 | 123.4 | 115.7 | 122.1 | 100.9 | 68.7 | 33.6 | 82.9 | 45.8 |
| 19. Operating Income | 100.0 | 134.8 | 175.3 | 170.1 | 171.4 | 140.6 | 147.3 | 107.9 | 184.0 | 154.9 |
| 20. Payments to Partners | 100.0 | 127.7 | 138.3 | 128.5 | 123.9 | 137.6 | 98.4 | 61.4 | 137.7 | 261.5 |
| **Selected Financial Statistics (Constant $, 1976 = 100)** | | | | | | | | | | |
| 21. Operating Income | 100.0 | 126.6 | 152.9 | 133.4 | 118.4 | 88.0 | 86.9 | 61.7 | 100.8 | 82.0 |
| 22. Payments to Partners | 100.0 | 119.9 | 120.7 | 100.8 | 85.6 | 86.1 | 58.0 | 35.1 | 75.5 | 138.4 |
| 23. Av. Payment, Partnership | 100.0 | 87.9 | 101.8 | 87.0 | 73.7 | 99.1 | 86.3 | 131.1 | 93.4 | 324.1 |
| 24. Av. Payment, Partner | 100.0 | 85.6 | 97.8 | 87.1 | 70.1 | 85.4 | 84.5 | 104.4 | 91.0 | 302.2 |

TABLE 3

CONTRACTORS NOT ELSEWHERE CLASSIFIED (041,043,044,046,047), WITH AND WITHOUT NET INCOME

| | 1976 | 1977 | 1978 | 1979 | 1980 | 1981 | 1982 | 1983 | 1984 | 1985 |
|---|---|---|---|---|---|---|---|---|---|---|
| 1. Number of Partnerships | 23,000 | 24,637 | 29,301 | 29,023 | 23,781 | 25,362 | 25,847 | 23,959 | 24,206 | 23,171 |
| 2. Number of Partners | 50,789 | 53,737 | 64,475 | 61,527 | 51,338 | 58,245 | 58,673 | 53,552 | 73,577 | 54,250 |
| **Selected Financial Statistics (Items 3 to 9 inclusive in 000's of dollars)** | | | | | | | | | | |
| 3. Operating Income | 2,461,104 | 2,794,982 | 3,531,985 | 3,668,259 | 3,519,236 | 4,183,939 | 4,070,614 | 3,982,810 | 4,828,877 | 5,156,551 |
| 4. Depreciation | 69,402 | 76,066 | 107,438 | 117,108 | 136,990 | n.a. | n.a. | n.a. | 228,996 | 228,795 |
| 5. Taxes Paid | 52,345 | 52,674 | 69,222 | 76,553 | 70,478 | 51,317 | 45,062 | 34,503 | 65,610 | 81,674 |
| 6. Interest Paid | 16,639 | 20,369 | 30,510 | 37,257 | 54,253 | 85,717 | 109,844 | 56,648 | 81,612 | 86,702 |
| 7. Payroll Deductions | 465,392 | 516,726 | 618,176 | 645,361 | 584,328 | 612,575 | 863,038 | n.a. | 638,241 | 793,759 |
| 8. Payments to Partners | 109,297 | 110,950 | 147,886 | 133,617 | 118,928 | 115,761 | 139,221 | 89,994 | 24,206 | 115,841 |
| 9. Net Income, less Deficit | 318,195 | 338,820 | 509,646 | 512,166 | 454,441 | 413,903 | 378,824 | 476,673 | 539,305 | 565,764 |
| **Selected Average Financial Statistics (Items 10 to 13 inclusive in $)** | | | | | | | | | | |
| 10. Av. Payment Partnership | 4,752 | 4,503 | 5,047 | 4,604 | 5,001 | 4,564 | 5,386 | 3,756 | 1,000 | 4,999 |
| 11. Av. Payment Partner | 2,152 | 2,065 | 2,294 | 2,172 | 2,317 | 1,987 | 2,373 | 1,680 | 329 | 2,135 |
| 12. Av. Income Partnership | 13,835 | 13,752 | 17,393 | 17,647 | 19,109 | 16,320 | 14,656 | 19,895 | 22,280 | 24,417 |
| 13. Av. Income Partner | 6,265 | 6,305 | 7,905 | 8,324 | 8,852 | 7,106 | 6,457 | 8,901 | 7,330 | 10,429 |
| **Selected Financial Statistics as Percent of Op. Income** | | | | | | | | | | |
| 14. Depreciation / Op. Income (%) | 2.8 | 2.7 | 3.0 | 3.2 | 3.9 | n.a. | n.a. | n.a. | 4.7 | 4.4 |
| 15. Interest / Op. Income (%) | 0.7 | 0.7 | 0.9 | 1.0 | 1.5 | 2.1 | 2.7 | 1.4 | 1.7 | 1.7 |
| 16. Payroll / Op. Income (%) | 18.9 | 18.5 | 17.5 | 17.6 | 16.6 | 14.6 | 21.2 | n.a. | 13.2 | 15.4 |
| **Selected Index Numbers (1976 = 100)** | | | | | | | | | | |
| 17. Partnerships | 100.0 | 107.1 | 127.4 | 126.2 | 103.4 | 110.3 | 112.4 | 104.2 | 105.2 | 100.7 |
| 18. Partners | 100.0 | 105.8 | 126.9 | 121.1 | 101.1 | 114.7 | 115.5 | 105.4 | 144.9 | 106.8 |
| 19. Operating Income | 100.0 | 113.6 | 143.5 | 149.0 | 143.0 | 170.0 | 165.4 | 161.8 | 196.2 | 209.5 |
| 20. Payments to Partners | 100.0 | 101.5 | 135.3 | 122.3 | 108.8 | 105.9 | 127.4 | 82.3 | 22.1 | 106.0 |
| **Selected Financial Statistics (Constant $, 1976 = 100)** | | | | | | | | | | |
| 21. Operating Income | 100.0 | 106.7 | 125.2 | 116.9 | 98.8 | 106.4 | 97.5 | 92.5 | 107.5 | 110.9 |
| 22. Payments to Partners | 100.0 | 95.4 | 118.1 | 95.9 | 75.2 | 66.3 | 75.1 | 47.0 | 12.1 | 56.1 |
| 23. Av. Payment, Partnership | 100.0 | 89.0 | 92.7 | 76.0 | 72.7 | 60.1 | 66.8 | 45.2 | 11.5 | 55.7 |
| 24. Av. Payment, Partner | 100.0 | 90.2 | 93.0 | 79.2 | 74.4 | 57.8 | 65.0 | 44.6 | 8.4 | 52.5 |

## TABLE 3

## 049: MANUFACTURING, WITH AND WITHOUT NET INCOME

| | 1976 | 1977 | 1978 | 1979 | 1980 | 1981 | 1982 | 1983 | 1984 | 1985 |
|---|---|---|---|---|---|---|---|---|---|---|
| 1. Number of Partnerships | 30,767 | 27,996 | 27,931 | 30,454 | 30,086 | 30,306 | 23,190 | 26,451 | 29,606 | 29,980 |
| 2. Number of Partners | 82,891 | 70,931 | 75,100 | 87,230 | 91,724 | 90,879 | 76,742 | 90,752 | 93,601 | 105,007 |
| **Selected Financial Statistics** | | | | | | | | | | |
| **(Items 3 to 9 inclusive in 000's of dollars)** | | | | | | | | | | |
| 3. Operating Income | 7,979,481 | 8,797,887 | 10,514,297 | 13,107,895 | 15,326,978 | 14,234,044 | 14,823,737 | 14,178,622 | 18,326,382 | 22,587,694 |
| 4. Depreciation | 306,468 | 305,960 | 374,102 | 453,956 | 763,980 | n.a. | n.a. | n.a. | 1,481,903 | 1,745,660 |
| 5. Taxes Paid | 155,614 | 169,236 | 201,709 | 239,104 | 233,577 | 180,156 | 166,564 | 152,667 | 209,394 | 250,427 |
| 6. Interest Paid | 99,176 | 141,591 | 166,251 | 281,775 | 392,393 | 403,990 | 424,301 | 400,236 | 614,043 | 842,224 |
| 7. Payroll Deductions | 1,455,295 | 1,350,571 | 1,641,227 | 2,003,046 | 2,024,797 | 1,788,734 | 1,923,374 | n.a. | 2,366,219 | 3,300,474 |
| 8. Payments to Partners | 152,169 | 115,461 | 132,976 | 167,831 | 158,553 | 188,996 | 119,274 | 107,781 | 132,861 | 154,209 |
| 9. Net Income, less Deficit | 470,054 | 461,000 | 660,015 | 484,564 | 47,204 | 44,064 | 81,563 | 74,406 | (1,100,943) | (1,085,187) |
| **Selected Average Financial Statistics** | | | | | | | | | | |
| **(Items 10 to 13 inclusive in $)** | | | | | | | | | | |
| 10. Av. Payment Partnership | 4,946 | 4,124 | 4,761 | 5,511 | 5,270 | 6,236 | 5,143 | 4,075 | 4,488 | 5,144 |
| 11. Av. Payment Partner | 1,836 | 1,628 | 1,771 | 1,924 | 1,729 | 2,080 | 1,554 | 1,188 | 1,419 | 1,469 |
| 12. Av. Income Partnership | 15,278 | 16,467 | 23,630 | 15,911 | 1,569 | 1,454 | 3,517 | 2,813 | (37,186) | (36,197) |
| 13. Av. Income Partner | 5,671 | 6,499 | 8,788 | 5,555 | 515 | 485 | 1,063 | 820 | (11,762) | (10,334) |
| **Selected Financial Statistics as Percent of Op. Income** | | | | | | | | | | |
| 14. Depreciation / Op. Income (%) | 3.8 | 3.5 | 3.6 | 3.5 | 5.0 | n.a. | n.a. | n.a. | 8.1 | 7.7 |
| 15. Interest / Op. Income (%) | 1.2 | 1.6 | 1.6 | 2.2 | 2.6 | 2.8 | 2.9 | 2.8 | 3.4 | 3.7 |
| 16. Payroll / Op. Income (%) | 18.2 | 15.4 | 15.6 | 15.3 | 13.2 | 12.6 | 13.0 | n.a. | 12.9 | 14.6 |
| **Selected Index Numbers (1976 = 100)** | | | | | | | | | | |
| 17. Partnerships | 100.0 | 91.0 | 90.8 | 99.0 | 97.8 | 98.5 | 75.4 | 86.0 | 96.2 | 97.4 |
| 18. Partners | 100.0 | 85.6 | 90.6 | 105.2 | 110.7 | 109.6 | 92.6 | 109.5 | 112.9 | 126.7 |
| 19. Operating Income | 100.0 | 110.3 | 131.8 | 164.3 | 192.1 | 178.4 | 185.8 | 177.7 | 229.7 | 283.1 |
| 20. Payments to Partners | 100.0 | 75.9 | 87.4 | 110.3 | 104.2 | 124.2 | 78.4 | 70.8 | 87.3 | 101.3 |
| **Selected Financial Statistics (Constant $, 1976 = 100)** | | | | | | | | | | |
| 21. Operating Income | 100.0 | 103.5 | 115.6 | 127.7 | 129.6 | 110.2 | 113.2 | 107.6 | 135.7 | 168.0 |
| 22. Payments to Partners | 100.0 | 71.3 | 76.3 | 86.5 | 72.0 | 77.7 | 46.2 | 40.5 | 47.9 | 53.6 |
| 23. Av. Payment, Partnership | 100.0 | 78.3 | 84.0 | 87.4 | 73.6 | 78.9 | 61.3 | 47.1 | 49.7 | 55.1 |
| 24. Av. Payment, Partner | 100.0 | 83.3 | 84.1 | 82.2 | 65.1 | 71.0 | 50.0 | 37.0 | 42.4 | 42.4 |

# TABLE 3

## 054: LUMBER AND WOOD PRODUCTS, EXCEPT FURNITURE, WITH AND WITHOUT NET INCOME

| | 1976 | 1977 | 1978 | 1979 | 1980 | 1981 | 1982 | 1983 | 1984 | 1985 |
|---|---|---|---|---|---|---|---|---|---|---|
| 1. Number of Partnerships | 6,564 | 4,763 | 5,472 | 5,972 | 5,821 | 4,466 | 4,025 | 4,389 | 2,162 | 1,324 |
| 2. Number of Partners | 15,979 | 12,119 | 13,690 | 14,386 | 14,576 | 11,262 | 10,162 | 12,265 | 6,534 | 7,080 |
| **Selected Financial Statistics** (Items 3 to 9 inclusive in 000's of dollars) | | | | | | | | | | |
| 3. Operating Income | 1,444,806 | 1,419,081 | 1,749,723 | 1,887,044 | 1,600,609 | 1,837,801 | 1,408,478 | 1,908,123 | 2,213,383 | 2,312,351 |
| 4. Depreciation | 65,468 | 56,920 | 63,272 | 86,506 | 93,288 | n.a. | n.a. | n.a. | 178,406 | 191,633 |
| 5. Taxes Paid | 33,894 | 28,181 | 33,993 | 38,990 | 30,217 | 23,444 | 22,952 | 19,046 | 43,364 | 27,943 |
| 6. Interest Paid | 22,858 | 22,355 | 23,208 | 40,092 | 45,995 | 101,491 | 94,119 | 99,233 | 146,083 | 145,947 |
| 7. Payroll Deductions | 213,479 | 225,140 | 254,724 | 294,775 | 242,693 | 295,408 | 227,395 | n.a. | 386,999 | 426,402 |
| 8. Payments to Partners | 30,445 | 17,822 | 26,195 | 32,620 | 28,757 | 19,418 | 28,479 | 28,617 | 18,488 | 18,994 |
| 9. Net Income, less Deficit | 109,102 | 99,210 | 125,617 | 69,138 | 8,875 | 8,854 | 15,776 | 12,617 | (219,853) | (151,373) |
| **Selected Average Financial Statistics** (Items 10 to 13 inclusive in $) | | | | | | | | | | |
| 10. Av. Payment Partnership | 4,638 | 3,742 | 4,787 | 5,462 | 4,940 | 4,348 | 7,076 | 6,520 | 8,551 | 14,346 |
| 11. Av. Payment Partner | 1,905 | 1,471 | 1,913 | 2,267 | 1,973 | 1,724 | 2,802 | 2,333 | 2,830 | 2,683 |
| 12. Av. Income Partnership | 16,621 | 20,829 | 22,956 | 11,577 | 1,525 | 1,983 | 3,920 | 2,875 | (101,690) | (114,330) |
| 13. Av. Income Partner | 6,828 | 8,186 | 9,176 | 4,806 | 609 | 786 | 1,552 | 1,029 | (33,648) | (21,380) |
| **Selected Financial Statistics as Percent of Op. Income** | | | | | | | | | | |
| 14. Depreciation / Op. Income (%) | 4.5 | 4.0 | 3.6 | 4.6 | 5.8 | n.a. | n.a. | n.a. | 8.1 | 8.3 |
| 15. Interest / Op. Income (%) | 1.6 | 1.6 | 1.3 | 2.1 | 2.9 | 5.5 | 6.7 | 5.2 | 6.6 | 6.3 |
| 16. Payroll / Op. Income (%) | 14.8 | 15.9 | 14.6 | 15.6 | 15.2 | 16.1 | 16.1 | n.a. | 17.5 | 18.4 |
| **Selected Index Numbers (1976 = 100)** | | | | | | | | | | |
| 17. Partnerships | 100.0 | 72.6 | 83.4 | 91.0 | 88.7 | 68.0 | 61.3 | 66.9 | 32.9 | 20.2 |
| 18. Partners | 100.0 | 75.8 | 85.7 | 90.0 | 91.2 | 70.5 | 63.6 | 76.8 | 40.9 | 44.3 |
| 19. Operating Income | 100.0 | 98.2 | 121.1 | 130.6 | 110.8 | 127.2 | 97.5 | 132.1 | 153.2 | 160.0 |
| 20. Payments to Partners | 100.0 | 58.5 | 86.0 | 107.1 | 94.5 | 63.8 | 93.5 | 94.0 | 60.7 | 62.4 |
| **Selected Financial Statistics (Constant $, 1976 = 100)** | | | | | | | | | | |
| 21. Operating Income | 100.0 | 92.2 | 106.2 | 101.6 | 74.7 | 78.6 | 59.4 | 80.0 | 90.5 | 95.0 |
| 22. Payments to Partners | 100.0 | 55.0 | 75.1 | 84.0 | 65.3 | 39.9 | 55.2 | 53.7 | 33.3 | 33.0 |
| 23. Av. Payment, Partnership | 100.0 | 75.8 | 90.1 | 92.3 | 73.6 | 58.7 | 90.0 | 80.3 | 101.1 | 163.7 |
| 24. Av. Payment, Partner | 100.0 | 72.5 | 87.6 | 93.3 | 71.5 | 56.6 | 86.7 | 70.0 | 81.4 | 74.5 |

TABLE 3

056:  PRINTING, PUBLISHING, AND ALLIED INDUSTRIES, WITH AND WITHOUT NET INCOME

| | 1976 | 1977 | 1978 | 1979 | 1980 | 1981 | 1982 | 1983 | 1984 | 1985 |
|---|---|---|---|---|---|---|---|---|---|---|
| 1. Number of Partnerships | 4,883 | 5,138 | 5,272 | 6,517 | 7,157 | 7,495 | 4,636 | 3,232 | 4,414 | 5,634 |
| 2. Number of Partners | 12,056 | 13,528 | 16,637 | 18,852 | 22,862 | 22,047 | 16,671 | 20,076 | 19,094 | 27,677 |
| **Selected Financial Statistics** | | | | | | | | | | |
| **(Items 3 to 9 inclusive in 000's of dollars)** | | | | | | | | | | |
| 3. Operating Income | 582,619 | 649,935 | 805,366 | 888,893 | 1,113,452 | 1,176,215 | 1,059,950 | 1,097,674 | 1,561,892 | 2,327,646 |
| 4. Depreciation | 12,632 | 19,479 | 17,003 | 58,134 | 131,825 | n.a. | n.a. | n.a. | 99,420 | 106,196 |
| 5. Taxes Paid | 14,807 | 22,058 | 19,472 | 20,446 | 27,636 | 27,161 | 23,800 | 24,644 | 29,026 | 47,020 |
| 6. Interest Paid | 5,052 | 9,071 | 7,652 | 17,595 | 26,484 | 34,489 | 33,743 | 24,919 | 42,849 | 57,970 |
| 7. Payroll Deductions | 126,821 | 163,701 | 149,336 | 165,877 | 201,498 | 248,352 | 201,312 | n.a. | 347,183 | 508,611 |
| 8. Payments to Partners | 19,285 | 17,261 | 16,070 | 22,216 | 24,603 | 39,167 | 35,884 | 26,040 | 38,559 | 34,597 |
| 9. Net Income, less Deficit | 95,335 | 59,295 | 139,588 | 86,802 | 37,350 | 3,656 | 4,381 | 1,361 | 34,818 | 118,397 |
| **Selected Average Financial Statistics** | | | | | | | | | | |
| **(Items 10 to 13 inclusive in $)** | | | | | | | | | | |
| 10. Av. Payment Partnership | 3,949 | 3,359 | 3,048 | 3,409 | 3,438 | 5,226 | 7,740 | 8,057 | 8,736 | 6,141 |
| 11. Av. Payment Partner | 1,600 | 1,276 | 966 | 1,178 | 1,076 | 1,777 | 2,152 | 1,297 | 2,019 | 1,250 |
| 12. Av. Income Partnership | 19,524 | 11,540 | 26,477 | 13,319 | 5,219 | 488 | 945 | 421 | 7,888 | 21,015 |
| 13. Av. Income Partner | 7,908 | 4,383 | 8,390 | 4,604 | 1,634 | 166 | 263 | 68 | 1,824 | 4,278 |
| **Selected Financial Statistics as Percent of Op. Income** | | | | | | | | | | |
| 14. Depreciation / Op. Income (%) | 2.2 | 3.0 | 2.1 | 6.5 | 11.8 | n.a. | n.a. | n.a. | 6.4 | 4.6 |
| 15. Interest / Op. Income (%) | 0.9 | 1.4 | 0.10 | 2.0 | 2.4 | 2.9 | 3.2 | 2.3 | 2.7 | 2.5 |
| 16. Payroll / Op. Income (%) | 21.8 | 25.2 | 18.5 | 18.7 | 18.1 | 21.1 | 19.0 | n.a. | 22.2 | 21.9 |
| **Selected Index Numbers (1976 = 100)** | | | | | | | | | | |
| 17. Partnerships | 100.0 | 105.2 | 108.0 | 133.5 | 146.6 | 153.5 | 94.9 | 66.2 | 90.4 | 115.4 |
| 18. Partners | 100.0 | 112.2 | 138.0 | 156.4 | 189.6 | 182.9 | 138.3 | 166.5 | 158.4 | 229.6 |
| 19. Operating Income | 100.0 | 111.6 | 138.2 | 152.6 | 191.1 | 201.9 | 181.9 | 188.4 | 268.1 | 399.5 |
| 20. Payments to Partners | 100.0 | 89.5 | 83.3 | 115.2 | 127.6 | 203.1 | 186.1 | 135.0 | 199.9 | 179.4 |
| **Selected Financial Statistics (Constant $, 1976 = 100)** | | | | | | | | | | |
| 21. Operating Income | 100.0 | 104.7 | 121.2 | 118.6 | 128.9 | 124.8 | 110.8 | 114.1 | 158.4 | 237.1 |
| 22. Payments to Partners | 100.0 | 84.1 | 72.7 | 90.3 | 88.1 | 127.1 | 109.7 | 77.2 | 109.6 | 94.9 |
| 23. Av. Payment, Partnership | 100.0 | 79.9 | 67.3 | 67.7 | 60.1 | 82.8 | 115.6 | 116.6 | 121.2 | 82.3 |
| 24. Av. Payment, Partner | 100.0 | 74.9 | 52.7 | 57.8 | 46.5 | 69.5 | 79.3 | 46.4 | 69.2 | 41.4 |

TABLE 3

062: MACHINERY, EXCEPT ELECTRICAL, WITH AND WITHOUT NET INCOME

| | 1976 | 1977 | 1978 | 1979 | 1980 | 1981 | 1982 | 1983 | 1984 | 1985 |
|---|---|---|---|---|---|---|---|---|---|---|
| 1. Number of Partnerships | 2,209 | 1,380 | 1,964 | 1,322 | 1,648 | 379 | 368 | 197 | 1,018 | 317 |
| 2. Number of Partners | 4,884 | 3,276 | 4,333 | 2,889 | 3,717 | 1,397 | 1,498 | 712 | 2,299 | 1,364 |
| **Selected Financial Statistics** (Items 3 to 9 inclusive in 000's of dollars) | | | | | | | | | | |
| 3. Operating Income | 485,727 | 548,493 | 623,798 | 647,738 | 795,827 | 482,205 | 376,253 | 276,938 | 168,348 | 508,661 |
| 4. Depreciation | 12,805 | 12,852 | 16,480 | 14,437 | 14,930 | n.a. | n.a. | n.a. | 8,467 | 62,227 |
| 5. Taxes Paid | 11,272 | 9,878 | 11,517 | 7,960 | 9,926 | 5,447 | 5,964 | 5,953 | 829 | 6,555 |
| 6. Interest Paid | 9,333 | 11,161 | 17,546 | 20,464 | 24,670 | 9,335 | 15,036 | 28,977 | 11,104 | 41,005 |
| 7. Payroll Deductions | 132,874 | 143,473 | 145,780 | 132,393 | 102,284 | 87,900 | 73,810 | n.a. | 13,920 | 81,260 |
| 8. Payments to Partners | 17,602 | 8,069 | 13,731 | 6,706 | 15,377 | 1,832 | 1,241 | 331 | 2,464 | 12,451 |
| 9. Net Income, less Deficit | 44,530 | 57,938 | 20,328 | 39,902 | 1,550 | 34,784 | 3,883 | 7,262 | 39,844 | (77,348) |
| **Selected Average Financial Statistics** (Items 10 to 13 inclusive in $) | | | | | | | | | | |
| 10. Av. Payment Partnership | 7,968 | 5,847 | 6,991 | 5,073 | 9,331 | 4,834 | 3,372 | 1,680 | 2,420 | 39,278 |
| 11. Av. Payment Partner | 3,604 | 2,463 | 3,169 | 2,321 | 4,137 | 1,311 | 828 | 465 | 1,072 | 9,128 |
| 12. Av. Income Partnership | 20,158 | 41,984 | 10,350 | 30,183 | 941 | 91,778 | 10,552 | 36,863 | 39,139 | (244,000) |
| 13. Av. Income Partner | 9,118 | 17,686 | 4,691 | 13,812 | 417 | 24,899 | 2,592 | 10,199 | 17,331 | (56,707) |
| **Selected Financial Statistics as Percent of Op. Income** | | | | | | | | | | |
| 14. Depreciation / Op. Income (%) | 2.6 | 2.3 | 2.6 | 2.2 | 1.9 | n.a. | n.a. | n.a. | 5.0 | 12.2 |
| 15. Interest / Op. Income (%) | 1.9 | 2.0 | 2.8 | 3.2 | 3.1 | 1.9 | 4.0 | 10.5 | 6.6 | 8.1 |
| 16. Payroll / Op. Income (%) | 27.4 | 26.2 | 23.4 | 20.4 | 12.9 | 18.2 | 19.6 | n.a. | 8.3 | 16.0 |
| **Selected Index Numbers (1976 = 100)** | | | | | | | | | | |
| 17. Partnerships | 100.0 | 62.5 | 88.9 | 59.8 | 74.6 | 17.2 | 16.7 | 8.9 | 46.1 | 14.4 |
| 18. Partners | 100.0 | 67.1 | 88.7 | 59.2 | 76.1 | 28.6 | 30.7 | 14.6 | 47.1 | 27.9 |
| 19. Operating Income | 100.0 | 112.9 | 128.4 | 133.4 | 163.8 | 99.3 | 77.5 | 57.0 | 34.7 | 104.7 |
| 20. Payments to Partners | 100.0 | 45.8 | 78.0 | 38.1 | 87.4 | 10.4 | 7.1 | 1.9 | 14.0 | 70.7 |
| **Selected Financial Statistics (Constant $, 1976 = 100)** | | | | | | | | | | |
| 21. Operating Income | 100.0 | 106.0 | 112.6 | 103.7 | 110.5 | 61.3 | 47.2 | 34.5 | 20.5 | 62.1 |
| 22. Payments to Partners | 100.0 | 43.1 | 68.1 | 29.9 | 60.4 | 6.5 | 4.2 | 1.1 | 7.7 | 37.4 |
| 23. Av. Payment, Partnership | 100.0 | 68.9 | 76.6 | 49.9 | 80.9 | 38.0 | 24.9 | 12.0 | 16.6 | 260.9 |
| 24. Av. Payment, Partner | 100.0 | 64.2 | 76.7 | 50.5 | 79.3 | 22.8 | 13.5 | 7.4 | 16.3 | 134.0 |

**TABLE 3**

**OTHER MANUFACTURING INDUSTRIES (050,053,055,057-061,063,064,065,066), WITH AND WITHOUT NET INCOME**

| | 1976 | 1977 | 1978 | 1979 | 1980 | 1981 | 1982 | 1983 | 1984 | 1985 |
|---|---|---|---|---|---|---|---|---|---|---|
| 1. Number of Partnerships | 17,111 | 16,715 | 15,223 | 16,643 | 15,461 | 17,965 | 14,161 | 18,632 | 22,012 | 22,705 |
| 2. Number of Partners | 49,972 | 42,008 | 40,440 | 51,103 | 50,569 | 56,172 | 48,413 | 57,700 | 65,673 | 68,886 |
| **Selected Financial Statistics** | | | | | | | | | | |
| **(Items 3 to 9 inclusive in 000's of dollars)** | | | | | | | | | | |
| 3. Operating Income | 5,466,329 | 6,180,378 | 7,335,412 | 9,684,219 | 11,817,091 | 10,737,821 | 11,979,056 | 10,895,887 | 14,382,759 | 17,439,037 |
| 4. Depreciation | 215,563 | 216,709 | 277,346 | 294,876 | 523,936 | n.a. | n.a. | n.a. | 1,188,643 | 1,373,343 |
| 5. Taxes Paid | 95,641 | 109,119 | 136,727 | 171,708 | 165,798 | 124,104 | 113,849 | 103,024 | 136,175 | 168,910 |
| 6. Interest Paid | 61,933 | 99,004 | 117,845 | 203,623 | 295,244 | 258,677 | 281,405 | 247,105 | 414,007 | 597,311 |
| 7. Payroll Deductions | 982,121 | 818,257 | 1,091,388 | 1,410,001 | 1,478,324 | 1,157,074 | 1,420,857 | n.a. | 4,400,620 | 2,237,172 |
| 8. Payments to Partners | 84,837 | 72,309 | 76,980 | 106,290 | 89,815 | 128,580 | 53,669 | 52,793 | 22,012 | 22,705 |
| 9. Net Income, less Deficit | 349,357 | 280,657 | 493,639 | 325,701 | 426,913 | 413,298 | 344,669 | 326,742 | (955,752) | (974,861) |
| **Selected Average Financial Statistics** | | | | | | | | | | |
| **(Items 10 to 13 inclusive in $)** | | | | | | | | | | |
| 10. Av. Payment Partnership | 4,958 | 4,326 | 5,057 | 6,386 | 5,809 | 7,157 | 3,790 | 2,833 | 1,000 | 1,000 |
| 11. Av. Payment Partner | 1,698 | 1,721 | 1,904 | 2,080 | 1,776 | 2,289 | 1,109 | 915 | 335 | 330 |
| 12. Av. Income Partnership | 20,417 | 16,791 | 32,427 | 19,570 | 27,612 | 23,006 | 24,339 | 17,537 | (43,420) | (42,936) |
| 13. Av. Income Partner | 6,991 | 6,681 | 12,207 | 6,373 | 8,442 | 7,358 | 7,119 | 5,663 | (14,553) | (14,152) |
| **Selected Financial Statistics as Percent of Op. Income** | | | | | | | | | | |
| 14. Depreciation / Op. Income (%) | 3.9 | 3.5 | 3.8 | 3.0 | 4.4 | n.a. | n.a. | n.a. | 8.3 | 7.9 |
| 15. Interest / Op. Income (%) | 1.1 | 1.6 | 1.6 | 2.1 | 2.5 | 2.4 | 2.4 | 2.3 | 2.9 | 3.4 |
| 16. Payroll / Op. Income (%) | 18.0 | 13.2 | 14.9 | 14.6 | 12.5 | 10.8 | 11.9 | n.a. | 30.6 | 12.8 |
| **Selected Index Numbers (1976 = 100)** | | | | | | | | | | |
| 17. Partnerships | 100.0 | 97.7 | 89.0 | 97.3 | 90.4 | 105.0 | 82.8 | 108.9 | 128.6 | 132.7 |
| 18. Partners | 100.0 | 84.1 | 80.9 | 102.3 | 101.2 | 112.4 | 96.9 | 115.5 | 131.4 | 137.8 |
| 19. Operating Income | 100.0 | 113.1 | 134.2 | 177.2 | 216.2 | 196.4 | 219.1 | 199.3 | 263.1 | 319.0 |
| 20. Payments to Partners | 100.0 | 85.2 | 90.7 | 125.3 | 105.9 | 151.6 | 63.3 | 62.2 | 25.9 | 26.8 |
| **Selected Financial Statistics (Constant $, 1976 = 100)** | | | | | | | | | | |
| 21. Operating Income | 100.0 | 106.1 | 117.7 | 137.8 | 145.8 | 121.4 | 133.5 | 120.7 | 155.5 | 189.3 |
| 22. Payments to Partners | 100.0 | 80.1 | 79.2 | 98.3 | 73.1 | 94.9 | 37.3 | 35.6 | 14.2 | 14.2 |
| 23. Av. Payment, Partnership | 100.0 | 81.9 | 89.0 | 101.0 | 81.0 | 90.3 | 45.1 | 32.6 | 11.0 | 10.7 |
| 24. Av. Payment, Partner | 100.0 | 95.2 | 97.8 | 96.1 | 72.3 | 84.4 | 38.6 | 30.8 | 10.8 | 10.2 |

# TABLE 3

## 067: TRANSPORTATION, COMMUNICATION ELECTRIC, GAS, AND SANITARY SERVICES, WITH AND WITHOUT NET INCOME

| | 1976 | 1977 | 1978 | 1979 | 1980 | 1981 | 1982 | 1983 | 1984 | 1985 |
|---|---|---|---|---|---|---|---|---|---|---|
| 1. Number of Partnerships | 16,860 | 16,837 | 19,886 | 19,778 | 20,417 | 21,711 | 18,448 | 20,132 | 20,578 | 24,970 |
| 2. Number of Partners | 49,079 | 45,022 | 55,480 | 61,036 | 73,192 | 73,005 | 93,329 | 103,035 | 142,091 | 186,326 |

### Selected Financial Statistics
(Items 3 to 9 inclusive in 000's of dollars)

| | 1976 | 1977 | 1978 | 1979 | 1980 | 1981 | 1982 | 1983 | 1984 | 1985 |
|---|---|---|---|---|---|---|---|---|---|---|
| 3. Operating Income | 2,542,612 | 3,817,903 | 4,486,154 | 5,409,055 | 5,868,413 | 6,239,972 | 6,569,555 | 7,154,727 | 10,732,715 | 11,252,973 |
| 4. Depreciation | 381,442 | 499,199 | 700,153 | 852,663 | 892,623 | n.a. | n.a. | n.a. | 2,112,716 | 2,865,803 |
| 5. Taxes Paid | 88,547 | 92,923 | 107,512 | 146,415 | 162,967 | 101,359 | 133,576 | 145,928 | 183,646 | 237,567 |
| 6. Interest Paid | 126,052 | 140,398 | 243,484 | 315,583 | 389,011 | 438,409 | 618,690 | 769,199 | 1,253,616 | 1,308,508 |
| 7. Payroll Deductions | 403,725 | 483,038 | 472,042 | 513,807 | 582,787 | 648,275 | 660,968 | n.a. | 949,704 | 1,061,249 |
| 8. Payments to Partners | 46,905 | 50,584 | 54,488 | 61,088 | 78,572 | 60,912 | 75,694 | 113,738 | 102,303 | 157,175 |
| 9. Net Income, less Deficit | 9,802 | 202,488 | 376,590 | 367,734 | 248,387 | 22,783 | 76,076 | 70,349 | (2,007,032) | (3,066,314) |

### Selected Average Financial Statistics
(Items 10 to 13 inclusive in $)

| | 1976 | 1977 | 1978 | 1979 | 1980 | 1981 | 1982 | 1983 | 1984 | 1985 |
|---|---|---|---|---|---|---|---|---|---|---|
| 10. Av. Payment Partnership | 2,782 | 3,004 | 2,740 | 3,089 | 3,848 | 2,806 | 4,103 | 5,650 | 4,971 | 6,295 |
| 11. Av. Payment Partner | 956 | 1,124 | 982 | 1,001 | 1,074 | 834 | 811 | 1,104 | 720 | 844 |
| 12. Av. Income Partnership | 581 | 12,026 | 18,937 | 18,593 | 12,166 | 1,049 | 4,124 | 3,494 | (97,533) | (122,800) |
| 13. Av. Income Partner | 200 | 4,498 | 6,788 | 6,025 | 3,394 | 312 | 815 | 683 | (14,125) | (16,457) |

### Selected Financial Statistics as Percent of Op. Income

| | 1976 | 1977 | 1978 | 1979 | 1980 | 1981 | 1982 | 1983 | 1984 | 1985 |
|---|---|---|---|---|---|---|---|---|---|---|
| 14. Depreciation / Op. Income (%) | 15.0 | 13.1 | 15.6 | 15.8 | 15.2 | n.a. | n.a. | n.a. | 19.7 | 25.5 |
| 15. Interest / Op. Income (%) | 5.0 | 3.7 | 5.4 | 5.8 | 6.6 | 7.0 | 9.4 | 10.8 | 11.7 | 11.6 |
| 16. Payroll / Op. Income (%) | 15.9 | 12.7 | 10.5 | 9.5 | 9.9 | 10.4 | 10.1 | n.a. | 8.9 | 9.4 |

### Selected Index Numbers (1976 = 100)

| | 1976 | 1977 | 1978 | 1979 | 1980 | 1981 | 1982 | 1983 | 1984 | 1985 |
|---|---|---|---|---|---|---|---|---|---|---|
| 17. Partnerships | 100.0 | 99.9 | 117.9 | 117.3 | 121.1 | 128.8 | 109.4 | 119.4 | 122.1 | 148.1 |
| 18. Partners | 100.0 | 91.7 | 113.0 | 124.4 | 149.1 | 148.7 | 190.2 | 209.9 | 289.5 | 379.6 |
| 19. Operating Income | 100.0 | 150.2 | 176.4 | 212.7 | 230.8 | 245.4 | 258.4 | 281.4 | 422.1 | 442.6 |
| 20. Payments to Partners | 100.0 | 107.8 | 116.2 | 130.2 | 167.5 | 129.9 | 161.4 | 242.5 | 218.1 | 335.1 |

### Selected Financial Statistics (Constant $, 1976 = 100)

| | 1976 | 1977 | 1978 | 1979 | 1980 | 1981 | 1982 | 1983 | 1984 | 1985 |
|---|---|---|---|---|---|---|---|---|---|---|
| 21. Operating Income | 100.0 | 141.1 | 154.0 | 166.8 | 159.4 | 153.6 | 152.4 | 160.8 | 231.3 | 234.2 |
| 22. Payments to Partners | 100.0 | 101.3 | 101.4 | 102.1 | 115.7 | 81.3 | 95.2 | 138.6 | 119.5 | 177.3 |
| 23. Av. Payment, Partnership | 100.0 | 101.4 | 85.9 | 87.1 | 95.5 | 63.1 | 87.0 | 116.0 | 97.9 | 119.8 |
| 24. Av. Payment, Partner | 100.0 | 110.4 | 89.7 | 82.1 | 77.6 | 54.6 | 50.1 | 66.0 | 41.2 | 46.7 |

## TABLE 3

### TRANSPORTATION, TOTAL (068,071,074,075,076), WITH AND WITHOUT NET INCOME

| | 1976 | 1977 | 1978 | 1979 | 1980 | 1981 | 1982 | 1983 | 1984 | 1985 |
|---|---|---|---|---|---|---|---|---|---|---|
| 1. Number of Partnerships | 13,364 | 13,942 | 16,611 | 16,781 | 16,675 | 17,790 | 12,231 | 13,097 | 13,783 | 17,406 |
| 2. Number of Partners | 36,365 | 33,970 | 44,392 | 44,277 | 52,612 | 52,523 | 44,523 | 41,674 | 54,697 | 61,722 |
| **Selected Financial Statistics** | | | | | | | | | | |
| (Items 3 to 9 inclusive in 000's of dollars) | | | | | | | | | | |
| 3. Operating Income | 2,001,255 | 3,176,057 | 3,310,610 | 3,832,870 | 4,440,157 | 4,530,256 | 4,296,710 | 4,895,213 | 6,765,928 | 5,924,007 |
| 4. Depreciation | 214,164 | 322,167 | 495,044 | 599,914 | 578,824 | n.a. | n.a. | n.a. | 825,649 | 1,009,309 |
| 5. Taxes Paid | 65,470 | 67,387 | 83,617 | 94,615 | 117,809 | 59,906 | 56,632 | 69,246 | 72,709 | 89,873 |
| 6. Interest Paid | 96,583 | 99,548 | 176,531 | 241,761 | 280,951 | 291,524 | 342,660 | 352,988 | 376,289 | 384,839 |
| 7. Payroll Deductions | 312,966 | 383,395 | 356,353 | 377,928 | 432,094 | 446,002 | 376,651 | n.a. | 459,742 | 481,267 |
| 8. Payments to Partners | 39,214 | 42,424 | 44,926 | 47,855 | 67,553 | 45,754 | 48,845 | 40,067 | 13,783 | 17,406 |
| 9. Net Income, less Deficit | 74,957 | 428,501 | 563,610 | 611,383 | 547,766 | 512,650 | 484,742 | 532,191 | 345,598 | 424,697 |
| **Selected Average Financial Statistics** | | | | | | | | | | |
| (Items 10 to 13 inclusive in $) | | | | | | | | | | |
| 10. Av. Payment Partnership | 2,934 | 3,043 | 2,705 | 2,852 | 4,051 | 2,572 | 3,994 | 3,059 | 1,000 | 1,000 |
| 11. Av. Payment Partner | 1,078 | 1,249 | 1,012 | 1,081 | 1,284 | 871 | 1,097 | 961 | 252 | 282 |
| 12. Av. Income Partnership | 5,609 | 30,735 | 33,930 | 36,433 | 32,850 | 28,817 | 39,632 | 40,635 | 25,074 | 24,399 |
| 13. Av. Income Partner | 2,061 | 12,614 | 12,696 | 13,808 | 10,411 | 9,760 | 10,887 | 12,770 | 6,318 | 6,881 |
| **Selected Financial Statistics as Percent of Op. Income** | | | | | | | | | | |
| 14. Depreciation / Op. Income (%) | 10.7 | 10.1 | 15.0 | 15.7 | 13.0 | n.a. | n.a. | n.a. | 12.2 | 17.0 |
| 15. Interest / Op. Income (%) | 4.8 | 3.1 | 5.3 | 6.3 | 6.3 | 6.4 | 8.0 | 7.2 | 5.6 | 6.5 |
| 16. Payroll / Op. Income (%) | 15.6 | 12.1 | 10.8 | 9.9 | 9.7 | 9.8 | 8.8 | n.a. | 6.8 | 8.1 |
| **Selected Index Numbers (1976 = 100)** | | | | | | | | | | |
| 17. Partnerships | 100.0 | 104.3 | 124.3 | 125.6 | 124.8 | 133.1 | 91.5 | 98.0 | 103.1 | 130.2 |
| 18. Partners | 100.0 | 93.4 | 122.1 | 121.8 | 144.7 | 144.4 | 122.4 | 114.6 | 150.4 | 169.7 |
| 19. Operating Income | 100.0 | 158.7 | 165.4 | 191.5 | 221.9 | 226.4 | 214.7 | 244.6 | 338.1 | 296.0 |
| 20. Payments to Partners | 100.0 | 108.2 | 114.6 | 122.0 | 172.3 | 116.7 | 124.6 | 102.2 | 35.1 | 44.4 |
| **Selected Financial Statistics (Constant $, 1976 = 100)** | | | | | | | | | | |
| 21. Operating Income | 100.0 | 149.1 | 144.3 | 150.2 | 153.3 | 141.7 | 126.6 | 139.8 | 185.3 | 156.6 |
| 22. Payments to Partners | 100.0 | 101.6 | 100.0 | 95.7 | 119.0 | 73.0 | 73.5 | 58.4 | 19.3 | 23.5 |
| 23. Av. Payment, Partnership | 100.0 | 97.4 | 80.4 | 76.2 | 95.4 | 54.9 | 80.3 | 59.6 | 18.7 | 18.0 |
| 24. Av. Payment, Partner | 100.0 | 108.8 | 81.9 | 78.6 | 82.2 | 50.6 | 59.9 | 50.9 | 12.8 | 13.9 |

## TABLE 3

### 071: TRUCKING AND WAREHOUSING, WITH AND WITHOUT NET INCOME

| | 1976 | 1977 | 1978 | 1979 | 1980 | 1981 | 1982 | 1983 | 1984 | 1985 |
|---|---|---|---|---|---|---|---|---|---|---|
| 1  Number of Partnerships | 8,164 | 9,016 | 12,075 | 11,136 | 10,777 | 12,199 | 8,260 | 10,185 | 8,980 | 12,992 |
| 2  Number of Partners | 19,860 | 20,086 | 30,830 | 25,806 | 29,770 | 29,339 | 20,431 | 23,241 | 33,285 | 41,750 |
| **Selected Financial Statistics** | | | | | | | | | | |
| **(Items 3 to 9 inclusive in 000's of dollars)** | | | | | | | | | | |
| 3.  Operating Income | 1,038,287 | 1,309,188 | 1,535,466 | 1,497,405 | 1,678,380 | 1,855,801 | 1,393,786 | 2,113,287 | 3,181,860 | 1,844,432 |
| 4.  Depreciation | 76,566 | 90,681 | 138,057 | 151,331 | 167,098 | n.a. | n.a. | n.a. | 223,804 | 283,901 |
| 5.  Taxes Paid | 48,284 | 52,514 | 63,332 | 55,929 | 59,669 | 43,108 | 35,715 | 47,201 | 46,178 | 47,316 |
| 6.  Interest Paid | 29,600 | 29,535 | 54,793 | 49,385 | 85,287 | 71,588 | 70,854 | 94,056 | 95,949 | 88,776 |
| 7.  Payroll Deductions | 224,387 | 244,128 | 242,654 | 235,503 | 288,021 | 289,962 | 205,035 | n.a. | 286,126 | 269,975 |
| 8.  Payments to Partners | 30,496 | 32,890 | 34,406 | 32,770 | 45,938 | 37,270 | 35,552 | 27,842 | 73,982 | 62,854 |
| 9.  Net Income, less Deficit | 57,169 | 104,884 | 135,493 | 114,214 | 116,415 | 131,446 | 27,196 | 78,748 | 116,856 | 148,274 |
| **Selected Average Financial Statistics** | | | | | | | | | | |
| **(Items 10 to 13 inclusive in $)** | | | | | | | | | | |
| 10. Av. Payment Partnership | 3,735 | 3,648 | 2,849 | 2,943 | 4,263 | 3,055 | 4,304 | 2,734 | 8,239 | 4,838 |
| 11. Av. Payment Partner | 1,536 | 1,637 | 1,116 | 1,270 | 1,543 | 1,270 | 1,740 | 1,198 | 2,223 | 1,505 |
| 12. Av. Income Partnership | 7,003 | 11,633 | 11,221 | 10,256 | 10,802 | 10,775 | 3,292 | 7,732 | 13,013 | 11,413 |
| 13. Av. Income Partner | 2,879 | 5,222 | 4,395 | 4,426 | 3,910 | 4,480 | 1,331 | 3,388 | 3,511 | 3,551 |
| **Selected Financial Statistics as Percent of Op. Income** | | | | | | | | | | |
| 14. Depreciation / Op. Income (%) | 7.4 | 6.9 | 9.0 | 10.1 | 1.0 | n.a. | n.a. | n.a. | 7.0 | 15.4 |
| 15. Interest / Op. Income (%) | 2.9 | 2.3 | 3.6 | 3.3 | 5.1 | 3.9 | 5.1 | 4.5 | 3.0 | 4.8 |
| 16. Payroll / Op. Income (%) | 21.6 | 18.7 | 15.8 | 15.7 | 17.2 | 15.6 | 14.7 | n.a. | 9.0 | 14.6 |
| **Selected Index Numbers (1976 = 100)** | | | | | | | | | | |
| 17. Partnerships | 100.0 | 110.4 | 147.9 | 136.4 | 132.0 | 149.4 | 101.2 | 124.8 | 110.0 | 159.1 |
| 18. Partners | 100.0 | 101.1 | 155.2 | 129.9 | 149.9 | 147.7 | 102.9 | 117.0 | 167.6 | 210.2 |
| 19. Operating Income | 100.0 | 126.1 | 147.9 | 144.2 | 161.6 | 178.7 | 134.2 | 203.5 | 306.5 | 177.6 |
| 20. Payments to Partners | 100.0 | 107.9 | 112.8 | 107.5 | 150.6 | 122.2 | 116.6 | 91.3 | 242.6 | 206.1 |
| **Selected Financial Statistics (Constant $, 1976 = 100)** | | | | | | | | | | |
| 21. Operating Income | 100.0 | 118.4 | 129.0 | 113.1 | 111.7 | 111.9 | 79.2 | 116.3 | 168.0 | 94.0 |
| 22. Payments to Partners | 100.0 | 101.3 | 98.4 | 84.3 | 104.1 | 76.5 | 68.8 | 52.2 | 133.0 | 109.1 |
| 23. Av. Payment, Partnership | 100.0 | 91.7 | 66.5 | 61.8 | 78.8 | 51.2 | 68.0 | 41.8 | 120.9 | 68.6 |
| 24. Av. Payment, Partner | 100.0 | 100.2 | 63.4 | 64.8 | 69.4 | 51.7 | 66.8 | 44.5 | 79.4 | 51.9 |

## TABLE 3

### OTHER TRANSPORTATION (069,070,074,075,076), WITH AND WITHOUT NET INCOME

| | 1976 | 1977 | 1978 | 1979 | 1980 | 1981 | 1982 | 1983 | 1984 | 1985 |
|---|---|---|---|---|---|---|---|---|---|---|
| 1. Number of Partnerships | 5,200 | 4,926 | 4,536 | 5,645 | 5,899 | 5,591 | 3,971 | 2,912 | 3,803 | 4,414 |
| 2. Number of Partners | 16,505 | 13,884 | 13,562 | 18,471 | 22,842 | 23,184 | 24,092 | 18,433 | 21,412 | 19,973 |
| **Selected Financial Statistics** | | | | | | | | | | |
| (Items 3 to 9 inclusive in 000's of dollars) | | | | | | | | | | |
| 3. Operating Income | 962,968 | 1,866,869 | 1,775,145 | 2,335,465 | 2,761,776 | 2,674,455 | 2,902,924 | 2,781,926 | 3,584,068 | 4,079,574 |
| 4. Depreciation | 137,598 | 231,486 | 356,986 | 448,583 | 411,727 | n.a. | n.a. | n.a. | 601,845 | 725,408 |
| 5. Taxes Paid | 17,186 | 14,873 | 20,285 | 38,686 | 58,139 | 16,798 | 20,916 | 22,045 | 26,530 | 42,557 |
| 6. Interest Paid | 66,983 | 70,013 | 121,738 | 192,377 | 195,664 | 219,936 | 271,806 | 258,932 | 280,340 | 296,062 |
| 7. Payroll Deductions | 88,579 | 139,267 | 113,699 | 142,425 | 144,074 | 156,040 | 171,616 | n.a. | 173,616 | 211,292 |
| 8. Payments to Partners | 8,718 | 9,534 | 10,520 | 15,086 | 21,614 | 8,484 | 13,293 | 12,225 | 7,466 | 36,554 |
| 9. Net Income, less Deficit | 17,788 | 323,617 | 428,117 | 497,170 | 431,390 | 383,930 | 457,546 | 453,443 | 228,742 | 276,422 |
| **Selected Average Financial Statistics** | | | | | | | | | | |
| (Items 10 to 13 inclusive in $) | | | | | | | | | | |
| 10. Av. Payment Partnership | 1,677 | 1,935 | 2,319 | 2,672 | 3,664 | 1,517 | 3,348 | 4,198 | 1,963 | 8,281 |
| 11. Av. Payment Partner | 528 | 687 | 776 | 817 | 946 | 366 | 552 | 663 | 349 | 1,830 |
| 12. Av. Income Partnership | 3,421 | 65,696 | 94,382 | 88,073 | 73,129 | 68,669 | 115,222 | 155,715 | 60,148 | 62,624 |
| 13. Av. Income Partner | 1,078 | 23,309 | 31,567 | 26,916 | 18,886 | 16,560 | 18,992 | 24,600 | 10,683 | 13,840 |
| **Selected Financial Statistics as Percent of Op. Income** | | | | | | | | | | |
| 14. Depreciation / Op. Income (%) | 14.3 | 12.4 | 20.1 | 19.2 | 14.9 | n.a. | n.a. | n.a. | 16.8 | 17.8 |
| 15. Interest / Op. Income (%) | 7.0 | 3.8 | 6.9 | 8.2 | 7.1 | 8.2 | 9.4 | 9.3 | 7.8 | 7.3 |
| 16. Payroll / Op. Income (%) | 9.2 | 7.5 | 6.4 | 6.1 | 5.2 | 5.8 | 5.9 | n.a. | 4.8 | 5.2 |
| **Selected Index Numbers (1976 = 100)** | | | | | | | | | | |
| 17. Partnerships | 100.0 | 94.7 | 87.2 | 108.6 | 113.4 | 107.5 | 76.4 | 56.0 | 73.1 | 84.9 |
| 18. Partners | 100.0 | 84.1 | 82.2 | 111.9 | 138.4 | 140.5 | 146.0 | 111.7 | 129.7 | 121.0 |
| 19. Operating Income | 100.0 | 193.9 | 184.3 | 242.5 | 286.8 | 277.7 | 301.5 | 288.9 | 372.2 | 423.6 |
| 20. Payments to Partners | 100.0 | 109.4 | 120.7 | 173.0 | 247.9 | 97.3 | 152.5 | 140.2 | 85.6 | 419.3 |
| **Selected Financial Statistics (Constant $, 1976 = 100)** | | | | | | | | | | |
| 21. Operating Income | 100.0 | 182.1 | 160.9 | 190.2 | 198.1 | 173.8 | 177.8 | 165.1 | 204.0 | 224.2 |
| 22. Payments to Partners | 100.0 | 102.7 | 105.3 | 135.7 | 171.3 | 60.9 | 89.9 | 80.1 | 46.9 | 221.9 |
| 23. Av. Payment, Partnership | 100.0 | 108.4 | 120.7 | 125.0 | 151.0 | 56.6 | 117.8 | 143.1 | 64.2 | 261.4 |
| 24. Av. Payment, Partner | 100.0 | 122.3 | 128.1 | 121.4 | 123.6 | 43.3 | 61.7 | 71.7 | 36.2 | 183.3 |

TABLE 3

COMMUNICATION, ELECTRIC, GAS AND SANITARY SERVICES (080,081,082), WITH AND WITHOUT NET INCOME

| | 1976 | 1977 | 1978 | 1979 | 1980 | 1981 | 1982 | 1983 | 1984 | 1985 |
|---|---|---|---|---|---|---|---|---|---|---|
| 1. Number of Partnerships | 3,496 | 2,895 | 3,275 | 2,997 | 3,742 | 3,921 | 6,216 | 7,035 | 6,795 | 7,564 |
| 2. Number of Partners | 12,714 | 11,052 | 11,088 | 16,759 | 20,578 | 20,481 | 48,807 | 61,360 | 87,393 | 124,603 |
| **Selected Financial Statistics** (Items 3 to 9 inclusive in 000's of dollars) | | | | | | | | | | |
| 3. Operating Income | 541,357 | 641,846 | 1,175,543 | 1,576,186 | 1,428,255 | 1,709,717 | 2,272,845 | 2,259,514 | 3,966,787 | 5,328,967 |
| 4. Depreciation | 167,278 | 177,032 | 205,109 | 252,749 | 313,799 | n.a. | n.a. | n.a. | 1,287,067 | 1,856,493 |
| 5. Taxes Paid | 23,077 | 25,536 | 23,895 | 51,803 | 45,159 | 41,453 | 76,944 | 76,680 | 110,937 | 147,695 |
| 6. Interest Paid | 29,469 | 40,850 | 66,952 | 73,822 | 108,061 | 146,884 | 276,030 | 416,211 | 877,327 | 923,670 |
| 7. Payroll Deductions | 90,759 | 99,643 | 115,688 | 135,879 | 150,693 | 202,273 | 284,318 | n.a. | 489,962 | 579,982 |
| 8. Payments to Partners | 7,691 | 8,160 | 9,561 | 13,233 | 11,018 | 15,157 | 26,849 | 73,671 | 20,855 | 57,767 |
| 9. Net Income, less Deficit | 25,004 | 43,179 | 35,104 | 40,735 | 63,186 | 87,526 | 160,911 | 149,954 | (2,352,630) | (3,491,010) |
| **Selected Average Financial Statistics** (Items 10 to 13 inclusive in $) | | | | | | | | | | |
| 10. Av. Payment Partnership | 2,200 | 2,819 | 2,919 | 4,415 | 2,944 | 3,866 | 4,319 | 10,472 | 3,069 | 7,637 |
| 11. Av. Payment Partner | 605 | 738 | 862 | 790 | 535 | 740 | 550 | 1,201 | 239 | 464 |
| 12. Av. Income Partnership | 7,152 | 14,915 | 10,719 | 13,592 | 16,886 | 22,322 | 25,887 | 21,315 | (346,230) | (461,530) |
| 13. Av. Income Partner | 1,967 | 3,907 | 3,166 | 2,431 | 3,071 | 4,274 | 3,297 | 2,444 | (26,920) | (28,017) |
| **Selected Financial Statistics as Percent of Op. Income** | | | | | | | | | | |
| 14. Depreciation / Op. Income (%) | 30.9 | 27.6 | 17.5 | 16.0 | 22.0 | n.a. | n.a. | n.a. | 32.5 | 34.8 |
| 15. Interest / Op. Income (%) | 5.4 | 6.4 | 5.7 | 4.7 | 7.6 | 8.6 | 12.1 | 18.4 | 22.1 | 17.3 |
| 16. Payroll / Op. Income (%) | 16.8 | 15.5 | 9.8 | 8.6 | 10.6 | 11.8 | 12.5 | n.a. | 12.4 | 10.9 |
| **Selected Index Numbers (1976 = 100)** | | | | | | | | | | |
| 17. Partnerships | 100.0 | 82.8 | 93.7 | 85.7 | 107.0 | 112.2 | 177.8 | 201.2 | 194.4 | 216.4 |
| 18. Partners | 100.0 | 86.9 | 87.2 | 131.8 | 161.9 | 161.1 | 383.9 | 482.6 | 687.4 | 980.0 |
| 19. Operating Income | 100.0 | 118.6 | 217.1 | 291.2 | 263.8 | 315.8 | 419.8 | 417.4 | 732.7 | 984.4 |
| 20. Payments to Partners | 100.0 | 106.1 | 124.3 | 172.1 | 143.3 | 197.1 | 349.1 | 957.9 | 271.2 | 751.1 |
| **Selected Financial Statistics (Constant $, 1976 = 100)** | | | | | | | | | | |
| 21. Operating Income | 100.0 | 111.4 | 189.5 | 228.3 | 182.3 | 197.7 | 247.6 | 238.5 | 401.6 | 520.9 |
| 22. Payments to Partners | 100.0 | 99.7 | 108.5 | 134.9 | 99.0 | 123.4 | 205.9 | 547.3 | 148.6 | 397.5 |
| 23. Av. Payment, Partnership | 100.0 | 120.4 | 115.8 | 157.4 | 92.5 | 110.0 | 115.8 | 272.0 | 76.4 | 183.7 |
| 24. Av. Payment, Partner | 100.0 | 114.7 | 124.3 | 102.3 | 61.2 | 76.7 | 53.6 | 113.3 | 21.7 | 40.6 |

*Page 227*

**TABLE 3**

**083: WHOLESALE AND RETAIL TRADE, WITH AND WITHOUT NET INCOME**

| | 1976 | 1977 | 1978 | 1979 | 1980 | 1981 | 1982 | 1983 | 1984 | 1985 |
|---|---|---|---|---|---|---|---|---|---|---|
| 1. Number of Partnerships | 195,014 | 193,312 | 200,195 | 204,916 | 200,273 | 216,808 | 205,142 | 194,360 | 184,841 | 200,532 |
| 2. Number of Partners | 468,773 | 498,871 | 478,481 | 487,819 | 487,363 | 528,483 | 490,863 | 478,893 | 443,712 | 492,511 |
| **Selected Financial Statistics** | | | | | | | | | | |
| **(Items 3 to 9 inclusive in 000's of dollars)** | | | | | | | | | | |
| 3. Operating Income | 46,073,078 | 48,616,283 | 52,920,233 | 58,229,310 | 65,793,083 | 70,442,389 | 69,736,174 | 59,879,912 | 72,335,387 | 69,079,237 |
| 4. Depreciation | 490,357 | 507,612 | 598,017 | 676,544 | 718,292 | n.a. | n.a. | n.a. | 1,199,719 | 1,172,399 |
| 5. Taxes Paid | 744,471 | 797,201 | 856,773 | 947,853 | 893,320 | 802,439 | 803,169 | 918,071 | 883,974 | 993,650 |
| 6. Interest Paid | 305,915 | 352,672 | 441,631 | 544,513 | 631,344 | 759,169 | 787,597 | 806,805 | 913,839 | 838,254 |
| 7. Payroll Deductions | 3,464,991 | 3,518,439 | 3,864,761 | 4,358,111 | 4,348,068 | 4,541,132 | 4,565,664 | n.a. | 5,221,006 | 5,526,742 |
| 8. Payments to Partners | 643,023 | 591,240 | 671,662 | 725,185 | 729,754 | 690,223 | 722,937 | 739,060 | 777,739 | 938,473 |
| 9. Net Income, less Deficit | 2,409,252 | 2,626,944 | 2,804,927 | 2,858,401 | 2,474,626 | 1,316,933 | 1,600,910 | 1,539,779 | 1,666,476 | 1,976,685 |
| **Selected Average Financial Statistics** | | | | | | | | | | |
| **(Items 10 to 13 inclusive in $)** | | | | | | | | | | |
| 10. Av. Payment Partnership | 3,297 | 3,058 | 3,355 | 3,539 | 3,644 | 3,184 | 3,524 | 3,803 | 4,208 | 4,680 |
| 11. Av. Payment Partner | 1,372 | 1,185 | 1,404 | 1,487 | 1,497 | 1,306 | 1,473 | 1,543 | 1,753 | 1,905 |
| 12. Av. Income Partnership | 12,354 | 13,589 | 14,011 | 13,949 | 12,356 | 6,074 | 7,804 | 7,922 | 9,016 | 9,857 |
| 13. Av. Income Partner | 5,139 | 5,266 | 5,862 | 5,860 | 5,078 | 2,492 | 3,261 | 3,215 | 3,756 | 4,013 |
| **Selected Financial Statistics as Percent of Op. Income** | | | | | | | | | | |
| 14. Depreciation / Op. Income (%) | 1.1 | 1.0 | 1.1 | 1.2 | 1.1 | n.a. | n.a. | n.a. | 1.7 | 1.7 |
| 15. Interest / Op. Income (%) | 0.7 | 0.7 | 0.8 | 0.9 | 0.10 | 1.1 | 1.1 | 1.4 | 1.3 | 1.2 |
| 16. Payroll / Op. Income (%) | 7.5 | 7.2 | 7.3 | 7.5 | 6.6 | 6.5 | 6.6 | n.a. | 7.2 | 8.0 |
| **Selected Index Numbers (1976 = 100)** | | | | | | | | | | |
| 17. Partnerships | 100.0 | 99.1 | 102.7 | 105.1 | 102.7 | 111.2 | 105.2 | 99.7 | 94.8 | 102.8 |
| 18. Partners | 100.0 | 106.4 | 102.1 | 104.1 | 104.0 | 112.7 | 104.7 | 102.2 | 94.7 | 105.1 |
| 19. Operating Income | 100.0 | 105.5 | 114.9 | 126.4 | 142.8 | 152.9 | 151.4 | 130.0 | 157.0 | 149.9 |
| 20. Payments to Partners | 100.0 | 91.9 | 104.5 | 112.8 | 113.5 | 107.3 | 112.4 | 114.9 | 121.0 | 145.9 |
| **Selected Financial Statistics (Constant $, 1976 = 100)** | | | | | | | | | | |
| 21. Operating Income | 100.0 | 99.1 | 100.2 | 99.1 | 98.7 | 95.7 | 89.3 | 74.3 | 86.0 | 79.3 |
| 22. Payments to Partners | 100.0 | 86.4 | 91.1 | 88.4 | 78.4 | 67.2 | 66.3 | 65.7 | 66.3 | 77.2 |
| 23. Av. Payment, Partnership | 100.0 | 87.1 | 88.8 | 84.2 | 76.3 | 60.4 | 63.0 | 65.9 | 70.0 | 75.1 |
| 24. Av. Payment, Partner | 100.0 | 81.2 | 89.4 | 85.0 | 75.4 | 59.5 | 63.4 | 64.3 | 70.0 | 73.5 |

*Page 228*

TABLE 3

084: WHOLESALE TRADE, WITH AND WITHOUT NET INCOME

| | 1976 | 1977 | 1978 | 1979 | 1980 | 1981 | 1982 | 1983 | 1984 | 1985 |
|---|---|---|---|---|---|---|---|---|---|---|
| 1. Number of Partnerships | 32,361 | 29,379 | 29,157 | 31,513 | 32,394 | 30,309 | 27,369 | 24,115 | 21,359 | 26,796 |
| 2. Number of Partners | 83,886 | 73,922 | 74,407 | 81,868 | 94,405 | 76,459 | 66,860 | 67,192 | 56,782 | 72,486 |
| **Selected Financial Statistics** (Items 3 to 9 inclusive in 000's of dollars) | | | | | | | | | | |
| 3. Operating Income | 16,011,459 | 16,624,409 | 17,818,552 | 20,512,475 | 28,426,030 | 29,601,718 | 30,187,403 | 17,224,243 | 28,169,882 | 23,531,460 |
| 4. Depreciation | 133,573 | 123,816 | 146,588 | 165,129 | 184,558 | n.a. | n.a. | n.a. | 301,714 | 241,416 |
| 5. Taxes Paid | 156,732 | 165,055 | 154,720 | 180,303 | 159,907 | 118,850 | 122,277 | 110,800 | 135,505 | 131,681 |
| 6. Interest Paid | 87,194 | 100,084 | 119,363 | 160,537 | 197,920 | 212,533 | 278,061 | 316,883 | 359,969 | 271,789 |
| 7. Payroll Deductions | 760,041 | 725,018 | 739,214 | 890,381 | 861,953 | 859,539 | 862,267 | n.a. | 1,026,075 | 896,081 |
| 8. Payments to Partners | 156,090 | 129,204 | 162,976 | 197,763 | 178,331 | 137,037 | 163,817 | 169,854 | 224,577 | 203,863 |
| 9. Net Income, less Deficit | 704,315 | 755,178 | 789,533 | 909,083 | 912,899 | 437,573 | 277,078 | 308,927 | 371,099 | 467,394 |
| **Selected Average Financial Statistics** (Items 10 to 13 inclusive in $) | | | | | | | | | | |
| 10. Av. Payment Partnership | 4,823 | 4,398 | 5,590 | 6,276 | 5,505 | 4,521 | 5,985 | 7,043 | 10,514 | 7,608 |
| 11. Av. Payment Partner | 1,861 | 1,748 | 2,190 | 2,416 | 1,889 | 1,792 | 2,450 | 2,528 | 3,955 | 2,812 |
| 12. Av. Income Partnership | 21,764 | 25,705 | 27,079 | 28,848 | 28,181 | 14,437 | 10,124 | 12,811 | 17,374 | 17,443 |
| 13. Av. Income Partner | 8,396 | 10,216 | 10,611 | 11,104 | 9,670 | 5,723 | 4,144 | 4,598 | 6,536 | 6,448 |
| **Selected Financial Statistics as Percent of Op. Income** | | | | | | | | | | |
| 14. Depreciation / Op. Income (%) | 0.8 | 0.7 | 0.8 | 0.8 | 0.7 | n.a. | n.a. | n.a. | 1.1 | 1.0 |
| 15. Interest / Op. Income (%) | 0.5 | 0.6 | 0.7 | 0.8 | 0.7 | 0.7 | 0.9 | 1.8 | 1.3 | 1.2 |
| 16. Payroll / Op. Income (%) | 4.8 | 4.4 | 4.2 | 4.3 | 3.0 | 2.9 | 2.9 | n.a. | 3.6 | 3.8 |
| **Selected Index Numbers (1976 = 100)** | | | | | | | | | | |
| 17. Partnerships | 100.0 | 90.8 | 90.1 | 97.4 | 100.1 | 93.7 | 84.6 | 74.5 | 66.0 | 82.8 |
| 18. Partners | 100.0 | 88.1 | 88.7 | 97.6 | 112.5 | 91.1 | 79.7 | 80.1 | 67.7 | 86.4 |
| 19. Operating Income | 100.0 | 103.8 | 111.3 | 128.1 | 177.5 | 184.9 | 188.5 | 107.6 | 175.9 | 147.0 |
| 20. Payments to Partners | 100.0 | 82.8 | 104.4 | 126.7 | 114.2 | 87.8 | 105.0 | 108.8 | 143.9 | 130.6 |
| **Selected Financial Statistics (Constant $, 1976 = 100)** | | | | | | | | | | |
| 21. Operating Income | 100.0 | 97.5 | 97.1 | 100.5 | 122.6 | 115.7 | 111.2 | 61.5 | 96.4 | 77.8 |
| 22. Payments to Partners | 100.0 | 77.8 | 91.1 | 99.4 | 78.9 | 55.0 | 61.9 | 62.2 | 78.9 | 69.1 |
| 23. Av. Payment, Partnership | 100.0 | 85.6 | 101.1 | 102.1 | 78.9 | 58.7 | 73.2 | 83.4 | 119.5 | 83.5 |
| 24. Av. Payment, Partner | 100.0 | 88.2 | 102.7 | 101.8 | 70.1 | 60.3 | 77.6 | 77.6 | 116.5 | 80.0 |

TABLE 3

100: RETAIL TRADE, WITH AND WITHOUT NET INCOME

| | 1976 | 1977 | 1978 | 1979 | 1980 | 1981 | 1982 | 1983 | 1984 | 1985 |
|---|---|---|---|---|---|---|---|---|---|---|
| 1. Number of Partnerships | 162,371 | 163,832 | 170,410 | 173,190 | 167,826 | 184,874 | 176,725 | 170,241 | 163,473 | 172,725 |
| 2. Number of Partners | 384,167 | 424,747 | 402,588 | 405,421 | 392,828 | 438,828 | 421,903 | 411,693 | 386,907 | 418,002 |

Selected Financial Statistics
(Items 3 to 9 inclusive in 000's of dollars)

| | 1976 | 1977 | 1978 | 1979 | 1980 | 1981 | 1982 | 1983 | 1984 | 1985 |
|---|---|---|---|---|---|---|---|---|---|---|
| 3. Operating Income | 30,032,594 | 31,983,372 | 35,025,060 | 37,702,076 | 37,307,313 | 40,143,385 | 39,385,129 | 42,639,667 | 44,132,987 | 45,486,151 |
| 4. Depreciation | 356,139 | 383,635 | 449,554 | 511,358 | 533,502 | n.a. | n.a. | n.a. | 897,894 | 930,983 |
| 5. Taxes Paid | 587,130 | 631,827 | 701,351 | 767,366 | 732,960 | 675,806 | 679,608 | 807,227 | 748,274 | 861,904 |
| 6. Interest Paid | 218,418 | 252,330 | 321,861 | 383,914 | 433,155 | 536,671 | 503,750 | 489,922 | 553,832 | 566,465 |
| 7. Payroll Deductions | 2,703,702 | 2,793,094 | 3,121,811 | 3,466,280 | 3,481,807 | 3,620,027 | 3,689,884 | n.a. | 4,193,347 | 4,630,347 |
| 8. Payments to Partners | 483,823 | 462,036 | 508,120 | 527,419 | 551,065 | 550,571 | 557,913 | 569,206 | 553,089 | 734,610 |
| 9. Net Income, less Deficit | 1,703,295 | 1,869,533 | 2,010,876 | 1,947,728 | 1,557,947 | 1,106,162 | 1,319,083 | 1,230,509 | 1,294,922 | 1,509,191 |

Selected Average Financial Statistics
(Items 10 to 13 inclusive in $)

| | 1976 | 1977 | 1978 | 1979 | 1980 | 1981 | 1982 | 1983 | 1984 | 1985 |
|---|---|---|---|---|---|---|---|---|---|---|
| 10. Av. Payment Partnership | 2,980 | 2,820 | 2,982 | 3,045 | 3,284 | 2,978 | 3,157 | 3,344 | 3,383 | 4,253 |
| 11. Av. Payment Partner | 1,259 | 1,088 | 1,262 | 1,301 | 1,403 | 1,255 | 1,322 | 1,383 | 1,430 | 1,757 |
| 12. Av. Income Partnership | 10,490 | 11,411 | 11,800 | 11,246 | 9,283 | 5,983 | 7,464 | 7,228 | 7,921 | 8,738 |
| 13. Av. Income Partner | 4,434 | 4,402 | 4,995 | 4,804 | 3,966 | 2,521 | 3,127 | 2,989 | 3,347 | 3,610 |

Selected Financial Statistics as Percent of Op. Income

| | 1976 | 1977 | 1978 | 1979 | 1980 | 1981 | 1982 | 1983 | 1984 | 1985 |
|---|---|---|---|---|---|---|---|---|---|---|
| 14. Depreciation / Op. Income (%) | 1.2 | 1.2 | 1.3 | 1.4 | 1.4 | n.a. | n.a. | n.a. | 2.0 | 2.1 |
| 15. Interest / Op. Income (%) | 0.7 | 0.8 | 0.9 | 1.0 | 1.2 | 1.3 | 1.3 | 1.2 | 1.3 | 1.3 |
| 16. Payroll / Op. Income (%) | 9.0 | 8.7 | 8.9 | 9.2 | 9.3 | 9.0 | 9.4 | n.a. | 9.5 | 10.2 |

Selected Index Numbers (1976 = 100)

| | 1976 | 1977 | 1978 | 1979 | 1980 | 1981 | 1982 | 1983 | 1984 | 1985 |
|---|---|---|---|---|---|---|---|---|---|---|
| 17. Partnerships | 100.0 | 100.9 | 105.0 | 106.7 | 103.4 | 113.9 | 108.8 | 104.8 | 100.7 | 106.4 |
| 18. Partners | 100.0 | 110.6 | 104.8 | 105.5 | 102.3 | 114.2 | 109.8 | 107.2 | 100.7 | 108.8 |
| 19. Operating Income | 100.0 | 106.5 | 116.6 | 125.5 | 124.2 | 133.7 | 131.1 | 142.0 | 147.0 | 151.5 |
| 20. Payments to Partners | 100.0 | 95.5 | 105.0 | 109.0 | 113.9 | 113.8 | 115.3 | 117.6 | 114.3 | 151.8 |

Selected Financial Statistics (Constant $, 1976 = 100)

| | 1976 | 1977 | 1978 | 1979 | 1980 | 1981 | 1982 | 1983 | 1984 | 1985 |
|---|---|---|---|---|---|---|---|---|---|---|
| 21. Operating Income | 100.0 | 100.0 | 101.8 | 98.5 | 85.8 | 83.7 | 77.3 | 81.1 | 80.5 | 80.1 |
| 22. Payments to Partners | 100.0 | 89.7 | 91.6 | 85.5 | 78.7 | 71.2 | 68.0 | 67.2 | 62.7 | 80.3 |
| 23. Av. Payment, Partnership | 100.0 | 88.9 | 87.3 | 80.2 | 76.2 | 62.5 | 62.5 | 64.1 | 62.2 | 75.5 |
| 24. Av. Payment, Partner | 100.0 | 81.1 | 87.5 | 81.0 | 76.9 | 62.4 | 61.9 | 62.7 | 62.3 | 73.8 |

TABLE 3

101: BUILDING MATERIALS, PAINT, HARDWARE, GARDEN SUPPLY, AND MOBILE HOME DEALERS, WITH AND WITHOUT NET INCOME

| | 1976 | 1977 | 1978 | 1979 | 1980 | 1981 | 1982 | 1983 | 1984 | 1985 |
|---|---|---|---|---|---|---|---|---|---|---|
| 1. Number of Partnerships | 8,545 | 8,483 | 9,366 | 8,525 | 7,215 | 7,297 | 9,815 | 10,737 | 7,992 | 8,567 |
| 2. Number of Partners | 20,672 | 21,577 | 23,035 | 21,193 | 17,867 | 18,645 | 24,810 | 28,359 | 18,927 | 20,836 |
| **Selected Financial Statistics** (Items 3 to 9 inclusive in 000's of dollars) | | | | | | | | | | |
| 3. Operating Income | 2,166,348 | 2,353,009 | 2,724,840 | 2,713,720 | 2,273,154 | 2,075,492 | 2,267,371 | 2,453,203 | 2,440,539 | 2,998,538 |
| 4. Depreciation | 26,928 | 26,222 | 36,826 | 38,729 | 35,538 | n.a. | n.a. | n.a. | 64,825 | 55,437 |
| 5. Taxes Paid | 43,132 | 40,717 | 49,208 | 49,875 | 44,183 | 29,559 | 36,795 | 40,433 | 42,941 | 51,371 |
| 6. Interest Paid | 20,995 | 20,834 | 36,199 | 37,153 | 36,429 | 40,066 | 40,063 | 58,673 | 46,144 | 47,682 |
| 7. Payroll Deductions | 192,699 | 194,151 | 210,888 | 214,963 | 209,620 | 176,852 | 196,395 | n.a. | 184,194 | 262,677 |
| 8. Payments to Partners | 41,067 | 39,902 | 48,226 | 47,211 | 47,595 | 45,495 | 63,293 | 49,302 | 54,335 | 77,009 |
| 9. Net Income, less Deficit | 158,645 | 185,340 | 203,246 | 183,011 | 118,656 | 103,919 | 81,316 | 33,305 | 156,633 | 92,298 |
| **Selected Average Financial Statistics** (Items 10 to 13 inclusive in $) | | | | | | | | | | |
| 10. Av. Payment Partnership | 4,806 | 4,704 | 5,149 | 5,538 | 6,597 | 6,235 | 6,449 | 4,592 | 6,799 | 8,989 |
| 11. Av. Payment Partner | 1,987 | 1,849 | 2,094 | 2,228 | 2,664 | 2,440 | 2,551 | 1,738 | 2,871 | 3,696 |
| 12. Av. Income Partnership | 18,566 | 21,848 | 21,700 | 21,468 | 16,446 | 14,241 | 8,285 | 3,102 | 19,599 | 10,774 |
| 13. Av. Income Partner | 7,674 | 8,590 | 8,823 | 8,635 | 6,641 | 5,574 | 3,278 | 1,174 | 8,276 | 4,430 |
| **Selected Financial Statistics as Percent of Op. Income** | | | | | | | | | | |
| 14. Depreciation / Op. Income (%) | 1.2 | 1.1 | 1.4 | 1.4 | 1.6 | n.a. | n.a. | n.a. | 2.7 | 1.9 |
| 15. Interest / Op. Income (%) | 0.10 | 0.9 | 1.3 | 1.4 | 1.6 | 1.9 | 1.8 | 2.4 | 1.9 | 1.6 |
| 16. Payroll / Op. Income (%) | 8.9 | 8.3 | 7.7 | 7.9 | 9.2 | 8.5 | 8.7 | n.a. | 7.6 | 8.8 |
| **Selected Index Numbers (1976 = 100)** | | | | | | | | | | |
| 17. Partnerships | 100.0 | 99.3 | 109.6 | 99.8 | 84.4 | 85.4 | 114.9 | 125.7 | 93.5 | 100.3 |
| 18. Partners | 100.0 | 104.4 | 111.4 | 102.5 | 86.4 | 90.2 | 120.0 | 137.2 | 91.6 | 100.8 |
| 19. Operating Income | 100.0 | 108.6 | 125.8 | 125.3 | 104.9 | 95.8 | 104.7 | 113.2 | 112.7 | 138.4 |
| 20. Payments to Partners | 100.0 | 97.2 | 117.4 | 115.0 | 115.9 | 110.8 | 154.1 | 120.1 | 132.3 | 187.5 |
| **Selected Financial Statistics (Constant $, 1976 = 100)** | | | | | | | | | | |
| 21. Operating Income | 100.0 | 102.0 | 109.8 | 98.2 | 72.5 | 60.0 | 61.7 | 64.7 | 61.7 | 73.2 |
| 22. Payments to Partners | 100.0 | 91.3 | 102.5 | 90.2 | 80.1 | 69.3 | 90.9 | 68.6 | 72.5 | 99.2 |
| 23. Av. Payment, Partnership | 100.0 | 92.0 | 93.5 | 90.4 | 94.8 | 81.2 | 79.1 | 54.6 | 77.5 | 99.0 |
| 24. Av. Payment, Partner | 100.0 | 87.5 | 92.0 | 88.0 | 92.6 | 76.9 | 75.7 | 50.0 | 79.2 | 98.4 |

TABLE 3

107: GENERAL MERCHANDISE STORES, WITH AND WITHOUT NET INCOME

| | 1976 | 1977 | 1978 | 1979 | 1980 | 1981 | 1982 | 1983 | 1984 | 1985 |
|---|---|---|---|---|---|---|---|---|---|---|
| 1. Number of Partnerships | 4,274 | 3,466 | 4,136 | 2,843 | 2,710 | 3,046 | 3,475 | 4,823 | 4,937 | 5,669 |
| 2. Number of Partners | 9,937 | 7,839 | 9,955 | 7,003 | 6,774 | 7,866 | 8,377 | 10,760 | 10,574 | 12,038 |
| **Selected Financial Statistics** | | | | | | | | | | |
| (Items 3 to 9 inclusive in 000's of dollars) | | | | | | | | | | |
| 3. Operating Income | 915,394 | 960,717 | 1,029,913 | 896,017 | 784,441 | 918,565 | 778,172 | 1,154,339 | 846,329 | 1,373,713 |
| 4. Depreciation | 8,461 | 9,094 | 9,143 | 7,525 | 7,855 | n.a. | n.a. | n.a. | 21,420 | 32,176 |
| 5. Taxes Paid | 17,249 | 15,944 | 17,296 | 13,500 | 13,216 | 13,861 | 11,915 | 19,046 | 15,126 | 28,144 |
| 6. Interest Paid | 6,635 | 5,842 | 6,911 | 7,312 | 8,961 | 10,448 | 8,396 | 21,096 | 10,634 | 12,529 |
| 7. Payroll Deductions | 72,289 | 78,269 | 80,645 | 66,794 | 67,835 | 71,098 | 61,909 | n.a. | 79,901 | 109,845 |
| 8. Payments to Partners | 15,638 | 16,323 | 13,986 | 13,809 | 11,085 | 14,168 | 13,262 | 23,059 | 23,129 | 25,071 |
| 9. Net Income, less Deficit | 53,318 | 54,947 | 59,224 | 53,503 | 33,879 | 48,918 | 1,931 | 10,566 | 5,757 | 40,662 |
| **Selected Average Financial Statistics** | | | | | | | | | | |
| (Items 10 to 13 inclusive in $) | | | | | | | | | | |
| 10. Av. Payment Partnership | 3,659 | 4,709 | 3,382 | 4,857 | 4,090 | 4,651 | 3,816 | 4,781 | 4,685 | 4,422 |
| 11. Av. Payment Partner | 1,574 | 2,082 | 1,405 | 1,972 | 1,636 | 1,801 | 1,583 | 2,143 | 2,187 | 2,083 |
| 12. Av. Income Partnership | 12,475 | 15,853 | 14,319 | 18,819 | 12,501 | 16,060 | 556 | 2,191 | 1,166 | 7,173 |
| 13. Av. Income Partner | 5,366 | 7,009 | 5,949 | 7,640 | 5,001 | 6,219 | 231 | 982 | 544 | 3,378 |
| **Selected Financial Statistics as Percent of Op. Income** | | | | | | | | | | |
| 14. Depreciation / Op. Income (%) | 0.9 | 0.10 | 0.9 | 0.8 | 1.0 | n.a. | n.a. | n.a. | 2.5 | 2.3 |
| 15. Interest / Op. Income (%) | 0.7 | 0.6 | 0.7 | 0.8 | 1.1 | 1.1 | 1.1 | 1.8 | 1.3 | 0.9 |
| 16. Payroll / Op. Income (%) | 7.9 | 8.2 | 7.8 | 7.5 | 8.7 | 7.7 | 8.0 | n.a. | 9.4 | 8.0 |
| **Selected Index Numbers (1976 = 100)** | | | | | | | | | | |
| 17. Partnerships | 100.0 | 81.1 | 96.8 | 66.5 | 63.4 | 71.3 | 81.3 | 112.8 | 115.5 | 132.6 |
| 18. Partners | 100.0 | 78.9 | 100.2 | 70.5 | 68.2 | 79.2 | 84.3 | 108.3 | 106.4 | 121.1 |
| 19. Operating Income | 100.0 | 105.0 | 112.5 | 97.9 | 85.7 | 100.3 | 85.0 | 126.1 | 92.5 | 150.1 |
| 20. Payments to Partners | 100.0 | 104.4 | 89.4 | 88.3 | 70.9 | 90.6 | 84.8 | 147.5 | 147.9 | 160.3 |
| **Selected Financial Statistics (Constant $, 1976 = 100)** | | | | | | | | | | |
| 21. Operating Income | 100.0 | 98.6 | 98.2 | 76.8 | 59.2 | 62.8 | 50.1 | 72.1 | 50.7 | 79.4 |
| 22. Payments to Partners | 100.0 | 98.1 | 78.0 | 69.3 | 49.0 | 56.7 | 50.0 | 84.3 | 81.1 | 84.8 |
| 23. Av. Payment, Partnership | 100.0 | 120.9 | 80.7 | 104.1 | 77.2 | 79.5 | 61.5 | 74.7 | 70.2 | 63.9 |
| 24. Av. Payment, Partner | 100.0 | 124.3 | 77.9 | 98.3 | 71.8 | 71.6 | 59.4 | 77.8 | 76.2 | 70.0 |

*Page 232*

## TABLE 3

## 110: FOOD STORES, WITH AND WITHOUT NET INCOME

| | 1976 | 1977 | 1978 | 1979 | 1980 | 1981 | 1982 | 1983 | 1984 | 1985 |
|---|---|---|---|---|---|---|---|---|---|---|
| 1. Number of Partnerships | 21,684 | 22,627 | 22,611 | 21,807 | 20,535 | 23,461 | 21,288 | 20,213 | 23,657 | 18,802 |
| 2. Number of Partners | 48,964 | 50,933 | 50,779 | 48,704 | 45,840 | 51,550 | 46,502 | 44,041 | 51,787 | 41,327 |
| **Selected Financial Statistics** (Items 3 to 9 inclusive in 000's of dollars) | | | | | | | | | | |
| 3. Operating Income | 5,912,641 | 6,409,065 | 6,842,724 | 6,854,311 | 7,341,731 | 7,406,263 | 7,460,137 | 7,167,664 | 8,802,217 | 8,017,754 |
| 4. Depreciation | 52,017 | 60,996 | 62,436 | 67,530 | 79,072 | n.a. | n.a. | n.a. | 106,353 | 110,161 |
| 5. Taxes Paid | 84,315 | 89,414 | 93,594 | 99,426 | 96,700 | 87,493 | 88,104 | 88,241 | 103,586 | 102,460 |
| 6. Interest Paid | 24,969 | 27,715 | 33,732 | 37,901 | 52,619 | 58,153 | 62,580 | 49,419 | 54,636 | 60,005 |
| 7. Payroll Deductions | 392,504 | 412,760 | 427,960 | 423,223 | 502,382 | 452,202 | 492,591 | n.a. | 618,280 | 584,991 |
| 8. Payments to Partners | 66,695 | 66,041 | 60,533 | 54,986 | 59,756 | 59,160 | 48,994 | 42,696 | 38,798 | 96,880 |
| 9. Net Income, less Deficit | 239,669 | 265,833 | 291,926 | 272,404 | 280,429 | 212,774 | 182,972 | 300,137 | 274,030 | 189,411 |
| **Selected Average Financial Statistics** (Items 10 to 13 inclusive in $) | | | | | | | | | | |
| 10. Av. Payment Partnership | 3,076 | 2,919 | 2,677 | 2,521 | 2,910 | 2,522 | 2,301 | 2,112 | 1,640 | 5,153 |
| 11. Av. Payment Partner | 1,362 | 1,297 | 1,192 | 1,129 | 1,304 | 1,148 | 1,054 | 969 | 749 | 2,344 |
| 12. Av. Income Partnership | 11,053 | 11,748 | 12,911 | 12,492 | 13,656 | 9,069 | 8,595 | 14,849 | 11,583 | 10,074 |
| 13. Av. Income Partner | 4,895 | 5,219 | 5,749 | 5,593 | 6,118 | 4,128 | 3,935 | 6,815 | 5,291 | 4,583 |
| **Selected Financial Statistics as Percent of Op. Income** | | | | | | | | | | |
| 14. Depreciation / Op. Income (%) | 0.9 | 0.10 | 0.9 | 0.10 | 1.1 | n.a. | n.a. | n.a. | 1.2 | 1.4 |
| 15. Interest / Op. Income (%) | 0.4 | 0.4 | 0.5 | 0.6 | 0.7 | 0.8 | 0.8 | 0.7 | 0.6 | 0.8 |
| 16. Payroll / Op. Income (%) | 6.6 | 6.4 | 6.3 | 6.2 | 6.8 | 6.1 | 6.6 | n.a. | 7.0 | 7.3 |
| **Selected Index Numbers (1976 = 100)** | | | | | | | | | | |
| 17. Partnerships | 100.0 | 104.3 | 104.3 | 100.6 | 94.7 | 108.2 | 98.2 | 93.2 | 109.1 | 86.7 |
| 18. Partners | 100.0 | 104.0 | 103.7 | 99.5 | 93.6 | 105.3 | 95.0 | 89.9 | 105.8 | 84.4 |
| 19. Operating Income | 100.0 | 108.4 | 115.7 | 115.9 | 124.2 | 125.3 | 126.2 | 121.2 | 148.9 | 135.6 |
| 20. Payments to Partners | 100.0 | 99.0 | 90.8 | 82.4 | 89.6 | 88.7 | 73.5 | 64.0 | 58.2 | 145.3 |
| **Selected Financial Statistics (Constant $, 1976 = 100)** | | | | | | | | | | |
| 21. Operating Income | 100.0 | 101.8 | 101.0 | 90.9 | 85.8 | 78.4 | 74.4 | 69.3 | 81.6 | 71.8 |
| 22. Payments to Partners | 100.0 | 93.0 | 79.2 | 64.7 | 61.9 | 55.5 | 43.3 | 36.6 | 31.9 | 76.9 |
| 23. Av. Payment, Partnership | 100.0 | 89.1 | 75.9 | 64.3 | 65.4 | 51.3 | 44.1 | 39.2 | 29.2 | 88.6 |
| 24. Av. Payment, Partner | 100.0 | 89.5 | 76.4 | 65.0 | 66.1 | 52.7 | 45.7 | 40.7 | 30.2 | 91.0 |

TABLE 3

111: GROCERY STORES, WITH AND WITHOUT NET INCOME

| | 1976 | 1977 | 1978 | 1979 | 1980 | 1981 | 1982 | 1983 | 1984 | 1985 |
|---|---|---|---|---|---|---|---|---|---|---|
| 1. Number of Partnerships | 14,687 | 15,180 | 14,666 | 14,530 | 13,101 | 12,995 | 11,898 | 10,952 | 11,674 | 11,299 |
| 2. Number of Partners | 33,351 | 33,732 | 32,753 | 32,090 | 28,980 | 28,769 | 25,911 | 24,568 | 25,461 | 24,175 |
| **Selected Financial Statistics (Items 3 to 9 inclusive in 000's of dollars)** | | | | | | | | | | |
| 3. Operating Income | 4,938,987 | 5,400,783 | 5,599,935 | 5,529,594 | 6,014,586 | 5,857,090 | 5,893,590 | 5,268,964 | 6,101,168 | 6,034,095 |
| 4. Depreciation | 36,744 | 43,501 | 46,079 | 47,168 | 54,437 | n.a. | n.a. | n.a. | 64,288 | 76,840 |
| 5. Taxes Paid | 66,543 | 73,471 | 73,801 | 79,158 | 76,598 | 66,957 | 65,598 | 61,716 | 63,421 | 72,874 |
| 6. Interest Paid | 18,527 | 22,016 | 26,427 | 27,744 | 35,786 | 41,254 | 45,117 | 36,612 | 37,757 | 42,461 |
| 7. Payroll Deductions | 295,140 | 321,694 | 326,315 | 309,682 | 394,888 | 351,000 | 369,746 | n.a. | 398,967 | 406,250 |
| 8. Payments to Partners | 49,282 | 41,821 | 37,590 | 35,785 | 38,281 | 38,042 | 33,382 | 25,190 | 26,383 | 35,025 |
| 9. Net Income, less Deficit | 176,995 | 210,642 | 216,560 | 222,331 | 222,257 | 167,953 | 149,437 | 172,428 | 143,159 | 156,579 |
| **Selected Average Financial Statistics (Items 10 to 13 inclusive in $)** | | | | | | | | | | |
| 10. Av. Payment Partnership | 3,355 | 2,755 | 2,563 | 2,463 | 2,922 | 2,927 | 2,806 | 2,300 | 2,260 | 3,100 |
| 11. Av. Payment Partner | 1,478 | 1,240 | 1,148 | 1,115 | 1,321 | 1,322 | 1,288 | 1,025 | 1,036 | 1,449 |
| 12. Av. Income Partnership | 12,051 | 13,876 | 14,766 | 15,302 | 16,965 | 12,924 | 12,560 | 15,744 | 12,263 | 13,858 |
| 13. Av. Income Partner | 5,307 | 6,245 | 6,612 | 6,928 | 7,669 | 5,838 | 5,767 | 7,018 | 5,623 | 6,477 |
| **Selected Financial Statistics as Percent of Op. Income** | | | | | | | | | | |
| 14. Depreciation / Op. Income (%) | 0.7 | 0.8 | 0.8 | 0.9 | 0.9 | n.a. | n.a. | n.a. | 1.1 | 1.3 |
| 15. Interest / Op. Income (%) | 0.4 | 0.4 | 0.5 | 0.5 | 0.6 | 0.7 | 0.8 | 0.7 | 0.6 | 0.7 |
| 16. Payroll / Op. Income (%) | 6.0 | 6.0 | 5.8 | 5.6 | 6.6 | 6.0 | 6.3 | n.a. | 6.5 | 6.7 |
| **Selected Index Numbers (1976 = 100)** | | | | | | | | | | |
| 17. Partnerships | 100.0 | 103.4 | 99.9 | 98.9 | 89.2 | 88.5 | 81.0 | 74.6 | 79.5 | 76.9 |
| 18. Partners | 100.0 | 101.1 | 98.2 | 96.2 | 86.9 | 86.3 | 77.7 | 73.7 | 76.3 | 72.5 |
| 19. Operating Income | 100.0 | 109.4 | 113.4 | 112.0 | 121.8 | 118.6 | 119.3 | 106.7 | 123.5 | 122.2 |
| 20. Payments to Partners | 100.0 | 84.9 | 76.3 | 72.6 | 77.7 | 77.2 | 67.7 | 51.1 | 53.5 | 71.1 |
| **Selected Financial Statistics (Constant $, 1976 = 100)** | | | | | | | | | | |
| 21. Operating Income | 100.0 | 102.7 | 98.9 | 87.8 | 84.1 | 74.2 | 70.4 | 61.0 | 67.7 | 64.7 |
| 22. Payments to Partners | 100.0 | 79.7 | 66.6 | 56.9 | 53.7 | 48.3 | 39.9 | 29.2 | 29.3 | 37.6 |
| 23. Av. Payment, Partnership | 100.0 | 77.1 | 66.7 | 57.6 | 60.2 | 54.6 | 49.3 | 39.2 | 36.9 | 48.9 |
| 24. Av. Payment, Partner | 100.0 | 78.8 | 67.8 | 59.2 | 61.7 | 56.0 | 51.5 | 39.6 | 38.4 | 51.9 |

TABLE 3

OTHER FOOD STORES (112,113,114,115,116,117), WITH AND WITHOUT NET INCOME

| | 1976 | 1977 | 1978 | 1979 | 1980 | 1981 | 1982 | 1983 | 1984 | 1985 |
|---|---|---|---|---|---|---|---|---|---|---|
| 1. Number of Partnerships | 6,997 | 7,447 | 7,945 | 7,277 | 7,433 | 10,466 | 9,389 | 9,261 | 11,982 | 7,503 |
| 2. Number of Partners | 15,613 | 17,201 | 18,026 | 16,614 | 16,859 | 22,781 | 20,590 | 19,473 | 26,327 | 17,152 |
| **Selected Financial Statistics** (Items 3 to 9 inclusive in 000's of dollars) | | | | | | | | | | |
| 3. Operating Income | 973,654 | 1,008,282 | 1,242,789 | 1,324,716 | 1,327,144 | 1,549,173 | 1,566,547 | 1,898,701 | 2,701,049 | 1,983,658 |
| 4. Depreciation | 15,273 | 17,495 | 16,357 | 20,363 | 24,635 | n.a. | n.a. | n.a. | 42,064 | 33,319 |
| 5. Taxes Paid | 17,772 | 15,943 | 19,793 | 20,269 | 20,100 | 20,536 | 22,504 | 26,525 | 40,165 | 29,586 |
| 6. Interest Paid | 6,442 | 5,699 | 7,304 | 10,156 | 16,832 | 16,899 | 17,464 | 12,911 | 16,879 | 17,544 |
| 7. Payroll Deductions | 97,364 | 91,066 | 101,644 | 113,540 | 107,494 | 101,201 | 122,846 | n.a. | 219,312 | 178,741 |
| 8. Payments to Partners | 17,413 | 24,220 | 22,943 | 19,200 | 21,476 | 21,118 | 15,612 | 17,507 | 12,415 | 61,854 |
| 9. Net Income, less Deficit | 62,674 | 55,191 | 75,366 | 51,676 | 60,398 | 65,899 | 91,020 | 133,261 | 130,871 | 32,833 |
| **Selected Average Financial Statistics** (Items 10 to 13 inclusive in $) | | | | | | | | | | |
| 10. Av. Payment Partnership | 2,489 | 3,252 | 2,888 | 2,638 | 2,889 | 2,018 | 1,663 | 1,890 | 1,036 | 8,244 |
| 11. Av. Payment Partner | 1,115 | 1,408 | 1,273 | 1,156 | 1,274 | 927 | 758 | 899 | 472 | 3,606 |
| 12. Av. Income Partnership | 8,957 | 7,411 | 9,486 | 7,101 | 8,126 | 6,296 | 9,694 | 14,389 | 10,922 | 4,376 |
| 13. Av. Income Partner | 4,014 | 3,209 | 4,181 | 3,110 | 3,583 | 2,893 | 4,421 | 6,843 | 4,971 | 1,914 |
| **Selected Financial Statistics as Percent of Op. Income** | | | | | | | | | | |
| 14. Depreciation / Op. Income (%) | 1.6 | 1.7 | 1.3 | 1.5 | 1.9 | n.a. | n.a. | n.a. | 1.6 | 1.7 |
| 15. Interest / Op. Income (%) | 0.7 | 0.6 | 0.6 | 0.8 | 1.3 | 1.1 | 1.1 | 0.7 | 0.6 | 0.9 |
| 16. Payroll / Op. Income (%) | 10.0 | 9.0 | 8.2 | 8.6 | 8.1 | 6.5 | 7.8 | n.a. | 8.1 | 9.0 |
| **Selected Index Numbers (1976 = 100)** | | | | | | | | | | |
| 17. Partnerships | 100.0 | 106.4 | 113.5 | 104.0 | 106.2 | 149.6 | 134.2 | 132.4 | 171.2 | 107.2 |
| 18. Partners | 100.0 | 110.2 | 115.5 | 106.4 | 108.0 | 145.9 | 131.9 | 124.7 | 168.6 | 109.9 |
| 19. Operating Income | 100.0 | 103.6 | 127.6 | 136.1 | 136.3 | 159.1 | 160.9 | 195.0 | 277.4 | 203.7 |
| 20. Payments to Partners | 100.0 | 139.1 | 131.8 | 110.3 | 123.3 | 121.3 | 89.7 | 100.5 | 71.3 | 355.2 |
| **Selected Financial Statistics (Constant $, 1976 = 100)** | | | | | | | | | | |
| 21. Operating Income | 100.0 | 97.3 | 111.4 | 106.7 | 94.2 | 99.6 | 94.9 | 111.4 | 152.0 | 107.8 |
| 22. Payments to Partners | 100.0 | 130.7 | 115.0 | 86.5 | 85.2 | 75.9 | 52.9 | 57.4 | 39.1 | 188.0 |
| 23. Av. Payment, Partnership | 100.0 | 122.8 | 101.3 | 83.1 | 80.2 | 50.8 | 39.4 | 43.4 | 22.8 | 175.3 |
| 24. Av. Payment, Partner | 100.0 | 118.6 | 99.5 | 81.3 | 78.9 | 52.0 | 40.1 | 46.0 | 23.2 | 171.1 |

## TABLE 3

## 118: AUTOMOTIVE DEALERS AND SERVICE STATIONS, WITH AND WITHOUT NET INCOME

| | 1976 | 1977 | 1978 | 1979 | 1980 | 1981 | 1982 | 1983 | 1984 | 1985 |
|---|---|---|---|---|---|---|---|---|---|---|
| 1. Number of Partnerships | 26,080 | 26,788 | 25,386 | 23,704 | 22,442 | 23,474 | 21,260 | 18,666 | 14,080 | 17,305 |
| 2. Number of Partners | 58,470 | 58,435 | 58,796 | 53,250 | 50,476 | 54,812 | 51,499 | 43,369 | 33,155 | 41,192 |
| **Selected Financial Statistics** | | | | | | | | | | |
| (Items 3 to 9 inclusive in 000's of dollars) | | | | | | | | | | |
| 3. Operating Income | 7,875,019 | 8,539,440 | 9,256,873 | 10,029,557 | 9,970,095 | 10,118,265 | 9,918,525 | 11,984,812 | 11,451,086 | 10,456,608 |
| 4. Depreciation | 54,664 | 61,033 | 65,657 | 75,222 | 67,107 | n.a. | n.a. | n.a. | 128,500 | 88,745 |
| 5. Taxes Paid | 109,932 | 121,677 | 124,454 | 143,570 | 121,435 | 100,933 | 93,995 | 102,680 | 93,558 | 103,247 |
| 6. Interest Paid | 50,910 | 62,575 | 72,818 | 87,921 | 88,799 | 104,934 | 92,153 | 81,984 | 108,165 | 90,661 |
| 7. Payroll Deductions | 430,373 | 429,903 | 444,690 | 485,928 | 457,344 | 450,223 | 442,106 | n.a. | 545,153 | 512,741 |
| 8. Payments to Partners | 81,521 | 89,978 | 99,918 | 99,809 | 95,145 | 86,490 | 95,064 | 129,422 | 132,512 | 131,373 |
| 9. Net Income, less Deficit | 347,800 | 371,014 | 360,483 | 421,102 | 272,703 | 191,562 | 189,940 | 265,897 | 251,547 | 275,483 |
| **Selected Average Financial Statistics** | | | | | | | | | | |
| (Items 10 to 13 inclusive in $) | | | | | | | | | | |
| 10. Av. Payment Partnership | 3,126 | 3,359 | 3,936 | 4,211 | 4,240 | 3,685 | 4,471 | 6,934 | 9,411 | 7,592 |
| 11. Av. Payment Partner | 1,394 | 1,540 | 1,699 | 1,874 | 1,885 | 1,578 | 1,846 | 2,984 | 3,997 | 3,189 |
| 12. Av. Income Partnership | 13,336 | 13,850 | 14,200 | 17,765 | 12,151 | 8,161 | 8,934 | 14,245 | 17,866 | 15,919 |
| 13. Av. Income Partner | 5,948 | 6,349 | 6,131 | 7,908 | 5,403 | 3,495 | 3,688 | 6,131 | 7,587 | 6,688 |
| **Selected Financial Statistics as Percent of Op. Income** | | | | | | | | | | |
| 14. Depreciation / Op. Income (%) | 0.7 | 0.7 | 0.7 | 0.8 | 0.7 | n.a. | n.a. | n.a. | 1.1 | 0.9 |
| 15. Interest / Op. Income (%) | 0.7 | 0.7 | 0.8 | 0.9 | 0.9 | 1.0 | 0.9 | 0.7 | 0.9 | 0.9 |
| 16. Payroll / Op. Income (%) | 5.5 | 5.0 | 4.8 | 4.8 | 4.6 | 4.5 | 4.5 | n.a. | 4.8 | 4.9 |
| **Selected Index Numbers (1976 = 100)** | | | | | | | | | | |
| 17. Partnerships | 100.0 | 102.7 | 97.3 | 90.9 | 86.1 | 90.0 | 81.5 | 71.6 | 54.0 | 66.4 |
| 18. Partners | 100.0 | 99.9 | 100.6 | 91.1 | 86.3 | 93.7 | 88.1 | 74.2 | 56.7 | 70.4 |
| 19. Operating Income | 100.0 | 108.4 | 117.5 | 127.4 | 126.6 | 128.5 | 125.9 | 152.2 | 145.4 | 132.8 |
| 20. Payments to Partners | 100.0 | 110.4 | 122.6 | 122.4 | 116.7 | 106.1 | 116.6 | 158.8 | 162.5 | 161.2 |
| **Selected Financial Statistics (Constant $, 1976 = 100)** | | | | | | | | | | |
| 21. Operating Income | 100.0 | 101.9 | 102.6 | 99.9 | 87.5 | 80.4 | 74.3 | 87.0 | 79.7 | 70.3 |
| 22. Payments to Partners | 100.0 | 103.7 | 106.9 | 96.0 | 80.6 | 66.4 | 68.8 | 90.7 | 89.1 | 85.3 |
| 23. Av. Payment, Partnership | 100.0 | 101.0 | 109.9 | 105.7 | 93.7 | 73.8 | 84.4 | 126.8 | 165.0 | 128.5 |
| 24. Av. Payment, Partner | 100.0 | 103.7 | 106.3 | 105.4 | 93.4 | 70.8 | 78.1 | 122.3 | 157.1 | 121.1 |

TABLE 3

MOTOR VEHICLE DEALERS (119,120), WITH AND WITHOUT NET INCOME

| | 1976 | 1977 | 1978 | 1979 | 1980 | 1981 | 1982 | 1983 | 1984 | 1985 |
|---|---|---|---|---|---|---|---|---|---|---|
| 1. Number of Partnerships | 5,920 | 6,227 | 6,452 | 4,892 | 4,451 | 4,281 | 5,014 | 3,120 | 3,982 | 4,920 |
| 2. Number of Partners | 13,067 | 13,582 | 14,019 | 10,779 | 9,721 | 12,362 | 15,690 | 7,176 | 8,964 | 12,256 |
| **Selected Financial Statistics** (Items 3 to 9 inclusive in 000's of dollars) | | | | | | | | | | |
| 3. Operating Income | 3,376,782 | 3,591,835 | 3,725,894 | 3,234,485 | 2,757,055 | 2,673,451 | 2,742,009 | 2,581,889 | 3,227,087 | 3,756,262 |
| 4. Depreciation | 17,658 | 17,118 | 18,599 | 22,896 | 16,182 | n.a. | n.a. | n.a. | 16,190 | 19,775 |
| 5. Taxes Paid | 26,327 | 31,256 | 28,126 | 24,078 | 20,047 | 19,397 | 17,573 | 16,441 | 20,721 | 26,214 |
| 6. Interest Paid | 29,195 | 31,963 | 37,769 | 48,517 | 44,458 | 46,478 | 45,476 | 22,138 | 34,892 | 34,654 |
| 7. Payroll Deductions | 159,792 | 167,125 | 157,398 | 150,480 | 137,815 | 151,204 | 142,801 | n.a. | 155,024 | 165,682 |
| 8. Payments to Partners | 24,176 | 26,568 | 26,016 | 27,525 | 29,034 | 15,151 | 16,277 | 13,877 | 25,372 | 24,487 |
| 9. Net Income, less Deficit | 104,287 | 109,549 | 109,276 | 77,793 | 36,662 | 53,349 | 48,313 | 72,158 | 117,925 | 126,703 |
| **Selected Average Financial Statistics** (Items 10 to 13 inclusive in $) | | | | | | | | | | |
| 10. Av. Payment Partnership | 4,084 | 4,267 | 4,032 | 5,627 | 6,523 | 3,539 | 3,246 | 4,448 | 6,372 | 4,977 |
| 11. Av. Payment Partner | 1,850 | 1,956 | 1,856 | 2,554 | 2,987 | 1,226 | 1,037 | 1,934 | 2,830 | 1,998 |
| 12. Av. Income Partnership | 17,616 | 17,593 | 16,937 | 15,902 | 8,237 | 12,462 | 9,636 | 23,128 | 29,615 | 25,753 |
| 13. Av. Income Partner | 7,981 | 8,066 | 7,795 | 7,217 | 3,771 | 4,316 | 3,079 | 10,055 | 13,155 | 10,338 |
| **Selected Financial Statistics as Percent of Op. Income** | | | | | | | | | | |
| 14. Depreciation / Op. Income (%) | 0.5 | 0.5 | 0.5 | 0.7 | 0.6 | n.a. | n.a. | n.a. | 0.5 | 0.5 |
| 15. Interest / Op. Income (%) | 0.9 | 0.9 | 1.0 | 1.5 | 1.6 | 1.7 | 1.7 | 0.9 | 1.1 | 0.9 |
| 16. Payroll / Op. Income (%) | 4.7 | 4.7 | 4.2 | 4.7 | 5.0 | 5.7 | 5.2 | n.a. | 4.8 | 4.4 |
| **Selected Index Numbers** (1976 = 100) | | | | | | | | | | |
| 17. Partnerships | 100.0 | 105.2 | 109.0 | 82.6 | 75.2 | 72.3 | 84.7 | 52.7 | 67.3 | 83.1 |
| 18. Partners | 100.0 | 103.9 | 107.3 | 82.5 | 74.4 | 94.6 | 120.1 | 54.9 | 68.6 | 93.8 |
| 19. Operating Income | 100.0 | 106.4 | 110.3 | 95.8 | 81.6 | 79.2 | 81.2 | 76.5 | 95.6 | 111.2 |
| 20. Payments to Partners | 100.0 | 109.9 | 107.6 | 113.9 | 120.1 | 62.7 | 67.3 | 57.4 | 104.9 | 101.3 |
| **Selected Financial Statistics** (Constant $, 1976 = 100) | | | | | | | | | | |
| 21. Operating Income | 100.0 | 99.9 | 96.3 | 75.1 | 56.4 | 49.6 | 47.9 | 43.7 | 52.4 | 58.9 |
| 22. Payments to Partners | 100.0 | 103.2 | 93.9 | 89.3 | 83.0 | 39.2 | 39.7 | 32.8 | 57.5 | 53.6 |
| 23. Av. Payment, Partnership | 100.0 | 98.2 | 86.1 | 108.1 | 110.3 | 54.2 | 46.9 | 62.2 | 85.5 | 64.5 |
| 24. Av. Payment, Partner | 100.0 | 99.3 | 87.5 | 108.3 | 111.5 | 41.5 | 33.1 | 59.7 | 83.9 | 57.1 |

*Page 237*

TABLE 3

122:  GASOLINE SERVICE STATIONS, WITH AND WITHOUT NET INCOME

| | 1976 | 1977 | 1978 | 1979 | 1980 | 1981 | 1982 | 1983 | 1984 | 1985 |
|---|---|---|---|---|---|---|---|---|---|---|
| 1. Number of Partnerships | 13,507 | 13,979 | 11,929 | 11,779 | 11,569 | 12,377 | 10,313 | 9,281 | 6,059 | 6,486 |
| 2. Number of Partners | 30,171 | 30,470 | 29,090 | 26,929 | 26,437 | 27,944 | 22,562 | 20,980 | 13,525 | 14,193 |
| **Selected Financial Statistics** | | | | | | | | | | |
| (Items 3 to 9 inclusive in 000's of dollars) | | | | | | | | | | |
| 3. Operating Income | 3,351,918 | 3,847,109 | 4,077,869 | 5,318,260 | 5,946,756 | 6,027,901 | 5,755,643 | 7,560,812 | 6,418,584 | 5,067,053 |
| 4. Depreciation | 24,101 | 29,216 | 30,465 | 32,781 | 35,382 | n.a. | n.a. | n.a. | 51,276 | 48,650 |
| 5. Taxes Paid | 64,074 | 68,572 | 72,711 | 91,851 | 81,492 | 61,099 | 59,367 | 64,769 | 52,897 | 54,851 |
| 6. Interest Paid | 8,928 | 13,623 | 15,024 | 17,849 | 22,573 | 27,837 | 24,296 | 39,648 | 39,451 | 25,485 |
| 7. Payroll Deductions | 183,670 | 176,573 | 198,627 | 225,192 | 210,723 | 190,662 | 187,610 | n.a. | 206,276 | 181,493 |
| 8. Payments to Partners | 37,867 | 42,318 | 42,282 | 44,692 | 42,017 | 41,672 | 38,836 | 56,115 | 50,037 | 40,457 |
| 9. Net Income, less Deficit | 160,600 | 202,297 | 173,679 | 274,219 | 206,741 | 78,116 | 131,046 | 107,936 | 78,974 | 122,815 |
| **Selected Average Financial Statistics** | | | | | | | | | | |
| (Items 10 to 13 inclusive in $) | | | | | | | | | | |
| 10. Av. Payment Partnership | 2,804 | 3,027 | 3,544 | 3,794 | 3,632 | 3,367 | 3,766 | 6,046 | 8,258 | 6,238 |
| 11. Av. Payment Partner | 1,255 | 1,389 | 1,453 | 1,660 | 1,589 | 1,491 | 1,721 | 2,675 | 3,700 | 2,850 |
| 12. Av. Income Partnership | 11,890 | 14,471 | 14,559 | 23,280 | 17,870 | 6,311 | 12,707 | 11,630 | 13,034 | 18,935 |
| 13. Av. Income Partner | 5,323 | 6,639 | 5,970 | 10,183 | 7,820 | 2,795 | 5,808 | 5,145 | 5,839 | 8,653 |
| **Selected Financial Statistics as Percent of Op. Income** | | | | | | | | | | |
| 14. Depreciation / Op. Income (%) | 0.7 | 0.8 | 0.8 | 0.6 | 0.6 | n.a. | n.a. | n.a. | 0.8 | 0.10 |
| 15. Interest / Op. Income (%) | 0.3 | 0.4 | 0.4 | 0.3 | 0.4 | 0.5 | 0.4 | 0.5 | 0.6 | 0.5 |
| 16. Payroll / Op. Income (%) | 5.5 | 4.6 | 4.9 | 4.2 | 3.5 | 3.2 | 3.3 | n.a. | 3.2 | 3.6 |
| **Selected Index Numbers (1976 = 100)** | | | | | | | | | | |
| 17. Partnerships | 100.0 | 103.5 | 88.3 | 87.2 | 85.7 | 91.6 | 76.4 | 68.7 | 44.9 | 48.0 |
| 18. Partners | 100.0 | 101.0 | 96.4 | 89.3 | 87.6 | 92.6 | 74.8 | 69.5 | 44.8 | 47.0 |
| 19. Operating Income | 100.0 | 114.8 | 121.7 | 158.7 | 177.4 | 179.8 | 171.7 | 225.6 | 191.5 | 151.2 |
| 20. Payments to Partners | 100.0 | 111.8 | 111.7 | 118.0 | 111.0 | 110.0 | 102.6 | 148.2 | 132.1 | 106.8 |
| **Selected Financial Statistics (Constant $, 1976 = 100)** | | | | | | | | | | |
| 21. Operating Income | 100.0 | 107.8 | 106.2 | 124.4 | 122.6 | 112.6 | 101.3 | 128.9 | 104.9 | 80.0 |
| 22. Payments to Partners | 100.0 | 105.0 | 97.4 | 92.6 | 76.7 | 68.9 | 60.5 | 84.7 | 72.4 | 56.5 |
| 23. Av. Payment, Partnership | 100.0 | 101.4 | 110.3 | 106.1 | 89.5 | 75.2 | 79.2 | 123.2 | 161.4 | 117.7 |
| 24. Av. Payment, Partner | 100.0 | 103.9 | 101.1 | 103.8 | 87.5 | 74.3 | 80.8 | 121.7 | 161.5 | 120.2 |

TABLE 3

OTHER AUTOMOTIVE DEALERS (121,123,124,125,126), WITH AND WITHOUT NET INCOME

| | 1976 | 1977 | 1978 | 1979 | 1980 | 1981 | 1982 | 1983 | 1984 | 1985 |
|---|---|---|---|---|---|---|---|---|---|---|
| 1. Number of Partnerships | 6,653 | 6,582 | 7,005 | 7,033 | 6,422 | 6,817 | 5,933 | 6,265 | 4,068 | 5,899 |
| 2. Number of Partners | 15,232 | 14,383 | 15,687 | 15,542 | 14,317 | 14,508 | 13,248 | 15,214 | 10,667 | 14,744 |
| **Selected Financial Statistics** (Items 3 to 9 inclusive in 000's of dollars) | | | | | | | | | | |
| 3. Operating Income | 1,146,319 | 1,100,496 | 1,453,110 | 1,476,813 | 1,266,273 | 1,416,913 | 1,420,874 | 1,842,112 | 1,805,415 | 1,633,293 |
| 4. Depreciation | 12,905 | 14,699 | 16,592 | 19,545 | 18,405 | n.a. | n.a. | n.a. | 61,032 | 20,320 |
| 5. Taxes Paid | 19,531 | 21,849 | 23,617 | 27,641 | 17,278 | 20,437 | 17,056 | 21,470 | 19,940 | 22,182 |
| 6. Interest Paid | 12,787 | 16,989 | 20,024 | 21,554 | 96,631 | 30,619 | 22,382 | 20,199 | 33,822 | 30,521 |
| 7. Payroll Deductions | 86,911 | 86,205 | 88,665 | 112,256 | 43,034 | 108,357 | 111,694 | n.a. | 183,851 | 165,566 |
| 8. Payments to Partners | 19,478 | 21,092 | 31,620 | 27,592 | 24,095 | 29,667 | 39,951 | 59,430 | 4,068 | 66,429 |
| 9. Net Income, less Deficit | 82,913 | 59,168 | 77,528 | 69,090 | 47,377 | 67,651 | 26,191 | 85,802 | 54,647 | 25,964 |
| **Selected Average Financial Statistics** (Items 10 to 13 inclusive in $) | | | | | | | | | | |
| 10. Av. Payment Partnership | 2,928 | 3,204 | 4,514 | 3,923 | 3,752 | 4,352 | 6,734 | 9,486 | 1,000 | 11,261 |
| 11. Av. Payment Partner | 1,279 | 1,466 | 2,016 | 1,775 | 1,683 | 2,045 | 3,016 | 3,906 | 381 | 4,505 |
| 12. Av. Income Partnership | 12,462 | 8,989 | 11,068 | 9,824 | 7,377 | 9,924 | 4,414 | 13,695 | 13,433 | 4,401 |
| 13. Av. Income Partner | 5,443 | 4,114 | 4,942 | 4,445 | 3,309 | 4,663 | 1,977 | 5,640 | 5,123 | 1,761 |
| **Selected Financial Statistics as Percent of Op. Income** | | | | | | | | | | |
| 14. Depreciation / Op. Income (%) | 1.1 | 1.3 | 1.1 | 1.3 | 1.5 | n.a. | n.a. | n.a. | 3.4 | 1.2 |
| 15. Interest / Op. Income (%) | 1.1 | 1.5 | 1.4 | 1.5 | 7.6 | 2.2 | 1.6 | 1.1 | 1.9 | 1.9 |
| 16. Payroll / Op. Income (%) | 7.6 | 7.8 | 6.1 | 7.6 | 3.4 | 7.7 | 7.9 | n.a. | 10.2 | 10.1 |
| **Selected Index Numbers** (1976 = 100) | | | | | | | | | | |
| 17. Partnerships | 100.0 | 98.9 | 105.3 | 105.7 | 96.5 | 102.5 | 89.2 | 94.2 | 61.1 | 88.7 |
| 18. Partners | 100.0 | 94.4 | 103.0 | 102.0 | 94.0 | 95.2 | 87.0 | 99.9 | 70.0 | 96.8 |
| 19. Operating Income | 100.0 | 96.0 | 126.8 | 128.8 | 110.5 | 123.6 | 124.0 | 160.7 | 157.5 | 142.5 |
| 20. Payments to Partners | 100.0 | 108.3 | 162.3 | 141.7 | 123.7 | 152.3 | 205.1 | 305.1 | 20.9 | 341.0 |
| **Selected Financial Statistics** (Constant $, 1976 = 100) | | | | | | | | | | |
| 21. Operating Income | 100.0 | 90.2 | 110.6 | 101.0 | 76.3 | 77.4 | 73.1 | 91.8 | 86.3 | 75.4 |
| 22. Payments to Partners | 100.0 | 101.7 | 141.7 | 111.1 | 85.5 | 95.3 | 121.0 | 174.3 | 11.4 | 180.5 |
| 23. Av. Payment, Partnership | 100.0 | 102.8 | 134.5 | 105.1 | 88.5 | 93.1 | 135.6 | 185.1 | 18.7 | 203.5 |
| 24. Av. Payment, Partner | 100.0 | 107.7 | 137.6 | 108.8 | 90.9 | 100.1 | 139.1 | 174.5 | 16.3 | 186.4 |

TABLE 3

127: APPAREL AND ACCESSORY STORES, WITH AND WITHOUT NET INCOME

| | 1976 | 1977 | 1978 | 1979 | 1980 | 1981 | 1982 | 1983 | 1984 | 1985 |
|---|---|---|---|---|---|---|---|---|---|---|
| 1. Number of Partnerships | 11,663 | 12,314 | 12,148 | 14,064 | 14,606 | 16,438 | 20,236 | 16,225 | 12,268 | 12,575 |
| 2. Number of Partners | 28,504 | 30,321 | 28,295 | 31,237 | 32,319 | 36,476 | 45,578 | 39,170 | 29,319 | 29,381 |
| **Selected Financial Statistics** (Items 3 to 9 inclusive in 000's of dollars) | | | | | | | | | | |
| 3. Operating Income | 1,456,942 | 1,533,296 | 1,593,498 | 1,808,224 | 1,831,703 | 1,793,717 | 2,022,570 | 3,186,589 | 1,739,302 | 1,749,204 |
| 4. Depreciation | 14,746 | 14,293 | 15,970 | 21,598 | 22,856 | n.a. | n.a. | n.a. | 71,091 | 28,323 |
| 5. Taxes Paid | 29,703 | 29,587 | 32,505 | 34,514 | 36,449 | 28,477 | 41,381 | 130,970 | 38,195 | 47,145 |
| 6. Interest Paid | 14,676 | 10,755 | 15,207 | 18,064 | 25,455 | 25,687 | 28,749 | 18,799 | 17,184 | 16,089 |
| 7. Payroll Deductions | 142,810 | 141,306 | 149,830 | 177,063 | 175,565 | 161,126 | 180,928 | n.a. | 173,148 | 157,004 |
| 8. Payments to Partners | 36,734 | 34,531 | 38,918 | 43,708 | 54,872 | 33,686 | 45,436 | 61,908 | 32,614 | 47,744 |
| 9. Net Income, less Deficit | 108,924 | 130,686 | 133,975 | 115,424 | 63,234 | 82,010 | 76,364 | 100,556 | 7,365 | 46,837 |
| **Selected Average Financial Statistics** (Items 10 to 13 inclusive in $) | | | | | | | | | | |
| 10. Av. Payment Partnership | 3,150 | 2,804 | 3,204 | 3,108 | 3,757 | 2,049 | 2,245 | 3,816 | 2,658 | 3,797 |
| 11. Av. Payment Partner | 1,289 | 1,139 | 1,375 | 1,399 | 1,698 | 924 | 997 | 1,580 | 1,112 | 1,625 |
| 12. Av. Income Partnership | 9,339 | 10,613 | 11,029 | 8,207 | 4,329 | 4,989 | 3,774 | 6,198 | 600 | 3,725 |
| 13. Av. Income Partner | 3,821 | 4,310 | 4,735 | 3,695 | 1,957 | 2,248 | 1,675 | 2,567 | 251 | 1,594 |
| **Selected Financial Statistics as Percent of Op. Income** | | | | | | | | | | |
| 14. Depreciation / Op. Income (%) | 1.0 | 0.9 | 1.0 | 1.2 | 1.3 | n.a. | n.a. | n.a. | 4.1 | 1.6 |
| 15. Interest / Op. Income (%) | 1.0 | 0.7 | 0.10 | 1.0 | 1.4 | 1.4 | 1.4 | 0.6 | 0.10 | 0.9 |
| 16. Payroll / Op. Income (%) | 9.8 | 9.2 | 9.4 | 9.8 | 9.6 | 9.0 | 9.0 | n.a. | 1.0 | 9.0 |
| **Selected Index Numbers** (1976 = 100) | | | | | | | | | | |
| 17. Partnerships | 100.0 | 105.6 | 104.2 | 120.6 | 125.2 | 140.9 | 173.5 | 139.1 | 105.2 | 107.8 |
| 18. Partners | 100.0 | 106.4 | 99.3 | 109.6 | 113.4 | 128.0 | 159.9 | 137.4 | 102.9 | 103.1 |
| 19. Operating Income | 100.0 | 105.2 | 109.4 | 124.1 | 125.7 | 123.1 | 138.8 | 218.7 | 119.4 | 120.1 |
| 20. Payments to Partners | 100.0 | 94.0 | 105.9 | 119.0 | 149.4 | 91.7 | 123.7 | 168.5 | 88.8 | 130.0 |
| **Selected Financial Statistics** (Constant $, 1976 = 100) | | | | | | | | | | |
| 21. Operating Income | 100.0 | 98.9 | 95.4 | 97.3 | 86.9 | 77.1 | 81.9 | 125.0 | 65.4 | 63.5 |
| 22. Payments to Partners | 100.0 | 88.3 | 92.4 | 93.3 | 103.2 | 57.4 | 72.9 | 96.3 | 48.7 | 68.8 |
| 23. Av. Payment, Partnership | 100.0 | 83.6 | 88.8 | 77.4 | 82.4 | 40.7 | 42.1 | 69.2 | 46.2 | 63.8 |
| 24. Av. Payment, Partner | 100.0 | 83.1 | 93.1 | 85.2 | 91.0 | 44.8 | 45.6 | 70.0 | 47.2 | 66.7 |

# TABLE 3

## 136: FURNITURE AND HOME FURNISHINGS STORES, WITH AND WITHOUT NET INCOME

| | 1976 | 1977 | 1978 | 1979 | 1980 | 1981 | 1982 | 1983 | 1984 | 1985 |
|---|---|---|---|---|---|---|---|---|---|---|
| 1. Number of Partnerships | 11,138 | 12,320 | 12,364 | 12,409 | 12,013 | 11,414 | 9,626 | 7,807 | 10,056 | 10,807 |
| 2. Number of Partners | 26,732 | 27,815 | 28,678 | 29,236 | 27,746 | 26,232 | 20,076 | 18,588 | 21,925 | 25,531 |
| **Selected Financial Statistics** | | | | | | | | | | |
| (Items 3 to 9 inclusive in 000's of dollars) | | | | | | | | | | |
| 3. Operating Income | 1,831,725 | 1,898,697 | 2,017,535 | 2,327,190 | 1,899,710 | 1,907,479 | 1,654,634 | 1,420,333 | 2,096,662 | 2,491,062 |
| 4. Depreciation | 17,724 | 21,728 | 31,968 | 29,791 | 23,078 | n.a. | n.a. | n.a. | 24,508 | 34,520 |
| 5. Taxes Paid | 33,727 | 36,563 | 38,711 | 47,249 | 36,250 | 35,340 | 28,717 | 24,829 | 30,237 | 39,247 |
| 6. Interest Paid | 13,314 | 16,803 | 21,638 | 26,618 | 23,926 | 25,357 | 24,129 | 18,171 | 22,505 | 28,846 |
| 7. Payroll Deductions | 157,887 | 157,107 | 205,965 | 259,961 | 173,870 | 182,036 | 146,296 | n.a. | 159,113 | 197,274 |
| 8. Payments to Partners | 42,623 | 35,921 | 45,769 | 61,892 | 49,014 | 72,065 | 36,043 | 25,624 | 25,038 | 50,161 |
| 9. Net Income, less Deficit | 130,347 | 161,746 | 166,838 | 145,062 | 147,056 | 69,287 | 144,679 | 124,519 | 151,633 | 172,942 |
| **Selected Average Financial Statistics** | | | | | | | | | | |
| (Items 10 to 13 inclusive in $) | | | | | | | | | | |
| 10. Av. Payment Partnership | 3,827 | 2,916 | 3,702 | 4,988 | 4,080 | 6,314 | 3,744 | 3,282 | 2,490 | 4,642 |
| 11. Av. Payment Partner | 1,594 | 1,291 | 1,596 | 2,117 | 1,767 | 2,747 | 1,795 | 1,379 | 1,142 | 1,965 |
| 12. Av. Income Partnership | 11,703 | 13,129 | 13,494 | 11,690 | 12,241 | 6,070 | 15,030 | 15,950 | 15,079 | 16,003 |
| 13. Av. Income Partner | 4,876 | 5,815 | 5,818 | 4,962 | 5,300 | 2,641 | 7,207 | 6,699 | 6,916 | 6,774 |
| **Selected Financial Statistics as Percent of Op. Income** | | | | | | | | | | |
| 14. Depreciation / Op. Income (%) | 0.10 | 1.1 | 1.6 | 1.3 | 1.2 | n.a. | n.a. | n.a. | 1.2 | 1.4 |
| 15. Interest / Op. Income (%) | 0.7 | 0.9 | 1.1 | 1.1 | 1.3 | 1.3 | 1.5 | 1.3 | 1.1 | 1.2 |
| 16. Payroll / Op. Income (%) | 8.6 | 8.3 | 10.2 | 11.2 | 9.2 | 9.5 | 8.8 | n.a. | 7.6 | 7.9 |
| **Selected Index Numbers (1976 = 100)** | | | | | | | | | | |
| 17. Partnerships | 100.0 | 110.6 | 111.0 | 111.4 | 107.9 | 102.5 | 86.4 | 70.1 | 90.3 | 97.0 |
| 18. Partners | 100.0 | 104.1 | 107.3 | 109.4 | 103.8 | 98.1 | 75.1 | 69.5 | 82.0 | 95.5 |
| 19. Operating Income | 100.0 | 103.7 | 110.1 | 127.0 | 103.7 | 104.1 | 90.3 | 77.5 | 114.5 | 136.0 |
| 20. Payments to Partners | 100.0 | 84.3 | 107.4 | 145.2 | 115.0 | 169.1 | 84.6 | 60.1 | 58.7 | 117.7 |
| **Selected Financial Statistics (Constant $, 1976 = 100)** | | | | | | | | | | |
| 21. Operating Income | 100.0 | 97.4 | 96.1 | 99.6 | 71.6 | 65.2 | 53.3 | 44.3 | 62.7 | 72.0 |
| 22. Payments to Partners | 100.0 | 79.2 | 93.7 | 113.9 | 79.4 | 105.8 | 49.9 | 34.4 | 32.2 | 62.3 |
| 23. Av. Payment, Partnership | 100.0 | 71.6 | 84.4 | 102.2 | 73.6 | 103.3 | 57.7 | 49.0 | 35.6 | 64.2 |
| 24. Av. Payment, Partner | 100.0 | 76.0 | 87.4 | 104.2 | 76.6 | 107.8 | 66.4 | 49.4 | 39.2 | 65.2 |

TABLE 3

## 145: EATING PLACES, WITH AND WITHOUT NET INCOME

| | 1976 | 1977 | 1978 | 1979 | 1980 | 1981 | 1982 | 1983 | 1984 | 1985 |
|---|---|---|---|---|---|---|---|---|---|---|
| 1. Number of Partnerships | 23,829 | 24,504 | 28,031 | 29,295 | 29,056 | 28,502 | 28,692 | 33,080 | 31,539 | 32,787 |
| 2. Number of Partners | 67,025 | 106,467 | 77,412 | 78,421 | 77,387 | 82,369 | 82,278 | 94,556 | 88,894 | 92,362 |
| **Selected Financial Statistics** (Items 3 to 9 inclusive in 000's of dollars) | | | | | | | | | | |
| 3. Operating Income | 3,653,341 | 4,011,934 | 5,140,585 | 5,855,760 | 6,073,396 | 6,622,192 | 6,791,809 | 7,390,186 | 8,297,935 | 8,753,696 |
| 4. Depreciation | 85,165 | 96,401 | 130,494 | 154,777 | 175,626 | n.a. | n.a. | n.a. | 289,984 | 315,332 |
| 5. Taxes Paid | 138,860 | 155,077 | 200,292 | 224,758 | 236,134 | 223,428 | 237,008 | 246,588 | 271,087 | 295,912 |
| 6. Interest Paid | 37,294 | 51,856 | 72,405 | 90,930 | 101,013 | 114,220 | 115,837 | 127,501 | 168,247 | 146,084 |
| 7. Payroll Deductions | 775,499 | 845,617 | 1,091,059 | 1,307,949 | 1,351,122 | 1,468,213 | 1,528,431 | n.a. | 1,743,598 | 1,925,285 |
| 8. Payments to Partners | 58,951 | 51,638 | 74,883 | 82,021 | 85,046 | 79,245 | 71,705 | 73,358 | 92,536 | 124,661 |
| 9. Net Income, less Deficit | 243,304 | 273,223 | 299,097 | 237,897 | 187,956 | 98,645 | 219,571 | 283,270 | 180,893 | 343,561 |
| **Selected Average Financial Statistics** (Items 10 to 13 inclusive in $) | | | | | | | | | | |
| 10. Av. Payment Partnership | 2,474 | 2,107 | 2,671 | 2,800 | 2,927 | 2,780 | 2,499 | 2,218 | 2,934 | 3,802 |
| 11. Av. Payment Partner | 880 | 485 | 967 | 1,046 | 1,099 | 962 | 871 | 776 | 1,041 | 1,350 |
| 12. Av. Income Partnership | 10,210 | 11,150 | 10,670 | 8,121 | 6,469 | 3,461 | 7,653 | 8,563 | 5,736 | 10,479 |
| 13. Av. Income Partner | 3,630 | 2,566 | 3,864 | 3,034 | 2,429 | 1,198 | 2,669 | 2,996 | 2,035 | 3,720 |
| **Selected Financial Statistics as Percent of Op. Income** | | | | | | | | | | |
| 14. Depreciation / Op. Income (%) | 2.3 | 2.4 | 2.5 | 2.6 | 2.9 | n.a. | n.a. | n.a. | 3.5 | 3.6 |
| 15. Interest / Op. Income (%) | 1.0 | 1.3 | 1.4 | 1.6 | 1.7 | 1.7 | 1.7 | 1.7 | 2.0 | 1.7 |
| 16. Payroll / Op. Income (%) | 21.2 | 21.1 | 21.2 | 22.3 | 22.3 | 22.2 | 22.5 | n.a. | 21.0 | 22.0 |
| **Selected Index Numbers (1976 = 100)** | | | | | | | | | | |
| 17. Partnerships | 100.0 | 102.8 | 117.6 | 122.9 | 121.9 | 119.6 | 120.4 | 138.8 | 132.4 | 137.6 |
| 18. Partners | 100.0 | 158.8 | 115.5 | 117.0 | 115.5 | 122.9 | 122.8 | 141.1 | 132.6 | 137.8 |
| 19. Operating Income | 100.0 | 109.8 | 140.7 | 160.3 | 166.2 | 181.3 | 185.9 | 202.3 | 227.1 | 239.6 |
| 20. Payments to Partners | 100.0 | 87.6 | 127.0 | 139.1 | 144.3 | 134.4 | 121.6 | 124.4 | 157.0 | 211.5 |
| **Selected Financial Statistics (Constant $, 1976 = 100)** | | | | | | | | | | |
| 21. Operating Income | 100.0 | 103.2 | 122.8 | 125.7 | 114.8 | 113.5 | 109.6 | 115.6 | 124.5 | 126.8 |
| 22. Payments to Partners | 100.0 | 82.3 | 110.8 | 109.1 | 99.7 | 84.1 | 71.7 | 71.1 | 86.0 | 111.9 |
| 23. Av. Payment, Partnership | 100.0 | 80.0 | 94.2 | 88.8 | 81.7 | 70.4 | 59.5 | 51.2 | 65.0 | 81.3 |
| 24. Av. Payment, Partner | 100.0 | 51.8 | 96.0 | 93.2 | 86.3 | 68.4 | 58.3 | 50.4 | 64.9 | 81.2 |

*Page 242*

TABLE 3

146: DRINKING PLACES, WITH AND WITHOUT NET INCOME

| | 1976 | 1977 | 1978 | 1979 | 1980 | 1981 | 1982 | 1983 | 1984 | 1985 |
|---|---|---|---|---|---|---|---|---|---|---|
| 1. Number of Partnerships | 7,996 | 8,524 | 8,562 | 9,048 | 8,227 | 6,749 | 6,957 | 5,615 | 3,591 | 4,778 |
| 2. Number of Partners | 18,628 | 19,110 | 18,407 | 21,050 | 18,155 | 14,718 | 15,667 | 13,085 | 7,631 | 10,055 |

Selected Financial Statistics
(Items 3 to 9 inclusive in 000's of dollars)

| | 1976 | 1977 | 1978 | 1979 | 1980 | 1981 | 1982 | 1983 | 1984 | 1985 |
|---|---|---|---|---|---|---|---|---|---|---|
| 3. Operating Income | 549,659 | 630,752 | 730,790 | 752,692 | 748,924 | 504,580 | 512,076 | 323,686 | 276,895 | 700,431 |
| 4. Depreciation | 15,554 | 18,016 | 18,459 | 28,272 | 24,733 | n.a. | n.a. | n.a. | 20,105 | 31,976 |
| 5. Taxes Paid | 26,530 | 31,123 | 35,699 | 34,244 | 35,551 | 22,134 | 20,586 | 25,651 | 15,110 | 29,798 |
| 6. Interest Paid | 9,609 | 10,872 | 11,994 | 17,450 | 19,634 | 9,511 | 7,639 | 6,852 | 10,874 | 8,442 |
| 7. Payroll Deductions | 79,564 | 96,536 | 94,408 | 85,037 | 89,626 | 62,473 | 74,372 | n.a. | 43,826 | 97,612 |
| 8. Payments to Partners | 19,522 | 13,298 | 11,656 | 15,669 | 16,825 | 9,699 | 9,432 | 14,451 | 5,225 | 4,778 |
| 9. Net Income, less Deficit | 45,264 | 51,855 | 72,833 | 59,317 | 53,984 | 28,555 | 11,937 | 531 | (999) | 60,540 |

Selected Average Financial Statistics
(Items 10 to 13 inclusive in $)

| | 1976 | 1977 | 1978 | 1979 | 1980 | 1981 | 1982 | 1983 | 1984 | 1985 |
|---|---|---|---|---|---|---|---|---|---|---|
| 10. Av. Payment Partnership | 2,441 | 1,560 | 1,361 | 1,732 | 2,045 | 1,437 | 1,356 | 2,574 | 1,455 | 1,000 |
| 11. Av. Payment Partner | 1,048 | 696 | 633 | 744 | 927 | 659 | 602 | 1,104 | 685 | 475 |
| 12. Av. Income Partnership | 5,661 | 6,083 | 8,507 | 6,556 | 6,562 | 4,231 | 1,716 | 95 | (278) | 12,671 |
| 13. Av. Income Partner | 2,430 | 2,714 | 3,957 | 2,818 | 2,974 | 1,940 | 762 | 41 | (131) | 6,021 |

Selected Financial Statistics as Percent of Op. Income

| | 1976 | 1977 | 1978 | 1979 | 1980 | 1981 | 1982 | 1983 | 1984 | 1985 |
|---|---|---|---|---|---|---|---|---|---|---|
| 14. Depreciation / Op. Income (%) | 2.8 | 2.9 | 2.5 | 3.8 | 3.3 | n.a. | n.a. | n.a. | 7.3 | 4.6 |
| 15. Interest / Op. Income (%) | 1.8 | 1.7 | 1.6 | 2.3 | 2.6 | 1.9 | 1.5 | 2.1 | 3.9 | 1.2 |
| 16. Payroll / Op. Income (%) | 14.5 | 15.3 | 12.9 | 11.3 | 12.0 | 12.4 | 14.5 | n.a. | 15.8 | 13.9 |

Selected Index Numbers (1976 = 100)

| | 1976 | 1977 | 1978 | 1979 | 1980 | 1981 | 1982 | 1983 | 1984 | 1985 |
|---|---|---|---|---|---|---|---|---|---|---|
| 17. Partnerships | 100.0 | 106.6 | 107.1 | 113.2 | 102.9 | 84.4 | 87.0 | 70.2 | 44.9 | 59.8 |
| 18. Partners | 100.0 | 102.6 | 98.8 | 113.0 | 97.5 | 79.0 | 84.1 | 70.2 | 41.0 | 54.0 |
| 19. Operating Income | 100.0 | 114.8 | 133.0 | 136.9 | 136.3 | 91.8 | 93.2 | 58.9 | 50.4 | 127.4 |
| 20. Payments to Partners | 100.0 | 68.1 | 59.7 | 80.3 | 86.2 | 49.7 | 48.3 | 74.0 | 26.8 | 24.5 |

Selected Financial Statistics (Constant $, 1976 = 100)

| | 1976 | 1977 | 1978 | 1979 | 1980 | 1981 | 1982 | 1983 | 1984 | 1985 |
|---|---|---|---|---|---|---|---|---|---|---|
| 21. Operating Income | 100.0 | 107.8 | 116.0 | 107.4 | 94.1 | 57.5 | 54.9 | 33.6 | 27.6 | 67.4 |
| 22. Payments to Partners | 100.0 | 64.0 | 52.1 | 62.9 | 59.5 | 31.1 | 28.5 | 42.3 | 14.7 | 13.0 |
| 23. Av. Payment, Partnership | 100.0 | 60.1 | 48.7 | 55.7 | 57.9 | 36.9 | 32.8 | 60.3 | 32.7 | 21.6 |
| 24. Av. Payment, Partner | 100.0 | 62.3 | 52.7 | 55.6 | 61.2 | 39.4 | 33.8 | 60.2 | 35.8 | 23.9 |

*Page 243*

TABLE 3

149: LIQUOR STORES, WITH AND WITHOUT NET INCOME

| | 1976 | 1977 | 1978 | 1979 | 1980 | 1981 | 1982 | 1983 | 1984 | 1985 |
|---|---|---|---|---|---|---|---|---|---|---|
| 1. Number of Partnerships | 4,730 | 4,151 | 3,791 | 3,746 | 3,347 | 3,926 | 4,275 | 3,807 | 3,167 | 3,024 |
| 2. Number of Partners | 10,226 | 8,859 | 8,986 | 9,414 | 8,376 | 8,969 | 9,210 | 8,766 | 7,176 | 6,728 |
| **Selected Financial Statistics** | | | | | | | | | | |
| (Items 3 to 9 inclusive in 000's of dollars) | | | | | | | | | | |
| 3. Operating Income | 1,017,914 | 1,025,305 | 1,083,083 | 1,172,420 | 1,271,121 | 1,352,713 | 1,272,628 | 1,242,983 | 1,515,271 | 1,091,206 |
| 4. Depreciation | 9,661 | 10,776 | 12,894 | 12,410 | 14,673 | n.a. | n.a. | n.a. | 32,721 | 14,089 |
| 5. Taxes Paid | 21,590 | 22,401 | 22,547 | 21,635 | 23,657 | 23,597 | 20,165 | 20,201 | 26,078 | 24,748 |
| 6. Interest Paid | 7,785 | 9,964 | 11,402 | 9,976 | 13,256 | 14,916 | 20,703 | 18,744 | 18,621 | 13,175 |
| 7. Payroll Deductions | 44,753 | 43,801 | 46,170 | 51,765 | 70,445 | 64,240 | 66,169 | n.a. | 88,391 | 52,872 |
| 8. Payments to Partners | 10,954 | 10,569 | 13,094 | 10,489 | 13,970 | 23,126 | 12,856 | 14,949 | 7,828 | 6,895 |
| 9. Net Income, less Deficit | 53,126 | 51,112 | 52,506 | 56,278 | 57,175 | 55,064 | 45,992 | 45,238 | 48,952 | 35,953 |
| **Selected Average Financial Statistics** | | | | | | | | | | |
| (Items 10 to 13 inclusive in $) | | | | | | | | | | |
| 10. Av. Payment Partnership | 2,316 | 2,546 | 3,454 | 2,800 | 4,174 | 5,890 | 3,007 | 3,927 | 2,472 | 2,280 |
| 11. Av. Payment Partner | 1,071 | 1,193 | 1,457 | 1,114 | 1,668 | 2,578 | 1,396 | 1,705 | 1,091 | 1,025 |
| 12. Av. Income Partnership | 11,232 | 12,313 | 13,850 | 15,023 | 17,082 | 14,025 | 10,758 | 11,883 | 15,457 | 11,889 |
| 13. Av. Income Partner | 5,195 | 5,769 | 5,843 | 5,978 | 6,826 | 6,139 | 4,994 | 5,161 | 6,822 | 5,344 |
| **Selected Financial Statistics as Percent of Op. Income** | | | | | | | | | | |
| 14. Depreciation / Op. Income (%) | 0.10 | 1.1 | 1.2 | 1.1 | 1.2 | n.a. | n.a. | n.a. | 2.2 | 1.3 |
| 15. Interest / Op. Income (%) | 0.8 | 0.10 | 1.1 | 0.9 | 1.0 | 1.1 | 1.6 | 1.5 | 1.2 | 1.2 |
| 16. Payroll / Op. Income (%) | 4.4 | 4.3 | 4.3 | 4.4 | 5.5 | 4.8 | 5.2 | n.a. | 5.8 | 4.9 |
| **Selected Index Numbers (1976 = 100)** | | | | | | | | | | |
| 17. Partnerships | 100.0 | 87.8 | 80.1 | 79.2 | 70.8 | 83.0 | 90.4 | 80.5 | 67.0 | 63.9 |
| 18. Partners | 100.0 | 86.6 | 87.9 | 92.1 | 81.9 | 87.7 | 90.1 | 85.7 | 70.2 | 65.8 |
| 19. Operating Income | 100.0 | 100.7 | 106.4 | 115.2 | 124.9 | 132.9 | 125.0 | 122.1 | 148.9 | 107.2 |
| 20. Payments to Partners | 100.0 | 96.5 | 119.5 | 95.8 | 127.5 | 211.1 | 117.4 | 136.5 | 71.5 | 62.9 |
| **Selected Financial Statistics (Constant $, 1976 = 100)** | | | | | | | | | | |
| 21. Operating Income | 100.0 | 94.6 | 92.8 | 90.3 | 86.3 | 83.2 | 73.7 | 69.8 | 81.6 | 56.7 |
| 22. Payments to Partners | 100.0 | 90.6 | 104.3 | 75.1 | 88.1 | 132.1 | 69.2 | 78.0 | 39.2 | 33.3 |
| 23. Av. Payment, Partnership | 100.0 | 103.3 | 130.2 | 94.8 | 124.5 | 159.2 | 76.6 | 96.9 | 58.5 | 52.1 |
| 24. Av. Payment, Partner | 100.0 | 104.6 | 118.7 | 81.5 | 107.6 | 150.6 | 76.9 | 90.9 | 55.9 | 50.6 |

## TABLE 3

### OTHER RETAIL STORES (148,150 TO 164,167,168,169,170), WITH AND WITHOUT NET INCOME

| | 1976 | 1977 | 1978 | 1979 | 1980 | 1981 | 1982 | 1983 | 1984 | 1985 |
|---|---|---|---|---|---|---|---|---|---|---|
| 1. Number of Partnerships | 37,952 | 36,104 | 40,522 | 44,308 | 43,970 | 56,428 | 47,247 | 46,581 | 52,186 | 58,412 |
| 2. Number of Partners | 85,189 | 83,412 | 90,997 | 98,584 | 100,207 | 128,804 | 110,026 | 105,462 | 117,518 | 138,552 |
| **Selected Financial Statistics** | | | | | | | | | | |
| **(Items 3 to 9 inclusive in 000's of dollars)** | | | | | | | | | | |
| 3. Operating Income | 4,369,137 | 4,229,207 | 4,277,147 | 4,916,162 | 4,703,973 | 6,976,761 | 6,298,739 | 6,040,164 | 6,666,751 | 7,853,942 |
| 4. Depreciation | 64,228 | 56,601 | 58,746 | 68,109 | 73,550 | n.a. | n.a. | n.a. | 132,154 | 206,427 |
| 5. Taxes Paid | 73,906 | 77,553 | 77,854 | 87,934 | 74,110 | 99,225 | 89,280 | 98,774 | 112,355 | 139,832 |
| 6. Interest Paid | 29,241 | 31,646 | 37,172 | 47,320 | 57,101 | 130,431 | 97,046 | 85,189 | 96,821 | 142,951 |
| 7. Payroll Deductions | 1,260,051 | 344,075 | 331,984 | 347,322 | 338,736 | 475,370 | 429,169 | n.a. | 536,867 | 693,402 |
| 8. Payments to Partners | 103,043 | 93,032 | 92,796 | 93,734 | 112,412 | 117,096 | 157,679 | 128,339 | 52,186 | 58,412 |
| 9. Net Income, less Deficit | 326,214 | 292,583 | 339,160 | 364,698 | 313,734 | 230,067 | 353,626 | 182,532 | 219,111 | 251,504 |
| **Selected Average Financial Statistics** | | | | | | | | | | |
| **(Items 10 to 13 inclusive in $)** | | | | | | | | | | |
| 10. Av. Payment Partnership | 2,715 | 2,577 | 2,290 | 2,116 | 2,557 | 2,075 | 3,337 | 2,755 | 1,000 | 1,000 |
| 11. Av. Payment Partner | 1,210 | 1,115 | 1,020 | 951 | 1,122 | 909 | 1,433 | 1,217 | 444 | 422 |
| 12. Av. Income Partnership | 8,595 | 8,104 | 8,370 | 8,231 | 7,135 | 4,077 | 7,485 | 3,919 | 4,199 | 4,306 |
| 13. Av. Income Partner | 3,829 | 3,508 | 3,727 | 3,699 | 3,131 | 1,786 | 3,214 | 1,731 | 1,864 | 1,815 |
| **Selected Financial Statistics as Percent of Op. Income** | | | | | | | | | | |
| 14. Depreciation / Op. Income (%) | 1.5 | 1.3 | 1.4 | 1.4 | 1.6 | n.a. | n.a. | n.a. | 2.0 | 2.6 |
| 15. Interest / Op. Income (%) | 0.7 | 0.8 | 0.9 | 0.10 | 1.2 | 1.9 | 1.5 | 1.4 | 1.5 | 1.8 |
| 16. Payroll / Op. Income (%) | 28.8 | 8.1 | 7.8 | 7.1 | 7.2 | 6.8 | 6.8 | n.a. | 8.1 | 8.8 |
| **Selected Index Numbers (1976 = 100)** | | | | | | | | | | |
| 17. Partnerships | 100.0 | 95.1 | 106.8 | 116.7 | 115.9 | 148.7 | 124.5 | 122.7 | 137.5 | 153.9 |
| 18. Partners | 100.0 | 97.9 | 106.8 | 115.7 | 117.6 | 151.2 | 129.2 | 123.8 | 137.9 | 162.6 |
| 19. Operating Income | 100.0 | 96.8 | 97.9 | 112.5 | 107.7 | 159.7 | 144.2 | 138.2 | 152.6 | 179.8 |
| 20. Payments to Partners | 100.0 | 90.3 | 90.1 | 91.0 | 109.1 | 113.6 | 153.0 | 124.5 | 50.6 | 56.7 |
| **Selected Financial Statistics (Constant $, 1976 = 100)** | | | | | | | | | | |
| 21. Operating Income | 100.0 | 90.9 | 85.4 | 88.2 | 74.4 | 99.9 | 85.0 | 79.0 | 83.6 | 95.1 |
| 22. Payments to Partners | 100.0 | 84.8 | 78.6 | 71.3 | 75.4 | 71.1 | 90.2 | 71.2 | 27.8 | 30.0 |
| 23. Av. Payment, Partnership | 100.0 | 89.2 | 73.6 | 61.1 | 65.1 | 47.9 | 72.5 | 58.0 | 20.2 | 19.5 |
| 24. Av. Payment, Partner | 100.0 | 86.5 | 73.6 | 61.6 | 64.1 | 47.1 | 69.9 | 57.5 | 20.2 | 18.5 |

TABLE 3

172: FINANCE, INSURANCE, AND REAL ESTATE, WITH AND WITHOUT NET INCOME

| | 1976 | 1977 | 1978 | 1979 | 1980 | 1981 | 1982 | 1983 | 1984 | 1985 |
|---|---|---|---|---|---|---|---|---|---|---|
| 1. Number of Partnerships | 446,988 | 476,390 | 516,135 | 577,336 | 637,480 | 681,638 | 725,622 | 730,067 | 790,902 | 843,867 |
| 2. Number of Partners | 3,250,369 | 3,814,396 | 3,782,421 | 4,271,344 | 5,566,294 | 5,326,300 | 5,756,896 | 5,926,901 | 7,408,313 | 7,754,557 |
| **Selected Financial Statistics** (Items 3 to 9 inclusive in 000's of dollars) | | | | | | | | | | |
| 3. Operating Income | 37,632,363 | 43,894,814 | 62,822,429 | 76,258,032 | 87,133,197 | 73,573,659 | 85,904,608 | 76,784,190 | 54,902,201 | 45,873,102 |
| 4. Depreciation | 5,998,739 | 6,639,837 | 7,562,135 | 9,537,785 | 11,608,309 | n.a. | n.a. | n.a. | 26,384,809 | 30,258,504 |
| 5. Taxes Paid | 3,712,130 | 3,939,317 | 4,034,690 | 4,485,561 | 5,267,825 | 1,416,746 | 1,395,789 | 1,654,042 | 1,859,838 | 2,187,992 |
| 6. Interest Paid | 9,670,652 | 10,413,334 | 12,093,787 | 16,119,115 | 21,549,095 | 13,497,742 | 13,970,129 | 14,611,942 | 15,487,083 | 17,772,393 |
| 7. Payroll Deductions | 2,071,045 | 2,220,388 | 2,502,571 | 3,090,122 | 4,109,553 | 2,772,865 | 3,035,967 | n.a. | 2,956,779 | 4,030,174 |
| 8. Payments to Partners | 545,151 | 516,300 | 616,382 | 817,772 | 1,079,628 | 1,306,257 | 1,407,991 | 1,324,310 | 1,392,157 | 843,867 |
| 9. Net Income, less Deficit | 226,851 | 97,044 | 113,206 | 52,092 | 424,877 | 536,004 | 1,115,589 | 1,310,521 | (19,243,718) | (25,928,668) |
| **Selected Average Financial Statistics** (Items 10 to 13 inclusive in $) | | | | | | | | | | |
| 10. Av. Payment Partnership | 1,220 | 1,084 | 1,194 | 1,416 | 1,694 | 1,916 | 1,940 | 1,814 | 1,760 | 1,000 |
| 11. Av. Payment Partner | 168 | 135 | 163 | 191 | 194 | 245 | 245 | 223 | 188 | 109 |
| 12. Av. Income Partnership | 508 | 204 | 219 | 90 | 666 | 786 | 1,537 | 1,795 | (24,331) | (30,726) |
| 13. Av. Income Partner | 70 | 25 | 30 | 12 | 76 | 101 | 194 | 221 | (2,598) | (3,344) |
| **Selected Financial Statistics as Percent of Op. Income** | | | | | | | | | | |
| 14. Depreciation / Op. Income (%) | 15.9 | 15.1 | 12.0 | 12.5 | 13.3 | n.a. | n.a. | n.a. | 48.1 | 66.0 |
| 15. Interest / Op. Income (%) | 25.7 | 23.7 | 19.3 | 21.1 | 24.7 | 18.4 | 16.3 | 19.0 | 28.2 | 38.7 |
| 16. Payroll / Op. Income (%) | 5.5 | 5.1 | 4.0 | 4.1 | 4.7 | 3.8 | 3.5 | n.a. | 5.4 | 8.8 |
| **Selected Index Numbers (1976 = 100)** | | | | | | | | | | |
| 17. Partnerships | 100.0 | 106.6 | 115.5 | 129.2 | 142.6 | 152.5 | 162.3 | 163.3 | 176.9 | 188.8 |
| 18. Partners | 100.0 | 117.4 | 116.4 | 131.4 | 171.3 | 163.9 | 177.1 | 182.3 | 227.9 | 238.6 |
| 19. Operating Income | 100.0 | 116.6 | 166.9 | 202.6 | 231.5 | 195.5 | 228.3 | 204.0 | 145.9 | 121.9 |
| 20. Payments to Partners | 100.0 | 94.7 | 113.1 | 150.0 | 198.0 | 239.6 | 258.3 | 242.9 | 255.4 | 154.8 |
| **Selected Financial Statistics (Constant $, 1976 = 100)** | | | | | | | | | | |
| 21. Operating Income | 100.0 | 109.6 | 145.7 | 158.9 | 160.0 | 122.4 | 134.6 | 116.6 | 80.0 | 64.5 |
| 22. Payments to Partners | 100.0 | 89.0 | 98.7 | 117.6 | 136.8 | 150.0 | 152.3 | 138.8 | 140.0 | 81.9 |
| 23. Av. Payment, Partnership | 100.0 | 83.5 | 85.4 | 91.0 | 95.9 | 98.3 | 93.8 | 85.0 | 79.1 | 43.3 |
| 24. Av. Payment, Partner | 100.0 | 75.2 | 84.4 | 89.5 | 80.3 | 91.5 | 86.4 | 76.2 | 61.0 | 34.6 |

# TABLE 3

## 173: FINANCE, WITH AND WITHOUT NET INCOME

| | 1976 | 1977 | 1978 | 1979 | 1980 | 1981 | 1982 | 1983 | 1984 | 1985 |
|---|---|---|---|---|---|---|---|---|---|---|
| 1. Number of Partnerships | 106,878 | 106,073 | 118,632 | 139,453 | 165,969 | 152,058 | 150,091 | 135,815 | 144,175 | 141,481 |
| 2. Number of Partners | 1,412,207 | 1,497,683 | 1,662,094 | 2,020,803 | 2,329,161 | 2,169,726 | 1,995,337 | 1,572,901 | 2,163,044 | 1,733,011 |
| **Selected Financial Statistics** (Items 3 to 9 inclusive in 000's of dollars) | | | | | | | | | | |
| 3. Operating Income | 5,568,751 | 6,990,481 | 18,451,234 | 21,185,327 | 23,379,400 | 39,890,980 | 48,572,944 | 32,405,016 | 26,170,236 | 15,244,569 |
| 4. Depreciation | 88,157 | 167,828 | 168,718 | 468,712 | 399,447 | n.a. | n.a. | n.a. | 1,217,707 | 1,115,853 |
| 5. Taxes Paid | 172,153 | 172,991 | 192,810 | 233,381 | 338,573 | 257,911 | 238,353 | 314,334 | 286,617 | 345,857 |
| 6. Interest Paid | 735,178 | 828,579 | 1,199,095 | 2,385,828 | 4,284,605 | 6,943,636 | 6,389,077 | 6,668,871 | 5,097,467 | 5,676,961 |
| 7. Payroll Deductions | 598,720 | 505,082 | 613,917 | 835,742 | 1,348,493 | 1,440,946 | 1,467,971 | n.a. | 1,331,159 | 1,741,423 |
| 8. Payments to Partners | 223,184 | 218,041 | 243,665 | 362,526 | 462,900 | 575,115 | 582,944 | 549,002 | 419,345 | 553,798 |
| 9. Net Income, less Deficit | 54,521 | 331,885 | 392,902 | 463,518 | 143,893 | 2,051,794 | 43,881 | 1,758,864 | 1,359,929 | 3,462,095 |
| **Selected Average Financial Statistics** (Items 10 to 13 inclusive in $) | | | | | | | | | | |
| 10. Av. Payment Partnership | 2,088 | 2,056 | 2,054 | 2,600 | 2,789 | 3,782 | 3,884 | 4,042 | 2,909 | 3,914 |
| 11. Av. Payment Partner | 158 | 146 | 147 | 179 | 199 | 265 | 292 | 349 | 194 | 320 |
| 12. Av. Income Partnership | 510 | 3,129 | 3,312 | 3,324 | 867 | 13,493 | 292 | 12,950 | 9,432 | 24,470 |
| 13. Av. Income Partner | 39 | 222 | 236 | 229 | 62 | 946 | 22 | 1,118 | 629 | 1,998 |
| **Selected Financial Statistics as Percent of Op. Income** | | | | | | | | | | |
| 14. Depreciation / Op. Income (%) | 1.6 | 2.4 | 0.9 | 2.2 | 1.7 | n.a. | n.a. | n.a. | 4.7 | 7.3 |
| 15. Interest / Op. Income (%) | 13.2 | 11.9 | 6.5 | 11.3 | 18.3 | 17.4 | 13.2 | 20.6 | 19.5 | 37.2 |
| 16. Payroll / Op. Income (%) | 10.8 | 7.2 | 3.3 | 3.9 | 5.8 | 3.6 | 3.0 | n.a. | 5.1 | 11.4 |
| **Selected Index Numbers (1976 = 100)** | | | | | | | | | | |
| 17. Partnerships | 100.0 | 99.2 | 111.0 | 130.5 | 155.3 | 142.3 | 140.4 | 127.1 | 134.9 | 132.4 |
| 18. Partners | 100.0 | 106.1 | 117.7 | 143.1 | 164.9 | 153.6 | 141.3 | 111.4 | 153.2 | 122.7 |
| 19. Operating Income | 100.0 | 125.5 | 331.3 | 380.4 | 419.8 | 716.3 | 872.2 | 581.9 | 469.9 | 273.8 |
| 20. Payments to Partners | 100.0 | 97.7 | 109.2 | 162.4 | 207.4 | 257.7 | 261.2 | 246.0 | 187.9 | 248.1 |
| **Selected Financial Statistics (Constant $, 1976 = 100)** | | | | | | | | | | |
| 21. Operating Income | 100.0 | 117.9 | 289.1 | 298.4 | 290.0 | 448.4 | 514.4 | 332.5 | 257.6 | 144.9 |
| 22. Payments to Partners | 100.0 | 91.8 | 95.3 | 127.4 | 143.3 | 161.3 | 154.0 | 140.6 | 103.0 | 131.3 |
| 23. Av. Payment, Partnership | 100.0 | 92.5 | 85.8 | 97.7 | 92.3 | 113.3 | 109.7 | 110.6 | 76.3 | 99.2 |
| 24. Av. Payment, Partner | 100.0 | 86.3 | 80.9 | 88.5 | 87.4 | 104.6 | 109.0 | 126.2 | 66.9 | 106.8 |

## TABLE 3

### BANKING AND CREDIT AGENCIES OTHER THAN BANKS (174,175), WITH AND WITHOUT NET INCOME

| | 1976 | 1977 | 1978 | 1979 | 1980 | 1981 | 1982 | 1983 | 1984 | 1985 |
|---|---|---|---|---|---|---|---|---|---|---|
| 1. Number of Partnerships | 2,756 | 2,412 | 2,336 | 3,385 | 2,428 | 2,559 | 1,708 | 2,160 | 3,708 | 4,066 |
| 2. Number of Partners | 15,856 | 19,798 | 50,107 | 28,318 | 15,628 | 24,080 | 19,090 | 27,125 | 252,898 | 40,391 |
| **Selected Financial Statistics** (Items 3 to 9 inclusive in 000's of dollars) | | | | | | | | | | |
| 3. Operating Income | 551,243 | 186,500 | 394,507 | 400,752 | 429,602 | 1,351,952 | 493,026 | 683,458 | 732,280 | 632,300 |
| 4. Depreciation | 5,552 | 6,882 | 6,880 | 4,599 | 8,357 | n.a. | n.a. | n.a. | 13,124 | 17,591 |
| 5. Taxes Paid | 6,045 | 4,400 | 6,452 | 5,819 | 7,342 | 3,953 | 2,250 | 2,910 | 5,908 | 3,696 |
| 6. Interest Paid | 29,664 | 29,050 | 52,496 | 68,339 | 92,204 | 126,290 | 88,078 | 113,849 | 212,081 | 389,031 |
| 7. Payroll Deductions | 33,946 | 31,084 | 36,046 | 40,228 | 57,685 | 65,055 | 55,286 | n.a. | 74,676 | 71,392 |
| 8. Payments to Partners | 9,069 | 6,510 | 10,577 | 6,787 | 9,016 | 12,577 | 6,728 | 7,442 | 3,708 | 6,301 |
| 9. Net Income, less Deficit | 42,916 | 24,845 | 43,400 | 153,959 | 86,015 | 114,600 | 37,910 | 160,062 | 577,292 | 120,065 |
| **Selected Average Financial Statistics** (Items 10 to 13 inclusive in $) | | | | | | | | | | |
| 10. Av. Payment Partnership | 3,291 | 2,699 | 4,528 | 2,005 | 3,713 | 4,915 | 3,939 | 3,445 | 1,000 | 1,550 |
| 11. Av. Payment Partner | 572 | 329 | 211 | 240 | 577 | 522 | 352 | 274 | 15 | 156 |
| 12. Av. Income Partnership | 15,572 | 10,301 | 18,579 | 45,483 | 35,426 | 44,783 | 22,196 | 74,103 | 155,688 | 29,529 |
| 13. Av. Income Partner | 2,707 | 1,255 | 866 | 5,437 | 5,504 | 4,759 | 1,986 | 5,901 | 2,283 | 2,973 |
| **Selected Financial Statistics as Percent of Op. Income** | | | | | | | | | | |
| 14. Depreciation / Op. Income (%) | 1.0 | 3.7 | 1.7 | 1.2 | 2.0 | n.a. | n.a. | n.a. | 1.8 | 2.8 |
| 15. Interest / Op. Income (%) | 5.4 | 15.6 | 13.3 | 17.1 | 21.5 | 9.3 | 17.9 | 16.7 | 29.0 | 61.5 |
| 16. Payroll / Op. Income (%) | 6.2 | 16.7 | 9.1 | 10.0 | 13.4 | 4.8 | 11.2 | n.a. | 10.2 | 11.3 |
| **Selected Index Numbers (1976 = 100)** | | | | | | | | | | |
| 17. Partnerships | 100.0 | 87.5 | 84.8 | 122.8 | 88.1 | 92.9 | 62.0 | 78.4 | 134.5 | 147.5 |
| 18. Partners | 100.0 | 124.9 | 316.0 | 178.6 | 98.6 | 151.9 | 120.4 | 171.1 | 1,595 | 254.7 |
| 19. Operating Income | 100.0 | 33.8 | 71.6 | 72.7 | 77.9 | 245.3 | 89.4 | 124.0 | 132.8 | 114.7 |
| 20. Payments to Partners | 100.0 | 71.8 | 116.6 | 74.8 | 99.4 | 138.7 | 74.2 | 82.1 | 40.9 | 69.5 |
| **Selected Financial Statistics (Constant $, 1976 = 100)** | | | | | | | | | | |
| 21. Operating Income | 100.0 | 31.8 | 62.4 | 57.0 | 53.8 | 153.5 | 52.7 | 70.8 | 72.8 | 60.7 |
| 22. Payments to Partners | 100.0 | 67.4 | 101.8 | 58.7 | 68.7 | 86.8 | 43.8 | 46.9 | 22.4 | 36.8 |
| 23. Av. Payment, Partnership | 100.0 | 77.0 | 120.1 | 47.8 | 77.9 | 93.5 | 70.6 | 59.8 | 16.6 | 24.9 |
| 24. Av. Payment, Partner | 100.0 | 54.0 | 32.2 | 32.8 | 69.8 | 57.2 | 36.4 | 27.4 | 1.5 | 14.3 |

# TABLE 3

## 176: SECURITY AND COMMODITY BROKERS AND SERVICES, WITH AND WITHOUT NET INCOME

| | 1976 | 1977 | 1978 | 1979 | 1980 | 1981 | 1982 | 1983 | 1984 | 1985 |
|---|---|---|---|---|---|---|---|---|---|---|
| 1. Number of Partnerships | 2,441 | 1,776 | 2,858 | 3,416 | 2,069 | 3,507 | 4,857 | 7,108 | 5,906 | 2,398 |
| 2. Number of Partners | 23,078 | 27,900 | 27,970 | 19,193 | 41,859 | 61,887 | 91,233 | 64,736 | 98,369 | 104,582 |
| **Selected Financial Statistics** (Items 3 to 9 inclusive in 000's of dollars) | | | | | | | | | | |
| 3. Operating Income | 2,461,756 | 3,841,521 | 13,863,464 | 14,150,440 | 12,663,076 | 22,999,310 | 34,369,142 | 20,473,574 | 22,699,407 | 11,158,778 |
| 4. Depreciation | 11,290 | 8,792 | 9,640 | 23,272 | 17,473 | n.a. | n.a. | n.a. | 26,954 | 34,403 |
| 5. Taxes Paid | 69,868 | 65,628 | 63,960 | 83,112 | 87,951 | 71,797 | 57,937 | 67,936 | 77,463 | 93,092 |
| 6. Interest Paid | 265,953 | 356,048 | 529,036 | 1,018,797 | 1,449,102 | 3,458,797 | 3,427,908 | 4,311,840 | 3,273,752 | 2,457,175 |
| 7. Payroll Deductions | 518,817 | 429,564 | 509,111 | 704,838 | 1,011,553 | 880,737 | 845,146 | n.a. | 999,579 | 1,129,412 |
| 8. Payments to Partners | 141,059 | 133,254 | 138,675 | 195,525 | 229,043 | 290,315 | 315,166 | 346,547 | 236,070 | 230,627 |
| 9. Net Income, less Deficit | 207,742 | 12,278 | 101,433 | 207,579 | 47,907 | 68,198 | 53,782 | 441,431 | (90,981) | 1,338,746 |
| **Selected Average Financial Statistics** (Items 10 to 13 inclusive in $) | | | | | | | | | | |
| 10. Av. Payment Partnership | 57,787 | 75,030 | 48,522 | 57,238 | 110,702 | 82,782 | 64,889 | 48,755 | 39,971 | 96,175 |
| 11. Av. Payment Partner | 6,112 | 4,776 | 4,958 | 10,187 | 5,472 | 4,691 | 3,455 | 5,353 | 2,400 | 2,205 |
| 12. Av. Income Partnership | 85,105 | 6,913 | 35,491 | 60,767 | 23,155 | 19,446 | 11,073 | 62,103 | (15,405) | 558,276 |
| 13. Av. Income Partner | 9,002 | 440 | 3,626 | 10,815 | 1,144 | 1,102 | 590 | 6,819 | (925) | 12,801 |
| **Selected Financial Statistics as Percent of Op. Income** | | | | | | | | | | |
| 14. Depreciation / Op. Income (%) | 0.5 | 0.2 | 0.1 | 0.2 | 0.1 | n.a. | n.a. | n.a. | 0.1 | 0.3 |
| 15. Interest / Op. Income (%) | 10.8 | 9.3 | 3.8 | 7.2 | 11.4 | 15.0 | 1.0 | 21.1 | 14.4 | 22.0 |
| 16. Payroll / Op. Income (%) | 21.1 | 11.2 | 3.7 | 5.0 | 8.0 | 3.8 | 2.5 | n.a. | 4.4 | 10.1 |
| **Selected Index Numbers (1976 = 100)** | | | | | | | | | | |
| 17. Partnerships | 100.0 | 72.8 | 117.1 | 139.9 | 84.8 | 143.7 | 199.0 | 291.2 | 242.0 | 98.2 |
| 18. Partners | 100.0 | 120.9 | 121.2 | 83.2 | 181.4 | 268.2 | 395.3 | 280.5 | 426.2 | 453.2 |
| 19. Operating Income | 100.0 | 156.0 | 563.2 | 574.8 | 514.4 | 934.3 | 1,396 | 831.7 | 922.1 | 453.3 |
| 20. Payments to Partners | 100.0 | 94.5 | 98.3 | 138.6 | 162.4 | 205.8 | 223.4 | 245.7 | 167.4 | 163.5 |
| **Selected Financial Statistics (Constant $, 1976 = 100)** | | | | | | | | | | |
| 21. Operating Income | 100.0 | 146.6 | 491.4 | 450.8 | 355.4 | 584.8 | 823.4 | 475.2 | 505.4 | 239.9 |
| 22. Payments to Partners | 100.0 | 88.7 | 85.8 | 108.7 | 112.2 | 128.8 | 131.8 | 140.4 | 91.7 | 86.5 |
| 23. Av. Payment, Partnership | 100.0 | 122.0 | 73.3 | 77.7 | 132.3 | 89.7 | 66.2 | 48.2 | 37.9 | 88.1 |
| 24. Av. Payment, Partner | 100.0 | 73.4 | 70.8 | 130.7 | 61.8 | 48.0 | 33.3 | 50.0 | 21.5 | 19.1 |

## TABLE 3

### 180: HOLDING AND INVESTMENT COMPANIES, WITH AND WITHOUT NET INCOME

| | 1976 | 1977 | 1978 | 1979 | 1980 | 1981 | 1982 | 1983 | 1984 | 1985 |
|---|---|---|---|---|---|---|---|---|---|---|
| 1. Number of Partnerships | 101,681 | 101,885 | 113,438 | 132,652 | 161,471 | 145,992 | 143,527 | 126,547 | 134,562 | 135,017 |
| 2. Number of Partners | 1,372,644 | 1,449,985 | 1,584,017 | 1,973,292 | 2,271,674 | 2,083,759 | 1,885,014 | 1,481,041 | 1,811,777 | 1,588,028 |
| **Selected Financial Statistics** (Items 3 to 9 inclusive in 000's of dollars) | | | | | | | | | | |
| 3. Operating Income | 2,555,752 | 2,962,460 | 4,193,263 | 6,634,135 | 10,286,722 | 15,539,719 | 13,710,777 | 11,247,984 | 2,738,548 | 3,453,490 |
| 4. Depreciation | 71,315 | 152,154 | 152,198 | 440,841 | 373,616 | n.a. | n.a. | n.a. | 1,177,630 | 1,063,860 |
| 5. Taxes Paid | 96,240 | 102,963 | 122,397 | 144,450 | 243,280 | 182,161 | 178,166 | 243,489 | 203,246 | 249,069 |
| 6. Interest Paid | 439,561 | 443,481 | 617,564 | 1,298,692 | 2,743,300 | 3,358,549 | 2,873,091 | 2,243,181 | 1,611,634 | 2,830,755 |
| 7. Payroll Deductions | 45,957 | 44,434 | 68,759 | 90,676 | 279,256 | 495,154 | 567,539 | n.a. | 256,903 | 540,619 |
| 8. Payments to Partners | 73,056 | 78,277 | 94,412 | 160,214 | 224,842 | 272,222 | 261,051 | 195,013 | 169,878 | 316,870 |
| 9. Net Income, less Deficit | 19,613 | 296,282 | 248,070 | 101,979 | 104,587 | 2,619,176 | 61,105 | 1,157,370 | 873,618 | 2,003,283 |
| **Selected Average Financial Statistics** (Items 10 to 13 inclusive in $) | | | | | | | | | | |
| 10. Av. Payment Partnership | 718 | 768 | 832 | 1,208 | 1,392 | 1,865 | 1,819 | 1,541 | 1,262 | 2,347 |
| 11. Av. Payment Partner | 53 | 54 | 60 | 81 | 99 | 131 | 138 | 132 | 94 | 200 |
| 12. Av. Income Partnership | 193 | 2,908 | 2,187 | 769 | 648 | 17,941 | 426 | 9,146 | 6,492 | 14,837 |
| 13. Av. Income Partner | 14 | 204 | 157 | 52 | 46 | 1,257 | 32 | 781 | 482 | 1,261 |
| **Selected Financial Statistics as Percent of Op. Income** | | | | | | | | | | |
| 14. Depreciation / Op. Income (%) | 2.8 | 5.1 | 3.6 | 6.7 | 3.6 | n.a. | n.a. | n.a. | 43.0 | 30.8 |
| 15. Interest / Op. Income (%) | 17.2 | 15.0 | 14.7 | 19.6 | 26.7 | 21.6 | 21.0 | 19.9 | 58.9 | 82.0 |
| 16. Payroll / Op. Income (%) | 1.8 | 1.5 | 1.6 | 1.4 | 2.7 | 3.2 | 4.1 | n.a. | 9.4 | 15.7 |
| **Selected Index Numbers (1976 = 100)** | | | | | | | | | | |
| 17. Partnerships | 100.0 | 100.2 | 111.6 | 130.5 | 158.8 | 143.6 | 141.2 | 124.5 | 132.3 | 132.8 |
| 18. Partners | 100.0 | 105.6 | 115.4 | 143.8 | 165.5 | 151.8 | 137.3 | 107.9 | 132.0 | 115.7 |
| 19. Operating Income | 100.0 | 115.9 | 164.1 | 259.6 | 402.5 | 608.0 | 536.5 | 440.1 | 107.2 | 135.1 |
| 20. Payments to Partners | 100.0 | 107.1 | 129.2 | 219.3 | 307.8 | 372.6 | 357.3 | 266.9 | 232.5 | 433.7 |
| **Selected Financial Statistics (Constant $, 1976 = 100)** | | | | | | | | | | |
| 21. Operating Income | 100.0 | 108.9 | 143.2 | 203.6 | 278.1 | 380.6 | 316.4 | 251.5 | 58.7 | 71.5 |
| 22. Payments to Partners | 100.0 | 100.7 | 112.8 | 172.0 | 212.6 | 233.2 | 210.7 | 152.5 | 127.4 | 229.5 |
| 23. Av. Payment, Partnership | 100.0 | 100.4 | 101.1 | 131.9 | 133.8 | 162.6 | 149.3 | 122.4 | 96.3 | 172.8 |
| 24. Av. Payment, Partner | 100.0 | 96.1 | 99.3 | 118.5 | 128.1 | 153.8 | 153.8 | 141.0 | 96.1 | 198.6 |

TABLE 3

184: INSURANCE AGENTS, BROKERS, AND SERVICES, WITH AND WITHOUT NET INCOME

| | 1976 | 1977 | 1978 | 1979 | 1980 | 1981 | 1982 | 1983 | 1984 | 1985 |
|---|---|---|---|---|---|---|---|---|---|---|
| 1. Number of Partnerships | 8,410 | 9,391 | 6,643 | 6,912 | 7,127 | 7,227 | 7,560 | 8,770 | 9,808 | 8,360 |
| 2. Number of Partners | 25,965 | 31,522 | 24,607 | 22,397 | 24,921 | 23,488 | 23,255 | 26,229 | 114,077 | 29,060 |
| **Selected Financial Statistics** (Items 3 to 9 inclusive in 000's of dollars) | | | | | | | | | | |
| 3. Operating Income | 2,291,915 | 2,284,451 | 2,120,870 | 3,235,738 | 3,116,599 | 3,157,085 | 3,342,832 | 3,023,935 | 2,720,885 | 2,019,801 |
| 4. Depreciation | 11,790 | 13,558 | 14,069 | 16,894 | 18,877 | n.a. | n.a. | n.a. | 36,266 | 40,111 |
| 5. Taxes Paid | 26,092 | 27,752 | 26,462 | 33,423 | 32,647 | 34,580 | 43,086 | 38,221 | 33,619 | 35,370 |
| 6. Interest Paid | 10,866 | 12,296 | 7,729 | 17,350 | 14,365 | 75,207 | 74,510 | 70,897 | 34,675 | 38,266 |
| 7. Payroll Deductions | 208,804 | 227,065 | 240,270 | 274,806 | 284,047 | 304,389 | 387,906 | n.a. | 221,707 | 258,520 |
| 8. Payments to Partners | 50,879 | 56,133 | 54,078 | 58,028 | 64,936 | 84,262 | 84,687 | 42,511 | 78,559 | 73,841 |
| 9. Net Income, less Deficit | 512,049 | 525,736 | 473,903 | 434,878 | 477,313 | 495,372 | 382,732 | 14,996 | 600,341 | 367,804 |
| **Selected Average Financial Statistics** (Items 10 to 13 inclusive in $) | | | | | | | | | | |
| 10. Av. Payment Partnership | 6,050 | 5,977 | 8,141 | 8,395 | 9,111 | 11,659 | 11,202 | 4,847 | 8,010 | 8,833 |
| 11. Av. Payment Partner | 1,960 | 1,781 | 2,198 | 2,591 | 2,606 | 3,587 | 3,642 | 1,621 | 689 | 2,541 |
| 12. Av. Income Partnership | 60,886 | 55,983 | 71,339 | 62,916 | 66,972 | 68,545 | 50,626 | 1,710 | 61,209 | 43,996 |
| 13. Av. Income Partner | 19,721 | 16,678 | 19,259 | 19,417 | 19,153 | 21,090 | 16,458 | 572 | 5,263 | 12,657 |
| **Selected Financial Statistics as Percent of Op. Income** | | | | | | | | | | |
| 14. Depreciation / Op. Income (%) | 0.5 | 0.6 | 0.7 | 0.5 | 0.6 | n.a. | n.a. | n.a. | 1.3 | 2.0 |
| 15. Interest / Op. Income (%) | 0.5 | 0.5 | 0.4 | 0.5 | 0.5 | 2.4 | 2.2 | 2.3 | 1.3 | 1.9 |
| 16. Payroll / Op. Income (%) | 9.1 | 9.9 | 11.3 | 8.5 | 9.1 | 9.6 | 11.6 | n.a. | 8.2 | 12.8 |
| **Selected Index Numbers (1976 = 100)** | | | | | | | | | | |
| 17. Partnerships | 100.0 | 111.7 | 79.0 | 82.2 | 84.7 | 85.9 | 89.9 | 104.3 | 116.6 | 99.4 |
| 18. Partners | 100.0 | 121.4 | 94.8 | 86.3 | 96.0 | 90.5 | 89.6 | 101.0 | 439.3 | 111.9 |
| 19. Operating Income | 100.0 | 99.7 | 92.5 | 141.2 | 136.0 | 137.7 | 145.9 | 131.9 | 118.7 | 88.1 |
| 20. Payments to Partners | 100.0 | 110.3 | 106.3 | 114.1 | 127.6 | 165.6 | 166.4 | 83.6 | 154.4 | 145.1 |
| **Selected Financial Statistics (Constant $, 1976 = 100)** | | | | | | | | | | |
| 21. Operating Income | 100.0 | 93.6 | 80.7 | 110.7 | 93.9 | 86.2 | 86.0 | 75.4 | 65.1 | 46.6 |
| 22. Payments to Partners | 100.0 | 103.6 | 92.7 | 89.4 | 88.2 | 103.7 | 98.2 | 47.7 | 84.6 | 76.8 |
| 23. Av. Payment, Partnership | 100.0 | 92.8 | 117.4 | 108.8 | 104.1 | 120.6 | 109.2 | 45.8 | 72.6 | 77.2 |
| 24. Av. Payment, Partner | 100.0 | 85.4 | 97.9 | 103.7 | 91.9 | 114.6 | 109.6 | 47.2 | 19.2 | 68.7 |

TABLE 3

185: REAL ESTATE, WITH AND WITHOUT NET INCOME

| | 1976 | 1977 | 1978 | 1979 | 1980 | 1981 | 1982 | 1983 | 1984 | 1985 |
|---|---|---|---|---|---|---|---|---|---|---|
| 1. Number of Partnerships | 331,700 | 360,926 | 390,860 | 430,971 | 464,384 | 522,352 | 567,971 | 585,481 | 636,920 | 694,027 |
| 2. Number of Partners | 1,812,197 | 2,285,191 | 2,015,720 | 2,228,144 | 3,212,213 | 3,133,086 | 3,738,304 | 4,327,771 | 5,131,192 | 5,992,476 |
| **Selected Financial Statistics** (Items 3 to 9 inclusive in 000's of dollars) | | | | | | | | | | |
| 3. Operating Income | 29,771,697 | 34,619,882 | 42,250,324 | 51,836,967 | 60,637,197 | 30,525,594 | 33,988,832 | 41,355,239 | 26,011,081 | 28,608,732 |
| 4. Depreciation | 5,898,792 | 6,458,451 | 7,379,347 | 9,052,179 | 11,189,986 | n.a. | n.a. | n.a. | 25,130,837 | 29,102,540 |
| 5. Taxes Paid | 3,513,885 | 3,738,574 | 3,815,418 | 4,218,757 | 4,896,605 | 1,124,254 | 1,114,350 | 1,301,486 | 1,539,602 | 1,806,764 |
| 6. Interest Paid | 8,924,608 | 9,572,459 | 10,886,964 | 13,715,938 | 17,250,125 | 6,478,899 | 7,506,542 | 7,872,174 | 10,354,941 | 12,057,165 |
| 7. Payroll Deductions | 1,263,521 | 1,488,241 | 1,648,383 | 1,979,575 | 2,477,014 | 1,027,530 | 1,180,090 | n.a. | 1,403,913 | 2,030,232 |
| 8. Payments to Partners | 271,088 | 242,126 | 318,639 | 397,218 | 551,792 | 646,880 | 740,360 | 732,797 | 894,253 | 929,829 |
| 9. Net Income, less Deficit | 283,508 | 182,806 | 753,599 | 141,932 | 328,715 | 790,721 | 1,109,981 | 1,487,907 | (21,203,988) | (29,758,568) |
| **Selected Average Financial Statistics** (Items 10 to 13 inclusive in $) | | | | | | | | | | |
| 10. Av. Payment Partnership | 817 | 671 | 815 | 922 | 1,188 | 1,238 | 1,304 | 1,252 | 1,404 | 1,340 |
| 11. Av. Payment Partner | 150 | 106 | 158 | 178 | 172 | 206 | 198 | 169 | 174 | 155 |
| 12. Av. Income Partnership | 855 | 506 | 1,928 | 329 | 708 | 1,514 | 1,954 | 2,541 | (33,291) | (42,878) |
| 13. Av. Income Partner | 156 | 80 | 374 | 64 | 102 | 252 | 297 | 344 | (4,132) | (4,966) |
| **Selected Financial Statistics as Percent of Op. Income** | | | | | | | | | | |
| 14. Depreciation / Op. Income (%) | 19.8 | 18.7 | 17.5 | 17.5 | 18.5 | n.a. | n.a. | n.a. | 96.6 | 101.7 |
| 15. Interest / Op. Income (%) | 30.0 | 27.7 | 25.8 | 26.5 | 28.5 | 21.2 | 22.1 | 19.0 | 39.8 | 42.2 |
| 16. Payroll / Op. Income (%) | 4.2 | 4.3 | 3.9 | 3.8 | 4.1 | 3.4 | 3.5 | n.a. | 5.4 | 7.1 |
| **Selected Index Numbers (1976 = 100)** | | | | | | | | | | |
| 17. Partnerships | 100.0 | 108.8 | 117.8 | 129.9 | 140.0 | 157.5 | 171.2 | 176.5 | 192.0 | 209.2 |
| 18. Partners | 100.0 | 126.1 | 111.2 | 123.0 | 177.3 | 172.9 | 206.3 | 238.8 | 283.1 | 330.7 |
| 19. Operating Income | 100.0 | 116.3 | 141.9 | 174.1 | 203.7 | 102.5 | 114.2 | 138.9 | 87.4 | 96.1 |
| 20. Payments to Partners | 100.0 | 89.3 | 117.5 | 146.5 | 203.5 | 238.6 | 273.1 | 270.3 | 329.9 | 343.0 |
| **Selected Financial Statistics (Constant $, 1976 = 100)** | | | | | | | | | | |
| 21. Operating Income | 100.0 | 109.2 | 123.8 | 136.6 | 140.7 | 64.2 | 67.3 | 79.4 | 47.9 | 50.9 |
| 22. Payments to Partners | 100.0 | 83.9 | 102.6 | 114.9 | 140.6 | 149.4 | 161.1 | 154.5 | 180.8 | 181.5 |
| 23. Av. Payment, Partnership | 100.0 | 77.2 | 87.0 | 88.5 | 100.3 | 94.7 | 94.1 | 87.6 | 94.1 | 86.8 |
| 24. Av. Payment, Partner | 100.0 | 66.1 | 92.3 | 93.5 | 79.8 | 86.6 | 77.5 | 65.0 | 63.8 | 54.7 |

TABLE 3

186: OPERATORS AND LESSORS OF BUILDINGS, WITH AND WITHOUT NET INCOME

| | 1976 | 1977 | 1978 | 1979 | 1980 | 1981 | 1982 | 1983 | 1984 | 1985 |
|---|---|---|---|---|---|---|---|---|---|---|
| 1. Number of Partnerships | 273,444 | 299,086 | 321,449 | 360,555 | 390,946 | 435,836 | 474,686 | 491,701 | 536,216 | 582,487 |
| 2. Number of Partners | 1,519,658 | 1,971,352 | 1,692,629 | 1,888,645 | 2,822,924 | 2,692,739 | 3,145,740 | 3,542,974 | 4,510,523 | 5,185,721 |
| **Selected Financial Statistics** | | | | | | | | | | |
| **(Items 3 to 9 inclusive in 000's of dollars)** | | | | | | | | | | |
| 3. Operating Income | 23,922,092 | 26,932,657 | 31,708,081 | 38,757,094 | 47,236,116 | 17,727,222 | 21,285,124 | 25,016,782 | 8,010,782 | 8,986,289 |
| 4. Depreciation | 5,697,610 | 6,213,022 | 7,122,350 | 8,777,647 | 10,773,849 | n.a. | n.a. | n.a. | 23,387,506 | 26,943,273 |
| 5. Taxes Paid | 3,282,793 | 3,498,308 | 3,566,352 | 3,972,647 | 4,599,676 | 875,673 | 842,899 | 994,567 | 1,120,793 | 1,373,908 |
| 6. Interest Paid | 8,095,138 | 8,714,746 | 9,978,486 | 12,540,071 | 15,571,594 | 4,091,219 | 4,701,885 | 5,228,168 | 7,050,216 | 8,348,764 |
| 7. Payroll Deductions | 991,493 | 1,121,742 | 1,238,884 | 1,473,508 | 1,961,065 | 571,333 | 586,237 | n.a. | 762,987 | 1,190,376 |
| 8. Payments to Partners | 177,198 | 139,244 | 183,630 | 230,835 | 383,826 | 370,367 | 475,780 | 551,958 | 611,115 | 701,846 |
| 9. Net Income, less Deficit | 273,021 | 230,841 | 1,856,285 | 263,327 | 389,803 | 672,091 | 849,140 | 1,374,200 | (18,885,837) | (26,204,238) |
| **Selected Average Financial Statistics** | | | | | | | | | | |
| **(Items 10 to 13 inclusive in $)** | | | | | | | | | | |
| 10. Av. Payment Partnership | 648 | 466 | 571 | 640 | 982 | 850 | 1,002 | 1,123 | 1,140 | 1,205 |
| 11. Av. Payment Partner | 117 | 71 | 108 | 122 | 136 | 138 | 151 | 152 | 135 | 135 |
| 12. Av. Income Partnership | 998 | 772 | 5,775 | 730 | 997 | 1,542 | 1,789 | 2,795 | (35,221) | (44,987) |
| 13. Av. Income Partner | 180 | 117 | 1,097 | 139 | 138 | 250 | 270 | 377 | (4,187) | (5,053) |
| **Selected Financial Statistics as Percent of Op. Income** | | | | | | | | | | |
| 14. Depreciation / Op. Income (%) | 23.8 | 23.1 | 22.5 | 22.7 | 22.8 | n.a. | n.a. | n.a. | 292.0 | 299.8 |
| 15. Interest / Op. Income (%) | 33.8 | 32.4 | 31.5 | 32.4 | 33.0 | 23.1 | 22.1 | 20.9 | 88.0 | 92.9 |
| 16. Payroll / Op. Income (%) | 4.1 | 4.2 | 3.9 | 3.8 | 4.2 | 3.2 | 2.8 | n.a. | 9.5 | 13.3 |
| **Selected Index Numbers (1976 = 100)** | | | | | | | | | | |
| 17. Partnerships | 100.0 | 109.4 | 117.6 | 131.9 | 143.0 | 159.4 | 173.6 | 179.8 | 196.1 | 213.0 |
| 18. Partners | 100.0 | 129.7 | 111.4 | 124.3 | 185.8 | 177.2 | 207.0 | 239.7 | 296.8 | 341.2 |
| 19. Operating Income | 100.0 | 112.6 | 132.5 | 162.0 | 197.5 | 74.1 | 89.0 | 104.6 | 33.5 | 37.6 |
| 20. Payments to Partners | 100.0 | 78.6 | 103.6 | 130.3 | 216.6 | 209.0 | 268.5 | 311.5 | 344.9 | 396.1 |
| **Selected Financial Statistics (Constant $, 1976 = 100)** | | | | | | | | | | |
| 21. Operating Income | 100.0 | 105.8 | 115.7 | 127.1 | 136.4 | 46.4 | 52.5 | 59.8 | 18.4 | 19.9 |
| 22. Payments to Partners | 100.0 | 73.8 | 90.4 | 102.2 | 149.6 | 130.8 | 158.4 | 178.0 | 189.0 | 209.6 |
| 23. Av. Payment, Partnership | 100.0 | 67.6 | 76.8 | 77.4 | 104.7 | 82.1 | 91.3 | 98.9 | 96.3 | 98.4 |
| 24. Av. Payment, Partner | 100.0 | 57.0 | 80.4 | 81.9 | 80.4 | 74.6 | 76.0 | 74.6 | 62.9 | 61.4 |

TABLE 3

187: LESSORS, OTHER THAN BUILDINGS, WITH AND WITHOUT NET INCOME

| | 1976 | 1977 | 1978 | 1979 | 1980 | 1981 | 1982 | 1983 | 1984 | 1985 |
|---|---|---|---|---|---|---|---|---|---|---|
| 1. Number of Partnerships | 25,637 | 26,303 | 28,216 | 27,130 | 30,689 | 30,808 | 30,217 | 32,218 | 32,558 | 37,589 |
| 2. Number of Partners | 131,266 | 135,954 | 137,419 | 130,195 | 145,767 | 168,988 | 205,044 | 245,388 | 214,681 | 253,820 |
| **Selected Financial Statistics** | | | | | | | | | | |
| **(Items 3 to 9 inclusive in 000's of dollars)** | | | | | | | | | | |
| 3. Operating Income | 539,386 | 533,174 | 730,390 | 772,140 | 1,065,132 | 706,983 | 759,455 | 1,002,954 | 227,656 | 326,234 |
| 4. Depreciation | 58,923 | 71,572 | 77,319 | 85,982 | 152,823 | n.a. | n.a. | n.a. | 766,442 | 908,931 |
| 5. Taxes Paid | 62,382 | 69,691 | 73,615 | 65,140 | 82,974 | 20,603 | 24,775 | 20,776 | 30,535 | 40,275 |
| 6. Interest Paid | 140,895 | 160,360 | 146,886 | 155,645 | 230,357 | 108,539 | 114,108 | 146,156 | 179,002 | 271,419 |
| 7. Payroll Deductions | 8,571 | 8,899 | 16,015 | 20,521 | 23,166 | 21,325 | 26,623 | n.a. | 28,967 | 37,441 |
| 8. Payments to Partners | 3,924 | 4,509 | 4,494 | 9,280 | 6,430 | 6,007 | 10,731 | 12,681 | 5,368 | 8,439 |
| 9. Net Income, less Deficit | 60,834 | 29,253 | 158,285 | 171,954 | 194,614 | 56,173 | 4,111 | 74,399 | (505,372) | (615,982) |
| **Selected Average Financial Statistics** | | | | | | | | | | |
| **(Items 10 to 13 inclusive in $)** | | | | | | | | | | |
| 10. Av. Payment Partnership | 153 | 171 | 159 | 342 | 210 | 195 | 355 | 394 | 165 | 225 |
| 11. Av. Payment Partner | 30 | 33 | 33 | 71 | 44 | 36 | 52 | 52 | 25 | 33 |
| 12. Av. Income Partnership | 2,373 | 1,112 | 5,610 | 6,338 | 6,341 | 1,823 | 136 | 2,309 | (15,522) | (16,387) |
| 13. Av. Income Partner | 463 | 215 | 1,152 | 1,321 | 1,335 | 332 | 20 | 303 | (2,354) | (2,427) |
| **Selected Financial Statistics as Percent of Op. Income** | | | | | | | | | | |
| 14. Depreciation / Op. Income (%) | 10.9 | 13.4 | 10.6 | 11.1 | 14.4 | n.a. | n.a. | n.a. | 336.7 | 278.6 |
| 15. Interest / Op. Income (%) | 26.1 | 30.1 | 20.1 | 20.2 | 21.6 | 15.4 | 15.0 | 14.6 | 78.6 | 83.2 |
| 16. Payroll / Op. Income (%) | 1.6 | 1.7 | 2.2 | 2.7 | 2.2 | 3.0 | 3.5 | n.a. | 12.7 | 11.5 |
| **Selected Index Numbers (1976 = 100)** | | | | | | | | | | |
| 17. Partnerships | 100.0 | 102.6 | 110.1 | 105.8 | 119.7 | 120.2 | 117.9 | 125.7 | 127.0 | 146.6 |
| 18. Partners | 100.0 | 103.6 | 104.7 | 99.2 | 111.0 | 128.7 | 156.2 | 186.9 | 163.5 | 193.4 |
| 19. Operating Income | 100.0 | 98.8 | 135.4 | 143.2 | 197.5 | 131.1 | 140.8 | 185.9 | 42.2 | 60.5 |
| 20. Payments to Partners | 100.0 | 114.9 | 114.5 | 236.5 | 163.9 | 153.1 | 273.5 | 323.2 | 136.8 | 215.1 |
| **Selected Financial Statistics (Constant $, 1976 = 100)** | | | | | | | | | | |
| 21. Operating Income | 100.0 | 92.9 | 118.2 | 112.3 | 136.4 | 82.0 | 83.0 | 106.2 | 23.1 | 32.0 |
| 22. Payments to Partners | 100.0 | 107.9 | 99.9 | 185.5 | 113.2 | 95.8 | 161.3 | 184.7 | 75.0 | 113.8 |
| 23. Av. Payment, Partnership | 100.0 | 104.7 | 90.2 | 174.9 | 94.7 | 80.2 | 137.0 | 147.0 | 59.0 | 78.0 |
| 24. Av. Payment, Partner | 100.0 | 102.7 | 97.0 | 188.2 | 102.7 | 74.1 | 102.7 | 97.0 | 45.6 | 57.0 |

## TABLE 3

### 188: REAL ESTATE AGENTS, BROKERS, AND MANAGERS, WITH AND WITHOUT NET INCOME

| | 1976 | 1977 | 1978 | 1979 | 1980 | 1981 | 1982 | 1983 | 1984 | 1985 |
|---|---|---|---|---|---|---|---|---|---|---|
| 1. Number of Partnerships | 17,478 | 17,998 | 18,932 | 21,161 | 19,043 | 19,018 | 17,854 | 17,027 | 18,049 | 17,707 |
| 2. Number of Partners | 77,813 | 78,968 | 86,534 | 110,962 | 79,768 | 72,128 | 124,944 | 116,869 | 168,403 | 166,541 |
| **Selected Financial Statistics** (Items 3 to 9 inclusive in 000's of dollars) | | | | | | | | | | |
| 3. Operating Income | 1,660,113 | 2,035,439 | 2,316,826 | 3,315,657 | 2,985,239 | 2,426,235 | 2,039,256 | 1,857,089 | 2,123,896 | 2,046,049 |
| 4. Depreciation | 57,150 | 95,710 | 68,119 | 87,804 | 145,349 | n.a. | n.a. | n.a. | 236,465 | 256,375 |
| 5. Taxes Paid | 61,528 | 69,845 | 58,829 | 66,196 | 87,557 | 63,486 | 53,429 | 59,518 | 65,114 | 64,215 |
| 6. Interest Paid | 184,084 | 206,346 | 177,765 | 295,601 | 366,359 | 302,028 | 362,588 | 248,978 | 324,876 | 358,554 |
| 7. Payroll Deductions | 152,310 | 200,245 | 179,435 | 262,389 | 245,052 | 165,941 | 199,055 | n.a. | 228,199 | 359,195 |
| 8. Payments to Partners | 60,179 | 56,016 | 59,294 | 86,365 | 75,002 | 147,185 | 82,616 | 51,288 | 140,573 | 36,768 |
| 9. Net Income, less Deficit | 3,895 | 107,993 | 170,948 | 176,525 | 76,110 | 17,238 | 38,427 | 35,444 | (221,749) | (347,198) |
| **Selected Average Financial Statistics** (Items 10 to 13 inclusive in $) | | | | | | | | | | |
| 10. Av. Payment Partnership | 3,443 | 3,112 | 3,132 | 4,081 | 3,939 | 7,759 | 4,627 | 3,012 | 7,788 | 2,076 |
| 11. Av. Payment Partner | 773 | 709 | 685 | 778 | 940 | 2,041 | 661 | 439 | 835 | 221 |
| 12. Av. Income Partnership | 223 | 6,000 | 9,030 | 8,342 | 3,997 | 906 | 2,152 | 2,082 | (12,286) | (19,608) |
| 13. Av. Income Partner | 50 | 1,368 | 1,976 | 1,591 | 954 | 239 | 308 | 303 | (1,317) | (2,085) |
| **Selected Financial Statistics as Percent of Op. Income** | | | | | | | | | | |
| 14. Depreciation / Op. Income (%) | 3.4 | 4.7 | 2.9 | 2.7 | 4.9 | n.a. | n.a. | n.a. | 11.1 | 12.5 |
| 15. Interest / Op. Income (%) | 11.1 | 10.1 | 7.7 | 8.9 | 12.3 | 12.5 | 17.8 | 13.4 | 15.3 | 17.5 |
| 16. Payroll / Op. Income (%) | 9.2 | 9.8 | 7.7 | 7.9 | 8.2 | 6.8 | 9.8 | n.a. | 10.7 | 17.6 |
| **Selected Index Numbers (1976 = 100)** | | | | | | | | | | |
| 17. Partnerships | 100.0 | 103.0 | 108.3 | 121.1 | 109.0 | 108.8 | 102.2 | 97.4 | 103.3 | 101.3 |
| 18. Partners | 100.0 | 101.5 | 111.2 | 142.6 | 102.5 | 92.7 | 160.6 | 150.2 | 216.4 | 214.0 |
| 19. Operating Income | 100.0 | 122.6 | 139.6 | 199.7 | 179.8 | 146.1 | 122.8 | 111.9 | 127.9 | 123.2 |
| 20. Payments to Partners | 100.0 | 93.1 | 98.5 | 143.5 | 124.6 | 244.6 | 137.3 | 85.2 | 233.6 | 61.1 |
| **Selected Financial Statistics (Constant $, 1976 = 100)** | | | | | | | | | | |
| 21. Operating Income | 100.0 | 115.2 | 121.8 | 156.6 | 124.2 | 91.5 | 72.4 | 63.9 | 70.1 | 65.2 |
| 22. Payments to Partners | 100.0 | 87.4 | 86.0 | 112.6 | 86.1 | 153.1 | 81.0 | 48.7 | 128.0 | 32.3 |
| 23. Av. Payment, Partnership | 100.0 | 84.9 | 79.4 | 92.9 | 79.0 | 140.7 | 79.2 | 50.0 | 123.9 | 31.9 |
| 24. Av. Payment, Partner | 100.0 | 86.2 | 77.4 | 78.9 | 84.0 | 165.1 | 50.5 | 32.4 | 59.1 | 15.2 |

TABLE 3

OTHER REAL ESTATE (189,190,191,192), WITH AND WITHOUT NET INCOME

| | 1976 | 1977 | 1978 | 1979 | 1980 | 1981 | 1982 | 1983 | 1984 | 1985 |
|---|---|---|---|---|---|---|---|---|---|---|
| 1. Number of Partnerships | 15,141 | 17,539 | 22,263 | 22,125 | 23,707 | 36,689 | 45,214 | 44,535 | 50,096 | 56,244 |
| 2. Number of Partners | 83,460 | 98,917 | 99,138 | 98,342 | 163,754 | 199,231 | 262,577 | 322,540 | 267,585 | 386,393 |
| **Selected Financial Statistics** (Items 3 to 9 inclusive in 000's of dollars) | | | | | | | | | | |
| 3. Operating Income | 3,650,106 | 5,118,612 | 7,495,026 | 8,992,076 | 9,350,710 | 9,665,155 | 9,904,996 | 13,478,414 | 15,648,747 | 17,250,160 |
| 4. Depreciation | 85,109 | 78,147 | 111,560 | 100,745 | 117,964 | n.a. | n.a. | n.a. | 740,424 | 993,961 |
| 5. Taxes Paid | 107,182 | 100,730 | 116,621 | 114,773 | 126,399 | 164,493 | 193,246 | 226,625 | 323,161 | 328,366 |
| 6. Interest Paid | 504,491 | 491,007 | 583,827 | 724,620 | 1,081,814 | 1,977,113 | 2,327,962 | 2,248,871 | 2,800,848 | 3,078,439 |
| 7. Payroll Deductions | 111,147 | 157,355 | 214,049 | 223,158 | 247,732 | 268,931 | 368,175 | n.a. | 383,760 | 443,220 |
| 8. Payments to Partners | 29,787 | 42,357 | 71,220 | 70,738 | 86,533 | 123,321 | 171,233 | 116,872 | 137,197 | 56,244 |
| 9. Net Income, less Deficit | 12,723 | 343,102 | 773,453 | 866,320 | 347,019 | 107,680 | 220,633 | 188,091 | (1,591,031) | (2,591,151) |
| **Selected Average Financial Statistics** (Items 10 to 13 inclusive in $) | | | | | | | | | | |
| 10. Av. Payment Partnership | 1,967 | 2,415 | 3,199 | 3,197 | 3,650 | 3,361 | 3,787 | 2,624 | 2,739 | 1,000 |
| 11. Av. Payment Partner | 357 | 428 | 718 | 719 | 528 | 619 | 652 | 362 | 513 | 146 |
| 12. Av. Income Partnership | 840 | 19,562 | 34,742 | 39,156 | 14,638 | 2,935 | 4,880 | 4,223 | (31,760) | (46,070) |
| 13. Av. Income Partner | 152 | 3,469 | 7,802 | 8,809 | 2,119 | 540 | 840 | 583 | (5,946) | (6,706) |
| **Selected Financial Statistics as Percent of Op. Income (%)** | | | | | | | | | | |
| 14. Depreciation / Op. Income (%) | 2.3 | 1.5 | 1.5 | 1.1 | 1.3 | n.a. | n.a. | n.a. | 4.7 | 5.8 |
| 15. Interest / Op. Income (%) | 13.8 | 9.6 | 7.8 | 8.1 | 11.6 | 20.5 | 23.5 | 16.7 | 17.9 | 17.9 |
| 16. Payroll / Op. Income (%) | 3.1 | 3.1 | 2.9 | 2.5 | 2.7 | 2.8 | 3.7 | n.a. | 2.5 | 2.6 |
| **Selected Index Numbers (1976 = 100)** | | | | | | | | | | |
| 17. Partnerships | 100.0 | 115.8 | 147.0 | 146.1 | 156.6 | 242.3 | 298.6 | 294.1 | 330.9 | 371.5 |
| 18. Partners | 100.0 | 118.5 | 118.8 | 117.8 | 196.2 | 238.7 | 314.6 | 386.5 | 320.6 | 463.0 |
| 19. Operating Income | 100.0 | 140.2 | 205.3 | 246.4 | 256.2 | 264.8 | 271.4 | 369.3 | 428.7 | 472.6 |
| 20. Payments to Partners | 100.0 | 142.2 | 239.1 | 237.5 | 290.5 | 414.0 | 574.9 | 392.4 | 460.6 | 188.8 |
| **Selected Financial Statistics (Constant $, 1976 = 100)** | | | | | | | | | | |
| 21. Operating Income | 100.0 | 131.7 | 179.2 | 193.2 | 177.0 | 165.7 | 160.0 | 211.0 | 235.0 | 250.1 |
| 22. Payments to Partners | 100.0 | 133.6 | 208.6 | 186.2 | 200.7 | 259.1 | 339.0 | 224.2 | 252.4 | 99.9 |
| 23. Av. Payment, Partnership | 100.0 | 115.4 | 141.9 | 127.5 | 128.2 | 106.9 | 113.5 | 76.2 | 76.3 | 26.9 |
| 24. Av. Payment, Partner | 100.0 | 112.7 | 175.3 | 158.1 | 102.2 | 108.4 | 108.0 | 57.8 | 78.8 | 21.5 |

TABLE 3

193: SERVICES, WITH AND WITHOUT NET INCOME

| | 1976 | 1977 | 1978 | 1979 | 1980 | 1981 | 1982 | 1983 | 1984 | 1985 |
|---|---|---|---|---|---|---|---|---|---|---|
| 1. Number of Partnerships | 207,248 | 226,638 | 241,313 | 238,716 | 263,400 | 262,932 | 279,171 | 306,294 | 331,103 | 341,295 |
| 2. Number of Partners | 676,915 | 752,041 | 783,163 | 813,459 | 938,027 | 1,024,751 | 1,146,522 | 1,274,934 | 1,577,704 | 1,713,060 |
| **Selected Financial Statistics** (Items 3 to 9 inclusive in 000's of dollars) | | | | | | | | | | |
| 3. Operating Income | 32,056,952 | 37,787,716 | 43,452,400 | 49,727,591 | 58,626,801 | 60,997,315 | 65,834,823 | 75,069,096 | 90,243,640 | 104,196,609 |
| 4. Depreciation | 2,114,488 | 2,398,789 | 2,996,898 | 3,362,246 | 4,137,512 | n.a. | n.a. | n.a. | 9,506,970 | 10,544,359 |
| 5. Taxes Paid | 994,036 | 1,144,146 | 1,331,725 | 1,491,595 | 1,706,247 | 1,710,381 | 1,906,894 | 2,043,104 | 2,583,201 | 2,992,718 |
| 6. Interest Paid | 1,096,517 | 1,183,269 | 1,525,567 | 1,890,824 | 2,478,040 | 2,689,365 | 3,291,559 | 3,625,926 | 4,817,213 | 5,887,018 |
| 7. Payroll Deductions | 7,607,275 | 8,741,484 | 9,934,238 | 11,456,000 | 13,560,867 | 14,760,645 | 15,890,604 | n.a. | 20,610,115 | 34,005,288 |
| 8. Payments to Partners | 1,126,888 | 1,215,790 | 1,372,472 | 1,631,674 | 1,981,433 | 2,164,698 | 2,168,132 | 2,683,618 | 2,998,483 | 341,295 |
| 9. Net Income, less Deficit | 7,802,578 | 9,244,749 | 10,344,281 | 11,339,292 | 12,424,161 | 11,618,171 | 11,902,165 | 12,456,811 | 15,583,256 | 16,541,329 |
| **Selected Average Financial Statistics** (Items 10 to 13 inclusive in $) | | | | | | | | | | |
| 10. Av. Payment Partnership | 5,437 | 5,364 | 5,688 | 6,835 | 7,523 | 8,233 | 7,766 | 8,762 | 9,056 | 1,000 |
| 11. Av. Payment Partner | 1,665 | 1,617 | 1,752 | 2,006 | 2,112 | 2,112 | 1,891 | 2,105 | 1,901 | 199 |
| 12. Av. Income Partnership | 37,649 | 40,791 | 42,867 | 47,501 | 47,168 | 44,187 | 42,634 | 40,669 | 47,065 | 48,466 |
| 13. Av. Income Partner | 11,527 | 12,293 | 13,208 | 13,940 | 13,245 | 11,338 | 10,381 | 9,771 | 9,877 | 9,656 |
| **Selected Financial Statistics as Percent of Op. Income** | | | | | | | | | | |
| 14. Depreciation / Op. Income (%) | 6.6 | 6.4 | 6.9 | 6.8 | 7.1 | n.a. | n.a. | n.a. | 10.5 | 10.1 |
| 15. Interest / Op. Income (%) | 3.4 | 3.1 | 3.5 | 3.8 | 4.2 | 4.4 | 5.0 | 4.8 | 5.3 | 5.7 |
| 16. Payroll / Op. Income (%) | 23.7 | 23.1 | 22.9 | 23.0 | 23.1 | 24.2 | 24.1 | n.a. | 22.8 | 32.6 |
| **Selected Index Numbers** (1976 = 100) | | | | | | | | | | |
| 17. Partnerships | 100.0 | 109.4 | 116.4 | 115.2 | 127.1 | 126.9 | 134.7 | 147.8 | 159.8 | 164.7 |
| 18. Partners | 100.0 | 111.1 | 115.7 | 120.2 | 138.6 | 151.4 | 169.4 | 188.3 | 233.1 | 253.1 |
| 19. Operating Income | 100.0 | 117.9 | 135.5 | 155.1 | 182.9 | 190.3 | 205.4 | 234.2 | 281.5 | 325.0 |
| 20. Payments to Partners | 100.0 | 107.9 | 121.8 | 144.8 | 175.8 | 192.1 | 192.4 | 238.1 | 266.1 | 30.3 |
| **Selected Financial Statistics** (Constant $, 1976 = 100) | | | | | | | | | | |
| 21. Operating Income | 100.0 | 110.7 | 118.3 | 121.7 | 126.3 | 119.1 | 121.1 | 133.8 | 154.3 | 172.0 |
| 22. Payments to Partners | 100.0 | 101.4 | 106.3 | 113.6 | 121.5 | 120.2 | 113.5 | 136.1 | 145.8 | 16.0 |
| 23. Av. Payment, Partnership | 100.0 | 92.7 | 91.3 | 98.6 | 95.6 | 94.8 | 84.2 | 92.1 | 91.3 | 9.7 |
| 24. Av. Payment, Partner | 100.0 | 91.3 | 91.9 | 94.5 | 87.7 | 79.4 | 67.0 | 72.2 | 62.6 | 6.3 |

*Page 257*

## TABLE 3

### 194: HOTELS AND OTHER LODGING PLACES, WITH AND WITHOUT NET INCOME

| | 1976 | 1977 | 1978 | 1979 | 1980 | 1981 | 1982 | 1983 | 1984 | 1985 |
|---|---|---|---|---|---|---|---|---|---|---|
| 1. Number of Partnerships | 14,917 | 13,463 | 17,735 | 16,952 | 16,040 | 19,569 | 18,321 | 18,196 | 18,917 | 21,794 |
| 2. Number of Partners | 69,360 | 66,444 | 74,306 | 81,916 | 89,597 | 122,183 | 118,329 | 123,373 | 241,166 | 189,576 |
| **Selected Financial Statistics (Items 3 to 9 inclusive in 000's of dollars)** | | | | | | | | | | |
| 3. Operating Income | 3,086,658 | 3,703,729 | 5,141,259 | 6,600,623 | 7,014,224 | 8,178,604 | 8,510,334 | 10,892,920 | 14,019,645 | 16,946,223 |
| 4. Depreciation | 358,517 | 395,969 | 551,454 | 692,965 | 763,095 | n.a. | n.a. | n.a. | 2,000,634 | 2,788,881 |
| 5. Taxes Paid | 219,628 | 239,124 | 305,652 | 366,183 | 384,415 | 389,120 | 469,254 | 514,996 | 636,313 | 824,752 |
| 6. Interest Paid | 433,328 | 455,007 | 640,113 | 826,667 | 942,425 | 1,189,509 | 1,566,460 | 1,741,888 | 2,463,792 | 3,205,772 |
| 7. Payroll Deductions | 666,091 | 785,964 | 1,017,649 | 1,261,299 | 1,434,281 | 1,640,506 | 1,896,854 | n.a. | 2,500,836 | 3,042,031 |
| 8. Payments to Partners | 37,323 | 35,598 | 40,443 | 55,354 | 67,821 | 72,850 | 137,715 | 103,922 | 90,669 | 116,418 |
| 9. Net Income, less Deficit | 6,222 | 13,283 | 108,270 | 102,429 | 1,140 | 35,248 | 102,738 | 126,136 | (2,109,805) | (3,383,463) |
| **Selected Average Financial Statistics (Items 10 to 13 inclusive in $)** | | | | | | | | | | |
| 10. Av. Payment Partnership | 2,502 | 2,644 | 2,280 | 3,265 | 4,228 | 3,723 | 7,517 | 5,711 | 4,793 | 5,342 |
| 11. Av. Payment Partner | 538 | 536 | 544 | 676 | 757 | 596 | 1,164 | 842 | 376 | 614 |
| 12. Av. Income Partnership | 417 | 987 | 6,105 | 6,042 | 71 | 1,801 | 5,608 | 6,932 | (111,530) | (155,247) |
| 13. Av. Income Partner | 90 | 200 | 1,457 | 1,250 | 13 | 288 | 868 | 1,022 | (8,748) | (17,848) |
| **Selected Financial Statistics as Percent of Op. Income** | | | | | | | | | | |
| 14. Depreciation / Op. Income (%) | 11.6 | 10.7 | 10.7 | 10.5 | 10.9 | n.a. | n.a. | n.a. | 14.3 | 16.5 |
| 15. Interest / Op. Income (%) | 14.0 | 12.3 | 12.5 | 12.5 | 13.4 | 14.5 | 18.4 | 16.0 | 17.6 | 18.9 |
| 16. Payroll / Op. Income (%) | 21.6 | 21.2 | 19.8 | 19.1 | 20.5 | 20.1 | 22.3 | n.a. | 17.8 | 18.0 |
| **Selected Index Numbers (1976 = 100)** | | | | | | | | | | |
| 17. Partnerships | 100.0 | 90.3 | 118.9 | 113.6 | 107.5 | 131.2 | 122.8 | 122.0 | 126.8 | 146.1 |
| 18. Partners | 100.0 | 95.8 | 107.1 | 118.1 | 129.2 | 176.2 | 170.6 | 177.9 | 347.7 | 273.3 |
| 19. Operating Income | 100.0 | 120.0 | 166.6 | 213.8 | 227.2 | 265.0 | 275.7 | 352.9 | 454.2 | 549.0 |
| 20. Payments to Partners | 100.0 | 95.4 | 108.4 | 148.3 | 181.7 | 195.2 | 369.0 | 278.4 | 242.9 | 311.9 |
| **Selected Financial Statistics (Constant $, 1976 = 100)** | | | | | | | | | | |
| 21. Operating Income | 100.0 | 112.7 | 145.3 | 167.7 | 157.0 | 165.8 | 162.6 | 201.6 | 248.9 | 290.5 |
| 22. Payments to Partners | 100.0 | 89.6 | 94.6 | 116.3 | 125.5 | 122.2 | 217.6 | 159.1 | 133.1 | 165.1 |
| 23. Av. Payment, Partnership | 100.0 | 99.3 | 79.5 | 102.4 | 116.7 | 93.2 | 177.2 | 130.4 | 105.0 | 113.0 |
| 24. Av. Payment, Partner | 100.0 | 93.5 | 88.1 | 98.5 | 97.3 | 69.4 | 127.7 | 89.4 | 38.3 | 60.5 |

## TABLE 3

### 196: MOTELS, MOTOR HOTELS, AND COURTS, WITH AND WITHOUT NET INCOME

| | 1976 | 1977 | 1978 | 1979 | 1980 | 1981 | 1982 | 1983 | 1984 | 1985 |
|---|---|---|---|---|---|---|---|---|---|---|
| 1. Number of Partnerships | 8,163 | 7,387 | 8,595 | 8,930 | 8,084 | 9,010 | 7,663 | 7,398 | 9,995 | 9,954 |
| 2. Number of Partners | 37,915 | 39,608 | 39,089 | 45,485 | 45,051 | 58,072 | 58,875 | 56,589 | 156,598 | 70,494 |
| **Selected Financial Statistics** (Items 3 to 9 inclusive in 000's of dollars) | | | | | | | | | | |
| 3. Operating Income | 1,551,371 | 1,869,406 | 2,478,116 | 3,377,928 | 3,109,649 | 3,010,457 | 3,258,909 | 3,874,536 | 3,957,395 | 4,517,161 |
| 4. Depreciation | 187,345 | 200,635 | 253,475 | 352,119 | 338,658 | n.a. | n.a. | n.a. | 646,973 | 805,449 |
| 5. Taxes Paid | 104,343 | 116,400 | 147,912 | 187,044 | 165,475 | 142,146 | 161,862 | 189,491 | 201,538 | 239,593 |
| 6. Interest Paid | 203,402 | 221,504 | 294,483 | 417,504 | 404,020 | 434,885 | 582,962 | 667,190 | 744,949 | 876,320 |
| 7. Payroll Deductions | 329,839 | 394,110 | 511,363 | 615,309 | 626,399 | 620,377 | 722,181 | n.a. | 801,896 | 899,922 |
| 8. Payments to Partners | 21,676 | 18,008 | 22,103 | 25,076 | 37,889 | 36,126 | 46,807 | 40,001 | 33,336 | 53,920 |
| 9. Net Income, less Deficit | 5,328 | 54,512 | 137,697 | 115,557 | 129,933 | 59,928 | 12,502 | 15,880 | (271,855) | (470,144) |
| **Selected Average Financial Statistics** (Items 10 to 13 inclusive in $) | | | | | | | | | | |
| 10. Av. Payment Partnership | 2,655 | 2,438 | 2,572 | 2,808 | 4,687 | 4,010 | 6,108 | 5,407 | 3,335 | 5,417 |
| 11. Av. Payment Partner | 572 | 455 | 565 | 551 | 841 | 622 | 795 | 707 | 213 | 765 |
| 12. Av. Income Partnership | 653 | 7,379 | 16,021 | 12,940 | 16,073 | 6,651 | 1,631 | 2,147 | (27,199) | (47,232) |
| 13. Av. Income Partner | 141 | 1,376 | 3,523 | 2,541 | 2,884 | 1,032 | 212 | 281 | (1,736) | (6,669) |
| **Selected Financial Statistics as Percent of Op. Income** | | | | | | | | | | |
| 14. Depreciation / Op. Income (%) | 12.1 | 10.7 | 10.2 | 10.4 | 10.9 | n.a. | n.a. | n.a. | 16.4 | 17.8 |
| 15. Interest / Op. Income (%) | 13.1 | 11.9 | 11.9 | 12.4 | 13.0 | 14.5 | 17.9 | 17.2 | 18.8 | 19.4 |
| 16. Payroll / Op. Income (%) | 21.3 | 21.1 | 20.6 | 18.2 | 20.1 | 20.6 | 22.2 | n.a. | 20.3 | 19.9 |
| **Selected Index Numbers** (1976 = 100) | | | | | | | | | | |
| 17. Partnerships | 100.0 | 90.5 | 105.3 | 109.4 | 99.0 | 110.4 | 93.9 | 90.6 | 122.4 | 121.9 |
| 18. Partners | 100.0 | 104.5 | 103.1 | 120.0 | 118.8 | 153.2 | 155.3 | 149.3 | 413.0 | 185.9 |
| 19. Operating Income | 100.0 | 120.5 | 159.7 | 217.7 | 200.4 | 194.1 | 210.1 | 249.7 | 255.1 | 291.2 |
| 20. Payments to Partners | 100.0 | 83.1 | 102.0 | 115.7 | 174.8 | 166.7 | 215.9 | 184.5 | 153.8 | 248.8 |
| **Selected Financial Statistics** (Constant $, 1976 = 100) | | | | | | | | | | |
| 21. Operating Income | 100.0 | 113.2 | 139.4 | 170.8 | 138.5 | 121.5 | 123.9 | 142.7 | 139.8 | 154.1 |
| 22. Payments to Partners | 100.0 | 78.0 | 89.0 | 90.7 | 120.8 | 104.3 | 127.4 | 105.4 | 84.3 | 131.6 |
| 23. Av. Payment, Partnership | 100.0 | 86.2 | 84.5 | 83.0 | 121.9 | 94.5 | 135.7 | 116.3 | 68.8 | 107.9 |
| 24. Av. Payment, Partner | 100.0 | 74.9 | 86.2 | 75.5 | 101.7 | 68.0 | 82.0 | 70.7 | 20.3 | 70.7 |

TABLE 3

OTHER LODGING PLACES (195,197,198,199,200), WITH AND WITHOUT NET INCOME

| | 1976 | 1977 | 1978 | 1979 | 1980 | 1981 | 1982 | 1983 | 1984 | 1985 |
|---|---|---|---|---|---|---|---|---|---|---|
| 1. Number of Partnerships | 6,754 | 6,076 | 9,140 | 8,022 | 7,955 | 10,559 | 10,657 | 10,798 | 8,922 | 11,840 |
| 2. Number of Partners | 31,445 | 26,836 | 35,217 | 36,431 | 44,546 | 64,110 | 59,454 | 66,784 | 84,567 | 119,082 |
| **Selected Financial Statistics** | | | | | | | | | | |
| (Items 3 to 9 inclusive in 000's of dollars) | | | | | | | | | | |
| 3. Operating Income | 1,535,287 | 1,834,323 | 2,663,142 | 3,222,695 | 3,904,575 | 5,168,146 | 5,251,425 | 7,018,383 | 10,062,251 | 12,429,062 |
| 4. Depreciation | 171,172 | 195,334 | 297,979 | 340,846 | 424,438 | n.a. | n.a. | n.a. | 1,353,661 | 1,983,433 |
| 5. Taxes Paid | 115,285 | 122,724 | 157,740 | 179,139 | 218,940 | 246,974 | 307,392 | 325,504 | 434,775 | 585,159 |
| 6. Interest Paid | 229,926 | 233,503 | 345,630 | 409,164 | 538,404 | 754,625 | 983,498 | 1,074,699 | 1,718,843 | 2,329,452 |
| 7. Payroll Deductions | 336,252 | 391,854 | 506,287 | 645,989 | 807,882 | 1,020,130 | 1,174,673 | n.a. | 1,698,940 | 2,142,108 |
| 8. Payments to Partners | 15,647 | 17,590 | 18,340 | 30,278 | 29,932 | 36,724 | 90,908 | 63,920 | 57,332 | 11,840 |
| 9. Net Income, less Deficit | 11,632 | 27,723 | 5,292 | 9,994 | 16,507 | 41,239 | 90,234 | 150,957 | (1,837,950) | (2,913,319) |
| **Selected Average Financial Statistics** | | | | | | | | | | |
| (Items 10 to 13 inclusive in $) | | | | | | | | | | |
| 10. Av. Payment Partnership | 2,317 | 2,895 | 2,007 | 3,774 | 3,763 | 3,478 | 8,530 | 5,920 | 6,426 | 1,000 |
| 11. Av. Payment Partner | 498 | 655 | 521 | 831 | 672 | 573 | 1,529 | 957 | 678 | 99 |
| 12. Av. Income Partnership | 1,722 | 4,563 | 579 | 1,246 | 2,075 | 3,906 | 8,467 | 13,980 | (206,002) | (246,057) |
| 13. Av. Income Partner | 370 | 1,033 | 150 | 274 | 371 | 643 | 1,518 | 2,260 | (21,734) | (24,465) |
| **Selected Financial Statistics as Percent of Op. Income** | | | | | | | | | | |
| 14. Depreciation / Op. Income (%) | 11.2 | 10.7 | 11.2 | 10.6 | 10.9 | n.a. | n.a. | n.a. | 13.5 | 16.0 |
| 15. Interest / Op. Income (%) | 15.0 | 12.7 | 13.0 | 12.7 | 13.8 | 14.6 | 18.7 | 15.3 | 17.1 | 18.7 |
| 16. Payroll / Op. Income (%) | 21.9 | 21.4 | 19.0 | 20.0 | 20.7 | 19.7 | 22.4 | n.a. | 16.9 | 17.2 |
| **Selected Index Numbers (1976 = 100)** | | | | | | | | | | |
| 17. Partnerships | 100.0 | 90.0 | 135.3 | 118.8 | 117.8 | 156.3 | 157.8 | 159.9 | 132.1 | 175.3 |
| 18. Partners | 100.0 | 85.3 | 112.0 | 115.9 | 141.7 | 203.9 | 189.1 | 212.4 | 268.9 | 378.7 |
| 19. Operating Income | 100.0 | 119.5 | 173.5 | 209.9 | 254.3 | 336.6 | 342.0 | 457.1 | 655.4 | 809.6 |
| 20. Payments to Partners | 100.0 | 112.4 | 117.2 | 193.5 | 191.3 | 234.7 | 581.0 | 408.5 | 366.4 | 75.7 |
| **Selected Financial Statistics (Constant $, 1976 = 100)** | | | | | | | | | | |
| 21. Operating Income | 100.0 | 112.2 | 151.4 | 164.6 | 175.7 | 210.7 | 201.7 | 261.2 | 359.2 | 428.4 |
| 22. Payments to Partners | 100.0 | 105.6 | 102.3 | 151.8 | 132.2 | 146.9 | 342.6 | 233.4 | 200.8 | 40.0 |
| 23. Av. Payment, Partnership | 100.0 | 117.4 | 75.6 | 127.8 | 112.2 | 94.0 | 217.2 | 146.0 | 152.0 | 22.8 |
| 24. Av. Payment, Partner | 100.0 | 123.7 | 91.5 | 130.9 | 93.2 | 72.0 | 181.3 | 110.0 | 74.7 | 10.6 |

TABLE 3

201: PERSONAL SERVICES, WITH AND WITHOUT NET INCOME

| | 1976 | 1977 | 1978 | 1979 | 1980 | 1981 | 1982 | 1983 | 1984 | 1985 |
|---|---|---|---|---|---|---|---|---|---|---|
| 1. Number of Partnerships | 22,666 | 23,300 | 26,604 | 24,266 | 25,607 | 27,840 | 30,179 | 31,165 | 33,282 | 34,967 |
| 2. Number of Partners | 52,274 | 55,538 | 57,632 | 54,324 | 57,187 | 62,564 | 69,213 | 79,574 | 79,816 | 86,106 |
| **Selected Financial Statistics** | | | | | | | | | | |
| (Items 3 to 9 inclusive in 000's of dollars) | | | | | | | | | | |
| 3. Operating Income | 1,239,128 | 1,304,412 | 1,475,278 | 1,467,295 | 1,661,812 | 1,714,784 | 1,925,522 | 2,010,864 | 2,245,631 | 2,481,308 |
| 4. Depreciation | 59,761 | 63,145 | 63,651 | 66,335 | 81,303 | n.a. | n.a. | n.a. | 157,697 | 178,561 |
| 5. Taxes Paid | 43,172 | 44,866 | 46,246 | 44,141 | 54,300 | 50,461 | 48,823 | 57,625 | 54,629 | 73,764 |
| 6. Interest Paid | 17,158 | 21,058 | 22,550 | 25,387 | 32,935 | 39,056 | 33,700 | 40,787 | 47,501 | 59,478 |
| 7. Payroll Deductions | 284,832 | 297,753 | 348,467 | 327,795 | 393,804 | 341,560 | 364,223 | n.a. | 477,145 | 516,201 |
| 8. Payments to Partners | 76,278 | 65,429 | 98,533 | 107,117 | 102,997 | 134,973 | 125,035 | 151,255 | 103,513 | 88,220 |
| 9. Net Income, less Deficit | 19,233 | 233,487 | 223,006 | 194,608 | 222,839 | 171,627 | 243,661 | 245,859 | 214,290 | 261,075 |
| **Selected Average Financial Statistics** | | | | | | | | | | |
| (Items 10 to 13 inclusive in $) | | | | | | | | | | |
| 10. Av. Payment Partnership | 3,365 | 2,808 | 3,704 | 4,414 | 4,022 | 4,848 | 4,143 | 4,853 | 3,110 | 2,523 |
| 11. Av. Payment Partner | 1,459 | 1,178 | 1,710 | 1,972 | 1,801 | 2,157 | 1,807 | 1,901 | 1,297 | 1,025 |
| 12. Av. Income Partnership | 849 | 10,021 | 8,382 | 8,020 | 8,702 | 6,165 | 8,074 | 7,889 | 6,439 | 7,466 |
| 13. Av. Income Partner | 368 | 4,204 | 3,869 | 3,582 | 3,897 | 2,743 | 3,520 | 3,090 | 2,685 | 3,032 |
| **Selected Financial Statistics as Percent of Op. Income** | | | | | | | | | | |
| 14. Depreciation / Op. Income (%) | 4.8 | 4.8 | 4.3 | 4.5 | 4.9 | n.a. | n.a. | n.a. | 7.0 | 7.2 |
| 15. Interest / Op. Income (%) | 1.4 | 1.6 | 1.5 | 1.7 | 2.0 | 2.3 | 1.8 | 2.0 | 2.1 | 2.4 |
| 16. Payroll / Op. Income (%) | 23.0 | 22.8 | 23.6 | 22.3 | 23.7 | 19.9 | 18.9 | n.a. | 21.3 | 20.8 |
| **Selected Index Numbers (1976 = 100)** | | | | | | | | | | |
| 17. Partnerships | 100.0 | 102.8 | 117.4 | 107.1 | 113.0 | 122.8 | 133.1 | 137.5 | 146.8 | 154.3 |
| 18. Partners | 100.0 | 106.2 | 110.2 | 103.9 | 109.4 | 119.7 | 132.4 | 152.2 | 152.7 | 164.7 |
| 19. Operating Income | 100.0 | 105.3 | 119.1 | 118.4 | 134.1 | 138.4 | 155.4 | 162.3 | 181.2 | 200.2 |
| 20. Payments to Partners | 100.0 | 85.8 | 129.2 | 140.4 | 135.0 | 176.9 | 163.9 | 198.3 | 135.7 | 115.7 |
| **Selected Financial Statistics (Constant $, 1976 = 100)** | | | | | | | | | | |
| 21. Operating Income | 100.0 | 98.9 | 103.9 | 92.9 | 92.6 | 86.6 | 91.6 | 92.7 | 99.3 | 106.0 |
| 22. Payments to Partners | 100.0 | 80.6 | 112.7 | 110.1 | 93.3 | 110.8 | 96.7 | 113.3 | 74.4 | 61.2 |
| 23. Av. Payment, Partnership | 100.0 | 78.4 | 96.1 | 102.8 | 82.6 | 90.2 | 72.6 | 82.4 | 50.7 | 39.7 |
| 24. Av. Payment, Partner | 100.0 | 75.8 | 102.2 | 106.0 | 85.3 | 92.5 | 73.0 | 74.4 | 48.7 | 37.2 |

## TABLE 3

### LAUNDRIES, DRY CLEANING, AND GARMENT SERVICES (202,203), WITH AND WITHOUT NET INCOME

|  | 1976 | 1977 | 1978 | 1979 | 1980 | 1981 | 1982 | 1983 | 1984 | 1985 |
|---|---|---|---|---|---|---|---|---|---|---|
| 1. Number of Partnerships | 7,211 | 7,431 | 6,950 | 6,807 | 6,614 | 5,692 | 7,248 | 5,673 | 6,940 | 8,854 |
| 2. Number of Partners | 15,905 | 18,467 | 15,260 | 15,117 | 14,531 | 12,040 | 16,389 | 12,554 | 15,170 | 20,296 |
| **Selected Financial Statistics** | | | | | | | | | | |
| **(Items 3 to 9 inclusive in 000's of dollars)** | | | | | | | | | | |
| 3. Operating Income | 447,259 | 457,944 | 445,974 | 490,490 | 525,032 | 557,965 | 583,152 | 560,676 | 654,959 | 741,506 |
| 4. Depreciation | 30,309 | 29,460 | 29,021 | 32,608 | 34,199 | n.a. | n.a. | n.a. | 56,403 | 85,580 |
| 5. Taxes Paid | 18,525 | 16,477 | 15,444 | 15,948 | 18,017 | 15,287 | 17,510 | 19,135 | 17,054 | 29,292 |
| 6. Interest Paid | 8,254 | 10,579 | 11,135 | 10,159 | 14,366 | 15,448 | 16,468 | 20,984 | 16,841 | 21,791 |
| 7. Payroll Deductions | 120,914 | 119,555 | 101,708 | 123,791 | 124,331 | 117,215 | 127,043 | n.a. | 131,569 | 138,191 |
| 8. Payments to Partners | 16,823 | 10,282 | 14,267 | 19,175 | 19,096 | 23,032 | 32,795 | 16,940 | 15,183 | 5,972 |
| 9. Net Income, less Deficit | 47,937 | 53,738 | 60,290 | 56,813 | 60,691 | 52,896 | 38,478 | 31,374 | 52,679 | 38,870 |
| **Selected Average Financial Statistics** | | | | | | | | | | |
| **(Items 10 to 13 inclusive in $)** | | | | | | | | | | |
| 10. Av. Payment Partnership | 2,333 | 1,384 | 2,053 | 2,817 | 2,887 | 4,046 | 4,525 | 2,986 | 2,188 | 674 |
| 11. Av. Payment Partner | 1,058 | 557 | 935 | 1,268 | 1,314 | 1,913 | 2,001 | 1,349 | 1,001 | 294 |
| 12. Av. Income Partnership | 6,648 | 7,232 | 8,675 | 8,346 | 9,176 | 9,293 | 5,309 | 5,530 | 7,591 | 4,390 |
| 13. Av. Income Partner | 3,014 | 2,910 | 3,951 | 3,758 | 4,177 | 4,393 | 2,348 | 2,499 | 3,473 | 1,915 |
| **Selected Financial Statistics as Percent of Op. Income** | | | | | | | | | | |
| 14. Depreciation / Op. Income (%) | 6.8 | 6.4 | 6.5 | 6.7 | 6.5 | n.a. | n.a. | n.a. | 8.6 | 11.5 |
| 15. Interest / Op. Income (%) | 1.9 | 2.3 | 2.5 | 2.1 | 2.7 | 2.8 | 2.8 | 3.7 | 2.6 | 2.9 |
| 16. Payroll / Op. Income (%) | 27.0 | 26.1 | 22.8 | 25.2 | 23.7 | 21.0 | 21.8 | n.a. | 20.1 | 18.6 |
| **Selected Index Numbers (1976 = 100)** | | | | | | | | | | |
| 17. Partnerships | 100.0 | 103.1 | 96.4 | 94.4 | 91.7 | 78.9 | 100.5 | 78.7 | 96.2 | 122.8 |
| 18. Partners | 100.0 | 116.1 | 95.9 | 95.0 | 91.4 | 75.7 | 103.0 | 78.9 | 95.4 | 127.6 |
| 19. Operating Income | 100.0 | 102.4 | 99.7 | 109.7 | 117.4 | 124.8 | 130.4 | 125.4 | 146.4 | 165.8 |
| 20. Payments to Partners | 100.0 | 61.1 | 84.8 | 114.0 | 113.5 | 136.9 | 194.9 | 100.7 | 90.3 | 35.5 |
| **Selected Financial Statistics (Constant $, 1976 = 100)** | | | | | | | | | | |
| 21. Operating Income | 100.0 | 96.2 | 87.0 | 86.0 | 81.1 | 78.1 | 76.9 | 71.6 | 80.3 | 87.7 |
| 22. Payments to Partners | 100.0 | 57.4 | 74.0 | 89.4 | 78.4 | 85.7 | 115.0 | 57.5 | 49.5 | 18.8 |
| 23. Av. Payment, Partnership | 100.0 | 55.8 | 76.8 | 94.7 | 85.5 | 108.5 | 114.4 | 73.2 | 51.4 | 15.3 |
| 24. Av. Payment, Partner | 100.0 | 49.5 | 77.2 | 94.0 | 85.8 | 113.2 | 111.5 | 72.9 | 51.9 | 14.7 |

TABLE 3

206: BEAUTY SHOPS, WITH AND WITHOUT NET INCOME

| | 1976 | 1977 | 1978 | 1979 | 1980 | 1981 | 1982 | 1983 | 1984 | 1985 |
|---|---|---|---|---|---|---|---|---|---|---|
| 1. Number of Partnerships | 6,205 | 7,058 | 8,572 | 7,970 | 8,829 | 6,382 | 6,978 | 9,158 | 10,200 | 9,357 |
| 2. Number of Partners | 13,361 | 15,861 | 18,081 | 16,604 | 18,794 | 13,356 | 16,028 | 22,733 | 23,702 | 20,486 |
| **Selected Financial Statistics** (Items 3 to 9 inclusive in 000's of dollars) | | | | | | | | | | |
| 3. Operating Income | 222,065 | 262,045 | 345,282 | 318,183 | 387,982 | 247,432 | 268,313 | 308,867 | 324,151 | 516,785 |
| 4. Depreciation | 7,262 | 7,177 | 9,882 | 8,849 | 11,165 | n.a. | n.a. | n.a. | 21,107 | 20,208 |
| 5. Taxes Paid | 7,993 | 10,934 | 11,542 | 10,837 | 13,343 | 6,510 | 8,962 | 10,210 | 13,723 | 14,060 |
| 6. Interest Paid | 2,099 | 2,294 | 2,091 | 2,868 | 3,652 | 5,328 | 4,364 | 6,776 | 12,884 | 10,560 |
| 7. Payroll Deductions | 71,752 | 84,918 | 112,433 | 97,695 | 133,971 | 70,404 | 91,231 | n.a. | 85,734 | 174,168 |
| 8. Payments to Partners | 23,754 | 18,421 | 37,660 | 35,786 | 37,043 | 46,913 | 24,699 | 58,215 | 48,396 | 36,493 |
| 9. Net Income, less Deficit | 38,829 | 48,865 | 47,165 | 35,018 | 46,288 | 25,001 | 27,137 | 20,679 | (5,523) | 16,261 |
| **Selected Average Financial Statistics** (Items 10 to 13 inclusive in $) | | | | | | | | | | |
| 10. Av. Payment Partnership | 3,828 | 2,610 | 4,393 | 4,490 | 4,196 | 7,351 | 3,540 | 6,357 | 4,745 | 3,900 |
| 11. Av. Payment Partner | 1,778 | 1,161 | 2,083 | 2,155 | 1,971 | 3,513 | 1,541 | 2,561 | 2,042 | 1,781 |
| 12. Av. Income Partnership | 6,258 | 6,923 | 5,502 | 4,394 | 5,243 | 3,917 | 3,889 | 2,258 | (541) | 1,738 |
| 13. Av. Income Partner | 2,906 | 3,081 | 2,609 | 2,109 | 2,463 | 1,872 | 1,693 | 910 | (233) | 794 |
| **Selected Financial Statistics as Percent of Op. Income** | | | | | | | | | | |
| 14. Depreciation / Op. Income (%) | 3.3 | 2.7 | 2.9 | 2.8 | 2.9 | n.a. | n.a. | n.a. | 6.5 | 3.9 |
| 15. Interest / Op. Income (%) | 0.10 | 0.9 | 0.6 | 0.9 | 0.9 | 2.2 | 1.6 | 2.2 | 4.0 | 2.0 |
| 16. Payroll / Op. Income (%) | 32.3 | 32.4 | 32.6 | 30.7 | 34.5 | 28.5 | 34.0 | n.a. | 26.5 | 33.7 |
| **Selected Index Numbers (1976 = 100)** | | | | | | | | | | |
| 17. Partnerships | 100.0 | 113.7 | 138.1 | 128.4 | 142.3 | 102.9 | 112.5 | 147.6 | 164.4 | 150.8 |
| 18. Partners | 100.0 | 118.7 | 135.3 | 124.3 | 140.7 | 100.0 | 120.0 | 170.1 | 177.4 | 153.3 |
| 19. Operating Income | 100.0 | 118.0 | 155.5 | 143.3 | 174.7 | 111.4 | 120.8 | 139.1 | 146.0 | 232.7 |
| 20. Payments to Partners | 100.0 | 77.5 | 158.5 | 150.7 | 155.9 | 197.5 | 104.0 | 245.1 | 203.7 | 153.6 |
| **Selected Financial Statistics (Constant $, 1976 = 100)** | | | | | | | | | | |
| 21. Operating Income | 100.0 | 110.9 | 135.7 | 112.4 | 120.7 | 69.7 | 71.3 | 79.5 | 80.0 | 123.1 |
| 22. Payments to Partners | 100.0 | 72.8 | 138.3 | 118.2 | 107.7 | 123.6 | 61.3 | 140.0 | 111.7 | 81.3 |
| 23. Av. Payment, Partnership | 100.0 | 64.0 | 100.1 | 92.0 | 75.7 | 120.2 | 54.5 | 94.9 | 67.9 | 53.9 |
| 24. Av. Payment, Partner | 100.0 | 61.4 | 102.2 | 95.0 | 76.6 | 123.7 | 51.1 | 82.3 | 62.9 | 53.0 |

TABLE 3

207: BARBER SHOPS, WITH AND WITHOUT NET INCOME

| | 1976 | 1977 | 1978 | 1979 | 1980 | 1981 | 1982 | 1983 | 1984 | 1985 |
|---|---|---|---|---|---|---|---|---|---|---|
| 1. Number of Partnerships | 2,461 | 2,255 | 2,778 | 2,628 | 2,570 | 1,992 | 2,766 | 3,982 | 3,528 | 4,234 |
| 2. Number of Partners | 5,696 | 5,129 | 5,724 | 5,350 | 5,228 | 3,984 | 5,698 | 10,914 | 9,086 | 13,813 |
| **Selected Financial Statistics** | | | | | | | | | | |
| **(Items 3 to 9 inclusive in 000's of dollars)** | | | | | | | | | | |
| 3. Operating Income | 95,494 | 93,747 | 116,790 | 112,519 | 111,448 | 115,260 | 153,303 | 265,718 | 306,775 | 280,826 |
| 4. Depreciation | 1,983 | 1,500 | 2,359 | 2,179 | 2,167 | n.a. | n.a. | n.a. | 6,002 | 7,574 |
| 5. Taxes Paid | 1,906 | 2,629 | 2,854 | 3,478 | 3,283 | 7,517 | 605 | 8,787 | 3,756 | 8,369 |
| 6. Interest Paid | 680 | 1,117 | 546 | 643 | 720 | 1,162 | 692 | 457 | n.a. | 2,621 |
| 7. Payroll Deductions | 24,394 | 26,627 | 37,651 | 29,799 | 23,129 | 38,919 | 52,648 | n.a. | 139,928 | 44,387 |
| 8. Payments to Partners | 13,038 | 13,533 | 21,855 | 25,426 | 26,989 | 18,875 | 3,625 | n.a. | n.a. | 4,234 |
| 9. Net Income, less Deficit | 22,481 | 25,429 | 24,058 | 25,561 | 27,746 | 20,867 | 38,720 | 48,689 | 31,743 | 116,458 |
| **Selected Average Financial Statistics** | | | | | | | | | | |
| **(Items 10 to 13 inclusive in $)** | | | | | | | | | | |
| 10. Av. Payment Partnership | 5,298 | 6,001 | 7,867 | 9,675 | 10,502 | 9,475 | 1,311 | n.a. | n.a. | 1,000 |
| 11. Av. Payment Partner | 2,289 | 2,639 | 3,818 | 4,753 | 5,162 | 4,738 | 636 | n.a. | n.a. | 307 |
| 12. Av. Income Partnership | 9,135 | 11,277 | 8,660 | 9,726 | 10,796 | 10,475 | 13,999 | 12,227 | 8,997 | 27,505 |
| 13. Av. Income Partner | 3,947 | 4,958 | 4,203 | 4,778 | 5,307 | 5,238 | 6,795 | 4,461 | 3,494 | 8,431 |
| **Selected Financial Statistics as Percent of Op. Income** | | | | | | | | | | |
| 14. Depreciation / Op. Income (%) | 2.1 | 1.6 | 2.0 | 1.9 | 1.9 | n.a. | n.a. | n.a. | 2.0 | 2.7 |
| 15. Interest / Op. Income (%) | 0.7 | 1.2 | 0.5 | 0.6 | 0.7 | 1.0 | 0.5 | 0.2 | n.a. | 0.9 |
| 16. Payroll / Op. Income (%) | 25.6 | 28.4 | 32.2 | 26.5 | 20.8 | 33.8 | 34.3 | n.a. | 45.6 | 15.8 |
| **Selected Index Numbers (1976 = 100)** | | | | | | | | | | |
| 17. Partnerships | 100.0 | 91.6 | 112.9 | 106.8 | 104.4 | 80.9 | 112.4 | 161.8 | 143.4 | 172.0 |
| 18. Partners | 100.0 | 90.0 | 100.5 | 93.9 | 91.8 | 69.9 | 100.0 | 191.6 | 159.5 | 242.5 |
| 19. Operating Income | 100.0 | 98.2 | 122.3 | 117.8 | 116.7 | 120.7 | 160.5 | 278.3 | 321.3 | 294.1 |
| 20. Payments to Partners | 100.0 | 103.8 | 167.6 | 195.0 | 207.0 | 144.8 | 27.8 | n.a. | n.a. | 32.5 |
| **Selected Financial Statistics (Constant $, 1976 = 100)** | | | | | | | | | | |
| 21. Operating Income | 100.0 | 92.2 | 106.7 | 92.4 | 80.6 | 75.5 | 94.7 | 159.0 | 176.1 | 155.6 |
| 22. Payments to Partners | 100.0 | 97.5 | 146.3 | 152.9 | 143.0 | 90.6 | 16.4 | n.a. | n.a. | 17.2 |
| 23. Av. Payment, Partnership | 100.0 | 106.4 | 129.6 | 143.2 | 136.9 | 111.9 | 14.6 | n.a. | n.a. | 10.0 |
| 24. Av. Payment, Partner | 100.0 | 108.3 | 145.5 | 162.8 | 155.8 | 129.5 | 16.4 | n.a. | n.a. | 7.1 |

## TABLE 3

### OTHER PERSONAL SERVICES (205,208,209,210), WITH AND WITHOUT NET INCOME

| | 1976 | 1977 | 1978 | 1979 | 1980 | 1981 | 1982 | 1983 | 1984 | 1985 |
|---|---|---|---|---|---|---|---|---|---|---|
| 1. Number of Partnerships | 6,789 | 6,556 | 8,304 | 6,861 | 7,594 | 13,773 | 13,188 | 12,352 | 12,614 | 12,522 |
| 2. Number of Partners | 17,312 | 16,081 | 18,567 | 17,253 | 18,633 | 33,183 | 31,097 | 33,372 | 31,858 | 31,510 |
| **Selected Financial Statistics** (Items 3 to 9 inclusive in 000's of dollars) | | | | | | | | | | |
| 3. Operating Income | 474,310 | 490,676 | 567,232 | 546,103 | 637,349 | 794,126 | 920,754 | 875,604 | 959,746 | 942,191 |
| 4. Depreciation | 20,207 | 25,008 | 22,389 | 22,699 | 33,773 | n.a. | n.a. | n.a. | 74,186 | 65,198 |
| 5. Taxes Paid | 14,748 | 14,826 | 16,405 | 13,878 | 19,657 | 21,146 | 21,744 | 19,494 | 20,096 | 22,043 |
| 6. Interest Paid | 6,125 | 7,068 | 8,778 | 11,717 | 14,197 | 17,118 | 12,177 | 12,571 | 17,777 | 24,506 |
| 7. Payroll Deductions | 67,772 | 66,653 | 96,674 | 76,511 | 112,373 | 115,022 | 93,302 | n.a. | 119,914 | 159,455 |
| 8. Payments to Partners | 22,663 | 23,193 | 24,749 | 26,731 | 19,869 | 46,154 | 63,916 | 76,099 | 39,934 | 44,741 |
| 9. Net Income, less Deficit | 151,258 | 95,455 | 91,492 | 77,216 | 91,112 | 74,788 | 139,325 | 152,757 | 135,391 | 89,486 |
| **Selected Average Financial Statistics** (Items 10 to 13 inclusive in $) | | | | | | | | | | |
| 10. Av. Payment Partnership | 3,338 | 3,538 | 2,980 | 3,896 | 2,616 | 3,351 | 4,847 | 6,161 | 3,166 | 3,573 |
| 11. Av. Payment Partner | 1,309 | 1,442 | 1,333 | 1,549 | 1,066 | 1,391 | 2,055 | 2,280 | 1,253 | 1,420 |
| 12. Av. Income Partnership | 22,280 | 14,560 | 11,018 | 11,254 | 11,998 | 5,430 | 10,565 | 12,367 | 10,733 | 7,146 |
| 13. Av. Income Partner | 8,737 | 5,936 | 4,928 | 4,476 | 4,890 | 2,254 | 4,480 | 4,577 | 4,250 | 2,840 |
| **Selected Financial Statistics as Percent of Op. Income** | | | | | | | | | | |
| 14. Depreciation / Op. Income (%) | 4.3 | 5.1 | 4.0 | 4.2 | 5.3 | n.a. | n.a. | n.a. | 7.7 | 6.9 |
| 15. Interest / Op. Income (%) | 1.3 | 1.4 | 1.6 | 2.2 | 2.2 | 2.2 | 1.3 | 1.4 | 1.9 | 2.6 |
| 16. Payroll / Op. Income (%) | 14.3 | 13.6 | 17.0 | 14.0 | 17.6 | 14.5 | 10.1 | n.a. | 12.5 | 16.9 |
| **Selected Index Numbers** (1976 = 100) | | | | | | | | | | |
| 17. Partnerships | 100.0 | 96.6 | 122.3 | 101.1 | 111.9 | 202.9 | 194.3 | 181.9 | 185.8 | 184.4 |
| 18. Partners | 100.0 | 92.9 | 107.2 | 99.7 | 107.6 | 191.7 | 179.6 | 192.8 | 184.0 | 182.0 |
| 19. Operating Income | 100.0 | 103.5 | 119.6 | 115.1 | 134.4 | 167.4 | 194.1 | 184.6 | 202.3 | 198.6 |
| 20. Payments to Partners | 100.0 | 102.3 | 109.2 | 117.9 | 87.7 | 203.7 | 282.0 | 335.8 | 176.2 | 197.4 |
| **Selected Financial Statistics** (Constant $, 1976 = 100) | | | | | | | | | | |
| 21. Operating Income | 100.0 | 97.2 | 104.4 | 90.3 | 92.8 | 104.8 | 114.5 | 105.5 | 110.9 | 105.1 |
| 22. Payments to Partners | 100.0 | 96.1 | 95.3 | 92.5 | 60.6 | 127.5 | 166.3 | 191.9 | 96.6 | 104.5 |
| 23. Av. Payment, Partnership | 100.0 | 99.5 | 77.9 | 91.5 | 54.1 | 62.8 | 85.7 | 105.5 | 52.0 | 56.6 |
| 24. Av. Payment, Partner | 100.0 | 103.4 | 88.8 | 92.9 | 56.3 | 66.6 | 92.6 | 99.5 | 52.5 | 57.4 |

## TABLE 3

### 211: BUSINESS SERVICES, WITH AND WITHOUT NET INCOME

| | 1976 | 1977 | 1978 | 1979 | 1980 | 1981 | 1982 | 1983 | 1984 | 1985 |
|---|---|---|---|---|---|---|---|---|---|---|
| 1. Number of Partnerships | 32,292 | 36,424 | 39,774 | 42,274 | 51,277 | 59,193 | 63,164 | 78,869 | 80,189 | 81,289 |
| 2. Number of Partners | 102,370 | 144,779 | 129,717 | 155,306 | 191,283 | 274,173 | 360,043 | 413,537 | 451,534 | 564,856 |
| **Selected Financial Statistics** (Items 3 to 9 inclusive in 000's of dollars) | | | | | | | | | | |
| 3. Operating Income | 2,416,771 | 3,101,180 | 3,748,145 | 4,009,392 | 5,256,460 | 4,898,639 | 5,259,821 | 6,438,694 | 7,278,916 | 8,192,931 |
| 4. Depreciation | 898,770 | 1,098,530 | 1,306,188 | 1,408,190 | 1,768,358 | n.a. | n.a. | n.a. | 3,495,424 | 3,977,830 |
| 5. Taxes Paid | 54,624 | 65,379 | 76,050 | 77,307 | 91,951 | 87,886 | 106,662 | 107,366 | 135,198 | 141,309 |
| 6. Interest Paid | 315,016 | 311,395 | 387,827 | 429,178 | 695,471 | 551,207 | 684,860 | 711,756 | 869,171 | 963,978 |
| 7. Payroll Deductions | 346,128 | 416,841 | 525,721 | 488,366 | 711,240 | 766,574 | 794,722 | n.a. | 1,105,678 | 1,153,448 |
| 8. Payments to Partners | 77,381 | 91,196 | 97,189 | 113,525 | 161,762 | 190,370 | 157,336 | 143,971 | 213,954 | 210,242 |
| 9. Net Income, less Deficit | 10,103 | 62,645 | 166,895 | 186,777 | 63,531 | 33,708 | 54,767 | 55,907 | 296,751 | 274,212 |
| **Selected Average Financial Statistics** (Items 10 to 13 inclusive in $) | | | | | | | | | | |
| 10. Av. Payment Partnership | 2,396 | 2,504 | 2,444 | 2,685 | 3,155 | 3,216 | 2,491 | 1,825 | 2,668 | 2,586 |
| 11. Av. Payment Partner | 756 | 630 | 749 | 731 | 846 | 694 | 437 | 348 | 474 | 372 |
| 12. Av. Income Partnership | 313 | 1,720 | 4,196 | 4,418 | 1,239 | 569 | 867 | 709 | 3,701 | 3,373 |
| 13. Av. Income Partner | 99 | 433 | 1,287 | 1,203 | 332 | 123 | 152 | 135 | 657 | 485 |
| **Selected Financial Statistics as Percent of Op. Income** | | | | | | | | | | |
| 14. Depreciation / Op. Income (%) | 37.2 | 35.4 | 34.9 | 35.1 | 33.6 | n.a. | n.a. | n.a. | 48.0 | 48.6 |
| 15. Interest / Op. Income (%) | 13.0 | 10.0 | 10.4 | 10.7 | 13.2 | 11.3 | 13.0 | 11.1 | 11.9 | 11.8 |
| 16. Payroll / Op. Income (%) | 14.3 | 13.4 | 14.0 | 12.2 | 13.5 | 15.7 | 15.1 | n.a. | 15.2 | 14.1 |
| **Selected Index Numbers (1976 = 100)** | | | | | | | | | | |
| 17. Partnerships | 100.0 | 112.8 | 123.2 | 130.9 | 158.8 | 183.3 | 195.6 | 244.2 | 248.3 | 251.7 |
| 18. Partners | 100.0 | 141.4 | 126.7 | 151.7 | 186.9 | 267.8 | 351.7 | 404.0 | 441.1 | 551.8 |
| 19. Operating Income | 100.0 | 128.3 | 155.1 | 165.9 | 217.5 | 202.7 | 217.6 | 266.4 | 301.2 | 339.0 |
| 20. Payments to Partners | 100.0 | 117.9 | 125.6 | 146.7 | 209.0 | 246.0 | 203.3 | 186.1 | 276.5 | 271.7 |
| **Selected Financial Statistics (Constant $, 1976 = 100)** | | | | | | | | | | |
| 21. Operating Income | 100.0 | 120.5 | 135.3 | 130.1 | 150.3 | 126.9 | 128.4 | 152.2 | 165.1 | 179.4 |
| 22. Payments to Partners | 100.0 | 110.7 | 109.6 | 115.1 | 144.4 | 154.0 | 119.9 | 106.3 | 151.5 | 143.8 |
| 23. Av. Payment, Partnership | 100.0 | 98.2 | 89.0 | 87.9 | 90.9 | 84.0 | 61.3 | 43.5 | 61.0 | 57.1 |
| 24. Av. Payment, Partner | 100.0 | 78.3 | 86.4 | 75.8 | 77.4 | 57.5 | 34.1 | 26.4 | 34.3 | 25.9 |

TABLE 3

218: AUTOMOTIVE REPAIR SERVICES, WITH AND WITHOUT NET INCOME

| | 1976 | 1977 | 1978 | 1979 | 1980 | 1981 | 1982 | 1983 | 1984 | 1985 |
|---|---|---|---|---|---|---|---|---|---|---|
| 1. Number of Partnerships | 21,219 | 23,259 | 24,176 | 22,070 | 22,752 | 25,190 | 23,154 | 28,287 | 35,396 | 30,188 |
| 2. Number of Partners | 46,452 | 51,599 | 55,145 | 54,242 | 54,730 | 59,205 | 52,656 | 67,505 | 76,991 | 67,760 |
| **Selected Financial Statistics** | | | | | | | | | | |
| (Items 3 to 9 inclusive in 000's of dollars) | | | | | | | | | | |
| 3. Operating Income | 1,519,879 | 1,760,055 | 2,311,183 | 2,165,301 | 2,415,045 | 3,104,175 | 2,554,385 | 3,092,570 | 3,808,690 | 4,171,445 |
| 4. Depreciation | 96,927 | 133,318 | 155,985 | 176,502 | 180,776 | n.a. | n.a. | n.a. | 257,020 | 242,747 |
| 5. Taxes Paid | 42,611 | 46,442 | 63,357 | 58,787 | 68,002 | 60,062 | 48,223 | 61,940 | 75,057 | 74,827 |
| 6. Interest Paid | 36,174 | 49,041 | 57,500 | 74,047 | 109,627 | 112,108 | 90,529 | 113,077 | 119,028 | 131,169 |
| 7. Payroll Deductions | 178,144 | 215,520 | 292,224 | 277,831 | 323,070 | 430,250 | 330,583 | n.a. | 514,649 | 529,787 |
| 8. Payments to Partners | 58,792 | 56,577 | 79,414 | 73,089 | 83,380 | 97,159 | 94,025 | 99,873 | 119,770 | 101,276 |
| 9. Net Income, less Deficit | 182,359 | 233,956 | 322,715 | 256,917 | 197,708 | 301,987 | 258,547 | 225,642 | 350,080 | 399,607 |
| **Selected Average Financial Statistics** | | | | | | | | | | |
| (Items 10 to 13 inclusive in $) | | | | | | | | | | |
| 10. Av. Payment Partnership | 2,771 | 2,432 | 3,285 | 3,312 | 3,665 | 3,857 | 4,061 | 3,531 | 3,384 | 3,355 |
| 11. Av. Payment Partner | 1,266 | 1,096 | 1,440 | 1,347 | 1,523 | 1,641 | 1,786 | 1,479 | 1,556 | 1,495 |
| 12. Av. Income Partnership | 8,594 | 10,059 | 13,349 | 11,641 | 8,690 | 11,988 | 11,166 | 7,977 | 9,890 | 13,237 |
| 13. Av. Income Partner | 3,926 | 4,534 | 5,852 | 4,736 | 3,612 | 5,101 | 4,910 | 3,343 | 4,547 | 5,897 |
| **Selected Financial Statistics as Percent of Op. Income** | | | | | | | | | | |
| 14. Depreciation / Op. Income (%) | 6.4 | 7.6 | 6.8 | 8.2 | 7.5 | n.a. | n.a. | n.a. | 6.8 | 5.8 |
| 15. Interest / Op. Income (%) | 2.4 | 2.8 | 2.5 | 3.4 | 4.5 | 3.6 | 3.5 | 3.7 | 3.1 | 3.1 |
| 16. Payroll / Op. Income (%) | 11.7 | 12.3 | 12.6 | 12.8 | 13.4 | 13.9 | 12.9 | n.a. | 13.5 | 12.7 |
| **Selected Index Numbers (1976 = 100)** | | | | | | | | | | |
| 17. Partnerships | 100.0 | 109.6 | 113.9 | 104.0 | 107.2 | 118.7 | 109.1 | 133.3 | 166.8 | 142.3 |
| 18. Partners | 100.0 | 111.1 | 118.7 | 116.8 | 117.8 | 127.5 | 113.4 | 145.3 | 165.7 | 145.9 |
| 19. Operating Income | 100.0 | 115.8 | 152.1 | 142.5 | 158.9 | 204.2 | 168.1 | 203.5 | 250.6 | 274.5 |
| 20. Payments to Partners | 100.0 | 96.2 | 135.1 | 124.3 | 141.8 | 165.3 | 159.9 | 169.9 | 203.7 | 172.3 |
| **Selected Financial Statistics (Constant $, 1976 = 100)** | | | | | | | | | | |
| 21. Operating Income | 100.0 | 108.8 | 132.7 | 111.7 | 109.8 | 127.8 | 99.1 | 116.3 | 137.3 | 145.2 |
| 22. Payments to Partners | 100.0 | 90.4 | 117.9 | 97.5 | 98.0 | 103.4 | 94.3 | 97.1 | 111.6 | 91.2 |
| 23. Av. Payment, Partnership | 100.0 | 82.5 | 103.4 | 93.7 | 91.4 | 87.1 | 86.5 | 72.8 | 67.0 | 64.1 |
| 24. Av. Payment, Partner | 100.0 | 81.4 | 99.3 | 83.5 | 83.1 | 81.1 | 83.3 | 66.8 | 67.4 | 62.5 |

TABLE 3

AUTOMOBILE REPAIR SHOPS, TOTAL (219,220,221,222,223), WITH AND WITHOUT NET INCOME

| | 1976 | 1977 | 1978 | 1979 | 1980 | 1981 | 1982 | 1983 | 1984 | 1985 |
|---|---|---|---|---|---|---|---|---|---|---|
| 1. Number of Partnerships | 17,760 | 19,541 | 19,473 | 17,975 | 17,907 | 21,694 | 19,630 | 23,853 | 25,707 | 20,561 |
| 2. Number of Partners | 38,862 | 43,707 | 44,299 | 44,771 | 42,346 | 50,211 | 44,848 | 57,669 | 55,462 | 45,051 |
| **Selected Financial Statistics** | | | | | | | | | | |
| **(Items 3 to 9 inclusive in 000's of dollars)** | | | | | | | | | | |
| 3. Operating Income | 1,251,025 | 1,487,098 | 1,954,791 | 1,864,582 | 1,980,843 | 2,724,253 | 2,288,625 | 2,585,914 | 2,741,347 | 2,968,998 |
| 4. Depreciation | 86,946 | 118,285 | 137,778 | 154,775 | 154,392 | n.a. | n.a. | n.a. | 223,822 | 203,789 |
| 5. Taxes Paid | 36,328 | 39,292 | 54,722 | 50,251 | 52,185 | 52,937 | 43,469 | 52,307 | 48,354 | 54,917 |
| 6. Interest Paid | 31,501 | 42,207 | 48,004 | 61,785 | 88,003 | 96,736 | 78,531 | 101,670 | 36,478 | 35,499 |
| 7. Payroll Deductions | 145,565 | 175,284 | 244,541 | 244,351 | 276,483 | 381,084 | 295,854 | n.a. | 414,747 | 435,686 |
| 8. Payments to Partners | 52,362 | 51,122 | 71,719 | 65,293 | 77,079 | 92,813 | 90,869 | 90,051 | 25,707 | 20,561 |
| 9. Net Income, less Deficit | 160,390 | 219,000 | 287,299 | 258,049 | 223,637 | 298,434 | 274,262 | 270,364 | 317,260 | 338,210 |
| **Selected Average Financial Statistics** | | | | | | | | | | |
| **(Items 10 to 13 inclusive in $)** | | | | | | | | | | |
| 10. Av. Payment Partnership | 2,948 | 2,616 | 3,683 | 3,632 | 4,304 | 4,278 | 4,629 | 3,775 | 1,000 | 1,000 |
| 11. Av. Payment Partner | 1,347 | 1,170 | 1,619 | 1,458 | 1,820 | 1,848 | 2,026 | 1,562 | 464 | 456 |
| 12. Av. Income Partnership | 9,031 | 11,207 | 14,754 | 14,356 | 12,489 | 13,757 | 13,972 | 11,335 | 12,341 | 16,449 |
| 13. Av. Income Partner | 4,127 | 5,011 | 6,485 | 5,764 | 5,281 | 5,944 | 6,115 | 4,688 | 5,720 | 7,507 |
| **Selected Financial Statistics as Percent of Op. Income** | | | | | | | | | | |
| 14. Depreciation / Op. Income (%) | 7.0 | 8.0 | 7.1 | 8.3 | 7.8 | n.a. | n.a. | n.a. | 8.2 | 6.9 |
| 15. Interest / Op. Income (%) | 2.5 | 2.8 | 2.5 | 3.3 | 4.4 | 3.6 | 3.4 | 3.9 | 1.3 | 1.2 |
| 16. Payroll / Op. Income (%) | 11.6 | 11.8 | 12.5 | 13.1 | 14.0 | 14.0 | 12.9 | n.a. | 15.1 | 14.7 |
| **Selected Index Numbers (1976 = 100)** | | | | | | | | | | |
| 17. Partnerships | 100.0 | 110.0 | 109.6 | 101.2 | 100.8 | 122.2 | 110.5 | 134.3 | 144.7 | 115.8 |
| 18. Partners | 100.0 | 112.5 | 114.0 | 115.2 | 109.0 | 129.2 | 115.4 | 148.4 | 142.7 | 115.9 |
| 19. Operating Income | 100.0 | 118.9 | 156.3 | 149.0 | 158.3 | 217.8 | 182.9 | 206.7 | 219.1 | 237.3 |
| 20. Payments to Partners | 100.0 | 97.6 | 137.0 | 124.7 | 147.2 | 177.3 | 173.5 | 172.0 | 49.1 | 39.3 |
| **Selected Financial Statistics (Constant $, 1976 = 100)** | | | | | | | | | | |
| 21. Operating Income | 100.0 | 111.7 | 136.3 | 116.9 | 109.4 | 136.3 | 107.9 | 118.1 | 120.1 | 125.6 |
| 22. Payments to Partners | 100.0 | 91.7 | 119.5 | 97.8 | 101.7 | 110.9 | 102.3 | 98.3 | 26.9 | 20.8 |
| 23. Av. Payment, Partnership | 100.0 | 83.3 | 109.0 | 96.6 | 100.9 | 90.8 | 92.6 | 73.2 | 18.6 | 17.9 |
| 24. Av. Payment, Partner | 100.0 | 81.6 | 104.9 | 84.9 | 93.3 | 85.8 | 88.7 | 66.2 | 18.9 | 18.0 |

# TABLE 3

## 222: GENERAL AUTOMOTIVE REPAIR SHOPS, WITH AND WITHOUT NET INCOME

| | 1976 | 1977 | 1978 | 1979 | 1980 | 1981 | 1982 | 1983 | 1984 | 1985 |
|---|---|---|---|---|---|---|---|---|---|---|
| 1. Number of Partnerships | 8,899 | 9,164 | 8,566 | 7,923 | 7,983 | 7,754 | 8,554 | 11,095 | 14,738 | 9,949 |
| 2. Number of Partners | 18,103 | 18,607 | 18,208 | 16,234 | 16,893 | 16,781 | 20,675 | 28,177 | 32,581 | 23,509 |
| **Selected Financial Statistics** (Items 3 to 9 inclusive in 000's of dollars) | | | | | | | | | | |
| 3. Operating Income | 571,917 | 638,774 | 814,211 | 757,285 | 820,336 | 1,090,545 | 936,862 | 1,183,472 | 1,401,086 | 1,546,039 |
| 4. Depreciation | 10,914 | 13,484 | 17,588 | 18,062 | 22,896 | n.a. | n.a. | n.a. | 33,270 | 26,381 |
| 5. Taxes Paid | 12,863 | 14,480 | 20,740 | 17,495 | 18,566 | 21,229 | 15,682 | 21,261 | 20,571 | 27,198 |
| 6. Interest Paid | 4,678 | 5,646 | 6,426 | 7,512 | 11,584 | 16,329 | 16,501 | 18,683 | 17,093 | 17,237 |
| 7. Payroll Deductions | 59,003 | 72,290 | 96,115 | 83,091 | 113,665 | 168,529 | 134,305 | n.a. | 148,200 | 194,200 |
| 8. Payments to Partners | 25,015 | 18,662 | 31,576 | 22,272 | 35,410 | 34,733 | 43,466 | 50,004 | 36,715 | 46,174 |
| 9. Net Income, less Deficit | 87,318 | 107,666 | 129,154 | 110,194 | 89,182 | 106,380 | 69,330 | 99,501 | 148,678 | 157,236 |
| **Selected Average Financial Statistics** (Items 10 to 13 inclusive in $) | | | | | | | | | | |
| 10. Av. Payment Partnership | 2,811 | 2,036 | 3,686 | 2,811 | 4,436 | 4,479 | 5,081 | 4,507 | 2,491 | 4,641 |
| 11. Av. Payment Partner | 1,382 | 1,003 | 1,734 | 1,372 | 2,096 | 2,070 | 2,102 | 1,775 | 1,127 | 1,964 |
| 12. Av. Income Partnership | 9,812 | 11,749 | 15,078 | 13,908 | 11,171 | 13,719 | 8,105 | 8,968 | 10,088 | 15,804 |
| 13. Av. Income Partner | 4,823 | 5,786 | 7,093 | 6,788 | 5,279 | 6,339 | 3,353 | 3,531 | 4,563 | 6,688 |
| **Selected Financial Statistics as Percent of Op. Income** | | | | | | | | | | |
| 14. Depreciation / Op. Income (%) | 1.9 | 2.1 | 2.2 | 2.4 | 2.8 | n.a. | n.a. | n.a. | 2.4 | 1.7 |
| 15. Interest / Op. Income (%) | 0.8 | 0.9 | 0.8 | 0.10 | 1.4 | 1.5 | 1.8 | 1.6 | 1.2 | 1.1 |
| 16. Payroll / Op. Income (%) | 10.3 | 11.3 | 11.8 | 11.0 | 13.9 | 15.5 | 14.3 | n.a. | 10.6 | 12.6 |
| **Selected Index Numbers (1976 = 100)** | | | | | | | | | | |
| 17. Partnerships | 100.0 | 103.0 | 96.3 | 89.0 | 89.7 | 87.1 | 96.1 | 124.7 | 165.6 | 111.8 |
| 18. Partners | 100.0 | 102.8 | 100.6 | 89.7 | 93.3 | 92.7 | 114.2 | 155.6 | 180.0 | 129.9 |
| 19. Operating Income | 100.0 | 111.7 | 142.4 | 132.4 | 143.4 | 190.7 | 163.8 | 206.9 | 245.0 | 270.3 |
| 20. Payments to Partners | 100.0 | 74.6 | 126.2 | 89.0 | 141.6 | 138.8 | 173.8 | 199.9 | 146.8 | 184.6 |
| **Selected Financial Statistics (Constant $, 1976 = 100)** | | | | | | | | | | |
| 21. Operating Income | 100.0 | 104.9 | 124.2 | 103.8 | 99.1 | 119.4 | 96.6 | 118.2 | 134.3 | 143.0 |
| 22. Payments to Partners | 100.0 | 70.1 | 110.1 | 69.8 | 97.8 | 86.9 | 102.5 | 114.2 | 80.4 | 97.7 |
| 23. Av. Payment, Partnership | 100.0 | 68.1 | 114.4 | 78.4 | 109.0 | 99.7 | 106.6 | 91.6 | 48.6 | 87.3 |
| 24. Av. Payment, Partner | 100.0 | 68.2 | 109.4 | 77.9 | 104.8 | 93.8 | 89.7 | 73.4 | 44.7 | 75.3 |

TABLE 3

OTHER AUTOMOBILE REPAIR (221,223), WITH AND WITHOUT NET INCOME

| | 1976 | 1977 | 1978 | 1979 | 1980 | 1981 | 1982 | 1983 | 1984 | 1985 |
|---|---|---|---|---|---|---|---|---|---|---|
| 1. Number of Partnerships | 6,070 | 6,736 | 8,142 | 7,586 | 7,608 | 11,318 | 8,482 | 10,196 | 10,969 | 10,612 |
| 2. Number of Partners | 12,861 | 14,004 | 17,989 | 19,674 | 16,010 | 25,398 | 17,169 | 20,513 | 22,881 | 21,542 |
| **Selected Financial Statistics** | | | | | | | | | | |
| (Items 3 to 9 inclusive in 000's of dollars) | | | | | | | | | | |
| 3. Operating Income | 449,758 | 585,449 | 829,695 | 783,024 | 801,392 | 1,294,402 | 1,081,252 | 1,084,477 | 1,340,261 | 1,422,959 |
| 4. Depreciation | 8,810 | 11,328 | 15,320 | 14,773 | 18,433 | n.a. | n.a. | n.a. | 45,110 | 28,915 |
| 5. Taxes Paid | 10,368 | 12,533 | 22,871 | 20,929 | 18,759 | 20,608 | 17,291 | 20,194 | 27,783 | 27,720 |
| 6. Interest Paid | 5,093 | 5,536 | 6,895 | 8,585 | 9,607 | 20,394 | 11,498 | 8,821 | 19,385 | 18,261 |
| 7. Payroll Deductions | 64,820 | 83,318 | 118,595 | 122,714 | 122,102 | 173,355 | 133,844 | n.a. | 237,625 | 222,811 |
| 8. Payments to Partners | 24,158 | 28,542 | 35,188 | 38,667 | 36,062 | 51,884 | 36,728 | 16,590 | 43,898 | 10,612 |
| 9. Net Income, less Deficit | 45,935 | 88,645 | 148,999 | 122,593 | 123,053 | 180,125 | 191,740 | 151,229 | 168,581 | 180,974 |
| **Selected Average Financial Statistics** | | | | | | | | | | |
| (Items 10 to 13 inclusive in $) | | | | | | | | | | |
| 10. Av. Payment Partnership | 3,980 | 4,237 | 4,322 | 5,097 | 4,740 | 4,584 | 4,330 | 1,627 | 4,002 | 1,000 |
| 11. Av. Payment Partner | 1,878 | 2,038 | 1,956 | 1,965 | 2,252 | 2,043 | 2,139 | 809 | 1,919 | 493 |
| 12. Av. Income Partnership | 7,568 | 13,160 | 18,300 | 16,160 | 16,174 | 15,915 | 22,606 | 14,832 | 15,369 | 17,054 |
| 13. Av. Income Partner | 3,572 | 6,330 | 8,283 | 6,231 | 7,686 | 7,092 | 11,168 | 7,372 | 7,368 | 8,401 |
| **Selected Financial Statistics as Percent of Op. Income** | | | | | | | | | | |
| 14. Depreciation / Op. Income (%) | 2.0 | 1.9 | 1.9 | 1.9 | 2.3 | n.a. | n.a. | n.a. | 3.4 | 2.0 |
| 15. Interest / Op. Income (%) | 1.1 | 0.10 | 0.8 | 1.1 | 1.2 | 1.6 | 1.1 | 0.8 | 1.5 | 1.3 |
| 16. Payroll / Op. Income (%) | 14.4 | 14.2 | 14.3 | 15.7 | 15.2 | 13.4 | 12.4 | n.a. | 17.7 | 15.7 |
| **Selected Index Numbers (1976 = 100)** | | | | | | | | | | |
| 17. Partnerships | 100.0 | 111.0 | 134.1 | 125.0 | 125.3 | 186.5 | 139.7 | 168.0 | 180.7 | 174.8 |
| 18. Partners | 100.0 | 108.9 | 139.9 | 153.0 | 124.5 | 197.5 | 133.5 | 159.5 | 177.9 | 167.5 |
| 19. Operating Income | 100.0 | 130.2 | 184.5 | 174.1 | 178.2 | 287.8 | 240.4 | 241.1 | 298.0 | 316.4 |
| 20. Payments to Partners | 100.0 | 118.1 | 145.7 | 160.1 | 149.3 | 214.8 | 152.0 | 68.7 | 181.7 | 43.9 |
| **Selected Financial Statistics (Constant $, 1976 = 100)** | | | | | | | | | | |
| 21. Operating Income | 100.0 | 122.3 | 161.0 | 136.5 | 123.1 | 180.1 | 141.8 | 137.8 | 163.3 | 167.4 |
| 22. Payments to Partners | 100.0 | 111.0 | 127.1 | 125.5 | 103.1 | 134.4 | 89.7 | 39.2 | 99.6 | 23.2 |
| 23. Av. Payment, Partnership | 100.0 | 100.0 | 94.8 | 100.5 | 82.3 | 72.1 | 64.2 | 23.3 | 55.1 | 13.3 |
| 24. Av. Payment, Partner | 100.0 | 101.9 | 90.9 | 82.1 | 82.8 | 68.1 | 67.2 | 24.6 | 56.0 | 13.9 |

TABLE 3

AUTOMOBILE PARKING AND OTHER SERVICES (219,220,224), WITH AND WITHOUT NET INCOME

| | 1976 | 1977 | 1978 | 1979 | 1980 | 1981 | 1982 | 1983 | 1984 | 1985 |
|---|---|---|---|---|---|---|---|---|---|---|
| 1. Number of Partnerships | 6,250 | 7,359 | 7,468 | 6,561 | 7,162 | 6,117 | 6,118 | 6,995 | 9,690 | 9,627 |
| 2. Number of Partners | 15,488 | 18,988 | 18,948 | 18,334 | 21,827 | 17,026 | 14,813 | 18,815 | 21,529 | 22,709 |
| **Selected Financial Statistics** (Items 3 to 9 inclusive in 000's of dollars) | | | | | | | | | | |
| 3. Operating Income | 498,204 | 535,832 | 667,277 | 624,991 | 793,317 | 719,229 | 536,270 | 824,621 | 1,067,343 | 1,202,448 |
| 4. Depreciation | 77,203 | 108,506 | 123,076 | 143,667 | 139,448 | n.a. | n.a. | n.a. | 178,640 | 187,451 |
| 5. Taxes Paid | 19,380 | 19,429 | 19,746 | 20,363 | 30,677 | 18,226 | 15,250 | 20,483 | 26,703 | 19,910 |
| 6. Interest Paid | 26,403 | 37,859 | 44,179 | 57,951 | 88,437 | 75,385 | 62,531 | 85,573 | 82,550 | 95,671 |
| 7. Payroll Deductions | 54,321 | 59,912 | 77,514 | 72,027 | 87,303 | 88,367 | 62,434 | n.a. | 128,824 | 112,776 |
| 8. Payments to Partners | 9,619 | 9,373 | 12,650 | 12,151 | 11,907 | 10,542 | 13,831 | 33,279 | 9,690 | 9,627 |
| 9. Net Income, less Deficit | 49,106 | 37,645 | 47,742 | 45,863 | 11,890 | 15,483 | 21,237 | 59,226 | 32,820 | 61,398 |
| **Selected Average Financial Statistics** (Items 10 to 13 inclusive in $) | | | | | | | | | | |
| 10. Av. Payment Partnership | 1,539 | 1,274 | 1,694 | 1,852 | 1,663 | 1,723 | 2,261 | 4,758 | 1,000 | 1,000 |
| 11. Av. Payment Partner | 621 | 494 | 668 | 663 | 546 | 619 | 934 | 1,769 | 450 | 424 |
| 12. Av. Income Partnership | 7,857 | 5,116 | 6,393 | 6,990 | 1,660 | 2,531 | 3,471 | 8,467 | 3,387 | 6,378 |
| 13. Av. Income Partner | 3,171 | 1,983 | 2,520 | 2,502 | 545 | 909 | 1,434 | 3,148 | 1,524 | 2,704 |
| **Selected Financial Statistics as Percent of Op. Income** | | | | | | | | | | |
| 14. Depreciation / Op. Income (%) | 15.5 | 20.3 | 18.4 | 23.0 | 17.6 | n.a. | n.a. | n.a. | 16.7 | 15.6 |
| 15. Interest / Op. Income (%) | 5.3 | 7.1 | 6.6 | 9.3 | 11.2 | 10.5 | 11.7 | 10.4 | 7.7 | 8.0 |
| 16. Payroll / Op. Income (%) | 10.9 | 11.2 | 11.6 | 11.5 | 11.0 | 12.3 | 11.6 | n.a. | 12.1 | 9.4 |
| **Selected Index Numbers (1976 = 100)** | | | | | | | | | | |
| 17. Partnerships | 100.0 | 117.7 | 119.5 | 105.0 | 114.6 | 97.9 | 97.9 | 111.9 | 155.0 | 154.0 |
| 18. Partners | 100.0 | 122.6 | 122.3 | 118.4 | 140.9 | 109.9 | 95.6 | 121.5 | 139.0 | 146.6 |
| 19. Operating Income | 100.0 | 107.6 | 133.9 | 125.4 | 159.2 | 144.4 | 107.6 | 165.5 | 214.2 | 241.4 |
| 20. Payments to Partners | 100.0 | 97.4 | 131.5 | 126.3 | 123.8 | 109.6 | 143.8 | 346.0 | 100.7 | 100.1 |
| **Selected Financial Statistics (Constant $, 1976 = 100)** | | | | | | | | | | |
| 21. Operating Income | 100.0 | 101.0 | 116.9 | 98.4 | 110.0 | 90.4 | 63.5 | 94.6 | 117.4 | 127.7 |
| 22. Payments to Partners | 100.0 | 91.5 | 114.8 | 99.1 | 85.5 | 68.6 | 84.8 | 197.7 | 55.2 | 53.0 |
| 23. Av. Payment, Partnership | 100.0 | 77.8 | 96.0 | 94.4 | 74.7 | 70.1 | 86.6 | 176.7 | 35.6 | 34.3 |
| 24. Av. Payment, Partner | 100.0 | 74.7 | 93.9 | 83.7 | 60.7 | 62.3 | 88.7 | 162.8 | 39.8 | 36.2 |

TABLE 3

225:  MISCELLANEOUS REPAIR SERVICES, WITH AND WITHOUT NET INCOME

| | 1976 | 1977 | 1978 | 1979 | 1980 | 1981 | 1982 | 1983 | 1984 | 1985 |
|---|---|---|---|---|---|---|---|---|---|---|
| 1.  Number of Partnerships | 8,630 | 10,055 | 9,447 | 9,094 | 10,306 | 10,722 | 11,284 | 13,497 | 11,300 | 7,778 |
| 2.  Number of Partners | 18,869 | 21,487 | 20,246 | 19,238 | 23,715 | 22,877 | 25,558 | 30,559 | 25,155 | 15,879 |
| **Selected Financial Statistics** | | | | | | | | | | |
| **(Items 3 to 9 inclusive in 000's of dollars)** | | | | | | | | | | |
| 3.  Operating Income | 426,216 | 514,451 | 734,315 | 643,018 | 809,444 | 1,088,388 | 1,023,458 | 1,360,630 | 1,026,279 | 954,065 |
| 4.  Depreciation | 10,059 | 13,338 | 15,226 | 13,511 | 24,292 | n.a. | n.a. | n.a. | 61,387 | 62,161 |
| 5.  Taxes Paid | 9,416 | 10,386 | 19,119 | 14,166 | 18,841 | 22,042 | 16,770 | 15,179 | 14,431 | 16,647 |
| 6.  Interest Paid | 3,922 | 5,051 | 6,252 | 5,964 | 10,087 | 11,273 | 12,119 | 12,745 | 19,690 | 16,517 |
| 7.  Payroll Deductions | 55,303 | 65,394 | 109,600 | 92,495 | 115,429 | 155,155 | 116,934 | n.a. | 104,846 | 150,525 |
| 8.  Payments to Partners | 19,695 | 20,519 | 39,887 | 28,500 | 35,043 | 44,958 | 21,272 | 40,719 | 25,025 | 34,695 |
| 9.  Net Income, less Deficit | 74,416 | 88,895 | 119,460 | 100,154 | 119,175 | 106,136 | 166,526 | 294,114 | 146,779 | 103,215 |
| **Selected Average Financial Statistics** | | | | | | | | | | |
| **(Items 10 to 13 inclusive in $)** | | | | | | | | | | |
| 10. Av. Payment Partnership | 2,282 | 2,041 | 4,222 | 3,134 | 3,400 | 4,193 | 1,885 | 3,017 | 2,215 | 4,461 |
| 11. Av. Payment Partner | 1,044 | 955 | 1,970 | 1,481 | 1,478 | 1,965 | 832 | 1,332 | 995 | 2,185 |
| 12. Av. Income Partnership | 8,623 | 8,841 | 12,645 | 11,013 | 11,564 | 9,899 | 14,758 | 21,791 | 12,989 | 13,270 |
| 13. Av. Income Partner | 3,944 | 4,137 | 5,900 | 5,206 | 5,025 | 4,639 | 6,516 | 9,624 | 5,835 | 6,500 |
| **Selected Financial Statistics as Percent of Op. Income** | | | | | | | | | | |
| 14. Depreciation / Op. Income (%) | 2.4 | 2.6 | 2.1 | 2.1 | 3.0 | n.a. | n.a. | n.a. | 6.0 | 6.5 |
| 15. Interest / Op. Income (%) | 0.9 | 0.10 | 0.9 | 0.9 | 1.3 | 1.0 | 1.2 | 0.9 | 1.9 | 1.7 |
| 16. Payroll / Op. Income (%) | 13.0 | 12.7 | 14.9 | 14.4 | 14.3 | 14.3 | 11.4 | n.a. | 10.2 | 15.8 |
| **Selected Index Numbers (1976 = 100)** | | | | | | | | | | |
| 17. Partnerships | 100.0 | 116.5 | 109.5 | 105.4 | 119.4 | 124.2 | 130.8 | 156.4 | 130.9 | 90.1 |
| 18. Partners | 100.0 | 113.9 | 107.3 | 102.0 | 125.7 | 121.2 | 135.4 | 162.0 | 133.3 | 84.2 |
| 19. Operating Income | 100.0 | 120.7 | 172.3 | 150.9 | 189.9 | 255.4 | 240.1 | 319.2 | 240.8 | 223.8 |
| 20. Payments to Partners | 100.0 | 104.2 | 202.5 | 144.7 | 177.9 | 228.3 | 108.0 | 206.7 | 127.1 | 176.2 |
| **Selected Financial Statistics (Constant $, 1976 = 100)** | | | | | | | | | | |
| 21. Operating Income | 100.0 | 113.4 | 150.3 | 118.3 | 131.2 | 159.8 | 141.6 | 182.4 | 132.0 | 118.5 |
| 22. Payments to Partners | 100.0 | 97.9 | 176.7 | 113.5 | 122.9 | 142.9 | 63.7 | 118.1 | 69.6 | 93.2 |
| 23. Av. Payment, Partnership | 100.0 | 84.0 | 161.4 | 107.7 | 103.0 | 115.0 | 48.7 | 75.5 | 53.2 | 103.5 |
| 24. Av. Payment, Partner | 100.0 | 85.9 | 164.7 | 111.2 | 97.8 | 117.8 | 47.0 | 72.9 | 52.3 | 110.8 |

## TABLE 3

### AMUSEMENT AND RECREATION SERVICES, INCLUDING MOTION PICTURES (230,233), WITH AND WITHOUT NET INCOME

| | 1976 | 1977 | 1978 | 1979 | 1980 | 1981 | 1982 | 1983 | 1984 | 1985 |
|---|---|---|---|---|---|---|---|---|---|---|
| 1. Number of Partnerships | 16,162 | 18,461 | 18,792 | 19,031 | 19,461 | 23,392 | 25,364 | 20,877 | 31,832 | 29,545 |
| 2. Number of Partners | 81,494 | 84,656 | 85,147 | 85,124 | 89,761 | 126,834 | 123,346 | 134,056 | 193,392 | 193,432 |
| **Selected Financial Statistics (Items 3 to 9 inclusive in 000's of dollars)** | | | | | | | | | | |
| 3. Operating Income | 1,689,856 | 2,052,504 | 2,592,633 | 3,195,270 | 3,632,958 | 4,266,083 | 5,282,993 | 5,488,840 | 7,209,284 | 8,533,253 |
| 4. Depreciation | 346,272 | 269,215 | 422,028 | 424,841 | 602,541 | n.a. | n.a. | n.a. | 1,727,721 | 1,434,812 |
| 5. Taxes Paid | 69,295 | 80,686 | 97,251 | 98,850 | 123,814 | 119,358 | 123,783 | 130,779 | 174,138 | 169,664 |
| 6. Interest Paid | 78,072 | 94,490 | 131,583 | 173,724 | 200,662 | 300,077 | 339,130 | 331,660 | 500,704 | 572,122 |
| 7. Payroll Deductions | 346,107 | 395,524 | 508,549 | 605,841 | 715,751 | 785,697 | 890,712 | n.a. | 1,206,164 | 1,354,515 |
| 8. Payments to Partners | 36,811 | 31,253 | 43,975 | 54,984 | 59,815 | 146,222 | 107,717 | 64,150 | 159,652 | 29,545 |
| 9. Net Income, less Deficit | 19,858 | 18,828 | 11,480 | 28,175 | 22,006 | 58,366 | 69,840 | 72,565 | (833,558) | (391,809) |
| **Selected Average Financial Statistics (Items 10 to 13 inclusive in $)** | | | | | | | | | | |
| 10. Av. Payment Partnership | 2,278 | 1,693 | 2,340 | 2,889 | 3,074 | 6,251 | 4,247 | 3,073 | 5,015 | 1,000 |
| 11. Av. Payment Partner | 452 | 369 | 516 | 646 | 666 | 1,153 | 873 | 479 | 826 | 153 |
| 12. Av. Income Partnership | 1,229 | 1,020 | 611 | 1,480 | 1,131 | 2,495 | 2,754 | 3,476 | (26,186) | (13,261) |
| 13. Av. Income Partner | 244 | 222 | 135 | 331 | 245 | 460 | 566 | 541 | (4,310) | (2,026) |
| **Selected Financial Statistics as Percent of Op. Income** | | | | | | | | | | |
| 14. Depreciation / Op. Income (%) | 20.5 | 13.1 | 16.3 | 13.3 | 16.6 | n.a. | n.a. | n.a. | 24.0 | 16.8 |
| 15. Interest / Op. Income (%) | 4.6 | 4.6 | 5.1 | 5.4 | 5.5 | 7.0 | 6.4 | 6.0 | 7.0 | 6.7 |
| 16. Payroll / Op. Income (%) | 20.5 | 19.3 | 19.6 | 19.0 | 19.7 | 18.4 | 16.9 | n.a. | 16.7 | 15.9 |
| **Selected Index Numbers (1976 = 100)** | | | | | | | | | | |
| 17. Partnerships | 100.0 | 114.2 | 116.3 | 117.8 | 120.4 | 144.7 | 156.9 | 129.2 | 197.0 | 182.8 |
| 18. Partners | 100.0 | 103.9 | 104.5 | 104.5 | 110.1 | 155.6 | 151.4 | 164.5 | 237.3 | 237.4 |
| 19. Operating Income | 100.0 | 121.5 | 153.4 | 189.1 | 215.0 | 252.5 | 312.6 | 324.8 | 426.6 | 505.0 |
| 20. Payments to Partners | 100.0 | 84.9 | 119.5 | 149.4 | 162.5 | 397.2 | 292.6 | 174.3 | 433.7 | 80.3 |
| **Selected Financial Statistics (Constant $, 1976 = 100)** | | | | | | | | | | |
| 21. Operating Income | 100.0 | 114.1 | 133.9 | 148.3 | 148.5 | 158.0 | 184.4 | 185.6 | 233.8 | 267.2 |
| 22. Payments to Partners | 100.0 | 79.8 | 104.2 | 117.1 | 112.3 | 248.6 | 172.6 | 99.6 | 237.7 | 42.5 |
| 23. Av. Payment, Partnership | 100.0 | 69.8 | 89.7 | 99.5 | 93.3 | 171.8 | 110.0 | 77.1 | 120.7 | 23.2 |
| 24. Av. Payment, Partner | 100.0 | 76.6 | 99.6 | 112.1 | 101.9 | 159.7 | 114.0 | 60.8 | 100.4 | 17.7 |

TABLE 3

240:  MEDICAL AND HEALTH SERVICES, WITH AND WITHOUT NET INCOME

| | 1976 | 1977 | 1978 | 1979 | 1980 | 1981 | 1982 | 1983 | 1984 | 1985 |
|---|---|---|---|---|---|---|---|---|---|---|
| 1. Number of Partnerships | 18,884 | 18,364 | 19,635 | 20,910 | 23,241 | 28,044 | 27,524 | 28,655 | 30,160 | 36,557 |
| 2. Number of Partners | 62,627 | 62,225 | 75,272 | 79,301 | 83,026 | 100,920 | 106,894 | 107,093 | 130,874 | 203,837 |
| **Selected Financial Statistics** | | | | | | | | | | |
| (Items 3 to 9 inclusive in 000's of dollars) | | | | | | | | | | |
| 3. Operating Income | 5,862,781 | 6,583,679 | 6,927,398 | 7,473,890 | 9,581,687 | 10,737,978 | 10,906,028 | 11,961,741 | 13,598,013 | 15,712,899 |
| 4. Depreciation | 98,078 | 107,942 | 131,886 | 144,088 | 175,325 | n.a. | n.a. | n.a. | 319,162 | 498,533 |
| 5. Taxes Paid | 152,222 | 184,540 | 204,964 | 198,294 | 245,204 | 262,931 | 275,852 | 268,187 | 315,158 | 381,754 |
| 6. Interest Paid | 80,311 | 88,630 | 109,208 | 126,963 | 147,238 | 177,680 | 201,209 | 257,907 | 612,796 | 440,328 |
| 7. Payroll Deductions | 1,393,239 | 1,645,659 | 1,805,404 | 1,850,291 | 2,456,486 | 2,713,022 | 2,759,430 | n.a. | 2,997,343 | 3,592,368 |
| 8. Payments to Partners | 196,496 | 190,929 | 143,572 | 235,377 | 304,124 | 296,302 | 336,589 | 662,745 | 416,461 | 958,378 |
| 9. Net Income, less Deficit | 1,993,158 | 2,161,737 | 2,242,059 | 2,369,104 | 3,037,490 | 3,639,265 | 3,854,253 | 3,472,752 | 4,639,983 | 4,413,387 |
| **Selected Average Financial Statistics** | | | | | | | | | | |
| (Items 10 to 13 inclusive in $) | | | | | | | | | | |
| 10. Av. Payment Partnership | 10,405 | 10,397 | 7,312 | 11,257 | 13,086 | 10,566 | 12,229 | 23,128 | 13,808 | 26,216 |
| 11. Av. Payment Partner | 3,138 | 3,068 | 1,907 | 2,968 | 3,663 | 2,936 | 3,149 | 6,188 | 3,182 | 4,702 |
| 12. Av. Income Partnership | 105,547 | 117,716 | 114,187 | 113,300 | 130,695 | 129,770 | 140,032 | 121,192 | 153,846 | 120,726 |
| 13. Av. Income Partner | 31,826 | 34,741 | 29,786 | 29,875 | 36,585 | 36,061 | 36,057 | 32,427 | 35,454 | 21,652 |
| **Selected Financial Statistics as Percent of Op. Income** | | | | | | | | | | |
| 14. Depreciation / Op. Income (%) | 1.7 | 1.6 | 1.9 | 1.9 | 1.8 | n.a. | n.a. | n.a. | 2.4 | 3.2 |
| 15. Interest / Op. Income (%) | 1.4 | 1.4 | 1.6 | 1.7 | 1.5 | 1.7 | 1.8 | 2.2 | 4.5 | 2.8 |
| 16. Payroll / Op. Income (%) | 23.8 | 25.0 | 26.1 | 24.8 | 25.6 | 25.3 | 25.3 | n.a. | 22.0 | 22.9 |
| **Selected Index Numbers (1976 = 100)** | | | | | | | | | | |
| 17. Partnerships | 100.0 | 97.2 | 104.0 | 110.7 | 123.1 | 148.5 | 145.8 | 151.7 | 159.7 | 193.6 |
| 18. Partners | 100.0 | 99.4 | 120.2 | 126.6 | 132.6 | 161.1 | 170.7 | 171.0 | 209.0 | 325.5 |
| 19. Operating Income | 100.0 | 112.3 | 118.2 | 127.5 | 163.4 | 183.2 | 186.0 | 204.0 | 231.9 | 268.0 |
| 20. Payments to Partners | 100.0 | 97.2 | 73.1 | 119.8 | 154.8 | 150.8 | 171.3 | 337.3 | 211.9 | 487.7 |
| **Selected Financial Statistics (Constant $, 1976 = 100)** | | | | | | | | | | |
| 21. Operating Income | 100.0 | 105.5 | 103.1 | 100.0 | 112.9 | 114.6 | 109.7 | 116.6 | 127.1 | 141.8 |
| 22. Payments to Partners | 100.0 | 91.3 | 63.8 | 93.9 | 106.9 | 94.4 | 101.0 | 192.7 | 116.2 | 258.1 |
| 23. Av. Payment, Partnership | 100.0 | 93.9 | 61.3 | 84.8 | 86.9 | 63.6 | 69.3 | 127.0 | 72.7 | 133.3 |
| 24. Av. Payment, Partner | 100.0 | 91.8 | 53.0 | 74.2 | 80.6 | 58.6 | 59.2 | 112.7 | 55.6 | 79.3 |

TABLE 3

241: OFFICES OF PHYSICIANS, WITH AND WITHOUT NET INCOME

| | 1976 | 1977 | 1978 | 1979 | 1980 | 1981 | 1982 | 1983 | 1984 | 1985 |
|---|---|---|---|---|---|---|---|---|---|---|
| 1. Number of Partnerships | 8,868 | 8,140 | 8,706 | 8,929 | 10,272 | 12,035 | 10,902 | 10,395 | 10,062 | 9,759 |
| 2. Number of Partners | 30,830 | 30,009 | 32,204 | 35,471 | 39,660 | 42,654 | 44,971 | 36,258 | 37,340 | 39,397 |
| **Selected Financial Statistics** (Items 3 to 9 inclusive in 000's of dollars) | | | | | | | | | | |
| 3. Operating Income | 3,196,198 | 3,551,972 | 3,724,684 | 3,815,379 | 5,578,657 | 5,392,794 | 5,069,573 | 5,353,575 | 6,289,003 | 6,451,832 |
| 4. Depreciation | 27,576 | 32,382 | 37,473 | 38,488 | 48,608 | n.a. | n.a. | n.a. | 64,680 | 95,591 |
| 5. Taxes Paid | 53,630 | 66,121 | 73,269 | 58,140 | 95,883 | 96,997 | 82,353 | 81,174 | 106,333 | 102,918 |
| 6. Interest Paid | 10,440 | 12,128 | 13,829 | 15,760 | 22,098 | 22,498 | 27,325 | 28,487 | 34,946 | 38,865 |
| 7. Payroll Deductions | 592,446 | 729,462 | 806,143 | 722,373 | 1,219,148 | 1,215,897 | 991,680 | n.a. | 1,284,428 | 1,279,576 |
| 8. Payments to Partners | 104,738 | 96,101 | 81,157 | 127,706 | 205,184 | 84,765 | 242,688 | 298,298 | 217,905 | 659,469 |
| 9. Net Income, less Deficit | 1,557,301 | 1,598,978 | 1,709,198 | 1,779,351 | 2,364,859 | 2,664,767 | 2,688,952 | 2,186,165 | 3,194,786 | 2,933,788 |
| **Selected Average Financial Statistics** (Items 10 to 13 inclusive in $) | | | | | | | | | | |
| 10. Av. Payment Partnership | 11,811 | 11,806 | 9,322 | 14,302 | 19,975 | 7,043 | 22,261 | 28,696 | 21,656 | 67,575 |
| 11. Av. Payment Partner | 3,397 | 3,202 | 2,520 | 3,600 | 5,174 | 1,987 | 5,397 | 8,227 | 5,836 | 16,739 |
| 12. Av. Income Partnership | 175,609 | 196,435 | 196,324 | 199,278 | 230,224 | 221,418 | 246,648 | 210,309 | 317,510 | 300,624 |
| 13. Av. Income Partner | 50,513 | 53,283 | 53,074 | 50,164 | 59,628 | 62,474 | 59,793 | 60,295 | 85,559 | 74,467 |
| **Selected Financial Statistics as Percent of Op. Income** | | | | | | | | | | |
| 14. Depreciation / Op. Income (%) | 0.9 | 0.9 | 1.0 | 1.0 | 0.9 | n.a. | n.a. | n.a. | 1.0 | 1.5 |
| 15. Interest / Op. Income (%) | 0.3 | 0.3 | 0.4 | 0.4 | 0.4 | 0.4 | 0.5 | 0.5 | 0.6 | 0.6 |
| 16. Payroll / Op. Income (%) | 18.5 | 20.5 | 21.6 | 18.9 | 21.9 | 22.6 | 19.6 | n.a. | 20.4 | 19.8 |
| **Selected Index Numbers (1976 = 100)** | | | | | | | | | | |
| 17. Partnerships | 100.0 | 91.8 | 98.2 | 100.7 | 115.8 | 135.7 | 122.9 | 117.2 | 113.5 | 110.0 |
| 18. Partners | 100.0 | 97.3 | 104.5 | 115.1 | 128.6 | 138.4 | 145.9 | 117.6 | 121.1 | 127.8 |
| 19. Operating Income | 100.0 | 111.1 | 116.5 | 119.4 | 174.5 | 168.7 | 158.6 | 167.5 | 196.8 | 201.9 |
| 20. Payments to Partners | 100.0 | 91.8 | 77.5 | 121.9 | 195.9 | 80.9 | 231.7 | 284.8 | 208.0 | 629.6 |
| **Selected Financial Statistics (Constant $, 1976 = 100)** | | | | | | | | | | |
| 21. Operating Income | 100.0 | 104.4 | 101.7 | 93.6 | 120.6 | 105.6 | 93.5 | 95.7 | 107.8 | 106.8 |
| 22. Payments to Partners | 100.0 | 86.2 | 67.6 | 95.6 | 135.3 | 50.7 | 136.7 | 162.7 | 114.0 | 333.2 |
| 23. Av. Payment, Partnership | 100.0 | 93.9 | 68.9 | 95.0 | 116.8 | 37.3 | 111.2 | 138.8 | 100.5 | 302.8 |
| 24. Av. Payment, Partner | 100.0 | 88.5 | 64.7 | 83.1 | 105.2 | 36.6 | 93.7 | 138.4 | 94.2 | 260.7 |

## TABLE 3

## OTHER MEDICAL AND HEALTH SERVICES (242 TO 251), WITH AND WITHOUT NET INCOME

| | 1976 | 1977 | 1978 | 1979 | 1980 | 1981 | 1982 | 1983 | 1984 | 1985 |
|---|---|---|---|---|---|---|---|---|---|---|
| 1. Number of Partnerships | 10,016 | 10,224 | 10,929 | 11,981 | 12,970 | 16,009 | 14,944 | 18,258 | 20,098 | 26,798 |
| 2. Number of Partners | 31,797 | 32,216 | 43,068 | 43,830 | 43,365 | 58,267 | 51,183 | 70,836 | 93,534 | 164,440 |
| **Selected Financial Statistics** | | | | | | | | | | |
| **(Items 3 to 9 inclusive in 000's of dollars)** | | | | | | | | | | |
| 3. Operating Income | 2,666,583 | 3,031,707 | 3,202,715 | 3,658,511 | 4,003,027 | 5,345,184 | 4,172,460 | 6,608,168 | 7,309,010 | 9,261,067 |
| 4. Depreciation | 70,502 | 75,560 | 94,413 | 105,600 | 126,717 | n.a. | n.a. | n.a. | 254,481 | 373,313 |
| 5. Taxes Paid | 98,592 | 118,419 | 131,694 | 140,155 | 149,320 | 165,933 | 103,783 | 187,012 | 208,825 | 278,836 |
| 6. Interest Paid | 69,871 | 76,502 | 95,380 | 111,204 | 125,140 | 155,181 | 77,772 | 229,420 | 277,850 | 401,463 |
| 7. Payroll Deductions | 800,793 | 916,197 | 999,261 | 1,127,919 | 1,237,339 | 1,497,126 | 1,082,311 | n.a. | 1,710,915 | 2,086,266 |
| 8. Payments to Partners | 91,758 | 94,828 | 62,415 | 107,672 | 98,939 | 211,537 | 80,966 | 364,447 | 198,556 | 26,798 |
| 9. Net Income, less Deficit | 435,857 | 564,552 | 532,862 | 589,752 | 673,745 | 974,498 | 1,098,067 | 1,286,586 | 1,445,196 | 1,479,599 |
| **Selected Average Financial Statistics** | | | | | | | | | | |
| **(Items 10 to 13 inclusive in $)** | | | | | | | | | | |
| 10. Av. Payment Partnership | 9,161 | 9,275 | 5,711 | 8,987 | 7,628 | 13,214 | 5,418 | 19,961 | 9,879 | 1,000 |
| 11. Av. Payment Partner | 2,886 | 2,944 | 1,449 | 2,457 | 2,282 | 3,630 | 1,582 | 5,145 | 2,123 | 163 |
| 12. Av. Income Partnership | 43,516 | 55,218 | 48,757 | 49,224 | 51,946 | 60,872 | 73,479 | 70,467 | 71,907 | 55,213 |
| 13. Av. Income Partner | 13,707 | 17,524 | 12,373 | 13,455 | 15,537 | 16,725 | 21,454 | 18,163 | 15,451 | 8,998 |
| **Selected Financial Statistics as Percent of Op. Income** | | | | | | | | | | |
| 14. Depreciation / Op. Income (%) | 2.6 | 2.5 | 3.0 | 2.9 | 3.2 | n.a. | n.a. | n.a. | 3.5 | 4.0 |
| 15. Interest / Op. Income (%) | 2.6 | 2.5 | 3.0 | 3.0 | 3.1 | 2.9 | 1.9 | 3.5 | 3.8 | 4.3 |
| 16. Payroll / Op. Income (%) | 30.0 | 30.2 | 31.2 | 30.8 | 30.9 | 28.0 | 25.9 | n.a. | 23.4 | 22.5 |
| **Selected Index Numbers (1976 = 100)** | | | | | | | | | | |
| 17. Partnerships | 100.0 | 102.1 | 109.1 | 119.6 | 129.5 | 159.8 | 149.2 | 182.3 | 200.7 | 267.6 |
| 18. Partners | 100.0 | 101.3 | 135.4 | 137.8 | 136.4 | 183.2 | 161.0 | 222.8 | 294.2 | 517.2 |
| 19. Operating Income | 100.0 | 113.7 | 120.1 | 137.2 | 150.1 | 200.5 | 156.5 | 247.8 | 274.1 | 347.3 |
| 20. Payments to Partners | 100.0 | 103.3 | 68.0 | 117.3 | 107.8 | 230.5 | 88.2 | 397.2 | 216.4 | 29.2 |
| **Selected Financial Statistics (Constant $, 1976 = 100)** | | | | | | | | | | |
| 21. Operating Income | 100.0 | 106.8 | 104.8 | 107.6 | 103.7 | 125.5 | 92.3 | 141.6 | 150.2 | 183.8 |
| 22. Payments to Partners | 100.0 | 97.1 | 59.4 | 92.0 | 74.5 | 144.3 | 52.0 | 226.9 | 118.6 | 15.5 |
| 23. Av. Payment, Partnership | 100.0 | 95.1 | 54.4 | 76.9 | 57.5 | 90.3 | 34.9 | 124.5 | 59.1 | 5.8 |
| 24. Av. Payment, Partner | 100.0 | 95.8 | 43.8 | 66.8 | 54.7 | 78.8 | 32.3 | 101.9 | 40.3 | 3.0 |

TABLE 3

252: LEGAL SERVICES, WITH AND WITHOUT NET INCOME

| | 1976 | 1977 | 1978 | 1979 | 1980 | 1981 | 1982 | 1983 | 1984 | 1985 |
|---|---|---|---|---|---|---|---|---|---|---|
| 1. Number of Partnerships | 26,909 | 26,964 | 28,623 | 28,836 | 29,524 | 25,446 | 26,535 | 24,821 | 25,152 | 30,795 |
| 2. Number of Partners | 93,311 | 97,809 | 105,288 | 105,273 | 118,113 | 106,410 | 114,702 | 111,703 | 121,066 | 132,861 |
| **Selected Financial Statistics** (Items 3 to 9 inclusive in 000's of dollars) | | | | | | | | | | |
| 3. Operating Income | 8,482,601 | 9,478,581 | 10,689,099 | 12,424,203 | 14,125,458 | 14,615,166 | 16,963,656 | 18,608,172 | 23,519,781 | 26,205,232 |
| 4. Depreciation | 100,820 | 116,418 | 149,812 | 181,952 | 222,170 | n.a. | n.a. | n.a. | 534,248 | 611,263 |
| 5. Taxes Paid | 199,651 | 223,424 | 255,722 | 308,042 | 336,759 | 377,762 | 445,981 | 478,360 | 634,875 | 705,496 |
| 6. Interest Paid | 21,210 | 27,166 | 40,251 | 53,755 | 75,977 | 107,579 | 154,428 | 134,069 | 184,177 | 207,523 |
| 7. Payroll Deductions | 1,935,947 | 2,178,541 | 2,450,755 | 2,954,311 | 3,400,667 | 3,789,694 | 4,436,668 | n.a. | 6,095,792 | 6,896,092 |
| 8. Payments to Partners | 226,457 | 264,786 | 276,018 | 302,095 | 362,743 | 453,658 | 437,885 | 393,483 | 638,068 | 724,164 |
| 9. Net Income, less Deficit | 4,131,342 | 4,590,659 | 5,130,920 | 5,841,940 | 6,596,160 | 6,297,277 | 7,363,339 | 8,243,477 | 10,006,130 | 10,654,560 |
| **Selected Average Financial Statistics** (Items 10 to 13 inclusive in $) | | | | | | | | | | |
| 10. Av. Payment Partnership | 8,416 | 9,820 | 9,643 | 10,476 | 12,286 | 17,828 | 16,502 | 15,853 | 25,368 | 23,516 |
| 11. Av. Payment Partner | 2,427 | 2,707 | 2,622 | 2,870 | 3,071 | 4,263 | 3,818 | 3,523 | 5,270 | 5,451 |
| 12. Av. Income Partnership | 153,530 | 170,251 | 179,259 | 202,592 | 223,417 | 247,476 | 277,495 | 332,117 | 397,826 | 345,983 |
| 13. Av. Income Partner | 44,275 | 46,935 | 48,732 | 55,493 | 55,846 | 59,179 | 64,195 | 73,798 | 82,650 | 80,193 |
| **Selected Financial Statistics as Percent of Op. Income** | | | | | | | | | | |
| 14. Depreciation / Op. Income (%) | 1.2 | 1.2 | 1.4 | 1.5 | 1.6 | n.a. | n.a. | n.a. | 2.3 | 2.3 |
| 15. Interest / Op. Income (%) | 0.3 | 0.3 | 0.4 | 0.4 | 0.5 | 0.7 | 0.9 | 0.7 | 0.8 | 0.8 |
| 16. Payroll / Op. Income (%) | 22.8 | 23.0 | 22.9 | 23.8 | 24.1 | 25.9 | 26.2 | n.a. | 25.9 | 26.3 |
| **Selected Index Numbers (1976 = 100)** | | | | | | | | | | |
| 17. Partnerships | 100.0 | 100.2 | 106.4 | 107.2 | 109.7 | 94.6 | 98.6 | 92.2 | 93.5 | 114.4 |
| 18. Partners | 100.0 | 104.8 | 112.8 | 112.8 | 126.6 | 114.0 | 122.9 | 119.7 | 129.7 | 142.4 |
| 19. Operating Income | 100.0 | 111.7 | 126.0 | 146.5 | 166.5 | 172.3 | 200.0 | 219.4 | 277.3 | 308.9 |
| 20. Payments to Partners | 100.0 | 116.9 | 121.9 | 133.4 | 160.2 | 200.3 | 193.4 | 173.8 | 281.8 | 319.8 |
| **Selected Financial Statistics (Constant $, 1976 = 100)** | | | | | | | | | | |
| 21. Operating Income | 100.0 | 105.0 | 110.0 | 114.9 | 115.0 | 107.8 | 117.9 | 125.3 | 152.0 | 163.5 |
| 22. Payments to Partners | 100.0 | 109.8 | 106.4 | 104.6 | 110.7 | 125.4 | 114.0 | 99.3 | 154.4 | 169.2 |
| 23. Av. Payment, Partnership | 100.0 | 109.6 | 100.0 | 97.6 | 100.9 | 132.6 | 115.6 | 107.6 | 165.2 | 147.9 |
| 24. Av. Payment, Partner | 100.0 | 104.7 | 94.3 | 92.7 | 87.4 | 109.9 | 92.8 | 83.0 | 119.0 | 118.9 |

# TABLE 3

## 255: ENGINEERING AND ARCHITECTURAL SERVICES, WITH AND WITHOUT NET INCOME

| | 1976 | 1977 | 1978 | 1979 | 1980 | 1981 | 1982 | 1983 | 1984 | 1985 |
|---|---|---|---|---|---|---|---|---|---|---|
| 1. Number of Partnerships | 5,594 | 6,297 | 6,558 | 7,370 | 6,675 | 6,342 | 7,873 | 10,352 | 6,704 | 10,922 |
| 2. Number of Partners | 14,164 | 15,867 | 17,715 | 20,624 | 15,939 | 16,014 | 21,451 | 25,385 | 18,166 | 28,253 |
| **Selected Financial Statistics** (Items 3 to 9 inclusive in 000's of dollars) | | | | | | | | | | |
| 3. Operating Income | 1,492,299 | 1,787,804 | 2,216,846 | 2,527,651 | 2,878,190 | 2,840,232 | 3,922,876 | 3,749,198 | 3,222,065 | 3,922,012 |
| 4. Depreciation | 14,235 | 17,869 | 22,693 | 28,299 | 33,216 | n.a. | n.a. | n.a. | 53,911 | 80,191 |
| 5. Taxes Paid | 32,624 | 41,658 | 62,529 | 59,500 | 66,727 | 64,816 | 97,983 | 80,277 | 75,984 | 89,807 |
| 6. Interest Paid | 6,339 | 9,015 | 9,232 | 11,643 | 16,757 | 24,320 | 38,048 | 39,523 | 31,802 | 26,107 |
| 7. Payroll Deductions | 471,554 | 565,389 | 675,873 | 745,386 | 819,471 | 848,437 | 1,250,755 | n.a. | 906,155 | 1,060,614 |
| 8. Payments to Partners | 43,103 | 51,923 | 80,218 | 111,492 | 129,726 | 138,715 | 108,942 | 207,550 | 217,438 | 280,087 |
| 9. Net Income, less Deficit | 261,016 | 314,040 | 391,911 | 396,188 | 447,074 | 373,871 | 535,000 | 410,215 | 337,863 | 456,343 |
| **Selected Average Financial Statistics** (Items 10 to 13 inclusive in $) | | | | | | | | | | |
| 10. Av. Payment Partnership | 7,705 | 8,246 | 12,232 | 15,128 | 19,435 | 21,872 | 13,837 | 20,049 | 32,434 | 25,644 |
| 11. Av. Payment Partner | 3,043 | 3,272 | 4,528 | 5,406 | 8,139 | 8,662 | 5,079 | 8,176 | 11,970 | 9,914 |
| 12. Av. Income Partnership | 46,660 | 49,871 | 59,761 | 53,757 | 66,977 | 58,952 | 67,954 | 39,627 | 50,397 | 41,782 |
| 13. Av. Income Partner | 18,428 | 19,792 | 22,123 | 19,210 | 28,049 | 23,347 | 24,941 | 16,160 | 18,599 | 16,152 |
| **Selected Financial Statistics as Percent of Op. Income** | | | | | | | | | | |
| 14. Depreciation / Op. Income (%) | 0.10 | 1.0 | 1.0 | 1.1 | 1.2 | n.a. | n.a. | n.a. | 1.7 | 2.0 |
| 15. Interest / Op. Income (%) | 0.4 | 0.5 | 0.4 | 0.5 | 0.6 | 0.9 | 0.10 | 1.1 | 0.10 | 0.7 |
| 16. Payroll / Op. Income (%) | 31.6 | 31.6 | 30.5 | 29.5 | 28.5 | 29.9 | 31.9 | n.a. | 28.1 | 27.0 |
| **Selected Index Numbers (1976 = 100)** | | | | | | | | | | |
| 17. Partnerships | 100.0 | 112.6 | 117.2 | 131.7 | 119.3 | 113.4 | 140.7 | 185.1 | 119.8 | 195.2 |
| 18. Partners | 100.0 | 112.0 | 125.1 | 145.6 | 112.5 | 113.1 | 151.4 | 179.2 | 128.3 | 199.5 |
| 19. Operating Income | 100.0 | 119.8 | 148.6 | 169.4 | 192.9 | 190.3 | 262.9 | 251.2 | 215.9 | 262.8 |
| 20. Payments to Partners | 100.0 | 120.5 | 186.1 | 258.7 | 301.0 | 321.8 | 252.7 | 481.5 | 504.5 | 649.8 |
| **Selected Financial Statistics (Constant $, 1976 = 100)** | | | | | | | | | | |
| 21. Operating Income | 100.0 | 112.5 | 129.6 | 132.8 | 133.2 | 119.1 | 155.0 | 143.6 | 118.3 | 139.1 |
| 22. Payments to Partners | 100.0 | 113.2 | 162.4 | 202.9 | 207.9 | 201.4 | 149.1 | 275.1 | 276.5 | 343.9 |
| 23. Av. Payment, Partnership | 100.0 | 100.5 | 138.5 | 154.0 | 174.3 | 177.7 | 105.9 | 148.7 | 230.7 | 176.1 |
| 24. Av. Payment, Partner | 100.0 | 101.0 | 129.8 | 139.3 | 184.8 | 178.2 | 98.4 | 153.5 | 215.6 | 172.4 |

## TABLE 3

### 256: ACCOUNTING, AUDITING, AND BOOKKEEPING SERVICES, WITH AND WITHOUT NET INCOME

| | 1976 | 1977 | 1978 | 1979 | 1980 | 1981 | 1982 | 1983 | 1984 | 1985 |
|---|---|---|---|---|---|---|---|---|---|---|
| 1. Number of Partnerships | 9,926 | 12,611 | 12,120 | 12,657 | 13,011 | 12,543 | 13,550 | 15,708 | 14,253 | 18,131 |
| 2. Number of Partners | 35,211 | 43,991 | 43,824 | 43,670 | 65,837 | 46,649 | 44,858 | 56,279 | 55,293 | 70,958 |
| **Selected Financial Statistics** (Items 3 to 9 inclusive in 000's of dollars) | | | | | | | | | | |
| 3. Operating Income | 4,083,117 | 4,612,392 | 5,450,519 | 6,305,001 | 7,077,452 | 7,595,965 | 7,457,855 | 8,671,311 | 10,383,136 | 13,901,548 |
| 4. Depreciation | 48,041 | 57,938 | 77,629 | 93,378 | 112,525 | n.a. | n.a. | n.a. | 207,705 | 290,202 |
| 5. Taxes Paid | 115,289 | 131,862 | 150,600 | 187,630 | 214,862 | 235,869 | 237,605 | 281,453 | 345,293 | 460,696 |
| 6. Interest Paid | 17,661 | 22,479 | 34,632 | 50,994 | 62,654 | 94,173 | 76,922 | 93,275 | 104,900 | 120,779 |
| 7. Payroll Deductions | 1,601,995 | 1,771,771 | 1,978,616 | 2,451,111 | 2,707,262 | 2,971,441 | 2,753,196 | n.a. | 3,812,341 | 5,107,812 |
| 8. Payments to Partners | 263,669 | 313,248 | 402,847 | 467,781 | 567,207 | 509,593 | 587,580 | 723,797 | 826,569 | 1,235,786 |
| 9. Net Income, less Deficit | 1,156,962 | 1,279,682 | 1,437,196 | 1,467,073 | 1,672,708 | 1,804,287 | 1,799,378 | 1,940,266 | 2,309,180 | 2,845,985 |
| **Selected Average Financial Statistics** (Items 10 to 13 inclusive in $) | | | | | | | | | | |
| 10. Av. Payment Partnership | 26,563 | 24,839 | 33,238 | 36,958 | 43,594 | 40,628 | 43,364 | 46,078 | 57,993 | 68,159 |
| 11. Av. Payment Partner | 7,488 | 7,121 | 9,192 | 10,712 | 8,615 | 10,924 | 13,099 | 12,861 | 14,949 | 17,416 |
| 12. Av. Income Partnership | 116,559 | 101,473 | 118,581 | 115,910 | 128,561 | 143,848 | 132,795 | 123,521 | 162,014 | 156,968 |
| 13. Av. Income Partner | 32,858 | 29,090 | 32,795 | 33,595 | 25,407 | 38,678 | 40,113 | 34,476 | 41,763 | 40,108 |
| **Selected Financial Statistics as Percent of Op. Income** | | | | | | | | | | |
| 14. Depreciation / Op. Income (%) | 1.2 | 1.3 | 1.4 | 1.5 | 1.6 | n.a. | n.a. | n.a. | 2.0 | 2.1 |
| 15. Interest / Op. Income (%) | 0.4 | 0.5 | 0.6 | 0.8 | 0.9 | 1.2 | 1.0 | 1.1 | 1.0 | 0.9 |
| 16. Payroll / Op. Income (%) | 39.2 | 38.4 | 36.3 | 38.9 | 38.3 | 39.1 | 36.9 | n.a. | 36.7 | 36.7 |
| **Selected Index Numbers (1976 = 100)** | | | | | | | | | | |
| 17. Partnerships | 100.0 | 127.1 | 122.1 | 127.5 | 131.1 | 126.4 | 136.5 | 158.3 | 143.6 | 182.7 |
| 18. Partners | 100.0 | 124.9 | 124.5 | 124.0 | 187.0 | 132.5 | 127.4 | 159.8 | 157.0 | 201.5 |
| 19. Operating Income | 100.0 | 113.0 | 133.5 | 154.4 | 173.3 | 186.0 | 182.7 | 212.4 | 254.3 | 340.5 |
| 20. Payments to Partners | 100.0 | 118.8 | 152.8 | 177.4 | 215.1 | 193.3 | 222.8 | 274.5 | 313.5 | 468.7 |
| **Selected Financial Statistics (Constant $, 1976 = 100)** | | | | | | | | | | |
| 21. Operating Income | 100.0 | 106.1 | 116.5 | 121.1 | 119.7 | 116.4 | 107.7 | 121.3 | 139.4 | 180.2 |
| 22. Payments to Partners | 100.0 | 111.6 | 133.3 | 139.1 | 148.6 | 121.0 | 131.4 | 156.8 | 171.8 | 248.0 |
| 23. Av. Payment, Partnership | 100.0 | 87.8 | 109.2 | 109.1 | 113.4 | 95.7 | 96.3 | 99.1 | 119.6 | 135.8 |
| 24. Av. Payment, Partner | 100.0 | 89.3 | 107.1 | 112.2 | 79.5 | 91.3 | 103.2 | 98.1 | 109.4 | 123.1 |

## TABLE 3

### 257: CERTIFIED PUBLIC ACCOUNTANTS, WITH AND WITHOUT NET INCOME

| | 1976 | 1977 | 1978 | 1979 | 1980 | 1981 | 1982 | 1983 | 1984 | 1985 |
|---|---|---|---|---|---|---|---|---|---|---|
| 1. Number of Partnerships | 6,668 | 6,995 | 7,722 | 8,430 | 8,228 | 6,865 | 8,755 | 8,026 | 8,233 | 11,034 |
| 2. Number of Partners | 27,590 | 29,302 | 31,996 | 34,123 | 53,274 | 34,313 | 34,702 | 36,819 | 39,319 | 53,251 |
| **Selected Financial Statistics** | | | | | | | | | | |
| **(Items 3 to 9 inclusive in 000's of dollars)** | | | | | | | | | | |
| 3. Operating Income | 3,786,222 | 3,880,854 | 4,666,960 | 5,953,069 | 6,583,430 | 7,141,221 | 6,948,023 | 8,126,392 | 9,743,642 | 13,113,393 |
| 4. Depreciation | 44,601 | 46,016 | 64,179 | 85,231 | 99,507 | n.a. | n.a. | n.a. | 185,976 | 263,122 |
| 5. Taxes Paid | 105,390 | 111,434 | 129,216 | 179,095 | 200,325 | 224,884 | 222,170 | 262,744 | 324,764 | 436,851 |
| 6. Interest Paid | 16,755 | 19,991 | 31,326 | 46,206 | 55,409 | 87,128 | 67,384 | 83,446 | 98,520 | 104,100 |
| 7. Payroll Deductions | 1,502,718 | 1,517,511 | 1,706,508 | 2,343,808 | 2,564,944 | 2,839,347 | 2,605,544 | n.a. | 3,612,766 | 4,875,571 |
| 8. Payments to Partners | 218,941 | 257,150 | 329,910 | 436,703 | 495,151 | 480,800 | 545,814 | 666,788 | 741,637 | 1,135,016 |
| 9. Net Income, less Deficit | 1,058,230 | 1,065,165 | 1,223,662 | 1,362,303 | 1,572,190 | 1,682,243 | 1,673,888 | 1,919,085 | 2,204,732 | 2,709,165 |
| **Selected Average Financial Statistics** | | | | | | | | | | |
| **(Items 10 to 13 inclusive in $)** | | | | | | | | | | |
| 10. Av. Payment Partnership | 32,835 | 36,762 | 42,723 | 51,803 | 60,179 | 70,036 | 62,343 | 83,078 | 90,081 | 102,865 |
| 11. Av. Payment Partner | 7,936 | 8,776 | 10,311 | 12,798 | 9,294 | 14,012 | 15,729 | 18,110 | 18,862 | 21,314 |
| 12. Av. Income Partnership | 158,703 | 152,275 | 158,464 | 161,602 | 191,078 | 245,046 | 191,192 | 239,109 | 267,792 | 245,529 |
| 13. Av. Income Partner | 38,356 | 36,351 | 38,244 | 39,923 | 29,511 | 49,026 | 48,236 | 52,122 | 56,073 | 50,875 |
| **Selected Financial Statistics as Percent of Op. Income** | | | | | | | | | | |
| 14. Depreciation / Op. Income (%) | 1.2 | 1.2 | 1.4 | 1.4 | 1.5 | n.a. | n.a. | n.a. | 1.9 | 2.0 |
| 15. Interest / Op. Income (%) | 0.4 | 0.5 | 0.7 | 0.8 | 0.8 | 1.2 | 0.10 | 1.0 | 1.0 | 0.8 |
| 16. Payroll / Op. Income (%) | 39.7 | 39.1 | 36.6 | 39.4 | 39.0 | 39.8 | 37.5 | n.a. | 37.1 | 37.2 |
| **Selected Index Numbers (1976 = 100)** | | | | | | | | | | |
| 17. Partnerships | 100.0 | 104.9 | 115.8 | 126.4 | 123.4 | 103.0 | 131.3 | 120.4 | 123.5 | 165.5 |
| 18. Partners | 100.0 | 106.2 | 116.0 | 123.7 | 193.1 | 124.4 | 125.8 | 133.5 | 142.5 | 193.0 |
| 19. Operating Income | 100.0 | 102.5 | 123.3 | 157.2 | 173.9 | 188.6 | 183.5 | 214.6 | 257.3 | 346.3 |
| 20. Payments to Partners | 100.0 | 117.5 | 150.7 | 199.5 | 226.2 | 219.6 | 249.3 | 304.6 | 338.7 | 518.4 |
| **Selected Financial Statistics (Constant $, 1976 = 100)** | | | | | | | | | | |
| 21. Operating Income | 100.0 | 96.3 | 107.6 | 123.3 | 120.1 | 118.1 | 108.2 | 122.6 | 141.0 | 183.3 |
| 22. Payments to Partners | 100.0 | 110.3 | 131.5 | 156.4 | 156.2 | 137.5 | 147.0 | 174.0 | 185.6 | 274.3 |
| 23. Av. Payment, Partnership | 100.0 | 105.2 | 113.5 | 123.7 | 126.6 | 133.5 | 112.0 | 144.6 | 150.4 | 165.8 |
| 24. Av. Payment, Partner | 100.0 | 103.9 | 113.4 | 126.5 | 80.9 | 110.5 | 116.9 | 130.4 | 130.3 | 142.1 |

## TABLE 3

### 258: OTHER ACCOUNTING, AUDITING, AND BOOKKEEPING SERVICES, WITH AND WITHOUT NET INCOME

| | 1976 | 1977 | 1978 | 1979 | 1980 | 1981 | 1982 | 1983 | 1984 | 1985 |
|---|---|---|---|---|---|---|---|---|---|---|
| 1. Number of Partnerships | 3,258 | 5,616 | 4,398 | 4,227 | 4,783 | 5,678 | 4,795 | 7,682 | 6,020 | 7,097 |
| 2. Number of Partners | 7,621 | 14,689 | 11,828 | 9,547 | 12,564 | 12,336 | 10,156 | 19,460 | 15,974 | 17,707 |
| **Selected Financial Statistics** | | | | | | | | | | |
| (Items 3 to 9 inclusive in 000's of dollars) | | | | | | | | | | |
| 3. Operating Income | 296,895 | 731,538 | 783,558 | 351,932 | 494,022 | 454,744 | 509,832 | 544,919 | 639,494 | 788,155 |
| 4. Depreciation | 3,440 | 11,922 | 13,450 | 8,147 | 13,018 | n.a. | n.a. | n.a. | 21,729 | 27,080 |
| 5. Taxes Paid | 9,899 | 20,428 | 21,383 | 8,535 | 14,537 | 10,985 | 15,435 | 18,709 | 20,529 | 23,845 |
| 6. Interest Paid | 906 | 2,488 | 3,306 | 4,787 | 7,245 | 7,045 | 9,539 | 9,829 | 6,380 | 16,678 |
| 7. Payroll Deductions | 99,277 | 254,260 | 272,109 | 107,304 | 142,318 | 132,094 | 147,652 | n.a. | 199,575 | 232,241 |
| 8. Payments to Partners | 44,728 | 56,098 | 72,937 | 31,078 | 72,057 | 28,793 | 41,766 | 57,010 | 84,932 | 100,770 |
| 9. Net Income, less Deficit | 98,732 | 214,517 | 213,534 | 104,770 | 100,519 | 122,045 | 125,490 | 21,182 | 104,448 | 136,819 |
| **Selected Average Financial Statistics** | | | | | | | | | | |
| (Items 10 to 13 inclusive in $) | | | | | | | | | | |
| 10. Av. Payment Partnership | 13,729 | 9,989 | 16,584 | 7,352 | 15,065 | 5,071 | 8,710 | 7,421 | 14,108 | 14,199 |
| 11. Av. Payment Partner | 5,869 | 3,819 | 6,166 | 3,255 | 5,735 | 2,334 | 4,112 | 2,930 | 5,317 | 5,691 |
| 12. Av. Income Partnership | 30,304 | 38,197 | 48,553 | 24,786 | 21,016 | 21,494 | 26,171 | 2,757 | 17,350 | 19,278 |
| 13. Av. Income Partner | 12,955 | 14,604 | 18,053 | 10,974 | 8,001 | 9,893 | 12,356 | 1,088 | 6,539 | 7,727 |
| **Selected Financial Statistics as Percent of Op. Income** | | | | | | | | | | |
| 14. Depreciation / Op. Income (%) | 1.2 | 1.6 | 1.7 | 2.3 | 2.6 | n.a. | n.a. | n.a. | 3.4 | 3.4 |
| 15. Interest / Op. Income (%) | 0.3 | 0.3 | 0.4 | 1.4 | 1.5 | 1.6 | 1.9 | 1.8 | 1.0 | 2.1 |
| 16. Payroll / Op. Income (%) | 33.4 | 34.8 | 34.7 | 30.5 | 28.8 | 29.1 | 29.0 | n.a. | 31.2 | 29.5 |
| **Selected Index Numbers (1976 = 100)** | | | | | | | | | | |
| 17. Partnerships | 100.0 | 172.4 | 135.0 | 129.7 | 146.8 | 174.3 | 147.2 | 235.8 | 184.8 | 217.8 |
| 18. Partners | 100.0 | 192.7 | 155.2 | 125.3 | 164.9 | 161.9 | 133.3 | 255.3 | 209.6 | 232.3 |
| 19. Operating Income | 100.0 | 246.4 | 263.9 | 118.5 | 166.4 | 153.2 | 171.7 | 183.5 | 215.4 | 265.5 |
| 20. Payments to Partners | 100.0 | 125.4 | 163.1 | 69.5 | 161.1 | 64.4 | 93.4 | 127.5 | 189.9 | 225.3 |
| **Selected Financial Statistics (Constant $, 1976 = 100)** | | | | | | | | | | |
| 21. Operating Income | 100.0 | 231.5 | 230.3 | 93.0 | 115.0 | 95.9 | 101.3 | 104.9 | 118.0 | 140.5 |
| 22. Payments to Partners | 100.0 | 117.8 | 142.3 | 54.5 | 111.3 | 40.3 | 55.1 | 72.8 | 104.1 | 119.2 |
| 23. Av. Payment, Partnership | 100.0 | 68.4 | 105.4 | 42.0 | 75.8 | 23.1 | 37.4 | 30.9 | 56.3 | 54.7 |
| 24. Av. Payment, Partner | 100.0 | 61.1 | 91.7 | 43.5 | 67.5 | 24.9 | 41.3 | 28.5 | 49.6 | 51.3 |

## TABLE 3

### OTHER SERVICES (253,259), WITH AND WITHOUT NET INCOME

| | 1976 | 1977 | 1978 | 1979 | 1980 | 1981 | 1982 | 1983 | 1984 | 1985 |
|---|---|---|---|---|---|---|---|---|---|---|
| 1. Number of Partnerships | 30,049 | 37,440 | 37,849 | 35,256 | 45,505 | 24,652 | 32,221 | 35,867 | 43,916 | 39,329 |
| 2. Number of Partners | 100,783 | 107,646 | 118,871 | 114,441 | 148,839 | 86,924 | 109,471 | 125,870 | 184,250 | 159,542 |
| **Selected Financial Statistics** | | | | | | | | | | |
| (Items 3 to 9 inclusive in 000's of dollars) | | | | | | | | | | |
| 3. Operating Income | 1,757,646 | 2,888,929 | 2,165,726 | 2,915,948 | 4,174,073 | 1,957,301 | 2,027,895 | 2,794,156 | 3,932,201 | 3,175,692 |
| 4. Depreciation | 83,008 | 125,107 | 100,346 | 132,184 | 173,911 | n.a. | n.a. | n.a. | 692,060 | 379,178 |
| 5. Taxes Paid | 55,504 | 75,779 | 50,234 | 78,694 | 101,371 | 40,076 | 35,959 | 46,943 | 122,125 | 54,003 |
| 6. Interest Paid | 87,325 | 99,937 | 86,420 | 112,501 | 184,208 | 82,382 | 94,153 | 149,239 | 163,650 | 143,246 |
| 7. Payroll Deductions | 327,935 | 403,128 | 221,379 | 401,271 | 483,406 | 318,309 | 296,527 | n.a. | 889,166 | 601,894 |
| 8. Payments to Partners | 90,883 | 94,332 | 70,377 | 82,360 | 106,818 | 79,899 | 54,037 | 92,154 | 187,364 | 150,499 |
| 9. Net Income, less Deficit | 172,838 | 247,537 | 316,656 | 443,847 | 298,941 | 196,957 | 10,568 | 182,821 | 225,564 | 908,217 |
| **Selected Average Financial Statistics** | | | | | | | | | | |
| (Items 10 to 13 inclusive in $) | | | | | | | | | | |
| 10. Av. Payment Partnership | 3,024 | 2,520 | 1,859 | 2,336 | 2,347 | 3,241 | 1,677 | 2,569 | 4,266 | 3,827 |
| 11. Av. Payment Partner | 902 | 876 | 592 | 720 | 718 | 919 | 494 | 732 | 1,017 | 943 |
| 12. Av. Income Partnership | 5,752 | 6,612 | 8,366 | 12,589 | 6,569 | 7,989 | 328 | 5,097 | 5,136 | 23,093 |
| 13. Av. Income Partner | 1,715 | 2,300 | 2,664 | 3,878 | 2,008 | 2,266 | 97 | 1,452 | 1,224 | 5,693 |
| **Selected Financial Statistics as Percent of Op. Income** | | | | | | | | | | |
| 14. Depreciation / Op. Income (%) | 4.7 | 4.3 | 4.6 | 4.5 | 4.2 | n.a. | n.a. | n.a. | 17.6 | 11.9 |
| 15. Interest / Op. Income (%) | 5.0 | 3.5 | 4.0 | 3.9 | 4.4 | 4.2 | 4.6 | 5.3 | 4.2 | 4.5 |
| 16. Payroll / Op. Income (%) | 18.7 | 14.0 | 10.2 | 13.8 | 11.6 | 16.3 | 14.6 | n.a. | 22.6 | 19.0 |
| **Selected Index Numbers (1976 = 100)** | | | | | | | | | | |
| 17. Partnerships | 100.0 | 124.6 | 126.0 | 117.3 | 151.4 | 82.0 | 107.2 | 119.4 | 146.1 | 130.9 |
| 18. Partners | 100.0 | 106.8 | 117.9 | 113.6 | 147.7 | 86.2 | 108.6 | 124.9 | 182.8 | 158.3 |
| 19. Operating Income | 100.0 | 164.4 | 123.2 | 165.9 | 237.5 | 111.4 | 115.4 | 159.0 | 223.7 | 180.7 |
| 20. Payments to Partners | 100.0 | 103.8 | 77.4 | 90.6 | 117.5 | 87.9 | 59.5 | 101.4 | 206.2 | 165.6 |
| **Selected Financial Statistics (Constant $, 1976 = 100)** | | | | | | | | | | |
| 21. Operating Income | 100.0 | 154.4 | 107.5 | 130.1 | 164.1 | 69.7 | 68.0 | 90.8 | 122.6 | 95.6 |
| 22. Payments to Partners | 100.0 | 97.5 | 67.6 | 71.1 | 81.2 | 55.0 | 35.1 | 57.9 | 113.0 | 87.6 |
| 23. Av. Payment, Partnership | 100.0 | 78.2 | 53.6 | 60.6 | 53.6 | 67.1 | 32.7 | 48.5 | 77.3 | 67.0 |
| 24. Av. Payment, Partner | 100.0 | 91.3 | 57.3 | 62.6 | 55.0 | 63.7 | 32.3 | 46.3 | 61.8 | 55.4 |

# APPENDIX
## SIC/Partnership Classification Numbers

## SIC CLASSIFICATION

*ALL INDUSTRIES*

AGRICULTURE, FORESTRY, AND
FISHING

N.A.
01 Agriculture production:
Crops
011 Grains
013 Other field crops
016 Vegetable and melons
017 Fruit and tree nuts
02 Agriculture production:
Livestock
018 Horticulture specialty
0211 Beef cattle, feedlots
0212 Beef cattle, except
feedlots
0213 Hogs
0214 Sheep and goats
024 Dairy farms
025 Poultry and eggs
029 General farms, primarily
livestock
027 Animal specialties
N.A.
07 Agricultural services
074 Veterinary services
N.A.
075 Animal services, except
veterinary

078 Landscape and horticultural
services
N.A.
08 Forestry
09 Fishing, hunting and trapping


MINING

10 Metal mining
11 Anthracite mining
12 Bituminous coal and
lignite mining
13 Oil and gas extraction
14 Mining and quarrying of
nonmetallic minerals except fuels

## PARTNERSHIP CLASSIFICATION

*001 ALL INDUSTRIES*

002 AGRICULTURE, FORESTRY, AND
FISHING

003 Farms

004 Field crops
Includes SIC industries 011 and
013.
005 Vegetable and melons
006 Fruit and tree nuts
N.A.

007 Horticulture specialty
008 Beef cattle, feedlots
009 Beef cattle, except
feedlots
N.A.
010 Hogs, sheep, and goats
011 Dairy farms
012 Poultry and eggs
013 General livestock,
except animal specialty
014 Animal specialty
015 Farms, not allocable
016 Agricultural services
017 Veterinary services
018 Livestock breeding
019 Animal services, except
livestock breeding and
veterinary
020 Landscape and
horticultural services
021 Miscellaneous services
022 Forestry
023 Fishing, hunting, and
trapping


026 MINING

027 Metal mining
028 Coal mining: SIC industries
11, and 12

029 Oil and gas extraction
030 Nonmetallic minerals except
fuels

| SIC CLASSIFICATION | PARTNERSHIP CLASSIFICATION |
|---|---|
| CONSTRUCTION | 031 CONSTRUCTION |
| 15 Building construction: general contactors and operative builders | 032 General building contractors and operative builders |
| 152 General bldg contractors, residential | 033 General building contractors. Includes SIC industries 152 and 154 |
| 154 General bldg contractors nonresidential | |
| 153 Operative builders | 034 Operative builders |
| 16 Construction other than building, general contractors | 035 General contractors other than building |
| 161 Highway and street construction | 036 Highway and street construction |
| 162 Heavy construction | 037 Heavy construction |
| 17 Construction: special trade contractors | 038 Special trade contractors |
| 171 Plumbing, heating (except electric), and air conditioning | 039 Plumbing, heating, and air conditioning |
| 172 Painting, paperhanging, and decorating | 040 Painting, paperhanging, decorating |
| 173 Electrical work | 041 Electrical work |
| 174 Masonry, stonework, tile setting, and plastering | 042 Masonry, stonework, tile setting, and plastering |
| 175 Carpeting and flooring | 043 Carpeting and flooring |
| 176 Roofing and sheet metal work | 044 Roofing and sheet metal work |
| 177 Concrete work | 045 Concrete work |
| 178 Water well drilling | 046 Water well drilling |
| 179 Misc. special trade contractors | 047 Misc. special trade contractors |
| N.A. | 048 Contractors not allocable |
| | |
| MANUFACTURING | 049 MANUFACTURING |
| 20 Food and kindred products | 050 Food and kindred products |
| 22 Textile mill products | 052 Textile mill products |
| 23 Apparel and other finished products made from fabric and similar stuff | 053 Apparel and other textile products |
| 24 Lumber and wood | 054 Lumber and wood products, except furniture |
| 25 Furniture and fixtures | 055 Furniture and fixtures |
| 26 Paper and allied products | N.A. |
| 27 Printing, publishing, and allied industries | 056 Printing, publishing, and allied industries |
| 28 Chemicals and allied products | 057 Chemicals and allied industries |
| 29 Petroleum, refining, and related industries | N.A. |

## SIC CLASSIFICATION

30 Rubber and misc. plastic
products
31 Leather and leather products
32 Stone, glass, clay,
and concrete products
33 Primary metal industries
34 Fabricated metal products, except
machinery and transportation
35 Machinery, except
electrical
36 Electrical and electronic
machinery equipment and supplies
37 Transportation equipment
38 Measuring, analyzing, and
controlling instruments
39 Misc. manufacturing
industries.

## TRANSPORTATION, COMMUNICATION, ELECTRIC, GAS, AND SANITARY SERVICES

40 Railroad transportation
41 Local and suburban
transit and interurban highway
passenger transport
4221 Taxicabs
N.A.
42 Motor freight transportation
and warehousing
421 Trucking

422 Public warehousing

44 Water transportation
45 Air transportation
46 Pipe lines except natural gas
47 Transportation services
4722 Arrangement of
passenger transportation
N.A.


N.A.

## 48 COMMUNICATIONS

49 Electric, gas, and
sanitary services

## PARTNERSHIP CLASSIFICATION

N.A.

058 Leather and leather products
059 Stone, clay, and glass
products
060 Primary metal industries
061 Fabricated metal products

062 Machinery, except
electrical
063 Electrical and
electronic equipment
064 Transportation equipment
N.A.

065 Other Manufacturing and
066 Manufacturing, not
allocable

## 067 TRANSPORTATION, COMMUNICATION, ELECTRIC, GAS, AND SANITARY SERVICES

N.A.
068 Local and interurban
passenger transit

069 Taxis
070 Other passenger transportation
071 Trucking and warehousing

072 Trucking, local and long
distance
073 Public warehousing and
trucking terminals
074 Water transportation
075 Air transportation
N.A.
076 Transportation services
077 Passenger transportation
arrangement
078 Freight transportation
arrangement
079 Other transportation services

## 080 COMMUNICATIONS

N.A.

| SIC CLASSIFICATION | PARTNERSHIP CLASSIFICATION |
|---|---|
| 491 Electric services | N.A. |
| 492 Gas production and distribution | N.A. |
| 493 Combination, electric, gas, and other utilities | 081 Electric, gas, and water services |
| 494 Water supply | N.A. |
| 495 Sanitary service | 082 Sanitary services |
| 496 Steam supply | Steam supply in 081 |
| 497 Irrigation systems | Irrigation in 081 |
| WHOLESALE AND RETAIL TRADE WHOLESALE TRADE | 083 WHOLESALE AND RETAIL TRADE 084 WHOLESALE TRADE |
| 501 Motor vehicles and automotive parts and supplies | 085 Motor vehicles and automotive equipment |
| 503 Lumber and other construction materials | 086 Lumber and construction materials |
| 506 Electrical goods | 087 Electrical goods |
| 507 Hardware, plumbing, heating, and supplies | 088 Hardware, plumbing, heating, and supplies |
| 5083 Farm and garden machinery and equipment | 089 Farm machinery and equipment |
| N.A. | 090 Other machinery |
| 502 Furniture and home furnishings | N.A. |
| 504 Sporting, recreational, photographic and hobby goods, toys and supplies | N.A. |
| 509 Miscellaneous durable goods | 091 Other durable goods |
| 511 Paper and paper products | Paper and paper products in 097 |
| 512 Drugs, drug proprietaries, and druggists' sundries | N.A. |
| 516 Chemicals and allied products | 092 Drugs, chemicals, and allied products |
| 513 Apparel, piece goods, and notions | 093 Apparel, piece goods, and notions |
| 514 Groceries and related products | 094 Groceries and related products |
| 515 Farm-products raw materials | 095 Farm-products raw materials |
| 517 Petroleum and petroleum products | Petroleum and petroleum products in 097 |
| 518 Beer, wine, and distilled alcoholic beverages | 096 Alcoholic beverages |

## SIC CLASSIFICATION

519 Miscellaneous nondurable
goods
N.A.

## RETAIL TRADE

52 Building materials,
hardware, garden supply, and
mobile home dealers
521 Lumber and other
building material dealers
523 Paint, glass, and
wallpaper stores
525 Hardware stores
526 Retail nurseries,
lawn and garden supply
stores
527 Mobile home dealers
53 General merchandise stores
533 Variety stores
539 Miscellaneous general
merchandise
54 Food stores
541 Grocery stores
542 Meat and fish markets
543 Fruit stores and
vegetable markets
544 Candy, nut, and
confectionery stores
545 Dairy products stores
546 Retail bakeries
549 Miscellaneous food
stores
55 Automobile dealers and
gasoline service stations
551 Motor vehicles (new and used)

552 Motor Vehicles (used only)

553 Auto and home supply stores
554 Gasoline service stations
555 Boat dealers
556 Recreational and
utility trailers dealers
557 Motorcycle dealers
559 Automotive
dealers, n.e.c.
56 Apparel and accessory
stores

## PARTNERSHIP CLASSIFICATION

097 Other nondurable goods
098 Wholesalers not allocable

## 100 RETAIL TRADE

101 Bldg material, paint, hardware,
garden supplies, and mobile home
dealers
102 Lumber and other
building materials
103 Paint, glass, and
wallpaper stores
104 Hardware stores
105 Retail nurseries, lawn and
garden supply
stores
106 Mobile home dealers
107 General merchandise
108 Variety stores
109 Other general
merchandise
110 Food Stores
111 Grocery stores
112 Meat and fish markets
113 Fruit stores and
vegetable markets
114 Candy, nut, and
confectionery stores
115 Dairy products stores
116 Retail bakeries
117 Miscellaneous food
stores
118 Automobile dealers and
service stations
119 Motor vehicle dealers (new
cars)
120 Motor vehicle dealers
(used cars)
121 Auto and home supply stores
122 Gasoline service stations
123 Boat dealers
124 Recreational
vehicles
125 Motorcycle dealers
126 Miscellaneous
aircraft and automotive
127 Apparel and
accessory stores

## SIC CLASSIFICATION

561 Men's and boys'
clothing stores
562 Ready-to-wear stores
(Women's)
563 Women's accessory
and specialty stores
564 Children and
infants' wear shops
565 Family clothing
stores
566 Shoe stores
568 Furriers and fur
shops
569 Miscellaneous apparel and
accessories
57 Furniture, home
furnishings, and equipment
stores
5712 Furniture stores
5713 Floor covering
stores
5714 Drapery, curtain,
and upholstery stores
5719 Miscellaneous
home furnishings

572 Household
appliance stores
5732 Radio and TV
stores
5733 Music stores
58 Eating and drinking places

59 Misc. retail stores
591 Drug and proprietary stores
592 Liquor stores
593 Used merchandise stores
5941 Sporting goods and bicycle shops
5942 Book stores
5943 Stationery stores
5944 Jewelry stores
5945 Hobby, toy, and
games
5946 Camera and
photographic supply
stores

## PARTNERSHIP CLASSIFICATION

128 Men's and boys' clothing
and furnishing stores
129 Women's ready-to-wear
stores
130 Women's accessory and
specialty shops
131 Children and infants' wear
stores
132 Family clothing
stores
133 Shoe stores
134 Furriers and fur
stores
135 Apparel and accessory
stores, n.e.c.
136 Furniture and home
furnishings stores

137 Furniture stores
138 Floor covering stores

139 Drapery, curtain, and
upholstery stores
140 Home furnishings and
equipment stores, except
appliances
141 Household appliance
stores
142 Radio and TV stores

143 Music stores
144 Eating and drinking places
145 Eating places
146 Drinking places
147 Misc. retail stores
148 Drug and proprietary stores
149 Liquor stores
150 Used merchandise stores
151 Sporting goods and bicycle
shops
152 Book stores
153 Stationery stores
154 Jewelry stores
155 Hobby, toys, and game shops

156 Camera and
photographic supply stores

## SIC CLASSIFICATION

5947 Gift, novelty, and souvenir shops
5948 Luggage and leather goods stores
5949 Sewing, needlework, and piece goods stores
5961 Mail order houses
5962 Automatic merchandise machine operators

5963 Direct selling establishments
598 Fuel and ice dealers (includes bottled gas)

5982 Fuel and ice dealers, except fuel oil and bottled gas dealers

5983 Fuel oil dealers
5984 Liquefied petroleum gas dealers
5992 Florists
5993 Cigar stands and stores
5994 News dealers and newsstand
N.A.
599 Retail stores, n.e.c.

## FINANCE, INSURANCE, AND REAL ESTATE

N.A.
60 Banking

61 Credit agencies other than banks
62 Security and commodity brokers, dealers, exchanges
621 Security brokers, dealers, and flotation companies

622 Commodity contracts brokers and dealers
623 Security and commodity exchanges
628 Allied services
67 Holding, and other investment companies

## PARTNERSHIP CLASSIFICATION

157 Gift, novelty, and souvenir shops
158 Luggage and leather goods stores
159 Sewing, needlework, and piece goods stores
160 Mail order houses
161 Merchandising machine operators

162 Direct selling establishments
N.A.

163 Fuel and ice dealers, except fuel oil and bottled gas

164 Fuel oil dealers
165 Liquefied petroleum gas dealers
166 Florists
167 Cigar stores and stands
168 News dealers and newsstands

169 Other retail stores

## 172 FINANCE, INSURANCE, AND REAL ESTATE

173 Finance
174 Banking and miscellaneous finance
175 Credit agencies other than banks
176 Security and commodity brokers and services
177 Security underwriting syndicates and 178
178 Security brokers, dealers, except underwriting
179 Commodity brokers, exchanges and allied services
SIC 622, 623, 628

180 Holding and investment companies

| SIC CLASSIFICATION | PARTNERSHIP CLASSIFICATION |
|---|---|
| N.A. | 181 Investment clubs |
| N.A. | 182 Common Trust funds |
| N.A. | 183 Other holding and investment companies |
| 64 Insurance agents, brokers, and services | 184 Insurance agents, brokers, and services |
| 65 Real estate | 18 Real estate |
| 651 Real estate operators and lessors | 186 Operators and lessors of buildings |
| 6512 Operators of nonresidential buildings | N.A. |
| 6513 Operators of apartment buildings | N.A. |
| 6514 Operators of residential buildings except apartments | N.A. |
| 6515 Operators of mobile homes | N.A. |
| 6517 Lessors of railroad property | N.A. |
| 6519 Lessors of real property, n.e.c. | 187 Lessors of other than buildings |
| 653 Real estate agents and managers | 188 Real estate agents, brokers, and managers |
| 654 Title abstract offices | 189 Title abstract companies |
| 6552 Subdividers and developers, except cemeteries | 190 Subdividers and developers, except cemeteries |
| 6553 Subdividers and developers of cemeteries | 191 Cemetery subdividers |
| 661 Combination of real estate, insurance loans, law offices | 192 Combined real estate, insurance, loan, law offices |
| SERVICES | SERVICES |
| 70 Hotels, rooming houses, camps, and other lodging places | 193 Hotels and other lodging |
| N.A. | 195 Hotels |
| 701 Hotels, motels, and tourist courts | 196 Motels, motor hotels, and tourist courts |
| 702 Rooming and boarding houses | 197 Rooming and boarding houses |
| 7032 Sporting and recreation camps | 198 Sporting and recreational camps |
| 7033 Trailer parks and campsites for transients | 199 Trailer parks and campsites |
| 7041 Organizational hotel and lodging houses | 200 Organizational hotels and lodging houses |
| 72 Personal services | 201 Personal services |
| 7215 Coin-operated laundries and dry cleaning | 202 Coin-operated laundries and dry cleaning |
| 7512 Garment pressing and agents for laundries and dry cleaning | 203 Laundries, dry cleaning, and garment services |

## SIC CLASSIFICATION

7221 Photographic studios,
portrait
7231 Beauty shops
7241 Barber shops
7251 Shoe repair, shoe shine,
and hat cleaning stores
7261 Funeral services
and crematoria
7299 Miscellaneous personal
services
73 Business services
731 Advertising
734 Services to dwelling and
other buildings
737 Computer and data processing

7392 Management, consulting, and
public relations
7394 Equipment rental and leasing
services
732 Consumer credit, mercantile
reporting agencies, and
collection agencies
733 Mailing, reproductions,
commercial art photography, and
steno services
735 News syndicates
736 Personal supply services
739 Miscellaneous business
services
75 Automobile repair services
and garages
751 Automotive rental and
leasing
752 Automobile parking
7531 Top and body repair shops

7538 General automotive repairs
7534 Tire retreading and repair
shops
7535 Paint shops
7538 General automotive repair
shops, n.e.c.
76 Miscellaneous repair services
7622 Radio and TV repair shops
7629 Electrical and electronic
repair shops
7641 Reupholstery and furniture
repair

## PARTNERSHIP CLASSIFICATION

205 Photographic studios,
portrait
206 Beauty shops
207 Barber shops
208 Shoe repair and hat
cleaning stores
209 Funeral services and
crematories
210 Miscellaneous personal
services
211 Business services
212 Advertising
213 Services to buildings

214 Computer and data
processing services
215 Management and public
relations
216 Equipment rental and
leasing
N.A.


N.A.


N.A.
N.A.
N.A.
217 Other business services
218 Automotive repair and
services
219 Automotive rentals and
leasing, no drivers
220 Automotive parking
221 Automotive top and body
repairs
222 General automobile repairs
223 Other automotive repair
shops. Includes SIC 7535

224 Automobile services,
except repair
225 Miscellaneous repair
226 Radio and TV repair shops
227 Electrical repair
shops, except radio and TV
228 Reupholstery and
furniture repair

## SIC CLASSIFICATION

769 Miscellaneous repair shops
and related services
78 Motion pictures
781 Motion picture production
and allied services
782 Motion picture distribution
and allied services
N.A.


783 Motion picture theatres
79 Amusement and recreation
services, except motion pictures
792 Theatrical producers,
orchestras, entertainers
7932 Billiards


7933 Bowling alleys
7941 Professional sport clubs


7948 Racing, including
track operations
799 Miscellaneous amusement and
recreation
80 Health services
801 Offices of physicians
802 Offices of dentists
803 Offices of osteopathic
physicians
8041 Offices of chiropractors
8042 Offices of optometrists
N.A.


805 Nursing and personal care
facilities
806 Hospitals
8071 Medical laboratories
8072 Dental laboratories
807 Health and allied services,
n.e.c.
811 Legal services
82 Educational services
8911 Engineering, architectural,
and surveying services
893 Accounting, auditing, and
bookkeeping services (Includes
Partnership 258 and 259).

## PARTNERSHIP CLASSIFICATION

229 Other miscellaneous
repair shops
230 Motion pictures
N.A.

N.A.

231 Motion picture production,
distribution, and services
232 Motion picture theatres
233 Amusement and recreation,
except motion pictures
234 Producers, orchestras,
entertainers
235 Billiard and pool
establishments
236 Bowling alleys
237 Professional sports
clubs and promoters
238 Racing, including track
operations
239 Other amusement and
recreation service
240 Medical and health services
241 Offices of physicians
242 Offices of dentists
243 Offices of osteopathic
physicians
244 Offices of chiropractors
245 Offices of optometrists
246 Registered and practical
nurses
247 Nursing and personal care
facilities
248 Hospitals
249 Medical laboratories
250 Dental laboratories
251 Other medical and health
services
252 Legal services
253 Educational services
255 Engineering and
architectural services
256 Accounting, auditing, and
bookkeeping services
257 Certified public
accountants

## SIC CLASSIFICATION

899 Services, n.e.c.

## PARTNERSHIP CLASSIFICATION

258 Other accounting, auditing,
and bookkeeping services
259 Services, n.e.c.